ANGUAGE
ARTS

LANGUAGE ARTS
Teaching Exceptional Students

GERALD WALLACE
The University of Virginia

SANDRA B. COHEN
The University of Virginia

EDWARD A. POLLOWAY
Lynchburg College

5341 Industrial Oaks Blvd.
Austin, Texas 78735

Copyright © 1987 by Gerald Wallace,
Sandra B. Cohen, and Edward A. Polloway

Printed in the United States of America

Library of Congress Cataloging in Publication Data

Wallace, Gerald, 1940-
   Language arts.

   Bibliography: p.
   Includes indexes.
   1. Exceptional children—Education—Language
arts.   2. Handicapped—Education—Language arts.   I. Cohen,
Sandra B.   II. Polloway, Edward A.   III. Title.
LC3975.W35   1987   371.9′044   87-6929
ISBN 0-89079-145-7

5341 Industrial Oaks Boulevard
Austin, Texas 78735

10   9   8   7   6   5   4   3   2   1   87   88   89   90   91   92

To our children,
Chris and T. J. Wallace,
Jeff and Julie Fowler,
and Lyndsay Polloway

CONTENTS

PREFACE

The development of language has often been seen as the essence of what makes us human. By our very nature, we strive to communicate with others in order to share our perceptions of the world, exercise social control, and acquire knowledge about our environment. Thus, for those individuals who experience language-related problems, the consequences can range from mild to profound disability in terms of academic, social, and vocational success.

Language Arts: Teaching Exceptional Students was written to assist practitioners in responding to the multitude of problems that can interfere with the acquisition of language and can confound the development of proficiency in the language arts. Our purpose is to provide the reader with a source that is conceptually sound as well as practically useful. Thus, we hope to contribute to the continuing efforts of educators to deliver effective instruction to those students who require adaptation in their educational programs.

For over a decade, the three of us have shared concerns about the language development of exceptional students and particularly about the quality of language arts instruction for these individuals. After dozens of informal conversations during this period of time, we finally found ourselves able to collaborate to develop a text within the area of language arts. This book represents our years of shared interests in these topics.

The book includes three sections related to language and language arts instruction for exceptional and remedial learners. The initial section is devoted to fundamentals. The first chapter addresses language and language development, while the second is concerned with central elements of language arts instruction for special populations.

The second section presents the core of the curriculum and methods discussion. Focused on mildly handicapped and remedial students, this section contains chapters devoted to the traditional language arts: listening, speaking, reading, and writing.

The third section is concerned with various adaptations to instruction necessary for successful programming for specific populations of exceptional individuals. Chapter 9, contributed by Sherryl Edwards, emphasizes language instruction for preschool handicapped children.

ix

Chapter 10, written by Jo Webber, addresses intervention with older severely handicapped individuals. Chapters 11 through 13 focus on several other groups of learners whose needs require significant modification of regular school programs: visually and hearing impaired students, culturally different learners, and gifted and talented pupils. Chapter 14, contributed by James Patton, provides a discussion of the instructional needs of disabled adults as those needs relate to the various domains of language arts.

The book is intended as a preservice or inservice source for teachers who work with a diverse population of students with needs for a modified language arts curriculum. It is essentially noncategorical in focus, although attention is given, where appropriate, to specific concepts, methods, and curriculums that have relevance to a given group of exceptional learners. We hope that the book will serve equally well as a core text both for special educators and for regular class teachers preparing themselves for the instructional realities of mainstreaming situations.

We would like to acknowledge the assistance of a number of individuals who have assisted us in the preparation of this book. Special thanks go to Betty Johnson, Donna Elliott, Patty Whitfield, Sarah Goldenberg, Fred Conner, Karen Dwier, Rebecca Shifflett, and Renita Parrish for help with the typing of the manuscript and the tracking down of references; to Carolyn Callahan for assistance with research related to the preparation of the chapter on gifted learners; to Chris Baxter and Stephanie Januta for help with the development of Chapters 2 and 10, respectively; and to Maggie McNergney for supplying examples of children's writings in Chapter 7. Finally, we would like to extend our appreciation to the management and staff of McGritz Restaurant in Lovingston, Virginia, who served as hosts for us in our numerous meetings during the development of this project.

Gerald Wallace
Sandra B. Cohen
Edward A. Polloway

Part One

FUNDAMENTALS OF
LANGUAGE

1
___

NATURE OF
LANGUAGE
DEVELOPMENT

We are surrounded by language. We talk, we sing, we discuss, we listen, we act out, we express with gestures, and we observe all that is around us. Through it all, we are involved with language. Although some of us are better at using language than others, we all can communicate. How language is acquired and why there is a difference among individuals in the use of language is what this chapter aims to explore. It is not necessary to become a linguist to understand the fundamental concepts of language development; however, as teachers we need to grasp the language acquisition process of the normal child before we can genuinely appreciate language differences. From this basic understanding the teacher should be able to perceive the range of language skills necessary for successful communication and independence.

As a child grows so does a facility with the language of the environment. In much the same way that it is impossible to precisely define the truly "typical" child's growth pattern—since there is a range that is exhibited by all normal children—it is also impossible to specify an exact sequence of developing language that will fit all cases. Children, as individuals, establish their own pace in acquiring language. This is evident in characteristics such as variations in vocabularies, intonation, and associated nonverbal features.

The power of language is felt by all children at an early age when they realize they can summon a parent with sound, receive a cookie on request, or interact with a sibling by speaking. By the age of 5, most children have generally achieved a basic competence in a language (including phonology, morphology, syntax, and semantics) and are able to communicate with those around them.

"The ability of children to think symbolically and to produce sound symbols makes it *possible* for children to learn language. The need to communicate makes it *necessary* for children to learn language" (Smith, Goodman, & Meredith, 1976, p. 11). This communication involves not only understanding others but also making one's own needs, thoughts, and wishes understandable.

WHAT IS LANGUAGE?

Language can most accurately be described as a social tool used to communicate information and to influence the actions of those around us. Human language is distinct from the communicative signals used by animals in that only our language features *discreteness, meaningfulness, productivity, and displacement* (Bootzin, Bower, Zajonc, & Hall, 1986). Language is discrete in that it is made up of separate units (words), which when combined form utterances that can expand the impact of the units themselves. These units or words are meaningful in ways that are derived from the society in which we function and may differ from time to time. This differentiates our language from animal communication in that a bird's call, for example, always stands for the same meaningful signal. In addition, there is an endless number of possible words and combinations, making language distinctively productive. We are limited only by the established rules that guide the production of our utterances. Finally, the versatility of language allows the communication to center on an object, event, or person that is not immediately present (displacement). As a result we can talk about the past, the future, and the hypothetical.

Keeping in mind the utility of language within a social system, it is important to understand both the structure (the component parts) and the function (application) of this tool. The structure of language is studied within the domain of *linguistics*, while its use or function is examined as part of *psycholinguistics*. To a teacher both areas are of importance in that the progress made during a child's education is highly influenced by the child's language production and use.

The fundamental components of language structure are (a) *phonemes,* (b) *morphemes,* (c) *semantics,* and (d) *syntax.* Phonemes are the total repertoire of speech sounds used within a language. The English language is limited to approximately 40 phonemes from which all words are created, and in almost all cases children learn these phonemes prior to any formal schooling. The phonemes, which correspond somewhat to the letters of the alphabet, are combined by a set of rules unique to the English language. A competent English speaker will know, for instance, that certain words such as *pretion* and *blik* are possible phoneme combinations but that *kgikd* and *bpoda* are not. This is because the speaker intuitively knows which words are acceptable according to the rules governing the combining of phonemes. In the latter two words, for example, the speaker knows that in English it is not possible to begin a word with two consecutive stop consonants. It is the combining and recombining of phonemes based upon established rules that enable us to effectively communicate in words with well-understood meanings and newly created words which will acquire meaning in the future.

The blending of phonemes results in the creation of meaningful units designated as morphemes. A morpheme, the smallest unit of meaning, must have a *referent* for which it clearly stands. Although many do, not all morphemes can stand alone as individual words. Those that do stand alone (e.g., *book, make,* and *idea*) are termed *free morphemes.* Morphemes such as prefixes and suffixes (e.g., *non-, pre-, -ed* and *-ing*), which must be attached or literally bound to other morphemes, are known as *bound morphemes.* Many words such as *unbreakable* are made up of more than one morpheme, leading to greater variety in the language system. The relative development of morphological constructions is found in Figure 1.1.

Semantics, the term often applied to the general meaning component of language, includes some, but not all, morphemes. At its simplest level semantics refers to a single word with a direct referent. But at the very complex level of language, semantics involves the interaction of words within a given context such as in the use of metaphor.

The way morphemes are put together represents the architectural plan, known as *syntax,* of the language. Phrases and sentences are the constructions resulting from the combinations of morphemes. There are a limited number of acceptable constructions in any language. For instance, in English we can say, "I want to go home now," or, "Now, I want to go home," but we cannot say, "Home now I go want to." Examples of syntactical rules in English are: (a) A noun phrase may consist of an article followed by a noun (e.g., *the man* or *an apple*), and (b) a sentence consists of at least a noun phrase and a verb phrase (e.g., *The man is eating*).

Rules of morphology have been tested in linguistic research following a method developed by Berko (1958). Children are asked to complete

FIGURE 1.1. The Relative Acquisition of Morphological Constructions

---

Initial Constructions | **Subsequent Constructions**

Singular nouns (cat) ⟶ Plural nouns (cats)

Regular plurals (dogs, cats) ⟶ Irregular plurals (children, men)

Regular adjectives (big) ⟶ Comparative adjectives (bigger)

Present progressive verbs (eating, playing) ⟶ Past tense verbs (played, ate)

Past tense irregular verbs (saw, ate, went, ran) ⟶ Past tense regular verbs (jumped, worked)

Past tense verbs (ate, went, jumped) ⟶ Future tense verbs (will go, is going to go)

First and second person pronouns (I, me) (mine, you) ⟶ Third person pronouns (he, she, her, him)

From Cole, M. & Cole, J. (1981). *Effective intervention with the language impaired child.* Rockville, MD: Aspen, p. 8. Reprinted with permission of Aspen Publishers, Inc.

sentences in which a significant morpheme is missing. Examples of sentences that will test a child's understanding are:

1. I have one glip. Now I have two _____.

2. Someone who netches is a _____.

3. Today I lom, yesterday I _____.

The close relationship that exists among the elements of the language is portrayed in Figure 1.2. The reader should examine the pyramid for both comprehension (movement up the pyramid) and production (movement down the pyramid) to understand the complete language picture. It is important to note that the apex represents the thought level. Although language is usually an integral part of a thought, it is

FIGURE 1.2. Language Construction Pyramid

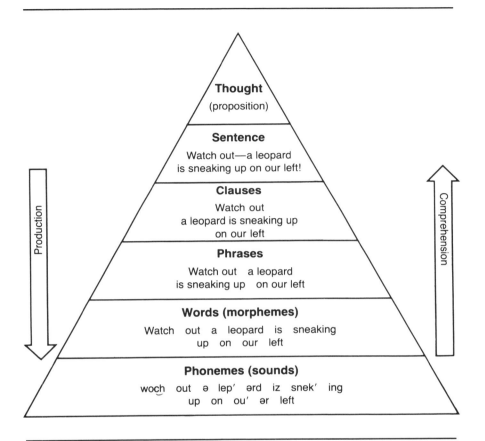

From Bootzin, R., Bower, G., Zajonc, R., & Hall, E. (1986). *Psychology today: An introduction* (6th ed.). New York: Random House, p. 398. Reprinted with permission of Random House.

not the same thing as the actual oral expression. The conscious thought exists in the form of a proposition consisting of a subject and a predicate. For example, in the sentence, "Sally is funny," *Sally* is the subject and *is funny* is the topical comment we are making about the subject. The pyramid also represents the psycholinguistic orientation. Remember that the word *psycholinguistic* is made up of *psycho*, referring to "thinking," and *linguistic*, indicating "language."

The interaction of phonology, morphology, semantics, and syntax increases as the child grows, allowing more and more sophisticated use of language. In the past, school curricula concentrated on the accuracy of the child's phoneme production in reading and spelling far more than morphographic knowledge. In fact, the concept of morphemes within linguistics did not develop until the 1940s, and only much more recently has the study of morphology been influential in curriculum materials and programs. The newer reading, language, and spelling programs tend to incorporate elements of language structure, specifically organizing around meaningful patterns of language which the child can learn and apply. An example of an instructional material using a morphographic orientation is found in Figure 1.3.

The development of syntactic understanding and use progresses in what appears to be an established sequence. Age 9 is now recognized as the time by which most children have mastered the language structure (Kean & Personke, 1976). Therefore, the elementary teacher should be aware of the expansion in syntactic structure which continues to need fostering as the child enters school.

LANGUAGE DEVELOPMENT

The developing child is also the developing communicator. Language is learned throughout the maturation process, and as Bloomfield (1933) states, this learning is "doubtless the greatest intellectual feat any one of us is ever required to perform" (p. 29). Educators, researchers, linguists, psychologists, and parents alike have appreciated the complexities of this enormous task and have searched for a means of explaining the phenomenon of language development.

In many ways the process by which language is acquired is still an enigma. We do know that there is a general sequence of language development: The infant first produces sounds, which later turn into single words, and in time these are linked together to form phrases and sentences. With the child's growth and experience, communication becomes longer and more complex. The process of passing through these stages includes not only the combination of sounds into words but the understanding of grammatical rules and what words actually mean. Examining language development from this perspective suggests that a series of rules influencing grammar, meaning, and application are essential components of the language process.

Association, Imitation, and Reinforcement

In the not-too-distant past, theories of language development have centered on the tenets of various psychologies of learning: association,

FIGURE 1.3. Academic Exercises Focusing on Morphographs

Part D

Add these morphographs together.
Remember, the morphograph y is a vowel letter.

1. ease + y = _____

2. fool + ish + ly = _____

3. form + al + ly = _____

4. store + age = _____

5. sleep + y = _____

6. length + y = _____

7. fate + al = _____

8. re + source + ful = _____

9. note + able = _____

10. straight + en = _____

Part E

Fill in the blanks to show the morphographs in each word.

1. _____ + _____ + _____ = designer

2. _____ + _____ + _____ = unplanned

3. _____ + _____ + _____ = strengthening

4. _____ + _____ = maddest

5. _____ + _____ + _____ = related

6. _____ + _____ = wreckage

7. _____ + _____ = really

8. _____ + _____ + _____ = unproven

From Dixon, R., & Engelmann, S. (1981). *Spelling Mastery: Level C, Student's Book,* Lesson 90. Chicago: Science Research. Reprinted with permission of Science Research Associates.

imitation, and reinforcement. Through observation of children's earliest utterances and analysis of experiments with nonsense syllables and other isolated materials, researchers first explained language acquisition by how a child associated words with agents. It was assumed that a child learned a word after having an agent labeled for him or her. This referential theory of language development emphasizes the importance of specific experiences for advancing language. A child can understand the meaning of the word *computer* only after having some contact either directly with a computer or with someone or something that is able to refer to the construct of computer in such a way as to make the learner aware of its properties. The referential theory, although explaining some significant aspects of language development, does not account for the multiple words associated with a singular meaning or cultural differences that influence meaning (Cohen & Plaskon, 1980).

Language acquisition has also been attributed to the use of imitation of adult speech. The belief is that the child hears the adult talk and then stores the language patterns for future use. This social learning theory of language emphasizes the parent's role as a language model in which children imitate both words and grammatical rules (Bandura, 1977).

Other theorists have insisted that reinforcement is the key to language development. According to this view, the child is believed to respond to external stimuli within the environment. Language is acquired through a stimulus-response paradigm in which language learning, like other forms of operant conditioning, is the direct result of reinforcement for one's behavior (Skinner, 1957). Language as a reinforcing agent begins with the mother's use of words to express affection and increases when other adults show attention and approval. Finally, as the child learns to use words to communicate needs, he or she is reinforced for mastery of the environment.

In too many cases the attempt to explain language acquisition was actually a means of explaining vocabulary development. Although children can learn a grammatical rule from imitation (Nelson, 1977), exact duplication of a response does not address the means by which children apply general rules to new utterances. Reinforcement and imitation clearly are involved in language acquisition but by themselves are unable to explain the complex use of language that children display.

Nativistic Orientation

In contrast to the theories of language development discussed above, the *generative theory* focuses on the innate language abilities of the child. In much the same way that a child learns to walk, so does the child learn to talk. Largely advanced by linguist Noam Chomsky (Chomsky,

1967), the generative theory (also known as a nativist or biological theory) states that the child deduces the language of the environment as a result of an intuitive mechanism, which Chomsky called the Language Acquisition Device (LAD). Language, it is believed, is not learned; rather, the LAD allows the child to abstract grammatical rules of the language to which he or she is exposed. Support for this nativistic orientation comes from the fact that children's language development is far in advance of their intellectual development. This theory explains why children are able to construct appropriate phrases and sentences they have never before heard. In fact, it is impractical to think that children are exposed to all possible phrases that they may at some time need to produce.

Important to this theory is the child's ability to distinguish differences expressed by sentences that are either similar in outward construction but varying in abstract meaning or that are different in construction but similar in meaning. The outward construction of a sentence is referred to as the surface structure and the underlying meaning as deep structure. In the following examples the differences the child must be able to discern in order to comprehend and produce language become evident.

1. Similar surface structure; different deep structure:

   "Sam plays dirty."
   "Sam plays in the dirt."

2. Different surface structure; similar deep structure:

   "Show me the picture."
   "Let me look at your painting."

Chomsky (1967) and others postulated that without an innate understanding of grammatical rules the child would be unable to handle language manipulations at such a sophisticated level. However, today even those who accept the idea that instinct may play a role in language development question Chomsky's assertion that any "sample of language encountered by an infant was enough for the LAD to dig down to the grammatical rules" (Bruner, 1978). The innate theory does not fully explain all aspects of a child's developing language. For instance, the following issues raised by Smith, Goodman, and Meredith (1970) illustrate the theory's weaknesses.

> 1. The innate theory does not sufficiently explain the errors that both learners and adults make in language (here an error is something that is outside the system of the language).

2. The theory does not account for or concern itself sufficiently with language change, a universal characteristic of language. The result is that significant differences between dialects are treated as unimportant.

3. The theory so minimizes the development of language as a learning process that it is counterproductive. If all children learn to talk, why be concerned about the process? (p. 17)

Psycholinguistic Orientation

Today, the psycholinguistic approach looks at the biological nature of language within the context of social interaction. Researchers and linguists are recognizing that language use during social interactions may play more of a role in language development than grammatical aspects (Bates, 1976; Bruner, 1978; Genishi, 1981). One interpretation of the psycholinguistic approach is espoused by Bruner (1978), who believes that the role of the mother, or primary caregiver, is the crucial component in the child's language acquisition. As Bruner (1978) states,

The child's entry into language is an entry into dialogue, and the dialogue is at first necessarily nonverbal and requires both members of the pair to interpret the communication and its intent. Their [mother and child] relationship is in the form of roles, and each "speech" is determined by a move of either partner. Initial control of the dialogue depends on the mother's interpretation, which is guided by a continually updated understanding of her child's competence. (p. 44)

The exchanges with the parent allow the child to develop an understanding of the nature of conversation and the context of language and eventually to learn the rules necessary for application. The turn-taking, the eye contact and the attention to another person involved in games, bouts of affection, and natural exchanges between the parent and child all build the foundation for developing language. The functions of language within the parent-child dyad are social interaction, requesting, indicating, and communicating possibilities such as imaginary roles or creatures (Bruner, 1978).

Bruner (1978), like others, is focused upon the pragmatic level of language development. Pragmatics is a key concept within the psycholinguistic orientation to language involving the use of language within a particular context. Another definition is offered by Muma (1978): "Pragmatics is a set of sociolinguistic rules one knows and uses in determining who says what to whom, how, why, when, and in what situations" (p. 137). The pragmatic aspect of language works as an organizing or governing component that binds the other psycholinguistic components of language together (Laughton & Hasenstab, 1986).

LANGUAGE ACQUISITION

Although the exact means by which children acquire language is still in question, there is a general understanding of the developmental sequence beginning with prelinguistic abilities and extending through mastery of complex language rules. Children of all cultures appear to go through the same stages, even though it is recognized that individual differences exist in children's rate and fluency of language acquisition.

Many factors affect language acquisition and must be considered when examining the variance among children. Three key factors identified by Marge (1972) are heredity, maturation, and environment. Heredity provides the range of possible language production, from poor to very good, that a child may demonstrate. Heredity includes intellectual components such as intelligence and innate language abilities as well as a child's anatomical and physiological structures concerned with speech production.

In addition to intellectual influences, a child's maturation subjects language development to biological considerations. As the child's neurological system develops, a readiness for language increases. Some evidence indicates that there is a sensitive period for language development extending from approximately age 2 to puberty. This sensitive period involves only first-language learning and does not relate to later language mastery. After puberty it would be extremely difficult, if not impossible, for a person to learn a first language (Bootzin et al., 1986).

The role of environmental influences in language acquisition has been recognized for some time. However, the extent of environmental effects is still an issue for debate. Language is not a natural result of growing up but rather a direct product of our environment interacting with our innate capacity to produce sounds. If left to grow in isolation, children do not acquire language. Environment has been held accountable for deprivation resulting in poorer language facility (Bernstein, 1961; Dennis, 1960; Skeels & Dye, 1939) as well as enrichment leading to language expansions (Heber & Garber, 1971; Skeels, 1966). Polloway and Smith (1982) delineate parenting practices, familial factors, social class variables, and bilingualism as specific environmental factors that play a significant part in the development of language. Figure 1.4 illustrates these various influences upon language development.

Prelinguistic Abilities

Language is believed to develop from the earliest cries of the newborn child who is signaling distress. The infant, at this point, is not intentionally trying to communicate, but such signaling informs the parents

FIGURE 1.4. Factors Influencing Language Development

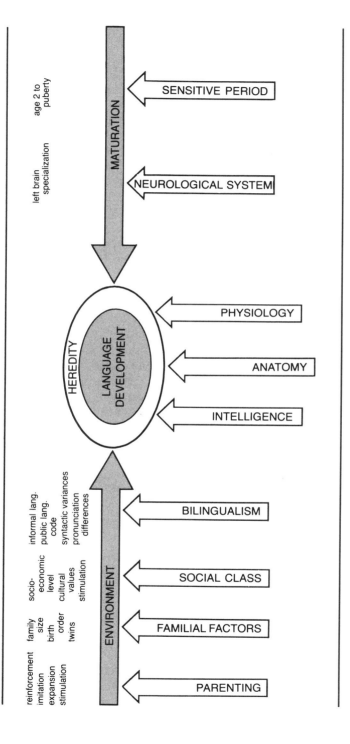

of a need for attention and results in specific actions. The child soon learns that cries are a means of controlling the environment (translated into adult action). As the randomness of the vocalizations decreases, babies develop distinct variations in their cries that can usually be interpreted by the parents as a cry resulting from hunger, pain, or anger (Wolff, 1969). It is only a matter of a few months before a baby begins to demonstrate other sounds, and clear babbling is evident by 6 months of age.

Also at an early age, children begin to sort out the language that they hear and to experience language in the context of the situation. This ability to understand receptive language originates with the infant's earliest discriminations of speech and nonspeech sounds and continues from vague associations to precise comprehension of large language units.

The following interaction illustrates the situational aspect of language in which the infant must learn to make associations.

Jeff, a 6-month-old, is in his crib crying when an adult appears. "Hi Sweetie, how's Mommy's best boy? Oh, you are wet. Let's change this diaper, then you and Daddy can play with a toy." Parent moves child to a change table while cooing to him and talking to a 4-year-old sibling who is playing with a doll. "Patrick, will you hand me a new box of Baby Wipes? Thanks. Okay, here's Daddy, and here is the new rattle. I'm going to read to Shana in the other room." (new voice is heard) "What do you see? Is it a rattle with a face of a clown? Make it shake. See, like this. Oh, what a big boy." The sound of the television in the next room can now be heard as the father continues to talk to Jeff.

This interaction is not a particularly complex or unique one. The baby has probably experienced many like it in the past and will repeatedly experience other variations of the situation in the future. Significant for language development is the child's ability to focus attention on some aspect of the encounter and from this to gain meaning. It is the context of the situation that will help the child to develop this comprehension. At first, meaning will relate to the experience as a whole (in this case to a general feeling of comfort) and later, as receptive abilities are refined, to individual aspects of the language situation (e.g., the change in voices and the change from talk about diapering to talk about play).

Although many vocalizations that occur during early babbling are apparently motor play, the intentional controlled production of speech sounds begins shortly after the 6-month mark, when children purposefully try to imitate the speech heard around them. The earliest babblings contain sounds found in all languages, whereas later babblings are clearly concentrations of the language to which the child is exposed.

The developing prelinguistic skills of the baby are also marked by the use of gestures and other nonverbal means of communication (Bootzin et al., 1986). The baby's use of a smile to keep an adult engaged in play is an early attempt at communication. Toward the end of the first year, children clearly use gestures to indicate needs or wants. A 10-month-old may stretch a hand out when wanting an adult to stay close by, or may look at a book and then combine an extended hand with a gutteral sound to indicate that the book is a wanted object. The intent to communicate is obvious, and the young child is using acceptable signals to convey meaning.

Finally, intonation begins to play a part in the child's developing language scheme. The variations in intonation signal a statement, a question, a demand, or a feeling such as joy or frustration. The patterns of intonation, like the patterns of sound, begin to resemble those the child hears (Bates, 1976). Intonation is an essential component of the language grammar the child will be expected to use. A simple variation in tone can change meaning dramatically, as is evident in many sarcastically spoken statements such as, "That's some present." Therefore, the mastery of intonation is important to the development of language itself.

The child eventually begins to participate in early language exchanges involving simple imitation of speech sounds and sound patterns. Known as *echolalia*, the imitation often occurs in a playful manner and coincides with an increase in the baby's desire to express needs and likes more fully.

Early Linguistic Abilities

The development of a one-word language system is the result of the baby's desire to meet his or her growing needs and to refine communication. Most often, the single words the baby uses are the names of objects and persons that have become important in the child's world. These understandable words, which appear about the time of the child's first birthday, are referred to as *holophrases*.

A holophrase is capable of serving multiple functions such as labeling, questioning, and demanding. For example the word *shoe* may mean: "That is a shoe," "Give me my shoe," or "Is that a shoe?" The function of the one-word sentence is indicated by variations in intonation, gestures, and situational variables. The success of the communication relies heavily on the ability of the listener to extract meaning from the situation. If, for instance, the child has lost a shoe, the listener would understand the word *shoe* to mean, "Put my shoe on."

An estimated 300 to 400 words make up the child's expressive vocabulary by the end of the second year (Lenneberg, 1966). The utility of this vocabulary is increased by the child's *overextension* of terms. That is, the child will commonly label similar but different objects with the same term. The 18-month-old may call all gray-haired older men "Grandpa," even though the child clearly recognizes his or her actual grandparent. Overextension allows the child to relate to an object for which he or she presently has no known label. As soon as a new and more appropriate label is learned, the correct substitution is made.

The child's ability with holophrases does not indicate his or her receptive vocabulary, which is far more advanced than the child's expressive skills. Interestingly, the use of holophrases does not indicate language competence, because by definition language involves the combining of words according to prescribed rules of grammar. Actual language competence appears only when the child has achieved a certain level of neurological maturation (Bootzin et al., 1986). Around the age of 2 the child will more frequently begin using two-word and three-word utterances. These word combinations, called *telegraphic speech*, are a highly condensed and efficient means of communicating. Basic function words are grouped together, with prepositions, articles, and conjunctions omitted. Therefore, a 2-year-old may say, "Go play," "Eat cookie," or "Read book Mommy."

By combining two-word phrases, the child can communicate a much more complex message ("Robyn tired. Go sleep"). From these simple grammatical combinations, the child develops the fundamentals of a rule-governed language system. Table 1.1 illustrates the sequence of two- and three-word constructions that the child masters (Brown, 1973). At this stage children can be observed saying simple sentences that they have never before heard, thus illustrating their ability to use grammatical rules to produce acceptable communication.

Advanced Linguistic Skills

The increase in a child's language facility is most evident in the expansion of expressive vocabulary. An average 1-year-old may have a speaking vocabulary of only 3 words; by 2 this has increased to 300 or more; and by age 5 the child is using a vocabulary of over 2,000 words (Smith, 1926).

The advance from telegraphic speech to the acquisition and mastery of complex language rules occurs fairly rapidly beginning with the third year of development, when the child demonstrates an understanding of word classes and incorporates inflectional and derivational forms. The child becomes an observant student of how adults use nouns and

TABLE 1.1. Types of Expressives Found in Two-Word Utterances

Meaning Category	Example
Identification	"Look ball." "Blue shoe."
Location	"Here car." "Bird up."
Recurrence	"More milk."
Negation	"No peas."
Nonexistence	"Milk all gone."
Possession	"Jeffrey car." "Daddy chair."
Agent, Object, Action	"Drink milk." "Mommy eat."
Attribution	"Green bug." "Go doggy."
Question	"What that?" "Why go?"

From Brown, R. (1973). *A first language: The early stages.* Cambridge, MA: Harvard University Press. Reprinted with permission.

verb endings in specific instances. The association of the utterance to the situation enables the child to acquire a basic set of rules that are generalizable to other situations.

Children are expected to apply rules such as word endings correctly even when there are exceptions to the rule. Children who at an early age may use an exception correctly will at a later time commonly make an error by *overgeneralizing* the basic rule. A noticeable example of overgeneralization is when children apply the rule for the past tense marker to irregular verb forms. As a result, the child may say, "I goed to the store yesterday." It is reassuring to note that the use of overgeneralizations is commonly dropped by the age of 7.

Advanced linguistic ability also includes the use of transformations in which surface structure is manipulated to convey specific meaning. A transformation is basically a set of rules that allows for a change in form without necessarily changing meaning. Examples of transformations are:

1. Give me the bucket.
   Give the bucket to me.

2. The boy chased the ball.
   The ball was chased by the boy.

3. The teacher told the girl to close the door.
   The teacher told her to close it.

Transformations provide variety to language by allowing for greater manipulation of word order. In some cases, as in the direct object transformation in example 3 above, transformations enable speakers to streamline the verbal message without altering the information (Cohen & Plaskon, 1980).

As the child reaches school age, language development becomes closely aligned with reading ability and the expansion of vocabulary and semantics which results from a variety of experiences. Language increases throughout the developmental period and coincides with the child's ability to use a range of cognitive processes such as discrimination, thinking, observing, and relating. The use of language allows children to gain control over the immediate environment as well as the future environments in which they will find themselves. Beyond age 9 the child will continue to show an increase in vocabulary and semantic ability as a result of experience. Although learning continues throughout school and beyond, the rate of learning will vary among individual children.

LANGUAGE AND THOUGHT

The relationship between the young child's developing language and cognitive processes begins with the child's world of experiences. As children interact with the family, shopkeepers, friends, and others who populate their world, they begin to search for and identify words that label, describe, request, or express a feeling related to some aspect of their experiences. By listening to the use of words and observing their associated consequences in actions, children begin to develop word concepts. As words are used in different and less familiar situations or ways, children expand their understanding and broaden their conceptual base.

The interrelationship between thinking and language is well acknowledged; however, the qualities of this relationship are often debated. Two theorists who have greatly influenced our understanding of the interplay of language and thought are the Swiss psychologist, Jean Piaget, and the Russian psychologist, Lev Vygotsky. Although not always contradictory, their views of language and thought do contain certain basic differences.

Piaget, who is a stage theorist, studied language within the context of children's developing cognitive abilities. Language, in Piaget's view, is secondary to abstract symbolic reasoning, and although language is fundamental to some learning, it is not so to all learning.

Piaget recognizes two types of speech in the young child: communicative, which is intended to transmit information, and egocentric, which is noncommunicative. Egocentric speech appears to be pleasurable for the young child and may result from the child's inability to separate words from acts. A young child's facility with big words resembling adult speech does not always indicate that he or she has developed the mental structures to deal with information and logic at an advanced level. According to Piaget, it is not possible to push a child from one stage to the next in language or in any other kind of learning (Kean & Personke, 1976).

Piaget perceives language learning as just one of many different kinds of learning. As the child develops, language and abstract symbolic learning become more closely aligned. The child is more influenced by formal language as a result of his or her growing ability to handle abstractions. Language becomes a major transmitter of thought, especially as the child begins to deal with the abstract or with the hypothetical possibilities of the future rather than with the concrete and immediate (Charles, 1974).

Vygotsky differs from Piaget in that he views language and thought as a unified process. Accordingly, language is involved in all cognitive processes, and, therefore, thought cannot occur without language. The young child's development from egocentric speech to inner speech at about school age is merely a continuation of the same function. The mental structures for each are similar and change only in that as the child matures, thought becomes more internalized (Vygotsky, 1962).

The Role of Language in Children's Thinking

Language and thought become more and more interrelated as the child grows. Three cognitive characteristics of the young child illustrate this developing relationship between language and thought: (a) egocentrism, (b) decentration, and (c) transformation (Yawkey et al., 1981). The maturing child's language and thinking increase qualitatively as well as quantitatively.

The young child sees the world from a singular view: directly from his or her own standpoint. Known as *egocentricity*, this characteristic denotes the child's inability to take the perspective of another person. All experiences are interpreted only from the point of view of the child. This means that when a book is dropped on a friend's toe and the friend cries, the child who dropped the book is unable to perceive of the experience as a painful one, since his or her observation was not painful. For the child to place himself or herself in the situation of another, it is necessary to develop abstract thought, and this has not yet been achieved. In addition, the egocentric child is unable to describe how someone else might feel in a situation.

The second characteristic, *decentration*, concerns the young child's focus upon superficial stimuli rather than attention to the salient characteristics. For instance, the child who is asked to watch a cook pour two half-cups of liquid, one into a tall glass and one into a cup, will not be able to determine that they are equal amounts of liquid. Instead, the child will respond when asked which has more liquid that, "The glass does." The child observed that the glass is taller and, therefore, must contain more liquid. It is interesting that this response will occur even though the child has observed the equal amounts that were poured. The child at this stage of development is unable to intellectually conceptualize and attend to the relevant feature of the amount of liquid and instead focuses on the irrelevant aspect of the container size. The child is not able to manipulate language and thought to frame the situation appropriately.

Transformation, the ability to closely associate a series of successive events across time and space, is the third cognitive trait that illustrates the relatedness of language and thought. The 3- or 4-year-old child altogether misses the relationships between events and views them instead as separate from each other. This is evident when a child sees an elephant walking outside at the zoo and later sees an elephant eating inside and exclaims that there are two big elephants. To the child who has seen the elephants at different times and places, the elephant inside cannot be the same as the one that was originally outside. The child lacks the conceptualization skills to associate these two events.

The growing child's thinking is characterized by nonegocentric thought, centration, and transformation abilities. The link between language and thought is obvious in the child's skill at building functional concepts and developing cognitive facility. It is apparent that language cannot be separated from the development of thinking and from the contexts in which it occurs (Genishi, 1981). As Jerome Bruner (1972) so aptly stated, "in children between the ages of four and twelve, language comes to play an increasingly powerful role as an instrument of knowing" (p. 165).

Developing Conceptual Understanding and Use

The use of concepts helps us to manage the multiple and complex stimuli found in our environment. In a sense, concepts are a simplification system which develops from the child's experiences and continues to grow as those experiences broaden. As children learn to attach symbolic labels to the objects, situations, feelings, and events around them, their facility with language increases. In this same way words become part of the thinking process. Conceptual theory applies to both concept formation, which involves the development of meaning, and concept use, which implies function. A concept exists as an abstraction only until language is applied to it, allowing us to refer to it, analyze it, and relate it to other concepts. Table 1.2 presents a possible sequence of manipulations the young learner goes through in the formation of a concept.

It is often asked, "Which comes first, the label or the concept?" According to most theorists, although the word is used to symbolize a concept, it will be correctly found in the child's vocabulary only after the concept is formed. That is, the concept precedes the linguistic label. A child will not use the terms *big* and *small*, for instance until he or she has a relative appreciation of size differences. Adults, however, have observed that a child's facility with words often predates the understanding of a concept. This is evident in situations in which the child uses a word but is unable to correctly apply the concept. For instance, a child playing a game of *Stop and Go* may cry, "Stop," but keep on going. Such occurrences have also been researched in studies of Piaget's concept of conservation, when children could describe the sequence but still could not conserve (DeStefano, 1978).

Concepts are formed, modified, enlarged, and used in an endless chain as the child's thinking continues to develop. It is interesting to note that concepts are inexact in that one person's understanding of a concept may vary from that of another person. However, the use of the concept will still permit communication, because, at the very least, we all hold a minimal level of shared understanding. A parent and an educator may not totally agree on the concept of learning, but what they do share allows them to discuss the child's progress. It is when our minimal levels of concept understanding do not match that we come into conflict.

Concepts perform many functions, including (a) organizing and simplifying learning, (b) facilitating communication, and (c) separating reality from fantasy. What makes up a concept is as important as what a concept does. Basically, a concept consists of a symbolic label, critical attributes (characteristics that are always associated with a member of the concept group), and rules (the means of combining attributes to

TABLE 1.2. The Process of Concept Formation

Step	Process	Example
Identification	The experience or thing is perceived as distinct from other experiences.	Child touches a *hot* stove and experiences *hot*.
Labeling	The identified experience or thing is given a name. Names may change as the concept is more accurately defined.	Child labels the stove as *hot*.
Description	The relevant features of the developing concept are isolated and recognized. These are the concept's critical attributes.	The child recognizes the tactile sensation of extreme heat and resulting discomfort.
Comparison and contrast	The learner relates the new experience to past experiences by the comparison of critical attributes. This may result in a modification of the description.	Child compares the sensation of *hot* stove to *hot* water and to touching other things such as a cup or cold snow.
Classification	The learner classifies the concept along with other experiences sharing the critical attributes.	*Hot* applies to stoves, water, food, fire, etc.
Relating	Covering all aspects of concept formation, the new concept is further associated with other experiences and extended to determine such things as quality, cause and effect, or implications.	*Hot* results from heat being applied to a "thing."
Manipulation	Concept usage or what the learner does with the concept is the result of this last step. Manipulation as well as the other step processes occurs through language.	Child thinks, "I will not touch the pot on the stove because it is *hot*."

Adapted with permission from Kean, J. M. & Personke, C. (1976). *The language arts: Teaching and learning in the elementary schools*. New York: St. Martin's Press, pp. 85–86.

describe the concept class). Examples of concepts delineated by attributes and rules are listed below.

Concept Label: Chair

Critical Attributes
1. furniture
2. used for sitting
3. has a seat and a back
4. seat raised off floor

Concept Rule: A chair is a piece of furniture that has a seat and a back which are raised off the floor and used for sitting.

Concept Label: Word

Critical Attributes
1. unit of speech that can stand alone
2. conveys meaning
3. made up of sound(s) or letters

Concept Rule: A word is the smallest unit of speech that, standing alone, has meaning and is made up of sound or sounds which are represented by letters in written form.

The way we classify concepts provides a piece of information about the parameters of the concept class. According to Martorella (1986), there are four primary ways to classify concepts: degrees of concreteness (concrete, abstract); context in which the concept is learned (formal or informal learning setting); nature of the critical attributes (singular combination, multiple combination, or relational); and form or manner in which the concept is learned (enactive, iconic, or symbolic). The teacher needs to analyze the concept to delineate any possible learning problems and to determine the best way to present the concept to reduce learning difficulty.

Although we all independently learn concepts in our daily lives, and continue to do so as we mature, concept teaching is fundamental to classroom instruction. During the early acquisition of a concept, the choice of examples and how the teacher models the use of the concept are two essential instructional features. Becker, Engelmann and Thomas (1975) specify that an efficient concept teaching program must meet four requirements.

> 1. A set of positive and negative instances [examples and nonexamples] is required. A concept cannot be taught with a single positive and a single negative instance, because any specific instance of a concept can be an example of another concept.

2. The set of instances should be selected so that *all* positive instances possess *all* relevant concept characteristics, and *all* negative instances possess *some* or *none* of these characteristics. If this is not done the teaching will provide contradictory information.

3. Irrelevant characteristics *within* positive and negative instances must be varied. Otherwise, a misrule may be taught.

4. The program must be cumulative so that all critical discriminations in the enlarging set of concepts are taught. A program cannot just teach something once and forget it. (p. 69)

Examples of a specific concept are as important as nonexamples taken from other concepts. Thus, an electric typewriter is significant not only as a member of the class of typewriters but as an example of what is not a word processor, a book, or a pencil.

Important for the purpose of instruction is that concepts allow the development of competencies that go beyond those that have been taught in specific tasks. The aim of concept teaching is to help the student acquire a *general case*. The general case denotes the application of the concept to items that have never been specifically taught. In other words, by learning only some members of the concept class of *dog*, the child can identify all unfamiliar animals that belong to the animal class, *dog*. Perhaps a more educationally relevant example is the concept of *division*. After the teacher illustrates a relatively limited number of problems, the student learns when it is appropriate to apply the concept of division to break a large unit into equal smaller units.

The most accurate test for whether a child has learned the general case and is able to apply the concept independently is to present concept instances which have not been used in the instructional sequence. A general case is established if the learner can correctly identify the unfamiliar items (Becker, Engelmann & Thomas, 1975). At a more advanced level of concept understanding the child should be able to relate the concept to other concepts (an island differs from a lake in that the former is surrounded by water, while the latter is surrounded by land) and/or apply the concept in a novel way ("Each man is an island . . ."). The teacher will want to test the level of concept understanding in order to ascertain the success of the instructional program and the need for further instruction.

LANGUAGE WITHIN THE SCHOOL ENVIRONMENT

The classroom represents a major portion of the child's daily environment, so the experiences encountered there should be designed with the intent of increasing language facility. Four essential elements of a

FIGURE 1.5. Language Environment Checklist

	Yes	No
A. Range of Experiences		
1. Does the experience build upon a previous experience?	___	___
2. Does the experience increase understanding of a new concept?	___	___
3. Does the experience increase vocabulary?	___	___
B. Meaningfulness of Instruction		
1. Can the learner state a reason for learning this skill/ concept?	___	___
2. Is there a plan for generalization of the skill or concept?	___	___
C. Learner participation		
1. Does the learner have sufficient practice trials for learning the skill or concept?	___	___
2. Does the learner have opportunity to apply the skill/ concept?	___	___
3. Does the learner receive corrective feedback when an error is made?	___	___
Modeling		
1. Are enough positive examples of the skill/concept demonstrated for the learner during initial instruction?	___	___
2. Is the skill/concept used as part of the instructional routine?	___	___

positive language environment in the classroom are (a) a range of experiences designed so that one often builds upon another, (b) meaningfulness of instruction, (c) active participation by all learners, and (d) appropriate modeling of language and language-related skills by the teacher and other leaders. The checklist provided in Figure 1.5 will help the teacher determine the overall appropriateness of the language environment within the classroom instructional routine.

The classroom that presents a positive language environment is one in which language is considered fundamental to the overall curriculum. As has already been indicated, language expansion results from experiences and from the opportunities to use language skills. Communication, which is the sharing of ideas and other personal thoughts, is increased if it occurs within an accepting environment which, although corrective at times, is never critical.

WHAT ARE THE LANGUAGE ARTS?

The language arts, sometimes referred to as the communication arts, are the basis of learning. They represent not only the input mechanism by which we receive information but also our means of expressing thought and understanding. The need for communication within any society emphasizes the necessity that each individual develop competence in oral and written forms of language. Those who, for one reason or another, do not develop such competence are at a distinct disadvantage and are often relegated to a lower status.

Anyone who has ever watched a child grow and learn to communicate through the early school years will be able to describe the hierarchical order of the language arts: listening, speaking, reading, and writing. Underlying these four broad areas is the learner's competence in language and thinking. These interactive components of the language arts are further illustrated in Figure 1.6, which more clearly shows the input and output aspects of each process. Listening and reading are considered receptive skills, while speaking and writing are productive in nature.

THE INTERRELATEDNESS OF LANGUAGE SKILLS

There is an obvious relationship between the development of language skills and the corresponding language arts. Table 1.3 highlights this association. The knowledge inherent in each language area becomes the basis for the instruction of individual language arts skills.

The benefit of learning to spell is appreciated only if the student is given the opportunity to write, listening in order to respond in a discussion is as important as listening for enjoyment, and the advantages of writing are discovered only through the wonders of reading. The overlap among the different areas of the language arts demonstrates their interrelatedness and emphasizes the necessity of providing an integrated curriculum. Unfortunately, language arts research and practice are often at odds. Although the integration of language skills is accepted as the key component of successful teaching, the individual language arts areas are more easily discussed as separate units. It is recognized that this separation is an artificial one, and throughout the reading of this text, or any other pertaining to language arts, the reader is cautioned to interpret the information in light of its importance to a total program. The classroom practice of segregating the language arts

FIGURE 1.6. Interrelationships of the Language Skills

	SPOKEN LANGUAGE		WRITTEN LANGUAGE	
	LISTENING (RECEIVED)	SPEAKING (PRODUCED)	READING (RECEIVED)	WRITING (PRODUCED)
	Hearing phonemes (language sounds)	Producing sounds		
	Understanding intonation meaning	Using intonation effectively		
	Discriminating among sounds	Producing meaningful words		
	Associating adult utterances with meaning	Speaking 2-word sentences grammatically		
	Understanding words	Speaking longer, more complex utterances	Seeing adults read	Observing adults writing
	Understanding more complex structures	Learning to modify speech to fit listener, context	Hearing stories read from books	"Scribble" writing
	Listening to stories	Learning appropriate registers	"Pretend reading" from books	
FORMAL SCHOOLING				
	Advanced listening skills	Learning to speak formally to group	Associating sounds with symbols	Learning to write symbols
	Continued development of knowledge of language	Polishing speaking abilities	Associating symbols with meaning (words)	Writing words
				Writing sentences
			Learning meaning of punctuation	Using punctuation
			Reading fluently	Learning different forms of writing
			Using advanced reading skills	Polishing writing skills
			Reading for pleasure and information independently	Writing with style

From Tiedt, M. (1983). *The language arts handbook.* Englewood Cliffs, NJ: Prentice-Hall, p. 8. Reprinted with permission of Prentice-Hall, Inc.

TABLE 1.3. Relationship Between Acquisition of Language Facility and the Language Arts

Area of Language Acquisition	Related Language Arts Area
Acquisition of syntax	Oral language development Question asking Functional writing skills Reading: comprehension
Development of semantics and pragmatics	Listening skills Vocabulary development Nonverbal language skills Reading: comprehension
Development of phonology	Spelling ability Reading: decoding

Adapted with permission from Cohen, S. B., & Plaskon, S. P. (1980). *Language arts for the mildly handicapped.* Columbus, OH: Charles E. Merrill, p. 78.

into individual skills as evidenced by 20-minute reading groups, 15-minute writing exercises, and a 5-minute handwriting activity is "probably a good indication of how teachers prefer to teach, rather than how children learn communication skills" (Genishi, 1981, p. 112).

HANDICAPPED
LEARNERS AND
LANGUAGE
INSTRUCTION

Language and the language arts constitute the core of the individual instructional programs provided to the majority of students identified as handicapped or remedial learners. Difficulties in the acquisition and refinement of oral language abilities, in the development of competence in reading, and in the achievement of proficiency in written communication represent major concerns for teachers intent on maximizing the success of their students in academic and social domains and ultimately in life adjustment. The purpose of this chapter is to provide an introduction to educational programming for students who have experienced problems within the various language domains. Each of the succeeding chapters focuses on specific methodology within a given language arts curricular area or for a particular population.

The chapter is divided into three major sections. The initial section provides an orientation to the population of handicapped and remedial learners for whom the book has been targeted. The second section is a discussion of the development of individualized education programs

(IEPs) for exceptional learners. The third section emphasizes selected general tenets of instruction that have relevance across the curriculum.

POPULATION PARAMETERS

Language-related problems are clearly not restricted to any one category or cluster of categories of exceptional individuals. Everyone can personally identify specific problems that they have encountered themselves within the broad reach of communicative skills, whether verbal expression difficulties such as getting lost in the middle of a sentence, slow or labored rate of reading, poor penmanship, erratic spelling habits, or writer's block coinciding with an attempt to write an introduction to a chapter. Such problems may have had their onset in childhood or later in life, may have been minor or serious, and may have been transitory or chronic. As a result we all have a basis for relating to those individuals who experience problems within this domain, even though obviously most persons either overcome their problem or develop compensatory strategies.

The target of this book is a heterogeneous population for whom language problems have contributed significantly to their difficulties in academic and social development. The language difficulties experienced by this group may have serious vocational implications as well. These students have been served at some point in their educational careers by special education and/or remedial services. The population includes (a) those individuals who are severely cognitively impaired and have serious problems in learning to communicate, even with relatively primitive systems of gesturing or other nonverbal means, (b) elementary school children struggling to comprehend reading assignments necessary for promotion to the next grade, and (c) bright, well-spoken adolescents and young adults whose writing deficits nevertheless prevent them from completing secondary or postsecondary diploma or degree requirements.

To provide information related to effective educational programming that is relevant to the problems experienced by students in the language domain, we have moved beyond the traditional—and somewhat awkward—structure of categorical special education. Thus, rather than deal with specific programs designed for mildly retarded or learning disabled students, for example, the core of the book (Part II, Chapters 3–9) essentially focuses on instructional approaches. These approaches are selected for their applicability to students who are considered mildly and moderately handicapped or who are currently being served in a remedial academic program. This population is further defined and described below. Part III then focuses on specific populations which can be grouped logically and which have language instruction needs that are likely to be different from those of the mildly/moderately handicapped population. These latter subgroups are organized in a way that facilitates discussion of programming within an educationally relevant framework. They include preschool handicapped, severely handicapped, sensory impaired, and gifted individuals and disabled adults. Each of these populations is defined and identified in the chapters in Part III. We turn our attention now to a discussion of those mildly/moderately handicapped and remedial students for whom the core of the book was specifically designed.

Mildly/Moderately Handicapped Learners

The generic term *mildly/moderately handicapped* has been used increasingly in recent years to refer to students who have been identified under the traditional special education categories of educable mental retardation, learning disabilities, and emotional disturbance/behavior disorders. It is important to note that the term is being used in this text as an argument neither for nor against the multifaceted issue of noncategorical special education. Rather, it acknowledges that students from among these three groups have a substantial overlap in educational needs in the area of language development; this would make the differential presentation of instructional curriculum and methods unnecessarily lengthy while at the same time redundant. Eloquent cases have been made both supporting the presumption of similarity of characteristics and needs of these three groups (e.g., Cohen & Plaskon, 1980; Hallahan & Kauffman, 1976, 1977) as well as questioning the congruence of needs (e.g., Polloway, Epstein, Polloway, Patton, & Ball, 1986). However, few of these arguments can detract from the basic premise that teachers should accumulate a substantial store of methods and materials from which to select to achieve a truly individualized program for each student. Regardless of whether the overlap among categories is substantial or limited, the reality in terms of programming needs must ultimately be based on the characteristics of the individual learner.

Let us return to the term mildly/moderately handicapped. Dependent on state identification guidelines, these students have been selected for special services within the respective categorical groups based typically on the following general criteria.

1. *Mental retardation:* subaverage general intellectual functioning (an IQ of approximately 70 or below) accompanied by deficits in adaptive behavior (see Grossman, 1983);

2. *Learning disabilities:* a discrepancy between educational achievement and expected levels of competency related to cognitive, linguistic, or perceptual processing variables not attributed to other specific handicapping conditions (see Federal Register, December 29, 1977, p. 65083);

3. *Emotional disturbance/behavior disorders:* demonstrated patterns of characteristics such as learning deficits, problems in maintaining satisfactory relationships, display of inappropriate behaviors in specified circumstances, a generally unhappy or depressed mood, and/or development of psychosomatic responses to personal or school problems (see Bower, 1981).

For the purpose of this book, of greater concern than traditional definitions are the specific characteristics of mildly/moderately handicapped individuals that have implications for language instruction and that are found more frequently among these three categories of children than in the general population. Consider the list below, which has been developed from a review of these traits provided by Cohen and Plaskon (1980), based in part on the work of Dexter (1977), Pasanella and Volkmor (1977), and Neff and Pilch (1976). The list represents a set of characteristics that *may* be found in students identified as mildly/moderately handicapped.

1. Cognitive Difficulties
   ❑ Learns at a reduced rate of speed
   ❑ Relies on concrete rather than abstract learning
   ❑ Has difficulty retaining information
   ❑ Lacks judgment and common sense
   ❑ Has a short attention span
   ❑ Has difficulty attending to relevant task dimensions; is distractible
   ❑ Experiences problems in learning basic concepts and forming conceptual relationships
   ❑ Is often unsuccessful at applying previous learning to new situation; generalizes poorly
   ❑ Acquires skills inefficiently and lacks strategies for problem solving

2. Basic Communication Problems
   ❑ Has difficulty with verbal expression
   ❑ Experiences problems with various aspects of verbal reception
   ❑ May find it difficult to carry on a conversation
   ❑ Does not respond in complete thoughts or may get "lost" in sentences

❑ Has problems expressing thoughts in written form
❑ Has difficulty remembering words and/or word attack strategies
❑ Experiences problems comprehending what was previously read

3. Auditory Problems
   ❑ Attends inefficiently when attempting to process verbal directions
   ❑ Gives inappropriate responses to verbal questions
   ❑ Prefers visual tasks that require very little listening
   ❑ Cannot determine the main idea from orally presented material
   ❑ Experiences difficulty in discriminating between similar sounding words (e.g., tap-top; pen-pin)
   ❑ Cannot accurately retell a story that was previously read out loud
   ❑ Has difficulty identifying and producing rhyming words
   ❑ Omits common prefixes and suffixes
   ❑ Cannot accurately repeat a series of words or digits that were orally presented
   ❑ Has trouble writing from dictation

4. Visual-Motor Problems
   ❑ Is easily distracted by visual stimuli
   ❑ Has difficulty discriminating shapes, colors, size relationships
   ❑ Has difficulty coordinating visual-motor skills for handwriting
   ❑ Makes letter reversals in handwriting
   ❑ Cannot remember the characteristics of something previously seen
   ❑ Reacts to parts rather than to the whole (e.g., letters rather than words)
   ❑ May have difficulty recognizing common objects or demonstrating their function
   ❑ Confuses similar letters (m-n; d-b; p-g; f-t) and numbers (1-7; 3-8, 6-9).

5. Social-Emotional Problems (related to communicative competence)
   ❑ May not be able to sit still for an appropriate amount of time; daydreams excessively
   ❑ Has difficulty making new friends
   ❑ Is aggressive toward peers
   ❑ Is withdrawn or hypoactive
   ❑ Is anxious when about to try new things
   ❑ Displays inconsistent behavior and experiences frequent mood changes
   ❑ Engages in excessive body movement or other self-stimulating activities

❑ Does not work well within a group setting
❑ Engages in inappropriate or excessive verbalizations
❑ Has difficulty ingratiating self to others

Remedial Learners

The population of students referred to as remedial learners represents a poorly defined group whose only common characteristic is likely to be that all have experienced difficulties related to school achievement. As mentioned earlier, among the most common areas of school achievement deficits are those within the various language domains.

The category of remedial learners is included as a target group of learners for this book for several reasons. First, slow learners now occupy what has already been termed the DMZ or "no man's land" between service delivery systems (Forness & Kavale, 1984; Smith, Polloway, & Smith, 1978). This diagnostic wasteland has been formed, and in some cases cultivated, by arbitrary adherence to IQ cutoff scores. Under such a system, an IQ of 70, for example, may be adopted as the formal ceiling score for mental retardation, while 80 or 85 may be used as a rigid basal level for learning disabilities. For those students who fall between the cracks, learning characteristics and educational needs may be quite consistent with the general population of mildly/moderately handicapped students, even though they are not eligible for services.

The second reason remedial learners are included within the focus of this text is that an increasing number of such individuals are students who have been declassified from specific special education categories. Most notable among those declassified are individuals formerly identified as mildly retarded. Recent research and government data (e.g., Algozzine & Korinek, 1985; Polloway & Smith, 1987; Reschly, in press) have described the decreasing number of students in programs serving this population and the coincidental likelihood that these students are simply placed in regular class programs. It is instructive to consider the appraisal of these students offered by MacMillan (in press), who describes this declassified population as "marginal achievers." It is clear that instructional adaptations and curricular modifications will frequently be necessary for this population to be successful; therefore, the methods described in this section of the book may prove relevant to their educational needs.

A third reason the group of remedial learners is included herein is that many of the methods and curricular modifications presented represent effective instructional techniques that can lead to the prevention of serious difficulties and, thus, to the avoidance of categorical placement within special education. Given the increasing numbers of individuals being served in programs for the learning disabled (e.g., Algozzine & Korinek, 1985; Gerber, 1984), it is apparent that the quality of education provided to slow learning children in the regular classroom must be enhanced to ensure that large numbers of otherwise poor achieving students are not routinely identified as learning disabled to permit them access to appropriate instruction. Among the many effective prereferral strategies that can help alleviate learning problems and thus result in the reduction of prevalence figures (e.g., Nevin & Thousand, in press), the improvement of instructional methods in the regular classroom is of primary significance.

The nature of *specialized* instructional programs must always be considered within the context of the *general* educational process. Obviously, before becoming concerned about the mastery of specialized techniques, one must first simply be able to teach. The best attributes of the special education program, especially as related to mildly/moderately handicapped and remedial learners, are essentially:

❑ the primary focus on the needs of the individual learner;

❑ curriculum designed to be relevant to students' current and long-term educational needs;

❑ an ever-expanding repertoire of empirically validated alternative teaching methods;

❑ an emphasis on the need for intensive instruction characterized by a high degree of teacher responsibility for learner outcomes.

Other than these considerations, the myriad of intangible traits that differentiate poor or mediocre from effective instruction apply as much to general as to special education.

INDIVIDUALIZED EDUCATION PROGRAMS

Subsequent to the passage of Public Law 94-142, the policy of developing Individualized Education Programs (IEPs) was mandated for all students enrolled in special education. The IEP was intended to establish a highly individualized structure for learning which would be dependent on the specific needs of each child. Although the concept has been interpreted and implemented, and used and abused, in a wide variety of ways, it nevertheless still serves as the appropriate beginning point for the discussion of instructional programming for students with exceptional learning needs.

The IEP can serve a variety of functions; three of these in particular offer the greatest benefit to teachers and students. First, by encouraging a focus on specific goals set for the child, the IEP can provide instructional direction. In this way the assignment of random exercises which do not have merit for the student's overall progress can be avoided, and programs can be seen within the context of long-term needs and thus provide appropriate instructional sequences.

Second, through the setting up of short-term objectives, IEPs provide a means of evaluating the effectiveness and efficiency of the teacher. In this sense, they introduce the concept of accountability into special education.

Finally, the IEP may increase communication among teacher, student, and family. No clear distinction should exist between home and school, because parental involvement should be an integral part of the IEP process.

To integrate the IEP into the prescriptive instructional process commonly used in the special education classroom, the following steps should be taken. Following the initial identification of students (child find), assessment data are collected. Next, the IEP is written specifying both the placement of the child (to be in the least restrictive and most appropriate setting) and the instructional goals and objectives. Following this, annual evaluation of placement and goals should occur with revision made frequently as needed.

In writing individual educational programs, a number of essential factors must be incorporated according to P.L. 94-142:

1. present level of performance

2. annual instructional goals

3. short-term objectives

4. statement of special services to be provided

5. rationale for special programs, consistent with the concept of the least restrictive alternative

6. schedule for initiation of services

7. schedule for evaluation of objectives

Of those factors listed, three—level of performance, annual goals, and short-term objectives—are essential for a functional IEP. Though no official structure for these three elements was established under the law, the following guidelines serve as a basis for the writing of the components. Each of the components of the IEP is illustrated in the sample provided in the appendix at the end of this chapter.

Performance Levels

The level of performance statements should clearly identify the student's present functioning level so that future goals can be established. Performance levels serve as a basis for both annual goals and short-term objectives, so they should be stated for all areas for which special instructional services will be provided. Included in these areas may be academic skills, overt behavioral patterns, self-help skills, vocational talents, and communication abilities and disabilities.

Performance levels represent summary statements which can take the form of formal test scores, descriptions of behaviors, or identification of specific abilities in relation to a sequence of skills in a specific area. In developing the statements, it is important to attend to two specific concerns. Pertinent and sufficient data must be supplied so that an appropriate basis is provided for setting annual goals; second, the statements should emphasize the positive aspects of the student rather than focusing on negative traits.

Annual Goals

The second part of the IEP of special importance is the section listing the *annual goals* (AGs). These goals, based on the previously stated performance levels, serve as long-term predictors of successes the child is anticipated to experience throughout the year. Annual goals are basically an "educated guess" on the part of the teacher as to what the child will accomplish and the degree to which he or she will be successful. These goals can be based on the child's chronological age, past learning profiles, and/or recent learning history.

The following example illustrates the relationship between performance levels and annual goals. If the current level of performance statement was *identifies only three initial consonant sounds* (t, g, b), then possible annual goals could include *identifies all initial consonant sounds* and/or *identifies short vowel sounds within cvc trigrams* (e.g., cat, pot).

When writing annual goals, three considerations should be made. First, these goals should be *positive*—providing an applicable guide for sequential instruction. It is important to restrict the use of negative comments so that beneficial communication will result among special educators, regular classroom teachers, students, and parents.

Next, annual goals should be *measurable*. To achieve this, they should incorporate precise, behavioral terms that indicate action, avoid difficulties in evaluation, and promote agreement among observers. The goals should be stated so it can be clearly determined that the goal has/ has not been reached.

Third, annual goals should be *student oriented*. The rationale for this attribute is that the only measure of success is what the student has learned, not what he or she allegedly has been taught. An example of an acceptable goal here could be: "The child will correctly differentiate between the letters /b/ and /d/." An unacceptable goal might be: "The child will be taught the difference between the letters /b/ and /d/."

Short-Term Objectives

The final major step involved in the construction of the IEP is the development of the *short-term objectives* (STOs). The STOs function as a path toward the achievement of the annual goals identified for each student. They supply the teacher with an outline to be followed during instruction to reach the annual goals. STOs are not, however, isolated skills; they must be consistent with the instructional direction provided by the annual goals. They essentially are stricter in their definition than those defined within the annual goals. Like annual goals, STOs should be measurable, student oriented, and positive; they also should reflect close attention to stated criteria for task success.

Because they are so closely related, it is important to restate the significance of the need for consistency between short-term objectives and annual goals. Since the STOs represent steps in the annual goal process, they should reflect major instructional accomplishments between the current levels of performance and the final goals. To accomplish this, three to eight objectives are usually identified and listed, each representing a skill that might be achievable in a time frame of perhaps one or two weeks to several months. The development of objectives from annual goals is a form of task analysis. In other words, STOs are formed through the breaking down of a more general goal (AG) into its more specific components (STOs). By extending this process, the teacher can then develop a unified set of objectives upon which weekly and daily instruction can be based.

The sample IEP at the end of this chapter is provided as a model. Although the format used for IEPs varies among states and localities, the necessary components are clearly included in this outline of a student's program.

INSTRUCTIONAL PROGRAMMING

The purpose of this section is to highlight a variety of principles and related considerations for the planning and implementation of instructional programs. This discussion emphasizes selected strategies of general relevance which can provide a basis for the specifically focused discussions within the remaining chapters of the book.

Two warnings are in order at this point. First, the list that follows makes no claims of being all-inclusive; rather, it is a representative sample of those strategies and concerns that are particularly significant for programming. Second, although the emphasis of this text is on the various domains of language, most of the basic principles of teaching apply across curricular content areas; therefore, while the following strategies are relevant to language programming, there is no presumption of exclusivity. The topics to be addressed include principles of assessment, elements of direct instruction, considerations with regard to grouping, stages of learning, other components of effective instruction and applications of the computer to instruction. The reader interested in further exploring general methods for assessment and instruction for handicapped students is referred to the following texts on assessment or instruction: Alley and Deshler (1979); Hammill and Bartel (1986); Otto and Smith (1980); Polloway, Payne, Patton, and Payne (1985); Wallace and Kauffman (1986); and Wallace and Larsen (1978).

Principles of Assessment

Assessment for instructional purposes is that portion of the evaluative process that moves beyond identification, classification, and labeling to focus on the data directly relevant to the implementation of intervention programs. For handicapped students and those not so-identified who nevertheless are experiencing difficulties in learning, it is important to match assessment data as closely as possible to the instructional program to be implemented. The discussion below provides an introduction to various approaches to assessment which will be further elaborated on in subsequent chapters.

Formal testing is the first step in the overall assessment sequence. In each of the chapters to follow, specific formal instruments that have been developed within particular curricular domains or for specific populations will be identified. However, in each case these formal tests should be seen primarily as beginning points within the evaluative process. Although they may present the teacher with information that assists in general decision making about programs to be implemented, such tests rarely provide the type of specific data that have direct implications for ongoing instruction. Table 2.1, adapted from Wallace and Kauffman (1986), provides a brief outline of the advantages and limitations of standardized, formal instruments.

To be useful for teaching, the primary source of information must be informal, daily assessment. Common and functional informal bases for assessment data include: the analysis of language samples, information relative to skill hierarchies, task analytic data, information gathered through the prescriptive teaching cycle, error analysis, and direct

TABLE 2.1. Standardized Tests: Advantages and Disadvantages

Advantages	Disadvantages
1. Comparisons to various normative groups	1. Specific teaching information and implications frequently lacking
2. Standardized procedures for administration and scoring	2. Risk of overgeneralizations and misuse of findings
3. Provides possible basis for pre/post-analysis to illustrate growth/learning	3. May discriminate against various groups with a given cultural background
4. Interpretation frequently aided by manual for examiner	4. Poor reliability and low validity found in some cases
5. Provide a measure of variability across specific areas	5. May lead to an emphasis on total scores rather than on the analysis of individual items
6. May include statistical data on reliability and validity	6. In some cases provide only, at best, confirmation of previously assumed hypotheses

Adapted from Wallace, G., & Kauffman, J. M. (1986). *Teaching students with learning and behavior problems* (3rd ed.). Columbus, OH: Charles E. Merrill. Reprinted with permission of Merrill Publishing Co.

and daily behavioral measurement. Each of these sources of data is discussed briefly below.

Analysis of Language Samples. The primary basis for language assessment as related to oral expression comes from spontaneous and elicited language samples. As opposed to the use of formal assessment instruments, the analysis of language samples obviously provides a potentially more valid approach to the determination of students' actual levels of language competence. While such analyses may be fraught with possible difficulties, not the least of which is simply soliciting an appropriate response to a stimulus or a situation, data from a student's own utterances are essential to an accurate assessment of strengths and weaknesses.

Skill Hierarchies. Information related to skill hierarchies can provide specific data on an individual student's strengths and weaknesses. Essentially, this approach is the basis for curriculum-based instruction in which the primary goal is to determine a student's skill level within the scope and sequence of the particular curricular area of concern. This information can be acquired through the use of checklists, which either may accompany the curriculum program or may need to be developed by the teacher, as well as through other teacher-made instruments.

Task Analysis. Task analysis involves the breaking down of an instructional objective into its component steps. This process enables the teacher to analyze important instructional tasks and determine the specific subskills that the student has already acquired as well as those that need to be taught. Once student performance has been determined on the particular tasks, a virtual blueprint for instruction has been laid out.

Prescriptive Teaching Cycle. The cycle of prescriptive teaching also provides an ongoing source of assessment information. Essentially, the prescriptive teaching cycle includes initial assessment, program planning, program implementation, and program evaluation leading to modifications in assessment. The intent of the prescriptive cycle is to enable the teacher to continually monitor a student's performance relative to daily and weekly instruction and thus serve as a basis for possible modifications in teaching.

Error Analysis. A fourth source of informal assessment data can come through the use of error analysis. By structuring specific tasks, teachers can probe for particular areas of difficulties being experienced by the student. For example, spelling is an area that lends itself well to error analysis. After presenting students with a series of dictated words to be spelled, the teacher can then determine the types of errors being made, develop hypotheses for reasons for the errors, and then use this information to design remedial programming.

Behavioral Measurement. Direct, daily measurement refers to a series of techniques that have been developed particularly for the evaluation of overt behavior. In each instance, these techniques represent alternative observational tools that can be used to provide accurate information about the occurrences of specific behaviors. Although a full discussion of these observational tools is beyond the scope of this chapter, they are briefly defined below. The reader who is interested in further information is referred to any of the series of excellent texts dealing with behavior analysis for educators (e.g., Alberto & Troutman, 1986; Kerr & Nelson, 1983; Walker & Shea, 1985).

The simplest form of behavioral observation is *event or frequency recording*. Frequency counts essentially require the notation of the number of times a child does or does not engage in a specific behavior. This approach is most applicable for individual behaviors that can be viewed as discrete occurrences (e.g., oral responses in class).

Duration recording provides a basis for describing an individual behavior by the cumulative amount of time in which it has occurred. This approach to measurement is most apt for behaviors that are not discrete and are more significant in terms of their time basis than the number of occurrences (e.g., on-task or in-seat behavior).

Interval recording is a more precise time-based system for direct measurement. Using this system, notation is made when a particular behavior occurs during a limited time frame (e.g., 10 or 15 seconds). Because of the nature of this recording system, it requires the assistance of a trained observer. Interval data are most commonly presented as a percentage figure reflecting the ratio of intervals in which the particular behavior did or did not occur to the total number of intervals. As with duration recording, interval recording is most appropriately used for behaviors that are not discrete (e.g., attention to teacher-directed instruction or to a specified independent seat-work activity).

Direct Instruction

A major contribution to the development of successful instructional programs in special and regular education in the last 20 years has come from the burgeoning research and curricular innovations based on direct instruction. As described by Carnine (1983), direct instruction is characterized by the following guidelines:

1. Cover large amounts of academic material and structure the school day so that a good proportion of class time is spent in core areas of reading, arithmetic, and language arts;

2. use teaching materials that are highly structured and elicit a high proportion of correct student responses;

3. conduct much of the instruction in small groups (as opposed to independent seatwork); and

4. provide immediate, academically oriented feedback to students. (p. 7)

An additional key characteristic is that direct instruction is typified as having fast-paced lessons allowing for frequent student responding and high rates of task engagement.

In its initial stages of development (e.g., Bereiter & Engelmann, 1966), direct instruction methodology produced perhaps the most substantial gains of any early education program implemented within the context of schools. Largely as an outgrowth of this research, and in order to have direct instruction curricula for use in Project Follow Through (a large-scale federal comparison of early intervention programs for disadvantaged children), the *Direct Instruction Systems for Teaching and Remediation* (DISTAR) were developed by Engelmann and associates. Reports of the evaluation of Project Follow Through indicated that those pupils exposed to the DISTAR program evidenced significant gains in academic skills (Becker & Carnine, 1980; Stebbins, St. Pierre, Proper, Anderson, & Cerva, 1977). Based on these data, Becker (1977) estimated that the implementation of the Direct Instruction model could result in children from low-income homes achieving in accordance with national norms by third grade. Efficacy data on other Direct Instruction (DI) programs have also been reported, most notably the *Corrective Reading Program* (Engelmann, Becker, Hanner, & Johnson, 1980), developed for use with older students experiencing difficulties in learning to read (Gerston, Brockway, & Henares, 1983; Lloyd, Epstein, & Cullinan, 1981; Polloway, Epstein, Polloway, Patton, & Ball, 1986). These programs are discussed further in Chapter 6.

More significant for our purposes here than these specific DI programs are the basic instructional principles that underlie them. Essentially, direct instructional methodology closely parallels the techniques that have been reported in both general and special education to represent effective instruction. As suggested by Stevens and Rosenshine (1981), the major attributes of effective instruction include group instruction, teacher-directed activities, academic focus, and individualization. These are briefly defined and discussed below.

Group Instruction. Group instruction is favored due to the reality of the learning needs of an entire classroom of students and the question of how to maximize time with the teacher. This issue is further discussed below in the separate section on grouping options.

Teacher-Directed Activities. Teacher-directed activities, as contrasted with those in which the student is functioning semi-independently, have been found generally more effective for slow learners and other low achievers. The key element is the organization and structure provided by the teacher, who must serve as the center of attention; this is the essence of direct instruction.

Academic Focus. The concept of academic focus is a reflection of the fact that "academic engaged time" has proven to be the best predictor of subsequent achievement. When students are actively involved in responding to specific instructional tasks, they are receiving instruction that is most likely to produce both short- and long-term benefits.

Individualization. Finally, individualization is a key element. Rather than being contradictory of the initial characteristic listed above of grouping, individualization refers to the acknowledgment that instructors are teaching children and not content. Once this acknowledgment of the individual is secured, individualization can be seen as being accomplished in large groups and small groups in addition to the more readily apparent one-to-one arrangement. This concern for grouping is discussed at length below.

Grouping Options[1]

Among the foremost principles upon which the field of special education was initially founded was the importance of individualized instructional programming. Frequently, the primary justification for the establishment of special services and subsequently for the referral of a particular child has been the assumption that instruction must be geared to a student's specific needs. Placement in a special education program has often been seen as a response to the prevalence of large group instructional methods in the regular classroom and the problems that may result for specific students. The requirement of Individual Educational Programs in P.L. 94-142 has further underscored this emphasis.

The literature in special education emphasizes the importance of instructional individualization. However, it is critical to distinguish between the nonequivalent concepts of *individualization* and *one-to-one instruction*. Payne, Polloway, Smith, and Payne (1981) note that individualization refers to

> instruction *appropriate* to the individual even though it is not always accomplished on a one-to-one basis. . . . In this sense, instruction can be accomplished through one-to-two ratios, in small groups, or even in large groups in some cases. Instruction should be organized in an efficient fashion to facilitate maximum learning by each student. (pp. 46–47)

In elaborating further on this concept, Stevens and Rosenshine (1981) added clarity: "Individualization is considered a characteristic of effective instruction if the term implies helping each student to succeed, to achieve a high percentage of correct responses, and to become confident of his or her competence" (p. 3).

---

[1]This section of the chapter is adapted in part from Polloway, E. A., Cronin, M. E., & Patton, J. R. (1986). The efficacy of one-to-one vs. group instruction: A review. *Remedial and Special Education, 7*(1), 22–30. Used with permission of the publisher, PRO-ED.

The special education literature has often reflected a preference on the part of teachers toward one-to-one as opposed to group instruction, though this tendency has not been adequately documented (Frankel & Graham, 1976). This assumption has been most apparent in research with severely handicapped persons, with 90% of the studies with severely handicapped persons reporting one-to-one instruction as the basis of training (Favell, Favell, & McGimsey, 1978). This trend has existed in spite of the fact that little research was available to support the relative efficacy of this approach as compared to small group intervention efforts (Reid & Favell, 1984).

To evaluate the merits of one-to-one versus small group training instructional arrangements, Polloway, Cronin, and Patton (1986) reviewed relevant research reported from studies involving a diversity of special populations and incorporating a variety of learning tasks. Their review focused on the three areas of concern of effectiveness, efficiency, and social benefits.

Effectiveness. Relative to this concern, the research reviewed was of an equivocal nature. In several cases, advantages for one-to-one training were reported (Alberto, Jobes, Sizemore, & Doran, 1980; Jenkins, Mayhall, Peschka, & Jenkins, 1974; Matson, DiLorenzo, & Esveldt-Dawson, 1981; Westling, Ferrell, & Swenson, 1982), while in other instances, group training procedures were reported to be more effective (Biberdorf & Pear, 1977; Kohl, Wilcox, & Karlan, 1978; Oliver, 1983; Orelove, 1982; Rincover & Koegel, 1977; Smith & Meyers, 1979). However, the more common finding was of essentially comparable results (Favell et al., 1978; Handleman & Harris, 1983; Ranieri, Ford, Vincent, & Brown, 1984).

Relatively few studies have compared group and one-to-one training models with mildly handicapped children and slow learners. However, as noted earlier, there has been substantial support for instructional strategies, such as those based on direct instruction, in which group arrangements are an essential element (Becker, 1977; Becker & Carnine, 1980; Gregory, Hackney, & Gregory, 1982; Stevens & Rosenshine, 1981).

Efficiency. In terms of efficiency, most reported research has been supportive of group training efforts (e.g., Elium & McCarver, 1980; Kazdin & Erickson, 1975; Kohl et al., 1978; Orelove, 1982; Ranieri et al., 1984; Rincover & Koegel, 1977). This finding reaffirms what many professionals in the field of special education have stated for years. It is instructive to consider Quay's (1966) comments of over two decades ago.

> The economics of public schools obviously requires the development of techniques that will allow children to be handled in a group situation.

. . . Even if the techniques of behavior remediation should prove to be very highly effective when applied on an individual basis, they are nevertheless likely to remain economically unfeasible unless they can be adapted for use in group settings such as the classroom. (p. 46)

An obvious undeniable benefit of group training is an increase in the number of students that can be served. Since one-to-one instruction is clearly more expensive, it could lead to a lack of services to children who might otherwise be eligible (Jenkins et al., 1974). An additional administrative benefit of group instruction that is particularly relevant to residential situations is that it facilitates compliance with federal standards (e.g., for medical assistance) by decreasing the "dead time" hours when no programming is provided (Storm & Willis, 1978).

Social Benefits. The third area relative to the efficacy of group versus one-to-one training efforts is the influence of these efforts on social outcomes—whether beneficial or detrimental. Benefits in this area are particularly important to subsequent language development, given the importance of social bases for the acquisition of both oral and written communication skills.

One social benefit of group training is simply the opportunity it affords for learning to participate in group activities. Fink and Sandall (1980) posited that the introduction of small group work with preschoolers would result in an increased ability to function in common school situations. Handleman and Harris (1983) stated that group work provides more normalizing experiences that eventually can lead to integration. Brown and his colleagues (Brown, Hermanson, Klemme, Hambrich, & Ora, 1970) indicated that group training resulted in the spontaneous development of social reinforcers as well as group enthusiasm.

The obverse of the situation may occur through an overemphasis on the one-to-one instructional model. Bryan (1983) stressed this point in discussing the social implications of the traditional resource model used with learning disabled students. She noted that given a primary focus on one-to-one instruction, handicapped children would be likely to encounter more difficulty in the process of being integrated into the regular class.

Benefits of Group Instruction. The research on grouping strategies supports an emphasis on a group training approach as a primary instructional basis for a significant portion of the programming efforts with handicapped students. Clearly, a variety of benefits can accrue from the use of group methodology. Johnson and colleagues aptly summarized these benefits as

better use of teacher time, more efficient student management, minimizing the effect of economic limitations, increased instructional time, increased peer-peer interaction, and increased generalization of skills. (Johnson, Flanagan, Burge, Kaufman-Debriere, & Spellman, 1980, p. 237)

Additionally, group instructional arrangements can assist in the development of observational learning, can facilitate overlearning and generalization, teach turn-taking and thus enhance pragmatic learning, and provide an option for the teacher's withholding attention for inappropriate behavior by attending to the other students in the group (Borus, Greenfield, Spiegel, & Daniels, 1973; Kohl et al., 1978; Oliver & Scott, 1981; Polloway, Cronin, & Patton, 1986).

Finally, it is worth noting again what seems to be the most critical variable favoring group instruction—increased teacher contact. To return to Stevens and Rosenshine's (1981) review of best practices, the importance of "academic engaged time" and its relationship to higher achievement levels has clearly been demonstrated and has consistently been supported by related research (Algozzine, Mirkin, Thurlow, & Graden, 1981; Denham & Lieberman, 1980; Thurlow, Ysseldyke, Graden, & Algozzine, 1983). Consequently, the increased opportunity afforded by small group instruction for teacher demonstration and corrective feedback represents a strong argument in favor of group instruction.

Stages of Learning

An overriding concern with implications for all instructional endeavors is the consideration of the specific stage or level of learning. Basically, there are four stages that can be identified as reflective of both different learning objectives and variant instructional techniques: acquisition, proficiency, maintenance, and generalization. These stages are briefly discussed below in addition to being schematically presented in Table 2.2.

Acquisition. This first stage refers to the initial learning of a specific skill, behavior, word, or construction. To achieve acquisition, disabled learners generally require these teaching behaviors to be utilized: demonstration, prompting, and supervised drill. With *demonstration*, the teacher provides to the student a model of, for example, the word to be pronounced, sentence to be written, or syllable to be decoded. Demonstration frequently includes a *prompt* provided to simplify the model, such as the addition of color coding to assist in distinguishing the letters *b* and *d*.

Supervised drill is essentially a verification process. It responds to the common lament of "they must know it because I certainly taught it" by giving each learner an opportunity to respond and thus demonstrate acquisition. Prompting again may be necessary here, such as the

TABLE 2.2. Stages of Learning

Learning Stage	Objective	Representative Teaching Strategies	Example: Proofreading for Capitalization Errors
Acquisition	Initial learning of a skill or behavior	Teacher demonstration (modeling) Verbal instructions Supervised drill	Directly instruct students, incorporating demonstration and explanation of editing process.
Proficiency	Development of mastery	Independent practice work Timed tests and related exercises	Increase the rate (i.e., number of errors found and corrected per unit of time).
Maintenance	Ability to retain acquired skill or behavior over time	Seatwork activities Instructional games Workbooks Computer activities	As the student moves on to other more advanced proofreading skills, continue to present review activities that require the use of this previously learned proofreading skill.
Generalization	Application of learned skill to new situation	Use of new instructional materials or activities that vary from original materials in terms of presentation. Instruction provided in other settings.	Require the use of this skill in written composition on a topic selected by the student.

Adapted from Polloway, E. A., Payne, J. S., Patton, J. R. & Payne, R. A. (1985). *Strategies for teaching retarded and special needs learners*. Columbus, OH: Charles E. Merrill. Reprinted with permission of Merrill Publishing Co.

response prompt of helping the child form his or her lips in the articulation of a specific sound or word.

Proficiency and Maintenance. These two stages present a degree of overlap in terms of instructional methodology. Technically, proficiency refers to the development of mastery and relates to the process of automaticity — that is, the level at which skills have developed so that the individual learner's responses are automatic. Maintenance, on the other hand, is defined as the retention of skills over time. The instructional practices most often associated with both of these stages are independent drill work. Examples include worksheets, learning and interest centers, instructional games, and computer-assisted instruction software geared to drill and practice.

Generalization. The ultimate test of successful learning comes at the application or generalization stage. For handicapped learners, especially in the various language domains, generalization learning is critical to independent functioning. Generalization is a generic term that measures learning across skills, across settings, and across instructors. The essential point is that with exceptional learners, teachers cannot adopt a "train and hope" philosophy (Stokes & Baer, 1977) but rather must provide for, and thus ensure, the occurrence of generalization.

Generalization is important not only for expanding a student's skill or behavioral repertoire, but also for its contribution to success in the mainstream environment and outside of the school setting, especially after the completion of secondary schooling. In order to support the process of language learning and transfer, a number of strategies are suggested below. These techniques are an expansion of the approaches provided by Alley and Deshler (1979).

❑ providing variance in the way that instructional lessons are presented;

❑ using varied examples to illustrate a skill to be learned (e.g., providing series of words to which a given phonics rule applies);

❑ setting up cooperative teaching arrangements in order to vary instructors;

❑ teaching students to cue others (e.g., regular class teachers) for feedback and reinforcement;

❑ varying physical and temporal settings to have the student apply the skill in other situations;

❑ organizing instruction within the community so that specific skills are used in the natural environment (e.g., ordering from a menu in a restaurant vs. in the classroom); and

❏ telling students to generalize by instructing them to use, for example, a particular strategy in a given situation (e.g., "When you are asked to proofread your paper, remember to first look at capitalization and punctuation errors").

To summarize these suggestions, generalization training should be based on two premises: It must be programmed for if it is to occur, and it will be most successful when students are actively involved in the process of learning to transfer.

The four stages or levels of learning dictate modification of instructional techniques. Critical learning objectives for students should be carefully tracked by the teacher to ensure that the instructional approach is consistent with the needs of the individual student.

Other Components of Effective Instruction

The three sections immediately above have highlighted significant *instructional dimensions* of effective instruction, with attention given to the importance of directive teaching strategies, appropriate grouping patterns, and teaching concerns related to the four stages of learning in students. Although these components clearly constitute major areas of concern for instruction, they by no means represent a total picture of the key aspects of programming. The purpose of this section is to briefly outline other antecedent components of effective instruction that warrant careful consideration.

A useful model for focusing on key variables related to instructional effectiveness was developed by Patton (see Polloway, Payne, Patton, & Payne, 1985). In presenting this model, he began by asking the critical questions that should be addressed before determining how instruction should proceed.

> On a general level, responding to the query "What is effective instruction?" is relatively easy. An answer to the question would probably imply that some type of learning takes place and probably would sound something like the definition of learning [that follows] . . . "the acquisition of knowledge or skills." Reflection obscures the meaning of this question, making it difficult to answer. Other related but more specific questions—To what specific skills are we referring: academic, social, or what? Does time come into play here? is rate of learning important?—are critical to any analysis of effective instruction. Moreover, effective instruction implies the most facile acquisition of a wide range of knowledge or skills in a psychologically healthy, appropriately structured learning environment. Furthermore, effective teachers do certain "things," called components of effective instruction. (p. 24)

The model itself is predicated on a division of the total instructional process into three major time-related areas: antecedents to teaching, teaching behaviors, and follow-ups to teaching.

Four dimensions constitute the antecedent component of this model: physical, social, organizational, and instructional. The reader should consult Polloway et al. (1985) for further information on the other elements of Patton's model. As can be seen in Figure 2.1, several of these (e.g., instructional dimensions, grouping) have been discussed previously in detail.

Physical Dimensions. Physical dimensions primarily refer to the structure and arrangement of the classroom. The key goal for teachers is to develop what Lindsley (1964) originally referred to as a *prosthetic environment* — that is, one specifically designed to facilitate successful student learning. To achieve the goal of a classroom environment as prosthetic support, teachers should consider structure that encourages and stimulates student responding while at the same time discourages distractibility; that provides space for teacher-directed instruction as well as age-appropriate forms of social interaction and sharing experiences; and that utilizes media equipment, technology, charts, and bulletin boards which enhance the instructional program without clashing with it. The reader is referred to Gray (1975), Polloway et al. (1985), and Zentall (1983) for further information relative to classroom design and structure.

Social Dimensions. Social dimensions of effective instruction refer to the psychological climate within the classroom. They relate to what Moos (1976) has conceptualized as the "personality" of the environment. Although social dimensions are somewhat more abstract than physical ones, they include

❏ the attitudes conveyed by the teacher toward the students, the teaching process, and the curricular conten

❏ the attitudes that students have brought to and/or developed within the instructional environment about the class, teacher, school, learning process, and overall curriculum;

❏ the characteristics of the teacher as related to, for example, reliance on specific interactive modes with students and consistency in instructional patterns and management strategies;

❏ the prior experiences of students and their impact on them not only in terms of knowledge gained and skills acquired but also in terms of the possible development of learning versus failure sets when presented with new content to be learned;

FIGURE 2.1. Components of Effective Instruction

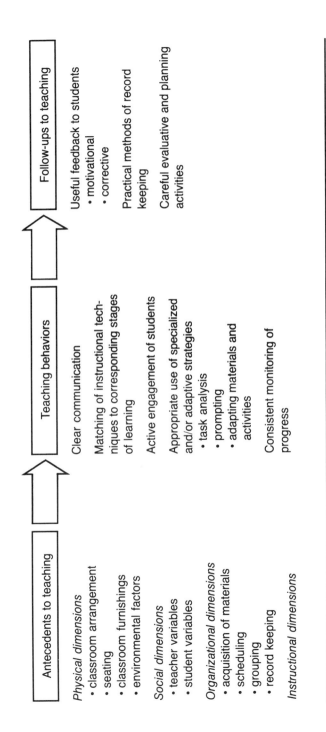

From Polloway, E. A., Payne, J. S., Patton, J. R., & Payne, R. A. (1985). *Strategies for teaching retarded and special needs learners.* Columbus, OH: Charles E. Merrill. Reprinted with permission of Merrill Publishing Co.

❑ the overall atmosphere of the school and the relative status of, for example, a given special program within the school's structure.

Organizational Dimensions. In addition to concerns relative to grouping, organizational dimensions also include materials acquisition, scheduling, and record keeping. Clearly the former is a critical concern in all curricular areas and is no less important in the various language domains. Its importance with handicapped or remedial learners is particularly underscored by the common assumption that there is no *one* best method or material for such students (Wallace & Kauffman, 1986). Regular review of the professional literature and commercial catalogues should be combined with a clear definition of objectives as to how specific materials can be used within an overall curriculum design to ensure that they are appropriate. Wilson (1982) has provided a useful analysis of the role of materials acquisition within the process of curricular design.

Scheduling is a second organizational dimension that must be addressed, since the daily schedule provides the basis for all instructional planning. When designed appropriately, schedules (a) can provide for relative emphases to critical versus less significant curricular areas, (b) can naturally build reinforcement via the Premack Principle into the instructional day (i.e., alternating demanding subjects with pleasurable activities), (c) can facilitate integration efforts with regular class programs, and (d) can provide students with an effective blend of routine and flexibility. More detailed discussions on scheduling can be found in Wiederholt, Hammill, and Brown (1983) and Smith and Payne (1980).

A third organizational dimension is record keeping. While numerous strategies have been developed in education to facilitate planning, monitoring, and evaluating instructional programming, the key element is not how record keeping is handled but that it is in fact incorporated into the instructional process. Thus, teachers should "locate, refine, personally adapt and practice using a system with which they are comfortable" (Polloway et al., 1985, p. 27). The system developed prior to actual teaching then clearly becomes the basis for evaluation subsequent to teaching.

Applications of the Computer to Instruction

Microcomputers have become an integral part of American education in the 1980s. Their use has expanded rapidly in the schools in the past decade to the point that it is rare to find a school that does not have microcomputers available for student use on at least an occasional basis if not within each classroom. As Hasselbring (1985) noted in evaluating the spirit of the times,

Parents and administrators alike are pressuring teachers to use computer technology in the teaching/learning process. Schools are increasingly seeking teachers with microcomputer expertise, while teachers lacking these skills are increasingly expected to acquire them. (p. 154)

Computer applications to specific language domains have been burgeoning particularly in recent years. Hardware and software development has been so rapid teachers have been forced to virtually redesign basic approaches for programming within specific areas and for specific populations (e.g., communication training for severely motorically involved persons). Although research on program effectiveness has not kept pace with these advances, nevertheless the empirical data base on microcomputer uses with handicapped students has increased more than 10-fold within the past five years.

The specific contributions that microcomputers can make to special education are as significant as they are varied. Hasselbring (1985), drawing on the work of Hannaford and Sloane (1982), identified the following uses:

1. provide a multisensory approach to learning

2. teach a wide range of content areas

3. provide interactive, individualized instruction

4. present a wide range of learning rates

5. record, store, and recall student responses on learning tasks

6. provide immediate feedback

7. provide varied forms of reinforcement

8. provide drill, repetition, and practice in a stimulating fashion

9. provide the teacher with diagnostic and prescriptive information on each student

10. assume many of the record-keeping and tedious caseload management responsibilities

11. assist in developing teaching materials

12. provide one-to-one tutoring on new concepts

13. present the learner with real-life problem-solving events through simulation. (pp. 159–160)

Specifically, the three major ways microcomputers have impacted on special education are computer-assisted instruction (CAI), computer-managed instruction (CMI), and materials generation. CAI is the aspect of microcomputer usage that has not often been associated with classroom instructional change. It includes the following forms: drill and practice, tutorial, simulation, problem solving, gaming, and tool application. The reader is referred to Behrmann (1984), Hasselbring (1985), and Taber (1983) for further information on these options.

CMI's purpose is to provide support to teachers in areas that often impinge upon their instructional (and leisure) time. Applications may include aides for diagnostic testing, assistance with the development of educational prescriptions, and record keeping.

Finally, microcomputers can assist in the generation of materials useful within the instructional process. Support for teachers for IEP writing and the creation of tests and work activities can be provided by word processing packages which can also be used in written language programs for students. Authoring languages have been designed to facilitate the development of instructional software programs, while authoring systems can further facilitate this process.

The remaining chapters provide, where relevant, specific discussion on microcomputer applications within various specific language domains. Further information on current microcomputer applications and potential avenues for the future can be obtained from any of the excellent chapters and texts on this topic that have recently been published, including those noted above. A particularly valuable resource is Project Retool, a microcomputer training program developed and disseminated by the Council for Exceptional Children (CEC). An excellent source book for software programs appropriate for special populations is the Specialware Directory (LINC Associates, 1986).

CONCLUDING COMMENTS

Language problems are the most commonly reported difficulties in handicapped and remedial learners. The majority of referrals for special services are initiated, at least in part, based upon the given individual's problems within one or several of the major language domains.

A philosophical and legal foundation for special services is the need for individualization in programming efforts. This foundation is reflected in the requirement that IEPs be developed for each child prior to placement into a specialized program. To ensure that IEPs serve a functional role in the educational process, teachers should stress the use of data reflected in present levels of performance as a basis for the establishment of relevant annual goals and short-term objectives.

General and specific instructional approaches are provided in each of the succeeding chapters. To provide an introduction to these discussions, this chapter has highlighted a number of important educational concerns, including an orientation to assessment, the nature of direct instruction, instructional grouping alternatives, stages of learning, important antecedents to learning, and the role of microcomputers in programming.

APPENDIX
Sample Individualized Education Program (IEP)

Student John Smith   DOB 8/22/77   Age 9

School(s) Yellow Branch Elementary   Parent/Guardian Ms. Mary Smith

Date Eligibility Determined 1/16/87   Date of IEP Meeting 1/20/87

Date of IEP Implementation 1/28/87   Date of IEP Completion 1/88

Participants in IEP meeting:

Date	Signature of Person Present	Relationship to Student
1/20/87	Ms. Mary Smith	mother
1/20/87	Mrs. L. Tweed	teacher (4th grade)
1/20/87	Mrs. J. Michael	principal
1/20/87	Mrs. Dana S. Bittner	sp. ed. teacher
1/20/87	Miss Alison Shoun	speech therapist
1/20/87	Mr. Edward Henry	p.e. teacher

I *GIVE* PERMISSION FOR MY CHILD _____
to be enrolled in the special program described in the Individualized Education Program. I understand that I have the right to review his/her records and to request a change in his/her Individualized Education Program at any time. I understand that I have the right to refuse this permission and to have my child continue in his/her present placement pending further action.

_____   _____
Date   Signature of Parent/Guardian

I *DO NOT GIVE* PERMISSION FOR MY CHILD _____
to be enrolled in the special education program described in the Individualized Education Program. I understand that I have the right to review his/her records and to request another placement. I understand that the action described above will not take place without my permission or until due process procedures have been exhausted. I understand that if my decision is appealed, I will be notified of my due process rights in this procedure.

_____   _____
Date   Signature of Parent/Guardian

DESCRIPTION OF SERVICES

1. Special Education Services

Placement/ Amt. of Time	Date to Begin	Anticipated Completion	Personnel	Location
5 hrs Special Class 5 days/wk. (Emotional Disburbance)	1/87	6/87	Special Ed. teacher	Yellow Branch

2. Related Services

½ hr. Speech Therapy 2d./wk.	1/87	6/87	Speech Therapist	Yellow Branch
½ hr. Movement Ed. 2d./wk.	1/87	6/87	Adaptive Phys. Ed. Teacher	Yellow Branch

3. Specialized Materials, Equipment, and Transportation

none required

4. Extent to which student can participate in regular educational programs (specify amount of time):

John can spend approximately one to one-and-a-half hours per day in the regular 4th grade class. During this time, he may participate in activities such as P.E., Music, Art, and watching films. John's lunch and recess time may also be spent with regular education programs daily.

PRESENT LEVELS OF PERFORMANCE
Summary of Assessment Information

1. Curricular Assessment Summary (test scores and skill descriptions):

John can successfully spell most CVC and CVCe words. He is able to recall specific details from a two-paragraph passage and answer literal questions. He sequences past events correctly when given a list of no more than six. John can subtract a 2-digit numeral from a 2-digit numeral without regrouping and knows all addition facts, regrouping included. John writes very legibly; he can transcribe paragraphs from print into cursive and can decode cursive handwriting when written clearly. He is able to perform all self-help skills adequately and needs only an occasional reminder to wash his hands before eating. John is presently reading on a 3.5 level, only slightly lower than grade level, and can tell the time from either a face or digital clock.

2. Personal-Social and Behavioral Assessment Summary:

John is usually a very quiet boy. He likes very much to be verbally complimented but withdraws when confronted with positive physical attention. He seems to exert himself only when angry or frustrated, and aggression often rules his association with classmates his own age. He successfully follows one-step directions and usually remembers to raise his hand before speaking. He performs very appropriately when asked to serve as a tutor or helper for the younger students who are having problems with their work, but has difficulty completing his own assignments. John has some trouble relating cause and effect in daily situations; it takes much explanation before John understands behavior-consequence relationships.

ANNUAL INSTRUCTIONAL GOALS

Goal #1: John will be able to accurately follow three-step directions when given orally or in writing by the teacher.

Goal #2: John will be able to independently complete 95% of his assigned work on time and with 90% accuracy.

Goal #3: John will be able to spell all regular CVCC and CCVC words containing familiar consonant blends and digraphs with 95% accuracy.

Goal #4: John will be able to subtract a 3-digit numeral from a 3-digit numeral requiring regrouping with 95% accuracy.

Goal #5: Given a short story (no more than 4 paragraphs), after reading silently, John will be able to answer written or oral inferential and conclusive questions and summarize the story verbally with 90% accuracy.

SHORT-TERM OBJECTIVES

Annual Goal #1: John will be able to accurately follow three-step directions when given orally or written by the teacher.

Objectives	Evaluation	Date Begun	Date Completed
1. will accurately follow oral and written one-step directions given by the teacher	teacher observation		
2. will accurately follow oral and written two-step directions given by the teacher	teacher observation		
3. will accurately follow three-step directions when given by the teacher in writing	teacher observation		
4. will accurately follow three-step directions when given orally by the teacher	teacher observation		
5. will accurately follow three-step directions when given orally or in writing by the teacher	teacher observation		

Annual Goal #2: John will be able to independently complete 95% of his assigned work on time and with 90% accuracy.

Objectives	Evaluation	Date Begun	Date Completed
1. will complete 95% of his assigned work on time with occasional physical and/or verbal prompting with 90% accuracy	observation & checklists		
2. will complete 95% of his assigned work on time, with verbal prompting only and with 90% accuracy	observation & checklists		
3. will independently complete 85% of his assigned work on time and with 85% accuracy	observation & checklists		
4. will independently complete 95% of his assigned work on time and with 90% accuracy	observation & checklists		

Annual Goal #3: John will be able to pronounce and spell all regular CCVC and CVCC words containing familiar consonant blends and digraphs with 95% accuracy.

Objectives	Evaluation	Date Begun	Date Completed
	flashcards		
1. will pronounce all regular CCVC	oral reading		
and CVCC words correctly 95% of	teacher		
the time	observation		
2. will spell, from dictation,			
all regular CCVC words with	spelling		
95% accuracy	tests		
3. will spell, from dictation,			
all regular CVCC words with	spelling		
95% accuracy	tests		
4. will pronounce and spell all	flashcards &		
regular CCVC and CVCC words	spelling		
with 95% accuracy	tests		

Annual Goal #4: John will be able to subtract a 3-digit numeral from a 3-digit numeral requiring regrouping with 95% accuracy.

1. will subtract a 1-digit numeral from	worksheets		
a 2-digit numeral requiring	teacher-made		
regrouping with 95% accuracy	tests		
2. will subtract a 2-digit numeral from	worksheets		
a 2-digit numeral requiring	teacher-made		
regrouping with 95% accuracy	tests		
3. will subtract a 2-digit numeral from	worksheets		
a 3-digit numeral without regroup-	teacher-made		
ing with 95% accuracy	tests		
4. will subtract a 3-digit numeral	worksheets		
from a 3-digit numeral requiring	teacher-made		
regrouping with 95% accuracy	tests		

Annual Goal #5: Given a short story (no more than 4 paragraphs), after reading silently, John will be able to answer written or oral inferential and conclusive questions and summarize the story verbally with 95% accuracy.

Objectives	Evaluation	Date Begun	Date Completed
1. after silent reading, John will accurately summarize the main idea of a 4-paragraph story in 2-3 sentences	oral tests		
2. after silent reading of a 4-paragraph story, John will be able to answer inferential questions with 95% accuracy	teacher-made oral and written tests		
3. after silent reading of a 4-paragraph passage, John will be able to draw accurate conclusions regarding the material 95% of the time	teacher-made oral and written tests		

The authors express their appreciation to Dana Satterwhite Bittner for her assistance in the development of this sample IEP.

Part Two

ASSESSMENT AND INSTRUCTION

3

LISTENING

Sound is everywhere. No matter what we do, where we work, or how we spend our free time, we need to listen. Unless one has an auditory handicap, listening is the most used language arts skill. As young children, listening helps us to learn the rules of language, to identify the functional aspects of our immediate environment, and to increase our emotional depth. Our earliest adventures are through orally read books, our sense of self develops along with the delivery of verbal messages from a parent, and our awareness of functional tasks grows from a pairing of visual demonstration and verbal expression. The complexity of the listening task increases as we grow older and are presented with an even greater barrage of auditory stimuli.

Upon school entrance, listening takes on new importance, and the child is expected to develop listening competence allowing for eventual critical analysis and appreciative thinking. In fact, it has been said that children enter school with listening as the most fully developed communication skill. However, 13 years later at the end of formal schooling, speaking ability has generally surpassed listening ability. What happens in between to cause the exchange in dominance of these two communication processes is a common neglect of listening within the elementary and secondary school curricula.

Although listening is the most used language arts skill, it is the least taught skill. Teachers assume that children listen, and that if speaking is taught, listening will follow. To some extent this is true. Good speaking enhances listening, and the intertwining of the two skills is inevitable. However, while listening occurs throughout the curriculum, its development cannot be left to chance. The extent to which we are asked to listen depends on the situation we are in. Several often cited, and now classic, studies demonstrate the importance of listening as a learning skill. Wilt (1950) found that elementary school children have been observed to spend as much as two and one-half hours listening within a five-hour day. An interesting point of Wilt's study is that this figure was twice as much time as elementary teachers had estimated. By secondary school, Markgraf (1957) found students were expected to spend nearly 46% of their school day listening to teachers, other students, and media. Rankin's (1930) early, but much-quoted, work found that Americans on the average spend 30% of their day speaking, 16% reading, 9% writing, and 45% listening. Keeping in mind the time period in which Rankin's study was conducted, it is probable that listening activities today have increased with the production and common use of television, telephones, videos, and other forms of mass media. In fact, Lundsteen (1979) reported that the average child spends 22,000 hours watching television between the ages of 3 and 18.

It is not that children need to do more listening, but rather that they need to learn to listen better. Children's absorption with television and other mass media involves passive listening. That is, children are expected to see and hear but not to speak back or react to the communication. Long-term passive listening can lead to poor listening habits, ultimately reducing learning experiences. Children need to be taught to listen; to clarify, to associate, to question, to react, to elaborate, and to evaluate what they hear.

IMPORTANCE OF LISTENING FOR THE PROBLEM LEARNER

The child who has difficulty learning in a traditional program is in critical need of good listening skills. Listening can compensate for deficits in reading and writing and can allow the child to progress through the curriculum at a normal rate. The good listener may acquire information through lecture, discussion, and media presentation that would otherwise have been lost. Unfortunately, one commonly cited characteristic of many handicapped children is poor listening. Most of the research related to exceptional children and listening deals with the learning disabled (LD) population. In comparison to the "normal" population, LD children exhibit lower levels of listening competence. LD students often demonstrate poor comprehension, do not seek clarification or feedback, and tend to remember less information (Bauer, 1977; Bryan, 1979; Kotsonis & Patterson, 1980).

It is not necessarily true that the act of "listening" will lead to good listening habits. What is true is that a poor listener will most likely be a poor learner. If a child cannot follow directions, understand a discussion, or pursue an argument, then it can be assumed that he or she will not be able to participate fully in the learning situation. Listening skills overlap considerably with skills in speaking, reading, and even writing. In fact, listening precedes these other language domains and is the foundational component for language development. Understanding language structure is fundamental to both listening and reading comprehension. Elementary children who are poor in listening comprehension when read aloud to tend to have similar difficulty in reading comprehension when confronted with the printed word. Since both listening and reading are decoding skills, it is probable that a lack of experience with basic language structure is at the root of such problems (Berger, 1978). The normal reader, regardless of his or her language environment, acquires these language structures through the act of reading itself. Interestingly, although poor readers are unable to learn these structures by reading, they can acquire them through listening. By giving such children repeated opportunities to be read to, it is possible to increase their listening comprehension as well as their reading comprehension (Temple & Gillet, 1984). Marlowe, Egner, and Foreman (1979) compared LD and normal children on story comprehension in two conditions: auditory presentation (listening) and visual presentation (reading). Under the auditory condition the LD subjects showed marked improvement in comprehension equaling the level of the normal group in the visual condition. The implication is that listening takes on even greater importance as a compensatory skill for deficient readers.

As the special student progresses to secondary level and then to adulthood, the importance of listening as a compensatory skill is increased. Alley and Deshler (1979) cite four reasons why listening should be taught within the secondary curriculum. Although Alley and Deshler address the LD curriculum, their points are relevant for all mildly handicapped students. First, there is increasing emphasis upon gaining information through the auditory channel. As one grows older, the language environment becomes more complex, with greater demands placed upon attention and critical listening. Second, information gathering and leisure time activities are largely involved with radios, televisions, and telephones, and the infusion of such technology has reduced the emphasis upon written communication in our daily lives. Third, most job and social situations demand good listening habits. Social acceptance is often related to one's ability to send and interpret verbal and nonverbal messages. Finally, it is evident that instruction in listening effectively improves listening ability. Therefore, it is not necessary to accept poor listening skills as a permanent performance level for exceptional children. A teacher who understands the importance of listening within the school setting as well as in social and job situations can enhance student listening skills.

THE LISTENING PROCESS

Listening is more than just hearing sound or the simple reception of a message. Listening involves deriving meaning from a message through a series of cognitive processes and as such differs from what we think of as hearing. The processing of a message (sound) allows the listener to respond in an appropriate way through words, gestures, or actions. Listening, therefore, is essential not only to human discourse but to almost any human interaction. When the listener responds the interaction that develops creates a continuity between the speaker and listener as each exchanges their role for the other's.

The act of *listening* is a complex one that begins with *hearing* and goes on to multiple sense perception. The listener must be able to hear the sounds of the environment, particularly the sounds of language. Images associated with sound also must be seen in order to appreciate the entire message. These images include facial expressions and other nonverbal elements of body language which influence human communication. Hennings (1979) extends the process beyond these basic impressions by:

1. Distinguishing language sounds and images from nonlanguage impressions being received.

2. Distinguishing among language sounds, for example the /b/ from the /h/ in the beginning of the words *bat* and *hat*.

3. Assigning meaning to language sounds and images and sorting significant from less significant ones.

4. Comprehending the factual content of an oral communication; in short, getting the facts straight about who, what, when, where, and how.

5. Analyzing relationships inherent in an oral communication—make comparisons and contrasts, grouping related points and ideas together, comprehending sequences, generalizing, determining cause and effect, hypothesizing consequences, making predictions based on the information received, and applying generalizations deductively to new situations.

6. Thinking of other points and ideas not mentioned by a speaker but related to what is being said.

7. Determining how the speaker feels about and views the facts.

8. Creating original ideas based on impressions received.

9. Formulating a personal opinion on the topic and developing reasons to support that opinion.

10. Evaluating aspects of communication—specifically the facts and ideas contained therein and the manner in which they are being communicated; perceiving distortions of the truth. (p. 3)

More attention is paid to the semantic aspect of the message than to either the phonological or syntactical components. When listening occurs, *thinking* and *feeling* also occur as the listener processes what is heard. Gaining full meaning from a message implies that the listener interacts with what is heard and integrates the message with past understanding and experience. Henning's list, provided above, clearly conveys the cognitive acts involved in the thinking component of listening, but what about the emotional component? How does what one feels influence what is heard and what is acted upon? Messages can excite, anger, arouse, amuse, confuse, please, or frighten. By simply listening to a story, a listener can react with a full range of emotions from laughter to tears providing evidence of emotional involvement. The listener's response is based upon the interplay of thinking and feeling and is a demonstration of how the message was comprehended. This final component of listening is known as *auding*, which denotes a higher level of mental processing, including categorizing, sequencing, comparing, and appreciating.

A basic model of listening which includes the three major components of *hearing*, *listening*, and *auding* (Taylor, 1973) is provided in Figure 3.1. Within the model several components are of such significance that they deserve our attention.

Auditory Discrimination

A child who looks up in the sky at the sound of an airplane overhead and looks down the road at the first sound of a motorcycle is demonstrating auditory discrimination. The ability to recognize differences among sounds leads to the development of appropriate responding. In the classroom a child learns to distinguish different "phonemes" such as the different g sounds in George and Glover; the b and p sounds; words such as pen and pin; and people's voices. Auditory discrimination is a broader concept than just speech sound discrimination, however. It includes the ability to distinguish the full range of sound, from nonlanguage sounds to subtle tonal differences in speech.

In all but a very few cases, children come to school able to recognize common environmental sounds. Those who cannot frequently have a

FIGURE 3.1. A Listening Model

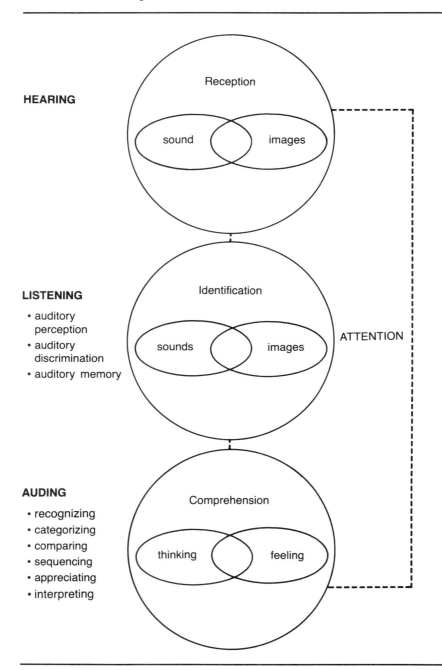

HEARING

Reception

sound   images

LISTENING

- auditory perception
- auditory discrimination
- auditory memory

Identification

sounds   images

ATTENTION

AUDING

- recognizing
- categorizing
- comparing
- sequencing
- appreciating
- interpreting

Comprehension

thinking   feeling

hearing loss or come from overcrowded homes and have learned at an early age to "tune out" or disregard sounds around them. Instruction for such children must begin with basic *sound awareness* in which the child learns to focus attention on particular sounds—in other words, to listen. Toward this end, activities that increase sound alertness and sound identification are advised. An example of such an activity would be to have the children cover their eyes while the teacher produces significant sounds (e.g., slams a book, closes a door, opens a window). The students have to locate the relevant sound's placement in the environment and identify the action.

Auditory Memory

The ability to store and retrieve sounds from past auditory experiences is known as auditory memory. For instance, when a child hears a fire engine on the street and then repeats the sound when playing with toy cars, she or he is demonstrating auditory memory. The importance of auditory memory for learning should be evident. Within the classroom, children often rely on auditory memory to repeat directions, imitate a counting sequence, or when using a phonics-oriented reading program. In phonics, children must be able to remember letter sounds as they "attack" unknown words and must then blend the sounds together in a meaningful way. Teachers who help children further develop their auditory memories are helping to establish a listening "set." Children who do not remember what they hear may do so as a result of (a) inattention, (b) auditory distortion, (c) visual modality preference, or (d) memory dysfunction.

Interpretation

Individual listeners bring their own personal experiences and backgrounds to each situation, and as a result what is heard, or rather, what is thought to be heard, is partly based upon individual interpretation. All teachers have had the experience of orally providing information and/or directions to a class only to find out that several members of the group have taken incorrect notes or worked on a project that emphasizes components the teacher did not focus upon. To avoid such experiences it is necessary to have listeners "reflect back" what they have heard. Teachers may ask students to repeat directions, summarize the main points of the lesson, provide an interpretation, or retell a story.

Attention

The attention factor within the model is of great importance to the classroom teacher, because its absence may preclude "good" listening. When a teacher straightens his or her stance and announces to a class, "I want you all to listen," the teacher is actually calling for the students to first pay attention so that they can listen. Psychologically, it is impossible for children, or anyone for that matter, to focus consistently for more than 20 seconds (Moray, 1969); therefore, a teacher must constantly pull his or her listeners' focus back to what is being said. In other words, the teacher must continually regain (maintain) student attention, which can be best achieved through active listening—listening that involves the listener in the creation of the message—or by demanding a response.

For many handicapped learners, listening problems begin with attending problems. Attention can be subdivided into two specific types: *selective attention*, the ability to focus upon a relevant stimulus, and *sustained attention*, the ability to maintain alertness over a period of time. It has been known for some time that poor attention is a major contributor to the lower amounts of learning of mentally retarded, emotionally disturbed, and (particularly) learning disabled students. The mildly handicapped often have difficulty separating relevant from irrelevant stimuli within the environment, resulting in inappropriate learning patterns.

The tendency to focus upon irrelevant stimuli, *distractibility*, is often mentioned as a characteristic of mildly handicapped learners. Teachers tend to apply this term to students who are unable to come to attention as well as those who cannot sustain attention. Distractibility within the oral environment may result from extraneous stimuli such as noise, lights, or movement as well as from more subtle distractors such as embedded meaning, flowery vocabulary, or garbled speech. Since good listening cannot result without good attending, it is important to recognize what factors influence attending behavior and to determine whether inadequate attending is at the root of the child's listening difficulty.

Factors that Promote Listening

Features of the environment and of the spoken message can be arranged to promote listening. Teachers should not expect that all children will "listen" just because they are told to do so, although it does help to alert students to the listening task. In fact, an analysis of the listening situation may reveal elements that make attending—and, therefore, listening—nearly impossible. Factors that are conducive to maintaining attention are listed below.

Listeners attend more when:

❑ the salience of elements is increased through repetition, vocal emphasis, and so forth;

❑ the oral message is meaningful, logical, and organized;

❑ messages are given in short units;

❑ the speaker can be clearly heard and understood;

❑ the speaker allows for listener participation in the form of clarification, feedback, responding, or other active strategies;

❑ the speaker has focused attention by telling the child to listen or by stating how the message will be of importance to the listener;

❑ reinforcement is given for attending in the form of participation, praise, or increased ability to perform a task;

❑ oral presentations are accompanied by visual aids which emphasize important points;

❑ the listener feels comfortable within the environment and has a positive attitude toward the speaker and the subsequent interaction;

❑ the listener knows there will be an opportunity to reflect upon and integrate the message before having to formulate a response.

Cognitive Levels

Listening occurs when we *want* to hear something and when we are involved in processing information to develop a response. In this manner, listening can be conceived of as a cyclical pattern involving receiving information, processing information, and responding. The way we cognitively process information and respond to the verbal stimulus depends on the mental effort and personal involvement we invest in each situation. As a result, listening levels will vary from one instance to another. DeHaven (1983) suggests several cognitive levels of listening teachers should be aware of: passive listening, listening for information, listening for understanding, critical listening, and appreciative listening (Table 3.1). Each of these categories is relevant for the instruction of handicapped learners. The handicapped child's learning characteristics are such that listening, at each cognitive level, may be a problem requiring direct instructional attention.

TABLE 3.1. Cognitive Levels of Listening

Listening Level	Behavioral Manifestations	Comments in Relation to Handicapped Learners
Passive Listening	• hearing sounds • no mental processing • no responding occurs	• child may appear attentive but may not be "tuned in" • teacher needs to gain child's attention before expecting a response
Listening for Information	• hearing • attending to specific information • ability to recall word meanings, facts, details, and directions • ability to form impressions, paraphrase, and deduce surface structure of sentences	• child may have difficulty focusing upon relevant information • child may attend to irrelevant information • child may not use memory strategies, therefore may not remember • attention to rehearsal, highlighting information and repetition of key points is important
Listening for Understanding	• attending and recall • linking ideas • associating old and new learning • summarizing • comparing and contrasting pieces of information • relationship building • locating main idea • predicting • using information for problem solving	• child may be unable to combine elements without a direct teaching approach • child may need to learn systematic strategies to use information for 'problem solving • child may need additional visual stimuli
Critical Listening	• includes understanding • information analysis • recognizes implications • separates fact from fantasy • notes bias or inconsistencies • evaluates information • draws conclusions	• child may have difficulty performing mental processes • child may need to prestate the reason for listening

TABLE 3.1. Continued

Listening Level	Behavioral Manifestations	Comments in Relation to Handicapped Learners
Appreciative Listening	• personal response to what is heard • crosses all other levels of listening • relates to reason for listening	• child may not understand this level due to limited past experiences • child may be out of touch with his or her own feelings and may react based upon peer group codes

LISTENING CHARACTERISTICS OF HANDICAPPED LEARNERS

The types and degrees of auditory dysfunction among handicapped learners vary greatly, much like the general population. Within any classroom a teacher may have a student whose difficulty in listening stems from perceptual problems, while another student's problems may result from a memory deficit, and still another may demonstrate auditory figure-ground confusion. A list of characteristics that may be displayed by handicapped children who have problems listening is delineated below.

❑ A mild hearing loss

❑ Deficient in sound awareness

❑ Difficulty in auditory discrimination

❑ Short attention span during oral presentations

❑ Difficulty following orally presented directions

❑ Problems in focusing upon significant information given within a body of orally presented material

❑ Inadequate mental organization of orally presented material

❑ Low frustration tolerance in oral language tasks

❑ Reliance upon visual stimuli

❑ Avoidance of oral language activities

❑ Inappropriate responding to oral questioning

❏ Inability to follow the logic of a debate or argument

❏ Sound distortions resulting in confusion, misinterpretations, and mispronunciation of words

❏ Inability to remember what is heard

ASSESSMENT OF LISTENING SKILLS

The variation in children's listening ability is the result of individual differences as well as situational factors. Assessment of listening skills will assist in the development of objectives and in the selection of appropriate teaching techniques. For instance, informal testing of spoken language retention may indicate that a child remembers material best when given a visual mediation strategy. If this is the case, the goal of retention is better served when the teacher helps the child visualize spoken language through word association, imagery, or pairing of visual and auditory stimuli. Assessment of listening skills, both formal and informal, is a preliminary step to instructional planning.

Formal Assessment

Formal assessment of listening is generally accomplished through tests designed to examine auditory retention and comprehension. Many listening tests are actually subtests of more comprehensive language assessments. Although the results of these subtests are important themselves for assessing a child's listening ability, their real importance is within the totality of the language assessment as a clue to how the child's listening skills interface with other language areas. Several of the most prominent formats for formally assessing listening ability, which are detailed by Wiig and Semel (1984), are outlined in Table 3.2. Formal tests that use these formats within their listening subtests are presented in Table 3.3.

Informal Assessment

Although formal tests do exist for pinpointing specific auditory skill deficits, listening assessment is most often carried out informally through diagnostic testing. Wallace and Larsen (1978) define *diagnostic testing* as, "the process that permits a teacher to analyze a child's behavior while

TABLE 3.2. Listening Assessment Approaches

Assessment Approach	Format	Information Gathered
Word Sequences	Child repeats a sequence of one to eight unrelated words or unordered digits in either a forward or backward presentation	Immediate auditory memory span is assessed as well as child's predominant strategies for recall (e.g., rehearsal, imagery)
Oral Directions	Child is expected to carry out a series of directions varying in number and complexity	Assesses memory efficiency (i.e., the synthesis of words resulting in meaningful perceptual-conceptual units)
Details in Spoken Paragraphs	Graded paragraphs increasing in sentence length and complexity are spoken to the child who, depending upon grade, is asked to recall details of names, places, events, and relationships	Assesses the child's ability to (a) sustain auditory attention, (b) selectively attend to detail, (c) recall and retrieve information and inferences

Adapted with permission from Wiig, E., & Semel, E. (1984). *Language assessment and intervention for the learning disabled* (2nd ed.). Columbus, OH: Charles E. Merrill. Reprinted with permission of Merrill Publishing Co.

the teacher engages in teaching" (p. 261). As oral material is presented in the classroom and whenever students engage in oral language activities, there are opportunities for the teacher to observe and evaluate the child's listening ability. Generally, a teacher is interested in promoting increased listening and, therefore, examines the language environment for elements that facilitate this process. However, in specific cases, it is necessary to assess areas that impede listening as a result of the child's skill development.

Two general approaches to informal listening assessment are (a) teacher checklist and (b) skill assessment. Each of these approaches offers specific information or a testing advantage that would advocate its use within certain situations. However, a case can be made for the benefits of combining the approaches and completing a more thorough assessment.

TABLE 3.3. Formal Tests of Listening Skills

Test Name	Publisher	Ages Appropriate	Administration	Relevant
McCarthy Scales of Children's Abilities (McCarthy, 1972)	Psychological Corporation	2–6 to 8–6	Individual	Verbal memory (Parts I, II), Numerical memory
Wechsler Intelligence Scale for Children–Revised (WISC–R) (Wechsler, 1974)	Psychological Corporation	6–0 to 17–0	Individual	Digit span
Detroit Tests of Learning Aptitude (DTLA-2) (Hammill, 1985)	PRO-ED	6–3 to 19–0	Individual	Auditory attention span for unrelated words; oral directions
Illinois Test of Psycholinguistic Abilities (ITPA) (Kirk, McCarthy, & Kirk, 1968)	University of Illinois Press	2–4 to 10–3	Individual	Auditory sequential memory
Clinical Evaluation of Language Functions (CELF) (Wiig & Semel, 1980)	Psychological Corporation	K–10 5–0 to 16–0	Individual	Processing oral directions; processing spoken paragraphs

FIGURE 3.2. Listening Checklist

Name _____ Date _____ Observer _____

Observation made during _____

LISTENING SKILLS	USES SKILL IN:			
	Informal Setting	Formal Academic Setting	Small Group	Large Group
1. appears to be paying attention				
2. discriminates and recognizes environmental sounds				
3. focuses upon relevant auditory stimuli				
4. seldom mispronounces common words				
5. follows directions given verbally				
6. can recall facts, events, etc., heard orally				
7. remembers concepts and sequences of materials presented orally				
8. responds appropriately to oral questions				
9. engages in appropriate dialogue				
10. participates in discussions				

Checklist. As a teacher presents information throughout the school day, multiple opportunities occur to observe a child's listening skills. Unfortunately, many teachers of exceptional children are so involved in the presentation of material and the development of the child's response that little attention is ever paid to how the child listens. A conscious effort to observe a child's listening ability will minimize this problem. Development of a checklist such as the one provided in Figure 3.2 will allow the teacher to assess listening skills. Two advantages to using a checklist are the easy adaptations of such instruments for particular settings and the relative ease of use and interpretation.

The focus of the checklist is upon student behaviors that indicate listening effectiveness. As such, the teacher is assessing the student's responses (expressions of learning) to the oral environment and relating these observations to listening ability.

Listening Skill Assessment. Another approach to listening assessment is to examine individual skill development. The aim of skill assessment is to determine if there are any significant deficits that may reduce the student's effectiveness in learning. Emphasis is placed upon the student's responding ability within the listening sequence (receiving-processing-responding). Therefore, listening assessments should be structured so that children need to respond. Discrimination, recall of information, and comprehension are examples of response categories that reflect listening ability. Each of these is briefly discussed below in regard to informal assessment of listening.

Discrimination involves the degree to which one sound is distinguished from other sounds. Stephens (1977) believes that auditory discrimination difficulties are evident in the mispronunciation of common words and the confusion of similar sounds. To assess discrimination, Stephens suggests:

1. Select material which is within the child's listening comprehension.

2. Set a criterion level below which performance is inadequate.

3. Pronounce the material one unit at a time; tell the (examinee) to repeat exactly what you say.

4. Note inaccuracies in pronunciation. (p. 162)

Recall of auditory stimuli is an essential skill of all learners. Success within both the regular and special education classrooms depends upon immediate and delayed recall of information. Be certain that during the assessment of auditory recall the learner uses only the auditory channel to gain information. A general procedure for the assessment of recall is given below.

1. Select a task(s) that is within the child's repertoire and that can be completed following oral directions.

2. Establish a criterion level.

3. Present the student with directions, providing all necessary materials for task completion.

4. Increase the number and complexity of the directions.

Delayed recall can be assessed in a similar manner with the completion of the task occurring 24 hours later. Other procedures, such as recall of story content, are just as appropriate for skill assessment and may even prove more adaptable for delayed recall diagnosis.

Comprehension, the ability to understand what is heard, is a more complex skill. A child who carries out an orally given direction is demonstrating not only auditory recall but also a basic level of comprehension. Higher order comprehension can be assessed by the following procedure:

1. Establish a criterion level for performance.

2. Select a series of verbal statements that reflect a variety of semantic relationships.

3. Say one statement at a time, having the student restate the phrase or retell the action in his or her own words.

TEACHING LISTENING SKILLS

Classroom practices involving the listening component of the language arts curriculum need to relate to the general features of daily listening activities. By maintaining a functional view, instruction can be directed at teaching the most generalizable elements of good listening. Examples of real-life listening activities include:

❑ listening to the news, a comedy show, or movie

❑ talking to a friend

❑ taking notes in class

❑ arguing with a sibling

❑ learning new information

❑ following a parent's directions

❑ responding to instructional questions

❑ listening to a story

❑ hearing a lecture

❑ listening to records

❑ making arrangements

❑ using the telephone

❑ taking orders for materials/services

❑ interviewing for a job

❑ listening to a joke

Assumptions About Listening Instruction

There are many inappropriate beliefs or myths about listening that interfere with the establishment of a good instructional program. One such myth is that listening is automatic and, therefore, cannot be taught. Teachers who understand the concepts of listening and the importance of this skill for problem learners are more inclined to develop a battery of activities directed at increasing listening ability. Some basic assumptions about listening instruction are:

1. Listening skills can be taught.

2. We cannot *give* students the ability to listen. We can aid, guide, and focus on listening by (a) setting an appropriate environment and (b) increasing the oral presentation impact.

3. Listening is an active transaction among an individual, the environment, and information. We listen best when we listen for a purpose.

4. Listening can be part of any subject curriculum.

5. There is not just one form of listening, and therefore students must be able to select and apply the appropriate listening strategy in any given situation.

Features of Listening that Are Important for Instruction

Ur (1984) examined daily listening tasks in an attempt to develop generalized features of the listening act. The result is a list of six essential features which are present in some combination within a listening activity. Although any listening situation may lack one or more of the features, no listening will occur with none of the characteristics present. The six generalizations specified by Ur that have direct teaching implications for problem learners are discussed below.

We Listen for a Purpose and with Certain Expectations. There are very few situations in which we are asked to listen that we don't have some idea of what we are going to hear. (Exceptions may be turning on a radio or television at random.) In the classroom, specific modes of talking associated with subject areas are known as *registers* and include the vocabulary, sentence structure, and relationships of the subject content.

Registers help us form expectations about what we are listening to. Richards (1978) makes a case for certain children's failure within individual subjects to be the result of never having learned the needed subject register. Teachers need to establish a means by which the child can perceive a purpose for listening. Problem learners can be helped to listen for relevant content through structuring statements and advanced organizers. The child who has difficulty focusing upon relevant stimuli will need to be prompted to seek certain information, to relate to previously learned concepts, and to remember vocabulary. It follows that expectations are closely linked to an understanding of purpose. That is, we hold certain expectations for a response when we ask a specific question, attend a lecture on a topic we know something about, or participate in a familiar group activity. When students listen to material that corresponds with their perceived expectations, the result is an increase in comprehension.

We Make an Immediate Response to What We Hear. Few person-to-person listening situations do not require some overt response. Even in cases of listening to electronic media such as television or a stereo, it is common to react by dancing to music, or laughing at a comedy routine. Within the classroom it is important to provide students with frequent opportunities to respond rather than waiting until the end of a cumbersome listening passage. Engaging students more frequently has been shown to increase achievement (Brophy & Good, 1986).

Providing students with instruction in active listening will help them to develop engagement strategies. Many mildly handicapped children have difficulty organizing information in a way that increases understanding and allows for retention. One technique to alleviate this problem is to teach association or mediation strategies. The listener is taught to silently manipulate the information by associating the material with already familiar material, posing a question, determining points of interest or agreement, and/or thinking of examples to apply the information. The teacher should also establish instructional breaks in the oral presentation which will help the student to cluster information into meaningful units.

We See the Person We Are Listening To. In nearly all cases we are able to visually relate to the speaker's characteristics (e.g., facial expression, dress, posture, gestures, etc.). Even while watching television the listener is afforded this opportunity to assess the influence of these personal attributes as part of the message. Visual memory often plays a similar role when conversing on the telephone. Research has consistently indicated that LD children and adolescents are less able than their normal peers to assess another person's affective state as expressed through nonverbal features (Bachara, 1976; Bryan, 1977; Wiig & Harris, 1974). In effect, they are not able to determine social cues which often significantly alter the meaning of an oral message. Classroom listening exercises need to help children recognize and assess the speaker's nonverbal characteristics which impact upon the message. Role playing, charades, and mime activities are excellent for achieving this goal.

The Environment Offers Clues to the Meaning of the Message. Most environmental clues, apart from those presented by the speaker, offer information about the situation, the atmosphere, and the general climate in which the oral message is being given. It is possible to determine intensity, formality, mood, and elements of relationship by observing the surroundings even with limited oral comprehension. An example of this is when one who travels in a foreign country is unable to speak the language. A great deal of information is gained from the environment—so much so that few travelers make outrageous mistakes. Speakers often highlight their statements with maps or emphasis upon the surroundings. Noises, smells and other stimuli that permeate our senses offer important background information.

The classroom implications of environmental cues being valuable to the listening act are clear. The problem learner needs to learn to observe and select relevant stimuli from the background. Although a great deal of attention has focused on the distractibility of many mildly handicapped children, it is possible to teach focusing skills. Within the classroom students need to focus upon visual materials such as overheads, charts, blackboards, and manipulatives. Such materials should be used to support oral presentations and should help the listener focus upon essential material. Environmental cues that interfere with listening by distracting, contradicting, or confusing the spoken message should be eliminated.

Stretches of Heard Discourse Come in Short Chunks. Listening alternates with responding in a series of repetitions, as in a classroom when the teacher interrupts the presentation with questions aimed at checking student comprehension. Periods of extended discourse are broken into smaller units by switching speakers, movement of the speaker or of an environmental cue, or listener reaction. Formal speeches such as lectures and broadcast reports are more continuous; however, the listener manages these stretches by relaxing attention, only to continually refocus as the verbal message goes on. As mentioned earlier, many mildly handicapped children experience problems in attention. Teachers can help these children by (a) breaking directions or lectures into short meaningful units which the listener can more easily comprehend; (b) pairing verbal messages with visual stimuli; (c) eliciting high levels of student participation and; (d) varying the presentation format.

Most Heard Discourse Is Spontaneous and Informal. Heard discourse, there-fore, differs from formal spoken prose in the amount of redundancy, noise, colloquialism, and auditory character. Spoken language can be described in terms of a formal-informal continuum covering such dis-course as political speeches to spontaneous conversation. Although the distinction between the extremes is evident, the majority of the spoken language we listen to lies in a somewhat grayer area containing elements of both formal and informal language. Within classrooms language tends to be informal in nature and contains (a) redundant speech in the form of rephrasings, corrections, repetitions and multiple stimuli; (b) collo-quial speech involving pronunciation, insertions, and slang expressions; (c) auditory character reflecting the number of pauses, uneven speed and pitch, hesitations, emotional exclamations, and interruptions; and (d) noise suggesting interference due to outside disturbances and mis-understood words and phrases.

Understanding the characteristics of the language a listener must attend to helps teachers to alter their discourse to achieve greater effectiveness. Mildly handicapped learners actually benefit from some of the characteristics of informal discourse. The number of repetitions and other redundant elements allow the problem listener to gather information even after a direction, description, or fact has been stated. When presenting oral information it is important for the teacher to provide multiple cues and to intersperse the discourse with colloquial-isms the child is most apt to comprehend. Pauses allow the listener to refocus attention and to mentally organize information for understand-ing and retrieval purposes. The speed with which information is pre-sented in classrooms also influences the message's impact. Research has dealt with the effect of compressed speech on the comprehension of mildly handicapped students. In studies with LDs, EMRs and normals, those students who listened to compressed speech learned the same amount of material in less time than students who listened to material presented at a normal rate. It appears we may be underestimating the amount of material mildly handicapped children are capable of listening to within a specified time period (D'Alonzo, 1981; D'Alonzo & Zucker, 1982). Robinson and Smith (1983) present a set of strategies designed to modify the speaker's message to increase listening effectiveness (Table 3.4).

Modifying Listening Behavior

Listening skills can be increased not only by amending the speaker's message but through direct instruction aimed at modifying the listener's behavior. Information regarding problems experienced by handicapped

TABLE 3.4. Strategies to Modify Input (The Message)

Input	Interventions
Attention—focusing the listener's attention on the speaker	1. Give direct instructions (Example: "Listen to what I'm going to say"). 2. Shorten input. 3. Use visual aid. 4. Reduce extraneous stimuli. 5. Increase proximity of speaker to listener.
Language	1. Simplify vocabulary. 2. Restate message. 3. Simplify syntax.
Memory—the speaker's facilitating listener recall	1. Use high-frequency words. 2. Disseminate group information in easily associated categories. 3. Use groupings categorized by semantic membership (what they are) rather than where or when. 4. Control message length. 5. Control linguistic (or surface) structure. 6. Control restatements—should be exact or will confuse. 7. Control serial position of information—information given last is remembered best, information given in the middle is forgotten most easily. 8. Use careful phrasing—can group words or elements for listener. 9. Increase relevance of material to listener—increases recall.
Comprehension	Provide practice at all levels of literal, critical, and appreciative comprehension.

From Robinson, S., & Smith, D. (1981). Listening skills: Teaching learning disabled students to be better listeners. *Focus on Exceptional Children, 13*(8), 1–15. Reprinted with permission of Love Publishing Company.

learners and remediation strategies have been provided throughout this chapter. However, a concise listing of instructional tactics may be helpful. Table 3.5 lists four areas of listening behavior that can be directly modified and provides associated objectives and intervention strategies.

TABLE 3.5. Modifying Listening Behaviors

Listening Behaviors	Objectives	Interventions
Attention	To increase the listener's ability to focus upon relevant stimuli and attention during extended discourse or oral presentation	1. Peer modeling 2. Teacher modeling 3. Verbal rehearsal 4. Reinforcement of physical guidance 5. Self-monitoring
Language	To increase understanding of what is being heard through expansion of the listener's conceptual and experiential background	1. Increase in vocabulary 2. Increase in knowledge of multiple word meanings 3. Increase in syntactic skills 4. Increase in experience 5. Role playing
Memory	To enhance memory processes so that the listening may store and retrieve essential information	1. Rehearsal during listening 2. Clustering or chunking information 3. Coding information 4. Visualization 5. Clarifying statements 6. Question asking 7. Identifying organizational cues (first, second) 8. Rehearsal after listening 9. Summarizing message after listening 10. Comparing information received to develop categories 11. Note taking
Comprehension	To increase meaningful listening by providing opportunities for (a) integrating information and (b) developing appropriate responses	1. Practice at all cognitive levels of listening 2. Practice in identifying nonverbal messages 3. Role playing 4. Discussion groups

Adapted from Robinson, S., & Smith, D. (1981). Listening skills: Teaching learning disabled students to be better listeners. *Focus on Exceptional Children, 13*(8), 1–15. Reprinted with permission of Love Publishing Company.

LISTENING ACTIVITIES

Listening can best be taught by integrating listening activities into the broader areas of the language arts and other content area curricula. Listening activities should not be conducted in isolation but instead should be used to enhance learning skills of reading, speaking, writing, and general knowledge. The selection of listening activities should be based upon practical considerations of individual and group character- istics and pre-established instructional objectives. Some general cate- gories of listening activities pertinent to the learning needs of many handicapped learners are:

❑ Distinguishing nonlanguage sounds

❑ Discriminating voices

❑ Following directions

❑ Remembering what you hear

❑ Organizing material

Each of these categories is discussed in more detail in the following sections.

Distinguishing Nonlanguage Sounds

Listening is learned by performing listening tasks more than by reading about listening skills, following flowcharts of good listening procedure, or discussing listener characteristics (Hennings, 1979). Children, at an early age, need to participate in activities that heighten the need for accurate listening. When children enter school, they already have devel- oped processing and responding skills. However, their listening expe- riences of the previous five or six years may not have developed their listening skills to the level required by the educational environment. Many special needs children enter school with levels of listening com- prehension lower than their average peers. Immediately, such children are placed at a disadvantage for learning to read, retrieving and retaining information presented orally, and participating fully in classroom dis- cussions and other oral activities.

Background noise can affect accuracy in discriminating among speech sounds (Hennings, 1979) as well as in comprehension of the environ- ment around us. A great deal of information is gained incidentally from understanding nonlanguage sounds. The listener must be aware of such sounds and learn to interpret them appropriately. Activities that can help a child develop comprehension of nonlanguage sounds are:

1. Make students aware of school sounds that transmit messages (e.g., bells, doors, footsteps, etc.).

2. Changes in weather conditions are often signaled by sounds. Have students discuss these sounds and establish their meanings.

3. Play a variety of musical instruments and have students associate each with a mood or feeling. Students may be asked to act out the feeling or draw a representational picture.

4. Read an oral passage while other environmental sounds can be heard. At the conclusion of the passage, discuss what effect sounds had on listening and what different students did to block out the extraneous noise.

5. Listen to a variety of environmental sounds and have children develop categories such as loud, soft, harsh, smooth, far, near, and so forth.

6. Have students listen to a taped story in which nonverbal sounds are significant to the context. Ask students to discuss (draw) significant features in the story.

Discriminating Voices

As we listen to speech, we process and respond to different elements within and among voices. For example, often children accustomed to a particular teacher's voice will pick that voice out and attend to it in a crowded and noisy area such as a playground. All listeners have a need to selectively attend to certain persons and must tune in to voice features which distinguish one voice from another. In addition, each speaker uses variations in tone, pitch, and pacing to convey significant messages. A harsh tone versus a soothing voice, an excited, cracking voice versus an even-pitched one, and a well-paced voice are examples of how voice elements influence message presentation. Often, differences in voices are too subtle for problem learners to detect and react to. Activities that focus upon interpretation of voice differences are extremely helpful.

1. Tape-record a story read in two or more different voices, changing elements such as tone or pitch. Have students discuss the different messages presented by the stories.

2. Ask the class to list characteristics of voices. Categorize the characteristics as pleasant, annoying, meaningful, nonmeaningful, and so forth.

3. When the class is in a noisy, crowded situation, the teacher should try to gain attention by speaking in a normal voice. Slowly, the teacher's voice should increase in loudness until members of the class are attending. A note should be made of when different children began to attend. Discuss the differences with the class.

4. Have three or four known people repeat the same statement on language master cards. Have a student label the cards and list what features distinguished each voice.

5. The teacher should use voice variations to present emotional aspects of a message. Then have the class label the emotion and identify the voice characteristics that conveyed it.

Following Directions

In and out of school settings listeners are asked to follow verbally given directions. The inability to do so commonly is listed as an identifying characteristic of handicapped learners. Following directions is essential to instructional accuracy. How a teacher presents task directions is as important as the listener's ability to attend to and implement the directions themselves. However, given any teacher's style and level of instructional competence, the learner is ultimately responsible for carrying out the directions. Students need to learn to listen for key directions and then to segment or sequence the directions appropriately. Activities that will help students learn to listen for and carry out directions are:

1. Play a command game in which children are expected to respond to a set of commands. Similar to "Simon Says," this game allows children to follow simple directions to increasingly more complex ones.

2. Have students work in pairs. One member of the pair is given a geometric picture, which must be described to the other partner. The description should be developed as a series of directions and given in such a way that the partner can reproduce the geometric design. The partner drawing the picture cannot ask any questions other than to have the direction repeated or rephrased.

3. Bring a new piece of equipment into the classroom and explain its possible uses (e.g., opaque projector, computer, or computer printer). Then orally give directions on how to operate the equipment. After a student has learned the operation procedure, he or she can be the one to direct the next learner.

4. Have students listen to a story for embedded directions that will lead to a "treasure." The child should write down each direction as it is given and at the end of the story follow all the directions to find the hidden object.

5. Provide each learner with a map of the local area or state. Present a series of directional commands to take them on a special trip. The listener who correctly follows the orally given route should be able to name the destination when the teacher announces, "We've arrived."

6. A variation on the previous activity is to have students work on a grid and arrive at a specific square by following directions. This activity can be done incorporating math sequences ("Move up 2 + 5 spaces") or other subject content ("Move to the left the number of spaces in the word *meeting*").

Remembering What You Hear

Information given orally needs to be instantly comprehended and remembered. The listener may need the information only for a short period of time, as in the case of following a verbal direction or when one engages in a brief social exchange (e.g., "I'm glad to hear you are doing well"). However, in many educational and social instances, the need to remember what we've heard over a longer period is paramount to the listening act itself. What is remembered is related to how the listener understands and organizes information as well as to such factors as motivation for listening, interest in what is being said, and affective components such as whether the speaker is liked. The complexity of the oral language situation makes it difficult to pinpoint activities or strategies that will clearly result in better recall. The suggestions that follow, however, are aimed at providing the listener with practice in short-term and/or long-term recall.

1. Read lists of elements that are contained within two or three different concept categories. Have different listeners remember components of their assigned category and then combine their lists.

2. Have students participating in a class discussion summarize the statements of the child who spoke immediately before them prior to adding their own comments.

3. Read a story aloud and ask students to try to remember as much detail as possible. At the end of the story, ask the class to make a list of key words. Wait one or two days before asking the students to "Look at these key words and remember the story details." Students

may need to add to the key word list at this time. After another day or two, provide the key word list again and direct students to reconstruct the story. For older children the delay from story to reconstruction may be increased.

4. Establish strings of rhyming words by stating a key word (e.g., *chair*) and having each child add a new rhyming word onto the string. A student who repeats an already-used word is out of the game.

5. Provide comprehension questions prior to reading a passage from a content area textbook. After listening to the reading students are to respond to the comprehension questions. An enhancement of this is to have students summarize the material or to evaluate the content.

6. Have the class listen to a radio news program. At the end of the broadcast, each student is to write a headline for each story he or she remembered.

7. A more advanced strategy related to a radio listening activity is to have students write an editorial concerning the most significant news story they heard.

Organizing Material

A significant aspect of the listening process concerns how one goes about organizing what is heard. Teaching handicapped learners to use prelistening and listening strategies (Table 3.6) leads to improved listening effectiveness. Such techniques as listening for a purpose, vocabulary awareness, clustering, and preparation for oral discourse allow the listener to structure the material for efficient responding, storage, and ultimately greater retrieval and recall.

Prelistening and listening skills are particularly important in the comprehension and retention of content area subject matter. Wiseman, Hartwell, and Hannafin, 1980) found that LD adolescents were able to attain as much, if not more, information from listening to content material as from direct reading of subject textbooks. The student who is successful at gathering information from an oral presentation or a taped reading of a textbook may be able to circumvent many of the problems associated with a reading disability. When large amounts of material are prescribed and the listener is expected to retain and apply the information, organizational skills become essential. Teachers can assist students in their listening organization by (a) using study guides to highlight main concepts; (b) teaching relevant vocabulary prior to the main lesson; (c) providing advanced organizers to establish a framework for the presentation; and (d) using prequestioning to direct listening.

TABLE 3.6. Organizational Skills Related to Listening

Stage of Listening Process	Organizational Skills

Prelistening	1. Mental preparedness
	   a. Review notes from previous class
	   b. Read/review information related to the topic
	   c. Relate topic to previous experiences
	   d. Examine study guides, outlines, etc.
	
	2. Semantic preparedness
	   a. Learn key vocabulary related to the topic
	   b. Isolate terms that should be focused upon
	
	3. Physical preparedness
	   a. Proximity to speaker
	   b. Position body toward speaker
	   c. Focus attention (eye contact) on speaker
	   d. Have necessary materials available (books, pencils, etc.)

Listening	1. Categorize or regroup information as it is heard
	
	2. Listen for verbal cues to the organization of the speaker
	
	3. Observe nonverbal cues that emphasize or highlight organization
	
	4. Identify main and supporting ideas
	
	5. Formulate questions
	
	6. Use memory strategies
	   a. Rehearsal strategies
	   b. Visualization techniques
	   c. Clustering techniques
	
	7. Notetaking

Postlistening	1. Review presented information, notes, and handouts 2. Seek information for unanswered questions 3. Summarize what has been said 4. Relate information to past learning 5. Review material for next session

Strategies that help to foster organized approaches to listening are:

1. *Prediction*: The teacher reads a story containing elements of sequence and logic to the class, leaving off the conclusion. Children are then asked to predict the outcome. Variations on this activity would include providing historical accounts, scientific experiments, and personal dialogue.

2. *Cloze Technique*: An adaptation of the old party game, *Mad Libs*, is a useful activity for helping students use context clues to determine missing parts. The teacher reads aloud a series of sentences, leaving out one relevant word. From the context of the sentence, the student must decide on what part of speech is appropriate for the missing element and what word to insert.

3. *Timelining*: Plotting timelines helps students to organize sequential material. As the student listens to a historical or fictional story which takes place across time, he or she plots the sequence of events on a timeline.

4. *Prequestioning*: Prior to providing oral information, the teacher asks one to three questions concerning the most relevant material. Students are expected to listen for the answers and to take notes which will help them respond.

5. *Study Guides*: The teacher provides each student with a study guide which is examined prior to listening to content material. Based on the information provided in the study guide, the student organizes (i.e., classifies, clusters) what is heard. Lesson components such as key vocabulary, basic facts, and essential concepts should be highlighted in the study guide.

6. *Outlining*: The student is asked to listen to a presentation and to use one of the suggested outlining techniques (see Table 3.7) to organize important information.

COMPUTER APPLICATIONS IN LISTENING

The integration of microcomputers into the classroom instructional routine has influenced all aspects of the language arts program including listening. Microcomputers are most important in developing comprehension related to listening. The student is given a series of procedural directions to follow or questions to respond to, and his or her responses are immediately and precisely recorded. The computer exercise allows

TABLE 3.7. Outlining Techniques for Oral Presentations

Type of Outline	Description	Example
Pictorial Outline	Listener makes spontaneous sketches to organize and remember details.	Child draws a series of pictures (using a minimum number of strokes) and arranges them in sequence.
Topical Outline	Listener records main idea and then details that support it.	The topic is identified before the listening experience and items are then recorded such as in a reporter's notebook.
Charting and Timelines	Listener organizes details around the temporal or spatial structure of an incident.	Timelines teach temporal relationships. Spatial relations are taught by quadrant charts or left-right, bottom-top charts.
Format Outlines	Listener is given a format for recording basic ideas, background information, and questions.	Child is directed to categorize information into topical ideas and supporting evidence and then records them into the given format.
Question Sets	Taxonomical sets of questions are provided prior to the narrative for listener to attend to.	The teacher asks Who? When? Why? How do you feel about _____?, etc.
Webbing	Listener identifies the central theme and supporting ideas.	

Hierarchical Outlining	Listener records superordinate categories under which subordinate details are identified.	Traditional
		I.
		  A.
		    1.
		    2.
		    3.
		  B.
		II.
		  A.
		    1.

Adapted with permission from Giordano, G. (1984). *Teaching writing to learning disabled students.* Rockville, MD: Aspen Publications.

for an accurate observation of the correctness of the response, the completeness of the response, and the student's knowledge base. The use of a teacher-made checklist for evaluating listening comprehension would further increase the computer's utility in this area.

BEST PRACTICES

Listening is a developmental skill which, although learned earliest among the language arts, needs to be practiced and improved throughout a child's school years to achieve mastery. Even as adults we experience ebbs and flows in our listening competence. Throughout this chapter, the case has been made for the inclusion of listening skills within the curriculum. The relationship between listening ability and spoken language is believed to be positive, implying the close link among the components of the language arts program.

The teacher of a mildly handicapped child can make a difference in whether or not oral discourse is understood and remembered. It is worth reviewing points made in the chapter that fall under the teacher's control and that promote listening. These include

1. breaking directions or lectures into short, meaningful units;

2. pairing verbal messages with visual stimuli;

3. eliciting frequent student participation;

4. varying the presentation format;

5. providing summary statements at the conclusion of a lesson;

6. using pauses and verbal cues to mark the most important information;

7. providing the student with a variety of situations in which different levels of listening will come into play;

8. teaching students to cluster and organize information for easy retrieval;

9. teaching rehearsal and mediation strategies which promote retention.

Two uncomplicated procedures advocated by Alley and Deshler (1979) as means to help mildly handicapped students listen actively and critically are Directed

Listening Activity, adapted from Cunningham and Cunningham (1976), and Guided Listening, adapted from Manzo (1975). Each technique is an adaptation of a reading procedure and is recommended here because of its utility for increasing listening.

Directed Listening Activity

This technique consists of basically three stages: readiness, listening-reciting, and follow-up. Suggested activities for each stage are as follows:

1. The Readiness Stage
   a. Establish motivation for the lesson.
   b. Introduce any new or difficult concepts.
   c. Introduce any new or difficult words.
   d. Set purposes for listening.

2. The Listening-Reciting Stage
   a. Students listen to satisfy the purposes for listening set during readiness.
   b. The teacher asks several literal and inferential questions that relate to the purposes set during readiness.
   c. The students volunteer interpretive and evaluative comments about the lesson. Some class discussion may ensue.
   d. If there are errors or gaps in the students' understanding of the lesson, the teacher directs the students to relisten to certain parts of the lesson.

3. The Follow-Up Stage
   a. The teacher provides opportunities for and encourages students to engage in activities that build on and develop concepts acquired during the lesson. These may include writing, reading, small group discussions, art activities, . . . (Cunningham & Cunningham, 1976, pp. 301–302)

Guided Listening

This procedure aims at increasing long-term recall and can be appropriately used every few weeks. After a 10- to 15-minute speech is presented (by tape or lecture), the teacher leads the class through the following steps:

1. The teacher sets the major purpose: "Listen to remember everything."

2. The teacher lectures, reads, or plays a recorded selection. If the teacher is lecturing, she records her lecture.

3. The teacher reminds the students that she asked them to listen to remember everything and lists what they remember on the board. (She may have two students perform this task.) During this stage the teacher accepts and writes everything the students contribute. She makes no corrections and asks no questions.

4. The teacher reads everything listed on the board, directing the students to look for incorrect or missing information.

5. The students listen again to the tape, record, or reading to correct wrong information and obtain missing information.

6. The information on the board is amended and added to as needed.

7. The teacher asks the students which ideas on the board seem to be the main ideas, the most important ideas, the ones they think they should remember for a long time. She marks these items.

8. Now that the students have mastered the literal level of the selections, the teacher raises any inferential questions she feels are vital for complete understanding.

9. The teacher erases the board and tests short-term memory with a test that is not dependent on reading or writing skills. (Oral true-false or multiple-choice items will do.)

10. Test long-term memory with a similar test containing different items several weeks later. (Manzo, 1975, pp. 302–303)

4

SPEAKING

Spoken language is essentially the vehicle for our expression of individuality. With the possible exception of occupational fields such as journalism, where writing is used to report facts, speaking is the primary form of communication that defines for others an individual's personality and abilities.

The creation of a simple division between the two oral language areas of listening and speaking clearly represents an artificially discrete separation. Although within this text they are presented in this fashion, this has been done primarily for ease in the presentation of assessment approaches and instructional strategies. In reality the oral decoding process known as listening and the oral encoding process known as speaking are obviously nearly inseparable. In instruction, teachers are advised to be cautious in allowing the two areas to become fragmented curricular concerns.

The emphasis of this chapter is on the specific instructional needs common to many mildly and moderately handicapped children in the schools as well as to those individuals who may be considered remedial or slow learners. Therefore, the focus is neither on those students who are identified as having a specific speech disorder (e.g., articulation problems, stuttering, or voice quality difficulties) nor on those identified as having language disorders of neurological origin (e.g., aphasia). Although many of the assessment approaches and instructional strategies presented may be applicable to these populations, they are not the major target for the chapter.

As previously noted, oral language has often been an overlooked curricular area for mildly and moderately handicapped students. For example, a 1982 survey of teachers of learning disabled students reported that oral language was their primary curricular concern, with their most common question being how to proceed with instructional programming in this area. The purpose of this chapter is to assist in remedying that concern by providing a further understanding of the typical difficulties experienced by exceptional students, identifying approaches for assessing these deficits, and discussing instructional programming strategies to develop spoken language skills and/or remediate specific problem areas.

DEVELOPMENT OF SPEAKING SKILLS

Chapters 1 and 3 provided an appropriate background for understanding the general developmental sequence for language acquisition, with specific attention given to early language milestones and to a sequence of oral receptive skills. In this section attention is given to those oral expressive skills that are most significant for instructional consideration. Because the emphasis of the chapter is on mildly/moderately handicapped children as well as on remedial and slow learning children within the school setting, the developmental sequence presented here is premised on the assumption that these students will enter school with at least a minimal level of competence in language production. Therefore, initial oral expressive skills such as simple one-word labeling and two-word constructions are not included in this sequence; they will be part of the discussion in the chapters in Part III that focus on preschool handicapped children and severely handicapped learners. Table 4.1 outlines specific spoken language skills in the area of structure by emphasizing the language dimensions of morphology and syntax. Table 4.2 focuses on a sequence of skill acquisition related to content and thus within the area of semantics. Finally, Table 4.3 is concerned with language usage and thus deals with pragmatics. The sequences in these tables are adapted from Cureton et al. (1983).

To evaluate an individual's competence, it is beneficial to consider the various levels of usage found in spoken and written language expression. According to Otto and Smith (1980), five levels can be identified with respect to grammar. Rather than one level being essentially correct, various levels may be appropriate in various situations. The five levels that Otto and Smith (1980) listed are described briefly in the following paragraphs.

The *illiterate level* includes language forms most often found in the speech patterns of persons lacking formal education. Examples include

TABLE 4.1. Developmental Sequence in Language Structure

Word Patterns
_____ 1. Uses present progressive verbs
_____ 2. Uses prepositional forms
_____ 3. Uses appropriate plural forms
_____ 4. Uses appropriate past forms
_____ 5. Uses appropriate possessive forms
_____ 6. Uses correct forms of the verb *to be*
_____ 7. Uses appropriate contractions

Sentence Patterns
_____ 1. Uses noun phrases with auxiliary paired with intransitive verb
_____ 2. Uses noun phrase and auxiliary paired with transitive verb and noun phrase as object
_____ 3. Uses noun phrase and form of the verb *to be* and noun object
_____ 4. Uses irregular past forms of verb tenses
_____ 5. Uses regular and irregular third person singular forms with verb agreement
_____ 6. Uses contracted and uncontracted auxiliary verbs
_____ 7. Uses various verbals such as gerunds, participles, and infinitives

Adapted with permission from *Developmental language instruction curriculum,* copyright 1984 by County School Board of Fairfax County, Fairfax County Public Schools, Fairfax, Virginia.

youse, ain't, and *knowed.* The illiterate level, though commonly used, is rarely considered acceptable in the school setting.

The *homely level* is essentially one step above the illiterate level. Included here are specific language forms reflective of dialectical patterns. Rather than being viewed as incorrect and therefore rejected, these forms may be quite acceptable in certain settings and can be modified for school usage over a period of time. Examples include confusion between the word pairs *take* and *carry, sit* and *set,* and *lie* and *lay* and the use of certain phrases such as *haven't hardly* and *light-complected.*

The next level, *standard informal English,* is the most common form of colloquial speech used by educated persons. It typically is the language of the classroom and thus will often be the goal in oral language training with school-age students. This language form includes acceptable use of pronouns such as *I, me, him,* and *her;* appropriate forms of the verb *to be* with respect to number and tense; appropriate use of past tenses of common irregular words such as *saw, gave,* and *took;* and the elimination of double negatives.

TABLE 4.2. Developmental Sequence in Semantics

_____ 1. Uses nouns as agents and objects
_____ 2. Uses action words appropriately
_____ 3. Uses courtesy words appropriately for greetings
_____ 4. Provides descriptive words
_____ 5. Uses agent-action-object constructions
_____ 6. Uses three word constructions to indicate location of objects
_____ 7. Coordinates two ideas into sentences with or without a conjunction
_____ 8. Correctly uses common pronouns
_____ 9. Responds verbally to questions
_____ 10. Uses nouns for a variety of specific cases
_____ 11. Uses forms of the verb _to be_ appropriately
_____ 12. Uses modifier words appropriately in a variety of cases (descriptive, locative, existence)
_____ 13. Uses adverbs in appropriate form (location, time, manner, comparison)
_____ 14. Appropriately uses prepositions for various purposes

Adapted with permission from _Developmental language instruction curriculum,_ copyright 1984 by County School Board of Fairfax County, Fairfax County Public Schools, Fairfax, Virginia.

The informal level is distinguished from the _formal level,_ because the latter includes closer scrutiny of the agreement of nouns and verbs, the word order of modifiers, and the tone of the words that are used. The formal level is typically characterized by a greater degree of care in usage and includes distinctions between _shall_ and _will,_ correct selection of _who_ versus _whom,_ and noun and verb agreement for words such as _neither_ and _was._

The last level is the _literary level._ According to Otto and Smith (1980), the purpose of this level is not only to communicate but also to achieve beauty through language. They cite Lincoln's Gettysburg Address as the classic example of the literary level; in this case language form was taken far beyond the clarity of expression that represents the basic nature of standard English. Certainly the use of language at the literary level would be desirable for anyone to achieve, though it is not a typical component of the special education curriculum.

SPEAKING CHARACTERISTICS OF HANDICAPPED LEARNERS

As discussed in Chapters 2 and 3, the language characteristics of mildly and moderately handicapped students suggest a wide diversity of

TABLE 4.3. Developmental Sequence in Pragmatics

_____ 1. Asks appropriate questions
_____ 2. Interrupts at appropriate times and in appropriate manner
_____ 3. Initiates appropriate verbal greetings and farewells
_____ 4. Identifies next speaker in a group by eye contact, gesture, or name
_____ 5. Responds appropriately by smiling, frowning, or otherwise responding to verbal stimulation
_____ 6. Modifies volume (loudness) for given social situation
_____ 7. Is able to clarify a topic for discussion
_____ 8. Requests clarification of topic or discussion
_____ 9. Can successfully participate in a discussion that requires turn-taking
_____ 10. Accepts momentary silence during a conversation
_____ 11. Back channels appropriately (provides short responses to keep conversation going with comments such as "really?," "why?," "uh huh")
_____ 12. Resists topic change when further discussion is desired
_____ 13. Closes conversation in appropriate manner
_____ 14. Uses politeness and tact
_____ 15. Is able to adjust to formality of language with regard to specific communicative situations
_____ 16. Communicates questions and commands
_____ 17. Communicates to facilitate a positive social environment
_____ 18. Communicates negative statements

Adapted with permission from *Developmental language instruction curriculum,* copyright 1984 by County School Board of Fairfax County, Fairfax County Public Schools, Fairfax, Virginia.

instructional needs. While some students can accurately be identified as language disordered, others simply have a need for an appropriate developmental program that reinforces the skills they are naturally acquiring. Specific characteristics of handicapped students with implications for intervention programs are discussed in the following sections according to the language dimensions of speech production (phonology), structure (morphology and syntax), content (semantics), usage (pragmatics), and how stages of development affect progress.

Problems with Phonology

Phonology relates primarily to the area of speech production. Typically, the problems that may be encountered have to do with the analysis and/or synthesis of specific speech sounds. Some of these problems may relate to motoric difficulties such as inability to perform necessary motor action or a problem in recalling precise motor patterns necessary for a particular utterance. Because these are not typically among the primary concerns or responsibilities of special and regular education classroom teachers, phonology will not be explored in any great length within this chapter. The reader is referred to any number of excellent texts on communication disorders and speech correction (e.g., Hixon, Shriberg, & Saxman, 1980) for further information on this topic.

Problems with Structure

Before considering the structural areas of *morphology* and *syntax*, it is illustrative to consider the relationship between surface structure and deep structure. Surface structure essentially refers to grammatical aspects of language; it provides a vehicle for understanding the true meaning, or deep structure, of an utterance. If students experience problems in decoding surface structure, there are clear implications for problems in comprehension and production of deep structure. Even in cases where students can comprehend surface structure, difficulties with or an inordinate amount of attention paid to surface structure can prevent them from fully understanding the meaning of the communication.

As an illustration of this concept, students who have problems with structure can find themselves lost in conversations and unable to follow the train of thought presented by the speaker. Although this represents a receptive problem, it ultimately can have implications for expressive oral language as well. An inability to follow structure can lead to difficulties in finding the correct formulation of words and sentences. Although this may manifest itself as an apparent search for a forgotten word, it actually may represent syntactical errors, as when the speaker tries to correct a grammatically inaccurate utterance but loses the train of thought, thus omitting words or using incorrect words. At any rate, problems in organization and form have frequently been cited as characteristics of exceptional students (e.g., Johnson & Myklebust, 1967). For example, learning disabled children have frequently been seen as using less complex language. This has been variously described as a generalized delay in acquisition, overall problems in syntax, specific problems in the use of complex sentences, and delay in the rate of acquisition of new grammatical structures (Boucher, 1984).

Several cautions must be considered in documenting the presence of structural errors in handicapped children. Bartel and Bryen (1982) noted that children typically exhibit a considerable amount of inconsistency in morphology. They cited vacillation in the use of *camed* and *come* as an example.

Second, caution must be exercised due to the dialectical variations often found in the structure of utterances of exceptional students. This can be particularly important for teachers working with students who speak black dialect, because it represents a formal system of morphological and syntactical rules at variance with standard English. It is important to therefore distinguish between specific linguistic deficiencies and differences based on dialect used in the home and/or community. This concern is further discussed in Chapter 12.

Problems with Semantics

One of the most frequently cited difficulties found in exceptional students in the area of semantics (or content) has been referred to as *dysonomia* or reauditorization problems. In spite of the ponderous sound of these words, they essentially refer to word retrieval problems experienced by a speaker, most often affecting nouns but also found with other parts of speech (Johnson & Myklebust, 1967). This lexical problem may be manifested (a) as delayed verbal responding, (b) as incorrect word choice where substitutions are made that do not accurately convey the intended message, (c) as the insertion of slang words or "filler" words such as *whatchamacallit* or *thingumajig,* or (d) as efforts to define the word. For other individuals, problems with word retrieval can lead to circumlocutions that are simply efforts to talk around the word. For example, consider the individual stuck at mid-sentence in the following: "I went to the baseball game the other night and I was really surprised how mad my uncle got at the . . . You know, the man who stands behind the catcher on the field . . . runs the game . . . calls people out . . . wears a blue coat."

Several other manifestations of problems with vocabulary are gestures and stereotyped or repetitive speech. In the case of gestures, the individual substitutes motor movements for specific words or phrases that are difficult for him or her to retrieve. In the case of stereotyped speech, there is limited variety in utterances because of an unexpanded vocabulary and hence restricted options for expressing similar concepts.

Wiig and Semel (1980) also identified the difficulty that some individuals have with multiple meanings. For example, the word *run* is best known in its basic verb form. However, there are numerous meanings of the word *run*, including references to stockings, streams, streaks (i.e., of good luck), playing cards, and scores in baseball. For some students the absence of the original meaning of the word as they have learned it can lead to confusion and create problems in understanding and using alternative meanings of the word. Similarly, it should not be surprising that handicapped students also regularly experience difficulties in responding to conversations laden with idiomatic expressions or slang ("Get down"; "up the creek without a paddle"; "not playing with a full deck") and metaphors and similes ("She eats like a bird"; "He's as skinny as a rail").

Hoskins (1983) indicated that although disabled children and adults may use adequate vocabulary in explanations or descriptions, they nevertheless may still have significant semantic difficulties. Areas that may present particular problems include the flexible use of words in various contexts, concepts not fully developed for words, and understanding idioms and sarcasm. The latter problem can have potentially serious social implications, Hoskins (1983) related the example of a woman in charge of a fund-raising project who changed her direction when told she was "barking up the wrong tree," which she assumed referred to the bark growing on the opposite side of the tree.

Another semantic concern has to do with the conceptual and cognitive bases for utterances. For individuals with difficulties in this area, expressive language can often take the form of what has been called "cocktail party speech" (Wiig & Semel, 1980). This term has been used to refer to expressions that may be structurally accurate but nevertheless conceptually weak and essentially vacuous. Similarly, individuals may have more difficulty with expression when dealing with abstract concepts as opposed to concrete objects.

Combined concerns for structural and content difficulties are considered in the concept of *automatic expressive processing*. For most individuals, speaking is a natural act that requires minimal prior consideration and limited emphasis on presentation. However, for those who may be experiencing difficulty in any of the specific skill areas previously explained, there is a strong likelihood of interference in the automatic nature of expressive language. In the same way that even an accomplished orator would need to prepare for a formal speech or presentation, it may be quite likely that a handicapped child would need similar preparation to converse in an acceptable fashion without evidencing linguistic difficulties. This leads to consideration of the final language dimension to consider relative to possible problems—pragmatics.

Problems with Pragmatics

The focus in pragmatics is on how the usage of language affects success both within and outside of the classroom. Although research has only relatively recently been reported on the acquisition of pragmatic skills by exceptional children, some studies, particularly in the area of learning disabilities, report that handicapped students are more likely to evidence difficulties related to the appropriate use of language for specific purposes such as making promises, requesting assistance, apologizing, warning, asserting, ingratiating oneself, and seeking clarification.

The most substantial research base has been developed by Tanis Bryan and her colleagues at the University of Illinois–Chicago Institute for Research in Learning Disabilities. Bryan, Donahue, and Pearl (1981) have summarized their research by noting that disabled children were less sensitive to the age differences of their listeners, less able to consider the perspective of their listener, more often failed to request clarification when given ambiguous messages, and in general were less skilled as conversational partners. Summarizing studies reported by Bryan and others, Boucher (1984) observed that learning disabled children were less competent than their nonhandicapped peers in terms of language complexity, typically were viewed negatively by peers, had poorly developed skills in role-taking, and had deficits in understanding social interactions.

In spite of this growing research base, however, both Boucher (1984) and Dudley-Marling (1985) have encouraged caution in wholehearted acceptance of these findings on pragmatics given the nature of the research that has been reported. Dudley-Marling (1985) expressed concern over the relatively limited research base, the virtual absence of replication, the few specific aspects of pragmatics researched, and the fact that most research has been conducted in contrived settings.

Boucher (1984) recently presented data relative to pragmatics indicating that LD children could adapt their language to different audiences and did engage in cooperative and questioning communicative styles. Other recent studies (e.g., Knight-Arest, 1984), however, have led to conclusions that LD boys were less effective than girls in taking the needs of the listener into consideration. Thus, the research in this area has mixed findings. It seems safest to conclude that many handicapped children will experience problems in language use, but at the same time caution should be exercised in characterizing the entire group as having pervasive deficits in this area.

Stages of Language Development

In consideration of the linguistic dimensions that may warrant intervention efforts, it is also useful to keep in mind the specific chronological periods that Wiig and Semel (1980) have indicated represent crucial stages of advanced language development. These include approximately the fourth grade level, the transition between junior and senior high school, and the transition between high school and postsecondary education or vocational placement. At each juncture, the complexity of language demands begins to increase significantly and thus can create special problems for students. Language difficulties can present problems not only in the elementary school. As Donahue and Bryan (1984) noted, LD adolescents, for example, do not grow out of their problems in the acquisition of vocabulary and syntactic and semantic structures, have continued difficulty in perceiving and interpreting social cues, and may be hindered in their ability to acquire linguistic rules due to their limited opportunities to observe and practice these skills in interactions with nonhandicapped peers. To further extend this point, Blalock (1982) reported that oral language problems persist into adulthood for LD individuals. Sixty-three of the 80 persons she studied had problems in oral language and auditory processing, including formulation, pronunciation of multisyllabic words, word retrieval, and extended explanations and narratives.

ASSESSMENT OF SPEAKING SKILLS

The purpose of assessment procedures in spoken language is to determine the specific learning needs of a student. Assessment is justified in spoken language both for students who primarily have developmental needs as well as for those whose problems dictate more intensive programming. Nelson (1981) indicates that intensive intervention efforts are justified particularly if an individual has a documented discrepancy between overall ability and current skill in at least two of the linguistic dimensions of phonology, morphology, syntax, semantics, and pragmatics.

Initially, attention in this section is given to formal assessment, including a review of the instruments that are available for use. However, as is true for all curricular areas, while formal tools provide a starting point for intervention programs, informal instruments provide the core data for the ongoing diagnostic process.

Formal Assessment

A number of formal tools available for the assessment of oral language skills were discussed in the previous chapter. In this chapter, we consider the tests and/or subtests that focus on the expressive component of language, although, as mentioned previously, it is somewhat artificial to divide expressive and receptive language into two discrete areas. Three initial observations concerning formal evaluation are warranted.

Initial Concerns. First, consideration must be given to the possible difficulty in determining competence through formal means. While language performance as defined by test results can obviously be measured, the possibility remains that such results may underestimate or distort the true picture of an individual's competence, especially since most evaluative formats are contrived rather than a reflection of the child's natural speaking abilities.

Second, no tests currently exist that truly evaluate the total spoken language domain. As Nelson (1981) states, no one test "can effectively encompass all aspects of psycholinguistic behavior. Rather a comprehensive language evaluation usually includes a broad sampling of communicative behaviors using one or more standardized assessment tools . . . followed by further testing in areas hypothesized to be particularly involved in the disorder" (p. 4). Subsequent to that effort, there will continue to be a need to supplement formal test data with systematic efforts to observe spontaneous language behavior.

Finally, consideration should be given to the traditional domination of process orientations toward spoken language assessment within special education. Essentially, a process approach to assessment focuses on the underlying factors purported to influence skill acquisition in a particular area; a product approach stresses the skill itself. In the case of spoken language, the most commonly used assessment tool in the 1970s was the *Illinois Test of Psycholinguistic Abilities* (ITPA) (Kirk, McCarthy, & Kirk, 1968).

The Process Approach.   The ITPA was designed as an assessment tool for evaluating psycholinguistic development. *Psycholinguistics* has been commonly defined as the field that encompasses concern for both psychological and language development or, more formally, the study of the mental processes that underlie the acquisition and use of language (Newcomer & Hammill, 1976). However, the definition of psycholinguistics used in the ITPA was derived from the communication model developed by Charles Osgood in 1954. Thus, the ITPA consists of subtests built on Osgood's model, including three processes of communication (reception, organization, and expression), two levels of communication (representational and automatic), and two channels of communication (auditory-vocal and visual-motor). The interaction of these components of the model produced an instrument with twelve subtests, including the following which have some relationship to oral expressive language: Verbal Expression, Grammatic Closure, Auditory Closure, Sound Blending, and Auditory Sequential Memory.

Compared to a true psycholinguistic model, the ITPA reflects an obvious absence in the area of pragmatics as well as limited assessment capabilities within other dimensions. Although some individual subtests offer useful assessment information (e.g., Grammatic Closure), the model itself has not been validated. Numerous researchers, most notably

Hammill and colleagues (Hammill & Larsen, 1974a; Newcomer & Hammill, 1976) have criticized the test. Newcomer and Hammill (1976) concluded that the ITPA should not be used for

❑ determining the etiology of academic failure;

❑ devising remedial instructional strategies for specific academic problems;

❑ selecting curricular programs designed to match instruction to a student's ITPA psycholinguistic profile;

❑ screening students deemed to be high risk for subsequent school failure.

The Product Approach. An alternative to the process approach to assessment is called a product approach. Tests that use the product approach focus on skills that have been acquired and also identify deficits that may warrant instruction in themselves. Product approaches make no presumptions about transfer; that is, the skills assessed are deemed important in themselves rather than for their contribution to, for example, other academic areas that may warrant attention to increase a student's overall achievement. The *Test of Language Development–Primary* (TOLD–P) (Newcomer & Hammill, 1982) and the *Test of Language Development–Intermediate* (TOLD–I) (Hammill & Newcomer, 1982) were developed as alternatives to the ITPA model. The TOLD–P and the TOLD–I each include seven subtests organized according to receptive and expressive elements combined with linguistic dimensions.

Specific Formal Instruments. Formal language tests are of two types: (a) comprehensive measures of all language functioning or (b) instruments focused on specific dimensions of language (Wallace & Larsen, 1978). Even when tests are considered comprehensive, they typically have two major deficiencies: they rarely attend to all linguistic dimensions—with pragmatics most often overlooked—and they rely heavily on contrived formats, which preclude evaluation of language within the natural environment. Comprehensive tools available for evaluation of oral expressive language include the ITPA, TOLD, the *Clinical Evaluation of Language Functions* (CELF) and the *Houston Test of Language Development* (see Table 4.4).

Several tests focus on specific language dimensions. These include the Developmental Sentence Analysis and the "Let's Talk" Inventory. In addition, subtests of some of the comprehensive tests address specific dimensions as well. Representative formal tests are listed in Table 4.4.

Informal Assessment

As noted previously, the diagnostic information central to intervention must come through informal evaluation. Muma and Pierce (1981) provide a clear discussion of the reasons why informally obtained data, such as descriptions of language samples, are more useful than formal test results.

> The major advancements in psychology and psycholinguistics have shown that language assessment in the clinical fields needed reorientation and revision in order to obtain evidence of an individual's problems rather than mere data. The reorientation that was warranted was a shift from such a strong reliance on the psychometric test model (normative tests and developmental profiles) to a reliance on a descriptive model. . . .
>
> The primary reason for the shift from a strong reliance on the psychometric normative test model to a reliance on the descriptive model is that the latter provides more appropriate evidence whereas the former imposes group criteria on an individual by virtue of a normative reference thereby obviating an assessment of an individual's own behaviors. This is somewhat of a paradox because the assessment process has been claimed to meet individual needs by virtue of individually administered tests, yet the tests themselves are group or norm referenced. Consequently, an assessment of an individual's needs is not likely to have been accomplished. (p. 2)

The two most commonly used sources of informal data on spoken language are language samples and structured language assessment exercises. Nelson (1981) noted that language samples can yield preliminary information on linguistic competence and knowledge for each of the linguistic dimensions related to probable remedial needs. There is little question that such an approach offers trained clinicians the most valid and reliable source of individual assessment data. However, for many classroom teachers, it is difficult to implement assessments that depend heavily on the interpretation of language samples, especially spontaneous samples. In these cases it is necessary to supplement the observation of a student's language with specifically designed though somewhat contrived assessment exercises. The following discussion highlights some examples of how both spontaneous, naturalistic observations and structured exercises can be used to provide data on the abilities of students within the various dimensions of language.

How to Conduct an Informal Assessment. The analysis of spoken language begins with simply listening to the student. The examiner should take the opportunity to observe and listen periodically throughout the day such as during instructional periods, structured recreation times, unstructured recess, and informal social times (Webber, 1981). Language samples then essentially become timed periods of conversation where the

TABLE 4.4. Formal Tests of Spoken Language

Test	Publisher	Appropriate Ages	Administration	Relevant Subtests or Focus of Assessment
Carrow Elicited Language Inventory (Carrow, 1974)	Learning Concepts	3 to 8	Individual	Sentence imitation
Clinical Evaluation of Language Functions (CELF) (Wiig & Semel, 1980)	Psychological Corporation	Two Levels: Grades K–5 and 5–12	Individual	Screening Tests (abbrev. list) Phoneme Discrimination and Production Sentence Formation and Recall Serial Recall Word Formation and Recall Diagnostic Battery (abbrev. list) Word Series Names on Confrontation Word Associations Model Sentences Formulated Sentences Speech Sounds
Developmental Sentence Analysis (Lee, 1974)	Northwestern University Press	2–0 to 6–11	Individual	Method of analysis of series of spontaneous language utterances

TABLE 4.4. Continued

Test	Publisher	Appropriate Ages	Administration	Relevant Subtests or Focus of Assessment
Environmental Language Inventory (MacDonald & Horstmeier, 1978)	Psychological Corporation	Verbal Children	Individual	Language samples of limited speech, prompted conversation, and spontaneous speech
Houston Test of Language Development (Crabtree, 1963)	Houston Press	6 months to 6 years	Individual	Consists of two parts including: checklist of varied language categories and materials kit for eliciting free speech for variety of linguistic skills
Illinois Test of Psycholinguistic Abilities (ITPA) (Kirk, McCarthy, & Kirk, 1968)	University of Illinois Press	2–4 to 10–3	Individual	Verbal Expression Grammatic Closure Auditory Closure Sound Blending Auditory Sequential Memory
"Let's Talk" Inventory for Adolescents	Charles E. Merrill	9 to adult	Individual	Picture presented to which student responds with sentence(s); measures pragmatics

TABLE 4.4. Continued

Test	Publisher	Appropriate Ages	Administration	Relevant Subtests or Focus of Assessment
Test of Adolescent Language–2 (TOAL–2) (Hammill, Brown, Larsen, & Wiederholt, 1987)	PRO-ED	11–0 to 18–5	Individual and Group	Speaking/Vocabulary Speaking/Grammar
Test of Language Development–Intermediate (TOLD–I) (Hammill & Newcomer, 1982)	PRO-ED	8–6 to 12–11	Individual	Generals Characteristics Sentence Combining Word Ordering Grammatic Comprehension
Test of Language Development–Primary (TOLD–P) (Newcomer & Hammill, 1982)	PRO-ED	4–0 to 8–11	Individual	Picture Vocabulary Oral Vocabulary Sentence Imitation Grammatic Understanding Grammatic Completion Word Articulation Word Discrimination

student is engaged in interaction with either peers or an adult. Transcription of language is very difficult while it is being produced, therefore, taping is encouraged to promote accuracy. While videotapes provide the advantage of a picture of the interaction, audiotapes are often preferred as the primary source or as a back-up to video, because the quality of audiotape allows more precise discriminations and thus can facilitate accurate transcription (Miller, 1981).

Spontaneous samples are easier to praise as a basis of assessment than they may be to obtain, especially with younger children. Miller (1981) provides the following suggestions for fruitful conversations with children:

1. *Listen*
   Focus on what the child means by what he or she says so your responses evidence shared focus.

2. *Be patient*
   Do not overpower the child with requests or actions. Allow the child space and time to perform. Do not be afraid of pauses.

3. *Follow the child's lead*
   Maintain the child's focus (topic, meaning) with your responses, comments, questions, and add new information where appropriate. Maintain the child's pace, do not rush on to the next activity.

4. *Value the child*
   Recognize the child's comments as important and worth your undivided attention. Do not patronize the child. Demonstrate unconditional positive regard. Be warm and friendly.

5. *Do not play the fool*
   A valued conversational partner has something to say worth listening to. Refrain from asking questions that the child knows you know the answer to, or from making the usual remarks children hear from adults.

6. *Learn to think like a child*
   Consider the child's perspective at different levels of cognitive development, and the child's awareness of the varying perspectives of action, time, and space. (p. 12)

Following from these basic suggestions, the teacher's role is to encourage the student's speech by avoiding overstructuring of verbal interactions such as can occur when children are asked a series of questions in order to elicit specific responses. Rather, it is preferable to allow the child to lead the conversation, thus increasing the likelihood of obtaining a valid sample (McLean & Snyder-McLean, 1978). To get children to talk, Miller (1981) makes the following suggestions, dependent on the student's developmental level:

❑ make a variety of toys and objects available for the child to interact with.

❑ encourage conversation toward topics about objects, people, and events that are not present or are of a different time (such as holidays, favorite activities, and the child's relatives).

❑ prompt the student to narrate a story about themes that are displaced in space or time such as relating a story about an event the child once participated in.

How to Use Informally Obtained Data. Data obtained from language samples can be used to provide an overview of the student's competence across linguistic dimensions as well as his or her abilities within specific skill areas. For example, in the area of structure, spontaneous samples can be used for determining mean length of utterance (MLU) and for the developmental analysis of sentences.

MLU is usually computed based on a sample of 50 utterances. It is a simple arithmetical average obtained by totaling the number of words in all of the utterances and dividing by 50. MLU can provide a reasonably accurate measure of language development and, since it can detect increases that occur over time, can provide a measure of acquisition and/or program success. Normative data are available, if desired, for children from below 2 years of age to 9½ years (Wiig & Semel, 1980). For children more advanced in language, morphemes are typically counted instead of whole words.

Wiig and Semel (1980) have also discussed the use of *developmental sentence analysis*, reviewing the work of Lee (1974). This approach focuses on quantitative measures of syntactical structures with attention to the following categories: indefinite pronouns and noun modifiers, personal pronouns, main verbs, secondary verbs, negatives, conjunctions, interrogative reversals, and *Wh-* questions. Further information on procedures for scoring and interpreting samples in this fashion can be found in Lee (1974) or Wiig and Semel (1980).

A full discussion of the analysis of spontaneous samples is beyond the scope of this chapter. The reader interested in more information is encouraged to consult Miller (1981) and McLean and Snyder-McLean (1978).

Other Informal Assessment Techniques. A variety of structured assessment activities can also be used to obtain data helpful in planning intervention programs. Wiig and Semel (1980) recommend rule extension for the assessment of morphological skills. Rule extension refers to the child's ability to modify base words to change meaning. Typically, morphological skills can be measured using sentence completion exercises or the cloze procedure. Either nonsense items or actual lexicon can be used. Another approach to the evaluation of morphology is to set up a series of pictures to be identified through the use of bound and free morphemes. Then a series of questions can be asked such as, "This dog is big, this one is bigger, but this one is the _____" and "Today I play ball, yesterday I _____ ball and tomorrow I will _____ ball."

Syntactical skills can be evaluated in various ways. Sentence imitation is often used, because a child's ability to repeat a sentence verbatim relies on his or her awareness of the structure of the sentence. This procedure can be complemented by having children repeat stories they have been told using their own words and structures; thus, the content is provided, and the student's use of syntax can be evaluated.

A variety of formats have been used for assessing semantics. These formats include identification and selection of objects that match spoken words; the obverse procedure of having a student judge a word's acceptability by stating a preference for a word in a given context; recognizing whether two phrases are similar or different in meaning; and providing to a peer instructional and/or descriptive information to lead him or her through a problem-solving task. However, as Wiig and Semel (1980) pointed out, the spontaneous use of words to describe actions, objects, and sequences provides more detailed information on the student's understanding of specific words and on the student's use of language within the social context. Other options include having the students discuss the elements of a picture shown to them, make up a story about the picture, and provide a list of words that can be used to describe the picture.

In concluding this section, a few comments are necessary concerning pragmatics. Within this dimension, assessment must be derived from natural usage, since that is essentially what pragmatics consist of.

In evaluating pragmatics, a key problem that professionals may face is that skills in this area are assumed to be easily acquired. However, it is important to note the absence of a particular skill in the area of pragmatics so that a student's needs can be addressed.

Bryan et al. (1981) note that it is important for professionals to be able to distinguish between a student who has deficits in language structures and a student who is experiencing social deficits and/or lack of confidence in linguistic skills. This distinction can be important in determining where to focus intervention and underscores the need for careful assessment. If students have pragmatic deficits, there is an increased likelihood that the assessment process will be more difficult.

To proceed with assessment, teachers can construct a checklist based on a list of pragmatic skills such as those listed in Table 4.3 and observe for the use of these skills throughout the day. Mercer and Mercer (1985) provide an illustration of this process. Teachers should consider the social context of an utterance to determine usage (e.g., "Daddy come" could be a request or an attempt to acquire information).

TEACHING SPEAKING SKILLS

Prior discussion in this text has identified the following dimensions of language: speech production (phonology), structure (morphology and syntax), content (semantics), and usage (pragmatics). The instructional strategies provided in this chapter follow a sequence that is consistent with this list of dimensions. To this list we have added the additional areas of *intention* and *public speaking*. Although clearly these added dimensions interrelate with the dimensions listed above, especially pragmatics, they are presented separately here to illustrate some strategies that can be used in programming. The section concludes with some other areas of concern: direct instruction, programming for adolescents, and computer applications.

General Considerations

Before focusing on specific areas, a number of general considerations need to be reviewed. These considerations provide a basis for the development of an instructional program in spoken language.

❑ Remedial work should not artificially separate the comprehension and production of language. Although specific needs may direct attention to one or the other aspect of language, overall programming should seek to integrate the decoding and encoding processes.

❑ Language intervention should be a regular part of the school day. Expression should be taught systematically rather than as a by-product of other subject areas (Morsink, 1984).

❑ Classroom situations should be provided that promote the natural use of language. Development can generally be facilitated by taking advantage of natural opportunities for speech rather than relying solely on overstructured environments or exercises stressing rote memory (Cureton et al., 1983).

❑ Intervention should not be confined to a designated instructional period. Reinforcement of skills attained should be an all-day effort. Since natural language learning is constantly taking place, any activity can be transformed into a language lesson (Cureton et al., 1983).

❑ Appropriate measures should also be taken to assure transfer between school and home, since parent involvement in the development of advanced skills is crucial (Mandell & Gold, 1984).

❑ Instruction through imitation can be used as a helpful basis for the acquisition of new words and structures. Although imitation must be considered a tool of limited value due to its contrived nature and the unlikelihood that it will promote generalization, its role cannot be overlooked.

❑ Teachers should act as models of appropriate language use and provide students with an opportunity to observe pronunciation patterns, grammatically accurate structure, appropriate word selection, and effective social usage.

❑ Input to students should be provided at a level slightly more complex than the student's level (Cureton et al., 1983).

❑ Where possible, peers should be included in programs to facilitate modeling. Peers are particularly important in helping a student to acquire language usage appropriate to their social group.

❑ Reinforcement, especially in terms of feedback from both adults and peers, can encourage and provide input into a student's appropriate use of language.

❑ Programming efforts should reflect the same emphasis on individualization that would be expected in any other curricular domain. Instructional efforts should take into consideration strengths, weaknesses, and future needs.

Intention

Intention refers to motivation in speaking. Although intention is related to pragmatics, it is dealt with separately here, because it provides a basis for all expression. For some handicapped children, in particular those who are younger or who have experienced a series of debilitating failures, the building of this basic language foundation may be the most critical instructional challenge that teachers face.

For most children, intention develops naturally through a series of common mechanisms in everyday life in the home, the school, and the community. The most basic mechanism for the development of intention is to use language for social control. At a very early age, most children realize how language can exercise a high degree of control over significant others in their lives. A second component of naturally developing intention comes from verbal and nonverbal stimulation. Exposure to interesting and exciting stimuli clearly encourages a child to respond.

A third naturally occurring mechanism that can develop intention is reinforcement. Reinforcement in this case can come through both external forms of encouragement such as praise and intrinsic reinforcement associated with the natural interest in hearing oneself speak.

For individuals experiencing difficulties in speaking that stem from a lack of motivation to speak, the three mechanisms listed above are obvious initial considerations. Although for most children the concepts of social control, stimulation, and reinforcement are a part of their daily existence, teachers should consider their possible absence in the environment of children who present themselves as extremely reluctant to engage in spoken language.

Wood (1976) and others have presented a number of suggestions for the promotion of linguistic intention. The suggestions include the following:

❑ Establish an environment that is low in pressure and promotes free speaking;

❑ Ensure that ample opportunities are available for oral exchange;

❑ Permit gesturing in reluctant speakers as an initial communicative vehicle but eventually move toward the preferred spoken expression while eliminating reliance on gestures;

❑ Express interest in a child's verbalization and probe for further expansions;

❑ Provide varied stimuli for students to interact with and respond to.

Instruction in Phonology

Phonological considerations in spoken language revolve around the presentation of specific speech sounds. Typically, the task of overcoming these problems is considered the direct instructional responsibility of neither regular nor special education classroom teachers but rather is placed on the speech/language therapist.

A full discussion of the strategies used to promote appropriate phonological production is beyond the scope of this chapter. However, although it is typically not the responsibility of classroom teachers to deal with speech difficulties, there is nevertheless a need for all professionals to be involved in ensuring the effectiveness of remedial programs. The cornerstone of a successful program is based on transdisciplinary efforts requiring ongoing communication among teachers and therapists. Once the program has been designed and implemented, the critical need is for consistency between the therapy setting and classroom usage. Teachers must play an important role in ensuring that gains made in the therapy situation are maintained and generalized both within and outside of the classroom. The lack of program integration between classroom instruction and therapy can result in the child's inability to integrate knowledge and use of language (Nelson, 1981). In addition to the common sense suggestion of providing models of good speech, teachers can also assist by prompting appropriate speech patterns and reinforcing accurate production.

Instruction in Language Structure

For ease in presentation, concerns for morphological and syntactical production are again grouped together under the heading of structure. While morphology requires the individual to focus on the relatively minor elements of word production such as prefixes, root words, and suffixes, syntax represents the more general area of grammar. A variety of specific activities can be helpful in promoting language development within these areas.

Several specific approaches represent intervention strategies that can be integrated into the student's own language. These approaches are alternatives to the *correction* model that is often used by adults to identify and correct the errors of children. For example, a correction form is illustrated by the following, "Mamma, doggie come." "No, not doggie come, here comes the doggie." The correction model at best may be ineffective and at worst may suppress language usage and should be used sparingly for the development of syntactic skills (Muma & Pierce, 1981). Muma (1971) outlined a series of alternatives to this model; several of the alternatives discussed below are drawn from this work.

Expansion. Expansion is particularly appropriate for structural learning in children. Expansion builds on short utterances by providing the child with a model of a longer alternative. The following dialogue illustrates how this process works in a natural setting: "Mama, doggie come." "Yes, dear, the doggie is coming." Although the distinction between expansion and correction may not always be a major one, the key element is that the child is receiving informative feedback in the context of encouragement which can assist the child in refining the structure.

Recasting Sentences. Recasting sentences (Filer, 1981) has also been recommended for language development in handicapped children and operates similarly to expansion. With this approach, the teacher responds to the child's utterance by recasting it in a different grammatical form. For example, the child who says, "The dog stayed home," might be answered by an adult with the following, "Yes, the dog did stay home."

Completion. Completion is based on the student's spontaneous language samples. Sentences derived from the student are represented to him or her with something missing. The student is then asked to complete the sentence in various ways.

Combination. As language develops further, an effective model to utilize is the combination approach. It is based on the presentation to the student of two to four short sentences, which the student then combines into longer and more complex sentences in any way desired. Any changes can be made, and structures can be added or deleted. It encourages the student to use grammatical structures that may not commonly be a part of his or her expressive language. The following dialogue illustrates this model: "The boy is riding his bicycle. The girl is riding her bicycle. The bicycles are both red." Response: "The boy and the girl are riding their red bicycles." As Muma and Pierce (1981) noted, such techniques "enable the child to explore his or her own language-exploitation in language learning" (p. 8).

Translation. An important concern for many teachers is the provision of appropriate instructional exercises for students whose primary language or dialect is not standard English. For example, for students who speak inner city black dialect, it would be most appropriate to develop a series of translation exercises where students are asked to provide the standard form for specific dialectical utterances. This approach can be useful in promoting an acquisition of standard English in such learners. This topic is discussed at greater length in Chapter 12.

Activities. Johnson and Myklebust (1967) encourage the arrangement of meaningful experiences for students as a basis for promoting accurate grammatical analysis. A student moves through specific motor movements or activities while the adult provides sentence structures that are descriptive of the action and which are subsequently associated with the act by the student.

Specific morphological forms can be developed by a series of oral language activities that require the student to complete phrases and sentences. The following list illustrates some examples of sentences for completion that emphasize different morphological patterns:

1. This is a child; these are two _____ .

2. This man farms; he is a _____ .

3. The paper was written and corrected; it now needs to be _____ .

4. The mother duck has five baby _____ .

The above formats can be used with nonsense words not only to assess a child's ability but also to provide instructional exercises. Nonsense words are useful, since they require that students understand appropriate syntax rather than just demonstrate an awareness of vocabulary words. For example, as a spin-off of Berko's (1958) "wug" format, the teacher can provide instruction on correct tense, superlatives, and other prefixes and suffixes. To illustrate this concept, consider the following sentences:

1. The mother tud was walking with her _____.

2. A woman who spends her working day dopping is a _____.

Fokes Sentence Builder. The Fokes program (Fokes, 1976) is included here because it illustrates an approach to assist children in learning the basic sentence structure of oral language. The program is designed to teach structure through the ordering of five grammatical categories: *who, what* (subject and direct object), *is doing* (verb), *which* (adjective), and *where* (preposition).

The Fokes program is based on the linguistic developmental needs of children identified as language disordered, learning disabled, hearing impaired, and mildly retarded as well as students classified as slow learners. It is to be used by teachers and/or therapists as a supplement to a core language program. As such, it was designed to provide children with the necessary instruction to assist them in producing and comprehending sentences and past, present, and future tenses while using articles, auxiliary verbs, plural nouns, verb forms, and pronouns. It presumes the prerequisite skills of combining two to three words into meaningful relationships, maintaining attention to activities for 20 minutes, and attention to picture items and the specific concepts reflected in them. The program was designed for either small group or one-to-one instruction. Individual lessons are approximately 20 to 30 minutes in duration, but they can be organized into several sections for students who experience attentional difficulties. Additional information on this program concerning its applicability to students with sensory impairments is provided in Chapter 13.

Instruction in Semantics

A primary focus of instructional strategies in the area of semantics has to do with the development of an expanded expressive vocabulary. This process involves the two related objectives of increasing usage of known words and introduction of additional words. In both cases the measure of improvement would be an increase in the variety of words that a student uses.

Several techniques suggested by Muma (Muma, 1971; Muma & Pierce, 1981) can be used effectively. *Expatiation* is an interactive model that focuses on semantic features by elaborating or broadening the topic of an utterance initiated by the child (Muma & Pierce, 1981). For example, consider the following dialogue: "Mama, doggie runs." "Yes, the dog is running around because he is hungry and wants something to eat."

A *revision* approach combines both semantic and structural elements. Using this technique, the teacher gives a sentence (or series of sentences) to the student and then asks her to retell it in her own words making any changes that she wishes. In addition to enhancing vocabulary usage, this technique can help to further develop a variety of linguistic forms.

A number of strategies can be employed to expand vocabulary. Timed or untimed naming exercises can enhance proficiency in the use of specific words. For example, students can be asked to name as many objects within the classroom as they can within 20 seconds. Stories read aloud to students can be interrupted briefly while students fill in the word or phrase that should logically follow. Using this exercise, students are developing not only their expressive vocabulary but also their listening comprehension.

Other teaching suggestions for students with word retrieval problems are provided by Johnson and Myklebust (1967). These strategies include: giving students sentences to provide a context that will ease recall ("I write with a _____"); putting pictures on cards paired with the sentences ("I sleep in a _____"); alerting students to cue off paired associates (e.g., bread and butter, salt and pepper); and teaching words as members of a series or sequence (e.g., hat, shirt, pants, socks, shoes).

One semantic concern that may present problems for handicapped children and has been documented for learning disabled children in particular is working with multiple meanings of words. For example, the word *diamond* refers essentially to the jewel and its shape but by association is also used to refer to a suit in cards, a baseball field, or as a synonym for a type of ring. Teachers should be alert to such words that may present problems to their students and should capitalize on natural opportunities for instruction. If necessary, instructional activities can be developed that note the alternative meanings of the word while teaching its root meaning. Students can be assisted in drawing conclusions for themselves and encouraged to incorporate the various meanings into their utterances.

Conceptual relationships among vocabulary words may also present problems for students. The development of exercises focusing on analogies can be particularly helpful for students to understand how words may be related. As an example, students can be given completion exercises such as the following.

1. Mondale: Carter:: Bush: _____

2. season: year:: quarter: _____

3. hot: cold:: tall: _____

Progress in the area of semantics also parallels cognitive development. For example, the ability to categorize clearly involves both linguistic and cognitive processes. To learn categorical structures, students can be provided with various sorting tasks (Hoskins, 1983). Samples of objects from two conceptual groups can be provided with children directed to sort according to nature or function of the objects (e.g., "Place together all the toys that are vehicles").

With each of the areas identified above, it is important to keep in mind that teachers must move beyond instructional exercises and drills and ensure that skills acquired and words learned are tied to the child's natural language patterns. Any instructional exercise necessarily represents a contrived, artificial language environment. Without efforts to encourage generalization to daily communicative exchanges, it is unlikely that the gains made in simple acquisition-type learning tasks such as these will be of any significant long-term value to the students.

Instruction in Pragmatics

As mentioned earlier, pragmatics is the study of that dimension of language associated with use and function. Pragmatics has particularly close ties with the area of social development; pragmatics and social development in combination can be seen as a major aspect of the concept of *communicative competence*.

Bryan (1983) illustrated the concept of communicative competence by emphasizing specific considerations that teachers should have for instruction. She noted that disabled students may have these specific needs for assistance:

❏ *Understanding a situation*: the ability to both socially and cognitively understand variables that are influencing conversational exchanges;

❏ *Making judgments*: the ability to determine what's been said and what will need to be said in order to complete a given thought or topic within a conversation; and

❏ *Appropriate participation*: the ability to be involved in communication exchanges through appropriate behaviors such as turn-taking.

Bruner (cited in Boucher, 1984) identified the teacher in the area of pragmatics as having an active role. The teacher must not only model appropriate language usage but must also help students understand the explicit and implicit intentions of language exchanges while helping them shape their expressions to fit appropriate social contexts. Teachers should take advantage of opportunities to encourage the use of pragmatic skills by modeling such exchanges as seeking help, greetings, saying farewells, and interrupting (Cureton et al., 1983).

The appendix following this chapter presents a list of activities for communicative intentions provided by Spekman and Roth (1984) with implications for instruction in the area of pragmatics. A series of communicative intentions (e.g., requests for information, greetings) are listed along with a facilitative context in which such intentions may be developed and suggested activities relevant for that area. The reader is referred to Spekman and Roth (1984) for further discussion of the topic.

Developing Public Speaking Skills

The skills discussed in the preceding sections have been presented as if they functioned somewhat in isolation. Obviously, this is not the case; rather, the primary concern is on coordination of all of the various skills subsumed within oral language to make the individual an effective communicator. Burns (1980) identified the following six areas in which students need to develop effective speaking skills: conversation, discussion, description-comparison-evaluation, reporting, story-telling, and creative drama and choral reading/speaking.

Burns (1980) also lists specific deficiencies in oral expression along with some suggestions for remediation. These areas include focus and logical organization, providing clarification and supporting details, strengthening description, subordination, and vocabulary. His suggestions follow:

❑ To strengthen focus and logical organization, children may:

1. arrange pictures in correct sequence in order to tell a story

2. describe events in a story in sequential order

3. list things seen on a field trip, organizing them in sequence by categories

4. outline the main points of a simple talk

5. tell stories, recalling events in the order in which they happened

6. dramatize stories in logical order

7. explain a process in science or give directions for a game

8. choose a topic and limit its scope to a certain number of points

❑ To strengthen clarification and supporting ideas, children may:

1. outline the main points of a simple talk, with supporting ideas for each main point

2. use incomplete stories or poems to invent endings which reveal relevancy of supporting details

3. expand a topic sentence into a short talk with supporting sentences

4. use functional speaking situations (announcements, giving directions, and explanations) for which supporting details may be developed.

❑ To strengthen description, subordination, and vocabulary, children may:

1. listen to and make lists of descriptive words (such as "quiet" words) or words that apply to different moods ("angry" words)

2. look for alternatives to tired words, such as *nice*

3. suggest words that aptly describe objects or events in a picture

4. study synonyms, antonyms, word histories

5. search in literature for figures of speech

6. focus on multiple or unusual meanings of common words, such as *run* and *fall*

7. listen for new or interesting words

8. practice expanding simple oral sentences through the use of modifiers

9. collect examples of the various sentence types

10. combine short sentences into compound or complex sentences or change a basic sentence into another form (transformations) (pp. 65–66)

Alley and Deshler (1979) emphasize strategies for public speaking skills as a primary focus of oral language instruction for disabled adolescents. The areas to which they directed their attention each have ties to the skills discussed earlier. Several are worthy of consideration.

Wait time can be taught to students who need to be reminded to collect their thoughts before speaking. It can help to counter the impulsive responding that is often noted in handicapped students. Additionally, it provides a way for individuals to begin preparation for their presentation.

Rehearsal is particularly relevant for those who have problems speaking in a spontaneous manner while retaining coherence. Through rehearsal training, students are encouraged to identify the information that they will be sharing and practice it before presenting it publicly.

Recognition of social impact encourages students to focus on pragmatic concerns by carefully assessing the social context in which a specific utterance or presentation will be delivered. Again, given the difficulties that some individuals have in perceiving subtle aspects of their social environment, attention to this area can be critical in effective public speaking.

Programming for Adolescents

In addition to the suggestions for public speaking as provided above, several other considerations are particularly apt for handicapped adolescents. The increasing need for programs designed for older students is as apparent in spoken language as in any other curricular area. Donahue and Bryan (1984) spoke to the particular needs of handicapped adolescents in addressing the form of programs that should be provided. They suggested that the successful development of social and communicative skills requires some special programming considerations.

❑ Will the acquisition of these skills allow students to meet peer as well as adult norms for appropriate communicative style? It is important to recognize that target behaviors are likely to be selected which appeal to adult expectations. For example, should educators be teaching rules for polite requests or how to engage in friendly exchanges of insults?

❑ Will this training program enable students to discern how and when to use their newly acquired skills in naturalistic settings?

❑ Will use of these communicative skills enhance the adolescent's social acceptance with peers and adults? (p. 19)

These considerations acknowledge the importance that language skills have for social survival of the adolescent both within and outside of the school environment. Relevant to this concern, Mandell and Gold (1984) aptly summarized skills for adolescents that are related to community social situations and vocational needs, expression of personal feelings, and participation in various interpersonal social exchanges. Their suggestions for skills to be taught include the following:

❑ how to order from a menu

❑ how to use the phone for local and long-distance calls

❑ how to make both formal and informal introductions

❑ how-to courtesies needed for specific social occasions, such as parties or school open houses

❑ how to set up job interviews

❑ how to participate in a job interview

❑ how to ask for help or clarification of tasks while on the job

❑ appropriate demonstrations of positive feelings for family, friends, and acquaintances

❑ socially acceptable methods for expressing negative feelings

❑ procedures for expressing personal opinions or offering suggestions

❑ giving directions, making announcements, and providing simple explanations

❑ reporting relevant and interesting information

❑ using appropriate gestures, intonations, and inflections to color meaning (loudness of voice, body language, etc.)

❑ sharing personal interests, hobbies, and experiences with adults and peers (in social and after-school interactions as well as in show-and-tell activities) (pp. 219–220)

Direct Instruction

This discussion on intervention strategies cannot conclude without considering the use of direct instructional programs for handicapped and remedial learners. Although such programs have sometimes been criticized for their tendency to conceptualize language development as limited to isolated skills acquisition, there remains little question of their effectiveness (Stebbins et al., 1977).

Engelmann and associates have published a series of direct instructional programs to teach arithmetic, reading, and language. The DISTAR language program (Engelmann & Osborn, 1971, 1972, 1976) was developed to provide instruction in the language of the school, including instructional language and the words and sentence structures relevant to success in reading comprehension. The program has three levels which systematically present group instruction to primary-aged students. The three levels are described by Osborn and Becker (1980) as follows:

Level One includes sequences in identity and action statements, prepositions, singular and plural statements, pronouns, verb tense, polars, comparatives, and-or, classification, part-whole relationships, some-all-none, same-different, before-after, if-then, who-where-when-what, as well as basic information such as days of the week, months and seasons of the year, colors, shapes, the names and definitions of different occupations, locations, and some natural phenomena.

Level Two devotes considerable time to tasks and word analysis skills, such as: definitions, descriptions, absurdities, analogies, if-then, true-false, questioning skills, statement analysis, synonyms, superlatives, and contractions. More general information is also presented, such as materials, part-whole objects, land forms (islands, peninsulas, continents), and some directional skills such as left-right, from-to, and map reading.

The application of the concepts and statements taught in both levels occurs in the problem-solving tasks and logical games that appear in almost every lesson.

The major focus of Level Three is on the analysis of sentences, both spoken and written. The emphasis is on analysis that deals with what a sentence says and what inferences can be logically drawn from that sentence. In the sequence of task activities, this kind of analysis is systematically extended to writing. The students spend a good part of almost every lesson writing sentences and then paragraphs. They also learn punctuation and capitalization rules and do some grammatical analysis as well. There are also sequences in which analogies and formal deductions are presented. By the end of the program students can identify subjects and predicates, can transform sentences from one verb tense to another and can identify statements, questions, and commands.[1]

BEST PRACTICES

The process of language development is complex and difficult to understand when we consider the progress made by typical children during the first 5 to 10 years of life. For parents, there is a blend of self-pride in having provided a model or cue that has worked along with continuing amazement over how the child acquires language structures and lexical items that have never been consciously taught. Given the almost miraculous progression of language development, the

[1]Reprinted by permission of the publisher from "Direct Instructional Language" by Jean Osborn and Wesley Becker in *Language Intervention for Exceptional Children,* in New Directions for Exceptional Children, Number 2, pp. 81–82, 1980.

magnitude of the task facing the teacher working with a child who experiences difficulty, delay, and/or disorders in oral language is obviously tremendous. Thus, while the "Best Practices" outlined in the following list provide a summary of this chapter and offer direction to those embarking on program development in oral language, it is important to keep in mind the complexity of the acquisition process for oral expressive language.

1. *Nature of Problem*: The population of handicapped and remedial learners which this text addresses is a varied group in terms of any attributes; oral expression is no exception. An initial concern must be to determine whether a significant problem is present as either a developmental delay or as a specific disorder.

2. *Assistance*: There may be no other area in which supportive services can be as valuable and as critical as in language development. Children and adolescents with problems should receive attention from speech/language professionals in addition to classroom teachers if they are to be successful in overcoming their difficulties.

3. *Coordination*: With assistance must come coordination of services. All persons involved in the program—special class teacher, regular educator, pathologist, parent, and often student—should be involved in goal-setting and in ensuring that there is programmatic continuity across learning environments.

4. *Assessment*: Formal instruments can afford teachers information of general interest concerning the strengths and deficits of an individual student. However, the evaluation of language samples, supplemented as needed by more structured informal assessments, should serve as the basis for decisions regarding programming.

5. *Naturalistic Focus*: Oral expressive language is best developed in the situation where it will be used—in the natural environment. Instruction within formal teaching periods must be related to these natural settings.

6. *Holistic Perspective*: Artificial separation of the language arts facilitates their presentation in this textbook. However, in reality, speaking and listening and reading and writing should be tied together as much as possible within the school curriculum.

7. *Nonstandard Speakers*: Dialectical variations should not be treated as substandard approximations of English.

Rather than being corrected, speakers of other dialects should be taught how to make the transition to standard form.

8. *Older Students*: Programs for oral expressive language development should be available for adolescent learners as well as for children. The focus of such efforts should be on the communication skills essential to successful speaking in class (secondary or postsecondary), on the job, in social settings, and in coordinating various other demands related to successful community living.

The above represent just a few key points about programming in the area of oral language. These should be combined with the concerns focused on in the previous chapter on Listening to build a comprehensive oral language curriculum.

APPENDIX
Intervention Activities for Communicative Intention

A. *Requests for Information:* Utterances that solicit information, permission, confirmation, or repetition (e.g., What's your name? What happened to your dog?)

Context: Situations in which someone wants or needs information

Activities

1. Introduce novel objects into the environment for which a child is likely to request a label (What is it?), information regarding function (What do you use it for?), operation (How do you make it work?), or construction (What's it made of?).

2. Play games such as Twenty Questions, Clue, scavenger hunts, or group acquaintance games (Find someone with your birthday. Find someone who has the same number of brothers as you).

3. Conduct interviews with different people (e.g., principal, librarian, fireman) for different purposes (e.g., to learn about an occupation, to learn about interests, opinions, etc.), and in different communication modes (face-to-face, telephone, mail).

4. Conduct science experiments that require a child to formulate specific questions regarding what might happen given certain conditions.

5. Engage in writing projects—Write to a pen pal and learn as much as you can. Write to your senator to learn his or her position on a current issue.

6. Use role-playing situations—Child goes to store (or restaurant) with $3.00. No prices are posted. Child gets lost and must ask someone for directions. Child is planning a trip and must gather information regarding bus schedule, fare, how much luggage is allowed, etc.

B. *Requests for Action:* Utterances that solicit action or cessation of action, that direct the behavior of others (e.g., Give me some cake. Don't do that. Why don't you come with me?)

Context: Situations in which someone wants or needs someone to perform, repeat, or cease some type of action or behavior

Activities

1. Introduce toys, technical equipment, and so on, that cannot be operated without assistance.

2. Utilize projects that require a minimum of two people and in which one student directs the behavior of another and tells what needs to be done.

3. Engage in pleasurable, amusing, entertaining and/or interesting activities

which a student is likely to request again (e.g., Read that story again. May I please have another cookie?).

4. Establish classroom rules that require a child to request actions of others (e.g., hall pass is required before leaving the room).

5. Create situations in which a child is likely to request a change of action or cessation of a behavior (e.g., stand in front of movie or TV screen, create loud noise when child is trying to concentrate).

C. *Response to Requests:* Utterances that supply solicited information or otherwise acknowledge preceding requests (e.g., My name is John. But I don't wanna go with you.)

Context: Situations in which requests for information or action are directed to someone

Activities

1. Utilize any of the activities listed above for A and B in which child is placed in the receiving or listener role and must respond appropriately to the specific requests of others.

2. Manipulate the form of a particular type of request. For example, when child's message is not understood, teacher might indicate confusion via a quizzical facial expression, shrugged shoulders, "Huh?," "I don't understand," or "Just where did you say you went?"

D. *Statements or Comments:* Utterances that state facts or rules, express belief, attitudes, or emotions, or describe environmental aspects (e.g., I don't like it when you yell at me. It sure is a nice sunny day today.)

Context: Situations in which someone is stimulated to comment or take a position

Activities

1. Introduce novel situations or interesting materials which are likely to gain a child's attention and stimulate comment (Gee, you moved all the desks around! The new bulletin board is neat.).

2. Utilize verbal and nonverbal incongruous situations (e.g., pictorial or verbal absurdities).

3. Discuss current events; have the child summarize the facts, determine the position of another, and/or state his or her own position.

4. Assign research projects that require a child to orally and/or in writing present his or her ideas.

5. Conduct debates, persuasive speeches.

E. *Attention Seeking:* Utterances that seek to gain and direct the attention of another—either to the child or some aspect of the environment (e.g., Hey, you! Mom! Look!)

Context: Situations in which someone wants or needs another's attention to progress with an activity or to achieve another communicative intention.

Activities

1. Utilize situations in which child must solicit attention of individuals at various distances (next to each other, across the aisle, across the room, in a different room).

2. Introduce role-playing situations—gaining attention of busy salesclerk. Interrupting an ongoing conversation among adults. Gaining attention of a peer in the school yard. Gaining attention in emergency situations.

F. *Protesting/Rejecting and Denying:* Utterances that express objection to ongoing or impending action or event or that contradict preceding utterances (e.g., I refuse to eat my spinach. I don't like you. I am not fat.)

Context: Situations in which someone is likely to object to some aspect of the environment or to deny a statement.

Activities

1. Request child to perform an undesired activity, eat a disliked food.

2. Establish arbitrary rules to determine a student's reactions.

3. Make blatantly untrue statements or false accusations.

4. Introduce role-playing situations—a younger student takes a toy away. A peer hits another on the playground. Parents take away TV privileges for three weeks.

5. Assign writing projects—write to toy company protesting poor construction of a toy. Write to congressman protesting elimination of services due to funding cuts.

G. *Greetings:* Utterances that express salutations and other conventionalized rituals (e.g., Hi, how are you? Bye.)

Context: Situations in which individuals meet, are introduced, and/or part

Activities

1. Develop situations in which a child must greet a partner in person, over the phone, and in a letter.

2. Role-play situations—Have student introduce friend to classmates, his mother to teacher or friend's mother, and so on. Student meets principal, clergyman, or teacher in store.

H. *Other Performatives:* Utterances that tease, warn, claim, exclaim or convey humor (e.g., You can't catch me. Watch out!)

Context: Situations in which an individual is likely to taunt or playfully provoke a listener, alert someone of impending harm, establish rights for the speaker, express surprise and delight, or cause humorous effect.

Activities

1. Have child develop legend for cartoon or fill in what characters in a cartoon might be saying.

2. Have child relate humorous experience.

3. Role-play situations — situation in which right to use a toy is contested (e.g., I'm using it now. It's my turn) or ownership is in question (e.g., That's mine). Games in which order of turns must be decided (e.g., I'm first). Situation in which child observes young child approaching fire, heavy object about to fall, or someone approaching a slippery area.

Adapted with permission from Spekman, N. J., & Roth, F. P. (1984). Intervention strategies for learning disabled children with oral communication disorders. *Learning Disability Quarterly, 7,* 10–13.

5

READING

As one part of the total communication process, reading is often regarded as the most important skill taught in our schools. Since the ability to read is essential for all types of academic success, difficulties in reading are usually considered a primary cause of school failure. The various problems encountered by the handicapped student in reading are often similar to the difficulties experienced by nonhandicapped learners. Nevertheless, the frequency of reading difficulties experienced by the handicapped is far greater than that found in students of normal development (Wallace, 1981). It is estimated that 85 to 90% of handicapped students have reading problems, while approximately 10 to 15% of the general school population have various degrees of reading difficulty (Kaluger & Kolson, 1978).

Many different reading materials, techniques, and methods are available for use in teaching the student experiencing reading difficulties. Due to the continuing search for a solution to the increasing number of disabled readers noted in this country, many materials have appeared in the educational marketplace during the past few years.

We are in agreement with most authorities in the field of reading who believe that there is no one best method of teaching reading. It is our viewpoint that teachers should be able to handle any number of reading problems after determining what will work for a particular pupil. Consequently, a variety of reading methods and materials is absolutely basic to the successful teaching of reading disabled students.

THE NATURE OF READING

The complicated process of learning how to read is reflected in the many definitions and theories of reading that are debated and discussed in the professional literature. Because each definition and model of reading represents a different theoretical position or philosophy, Spache and Spache (1986) believe that no one definition of reading will be accepted unanimously. These authors describe reading as a multifaceted process which can be viewed at various developmental stages in terms of skill development, as a visual art, a perceptual process, a communication component, a reflection of economic and cultural background, or a psycholinguistic process, as information processing, or as a thinking process. Reading changes from what is considered primarily word recognition at one stage, through the development of sight vocabulary and word analysis skills, through various degrees of comprehension, to a mature act involving many of the higher mental processes.

Most models of the reading process can be classified as *bottom-up* models, *top-down* models, or *interactive* models. In the bottom-up models, reading is basically a translating, decoding, and encoding process. In these models, the reader attends to letters, anticipates the words the letters will spell, and identifies the words with further expectations as to how they will be strung together and what they will mean when assembled into phrases and sentences (Spache & Spache, 1986). Reading comprehension, in the bottom-up models, is essentially viewed as an automatic outcome of accurate word recognition.

On the other hand, most of the top-down models of the reading process are based on psycholinguistic concepts involving interaction between thought and language. The reader's cognitive and language competence plays the key role in the construction of meaning from printed material. Unlike bottom-up models, in the top-down models graphic information is used only to support or reject hypotheses about meaning.

Interactive models claim that bottom-up and top-down processes occur simultaneously for skilled readers. Thus, the graphic information in the text and the information in the reader's mind are both important in describing interactive models.

Although most reading approaches developed for disabled readers have been based on a bottom-up orientation (Hammill & Bartel, 1986), the premise of this chapter is that the interactive model best defines the nature of reading, since most beginning readers rely on their own linguistic competence along with various word analysis skills. Furthermore, as noted by Spache and Spache (1986), top-down and bottom-up models present problems when followed strictly, because too much attention to decoding affects both meaning and rate of reading, while random guessing about the meanings of words and sentences is not really reading.

DEVELOPMENT OF READING SKILLS

A number of writers in the field of reading suggest that individuals learn to read as they acquire certain sequential skills. The multitude of skills required to become an efficient reader are usually classified as either word recognition or comprehension skills. Although the purpose of reading is to gather meaning from the printed page, this cannot be accomplished unless the individual can recognize the words that compose the reading passage. Word recognition skills are needed to decode the printed letters and to match the letters and words with sounds, while comprehension skills are needed to understand the meaning of what is read. Both types of skills are certainly needed for an individual to learn how to read.

Although most individuals learning to read are taught using a sequence of skills, no one sequence of skills is common to all reading programs. Moreover, Bourque (1980) points out that most skill sequences have not yet been validated and are based on expert judgment. Therefore, the skills listed in Table 5.1 should be considered a general guide to the sequence of reading skills usually taught in most schools. More important, the skills listed in Table 5.1 will provide a means for both locating and assessing specific reading deficiencies.

The Reading Stages

The process of sequential skill acquisition is also reflected in a series of developmental stages through which most efficient readers progress. Although it is difficult to establish absolute stages of development and skill sequences for any one student, we have found the five reading stages outlined by Harris and Sipay (1980) to be a valuable description. These are discussed briefly in the following paragraphs.

Reading Readiness. This stage serves as a foundational phase for subsequent growth in reading, and it usually occurs from birth to age 6. Although readiness has been long recognized as an important concept, confusion persists regarding its exact nature. Some writers insist that readiness is largely a matter of maturation, while others view readiness in terms of a particular facet of development. We agree with Anastasi's

TABLE 5.1. Sequence of Reading Skill Development

Grade	Skills Acquired
Kindergarten	Identify sounds and pictures
	Express ideas in complete verbal sentences
	Understand meaning of words such as *above* and *far.*
	Understand concepts of size, small, etc.
	Recognize and identify colors
	Organize objects into groups
	Match forms
	Understand beginning concepts of number
Grade 1	Recognize letters of alphabet; can write and give sound
	Auditory and visual perception and discrimination of initial and final consonants
	Observe left to right progression
	Recall what has been read
	Aware of medial consonants, consonant blends, digraphs
	Recognize long sound of vowels; root words; plural forms; verb endings *-s, -ed, -d, -ing;* opposites; pronouns *he, she*
	Understand concept of synonyms, homonyms, antonyms
	Understand simple compound words
	Copy simple sentences, fill-ins
Grade 2	Comprehension and analysis of what has been read
	Identify vowel digraphs
	Understand varient sounds of *y*
	Identify medial vowels
	Identify diphthongs
	Understand influence of *r* on preceding vowel
	Identify three-letter blends
	Understand use of suffix *-er*
	Understand verb endings (e.g., *stop, stopped*)
Grade 3	Recognize multiple sounds of long *a* as in *ei, ei, ay, ey*
	Understand silent *e* in *-le* endings
	Understand use of suffix *-est*
	Know how to change *y* to *i* before adding *er, est*
	Understand comparative and superlative forms of adjectives
	Understand possessive form using *s*
	Use contractions
	Identify syllabic breaks

TABLE 5.1. Continued

Grade	Skills Acquired
Grade 4	Recognize main and subordinate parts
	Recognize unknown words using configuration and other word attack skills
	Identify various sounds of *ch*
	Recognize various phonetic values of *gh*
	Identify rounded *o* sound formed by *au, aw, al*
	Use and interpret diacritical markings
	Discriminate among multiple meanings of words
Grade 5	Read critically to evaluate
	Identify digraphs *gn, mb, bt*
	Recognize that *augh* and *ough* may have round *o* sound
	Recognize and pronounce muted vowels in *el, al, le*
	Recognize secondary and primary accents
	Use of apostrophe
	Understand suffixes *-al, -hand, -ship, -ist, -ling, -an, -ian, -dom, -ern*
	Understand use of figures of speech: metaphor, simile
	Ability to paraphrase main idea
	Know ways paragraphs are developed
	Outline using two or three main heads and subheadings
	Use graphic material
Grade 6	Develop ability for critical analysis
	Recognize and use Latin, Greek roots, such as *photo, tele, graph, geo, auto*
	Develop generalization that some suffixes can change part of speech, such as *-ure* changing an adjective to noun (*moist-moisture*)
	Understand meaning and pronunciation of homographs
	Develop awareness of shifting accents

From Guerin, G. R., & Maier, A. S. (1983). *Informal assessment in education.* Palo Alto, CA: Mayfield, pp. 245–246. Reproduced with permission of Mayfield Publishing Co.

(1982) use of the term as the attainment of prerequisite skills, knowledge, attitudes, motivation, and other appropriate behavioral traits that enable the learner to profit maximally from instruction.

Among the important factors that contribute to reading readiness, Kirk, Kliebhan, and Lerner (1978) point to the following: (a) mental maturity, (b) visual abilities, (c) auditory abilities, (d) speech and language development, (e) thinking skills, (f) physical fitness and motor

FIGURE 5.1. Components of Reading Readiness

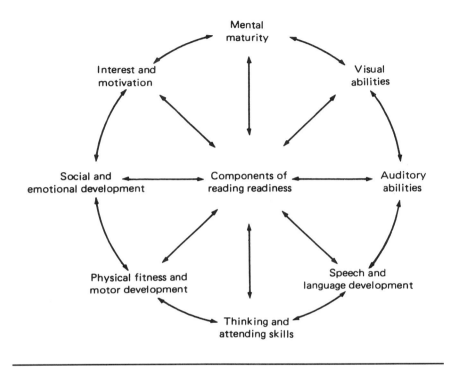

From Kirk, S. A., Kliebhan, S. J. M., & Lerner, J. W. (1978). *Teaching reading to slow and disabled learners*. Boston: Houghton Mifflin, p. 33. Reprinted with permission of Houghton Mifflin Company.

development, (g) social and emotional development, and (h) interest and motivation. Although each of these factors is involved in reading readiness, they vary considerably in importance, and no factor by itself guarantees success or failure. Figure 5.1 illustrates how these reading readiness factors operate as a total system.

Reading readiness does not occur at an exact point in a child's development in the sense that a child is "ready" for reading one day but not the day before. Reading readiness is not an all-or-nothing characteristic but actually a transitional period where the child gradually develops the skills necessary for beginning reading success. Harris and Sipay (1985) suggest that it is better to ask what the child is ready to learn, and at what rate, rather than to conceive of reading readiness as a fixed state. Moreover, readiness activities are an important component of formal initial reading instruction.

Initial Stage of Learning to Read. This period is considered the start of the formal reading program, and it usually occurs in the first grade, although some children may learn to read before or considerably after this time. The emphasis during this particular stage is most often on building a basic sight vocabulary. Sight words frequently appear in beginning reading material and should be recognized automatically without additional analysis. In addition to building a basic sight vocabulary, the emphasis during this period is on developing confidence in the reading situation and on beginning instruction in various word analysis skills. Among the word analysis techniques introduced during this stage, phonetic analysis is probably the most widely used. However, other important word analysis techniques are also introduced during this period, including *configuration*, which helps to identify words by their length and shape; *structural analysis*, which refers to the identification of words by using word parts such as prefixes, suffixes, root words, and inflections; *contextual analysis*, which emphasizes the context in which a word is used; and *picture clues*. Although some word analysis techniques, such as configuration, have only limited value, the use of a variety of analysis techniques should be the goal of most reading programs.

Rapid Development of Reading Skills. During this stage, which normally occurs in the second and third grades, the emphasis is on providing a thorough coverage of the basic reading skills. For example, stress is placed on the extension of a sight vocabulary, improvement of reading comprehension, building competence in independent word analysis, building interest in reading, and encouraging wider reading in a variety of materials. Developmental reading lessons still form the major part of the reading program for typical learners, although functional reading and recreational reading gradually increase in importance.

The student with reading difficulties will find this stage to be a particularly difficult period due to the rapid introduction of a tremendous number of skills during this period. Consequently, this stage of reading development usually extends into the intermediate grades and beyond for the student with reading difficulties.

Wide Reading Stage. This stage, which usually occurs during the intermediate grades, is characterized by the use of a broader range of reading methods and materials. Voluntary reading and reading for pleasure are emphasized during this period, along with continuing expansion of vocabulary and constant review of various word analysis skills. The focus of this stage, however, is on the broadening of comprehension skills and abilities. The three levels of comprehension usually emphasized are *literal*, *interpretive*, and *critical*.

Literal comprehension refers to the recall of directly stated facts. At this level, the reader can outline, paraphrase, or summarize the ideas expressed by the author of a text. The interpretive level of comprehension, on the other hand, involves skills that go beyond the printed page. Karlin (1980) points out that interpretive comprehension involves implied meaning or "reading between and beyond the lines." The third level of comprehension, critical reading, is an extension of the interpretive level and also involves subjective judgments based on attitudes and experiences of the reader. Critical reading is usually considered the highest level of comprehension—the level at which the reader compares the material with his or her total conceptual background.

The Barrett taxonomy of cognition and effective dimensions of reading comprehension further divides comprehension into four major skill categories or levels, including literal recognition or recall, inference evaluation, and appreciation. Table 5.2 provides an outline of this taxonomy.

Refinement of Reading. This stage typically occurs during junior high school, senior high school, and college. The emphases during this stage include refining comprehension skills, increasing reading rate, achieving flexibility in reading for different purposes, and developing proficient study skills. Polloway and Smith (1982) observe that the interrelationship among reading and various content areas such as history and science reaches its peak during this stage. They recommend close evaluation of student difficulties in various content areas to determine whether reading deficits might be contributing to a problem.

Chall's Classification of Reading Stages

In addition to this five-stage process of learning to read, Chall (1983) has recently proposed six stages of classification which may overlap and are not fixed. These stages include:

Stage 0: Prereading Stage. The child develops the prerequisite skills for reading. This stage usually occurs during preschool and kindergarten.

Stage 1: Initial Reading and Decoding Stage. This stage typically occurs in first grade and the beginning of second grade, when the child learns the relationship between letters and sounds and between printed and spoken words.

Stage 2: Confirmation and Fluency Stage. The child in this stage confirms what he or she already knows by reading familiar stories with increasing

TABLE 5.2. The Barrett Taxonomy: Cognitive and Affective Dimensions of Reading Comprehension

1.0 Literal recognition or recall
   1.1 Recognition or recall of details
   1.2 Recognition or recall of main ideas
   1.3 Recognition or recall of sequence
   1.4 Recognition or recall of comparisons
   1.5 Recognition or recall of cause and effect relationships
   1.6 Recognition or recall of character traits

2.0 Inference
   2.1 Inferring supporting details
   2.2 Inferring the main idea
   2.3 Inferring sequence
   2.4 Inferring comparisons
   2.5 Inferring cause and effect relationships
   2.6 Inferring character traits
   2.7 Predicting outcomes
   2.8 Inferring about figurative language

3.0 Evaluation
   3.1 Judgments of reality or fantasy
   3.2 Judgments of fact or opinion
   3.3 Judgments of adequacy or validity
   3.4 Judgments of appropriateness
   3.5 Judgments of worth, desirability, or acceptability

4.0 Appreciation
   4.1 Emotional response to plot or theme
   4.2 Identification with characters and incidents
   4.3 Reactions to the author's use of language
   4.4 Imagery

From Smith, R. J., & Barrett, T. C. (1979). *Teaching reading in the middle grades.* Reading, MA: Addison-Wesley. Reprinted with permission of Addison-Wesley Publishing Co.

fluency and by using decoding skills. This stage usually occurs in the second and third grades.

Stage 3: Reading for Learning the New: A First Step.   Although Chall (1983) did not designate grade or age levels for this stage, it is thought to occur in grades 4 through 9 when students learn new ideas, gain new knowledge, and experience new feelings. Reading activities usually refine and improve skills already started.

Stage 4: Multiple Viewpoints: High School. Skills are acquired at this stage by reading and studying materials that vary widely in type, content, and style.

Stage 5: Construction and Reconstruction—A World View: College. The reading program at this stage, usually occurring after high school, takes many different forms and may be either developmental or remedial.

READING CHARACTERISTICS OF HANDICAPPED LEARNERS

Throughout history, students with reading disabilities have been classified by a variety of terms. According to Wallace and McLoughlin (1979), one of the earliest terms used to describe handicapped readers was *strephosymbolia*, which referred to the pupil with "twisted symbol" difficulty. Later, *alexia*, *word blindness*, and *minimal brain dysfunction* were used. Recently, students with reading problems are often labeled *dyslexic*. This term was originally proposed to denote those students with reading disturbances due to neurological involvement. However, dyslexia has evolved in practice to its use in a variety of ways, including, for example, the indication of a generic cause for reading disturbance.

Notwithstanding the importance of terminology for some situations, the major concern of educators working with disabled readers should be to identify the deficient reading behaviors and consequently teach appropriate reading skills. Furthermore, it is our belief that the complex nature of the reading process, coupled with the vast number of skills required of the efficient reader, certainly contributes to the many different reading problems experienced by the learner handicapped in reading. Some of the prevalent reading difficulties are summarized in the following paragraphs.

1. *Readiness skills* may be lacking, including visual discrimination, auditory discrimination, sound blending, memory skills, directionality, and language facility.

2. *Word analysis* and *word recognition* are often faulty. Some of the specific difficulties involve problems with letter and word reversals, phonics, structural analysis, contextual analysis, and sight words.

3. *Comprehension* abilities may be deficient. Students often experience problems at the literal, interpretive, and critical levels of comprehension along with more specific difficulties in noting main ideas and details, determining sequences, seeing relationships, comparing and contrasting, anticipating outcomes, following directions, and evaluating and making judgments.

4. *Study skills* are actually necessary at all levels of schooling. Some important study skills include using the table of contents and index, locating and using basic reference materials, note-taking, and using various graphic aids such as maps, graphs, tables, and so forth.

5. *Oral reading skills* may be deficient, including difficulties with word-by-word reading, mispronunciations, phrasing problems, and repetitions.

6. *Literacy interests* are an often overlooked area of reading difficulties. Some students have problems in the appreciation of literature, making good use of library time and free reading of books, and enjoying storytelling and creative drama.

In the initial sections of this chapter we have discussed the varied nature of reading and the developmental sequence of reading skills. The preceding discussion of the characteristics of disabled readers should serve as a useful guide for the following section, which outlines the various assessment tools utilized with the reading handicapped.

ASSESSMENT OF READING SKILLS

A number of very different assessment techniques are commonly used to appraise the reading abilities of handicapped learners. Standardized tests are administered in many cases, while information gathered from systematic observations and informal tests also is used in planning appropriate instructional strategies. Nevertheless, in most cases we have found that the most efficient measurement processes employ a variety of appraisal techniques, including both formal and informal assessment.

Formal Reading Tests

Among the various reading assessment approaches, formal techniques are those formally-developed reading tests that are commercially available. Many formal reading tests are norm-referenced or standardized, while others are commercially published criterion-referenced tests. Formal reading test scores are usually reported in a variety of ways, including grade-level scores, percentiles, stanines, and age equivalent scores. In addition, most formal assessment techniques in reading include specific directions for administering, scoring, and interpreting the results of the test. In this section we discuss three types of formal assessment procedures in reading: (a) diagnostic tests, (b) word recognition tests, and (c) criterion-referenced tests.

Diagnostic Reading Tests. Diagnostic reading tests usually consist of multiple subtests, each appraising a specific reading skill. The diagnostic reading batteries listed in Table 5.3 provide detailed information concerning a pupil's skills and abilities in various areas of reading. The skills most often evaluated by these tests include word analysis, word recognition, sight vocabulary, and related reading skills such as visual discrimination and sound blending. A number of diagnostic tests also include an oral reading subtest. Most diagnostic tests are intended for individual administration by professionals trained in appraising handicapped and/or remedial learners. It is important to note that while many diagnostic reading tests are norm-referenced, the norms for these batteries are seldom constructed as carefully as are those for other reading tests (Richek, List, & Lerner, 1983). Therefore, the standardization procedures and norms of these tests should be carefully examined before they are used by the teacher.

According to Ramsey (1967), diagnostic reading tests may be judged according to several of the following criteria. *Reality* refers to skills and concepts being evaluated in a manner similar to their usage in actual reading. *Guessing* means that correct guessing should not be possible. *Active* describes the student who responds with overt, observable behavior. *Specificity* implies that success or failure on an item should be attributable to only one ability rather than to a combination of abilities. *Comprehension* suggests that questions on comprehension should require understanding and interpretation rather than mere recall of directly stated details. According to these criteria, Harris and Sipay (1985) point out that none of the diagnostic reading batteries listed in Table 5.3 are fully satisfactory. Nevertheless, all five tests are useful and recommended for appraising reading skills. Of the five batteries discussed, the *Gates-McKillop-Horowitz Reading Diagnostic Tests* (Gates, McKillop, & Horowitz, 1981) and the *Diagnostic Reading Scales* (DRS) (Spache, 1981) adequately cover the widest range of reading ability, with the *Gates-McKillop-Horowitz* probably being the most comprehensive of all the batteries. The *Durrell Analysis of Reading Difficulty* (Durrell & Catterson, 1980) is considered to be the most appropriate for use with less severe cases of reading disability and for students reading at or above the third grade level (Bond, Tinker, & Wasson, 1979; Harris & Sipay, 1985), while the *Stanford Diagnostic Reading Test* (Karlsen, Madden, & Gardner, 1974, 1977) is best suited to determine appropriate reading placements for students, because it is a group administered test. According to Dwyer (1978), the *Woodcock Reading Mastery Test* is probably best used as a global measure for reading difficulties and not for any precise diagnostic decisions. The *DRS* is considered to be significantly improved over the earlier edition and is useful in the evaluation of various phonics skills (Ekwall & Shanker, 1983). In sum, however, it is wise to consider the

TABLE 5.3. Diagnostic Reading Scales

Test	Publisher	Grade Level	Administration	Subtests
Diagnostic Reading Scales (DRS) (Spache, 1981)	CTB/McGraw-Hill	1–7	Individual	Word recognition lists, graded reading passages, word analysis, and phonics tests
Durrell Analysis of Reading Difficulty (Durrell & Catterson, 1980)	Harcourt Brace Jovanovich	nonreading–6	Individual	Oral reading, silent reading, listening comprehension, word recognition and word analysis, listening vocabulary, pronunciation of word elements, spelling, visual memory of words, auditory analysis of words and elements, and prereading phonics abilities inventories
Gates-McKillop-Horowitz Reading Diagnostic Tests (Gates, McKillop, & Horowitz, 1981)	Harper & Row	1–6	Individual	Oral reading, reading sentences, words-flash, words-continued, syllabication, recognizing, reorganizing, and blending common word parts, reading words, giving letter sounds, naming capital letters, recognizing the visual forms of auditory discrimination, spelling, and informal writing sample
Stanford Diagnostic Reading Test (SDRT) (Karlsen, Madden, & Gardner, 1974, 1977)	Harcourt Brace Jovanovich	1–12	Group	Auditory vocabulary, auditory discrimination, phonetic analysis, structural analysis, word reading, reading comprehension, and rate
Woodcock Reading Mastery Tests (Woodcock, 1973)	American Guidance Service	K–12	Individual	Letter identification, word identification, word attack, word comprehension, and passage comprehension

observation by Harris and Sipay (1985) that it is more practical to become thoroughly familiar with one diagnostic battery and use it repeatedly than to attempt to master all of these tests, since examiners derive additional insights from a test as they become familiar with it. Some additional diagnostic tests designed to provide a concentrated appraisal of specific reading skills are listed in Table 5.4.

Word Recognition Tests. Graded word lists, which estimate a student's general reading level in relation to word knowledge, are a relatively recent addition to the broad array of reading assessment approaches. According to Hammill and Bartel (1986), graded word lists serve three purposes. First, they serve as a sample of a student's sight vocabulary; second, the lists provide clues to the word analysis skills that students use as they attack unfamiliar words; and third, the word list gives some indication of where to initiate reading instruction with the student.

Most graded word lists consist of 10 to 15 words of each reading level from primer through high school. Testing is usually initiated with the word list at least two years below the student's grade assignment and continued to more difficult lists until the student misses at least three words in any given list. Betts (1956) recommends that a student achieve a score of approximately 95% at any given reading level before he or she is considered ready for the next level.

Graded word lists are helpful as a quick estimate of word recognition and general levels of reading ability. Harris and Sipay (1985) report that scores on these tests correlate highly with more complete measures of reading ability at primary levels; this correlation is less high in upper grades. Nevertheless, Ekwall and Shanker (1983) suggest that students who are very good at word attack skills may tend to correctly pronounce quite a few words that are not in their sight vocabularies. These authors also point out that the graded word list is quite likely to be inaccurate in terms of placement levels for the student with reading comprehension difficulties. Most important, however, graded word lists provide only limited information in regard to understanding the specific difficulties of learners who are handicapped in reading.

San Diego Quick Assessment. The *San Diego Quick Assessment* (LaPray & Ross, 1969) is considered to be an extremely useful graded word list. The list is shown in Figure 5.2. The *San Diego* is composed of words from basal reader glossaries and from the Thorndike Word List. In administering the list, the examiner should type out each list of 10 words on an index card. The test is usually initiated at the list that is at least two years below the pupil's grade level assignment. The student is asked to read the words aloud. If he or she misreads any words on the list, the examiner should drop to easier lists until no errors are made. Students should be encouraged to read unknown words in order for

TABLE 5.4. Tests of Specific Reading Skills

Test	Publisher	Grade Level	Administration	Subtests
Gilmore Oral Reading Test (Gilmore & Gilmore, 1968)	Harcourt Brace Jovanovich	1–8	Individual	Accuracy comprehension and rate of oral reading
Gray Oral Reading Tests–Revised (GORT–R) (Wiederholt & Bryant, 1986)	PRO-ED	1–college	Individual	Speed and accuracy of oral reading and specific error classification
McCullough Word Analysis Tests (McCullough, 1963)	Ginn	4–6	Individual or Group	Identifying initial blends and digraphs, using phonetic discrimination, matching letters to vowel sounds, sounding whole words, interpreting phonetic symbols, dividing words into syllables, and identifying root words in affixed forms
Test of Reading Comprehension (TORC) (Brown, Hammill, & Wiederholt, 1986)	PRO-ED	2–12	Individual	General vocabulary, syntactic similarities, paragraph reading, sentence sequencing, more specific vocabulary needed to read in content areas

the examiner to identify word analysis techniques used by the student for word identification. Increasingly difficult lists are read until at least three words are missed.

The results of the test may be used to determine reading levels and also to detect specific analysis errors. The list on which a pupil misses no more than one of the 10 words is the independent reading level. Two errors on the list indicate the instructional level, and three or more errors identify the level at which reading material will be too difficult.

Slosson Oral Reading Test. The *Slosson Oral Reading Test (SORT)* (Slosson, 1963) is individually administered and is based on the ability to pronounce words at different levels of difficulty. The *SORT* consists of ten lists of 20 words from the primer level through the eighth grade, with an additional list for high school students. Words on each list were taken from "standardized school readers."

The test is administered by initially finding the word list for which the student can pronounce all words correctly (called the *starting list*) and continuing until the *stopping list*, or the list where the student mispronounces or is unable to read all 20 words. Omitted words as well as words that take more than about 5 seconds to pronounce are counted as errors. The number of correct words plus the words below the starting list, for which automatic credit is given, is considered the raw score. Raw scores can be converted to reading grade levels.

The author reports a correlation coefficient of .96 with the *Gray Oral Reading Test* (Gray & Robinson, 1967). A test-retest reliability coefficient of .99 is also reported, but no further information regarding these scores is provided.

The *SORT* provides a relatively quick estimate (average testing time is approximately 3 minutes) of a student's reading level. However, a more thorough appraisal will be necessary for most students experiencing reading difficulties.

Criterion-Referenced Tests. Criterion-referenced testing has recently become a widely used alternative to norm-referenced testing. In criterion-referenced testing, performance is evaluated in terms of an absolute or specific criterion that has been set for the student without comparison to the performance of other students. Whereas most norm-referenced testing is a global measure of reading ability, yielding scores in such areas as word recognition and comprehension, most criterion-referenced tests measure mastery of specific skills. Recognition of 90% of the root words in a list of 50 words, for example, might be the criterion set for one student. On the other hand, recognition of the initial consonant *b* at the 80% level in a list of 10 words might be the criterion for another student.

Criterion-referenced testing can provide a number of distinct advantages for planning instruction. The flexibility of assessing a large number

FIGURE 5.2. The San Diego Quick Assessment Word List

PP	Primer	1	2
see	you	road	our
play	come	live	please
me	not	thank	myself
at	with	when	town
run	jump	bigger	early
go	help	how	send
and	is	always	wide
look	work	night	believe
can	are	spring	quietly
here	this	today	carefully

3	4	5	6
city	decided	scanty	bridge
middle	served	business	commercial
moment	amazed	develop	abolish
frightened	silent	considered	trucker
exclaimed	wrecked	discussed	apparatus
several	improved	behaved	elementary
lonely	certainly	splendid	comment
drew	entered	acquainted	necessity
since	realized	escaped	gallery
straight	interrupted	grim	relativity

7	8	9	10	11
amber	capacious	conscientious	zany	galore
dominion	limitation	isolation	jerkin	rotunda
sundry	pretext	molecule	nausea	capitalism
capillary	intrigue	ritual	gratuitous	prevaricate
impetuous	delusion	momentous	linear	risible
blight	immaculate	vulnerable	inept	exonerate
wrest	ascent	kinship	legality	superannuate
enumerate	acrid	conservatism	aspen	luxuriate
daunted	binocular	jaunty	amnesty	piebald
condescend	embankment	inventive	barometer	crunch

From LaPray, M., & Ross, R. (1969). The graded word list: A quick gauge of reading ability. *Journal of Reading, 12,* 305–307. Reproduced with permission of M. LaPray and the International Reading Association.

of reading skills that provide information directly applicable to remedial programs is probably the most noteworthy benefit for teachers. However, examiners using criterion-referenced testing should be aware of the limitations of these tests. As noted by Otto and Smith (1980), criterion-referenced testing can be both complex and time consuming. The setting of inappropriate criteria for individual pupils is another major disadvantage of this approach, since there is little empirical evidence to substantiate the commonly used standards of 80 or 90%.

Criterion-referenced and norm-referenced tests both provide the teacher with usable information for planning instructional programs; therefore, the use of criterion-referenced or norm-referenced tests should not be an either/or proposition. Norm-referenced tests can provide information regarding estimates of achievement gains and whether students are achieving at a level commensurate with their ability, whereas criterion-referenced tests are usually preferred in situations assessing whether or not a student has acquired a particular skill or knowledge.

Although many criterion-referenced reading tests are part of a complete reading program, a wide variety of systems independent of specific reading programs have been published in the last two decades. Two such systems are reviewed in the following section.

Fountain Valley Teacher Support System in Reading. The *Fountain Valley Teacher Support System in Reading* (Zweig & Associates, 1971) is composed of 77 self-scoring criterion-referenced tests covering 367 behavioral objectives in the reading skills areas of phonic analysis, structural analysis, vocabulary, comprehension, and study skills. The tests are arranged in order of difficulty, and they may be individually or group administered.

The results of the *Fountain Valley* provide information regarding each student's strengths and weaknesses in reading. In addition, continuous pupil profiles are included so that teachers might record individual student achievement over a period of time. A cross-referenced guide to various basal reading series is also included for locating pages specific to particular instructional objectives.

Reliability, validity, and normative data are not provided, since the *Fountain Valley* is a criterion-referenced system. However, the tests do enable teachers to determine a pupil's strengths and weaknesses in the developmental sequence of reading. Moreover, the ability to link specific instructional objectives with appropriate reading methods and materials must certainly be considered a prime advantage of the *Fountain Valley* system.

Wisconsin Tests of Reading Skill Development. The *Wisconsin Tests of Reading Skill Development* (Kamm, Miles, Van Blaricom, Harris, & Stewart, 1972) consists of six components: Word Attack, Comprehension, Study Skills, Self-Directed Reading, Interpretive Reading, and Creative Reading. The tests are available at seven levels of difficulty, all of which are

TABLE 5.5. Skills by Area and Grade Level for the Wisconsin Test of Reading Skills Development

Skill Area	K	1	2	3	4	5	6
				Grade			
Word Attack	A	B	C	D	–	–	–
Comprehension	A	B	C	D	E	F	G
Study Skills	A	B	C	D	E	F	G
Self-Directed Reading		A–C			D–E		F–G
Interpretive Reading		A–C			D–E		F–G
Creative Reading		A–C			D–E		F–G

appropriate for individual or group administration. Time limits are not imposed. The tests focus upon a pupil's performance of the task, not the rate of response. The six areas and traditional grade level equivalents of the various levels are shown in Table 5.5.

The Word Attack area, for example, is composed of 38 brief tests, each of which is keyed to specific word attack objectives so that each test is an independent unit. The word attack skills correspond to those skills usually taught in the primary grades, including sight vocabulary, rhyming, consonants, vowels, base words, plurals, and syllabication. The terminal, or broad, objective for the Word Attack element is as follows: Upon completion of all four Word Attack skill levels, the student will be able to attack independently phonetically and/or structurally regular words and will recognize all common irregular Dolch list words (Dolch, 1953). Pupils of average or above average ability will attain this objective at least by the end of the fourth grade, while others will attain this objective by the end of the sixth grade.

The comprehension component of the *Wisconsin*, on the other hand, emphasizes reading comprehension skills requiring convergent thinking. The comprehension skills are arranged by strands, and each strand has a hierarchy. The strands include main idea, sequences, context clues, affixes, reasoning, and reading for detail. Each step within a strand represents a different and discrete skill built on, or subsuming, previous skills within that strand. The comprehension tests generally correspond to those skills taught in kindergarten through sixth grade. An 80% criterion is frequently used throughout the tests.

The authors of the *Wisconsin* report that each of the tests had demonstrated reliability at a reasonably high level of .80 or better. However, no other information regarding reliability or validity is available.

The *Wisconsin* tests are a good example of a criterion-referenced testing system in reading. The tests ably identify various reading skills which appear essential for achievement in school. The information provided allows conscientious teachers to plan appropriate instruction and to monitor each pupil's progress.

Informal Reading Assessment

Informal methods are widely used in appraising the reading skills of handicapped learners. Farr (1969), for example, notes that despite the lack of norms, informal tests can be reliable and valid measures of reading, since more samples of reading behavior are likely to be taken with informal measures than with formal ones. Among the wide variety of informal assessment techniques in reading, *observations*, *oral questioning and interviews*, *informal reading inventories*, the *cloze procedure*, and *informal teacher-constructed tests* are among the most widely used and the most beneficial. Each of these is discussed in this section.

Observation. Various observational techniques have recently been widely recommended as important components of the informal assessment process. Observational procedures are often used to confirm the findings of both formal and informal tests, while at other times observations are used to study certain skills and behaviors untapped by formal tests.

Teachers are afforded many excellent opportunities throughout the school day to observe pupils in reading-related activities. Seatwork assignments, class discussions, group instruction, and silent and oral reading periods seem to be the most advantageous times for observing a pupil's reading skills and abilities. Wallace and McLoughlin (1979) note that an analysis of observed reading skills often provides answers to the following questions:

❑ What word analysis does the child utilize?

❑ How extensive is the child's sight vocabulary?

❑ What *consistent* word analysis errors are made by the child?

❑ Does the child depend upon one analysis skill (e.g., sounding words out)?

❑ Are factual questions answered correctly?

❑ Is the child able to answer comprehension questions requiring inferential and critical reading ability? (p. 163)

It is usually helpful to have some type of systematic recording of observations. Recordings may be kept as dated observations through use of anecdotal records. Checklists are also used to note reading difficulties and for monitoring student progress in reading. A number of the diagnostic reading tests described earlier in this chapter (e.g., *Durrell Analysis of Reading Difficulty* and the *Gates-McKillop-Horowitz Reading Diagnostic Tests*) contain checklists that may be used in observing various reading behaviors. In addition, the *Barbe Reading Skills Checklists* (Barbe, 1975) are commercially available for observing the following skills: vocabulary, perception, word analysis, word attack, study skills, comprehension, oral expression, oral and silent reading, and creative reading. Another sample observational checklist is shown in Figure 5.3.

Observations are an excellent additional source of assessment data that may be used in conjunction with other evaluative information to provide the best possible program of instruction for the student with reading difficulties. Pasanella and Volkmar (1981) indicate that the rigorous application of observational techniques may provide an almost sufficient data base for beginning to plan instruction. Nonetheless, observations must be carefully interpreted. Observational interpretations should be based upon current, multiple observations that have occurred over an extended time period.

Interviews and Oral Questioning. Interviews and oral questioning are additional informal assessment techniques used in measuring various reading skills. For the most part, these techniques are utilized in appraising reading interests and attitudes and in gathering data concerning word analysis, word recognition, and reading comprehension skills.

We strongly recommend the use of interviews as an excellent technique to use in the determination of a student's reading interests. For the student encountering reading difficulties, assessing interests will be a crucial consideration in selecting instructional materials and planning corrective programming. During the interview, it is suggested that the teacher encourage students to talk about their likes and dislikes in games, movies, television programs, books, and future career goals.

Very limited training is provided to educators in regard to the skill of interviewing, even though teachers are frequently involved in conversations with students, parents, and other professionals (Guerin & Maier, 1983). These authors note that a successful interview calls for a clear purpose and direction. From beginning to end, the interview should be designed to elicit information; to convey concerns, understanding, and information; and to arrive at a plan or achieve closure.

On the other hand, a number of writers believe that the most important use of comprehension testing is accomplished by means of oral questions and answers during daily work in silent reading. Often, teachers will give students an initial purpose for reading a particular story by providing a guiding question. Following the silent reading of

FIGURE 5.3. Observation Checklist

AREA	ADEQUATE	SOMEWHAT ADEQUATE	INADEQUATE	COMMENTS
Work Habits				
Quality of classwork				
Independent working habits				
Impulsivity				
Response to teacher questions				
Following directions				
Participation in class				
General health and nutrition				
Reading Habits				
Oral reading fluency				
Repetitions				
Stress during oral reading				
Relies on teacher aid				
Sight words:				
function (high-utility) words				
other words				
Phonics				
Consonants				
Consonant blends and digraphs				
Vowels				
Other				
Multisyllable words				
Blends sounds together				
Reversals (letters, words)				
Comprehension				
Factual				
Higher level				
Word meanings				
Loses place in reading				
Visual problems in reading				
Other				

From Richek, M. A., List, L. K., & Lerner, J. W. (1983). *Reading problems: Diagnosis and remediation.* Englewood Cliffs, NJ: Prentice-Hall, p. 115. Reprinted with permission of the publisher.

the passage, further aspects of comprehension such as noting specific details, recognizing feelings and moods, following a sequence, and predicting outcomes can be checked by additional oral questions and answers. Harris and Sipay (1985) believe that the major advantages of oral questioning are that (a) oral questions allow freedom of response not characteristic of the more time-consuming written answer; (b) errors in understanding can be immediately detected and corrected; and (c) further discussion and exchanges of opinion are possible with oral questioning. Nonetheless, we recommend that some type of written record be kept of oral questioning responses; otherwise, the teacher is too dependent upon incidental learnings, memory, and haphazard measurement samples (Bush & Huebner, 1979).

Informal Reading Inventories.   An informal reading inventory, commonly referred to as an IRI, consists of a series of carefully graded reading passages for reading levels from preprimer through eighth grade. The IRI, which can be either purchased or teacher-made, is widely used for informally determining a student's general reading level. An example of an IRI reading passage with comprehension questions is illustrated in Figure 5.4.

Constructing an IRI.   An excellent outline for developing an IRI has been provided by Hammill and Bartel (1986). The directions include:

1. Selection of a standard basal series
   a. Choose any series that goes from preprimer to the sixth level.
   b. Select materials that the child has not previously used.

2. Selection of passages from the basal reader
   a. Choose a selection that makes a complete story.
   b. Choose selections of about 50 words at the preprimer level; 100 words at the primer, first, and second levels, and 100–150 words at the upper levels.
   c. Choose two selections at each level: plan to use one for oral reading and one for silent reading, and take the selections from the middle of the book.

3. Construction of questions
   a. Build five questions for each selection at the preprimer level; six questions for each selection at primer, first, and second levels; and ten questions from each selection at level three and above.
   b. Avoid "yes" and "no" questions.
   c. Include vocabulary in the questions that is at the same level as vocabulary in the selection.
   d. Construct three kinds of questions at each level in about the following percentages: factual, 40 percent; inferential, 40 percent; vocabulary, 20 percent.

4. Construction and preparation of test
   a. Cut and mount the selection on oaktag *or*
   b. Note the pages in the book, print the questions on separate cards, and have the child read the selection from the text itself. (pp. 41–42)

Administering an IRI.   In administering an IRI, the examiner asks the student to read orally from the graded reading passages until the

FIGURE 5.4. Sample IRI Reading Passage

○PP PASSAGE ━━━ FORM C ━━━ TEACHER PP○

MOTIVATIONAL STATEMENT: Read this story to find out what Joe did.

Joe was not happy.
He wanted a pet.
He found a pet.
It was a goat.

Mom said, "No."
Dad said, "No!
No! No!"
No goat for Joe.

Joe heard a sound.
He looked around.
It was a dog.
A little dog.

Joe patted the dog.
"Hello!" Joe said.
"I like you."
"Bow-wow!" said the dog.

"Nice dog!" said Joe.
"Come with me.
Be my dog.
Be my pet."

SCORING AID

WORD RECOGNITION

% MISCUES	
99	1
95	3
90	6
85	9

COMPREHENSION

% ERRORS	
100	0
87.5	1
75	2
62.5	3
50	4
37.5	5
25	6
12.5	7
0	8

61 WORDS

WPM

3660 /

COMPREHENSION QUESTIONS

___ main idea
1. What would be a good title for this story? (Joe Finds a Dog; Joe Finds a Pet)

___ detail
2. How did Joe feel at the beginning of the story? (sad; not happy)

___ sequence
3. What was the first pet Joe found? (a goat)

___ cause and effect/inference
4. Why was Joe sad at the beginning of the story? (He wanted a pet; his mom and dad wouldn't let him keep the goat.)

___ detail
5. What did Joe hear? (a sound; a dog)

___ detail
6. What size was the dog? (little)

___ sequence
7. What was the first thing Joe did to the dog? (He patted it.)

___ inference
8. How did Joe feel at the end of the story? (happy; better) Why do you say that? (He had found a pet and he had wanted one badly.)

[Note: Do not count as a miscue mispronunciation of the name Joe. You may pronounce this word for the student if needed.]

From Burns, P. C., & Roe, B. D. (1985). *Informal Reading Inventory.* Boston: Houghton Mifflin, p. 108. Used with permission.

material becomes too difficult. A silent reading passage is also typically read at each grade level. The student is usually asked a series of comprehension questions following each reading passage.

Two major types of information can be generally obtained from the IRI: (a) quantitative information expressed in grade equivalent scores to indicate the reader's *independent* reading level, *instructional* reading level, *frustration* level, and *capacity* level and (b) qualitative information concerning the reader's word recognition and comprehension skills (Burns & Roe, 1980).

The independent reading level is the level at which a student can read with understanding and ease and without assistance. At this level, reading is not usually accompanied by any symptoms of difficulty, such as finger pointing or lip moving. Material at this level is read with 99% or better word recognition (misses no more than one word in a hundred) and 90% or better comprehension (misses no more than one question in 10).

The instructional reading level is the level at which a student can read with understanding under teacher guidance. This is the level at which the student should be placed for reading instruction. At this level, the pupil reads with 90% or better word recognition (misses no more than one word in 10) and 75% or better comprehension (misses no more than 2 questions in 8).

At the frustration level, the reading material is too difficult for the pupil. Fluency usually breaks down at this level, and the student makes many errors. Word recognition is less than 90% (misses more than 10 words in 100), and comprehension is less than 50% (misses more than 5 questions in 10) at this level.

The capacity or the listening comprehension level is the level at which a student comprehends at least 75% of material read aloud by the teacher. This level indicates the student's understanding of language. Some teachers also use this level as a measure of reading potential.

Scoring an IRI. In addition to determining a pupil's reading level, an IRI can be used for detecting various word recognition, word analysis, and comprehension difficulties. A marking system for recording a pupil's oral reading errors is usually recommended. Figure 5.5 provides an example of a system for both designating and scoring specific errors. Analysis of a pupil's IRI performance will help to pinpoint specific difficulties that the student is encountering and often will suggest instructional strategies for overcoming these difficulties.

Commercial reading inventories. A number of teachers find it more convenient to use commercially prepared reading inventories rather than constructing their own IRI. Table 5.6 lists some commercial reading inventories.

On the whole, the available commercial inventories are well constructed. However, Richek, List, and Lerner (1983) suggest that the

FIGURE 5.5. Recording System for Oral Reading Errors

Error	Marking	Comment
Mispronunciation	*wert* / *went*	The student attempts to pronounce the word but produces a nonsense word, rather than a real one.
Substitution	*want* / *went*	The student substitutes a real word that is incorrect.
Refusal to pronounce	*TP* / went	The student neither pronounces the word nor attempts to do so. The teacher supplies the word so that testing can continue.
Insertion	*on* / sent to	The student inserts a word that does not appear in the text.
Omission	to (the) school	The student omits a word in the text but continues to read.
Repetition	in the little house	The student repeats one or more words that have been read.
Reversal	that (he saw)	The student reverses the order of words or letters.

From Burns, P. C., & Roe, B. D. (1985). *Informal Reading Inventory.* Boston: Houghton Mifflin, p. 3. Used with permission.

following features of a commercial reading inventory need to be considered: (a) Are the passages long enough to permit oral reading patterns to stabilize? (b) Is there a provision of more than one form to allow for retesting of silent reading? (c) Does the test provide a breakdown of oral reading miscues and the coding of different types of comprehension questions? (d) Does the test permit photocopying of material for classroom use? and (e) Is the difficulty level of the reading passages verified through a readability formula?

TABLE 5.6. Commercial Reading Inventories

Inventory	Publisher
Analytical Reading Inventory	Charles E. Merrill
Classroom Reading Inventory	William C. Brown
Diagnostic Reading Inventory	Kendall/Hunt
Ekwall Reading Inventory	Allyn & Bacon
Informal Reading Assessment	Rand McNally
Reading Miscue Inventory	Macmillan
Standard Reading Inventory	Klamath Printing
Sucher-Allred Reading Placement Inventory	Economy

Miscue analysis. Another method for recording and analyzing oral reading in a systematic fashion is called the *reading miscue* procedure. According to Goodman (1973), a miscue is an actual observed response in oral reading which does not match the expected outcome. In analyzing oral reading, the emphasis is placed on the nature of the miscue rather than on the number of oral reading errors. Since the miscues are analyzed quantitatively, information concerning the student's language patterns and reasoning skills is usually provided. The focus of miscue analysis is on how the student's responses affect the actual meaning of a sentence or reading passage.

The reading miscue assessment technique is presented in the *Reading Miscue Inventory* (Goodman & Burke, 1972), which contains reading passages and scoring sheets that are used for applying miscue analysis. The *Inventory* analyzes miscues according to graphic, syntactic, and semantic characteristics (see Figure 5.6). Hammill and Bartel (1986) indicate that by rating the relative proportion of miscues in each category, a teacher can form some idea of whether the student's difficulty is more of the word analysis type (mostly graphic miscues) or whether the pupil has linguistic or cognitive difficulty in forming hypotheses about the meaning of the material being read (mostly syntactic and semantic miscues).

Advantages and limitations of the IRI. According to Wallace and McLoughlin (1979), the IRI is relatively easy to construct, does not take very long to administer, and is comparatively inexpensive. Savage and Mooney (1979) point out that the IRI is a manageable tool that the teacher can use in placement, selection of reading materials, and prescriptive planning for students encountering reading difficulties. Most important, the results from an IRI can be readily used during classroom

FIGURE 5.6. Questions in the *Reading Miscue Inventory*

---

1 DIALECT: Is a dialect variation involved in the miscue?

2 INTONATION: Is a shift in intonation involved in the miscue?

3 GRAPHIC SIMILARITY: How much does the miscue look like what was expected?

4 SOUND SIMILARITY: How much does the miscue sound like what was expected?

5 GRAMMATICAL FUNCTION: Is the grammatical function of the miscue the same as the grammatical function of the word in the text?

6 CORRECTION: Is the miscue corrected?

7 GRAMMATICAL ACCEPTABILITY: Does the miscue occur in a structure which is grammatically acceptable?

8 SEMANTIC ACCEPTABILITY: Does the miscue occur in a structure which is semantically acceptable?

9 MEANING CHANGE: Does the miscue result in a change of meaning?

From Goodman, Y. M., Watson, D. J., & Burke, C. L. (1987). *Reading miscue inventory: Alternative procedures.* New Yo.k: Richard C. Owen Publishers Inc. Reprinted with permission.

instruction. Although the IRI can serve as an excellent assessment tool, a number of limitations of this approach should be mentioned.

A number of writers feel that the criteria for determining IRI reading levels are arbitrary, rigid, and too high (Savage & Mooney, 1979). In addition, they point out that the IRI assumes that the readability measures applied to reading passages are firm and accurate, yet research suggests that this assumption is questionable. Several studies have found that some standardized reading achievement tests tend to give grade-equivalent scores higher than the instructional level determined by an IRI. Harris and Sipay (1985) point out, however, that the results of such comparison will be determined by (a) the standardized test used; (b) the material on which the IRI is based; (c) how well the IRI is constructed, administered, scored, and interpreted; and (d) the criteria used to determine the functional reading levels. Nonetheless, when there is disagreement between the estimate provided by a standardized test and the results of an IRI, these authors recommended the latter as a more dependable guide in the choice of reading materials.

FIGURE 5.7. Cloze Selection

Children love to go to the circus. The clowns are probably ___1___ best part of the ___2___ for many children. The ___3___ often look funny and ___4___ crazy things during all ___5___ the performances. All of ___6___ different animals at the ___7___ are also exciting. Sometimes ___8___ performers ride on the ___9___ and do tricks with ___10___. The circus is probably ___11___ of the best types ___12___ entertainment for children of ___13___ ages.

Correct Answers: 1. the 2. circus 3. clowns 4. do 5. of 6. the 7. circus
8. the 9. animals 10. them 11. one 12. of 13. all

Cloze Procedure. The cloze procedure is an informal assessment approach that may be used to estimate the readability level of reading materials or to estimate a pupil's instructional reading level. The procedure is also used as an instructional technique for teaching reading comprehension.

Based on the gestalt term *closure,* the cloze procedure consists of deleting every *n*th word (usually every fifth word) from a reading passage and replacing it with a blank line. Pupils are then expected to read the passage and fill in the blanks by using the correct word according to the proper context of the sentence. Figure 5.7 shows an example of the cloze procedure. The steps for designing a cloze test are listed below.

1. Randomly select a minimum of two reading passages of approximately 250 words in length from each graded reading selection to be assessed. Reading passages should begin a new paragraph.

2. Delete every fifth word from the passage starting with the second sentence and replace the deleted words with lines of equal length.

3. Duplicate the passages. For individual administration, pupils may simply say the word. In a group administration, the students are instructed to fill in the missing word.

The cloze score is the number of correct responses divided by the number of deleted words and usually is expressed as a percentage. Most authors suggest that only the exact deleted word should be counted as a correct response. However, some writers, believing that supplying synonyms indicates comprehension, accept the synonym as a correct response. The percentages of the various reading levels, according to Ekwall and Shanker (1983), include

Reading Level	Cloze Score
Free or independent level	58–100%
Instructional level	44–57%
Frustration level	43% or below

Harris and Sipay (1985) point out that the main advantages of the cloze procedure are that (a) it is easier and quicker to construct, administer, score, and interpret than the IRI; (b) its use requires less expertise; (c) it can be group administered; (d) it provides a good measurement of the ability to use semantic and syntactic cues; and (e) research findings regarding its reliability and validity for pupils over age 8 are impressive. Others feel that the cloze procedure is a good measure of comprehension, because readers who understand the structure and content of the written text should be able to fill in the missing words correctly (Dieterich, Freeman, & Griffin, 1978).

It is important to note that the cloze procedure provides only limited diagnostic data. Information regarding a pupil's word recognition, decoding skills, or specific strengths and weaknesses in various reading comprehension skills is essentially available through the cloze procedure. Therefore, we recommend that the procedure be used carefully.

Informal Teacher-Constructed Tests. An informal teacher-constructed test is another excellent method for assessing a pupil's reading skills. We have found that these tests usually measure skills that are directly related to classroom instruction and consequently provide information concerning specific reading skills. Polloway and Smith (1982) suggest that when used appropriately, informal teacher-constructed tests provide for direct conversion of results into remedial activities.

Teacher-constructed tests are typically designed by using published tests and workbook exercises as guides. Hammill and Bartel (1986) note that a good scope-and-sequence chart outlining the major reading skill areas in the recommended order of presentation may also be used as the framework for building an informal test. In addition, Otto (1973) describes the sequence of steps in constructing an informal test:

1. Decide exactly what information is desired and what this means in terms of observable behavior;

2. devise new test items, materials, or situations to sample the behavior to be evaluated, or adapt existing ones;

3. keep a record of the student's behavior and responses;

4. analyze the obtained information; and

5. make judgments as to how the information fits the total pictures and how well it fills the gap for which it was intended.

Informal teacher-constructed tests can be designed to measure almost any specific reading skill. Various word analysis and word recognition skills are ideally suited to the objective-type formats typically used in informal tests. On the other hand, teacher-constructed tests in reading comprehension are considered a bit difficult to construct, because comprehension skills are not as clearly observable as word analysis skills. In all cases, however, the teacher should be careful to include a sufficient number of test items to adequately measure the reading skills. Figure 5.8 illustrates two informal teacher-constructed tests.

TEACHING READING SKILLS

Effective instructional programs for the disabled reader are based upon systematic planning and the most efficient teaching procedures. Some important guidelines considered in teaching reading to the handicapped are discussed in this section.

Continuous Assessment

As an integral part of the remedial process, assessment must be considered an ongoing procedure for continually gathering relevant information (Wallace & Larsen, 1978). Initial assessment results provide information helpful in organizing remedial programs but, as the student progresses, many of the initial recommendations can be modified or eliminated based upon the student's changing needs.

Continuous assessment is the basis upon which clinical or diagnostic teaching is formulated. Harris and Sipay (1985) describe clinical teaching as an alternating test-teach-retest-reteach process whereby the remedial teacher starts by determining what has been mastered and what needs to be improved. After proceeding with the instructional plan for a brief period of time, it usually becomes necessary to determine whether the instruction has been effective. If the instruction has been

FIGURE 5.8. Samples of Teacher-Constructed Tests

Test 1: Root Words

Objective: To assess knowledge of root words

Directions: Direct the student to underline the root word in each of the listed words.

1. reread	11. childhood
2. jumped	12. quickly
3. spotless	13. disobey
4. inactive	14. cupful
5. singing	15. semicircle
6. preschool	16. uneven
7. smallest	17. friendship
8. joyful	18. uncomfortable
9. worthless	19. actor
10. unwanted	20. imperfectly

Test 2: Vowel Sounds

Objective: To assess knowledge of vowel sounds

Directions: Direct the student to underline the word that you pronounce.

1. tan	2. but	3. ring	4. slick	5. cap
ten	bat	rung	slack	cup
tin	bet	rang	slock	cop

6. ball	7. tug	8. king	9. pup	10. beck
bull	tag	kong	pep	back
bill	tig	kung	pop	buck

effective, new skills or strategies can be introduced; if not, either additional instruction and practice are indicated or a different instructional approach may be needed.

Continuous assessment does not refer to a series of formal tests that are administered to the student. Rather, continuous assessment involves the many opportunities that teachers have throughout the school day to evaluate a student's achievement (Wallace & Kauffman, 1986). Oral reading, for example, can provide a good indication of a student's understanding of certain word analysis skills. Similarly, other reading difficulties can be noted by checking seatwork assignments. Using this type of information in planning teaching programs is a primary goal of clinical teaching. As noted by Lerner (1985), continuous assessment actually is a part of the entire teaching process, not simply a prelude to remedial instruction.

Selecting and Adapting Materials

As noted earlier, this chapter is based on the premise that there is no one best instructional material for teaching reading to handicapped learners. Articulate arguments and occasional empirical evidence can be cited in support of certain reading materials and techniques. Nonetheless, Heilman, Blair, and Rupley (1986) have recently reported that virtually every method and procedure described in the vast literature on reading is reported to have been successful with some students and unsuccessful with others. The evidence indicates that no one method is clearly superior to another. These authors suggest that because there are significant individual differences in the way students learn to read, it follows that the different utilization of approaches is advisable.

Selecting appropriate reading materials is a crucial component in the remediation process, and the current proliferation of available instructional materials has certainly added to the teacher's dilemma about which materials to choose. Information about reading materials can be obtained from publishers, material resource centers, colleges and universities, and various retrieval systems. One federally funded retrieval system, the National Instructional Materials Information System, is part of the National Center for Educational Media/Materials for Handicapped in Columbus, Ohio. This system includes abstracts of media and materials appropriate for students with reading problems (Wallace & Kauffman, 1986).

Many instructional materials in reading will need to be adapted for use with the handicapped learner because of their complex directions, fast pace, too high reading level, boring content, or confusing format (Mercer & Mercer, 1985). Some suggestions for adapting reading materials listed by Mandall and Gold (1984) and Lerner (1985) include:

❑ increase the amount of repetition

❑ provide more examples or activities

❑ provide more review

❑ introduce the work more slowly

❑ rewrite material

❑ paraphrase written direction

❑ tape-record directions and assignments

❑ provide study guides for terms, definitions, and so forth

❑ allow students to respond orally rather than in writing

❑ provide periodic practice for review

Organized Instruction

Students with reading handicaps usually respond favorably to an organized classroom situation with an emphasis on systematic and direct instruction. Kauffman (1985), for example, notes that situations in which students do not know what is expected of them often reinforce the behaviors that originally contributed to the reading difficulty. The following guidelines have been offered by Otto and Smith (1980), Polloway and Smith (1982), and Richek, List, and Lerner (1983) for planning organized remedial instruction:

❑ Reduce anxiety by establishing rapport, selecting materials not associated with past failures, and removing any tension from the reading process.

❑ Provide success as a first step to motivating students to perform. Learning seems to improve the most when students have successful experiences in the classroom.

❑ Provide specific feedback to the student on what is both correct and incorrect in order to continually improve the student's performance.

❑ Encourage student involvement in planning and implementing instruction by sharing responsibility and thereby building a sense of ownership in the student.

❑ Establish a positive learning environment to assist in the promotion of productive gains for handicapped readers. Lovitt (1977), for example, found that positive behaviors on the part of the teacher resulted in improved academic performance for children.

❑ Chart a pupil's progress by keeping accurate and current records that monitor daily assignments. Students can also be provided with a sense of accomplishment by charting their own progress.

❑ Maintain interest in learning by designing flexible programs which provide support and encouragement for the student while motivating the pupil to succeed at specific tasks.

Direct Instruction

Considerable research (e.g., Medley, 1977) consistently demonstrates that direct teacher instruction positively enhances student achievement. Direct instruction has been described by Rosenshine (1977) as

> teaching activities focused on academic matters where goals are clear to students; time allocated for instruction is sufficient and continuous; content coverage is extensive; student performance is monitored; questions are at a low cognitive level and produce many correct responses; and feedback to students is immediate and academically oriented. (p. 9a)

Direct instruction has been characterized as *active* teaching. Teachers demonstrate, model, prompt, illustrate, and give feedback during direct instruction. Although materials, aids, and games are used to facilitate teaching, the teacher is always recognized as the major variable for determining the effectiveness of instruction.

For the student handicapped in reading, direct instruction focuses on the specific behaviors and skills that are lacking and that require further development. Rather than devoting an inordinate amount of time to peripheral skill development, direct instruction provides students with systematic and structured learning activities appropriate for their specific academic needs. Consequently, direct instruction has proven to be an effective teaching model for reading disabled students (Lloyd, Epstein, & Cullinan, 1980; Polloway, Epstein, Polloway, Patton, & Ball, 1986).

TEACHING READING READINESS

As noted earlier, readiness for reading has been long recognized as an important concept and one that clearly serves as a foundational phase for subsequent growth in reading. Reading readiness is considered by many to be a complex concept involving many different contributing factors that develops through the intimate interplay of learning with biological growth.

In attempting to develop the specific skills noted to be an important part of readiness for reading, teachers should provide a positive and supportive learning environment. In addition, Heilman, Blair, and Rupley (1986) suggest the following instructional considerations in planning a reading readiness program:

❏ Design activities around a language arts base that takes advantage of and extends the rich language background of children.

❏ Develop in students the concept that reading is communication and that meaning is essential.

❏ Arrange a planned program to teach word meanings through the use of both oral and written context.

❏ Allow students varied opportunities to read and to be involved with meaningful reading activities.

❏ Teach students in an integrated fashion essential reading technology and concepts such as *word, letter, sound, sentence, left-to-right progression,* and *letter names.*

❏ Stimulate interest in reading by reading a variety of stories aloud to children.

❏ Incorporate the arts (music, art, and drama) into your program to increase motivation and to foster language growth.

❏ Prepare systematic activities to teach good listening skills.

❏ Set short-term goals that children can readily achieve.

❏ Do not give children tasks that they do not understand or cannot do.

❏ Give responsibility to all children and not just to those who are already confident and at ease.

❏ Select goals for your program in relation to what children need — not in relation to what a commercially prepared reading readiness program states.

Specific readiness teaching activities usually involve skill development in listening, auditory discrimination, visual discrimination, sound blending, and left-right orientation. The appendix at the end of this chapter provides some examples of instructional activities used to enhance a student's probability for success in beginning reading.

WORD ANALYSIS

Word analysis or decoding skills are used by the reader to pronounce words not recognized instantly and automatically. Included among word analysis techniques are phonetic analysis, structural analysis, configuration, picture clues, and contextual analysis. Sight word recognition is also considered a word recognition technique, although not a word analysis skill per se.

Adequate word analysis skills are considered an essential part of reading development for all students; however, many reading disabled students experience difficulties learning these skills. These students are usually severely limited in reading and often develop a number of inappropriate reading habits such as wild guessing, substituting words, very slow reading, and constantly losing their place.

Since all word analysis techniques are not of equal value in learning new words, these skills should be used flexibly. If one method does not work, other techniques should be utilized. Students should develop independence and mastery in all areas of word analysis in order to focus on the meaning of what is read. Table 5.7 provides a listing of decoding skills to be learned by reading levels. The table is intended as a list from which behavioral objectives can be derived or as an instructional checklist to determine what needs to be taught rather than to provide an instructional sequence (Harris & Sipay, 1985). A separate sequence for teaching phonic skills is provided in Table 5.10.

Sight Words

Sight words are those words that are recognized instantly without any additional analysis. The ability to automatically recognize words that are frequently used in basic reading material (*the*, *you*, *said*, *in*, etc.) is an important goal for all readers. Early recognition of some sight words does facilitate achievement in beginning reading. A widely known source for common sight words is the Dolch list (Dolch, 1953), which was updated by Johnson (1971) to reflect currently used words. The revised list, as shown in Table 5.8, is divided into five groups which represent words for the first five respective reading levels.

In working with reading disabled students, sight words should be gradually and carefully introduced. Extended systematic practice which provides for constant review of sight words is also recommended. The use of high interest–low vocabulary books, the language experience approach, and various multisensory tracing methods—all of which are described in this chapter—are sources of excellent opportunities for

TABLE 5.7. Desirable Decoding Skills by Reader Level

Pre-primer

Grapheme–phoneme associations for consonants: *b, c /k/, d, f, g /g/, h, j, l, m, n, p, r, s, t, w*
Substitution: substituting initial and final consonants in known words
Context cues: using context and consonants to recognize unknown words
Morphemic analysis: inflectional endings *s* (plural marker—*dogs*) and *ed* (*called*)

Primer

Grapheme–phoneme associations:
  consonants: *k, v, y, z*
  consonant digraphs: *ch, sh, th*
  consonant blends: *pl, st, tr*
  short vowels: *a, e, i, o, u*
  spelling patterns: *er, or, ur, ar, ow, et, an, ight, at, ay, all*
Substitution: using grapheme–phoneme associations and parts of known
  words to recognize unknown words
Context cues: using semantic and syntactic cues to monitor responses to
  unknown printed words
Morphemic analysis:
  inflectional endings: *s* (3rd person singular verbs—*eats*), *d* (*liked*), *es* (*boxes*), *'s*
  (possessive—*Ann's*), *er* (comparative—*faster*)
  suffix: *er* (as agent—*farmer*)

First Reader

Grapheme–phoneme associations:
  consonant: *x*
  consonant digraphs:[a] *wh, kn /n/, wr /r/, ck /k/*
  consonant blends: *br, cr, dr, fr, gr, bl, cl, fl, sl, sc, tw, ld, nd*
  short vowels: *y*
  long vowels: *a, e, i, o, u, y*
  vowel digraphs: *ay, ea /ē/ & /ĕ/, ee, oa, ow /ō/*
  vowel diphthongs: *oi, oy, ow, /ou/*
  spelling patterns: *alk, eigh, ind, old, ook*
  generalization: In the initial position, *y* represents a consonant sound; in
  other positions, a vowel sound
Morphemic analysis:
  inflectional endings: *ing* (*walking*), *est* (*fastest*)
  compound words: compounds comprised of 2 known words
  contractions: *not = n't* (*doesn't*), *will/shall = 'll* (*I'll*)[b]
Structural analysis:
  separating monosyllables into parts
  counting the number of vowel sounds in a word as a clue to the number of
  syllables
Synthesis: blending sounds into syllables; syllables into words

---

TABLE 5.7. Continued

Second Reader

Grapheme–phoneme associations:
consonants: *c* /s/, *g* /j/
consonant digraphs: *ph* /f/, *tch* /ch/, *gn* /n/, *mb* /m/, *dge* /j/
consonant blends: *gl, pr, qu* /kw/, *sk, sm, sn, sp, sw, scr, sch, str, squ, thr, lk, nk*
vowel digraphs: *ai,* /oo/ & /oo/, *ey, ew, ei, ie, ue*
vowel diphthongs: *ou, au, aw*
schwa: /ə/ as represented by an initial vowel (*ago*)
r-controlled vowels: *ar, er, ir, or, ur, oor* (*door, poor*) *ear* (*year, earn, bear, heart*),
   our (*hour, four*)
spelling pattern: *ough,* (*through, though, thought, rough*)
generalizations:
   1. When *c* and *g* are followed by *e, i,* or *y* they usually represent soft
      sounds
   2. A single vowel letter at the end of an accented syllable usually repre-
      sents its long sound
   3. A single vowel letter followed by a consonant other than *r* usually
      represents its short sound in an accented syllable
   4. A single vowel letter followed by a single consonant, other than *v,* and
      a final *e* usually represents its long sound and the *e* is silent
Morphemic analysis:
inflectional endings: *s'* (*boys'*), *en* (*beaten*)
prefix: *un*
suffixes: *ful, fully, ish, less, ly, ness, self, y*
contraction: *have* = *'ve* (*I've*)[b]
generalizations:
   1. Divide between the words that form a compound; other divisions may
      occur in either or both parts
   2. Divide between the root word and an affix; other divisions may occur
      in either the root or affix
recognizing words with spelling changes made by adding suffixes when: the
   final *e* has been dropped (*hide—hiding*), *y* has been changed to *i* (*baby—
   babies*), and a final consonant has been doubled (*sit—sitting*)
Accenting: hearing and marking accented syllables

Third Reader

Grapheme–phoneme associations:
consonant blends: *spl, spr, ng, nt*
generalization: A single vowel letter or vowel combination (danger*ous*) represents a schwa sound in many unaccented syllables
Morphemic analysis:
prefixes: *dis, ex, im, in, post, pre, re, sub, super, trans*
suffixes: *or* (as agent—*actor*), *ous, tion, sion, ment, ty, ic, al, able*
contractions: *are* = *'re* (*they're*),[b] *would/had* = *'d* (*I'd*)[c]

TABLE 5.7. Continued

<table>
<tr><th colspan="2">Second Reader</th></tr>
</table>

Structural analysis: Syllabicating words of more than 2 syllables
Accenting generalizations:
  1. Usually the first syllable in a 2-syllable word is accented
  2. Usually affixes are not accented

---

[a] Silent consonants are included under consonant digraphs.
[b] More words with this contraction are likely to be encountered at higher reader levels.
[c] Most contractions of *would/should* ('d) and *is/has* ('s) are likely to be encountered above the third reader level.

From Harris, A. J., & Sipay, E. R. (1985). *How to increase reading ability* (8th ed.). New York: Longman. Reprinted with permission.

practicing sight words. Some of the following specific techniques are also used for developing sight word proficiency.

❑ Label objects around the classroom.

❑ Develop picture dictionaries using magazine photographs and illustrations.

❑ Use word games that emphasize common sight words.

❑ Have students listen to a tape recording of sight words while following a worksheet of the same words.

❑ Make flash cards for individual or group practice sessions.

❑ Always introduce sight words in a sentence.

❑ Point out unusual configurations of various sight words.

❑ Classify sight words by categories (people, things, animals, etc.).

Phonics

Phonics instruction has been the center of controversy for many years Some writers view phonics as a panacea for solving all reading problems encountered by a student, while others condemn phonics as a destructive method leading to slow, word-by-word reading with little comprehension gained from the printed page (Matthes, 1972).

Our viewpoint is that phonics should be considered one method for teaching word analysis. As such, phonics instruction for any student

TABLE 5.8. Basic Sight Words

preprimer	primer	first	second	third
1. the	45. when	89. many	133. know	177. don't
2. of	46. who	90. before	134. while	178. does
3. and	47. will	91. must	135. last	179. got
4. to	48. more	92. through	136. might	180. united
5. a	49. no	93. back	137. us	181. left
6. in	50. if	94. years	138. great	182. number
7. that	51. out	95. where	139. old	183. course
8. is	52. so	96. much	140. year	184. war
9. was	53. said	97. your	141. off	185. until
10. he	54. what	98. may	142. come	186. always
11. for	55. up	99. well	143. since	187. away
12. it	56. its	100. down	144. against	188. something
13. with	57. about	101. should	145. go	189. fact
14. as	58. into	102. because	146. came	190. through
15. his	59. than	103. each	147. right	191. water
16. on	60. them	104. just	148. used	192. less
17. be	61. can	105. those	149. take	193. public
18. at	62. only	106. people	150. three	194. put
19. by	63. other	107. Mr.	151. states	195. thing
20. I	64. new	108. how	152. himself	196. almost
21. this	65. some	109. too	153. few	197. hand
22. had	66. could	110. little	154. house	198. enough
23. not	67. time	111. state	155. use	199. far
24. are	68. these	112. good	156. during	200. took
25. but	69. two	113. very	157. without	201. head
26. from	70. may	114. make	158. again	202. yet
27. or	71. then	115. would	159. place	203. government
28. have	72. do	116. still	160. American	204. system
29. an	73. first	117. own	161. around	205. better
30. they	74. any	118. see	162. however	206. set
31. which	75. my	119. men	163. home	207. told
32. one	76. now	120. work	164. small	208. nothing
33. you	77. such	121. long	165. found	209. night
34. were	78. like	122. get	166. Mrs.	210. end
35. her	79. our	123. here	167. thought	211. why
36. all	80. over	124. between	168. went	212. called
37. she	81. man	125. both	169. say	213. didn't
38. there	82. me	126. life	170. part	214. eyes
39. would	83. even	127. being	171. once	215. find
40. their	84. most	128. under	172. general	216. going
41. we	85. made	129. never	173. high	217. look
42. him	86. after	130. day	174. upon	218. asked
43. been	87. also	131. same	175. school	219. later
44. has	88. did	132. another	176. every	220. knew

cannot be considered as an end in itself. Rather, it must be viewed as a means to independent reading. As such, Heilman, Blair, and Rupley (1986) note that the optimum amount of phonics instruction for any learner is the minimum needed to become an independent reader.

Phonics is actually a method for teaching sound-symbol (phoneme-grapheme) relationships. Although most phonics programs differ in content, the methodology employed in teaching phonics is usually either the *synthetic* or the *analytic* approach.

The synthetic method of phonics instruction involves teaching individual letter sounds that are subsequently synthesized or blended together into words. This approach to teaching phonics usually involves the introduction of a number of phonics rules and regulations. It is the approach that is most often associated with phonics instruction programs.

The analytic approach, on the other hand, makes sound generalizations from words that have been learned as sight words. Rather than identify individual letter sounds, students initially learn words by sight or linguistic elements. Actual phonics instruction in the analytic method is not introduced until the student has learned enough words to provide examples of letter-sound relationships.

The actual ingredients or elements of phonics include *consonants* (all letters except vowels); *consonant blends* (two- or three-consonant letter combinations that produce blended sounds); *consonant digraphs* (consonant combinations that represent one sound); *silent comments* (consonants that, when combined with other specific letters, are not pronounced); *vowels* (*a, e, i, o, u,* and sometimes *y*); *vowel digraphs* (vowel combinations that represent a single sound); *vowel diphthongs* (vowel combinations that represent a blended sound); and the *schwa sound* (vowel sound in an unaccented syllable). Table 5.9 provides a listing of these phonic elements with specific examples. Lerner (1985) cites evidence demonstrating that many teachers are not well grounded in these phonic elements. Also, she posits that many teachers receive inadequate phonics instruction in preservice teacher education programs.

In teaching phonics to reading disabled students, it is imperative that teachers follow a sequence of instruction that provides for repeated opportunities to practice various phonics principles and rules. The following sequence of instruction is often used in teaching phonics to the handicapped learner.

1. initial and final consonants

2. consonant blends and digraphs

3. short vowels

4. long vowels

5. silent letters

6. vowel digraphs

7. vowel diphthongs

The specific letters for this suggested sequence of phonic skills are listed in Table 5.10.

Phonics programs can be used in combination with other reading materials (basal readers, programmed instruction, etc.) to provide needed supplementary instruction in phonetic analysis. Many phonics programs include workbooks, teachers' manuals, duplicating masters, and other supplementary aids. Some commercially available phonics programs often used with disabled readers include:

Merrill Phonics Skilltext Series (Merrill)

Individualized Reading Skills Program (Science Research Associates)

Webster Word Wheels (McGraw-Hill)

Phonics We Use (Lyons & Carnhan)

Schoolhouse Reading Kits (Science Research Associates)

Phonetic Key to Reading (Economy)

Phonovisual Method (Phonovisual Products)

Phonic Remedial Reading Lessons (Academic Therapy Publications)

Although phonics instruction is often recommended as a word analysis technique for students with reading problems, it would be wise to use it judiciously with many of these students because they may have been previously exposed to this approach with unsuccessful results. Some students experience failure in phonics due to the emphasis on letter and word pronunciation without stressing meaning and due to the confusion that arises with words that are exceptions to the rules (Kaluger & Kolson, 1978). In addition, Gillespie-Silver (1979) points out that some phonics programs give the student the impression that reading is merely a process of sounding out and blending letters into words. On the contrary, we believe that reading is a thinking process which involves the flexible use of different word analysis techniques to reach the ultimate goal of comprehending what is read. Consequently, phonics should be used in combination with all other word analysis techniques.

Structural Analysis

Structural analysis refers to the identification of words by using the meaningful parts within words such as prefixes (*un*tie, *re*print, *pre*pay); suffixes (jump*ing*, blame*less*, move*ment*); compound words (railroad, firefighter, battleground); roots (un*fair*, anti*climax*, re*mark*able); contractions (don't, we'll, you've); and syllabication (mus-cle, zip-per, vis-i-ble).

TABLE 5.9. Phonic Elements

Consonants				Vowels	
Single	Blend	Digraph	Silent	Single	Adjacent pairs
b	bl	sh	-ight	**Short (unglided) in VC, CVC patterns**	**Digraphs** (Sound of one of the vowels or another vowel is heard)
d	cl	ch	write	a (at, can)	ai (hail, again)
f	fl	th[6]	know	i (in, fin)	ay (say, says)
h	gl	wh	chick	e (bet)	ea (each, great)
j	sl	ph	bomb	o (oz, top)	ei (believe, lie)
k	br	-nk		u (up, tug)[7]	
l	cr	-ng			**Diphthongs** (Sound of both vowels is heard)
m	dr	-ck		**Long (glided) in CVCe, CV patterns**	oi (boil)
n	gr			a (rate, vapor)	ou (out)
p	pr			i (hide, bicycle)	au (audio)
r	tr			e (fete, he)	
t	sc			o (hope, motel)	
v	sk			y (by)	
w	sm				
y	sn				
z	sp				
c[1]	scr				

TABLE 5.9. Continued

Consonants				Vowels	
Single	Blend	Digraph	Silent	Single	Adjacent pairs
g^2	spr			**Variant sounds in various**	
s^3	str			**patterns**	
q^4				a (bār, bȧll, fâre, ȧkin)	
x^5				e (hêr)	
				i (fîr)	
				o (wŏn, fôr)	
				u (tûrn)	

[1]The letter c tends to be associated with a hard sound when it precedes the letters a, o, or u and a soft sound when preceding i, e, and y: cake, city.

[2]The letter g tends to be associated with a hard sound when it precedes the letters a, o, or u and a soft sound when preceding e and i: go, gem.

[3]The letter s is associated with three different sounds: s as in so, z as in his, and sh as in sugar.

[4]The letter q is normally associated with the sound of kw when it occurs (followed by u) at the beginning of a word.

[5]The letter x is normally associated with the sound of z when it occurs at the beginning of a word.

[6]The letters th are represented by two different sounds: thin, then.

[7]The short or unglided sound associated with u is also produced by other letters occurring in unaccented syllables: hasten, charity. This is called the schwa sound and is represented by the symbol ə in dictionaries and glossaries.

From Guszak, F. J. (1985). Diagnostic reading instruction in the elementary school. New York: Harper & Row, p. 90. Reprinted with permission of the publisher.

TABLE 5.10. Sequence for Teaching Phonics

SIMPLE CONSONANTS
b, p, m, w, h, d, t, n, hard *g* (gate), *k,* hard *c* (cake), *y* (yet), *f* (for)

MORE DIFFICULT CONSONANTS
v, l, z (zoo), *s* (sat), *r, c,* (cent), *q* (kw), *x* (ks), *j, g* (engine), *s* (as)

CONSONANT BLENDS AND DIGRAPHS
ck, ng, th (the), *zh, sh, th* (thin), wh, ch

SIMPLE CONSONANT BLENDS
with *l, r, p,* or *t,* as *bl, pl, gr, br, sp, st, tr, thr, str, spl, scr,* and others as they
appear

SHORT VOWELS
a (hat), *e* (get), *i* (sit), *o* (top), *u* (cup), *y* (happy)

LONG VOWELS
a (cake), *e* (be), *i* (five), *o* (old), *u* (mule), *y* (cry)

SILENT LETTERS
k (knife), *w* (write), *l* (talk), *t* (catch), *g* (gnat), *c* (black), *h* (hour)

VOWEL DIGRAPHS
ai (pail), *ea* (each), *oa* (boat), *ee* (bee), *ay* (say), *ea* (dead)

VOWEL DIPHTHONGS
au (auto), *aw* (awful), *oo* (moon), *oo* (wood), *ow* (cow), *ou* (out), *oi* (oil), *oy*
(boy), *ow* (low)

VOWELS WITH *r*
ar (car), *er* (her), *ir* (bird), *or* (corn), *ur* (burn)
Same with *l* and *w*

PHONOGRAMS (WORD PATTERNS)
ail, ain, all, and, ate, ay, con, eep, ell, en, ent, er, est, ick, ight, ill, in, ing, ock, ter,
tion
Alternates—*ake, ide, ile, ine, it, ite, le, re, ble*

From Spache, G. D., & Spache, E. B. (1986). *Reading in the elementary school* (5th ed.).
Boston: Allyn & Bacon, pp. 478–479. Reprinted with permission of Allyn & Bacon.

As with other word analysis skills, drill activities followed by the
application of structural analysis skills to actual reading opportunities
are important components of remedial instruction. Richek, List, and
Lerner (1983) mention that because structural analysis elements are so
frequent in text, most reading material will give substantial opportunity
to apply this knowledge in the reading situation.

Some instructional activities to provide structural analysis practice follow.

❑ Color cue parts of words as a help in remembering them.

❑ Have students count the number of syllables in words read by the teacher.

❑ Make a book of prefixes, suffixes, or compound words that students come across in reading.

❑ Have students invent and define their own compound words.

❑ Call out contractions and have students give the words that make up the contractions.

❑ Give students lists of words in which they must identify roots, prefixes, or suffixes.

❑ Have students arrange lists of words in columns according to the number of syllables in each word.

❑ Allow students to make as many words as possible from an envelope of root words and another envelope of prefixes or suffixes.

Context Clues

The context in which a word is used can also be helpful in the analysis of some unknown words. In using contextual analysis, the reader relies on the sense of the sentence to figure out an unknown word. The student is actually predicting the unknown word based on syntactic and semantic cues which evolve from the other words in the passage. Cohen and Plaskon (1980) point out that, in most cases, the pupil must have the decoding skills to identify the majority of words in the sentence. More important, using context encourages the student to view reading as a meaningful language process (Richek, List, & Lerner, 1983).

Disabled readers often experience difficulty in using context clues as a word analysis procedure because of inadequate word recognition skills which cause them to focus on decoding the words rather than on obtaining meaning. In addition, Harris and Sipay (1985) suggest that poor readers make more miscues, are less aware of the extent to which their miscues disrupt meaning, and are less effective in using multiple cues and alternative strategies in preserving the meaning of the text.

To help students use contextual analysis, Dahl and Samuels (1977) suggest a hypothesis-test strategy including the following steps: (a) Use information from the passage; (b) make a prediction as to which word is most likely to occur; (c) compare the printed and predicted words (testing the hypothesis); and (d) accept or reject the prediction. When a word is rejected, the student should attempt another word.

In addition to the hypothesis-testing strategy, some of the following activities are also used to develop contextual analysis skills:

❑ Give students passages with words omitted and replaced with blanks. Have students complete the passage by filling in the blanks.

❑ Read stories to students and periodically pause so that students can complete the thought.

❑ Make tape recordings in which key words are omitted and have the students fill in the blank spaces as the tape is played (Ekwall, 1985).

❑ Use nonsense words in sentences and ask students to define them.

❑ Have students select the most appropriate word from multiple choices provided for a series of sentences.

❑ Use pictures or rebuses for certain words in a sentence and ask students to substitute the appropriate word.

❑ Provide riddles in written form and ask students to identify what is being described.

COMPREHENSION

Reading comprehension is usually a major area of difficulty for the handicapped student. As Savage and Mooney (1979) observe, comprehension is a cognitive activity; therefore, it stands to reason that the student whose learning problem is primarily cognitively based will experience difficulties with this area of reading.

Although reading comprehension is a multifaceted process, most experts (e.g., Ekwall & Shanker, 1983) suggest that four specific factors seem particularly critical to the development of reading comprehension skills.

1. The knowledge the reader brings to the printed page will affect reading comprehension. This includes past experiences, special vocabulary, and previous learning about a subject.

2. The reader's interest in the subject is another important variable. The more a student is interested in a subject, the more he or she will want to learn about the topic.

3. The purpose for reading is a factor which affects all levels of comprehension. Individuals who read with a specific purpose in mind will certainly comprehend more than students who are uncertain about why they are reading a particular passage.

4. The reader's word recognition skills will also affect the degree of comprehension. Students will be unable to comprehend material that includes difficult decoding demands. The amount of time and energy devoted to decoding new words is often a primary problem for the handicapped reader.

Although there is agreement that comprehension is *the* vital component of the reading process, there is little consensus on how to teach reading comprehension. The reason for this, according to Harris and Sipay (1985), is that until fairly recently very little has been known about the reading comprehension process that could be translated into instructional practices.

Some general procedures for developing reading comprehension among the handicapped follow. Three specific reading comprehension strategies are also discussed in this section.

❑ Have students answer *when, where, who, what,* and *why* questions as they read.

❑ Encourage students to predict what may happen in a story based upon what was already read.

❑ Have students ask comprehension questions of the teacher or other students.

❑ Allow at least 5 seconds after each question for the student to think of the response.

❑ Teach students to follow an author's organization by pointing out signals, markers, and headings.

❑ Have students retell a particular passage in their own words.

❑ Teach students to reread sections that they do not understand.

❑ Discuss pictures or illustrations in the text as a clue to comprehension.

❑ Practice the ability to read in phrases or "chunking" to process thought units within a sentence.

❑ Teach students to form a mental image of what they read about.

❑ Provide direct instructions on meanings of words in the reading passage.

❏ Have students locate nonsense material purposely placed in a passage.

Directed Reading-Thinking Activity

The Directed Reading-Thinking Activity (DRTA) is an instructional approach to teaching reading comprehension in which students first predict what they will read and then check their prediction through subsequent reading. The method was developed by Stauffer (1975) based upon his beliefs that reading should be taught as a thinking activity. He comments that both reading and thinking require a context to be read or thought about, both embody the dynamics of discovery, and both entail a systematic examination of ideas.

The DRTA can be used with virtually any kind of reading material, including basals and various content area textbooks. Regardless of the grade level, Aulls (1982) points out that the teacher's role is to act as a facilitator for thinking about a story. The goals are to teach pupils (a) to examine, (b) to hypothesize, (c) to find proof, (d) to suspend judgment, and (e) to make decisions (Lerner, 1985).

The stages for using DRTA, as outlined by Mason and Au (1986), follow.

Step 1. Tell the students the title of the selection or show them an illustration. On the basis of this information, have them make predictions about the story. If an informational text is being used, an alternative is to have students tell what they already know about the topic. Write predictions and other ideas on the chalkboard.

Step 2. Pointing out to the students that they will be reading to see if the text verifies the information on the chalkboard, have them read a portion of the text silently.

Step 3. Reopen the discussion by having the students go down the list of predictions and ideas on the board, telling which were verified. Point out to the students that there are several possibilities. The idea could be

a. verified by the text (in which case you can have a pupil read the relevant sentence aloud);

b. disproved by the text (again, a pupil might read the relevant sentence aloud);

c. only partially verified or disproved, with more information being required to make a definite decision about whether the idea is right or wrong;

d. shown to be only partially right or wrong, but definitely requiring revision on the basis of text information; or

e. not mentioned.

Items in the list are rewritten, marked as true, crossed off if false, and so on. New hypotheses may also be added. Thus, the list should become a running record of important text information.

Step 4. Alternate periods of silent reading and discussion until the whole text has been read. Older students who have participated in this procedure before may be asked to copy the original list from the board and directed to read and then revise the list on their own for seatwork. In all cases, emphasize the quality of reasoning students are doing rather than just the correctness of their initial hypotheses. Point out how the process of mentally generating and revising hypotheses is something that should always be done while reading.

DRTA has been noted to be highly effective with many disabled readers, because the novelty of the approach captures student attention and encourages them to take an active role in learning (Richek, List, & Lerner, 1983). In addition, DRTA can be helpful for the student whose primary reading difficulties are associated with attentional problems.

SQ3R Method

One of the best known and most widely used reading comprehension strategies is the SQ3R (Survey, Question, Read, Recite, Review) method. This technique, developed originally by Robinson (1961) as an independent study skill approach, can be used with most content material. It involves five steps: (a) *Survey* the headings and summarize quickly to get the general ideas that will be developed in the assignment; (b) turn headings and subheadings into *questions*; (c) *read* to answer questions formulated in the previous stage; (d) attempt to *recite* from memory the answers to previously formulated questions; and (e) upon completion of the assignment, *review* the lesson to organize ideas. A more complete description of this approach is outlined in Table 5.11.

According to Robinson (1961), the SQ3R method is not learned by simply reading about it—it must be practiced under supervision. Furthermore, Tadlock (1978) recommends that students should also be told why and how the SQ3R method will aid in their retention of content material.

Comprehension strategies such as DRTA and SQ3R seem particularly useful for reading disabled students, since these pupils often require a systematic approach or structure for learning various skills. In addition, the active involvement of the reader that is an inherent component of each strategy promotes learning of reading skills.

Repeated Readings

Repeated readings is another method often used to improve both oral reading fluency and reading comprehension. The method consists of

TABLE 5.11. How SQ3R Works

Step	Description
S Survey	Here is where you skim or survey the material. It means looking over the whole assignment *before* you actually start to read it. 1. Check the title first to get an idea of what the material is about. 2. Note the beginning and end to get a notion of how much material the author uses to get across the ideas. 3. Pay attention to headings and subheadings. They can help you get an over-all picture of the author's plan. 4. Look at charts, pictures, graphs, and other illustrative material. Check the captions under each. These can also help give you clues to the over-all plan. 5. Quickly read any headnotes, introductory paragraphs, and summary sections. They can give you a better overview.
Q Question	This is the crucial stage in personalizing the assignment, making it really yours. On a separate sheet of paper, jot down the questions that you, personally, want answered. What might the author be able to tell you about the topic that you don't already know? What are *you* curious about here? Sometimes, turning the headings and subheadings into questions helps.
R Read	Now you are ready to actually read the assignment. 1. Read the introductory paragraphs rather carefully. 2. Add to your personal list of questions if you need to. 3. Skim the less important points. 4. Add difficult words to your question sheet so that you can verify the meanings later. 5. Keep asking yourself: What is the author's main purpose in writing this material?
R Review	After you have completed the reading, try to remember each section. What was the author's main purpose? What were the chief points? What was the over-all plan? Try to keep the key points in mind.
R Recite	One of the best ways of understanding anything is to tell it to someone else in your own words. At this final stage, "tell" your answers to the questions, either to yourself in writing or to another student in conversation. Making a synopsis or summary (which includes answers to your questions) is also a powerful learning method.

From Devine, T. G. (1981). *Teaching study skills: A guide for teachers.* Boston: Allyn & Bacon, p. 45. Reprinted with permission of Allyn & Bacon.

reading orally a 50- to 200-word selection while simultaneously listening to a taped version of the same material. The selection is read repeatedly until some specific criterion of speed and accuracy is obtained. A criterion of 85 words per minute is most often used to determine adequate fluency. Another selection is usually provided once the student reaches the desired level of speed and accuracy.

According to Samuels (1979), students required fewer readings with each new selection after practice with this technique. Samuels indicates that comprehension improves with repeated readings, because the student's attention to decoding is minimized. Ekwall and Shanker (1983) mention that disabled readers often try to read too fast in using the repeated readings technique. These writers recommend that the teacher encourage students first to read accurately and then work to improve speed.

A combination of repeated readings and the neurological impress method (a system described later in this chapter of unison reading where the student and the teacher read aloud simultaneously at a rapid rate) has been reported to improve word recognition and comprehension skills for intermediate and junior high school age students reading at the primary level (Bos, 1982). In a study with learning disabled students, Rashotte and Torgesen (1985) found that when reading selections have few shared vocabulary words, little generalization occurs, and reading fluency is not markedly improved.

In sum, repeated readings seem to be effective, because the method seems to help students discover the appropriate prosodic pattern of the material or because the repeated practice helps students transfer the assignment of the appropriate prosodic features to new passages (Schreiber, 1980).

DEVELOPMENTAL READING APPROACHES

A number of reading approaches used with the student handicapped in reading are basically developmental methods and materials individually adapted for use with this population. Lerner (1985) suggests that sometimes a developmental approach will be successful with disabled readers, because it is taught at another time, in another place, or by a different teacher in various special education settings. The developmental approaches discussed in this section are (a) basal readers, (b) linguistic approach, (c) language experience approach, (d) individualized reading, and (e) programmed instruction.

Basal Readers

Because basal reading programs are widely used in the United States, they have been called the backbone of American reading instruction. According to Spache and Spache (1986), approximately 95 to 98% of primary teachers and at least 80% of intermediate-grade teachers use basal readers almost every school day.

Basal readers are a preplanned, sequentially organized and correlated set of methods and materials designed to teach developmental reading skills systematically (Harris & Sipay, 1985). According to Aukerman (1981), there are approximately 15 American basal reading series. All of these basal programs include a series of graded readers ranging from the readiness through sixth- or eighth-grade level. The following features are among those that Aukerman (1981) lists as common to most basal series.

1. A readiness component

2. Preprimers, beginning with picture books that have very few words and gradually increasing to real stories

3. Instruction in word analysis skills running concurrently with the basal stories

4. A complete set of comprehension questions for each story

5. A teacher's manual with detailed lesson plans

6. Suggestions for teaching the other language arts skills (listening, speaking, and writing)

7. A wide range of literacy selections, including both fiction and nonfiction

8. Study skills instruction

9. Outstanding art work

10. Student workbooks for follow-up practice

11. Provision for students who fail to master new skills the first time they are taught

12. Various testing devices for assessment and evaluation

Most basal reading series tended to be very much alike through the early 1960s. At about that time, however, these series became the targets of severe criticism as being sexist or because of cultural or ethnic bias. Consequently, more recently developed basals have better balance in

TABLE 5.12. Publishers of Different Types of Basal Reading Programs

Eclectic, balanced, or meaning-based (usually core vocabulary with analytic phonics)	Phonics-based
• Allyn & Bacon	*Analytic Phonics*
• American Guidance Service	• Economy
• Ginn	
• Harcourt Brace	*Synthetic Phonics*
• Harper & Row	• Open Court
• Holt	
• Houghton Mifflin	*Linguistic*
• Laidlaw	• Lippincott
• Macmillan	• Charles E. Merrill
• Riverside (Rand-McNally)	
• Scott Foresman	

From Ekwall, E. E., & Shanker, J. L. (1985). *Teaching reading in the elementary school.* Columbus, OH: Charles E. Merrill, p. 32. Reprinted with permission of Merrill Publishing Co.

racial and ethnic characters; male and female characters; urban, suburban, and rural settings; and story settings (e.g., apartment house, trailer park, etc.) as compared to earlier published basals. According to Aukerman (1981) and Harris and Sipay (1985), basals now include more handicapped characters and senior citizens who are depicted favorably, and their literary quality and artwork have improved. Furthermore, violence seems to have been avoided in most basal reading stories.

Another significant change in basals has been the addition of various word analysis techniques other than sight word approaches. Nonetheless, most basal readers still fit into the broad categories of either the eclectic programs that rely on a core vocabulary and analytic phonics or phonics-based programs (Ekwall & Shanker, 1983). Table 5.12 provides a summary of the different types of basal programs.

All of these recent changes have helped to make basals more acceptable to teachers working with reading disabled students. Nevertheless, basal readers continue to be criticized by many special educators. Gillespie-Silver (1979), for example, noted that the basal approach tends to encourage group instruction, possibly causing neglect of the unique, individual needs of handicapped students. Furthermore, many students disabled in reading are frequently subjected to the same basal readers year after year without any appreciable success, but with ever increasing resistance and frustration in regard to reading in general (Kaluger

& Kolson, 1978). Table 5.13 lists some of the prominent strengths and weaknesses of the basal reader approach.

In summary, we believe that many basal reading series can be used effectively with the student handicapped in reading. As a first step, basals should be judiciously reviewed before being used with these students. Since many disabled students will have been unsuccessfully exposed to basals before receiving remedial assistance, it is also important to consider the student's attitude toward using various basals.

Furthermore, teachers should consider a great deal of supplementary material or the simultaneous use of several basals with handicapped pupils. Both of these considerations permit teachers to provide varied instruction for pupils with diverse reading difficulties.

Linguistic Approach

Some linguistic principles are often applied to reading instruction, because linguists are primarily concerned with the structure of language, and reading is viewed as part of the language process. Even so, some experts in this area (Goodman, 1972) state that there is no such thing as a linguistic reading program but only reading programs written by linguists.

According to Ekwall and Shanker (1983), most so-called linguistic reading programs focus on only a narrow aspect of linguistic science — instruction that emphasizes the regularity of letter-sound associations through consistent spelling patterns. Most of the programs use a whole-word method and the principle of minimal variation. Beginning reading words usually consist of three-letter words which follow a consonant-vowel-consonant pattern (CVC) containing only short vowels (e.g., *fin, sat, man, hit*). The principle of minimal variation refers to words that are alike except for one letter (e.g., *cop, mop, top*). Figure 5.9 provides an example of a story from a linguistic reader.

Nevertheless, not all linguistic programs are alike. Programs differ on such factors as the use and teaching of high-frequency words (e.g., *the*) that are not phonemically regular. In addition, Ekwall and Shanker (1985) note that some programs use nonsense words, while others do not. Some programs include illustrations, while others omit them because they might distract students from focusing on the words. In sum, no two linguistic series seem to agree closely on details.

The obvious advantages of this approach for students disabled in reading, as summarized by Cohen and Plaskon (1980), include the following:

1. Stresses the transition from spoken to written talk by showing the child the relationship between phonemes and graphemes.

TABLE 5.13. Strengths and Weaknesses of the Basal Reader Approach

Strengths

1. Basal readers provide a comprehensive program with numerous materials.
2. Basal readers provide a sequential, systematic presentation of vocabulary, decoding, comprehension, and study skills.
3. Basal readers provide for a systematic review of skills as students progress through the program.
4. Controlled vocabulary in the early stages helps students achieve initial success with decoding.
5. A system for placing students and evaluating their progress is included.
6. Workbooks and other reinforcement materials are included to aid the teacher in planning and carrying out instruction.
7. The teacher's manuals provide daily lesson plans and a wealth of other instructional resources.
8. Basal readers are designed for small-group instruction.
9. The programs are written by reading experts.
10. Basal readers are attractive and carefully packaged.
11. Basal readers provide a variety of literary forms carefully selected from outstanding children's literature.

Weaknesses

1. Vocabulary may be either too restricted or not restricted enough. Ranges in readability increase as levels become more difficult.
2. Language patterns of basal stories at the earliest levels may not match children's oral language.
3. The variety and number of selections cannot be as great as that found in actual trade books. Some selections lack literary merit.
4. The systematic, sequential approach to skill development is considered inappropriate by some.
5. The structured nature of basal programs may decrease individualized instruction and limit a teacher's choices.
6. Basal programs tend to be less effective for both the very able and the slowest readers.
7. Teacher's manuals may contain too much information, requiring the teacher to determine which parts of the lesson are essential and which are supplementary.
8. Workbook materials can be misused because there are so many inappropriate pages.
9. Basal selections have been criticized for inadequate or inappropriate portrayal of ethnic and racial minorities, women, and the handicapped.

From Ekwall, E. E., & Shanker, J. L. (1985). *Teaching reading in the elementary school.* Columbus, OH: Charles E. Merrill. Reprinted with permission of Merrill Publishing Co.

FIGURE 5.9. Linguistic Examples

The cat had a nap.

He sat on the mat.

The cat is fat.

Fat cat!

The ham is hot.

Sam has a fan.

Hot ham!

---

2. Arranges learning from familiar, phonemically regular words to those of irregular spelling. This encourages recognition of consistent visual patterns.

3. The student learns to spell and read the word as a whole unit.

4. Creates an awareness of sentence structure, so the pupil learns that words are arranged to form sentences.

5. Teaches reading by association with the student's natural language facility. (pp. 398–399)

Major disadvantages of the linguistic approach include the lack of initial emphasis on comprehension and the use of stilted unnatural language in stories. In addition, linguistic approaches assume that students are able to discover for themselves the relationship between sounds and letters (Kirk, Kliebhan, & Lerner, 1978). This assumption may not hold for many disabled readers, who often experience difficulty generalizing.

Some reading materials based on a linguistic approach which have been used with students handicapped in reading include:

Let's Read (Clarence L. Barnhart)

Linguistic Readers (Harper & Row)

Merrill Linguistic Readers (Merrill)

Miami Linguistic Readers (D. C. Heath)

Palo Alto Program (Harcourt Brace Jovanovich)

SRA Basic Reading Series (Science Research Associates)

Structural Reading Series (L. W. Singer)

Language Experience Approach

The language experience approach (LEA), more than any other approach to the teaching of reading, conceives of learning to read as part of the process of language development (Spache & Spache, 1986). The development of reading skills in this approach is interrelated with the development of skills in listening, speaking, and writing. The oral and written expressions of each student serve as the primary reading materials in this approach, since reading is considered a by-product of thinking and oral expression.

The rationale for this approach is stated very concisely by Allen and Allen (1982):

What I can think about, I can talk about.

What I can say, I can write—or someone can write for me.

What I can write, I can read.

I can read what I can write and what other people can write for me.

According to Ekwall and Shanker (1985), there are five main LEA techniques: the key vocabulary approach, the group experience chart, individual descriptions of illustrations done in a group setting, the individual experience story, and individual experience stories using the tape recorder. Each of these techniques is described in the following paragraphs.

Key Vocabulary. In the key vocabulary approach to LEA, words that have special meaning to a student are elicited by the teacher. Ekwall and Shanker (1985) suggest that words are drawn from the student one at a time and gradually expanded to whole sentences that the student learns to write down. This leads to the first child-authored stories, which are often shared with other students.

Group Experience Chart. The group experience chart approach usually has an entire class or group of students develop a story that the teacher prints on a large chart or the chalkboard. Students subsequently read the story as a group or individually with the teacher.

Descriptions of Illustrations. A third type of LEA activity is individual descriptions of illustrations done in a group setting. In this activity, students draw pictures following the discussions of some topic (e.g., My favorite animal, I like to, etc.). Students complete illustrations of the topic, and teachers caption the drawings using each student's exact words. The illustrations are usually bound into a book that students can later read.

Individual Experience Story. The most common type of LEA activity is the individual experience story. Initially, the teacher will write down sentences and stories dictated by the student. During the dictation, the teacher can discuss word choice, sentence structure, and the sounds of letters and words, but the story is not censored in any way. As the student progresses, dictated stories are followed by individually written compositions. Table 5.14 provides some examples of topics used for LEA stories.

Individual Experience Story Using Tape Recorder. The fifth type of LEA activity is actually a variation of the individual experience story that has the student use a tape recorder to dictate the story. The stories are later transcribed into a printed or typed form by the teacher. Ekwall and Shanker (1985) point out that this approach lacks the intimacy and immediacy of a person-to-person dictation and is therefore not often used with beginning readers.

There is no predetermined, rigid control over vocabulary, syntax, punctuation, spelling, or content in LEA, because each student's own experiences are considered uniquely in the application of the approach. The emphasis is essentially on reading material that grows out of each student's experience and that student's own language in expressing these thoughts (Lerner, 1985).

In LEA evaluation of pupil progress is based upon growth in clarity and depth of thinking, sentence sense, mechanics, and spelling as revealed in the student's own productions. In addition, pupil growth in the ability to express ideas in oral and written form and to comprehend the writings of others is constantly observed (Spache & Spache, 1986).

Although LEA has been considered primarily an approach to teaching beginning reading, it can be an effective teaching tool for students of any age who are disabled in reading, because it attempts to relate reading to other communication skills in an instructional program. Some additional advantages listed by Ekwall and Shanker (1985) include:

TABLE 5.14. Examples of Topics for LEA Stories

- what they have learned about Thanksgiving or Christmas
- what places they would like to visit
- what stories they enjoy, and why
- how they like to spend their free time
- how their brothers and sisters spend their free time
- what they liked about a school art exhibit or trip
- what they dream about
- who their favorite television characters are
- how to make a kite or paper airplane
- what there is to see at a zoo
- what ideas puzzle them
- what jobs their parents have
- how they learned to ride a bicycle or to swim
- what to look and listen for on a walk through the woods
- what kinds of transportation they see in the neighborhood
- what outdoor games they enjoy
- which foods they prefer and which ones are good for them
- how to train house pets
- why and when they should wash their hands or brush their teeth
- what riddles they like

From Karlin, R. (1980). *Teaching elementary reading* (3rd ed.). New York: Harcourt Brace Jovanovich, p. 205. Reproduced with permission of the publisher.

❏ LEA matches the students' interests with learning activities and is highly motivating.

❏ The approach is individualized, and slower students can progress at their own rates.

❏ The approach is especially appropriate for students who speak a second language or dialect.

❏ Pupils become self-directed learners.

❏ Expensive materials are not required with LEA.

The available research evidence, as summarized by Spache and Spache (1986), indicates that LEA is a successful method of teaching reading to widely different groups of individuals. In one study these writers cite, retarded readers gained significantly more sight words in 15 weeks than matched basal students. In another study vocabulary tests showed significant gains for pupils with severe reading deficits in a 3-week summer camp that used LEA. Nevertheless, it is important to note that this approach demands a great deal from the teacher. Ekwall and Shanker (1985) point out that the teacher must organize instruction, take dictation, plan individual students' programs, and monitor their progress. Also teachers must have an excellent working knowledge of the reading process. Otherwise, sequential reading skills may not be learned. Since most students disabled in reading require a structured and systematic approach to learning how to read, teachers of these pupils cannot depend upon the incidental learning of reading skills.

Individualized Reading

As a specific developmental reading approach, individualized reading has various meanings among users of the term. Nonetheless, over the years a number of practices have become associated with individualized reading. These include self-selection of materials by pupils, self-pacing in reading, individual student conferences with the teacher, and emphasis on record keeping by the teacher, pupil, or both (Heilman, Blair, & Rupley, 1986).

Fundamental to the individualized reading approach is the belief that students naturally will select reading materials that are suited to their own interests and reading levels and thereby increase their enthusiasm for reading. Obviously, the success of self-selection is influenced by the assumptions that students have interests they wish to explore further, that there are sufficient materials available that fit their interests, and that the available materials can be read independently (Heilman, Blair, & Rupley, 1986). A wide variety of materials, including trade books, basals, newspapers, and magazines at different reading levels, should be available for appropriate self-selection.

Following the selection of materials, students pace themselves and record both their progress and any problems that are encountered. Specific problems can be then discussed at scheduled pupil-teacher conferences which provide time for checking word recognition skills and reading comprehension. The conferences are considered a major strength of the individualized reading approach, because they involve the pupil in the reading process through discussion of a book, oral reading, skill practice, or completion of record books. The frequency, length, and format for pupil-teacher conferences vary from classroom to classroom.

Careful record keeping is another important component of individualized reading. Records can take a variety of forms, but they usually include a listing of books read, a brief summary of each book, and some listing of new or unknown words encountered in reading. Records concerning the student's reading material, level of performance, and reading strengths and weaknesses are also kept by the teacher from information gathered during pupil-teacher conferences.

Although individualized reading has many merits for students progressing well in reading, it remains questionable for pupils disabled in reading. One of the major disadvantages for this population is the lack of self-pacing skills on the part of many handicapped students. As noted by Kirk, Kliebhan, and Lerner (1978), too much is left to self-learning with individualized reading, and the approach lacks structure and organization for developing specific reading skills. Students disabled in reading will require a more systematic approach for learning these skills.

Programmed Reading Approach

Programmed instruction (PI) is a reading approach with a format that is unusual to most readers. In reading, PI most often takes the form of workbooks and teaching machines. The information in most programs is presented to the student through a series of small, sequential steps, each of which is referred to as a frame. Each frame may be a picture, a word or sentence, or any specific unit that illustrates a single idea. The student is usually required to respond in some way to each frame. The response may involve filling in a blank space or answering a specific question. In almost all cases, answers to questions are readily available following the student's response. Answers are frequently given in the margins of workbooks, while on teaching machines a light or sound often gives the student the immediate feedback.

According to Wallace (1981), PI in reading is presented in either a *linear* or a *branching* format. In linear programming, the student simply moves from one frame to the next. On the other hand, branching programs direct the pupil to another page or section of the workbook for review material when a response to a frame is incorrect.

Most presently available PI materials rely heavily on a phonic-linguistic approach to word recognition. Perhaps the best-known PI reading material is the Sullivan Associates' *Programmed Reading* (Buchanan, 1966). This series is a programmed workbook approach for teaching reading to students through the sixth grade. The program consists of a language arts readiness kit and three PI reading series. Additional resource materials include teacher guides, tests, activity books, and duplicating masters. Series I focuses on word analysis, and Series II and Series III emphasize comprehension. Using a phonic-linguistic approach, students are taught to write and spell each word and also to read vocabulary words that are presented. A sample page from this program is shown in Figure 5.10.

FIGURE 5.10. Example of Programmed Reading

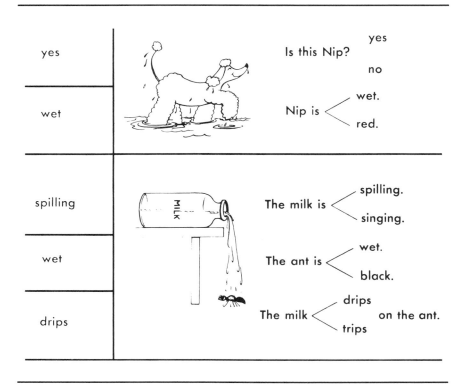

From *Programmed Reading,* Book 4, Revised edition. (1968). New York: McGraw-Hill. Reprinted by permission of McGraw-Hill Book Company.

Although the format of PI may prove to be motivating for some disabled readers because it allows each student to move at his or her own pace, we feel that some caution should be exercised in using PI with students experiencing reading difficulties. Many disabled readers lack the skills required to use the self-pacing format. In addition, Beck (1977) observes that comprehension is often interrupted when the pupil stops to fill in a response. Finally, it is important to note that PI reading materials do not provide the personalized, direct teacher interaction so often necessary for the student requiring basic skills instruction.

In our view, programmed reading instruction is best used as a supplement to the more traditional reading approaches. PI can be quite useful, in particular, for drill and practice of various word analysis skills, especially phonetics and structural analysis.

REMEDIAL PROGRAMS AND APPROACHES

The reading methods discussed in this section are special approaches designed for use with the reading disabled student. Many of these programs are highly specialized methods for teaching reading and are not ordinarily intended for developmental use in the regular classroom.

High Interest–Low Vocabulary Materials

A major source of frustration for both students experiencing reading problems and their teachers has been the unavailability of interesting and relevant materials at levels of difficulty appropriate to various abilities. Many students with reading difficulties are frustrated because books geared to their interest level are beyond their reading ability. Fortunately, as noted by Polloway and Smith (1982), the phenomenal increase during the last decade in the number of high interest–low vocabulary materials has helped to solve this basic curricular problem.

High interest–low vocabulary materials are designed with a relatively easy vocabulary and style but with an interest level that would maintain the interest of an older student (Kirk, Kliebhan, & Lerner, 1978). Materials are available that focus on adolescent subjects, such as sports, dating, adventure, and cars, while maintaining a highly controlled vocabulary (Mandell & Gold, 1984). Table 5.15 provides examples of the different books that are available. A more extensive list is provided by Harris and Sipay (1985).

In selecting high interest–low vocabulary materials, Thypin (1979) suggests the following as important characteristics:

❑ Relevance to the interests and needs of the particular student;

❑ Content level of difficulty appropriate for the pupil;

❑ Within the grasp of the student's cognitive skills;

❑ Vocabulary consistent with the student's oral language and phonetic skills;

❑ Syntactic level that parallels the pupil's competence;

❑ Interesting appearance that appeals to the student, especially in terms of the implied level of maturity.

A number of procedures are available to the teacher attempting to estimate the reading level of a book or material wthout a clearly designated level. One of the most common procedures is using one of many

TABLE 5.15. High Interest–Low Vocabulary Materials

Title	Focus	Number	Reading	Interest	Publisher
Cowboys of Many Races	Racial/ethnics cowboys on frontier	7	pp–5	1–7	Benefic Press
Jim Hunter Books	Adventures of a secret agent	16	2–3	6–adult	Fearon
Deep Sea Adventure Series	Sea Adventures and mysteries	12	2–5	3–8	Addison
Fastback Romance Books	Romantic adventures	10	4–5	7–adult	Fearon
Dan Frontier	Early pioneer life	10	pp–3	1–6	Benefic Press
Prime Time Adventures	Mystery and adventure tales	10	2	4–12	Children's Press
Cowboy Sam	Western content	15	pp–3	1–6	Benefic Press
Hi-ho Paperbacks	Contemporary adventure and mystery	14	2–3	7–12	Bantam Books
Everyreader Series	Classics and short stories	20	4	6–8	Webster
Indians	Indian biographies	13	3	4–6	Garrard
Turning Point	Varied topics	30	2–6	5–10	McCormick
Mystery Adventure Series	Young adults solve mysteries	6	2–6	4–12	Benefic Press
Crisis Series	Teenagers facing crisis	6	2–4	6–adult	Fearon
Specter	Ghost stories	8	2–3	6–adult	Fearon
Ready, Get Set, Go Books	Varied topics	24	1–3	1–6	Children's Press
Moonbeam Series	Adventures of a monkey	10	pp–3	1–6	Benefic Press

TABLE 5.15. Continued

Title	Focus	Number	Reading	Interest	Publisher
Mania Books	Varied topics	16	1	1–5	Children's Press
Space Police	Space-age police	6	2–3	6–adult	Fearon
Exploring and Understanding Series	Science processes	13	4	4–9	Benefic Press
Tom Logan Series	Old west adventures of boy growing to manhood	10	pp–1	1–6	Benefic Press
A Book About	Science	16	2	2–4	Raintree
Hiway Books	Mystery, racing and interpersonal relationships	17	2–4	7–12	Westminister
Emergency Series	Paramedic team adventures	6	2–4	2–9	Benefic Press
Pacemaker True Adventures	True stories of spies, pirates, etc.	11	2–3	5–adult	Fearon
Discovery	Biographies of different people	60	2–3	4–6	Garrard
Laura Brewster Books	Adventures of an insurance investigator	6	2–3	6–adult	Fearon
Landmark Books	Historical events and important people themes	65	4–6	5–9	Random
Famous Animal Stories	Animal stories	17	3	4–6	Garrard

available readability formulas. In addition, Mercer and Mercer (1985) briefly discuss a computer software program, *Readability Formulas* (produced by Encyclopaedia Britannica Corporation), which allows the user to simultaneously apply seven different readability formulas to any reading selection to determine reading level.

An easy-to-use and quick to compute readability formula is the Fry Readability Formula. As shown in Figure 5.11, this procedure calculates a book's reading level by the following method:

1. Randomly select three 100-word passages, one each from the beginning, middle, and end of the book. Count proper names, initializations, and numerals in the 100-word selections.

2. Count the total number of sentences in each 100-word passage. Estimate the number of sentences to the nearest tenth of a sentence. Average the total number of sentences in the beginning, middle, and ending passages so that you have one number to represent the number of sentences per 100 words.

3. Count the total number of syllables in each of the three 100-word passages. A quick and easy method to count syllables is to simply tabulate every syllable over one in each word and add that number to 100 at the end of the passage. Average the total number of syllables for the three 100-word passages.

4. Plot on the graph the average number of sentences per 100 words and the average number of syllables per 100 words. The area where the dot is plotted provides the approximate grade level (seventh grade level for the example in Figure 5.12).

Multisensory Approaches

Multisensory approaches to reading instruction usually teach skills through kinesthetic (movement) and tactile (touch) stimulation, along with the visual and auditory modalities. Two widely known multisensory methods for teaching reading are discussed in this section.

The Fernald Method. The Fernald technique, which has become almost synonymous with multisensory techniques, was first described by Grace Fernald and Helen B. Keller in 1921. A full description of the Fernald method is provided in Idol's (1988) edited revision of Grace Fernald's (1943) classic, *Remedial Techniques in Basic School Subjects.*

　　This remedial method utilizes the visual, auditory, kinesthetic, and tactile (VAKT) modalities to teach reading. Although the technique has

FIGURE 5.11. Fry Readability Graph

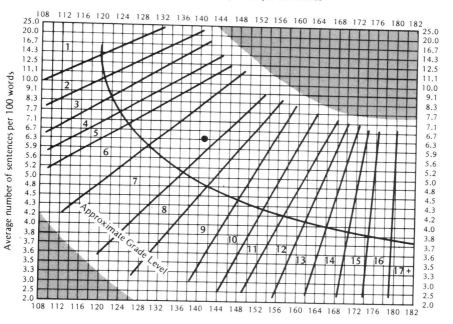

DIRECTIONS: Randomly select 3 one hundred word passages from a book or an article. Plot average number of syllables and average number of sentences per 100 words on graph to determine the grade level of the material. Choose more passages per book if great variability is observed, and conclude that the book has uneven readability. Few books will fall in gray area, but when they do, grade level scores are invalid.

Count proper nouns, numerals, and initializations as words. Count a syllable for each symbol. For example, "1945" is 1 word and 4 syllables and "IRA" is 1 word and 3 syllables.

EXAMPLE:

	SYLLABLES	SENTENCES
1st Hundred Words	124	6.6
2nd Hundred Words	141	5.5
3rd Hundred Words	158	6.8
AVERAGE	141	6.3

READABILITY 7th GRADE (see dot plotted on graph)

From Fry, E. (1972). *Reading instruction for classroom and clinic* (p. 232). New York: McGraw-Hill.

been utilized largely in reading, the procedures have also been successful in ameliorating spelling difficulties in handicapped students.

At the beginning, the student is asked to tell the teacher a few words he or she would like to learn. Once a few words have been mastered, the student is encouraged to compose a story. The stories are at first dictated to the teacher and later written by the student. The dictated stories then provide material from which additional words are learned. Stories are typed by the teacher so that the students can read them the following day.

The specific method for teaching words gradually changes as the student's ability to learn words improves. Four stages for teaching words are identified by Fernald (1943).

Stage 1. Tracing. The word is written for the student in large manuscript or cursive writing on either the chalkboard or on a strip of paper measuring approximately 4 inches by 10 inches. The student traces the words with finger contact, saying each part of the word as it is traced. This procedure is repeated until the word can be traced from memory. Each new word is typed on a card and filed alphabetically in a box by the student. During this stage, the following points are stressed: (a) Finger contact is important in tracing; (b) the student should always write the word from memory; (c) the whole word should always be written as a unit; (d) each word should be said aloud as it is traced or written; (e) whatever the student writes must be typed and read before too long an interval, since this provides transfer from the written to the printed form; and (f) words should be meaningful to the pupil and used in context.

Stage 2. Writing without tracing. At this stage, the tracing of words is eliminated. The student learns a word by looking at the manuscript or cursive copy, saying the word to himself several times, and writing the word from memory. If an error is made, the student compares the result with the model, paying particular attention to the part or parts that were missed. Words are written on index cards and filed alphabetically as in the first stage.

Stage 3. Recognition in print. After some period of time, the student learns directly from the printed page without having each word written on a card. At this stage, the pupil looks at the word, pronounces it, and writes the word from memory. Unknown words are told to the student. Reading in books is usually initiated during this stage.

Stage 4. Word analysis. New words are learned by generalizing from words already known. Fernald felt that as the student looks at the word, the simultaneous association by similarity with known words, together with the meanings inferred from the context, gives the student an instant perception of the word. Unknown words are again told to the pupil. Sounding out words is discouraged. During this final stage, students are encouraged to read widely from many different reading materials.

It is advised that the nonreader start at Stage 1 and students with partial disabilities at Stage 2. Fernald does not offer any special procedures for overcoming specific difficulties such as reversals or omissions, since the method enforces a consistent left-to-right sequence and requires correct reproduction of the entire word.

The Fernald method is intended to be used with the student who fails to learn by more commonly used methods; it is not intended for use with large groups of students. Some authorities have suggested that the success of the method may not be a result so much of the tracing and writing of words as of the careful attention and concentration given to the word.

According to Harris and Sipay (1985), the Fernald method has several desirable features for students with reading disabilities: (a) careful and systematic observations and study of words; (b) consistent left-to-right direction in reading; (c) repetition; (d) errors immediately noted and corrected; (e) progress noted by the pupil at practically every lesson; and (f) visual impressions reinforced by sensory impressions from tracing, writing, and saying the words.

Although research evidence regarding the merits and shortcomings of the Fernald method compared with other approaches is inconclusive, the method is highly recommended as a very successful approach for students who are severely handicapped in reading.

The Gillingham Method. The Gillingham technique (Gillingham & Stillman, 1968) is a highly structured synthetic phonics approach that uses a multisensory technique for teaching reading, spelling, and writing. The method is based on the theoretical work of Orton (1937), who was interested in the relationship between cerebral dominance and reading and language disorders. A detailed manual adapting the method for classroom use by primary-grade teachers is also available (Slingerland, 1974). Another set of materials based on the Gillingham approach has been developed by Traub and Bloom (1970). In addition, a guide for teaching spelling in a way consistent with Orton's procedures has been written by Childs and Childs (1971).

The Gillingham method emphasizes a multisensory approach for learning specific reading skills. Students are taught letter sounds, visual symbols, and various sensory associations through tracing, copying, and writing specific letters. Phonograms are introduced by the teacher through the following highly structured procedures:

a. A small card with one letter printed on it is exposed to the student, and the *name* of the letter is spoken by the teacher. The name of the letter is repeated by the student. As soon as the name of the letter is mastered, the *sound* is made by the teacher and repeated by the student. This card is then exposed and the teacher asks, "What does this letter say?" The student is expected to give the sound.

b. With the card not being exposed, the teacher makes the sound represented by the letter and says, "Tell me the name of the letter that has this sound." The student is expected to give the name of the letter.

c. The letter is carefully made by the teacher and its form explained to the student. The letter is traced by the student on the teacher's lines, then copied, written from memory, then written again without looking at the previously written letters. Finally, the teacher makes the sound and asks the student to "Write the letter that has this sound." (Wallace & McLoughlin, 1979, pp. 179–180)

The first group of letters taught includes *a, b, f, h, i, j, k, m, p,* and *t.* After these letters have been learned through the procedures outlined above, the process of blending is introduced using CVC (consonant-vowel-consonant) words (e.g., *bat, fib, it, Jim, map,* etc.). Gillingham preferred to sound the initial consonant and vowel together, then add the final consonant (/*ma*/*p*/). These regularly spelled words are then used for various sentences and stories as specified in the manual. The words and sentences are also used for spelling, which is introduced following blending. Nonphonetic words are taught through kinesthetic procedures.

Materials developed for use with the Gillingham method include phonetic drill cards, phonetic word cards, syllable concept cards, and "little" stories. The authors of the program strongly believe that the use of these materials is absolutely essential for the method to be successful. More important, the authors insist that the procedure be followed rigidly, since the steps are considered to be sequentially based. According to the authors, the method requires five lessons per week for a minimum of two years, and no other reading and spelling instruction should be used with the student while the Gillingham procedures are being used.

According to Kirk, Kleibhan, and Lerner (1978), the Gillingham method has been criticized for several reasons including: (a) overly rigid procedures; (b) uninteresting reading material; (c) lack of accommodation for pupils with auditory discrimination and auditory perception problems; and (d) delay in the reading of other materials.

On the other hand, Otto and Smith (1980) point out that the Gillingham method has been reported to be successful when used with modifications according to each student's specific needs. These writers urge that teachers use only those aspects of the method that can be implemented practically.

Phonics-Related Methods

The reading approaches discussed in this section are all considered to be special techniques for teaching phonics as a word analysis method. *Reading Mastery: DISTAR* programs can also be used as a complete reading program.

Phonic Remedial Reading Lessons. The *Lessons* (Kirk, Kirk, & Minskoff, 1985) are specifically designed to teach phonic skills to students reading below the third grade level and who also require remedial assistance. The *Lessons* are based on the *Remedial Reading Drills* (Hegge, Kirk, & Kirk, 1955), which were devised for teaching reading to handicapped students. According to Kirk et al. (1985), the *Lessons* are most appropriate for pupils who have failed to learn to read after a number of years in school.

The 77 phonic lessons are composed of various letter sounds which are systematically presented in sequential order. The method provides repeated practice in blending specific sounds through lists of words. Each word is read orally, and the student is required to sound out each phonetic element before blending it into a word. The teacher is also encouraged to have the pupil write the letter from memory as the sound is produced by the student.

The *Lessons* are divided into six parts: (a) Part I presents single letters to be associated with single sounds; (b) Part II consists of two- and three-letter sequences that have a single sound; (c) no new sound-symbol associations are introduced in Part III, but symbols are integrated into consonant blends and common syllables; (d) Part IV presents new configurations which are more difficult or larger units of graphemes; (e) Part V consists of sounds that are exceptions to the sounds previously taught; and (f) Part VI merges into some grammatical understanding of plurals, possessives, past tense, present progressive, affixes, compound words, and syllabication. The lesson for /ck/ is shown in Figure 5.12.

The *Lessons* have proven successful with students who have failed to profit from conventional reading methods yet can be educated in phonic principles. The *Lessons* do provide much-needed repetition and practice for the student handicapped in reading. In addition, the well-organized and sequential order of sound-symbol presentations have been also mentioned as advantages of the *Lessons*.

Phonovisual Method. This method (Schoolfield & Timberlake, 1960) is a structured approach for teaching phonics. The program is intended to be used as a supplement to the sight-word method of teaching word analysis. The two main components of the program are the consonant

FIGURE 5.12. Example of *Phonic Remedial Reading Lessons*

Lesson 12
ck

b a ck	s a ck	sh a ck	p a ck	t a ck
p i ck	s i ck	N i ck	k i ck	l i ck
r o ck	s o ck	d o ck	sh o ck	l o ck
t u ck	l u ck	b u ck	d u ck	m u ck
p e ck	ch e ck	n e ck	d e ck	b e ck

p i ck	p e ck	p a ck	p u ck
r o ck	r a ck	R i ck	r u ck
d u ck	d o ck	d e ck	D i ck
l o ck	l a ck	l u ck	l i ck

w i ck	w i tch	p i t	p i tch
h a t	h a tch	p a ck	p a tch
s i ck	s a ck	s t i tch	s t i ck
l a tch	l a ck	R i ck	r i ch
b a ck	b a tch	l i ck	l u ck
D u tch	d u ck	s h ock	s o ck

kick	chick	suck	luck	tick	check
Dick	puck	wick	check	sock	catch
buck	block	shock	chuck	shack	peck
muck	neck	rock	peck	lock	buck

From Kirk, S. A., Kirk, W. D., & Minskoff, E. (1985). *Phonic remedial reading lessons* Novato, CA: Academic Therapy Publications. Reprinted with permission.

chart and the vowel chart. Pictures are used to represent each sound on the charts. In addition, the charts serve as a means for the student to recognize each letter, the sound it signals, and the position of speech organs (lips, tongue, etc.) when the sound is produced. All other materials are based on and used in conjunction with the charts. They are the essence of the Phonovisual Method.

The 26 sounds on the consonant chart are organized both vertically and horizontally. In the first vertical column are the breath (voiceless) sounds (*p, t, ch,* etc.); in the second column are the voiced consonant sounds (*b, v, d,* etc.); the third column contains nasal sounds (*m, n,* etc.); and the last column has the remaining consonant sounds (*r, y, l,* etc.).

Horizontally, the sounds are spaced to indicate the phonetic relationship with the sounds in the first vertical column. For example, the *b* at the top of the second column is the voiced equivalent (or cognate) of the breath sound of the *p* in the first column, etc.

The vowel chart consists of 18 vowel sounds. Horizontally, the top row gives the five long vowels, and the next row gives the five short vowel sounds. The remaining eight vowel sounds (*aw, oo, oy,* etc.) are spaced throughout the chart.

The consonant chart is taught first, because there are more consonants than vowels. Vowels and consonant blends are taught after the pupil has mastered the initial and final consonant positions. Syllabication, compound words, and nonphonetic spelling is also introduced in the latter part of the program. The complete set of phonovisual materials includes teacher manuals, cassette tapes, workbooks, games, filmstrips, and various other practice materials.

The Phonovisual Method is a concise and well-organized approach to teaching phonic skills. In addition, the authors provide some excellent suggestions for using the method with reading disabled students, including a number of case histories.

Reading Mastery: DISTAR. The Direct Instructional System for Teaching Arithmetic and Reading (DISTAR) (Engelmann & Bruner, 1969) was originally developed to teach beginning reading to culturally disadvantaged and slow-learning students. The program has since been revised and reorganized (*Reading Mastery: DISTAR,* Engelmann & Bruner, 1984) and is now suitable for reading disabled students at all levels of instruction. The program is based on the belief that students will learn to read if they are carefully taught. Consequently, the approach emphasizes a direct instruction model. Students are taught in small, homogeneous groups, and lessons are highly structured, fast paced, and intensive. Students receive continuous positive reinforcement throughout the program. Their mastery of specific skills is appraised through criterion-referenced tests. Special lessons are also available for skills that have not been mastered.

Initially, the program emphasizes sequencing, left-right progression, and sound-symbol associations. Sequencing skills are taught through symbol-action games. Blending exercises are designed to teach the synthetic relationships of sounds and words. Students are taught to blend through a *say-it-fast* procedure, whereas spelling words by sounds teaches the reverse procedure. Following mastery of approximately 20 phonemes, storybooks are introduced for textual reading purposes.

The DISTAR program is a complete reading program which consists of a number of different materials. The program is recommended for any pupil who has not mastered basic decoding and comprehension skills or any student requiring remedial assistance in these areas. The program teaches the pupil to use a variety of word analysis skills. Literal and inferential skills are also employed. The accompanying DISTAR library series is intended to supplement and reinforce skills developed in the program.

Although Kirk, Kliebhan, and Lerner (1978) have criticized the emphasis on auditory skills and the rigidity of the DISTAR program, other writers have found the material to be well-organized and highly effective in teaching students to read. In addition, Haring and Bateman (1977) report a substantial amount of empirical support for using DISTAR materials with populations that previously have had many school failures. In sum, the evidence clearly suggests that the DISTAR program can be an effective tool for teaching reading to handicapped students.

SRA Corrective Reading Program. The SRA Corrective Reading Program (CRP) (Engelmann, Becker, Hanner, & Johnson, 1980) is based on DISTAR concepts and designed for students in grades 4 through 12. This program is divided into decoding and comprehension sections, each with 340 lessons. The lessons include teacher-directed activities, independent seatwork, and tests of student performance. Each lesson lasts approximately 35 to 40 minutes and includes a built-in reinforcement system. Student contracts and progress charts also accompany the program.

Recently, Polloway et al. (1986) used the CRP with a group of learning disabled and educable mentally retarded adolescents with data collected on the achievement of these students in the domains of reading recognition and comprehension. When compared to reading progress in prior years, both groups showed significantly greater improvements. On the whole, the CRP seems to be a very effective program for teaching reading to older students continuing to experience difficulties in basic reading recognition and comprehension skills.

Sight-Word Methods

The two reading approaches discussed in this section were specifically designed for teaching students handicapped in reading. Both techniques have been used successfully with this population.

Edmark Reading Program. The Edmark program (Edmark Associates, 1972) was designed to teach retarded and nonreading students a 150-word sight vocabulary. The only student prerequisites for the program are an ability to repeat a word that the teacher says and the ability to make gestural or verbal responses. The program is based upon operant learning principles and incorporates training in errorless discrimination, shaping, fading, and stimulus-response chaining.

The 227 lessons in the program focus on (a) word recognition exercises, which teach one or two words per lesson; (b) direction books, which teach the student to follow directions; (c) picture-phrase matching; and (d) storybooks, which are read orally by the student. A whole-word approach to word recognition is utilized throughout the program.

Among the advantages of the program are: (a) each lesson is broken down into small, discrete, sequential steps; (b) students progress at their own rate; and (c) teachers are encouraged to use either verbal praise or token reinforcement. Review tests and procedures for charting reading progress are also included.

The authors reported considerable success in using the program with retarded individuals. According to Lent (1968), students with IQs lower than 35 have been able to read the 150-word vocabulary and use the words functionally. In addition, research studies by Walsh and Lamberts (1979) and Vandever and Stubbs (1977) reported that moderately-severely handicapped students made progress with the Edmark program.

Neurological Impress Method. The NIM (Heckelman, 1969) was designed for students with severe reading handicaps. Basically, the method is a system of unison reading whereby the student and the teacher read aloud simultaneously at a rapid rate. The method is based on the theory that a new learning process, a neurological memory trace, is established when students see the words in print and hear both the teacher's and their own voices saying the words. According to the author, the NIM exposes pupils to accurate, fluid oral reading while enabling them to contribute to the reading process.

To implement the NIM approach, the student is seated slightly to the front of the teacher with the student and the teacher holding the book jointly. As the student and teacher read the materials in unison, the voice of the teacher is directed into the student's ear. The teacher accompanies the reading by moving his or her index finger under the words being read. Later, the student is taught how to use his or her own finger as a locator for each word read. At times the teacher may read slightly louder and faster than the student in order to imprint the correct responses in the student. As the student gains fluency and confidence, the teacher reads more softly and slower than the student. Comprehension of the material is not a concern, nor is the teaching of phonics or any other word analysis technique.

Very limited research indicates some success with this approach. Bos (1982), for example, felt that the NIM resulted in significant word recognition and comprehension gains for disabled readers, though the studies used small samples and often lacked control groups. Otto, McMenemy, and Smith (1973) report that certain handicapped readers with serious phrasing problems were helped substantially by the NIM. Finally, Richek, List, and Lerner (1983) believe that this method may improve oral reading very quickly.

Special Alphabet Programs

Some educators believe that irregularities in the English sound-symbol system are responsible for the difficulties encountered by many pupils in learning to read. According to Harris and Sipay (1985), many of these educators believe that a one-to-one correspondence, in which each grapheme always represents the same phoneme (and vice versa), would make it easier to learn the code and would facilitate the acquisition of reading ability. The programs that follow are based on this assumption.

Initial Teaching Alphabet.   Probably the best known of the special alphabets is the Initial Teaching Alphabet (i.t.a.) (Downing, 1965). The i.t.a. system employs a 44-character alphabet in which each of the 44 symbols represents one sound. The i.t.a. is actually composed of 24 traditional letters from the conventional alphabet (*q* and *x* are eliminated) and 20 additional letters, some of which resemble two familiar letters joined together. Also, in i.t.a. the larger version of a letter becomes its capital. Some examples of words in i.t.a. include *cors* (course), *sum* (some), *aulmoest* (almost), and *akwaerium* (aquarium).

The authors of i.t.a. clearly proposed the special alphabet as an alternative medium and not as a method for teaching reading. It is intended for use primarily in the early stages of learning to read. Pupils are expected to transfer to traditional orthography (TO) by the end of the first year.

The i.t.a. system has not been used extensively with reading disabled students for a number of reasons. Kirk, Kliebhan, and Lerner (1978) suggest that transfer to regular print is inherently difficult for disabled readers because of poor transfer and generalization abilities. Although i.t.a. was fairly popular at one time, Harris and Sipay (1985) state that the use of this alphabet has declined markedly in the United States, where i.t.a. materials are no longer published.

Words in Color.   Another special alphabet program for teaching reading is *Words in Color* (Gattegno, 1962), which uses color to represent 47

English phonemes. Each phoneme, regardless of spelling, is assigned a different color in this system. Large wall charts with black background are used to teach each of the different sounds and colors. Sounds are learned by drilling the sounds in isolation and blending them together.

Words in Color does not seem to offer the reading disabled student any particular advantage compared to other reading approaches. In fact, it is generally concluded that the system is more confusing than helpful to students already disabled in reading.

COMPUTER APPLICATIONS IN READING

During the last decade, American schools have witnessed an explosive interest in the use of computers for various educational purposes. In reading, computer applications include programs for drill and practice of skills, presentation of information in tutorial format, and other uses such as simulations and problem solving. However, most studies indicate that computers are used primarily for drill and practice activities (Sapona, 1985). For example, Becker (1983) found that the most common computer application among his nationwide survey of elementary schools was drill and practice activities.

Using the computer for the drill and practice of reading skills serves as a supplement to other forms of instruction. It also helps to integrate and consolidate previously learned material through practice on the computer. A number of studies suggest that using the computer for drill activities may be more interesting to students when the software is in a gamelike format (Schiffman, Tobin, & Buchanan, 1982). In addition, Ekwall and Shanker (1983) point out that drill and practice programs focus on specific vocabulary and decoding skills such as basic sight words, basal reader vocabulary words, and phonic skills.

A number of other computer uses for the reading disabled have been suggested. Maddux (1984) offers a useful distinction between what he referred to as Type I and Type II uses of microcomputers. Type I uses, such as drill and practice of skills, tutorials, and data management, are uses that help teachers deliver instruction as they have in the past. In contrast, Type II uses, such as word processing and simulation programs, are those that enhance and improve teacher-delivered instruction. Maddux (1984) believes that while Type I uses are valuable and helpful to teachers, successful long-term use of computers in the classroom is dependent upon the development and implementation of Type II uses (Sapona, 1985).

The computer can be of great value to the teacher of reading. Like any other reading material, the computer, as noted by Heilman, Blair, and Rupley (1986), is a tool to help the teacher to teach students how to read. Among the specific advantages of using computers with the reading disabled, Lerner (1985) mentions the following: (a) Individual instruction is provided; (b) nonthreatening feedback and corrective procedures are used; (c) opportunity for as much drill and repetition as the student needs and wants is afforded, since the computer has infinite patience; and (d) a large amount of skills-oriented practice is provided.

On the other hand, Harris and Sipay (1985) contend that computer hardware is better developed than the software and believe that most of the available reading software does little that could not be done without a computer. In addition, at the present time there is no empirical evidence of what effect computer use for drill and practice activities has on the achievement of reading disabled students (Sapona, 1985). Because of the rapidly developing nature of this field, we recommend that teachers keep abreast of current findings through professional journals and publications. Meanwhile, there is a definite need for increased documentation before computers are widely used as a basis for reading remediation programs.

BEST PRACTICES

Successful reading development is regarded as the most significant common denominator of achievement in many areas of the curriculum. Consequently, reading has been widely emphasized in special education classrooms during the past few years. Nonetheless, many handicapped students, regardless of age, tend to read below their mental age reading expectancy level.

It is our viewpoint that successful instructional programming for students with reading problems depends upon a thorough appraisal of each pupil's reading strengths and weaknesses. Individual circumstances will affect exactly what is included in the appraisal process, which assessment procedures are used, and who will be involved in the process. Moreover, the most proficient assessment of the reading disabled includes a variety of appraisal techniques.

Clearly, the best evaluation will be ineffectual if the results are not used in planning instructional programs (Wallace, 1981). Although many developmental reading approaches and specialized techniques are available, it is our belief that successful reading remediation is based upon the use of a variety of instructional methods and materials suited to individual student characteristics. As noted throughout the chapter, no one method of reading instruction has been demonstrated to be clearly superior for teaching handicapped readers. On the contrary, Kirk, Kliebhan, and Lerner (1978) hypothesize that teacher effectiveness often is of greater importance than the method. Wallace and Kauffman (1986) indicate that a conscientious and skillful effort on the part of the teacher is the primary factor in successful teaching.

In sum, the best practices in reading (a) employ ongoing diagnosis of pupils' reading development, (b) structure and direct pupils' learning, (c) provide opportunities for pupils to practice and apply skills in meaningful context, and (d) attend to maintaining a high level of pupil involvement in learning (Heilman, Blair, & Rupley, 1986).

APPENDIX
Instructional Activities for Reading Readiness

I. Skill: COMPREHENSION
  A. Listening Comprehension
    1. *Outcome:* The ability to understand and recall what one hears.
    2. *Teaching Tasks:*
      a. Read a simple story to the children showing pictures of each of the main characters and/or events. After the story is completed ask them to name each character or event and tell something that happened in the story.
      b. Using a flannel board, illustrate a story as you tell it. Have the children recreate the story in their own words using the flannel board pieces.
      c. Use either of the above techniques and ask the children to infer a relationship between the characters or a new ending for the story line. Children who can infer relationships and future events are functioning at a higher order comprehension skill.
      d. Orally present directions to the children to carry out a task: "Clap your hands two times" or "Color the circle blue."
  B. Visual Comprehension
    1. *Outcome:* The ability to understand and recall what one sees.
    2. *Teaching Tasks:*
      a. Show the children a drawing of an activity being performed by another child. Ask them to tell you what the child in the drawing is doing: "What does the picture say?"
      b. After looking at a nonsense picture, or a drawing of a common object, person, or animal with a missing part, ask the children to tell you: "What's wrong here?"
      c. Show the children a sequenced cartoon strip with the words cut out or covered over. Ask the children to provide appropriate dialogue. (Peanuts or Henry comics are excellent for this activity.)
II. Skill: DISCRIMINATION
  A. Auditory Discrimination
    1. *Outcome:* The ability to discriminate likenesses and differences among sounds.
    2. *Teaching Tasks:*
      a. After teaching the concept of rhyming words have the children name a color that rhymes with _____ :
         head and bread _____(red)
         fellow and bellow _____(yellow)
         bean and teen _____(green)
         fight and light _____(white)
         or name an object word that rhymes with _____ :
         hair and fair _____(chair)
         up and pup _____(cup)

fish and wish _____(dish)
goat and moat _____(coat)

The same type of activity can be done with number words, animal words, and names of children in the class.

b. Present the children with objects or pictures and ask them to match names beginning with the same sound.

(bat)   (bear)   (house)   (chair)

c. Provide the children with the key sound and ask them to clap their hands whenever they hear it. For example, if the sound is "t" they would clap once for table and twice for tattle.

B. Visual Discrimination
   1. *Outcome:* The ability to discriminate printed symbols from each other.
   2. *Teaching Tasks:*
      a. Ask the children to match similar shapes and patterns:

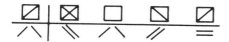

b. Progress from shapes and patterns to letters and numerals:

7	2	3	7	5
f	t	h	e	f

c. Finally the children should be able to match identical words (letter patterns):

who	yes	who	where	now
can	cat	cast	can	come

III. Skill: MEMORY
   A. Auditory Memory
      1. *Outcome:* The ability to remember what one hears.
      2. *Teaching Tasks:*
         a. Using the direction activity suggested under the auditory comprehension skill increase the number of tasks the children must do. For example:
            Clap your hands.
            Clap your hands and stand up.

Clap your hands, stand up, and go to the door.

Clap your hands, stand up, go to the door, and turn around.

    b. After listening to a story involving a series of events, ask the children to tell or draw a picture of the proper story sequence.

B. Visual Memory
  1. *Outcome:* The ability to remember what one sees.
  2. *Teaching Tasks:*
    a. Show the children a string of large beads of various colors. Start with only a few and ask the children to look at the beads (about five seconds) and then to make a string just like it. Increase the number of beads on the string, giving the children the chance to model each new addition.
    b. Show the children a picture of common objects. Remove the stimulus picture and have them name each of the objects (or animals) in the picture that they remember.

IV. Skill: ASSOCIATION
  A. Letter Name to Letter Symbol Association
    1. *Outcome:* The ability to identify letters by name.
    2. *Teaching Tasks:*
      a. Use as many modalities as possible when introducing each letter. For instance, have the children see "a," say "a," cut out "a," color over "a," make an "a" out of clay, and paint or write "a."
  B. Phoneme to Grapheme Association
    1. *Outcome:* The ability to associate a sound with its representative symbol.
    2. *Teaching Tasks:*
      a. Present each letter with a word and associated picture stimulus that begins with its representative sound. For example, sand-s, book-b, fish-f. The children should be able to identify each letter when given the appropriate key word.

V. Skill: ORIENTATION
  A. Visual Tracking
    1. *Outcome:* The ability to follow an object or a line of print across space.
    2. *Teaching Tasks:*
      a. Present a line of pictures of common objects for the child to name in order as the teacher points to them.

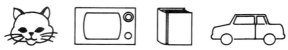

      b. Ask the children to complete a simple maze by moving a finger along the route.

      c. Have the children trace different lines and shapes following from a marked starting point to a predetermined finish.

B. Left to Right Orientation
  1. *Outcome:* The ability to read across a page from left to right.
  2. *Teaching Tasks:*
     a. Present materials with a green line drawn on one side and a red line on the other. Tell the children that we always begin reading on the side of the green line and move across the page until we reach the red line. Have the children practice this by moving a finger across the page.
     b. Have the children draw a series of lines across the page from left to right.
     c. Have the children *read* colored dots from left to right across a page.

(Represented in colors: red, green, blue, blue, red.)

From Cohen, S. B., & Plaskon, S. P. (1980). *Language arts for the mildly handicapped.* Columbus, OH: Charles E. Merrill, pp. 370–373. Reprinted with permission.

6

HANDWRITING

Written language is the third major linguistic area that students are introduced to in school. The sequence as presented in this book—oral language (listening and speaking), reading, and writing—represents the chronological sequence of learning these skills. However, this sequence is not intended to suggest that teachers should wait until other areas are well established before introducing writing—clearly, written language, oral language, and reading have important interactive relationships.

The three major skill domains involved in written language are handwriting, spelling, and written expression. Within these three areas, the proficiency of exceptional students varies significantly. For some pupils the task of writing their own names may present a major obstacle, while some mildly handicapped adolescents may focus on learning those higher level writing skills that will facilitate success in postsecondary education.

In emphasizing handwriting skills in this chapter, it must first be noted that not all handicapped and remedial students experience problems in handwriting. This is particularly important when one considers the nature of successful performance in handwriting. Tradition in American schools has often been to strive for "perfection." Of course, this is an unattainable goal, and it is questionable whether it should even be sought. Therefore, the realistic goal that teachers should undertake is that of legibility. It is safe to assume that for most adults, the development of a personal style that might regularly, or at least sporadically, include illegible or semilegible letters and words is quite common. The classic example of physicians' prescriptions underscores this point. Therefore, instructional programs should eschew stressing the perfect reproduction of some recognized standard and encourage instead a legible, yet perhaps unique style. Such an emphasis has not traditionally been a feature of handwriting instruction (Tagartz, Otto, Klausmeier, Goodwin, & Cook, 1968).

Given the variety of skills and needs that students may present in the area of handwriting, the role of the teacher will vary greatly. However, two major distinctions can be made. For some students their instructional needs are essentially of a developmental nature. All young children need some help in handwriting, even though they may not experience any specific problems; this need is reflected in the fact that 98% of elementary teachers provide some formal instruction in this area (Burns, 1974). However, other children may exhibit what can accurately be termed handwriting disorders. Although to some extent the types of instructional programs used will have some similar features, clearly the intensity of instruction would be increased for the student with specific problems, as would the requirement for individualization of programs matched to the student's needs.

DEVELOPMENT OF HANDWRITING SKILLS

The developmental sequence of skills in written language includes specific milestones in four areas: prerequisite writing skills or readiness abilities, handwriting, spelling, and written expression. Table 6.1 outlines a developmental progression for these four areas. The focus for this chapter is on the first two—prerequisite skills and handwriting skills.

Several considerations regarding prerequisite and handwriting skills warrant further attention at this point. The first concerns the topic of handedness—that is, a child's development of hand dominance. Handedness has been seen as affected by genetic variables, hemispheric determination, or both. In some cases handedness is considered to be learned through early practice and reinforcement (Cohen & Plaskon, 1980). For example, a child can be taught a specific task such as waving bye-bye with the right or left hand and then may choose whether or not to change hands. Kaufman, Zalma, and Kaufman (1978) reported in their study on this trait that approximately 72% of their sample of children aged from 2–6 to 4–6 had established handedness as measured by consistent responding with a given hand to McCarthy Scale motor items (bouncing a ball, catching and throwing a beanbag, and drawing with a pencil). This number was slightly higher for children between

TABLE 6.1. Written Language Developmental Sequence

Prerequisite skills for handwriting
1. able to touch, reach, grasp, and release objects
2. able to distinguish similarities and differences in objects and designs
3. has established handedness

Handwriting skills:
1. grasps writing utensil
2. moves writing utensil in up/down fashion
3. moves writing utensil in left to right direction
4. moves writing utensil in a circular manner
5. copies letters
6. copies own name in manuscript form
7. writes own name in manuscript form
8. copies words and sentences in manuscript form
9. copies manuscript from far-point
10. copies letters and words in cursive writing
11. copies sentences in cursive writing
12. copies cursive from far-point

Spelling skills:
1. recognizes letters of the alphabet
2. recognizes words
3. says words that can be recognized
4. recognizes similarities and differences in words
5. differentiates between different sounds in words
6. associates certain sounds (phonemes) with symbols or letters
7. spells phonetically regular words
8. spells phonetically irregular words
9. generates rules for spelling various words and word problems
10. uses correctly spelled words in written compositions

Written expression skills:
1. writes phrases and sentences
2. begins sentences with a capital letter
3. ends sentences with correct punctuation
4. uses proper punctuation in other instances
5. demonstrates simple rules for sentence structure
6. writes complete paragraphs
7. writes notes and letters
8. expresses creative ideas in writing
9. utilizes writing as a functional means of communication

From Polloway, E. A., Payne, J. S., Patton, J. R., & Payne, R. A. (1985). *Strategies for teaching retarded and special needs learners*. Columbus, OH: Charles E. Merrill, p. 266. Reprinted with permission of National Council of Teachers of English.

5–0 and 8–6. Therefore, it can be concluded that most children will come to school with hand dominance and obviously should not be encouraged to change (Burns, 1974). For those relatively few individuals for whom there are doubts concerning preferred hand, teachers should plan to evaluate for dominant hand. Information on this topic is discussed later in the chapter.

A second consideration related to the sequence of skills involves the importance of legibility. As noted earlier, the stress in this chapter is on the production of written language that can be clearly understood rather than on writing for its aesthetic appeal. Such an emphasis thus tends to equate legibility with quality in that effective communication rather than good handwriting is the goal (Otto, McMenemy, & Smith, 1973).

Another concern is speed. While legibility and thus accuracy of production is foremost, rate must not be overlooked as a secondary objective. Slow, labored writing efforts that impede task completion and thus communication can become an instructional focus. For illustrative purposes, Table 7.2 provides a breakdown of writing speeds for students in grades 4 through 6 which can be used for comparative purposes. Groff (1961) contends that his figures more nearly approach the actual speeds that students were able to maintain under normal writing conditions than did the earlier data presented by Ayres (cited in Groff, 1961) and also summarized in Table 6.2.

A final consideration stemming from Table 7.1 that needs explanation is the sequence from manuscript to cursive writing. Manuscript was introduced into this country in the early 1900s and by the 1920s was generally accepted in the schools as the preferred form of initial writing. Transition to cursive writing was then effected by third grade (Early, Nelson, Kleber, Treegoob, Huffman, & Cass, 1976; Hagin, 1983; Rubin, 1975). This sequence is still commonly followed in the schools today—probably based more on tradition than empirical data (Early et al., 1976). For this reason the sequence from manuscript to cursive handwriting is followed in this chapter. A subsequent section addresses the relative merits of manuscript versus cursive as the preferred initial approach.

HANDWRITING CHARACTERISTICS OF HANDICAPPED LEARNERS

Problems in handwriting can range from severe eye-hand motor dysfunctions to relatively minor difficulties with specific strokes or letters. Each student should be carefully evaluated to determine if problems exist and, if so, the severity of the difficulty being experienced should be appraised.

TABLE 6.2. Handwriting Speeds (Letters/Minute) of Pupils Studied by Ayres and Groff

Letters per Minute	Percent of Pupils					
	Grade		Grade		Grade	
	4 Ayres	4 Groff (N = 1563)	5 Ayres	5 Groff (N = 1522)	6 Ayres	6 Groff (N = 1749)
10–19	Not reported	6.8	1	3.8		1.5
20–29		25.4	2	13.5	2	5.5
30–39		31.5	5	31.5	3	18.4
40–49		21.3	12	26.0	8	27.1
50–59		9.9	20	12.6	14	21.2
60–69		3.6	22	7.6	19	12.9
70–79		.8	19	3.2	21	7.9
80–89		.3	12	.8	16	3.6
90–99		.1	5	.4	10	.9
100–109			2	.4	5	.8
110–119					2	.4
	M = 55	M = 35.06	M = 64	M = 40.65	M = 71	M = 49.65

From Groff, P. J. (1961). New speeds of handwriting. *Elementary English, 38,* 565. Reprinted with permission of National Council of Teachers of English.

Figure 6.1 provides an illustration of a severe problem with the motor coordination necessary for accurate writing. The 8-year-old child from whom the sample was elicited was labeled *dysgraphic* to indicate the severity of the writing difficulty. Johnson and Myklebust (1967) suggest that the term could apply to students whose problems range from the inability to hold a pencil to difficulties in drawing a straight line. As with other medico-clinical terms such as *dyslexia* or *aphasia*, it seems appropriate to avoid usage of the term except in cases where pronounced problems are evident and physiological sources can be either documented or at least reasonably theorized to exist.

More important than the label are the effects of serious writing disorders. In addition to the obvious interference with legibility, Siegel and Gold (1982) note that the concentration required for the production of written forms can have adverse effects on the content. These writers hypothesize that the energy necessary for the physical act of writing can leave little in reserve for the higher level cognitive demands of the

FIGURE 6.1. Copying of an 8-year-old Labeled Dysgraphic

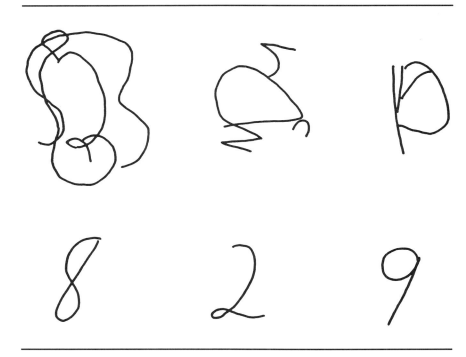

From Johnson, D. J., & Myklebust, H. R. (1964). *Learning disabilities: Educational principles and practices.* New York: Grune & Stratton, p. 201. Reprinted with permission.

task, hence writing styles of disordered learners are often characterized by short sentences, restricted vocabulary, and simplistic syntax.

For most exceptional children, however, possible problems are more likely to be of less magnitude than those described in the preceding paragraph and often are linked to specific deficits in visual memory, fine motor coordination difficulties, poor teaching, or perhaps simply carelessness. Graham and Miller (1980), in their review of research, indicate that inadequate instruction was the most visible explanation for subsequent writing difficulties. Although cause will seldom be determined, even if it is, it will often not be helpful in instruction. Nevertheless, as Mandell and Gold (1984) note, it is important to differentiate actual disorders from carelessness or lack of motivation.

For the majority of students, the focus will be on the specific problems that are encountered in legible writing. A classic study of illegibilities was reported by Newland (1932), who supervised the analysis of over one million letters written by 2,381 individuals ranging from first grade to adulthood. Over 42,000 illegibilities were tabulated, and a set of specific conclusions was drawn. As Newland (1932) reports:

1. There were more forms of illegibilities peculiar to the different age groups than there were common to two or more age levels.

2. The illegibilities of only four letters (a, e, r, t) contributed 45, 46, and 47 percent to the elementary, high-school and adult groups respectively.

3. Only fourteen forms of illegibilities in the elementary and high school levels and nine in the adult group contributed 50 percent of all the illegibilities recorded.

4. Only four types of difficulties in the formation of letters caused over one-half of all illegibilities.

5. The gross frequency with which illegibilities appeared tended to increase with age. (p. 249)

Newland (1932) continues by drawing these implications:

These results indicate that while remedial or preventive work should be adapted to the different age levels, either the prevention of illegibilities in the writing of the letters "a," "e," "r," and "t," the correction of from nine to fourteen forms of illegibilities, or the correction or prevention of four types of bad letter-formation habits would decrease the number of illegibilities by one-half. Corrective or preventive work directed along all three of these lines would probably eliminate at least three-fourths of all illegibilities. (p. 239)

For identified handicapped students, there is no comparable data base available. Nevertheless, there is little reason to believe that these patterns would not represent appropriate analysis for exceptional learners as well. Mercer and Mercer (1985) identified common eligibilities in disabled learners which are presented in Figure 6.2. In addition, they have highlighted the most common problems experienced by children and adolescents with learning problems as slowness, letter and number directionality errors, inappropriate slant, spacing problems, reversals, inability to remain on the line, and general messiness.

ASSESSMENT OF HANDWRITING SKILLS

Given the variety of severe, generalized problems as well as the specific difficulties that may be exhibited within a given group of handicapped and remedial learners, individual assessment is essential for the development of a responsive instructional program. This section reviews

FIGURE 6.2. Common Illegibilities

a like u	*Ce*	m like n	*n*
a like o	*Ce*	n like u	*uu*
a like ce	*Ce*	o like a	*a*
b like li	*li*	o like v	*v*
be like bl	*bl*	p like js	*js*
b like k	*k*	r like n	*n*
c like e	*e*	r like v	*v*
c like a	*ci*	r like i	*i*
d like cl	*cl*	t like i	*i*
e like i	*i*	t like l	*l*
g like y	*y*	u like ee	*ee*
g like q	*q*	u like ei	*ei*
i like e	*e*	w like n	*n*
h like li	*li*	w like ue	*ue*
h like k	*k*	w like eu	*eu*
k like ls	*ls*	x like v	*v*
m like w	*uu*	y like ij	*y*

From Mercer, C. D., & Mercer, A. (1985). *Teaching students with learning problems.* Columbus, OH: Charles E. Merrill, p. 429. Reprinted with permission.

available formal assessment measures and then discusses approaches to informal evaluation within this curricular domain.

Formal Assessment

Handwriting assessment has not received a significant amount of attention in education. As Graham (1982) notes, there are three possible reasons why evaluation has been either nonexistent or at least nonsystematic: Most programs are designed to instruct but not to evaluate; the subject has received limited attention in research and training; and standardized procedures have not been readily available.

In spite of this dearth of information on assessment and specifically of instruments for appraisal, there are nevertheless several tools available for use in regular and special education that can contribute to the evaluative process.

Zaner-Bloser Evaluation Scale.   The *Zaner-Bloser Evaluation Scales* (Zaner-Bloser, 1979) are a series of graded writing samples that can be used as a basis for comparison with a child's writing. At succeeding grade levels (1–8), the Scales present five examples of writing which represent excellent, good, average, fair, and poor levels of competence respectively. Ratings of these examples were arrived at through observation of the following elements of handwriting: letter formation, verticality (for manuscript) or slant (for cursive), spacing, alignment and proportion, and line quality. Samples taken from the sixth grade evaluation scale are presented in Figure 6.3; similar samples are available for manuscript form for grades 1 through 2 and cursive for grades 3 through 8. The evaluator's task is to select the sample that most closely matches the performance of the individual student.

Test of Written Language.   Another formal instrument available for the assessment of handwriting as well as other areas of written language is the *Test of Written Language* (TOWL) (Hammill & Larsen, 1983). The revised TOWL includes six subtests, with the one concerning handwriting based on the evaluation of the penmanship exhibited by the student in a spontaneous writing sample. This subtest scale has acknowledged linkage with the Zaner-Bloser scale and similarly presents writing samples for comparative purposes. Samples are available only for cursive writing on the TOWL. Scoring is based on the absolute criterion of the writing samples (Figure 6.4). Each student's performance, regardless of age, is rated from 1 to 10, with average skill at a given age determined through reference to the normative tables.

Both of these tools obviously rely on the use of rating scales for assessing writing. Although scales can be very useful in providing a

FIGURE 6.3. Zaner-Bloser Grade 5 Evaluation Scale

Example 1—Excellent for Grade Six

The North Wind lives
in a cold, dark cave
in the land of ice-and-snow.
The East Wind lives
in a roofless cell
through which the bright stars glow.

Example 2—Good for Grade Six

The North Wind lives
in a cold, dark cave
in the land of ice-and-snow.
The East Wind lives
in a roofless cell
through which the bright stars glow.

Example 3—Average for Grade Six

The North Wind lives
in a cold, dark cave
in the land of ice-and-snow.
The East Wind lives
in a roofless cell
through which the bright stars glow.

Example 4—Fair for Grade Six

The North Wind lives
in a cold, dark cave
in the land of ice-and snow.
The East Wind lives
in a roofless cell
through which the bright stars glow.

Example 5—Poor for Grade Six

The North Wind lives
in a cold, dark cave
in the land of ice-and-snow.
The East Wind lives
in a roofless cell through
which the bright stars glow.

From *Creative growth with handwriting* (2nd ed.) (1979). Columbus, OH: Zaner-Bloser. Reprinted with permission.

FIGURE 6.4. Rating Scales from the Test of Written Language

Rating 10

Rating 9

Once upon a time there was a mars club around the corner where every day most of the people in my class went to after school at three o'clock every. Soon later on in the year five people had joined. Soon

Rating 8

Rating 7

The first picture is about scientist have notice that the earth is starting to explode. Because the earth is cracking. They got all of the people together because they have notice that there

Rating 6

Rating 5

Once upon a time in a galaxy far away on the planet of Ounbee. Ounbebeen shaken by a series of Ounbee quacks. This planet has a very well advanced science department it claims the planet will be

Rating 4

Rating 3

Once upon a time some space ships landed on some planet were there was elephants, mice, ducks, turtles, pigs and hipptalpatimos and the people started digging halls in the the

Rating 2

Rating 1

onet a time that was is popued fonae meme and the tiny and tiny to git the aila forn aut papod and the was mot art con foune popsone they was not

Rating 0

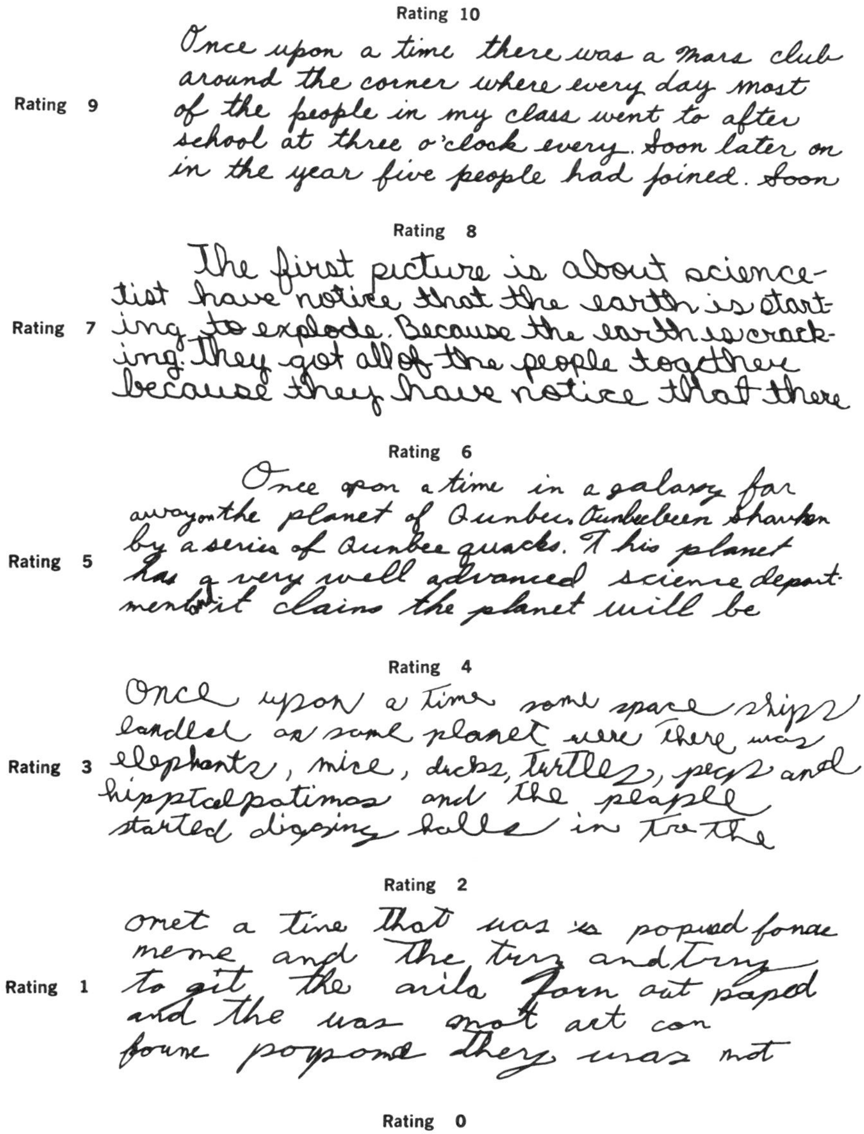

From Hammill, D. D., & Larsen, S. C. (1983). *Test of Written Language.* Austin, TX: PRO-ED, p. 24. Reprinted with permission.

general appraisal of writing proficiency, it is wise to also consider their possible limitations. As Graham (1982) notes, scales "may only be useful for obtaining a rough estimate of handwriting competence or selecting a classroom's best or worst specimens. They should not be used to assess performance on a daily basis or to identify specific handwriting strengths and weaknesses" (p. 37).

Two other recently developed tools are briefly discussed within this section on formal assessment, although each could be as accurately considered informal in nature.

Denver Handwriting Analysis. The *Denver Handwriting Analysis* (DHA) (Anderson, 1983) is described as a "method of handwriting evaluation that offers a detailed analysis of the student's performance and provides results that are relevant to instructional programming" (p. 9). It is intended to serve as a criterion-referenced test for students in grades 3 through 8 and could possibly be extended for use with both older and younger students.

The DHA is presented as a task analysis approach to handwriting assessment and is an alternative to instruments that are essentially only generally concerned with level of legibility. The objectives of the DHA include assessing handwriting across a classroom-relevant multitask format, identifying specific forms of errors that interfere with legibility and efficiency, and translating assessment data into remedial planning. Clearly, the DHA is quite different in purpose from the more global focus of assessment tools such as the Handwriting subtest of the TOWL (Hammill & Larsen, 1983).

The DHA contains five parts: (a) near-point copying, which requires the student to copy a four-line poem; (b) writing the alphabet, which includes two sections for writing the upper case and lower case letters from memory; (c) far-point copying, based on a three-sentence story posted on a wall chart; (d) manuscript-cursive transition, which requires production of cursive letters when presented with their manuscript counterpart; and (e) dictation, which includes directions to students to write sequences of from two to nine letters per line (Polloway, in press-a).

Diagnosis and Remediation of Handwriting Problems. The *Diagnosis and Remediation of Handwriting Problems* (DRHP) (Stott, Moyes, & Henderson, 1985) was designed to assess handwriting deficits as a basis for remedial programming. It is intended as a measure of legibility appropriate for children who have had a minimum of two years of handwriting instruction. The DRHP focuses on the detection of patterns in three types of faults that result in poor legibility or poor performance.

The first type, faults of concept and style, include conceptual errors such as incorrect letter forms and improper joining of letters; inappropriate spacing between or within words; stylistic distractors such as extreme slants or unusual letter size; and slurring, defined as the degeneration of letters (i.e., partial or total elimination). The second part of the DRHP focuses on faults suggestive of perceptual or motor problems, including: inconsistency of slant, inconsistency of letter size, irregular word alignment, random letter distortion, and tremor. The third part, faults of writing position, focuses on diagnostic indicators such as posture, physical disadvantages (e.g., vision defects, compulsive movements), and faults in the way the task is addressed (e.g., impulsivity, haste, overcaution) (Polloway, in press-b).

Informal Assessment

Other than the general assessment of overall competence, handwriting lends itself more readily to informal evaluation. The most effective way to derive educationally useful information is to plan systematic observations of elicited writing samples to ascertain instructional needs as well as to document student improvement. The following discussion focuses on several concerns for informal evaluation.

As noted earlier, for a limited number of students, hand dominance may not be established or at least may not be apparent to the teacher. In such instances, Burns (1980) recommends using an informal screening sequence to determine preferred hand. Burns reiterates the procedures initially suggested by Monroe (1951) and provided in Figure 6.5.

For students who are writing, Otto, McMenemy, and Smith (1973) identified three initial observations that should be considered to begin the process of screening. Each of the three represents a concern of direct relevance for instructional programming.

❑ the student's handwriting is generally of poor quality;

❑ the handwriting is generally acceptable when the student determines the pace but deteriorates when there is pressure to increase pace; and

❑ the student habitually writes at a slow pace.

After initial consideration of these variables, further analysis should concentrate on possible correlates such as poor memory for letters as a source of slow rate or inappropriate pencil grip as a basis for poor quality. Kaminsky and Powers (1981) offer a more comprehensive list of indicators which the reader may wish to consult.

FIGURE 6.5. Determining Hand Dominance

1. Place a pencil on a table before the seated child, vertically in front of him, point of pencil midway between right and left hands. Observe the hand with which he or she grasps it.

2. Have the child put a dot in each square of cross-section (1-inch squares may be mimeographed for an entire class) and count the number he can mark in one minute. Is he or she among the best or the poorest in the class? Does he or she shift handedness during this performance?

3. Have the child repeat the performance with his unpreferred hand. Compare speed and quality with the previous record and with the class. Ambidextrous children are often low in the class in the preferred hand test, but high in the unpreferred-hand test. The quality of work of two hands is more similar than those of the majority of children.

4. Note hand used in pretending to throw a ball.

5. Note hand used in pretending to thread a needle.

6. Note hand used in pretending to comb hair.

7. Note hand used in pretending to brush teeth.

8. Note hand used in pretending to eat.

9. Note hand used in pointing to an object across the room.

From Monroe, M. (1951). *Growing into reading.* New York: Scott, Foresman, p. 50. Reprinted with permission.

At this point in the diagnostic process, assessment should be used to analyze the specific features of writing that interfere with communication. Given again that the focus is on legibility, it is wise to consider the traits that have been identified as most significantly influencing legibility: general neatness, uniform arrangement, well-proportioned and properly formed letters, even alignment of words with proper spacing between them, and regular slant (Graham & Miller, 1980).

To target specific sub-skills, a checklist should be developed to provide for an analysis of possible difficulties. Two examples are provided. The survey presented in Figure 6.6 was developed by Bain (1982) to record and describe various handwriting problems. To use it, teachers would need to select several activities for in-class writing that will generate a set of writing samples to be observed.

The second sample is presented as a progress chart. Given the relative tedium of handwriting instruction, it is wise for teachers to

FIGURE 6.6.   Handwriting Survey

Student Name: Age: Grade:

Hand used: Examiner: Date:

Handwriting skills (if known, both cursive and manuscript) should be compared on the following tasks to determine the nature of the problem and extent of difficulty.

1. Write lower case alphabet
2. Write upper and lower case letters from dictation
3. Write single words from dication
4. Near point copy
5. Far point copy
6. Spontaneous writing
7. Note taking

Organization of the paper: Pencil grip:

Pencil pressure: Position of the paper:

Anchor hand position:

Letter formation: Letter size:

Letter slant: Letter spacing:

Letter alignment:

Word spacing: Word slant:

Omissions: Substitutions: Additions:

Mixed (cursive/manuscript):   Mixed (lower/upper case):

Erasing: Writing over:

Speed: Fluency:

Attention to task:

Student's attitude toward handwriting:

Additional comments:

From Bain, A. M. (1982) Written expression: Assessment and remediation for learning disabled students. *Learning Disabilities, 1*(5), 52. Reprinted with permission.

FIGURE 6.7. Handwriting Progress Chart

Pupil Name _____	Oct.	Dec.	Feb.	April
Letter size and form				
Spacing within words				
Spacing between words				
Spacing between sentences				
Alignment				
Slant				
Line quality				
Letter joinings				
Letter endings				
Margins and arrangement				
Neatness				
Position				
Rate of writing				

Key: X-Deficiency noted
    ✔-Improvement shown
    O-Satisfactory				

From Burns, P. C. (1980). *Assessment and correction of language arts difficulties.* Columbus, OH: Charles E. Merrill, p. 219. Reprinted with permission.

monitor performance so that evidence of improvement can be collected throughout the school year. Figure 6.7, in combination with a record of written permanent products, can be useful for communication with parents and students themselves in addition to providing an evaluative measure for instruction.

FIGURE 6.8. Error Analysis Chart

Problem	Causation	Example
Excess in stroke:		
1. Heaviness	Too much pressure on pencil from the index finger Incorrect writing instrument	nice
2. Lightness	Pencil held too straight Incorrect writing instrument	we
3. Straightness	Arm held too close to the body Finger too close to pencil nib Pencil guided by index finger only Incorrect paper position Fingers too stiff Writing tool held too tightly	Susan
4. Slant	Writing too close to the body Fingers too far from writing tool point Incorrect paper position Misunderstands direction of stroke	come
5. Size/width	Lacks understanding of proportion Hand and arm movement too slow Inflexible movements	house
6. Spacing	Pencil moves too fast or too slow Misunderstands purpose of spacing (e.g., between letters, words, etc.)	c ar

From Cohen, S. B., & Plaskon, S. P. (1980). *Language arts for the mildly handicapped.* Columbus, OH: Charles E. Merrill, p. 250. Reprinted with permission.

One other source of informal diagnostic information can be an understanding of the common stroke errors that students make and their possible causes. Each of the six samples presented in Figure 6.8 can have implications for specific remedial instructional procedures.

TEACHING HANDWRITING SKILLS

Handwriting is commonly taught in virtually all elementary classrooms and in the majority of special classes at this school level as well. Traditionally, two characteristics have been common in instruction: Programming has been implemented as a large group activity, and the time spent on instruction has typically been recommended to be approximately 10 to 15 minutes per day (Wiederholt, Hammill, & Brown, 1983). While the time frame should be generally appropriate for most children, the emphasis on group instruction must be reconsidered for exceptional children, with individualization often necessary to meet the needs of these students.

In the development of programs in writing, several assumptions bear consideration. Morsink (1984), in reviewing the limited existing literature on handwriting for handicapped learners, concluded that:

❏ teachers must realize that some students will never develop beautiful writing, thus teaching should proceed accordingly with reduced objectives;

❏ consistent feedback is the key to continued improvement by students; and

❏ continued failure, especially when paired with criticism, will not lead to improvement.

In the succeeding section we discuss instructional methods, materials, and considerations for the full sequence of skills within this curricular domain. Attention is given to prewriting concerns, beginning writing, manuscript and cursive writing, and alteratives to writing. Special topics including left-handedness and computer applications conclude the chapter.

Prewriting Skills

Prior to the development of legible handwriting skills, every child needs to have achieved two general objectives. The first is the need to establish a preferred hand for writing as well as for other related motor acts. The second purpose associated with the prewriting stage is coordinating vision with specific fine motor skills.

In order to achieve these two goals, a variety of skills have typically been suggested as readiness for the acquisition of actual handwriting skills. The following list summarizes some of the common activities that have been utilized at this stage.

❏ manipulation of objects such as beads, nuts, and bolts

❏ tracing of objects with the index finger in sand

❏ placing rings on a long rod according to size and/or color

❏ manipulation of scissors for cutting paper and cloth

❏ putting together various types of puzzles

❏ crayon and finger painting

❏ drawing simple pictures

❏ placing forms in proper holes in form boxes

❏ building with tinker toys or similar objects

❏ connecting dots and completing figures

❏ playing jacks and other similar games such as pick-up sticks

It is important to note several things about this list of activities. First, some of the activities are clearly of importance simply for their own worth (e.g., cutting with scissors) and thus may have merit regardless of their relationship to writing. On the other hand, given that the activities do not require that true writing skills be applied, it must be noted that there is no empirical support that these types of exercises will assist in the refinement of existing handwriting skills. It can be argued to the contrary that the focus on nonwriting fine motor skill development will simply take time away from the direct instruction of writing skills. Another caution concerns the use of prewriting activities for those children who have no skills or only a primitive ability level. Again, an overemphasis on fine motor skills in many cases will not be beneficial. It is important for teachers to realize that the handwriting process itself does provide fine motor practice and thus accomplishes both linguistically relevant goals in the area of writing as well as the motoric goal of enhancing fine motor coordination. As Hammill (1982) notes, so-called prerequisite skills can be naturally developed in many cases simply through directing students to write letters and words rather than through extensive prewriting instruction.

Beginning Writing

The beginning writing stage is focused on the refinement of fine motor skills into coordinated communicative ability. As such, the initial concerns for instruction are most often on the specific motor acts that may present difficulty to the individual beginning writer.

In order to confirm a student's readiness to learn to write, Burns (1980) listed the following items as worthy of consideration. The child who is ready to write:

1. Exhibits an easy three-finger grasp near the end of the pencil.
2. Maintains a reasonable sitting and writing position.
3. Can copy a model of a triangle with three sharp angles and no openings.
4. Can draw a picture of a person with four body parts: head, body, arms, and legs.
5. Can copy a word, such as his or her own name, from a model card.
6. Proceeds basically from left-to-right sequence in writing.
7. Can copy a common word from the chalkboard. (pp. 212–213)

Consistent with the above discussion on prewriting skills, the teacher should use these sources of information as a basis for designing appropriate instruction rather than as an absolute criterion for determining whether or not to proceed with instruction.

From a task analytic prospective, the process of determining which components of the writing act can create difficulties should begin with consideration of reaching for the writing utensil, grasping the writing utensil, slanting the utensil in the appropriate angle, and arranging fingers around the utensil. For many children, especially those who are young and/or developmentally delayed, the greatest problem that they will have at this stage is with the correct grip on the writing utensil. For this reason a variety of prosthetic aids have been used to facilitate appropriate grip. These aids include the larger primary-sized pencils common to many kindergarten and first grade classrooms, the wrapping of the pencil with tape, the use of a multisided large pencil, and the adaptation of a standard pencil with a Hoyle gripper—a three-sided rubber or plastic device that encourages the student to place two fingers and the thumb in the proper position. It should be noted that Graham and Miller's (1980) review of research on handwriting instruction indicates that it is not necessary in many cases to modify the writing utensils through the use of such prosthetic tools. Norton (1980) suggests that, given the absence of supportive research for adapted pencils, students should be allowed to select whichever size is most comfortable for them. However, since most of the handwriting data base has not been generated from problem learners, it is important that teachers consciously assess the grip of individual students who are experiencing problems in order to determine what difficulties are contributing and whether these adaptations are warranted. Anecdotal data obtained on classrooms of elementary-aged mildly handicapped children indicate a prevalence

FIGURE 6.9. Story Statements Corresponding to Manuscript Strokes

1. Here is the flag. Can you draw the pole?
2. The road is very long and flat. Draw a road.
3. The teeter-totter goes up and down. First make it go this way ⬂ and then that way ⬀ .
4. The sun is nice and round. Draw the sun.
5. Sometimes the moon looks like this. ((

   Can you make half of that moon, (?
6. There are times when the moon looks as though it faces the other way 🌙 . Now make half of this moon) .

From Cohen, S. B., & Plaskon, S. P. (1980). *Language arts for the mildly handicapped.* Columbus, OH: Charles E. Merrill, p. 244. Reprinted with permission.

of over 20% of students experiencing difficulty in assuming the proper writing grip.

The next consideration in the transition to true writing is the integration of visual-motor skills into actual writing. An activity that may be useful for some children is an opportunity to engage in some directionality exercises. The purpose for these activities is to reinforce the concept of left to right progression. Guided exercises where students are asked to draw lines from left to right can be offered in a variety of ways to reinforce this skill.

Another activity to encourage beginning writing is the introduction of specific shapes and strokes by focusing on the most common forms that students need to learn to write legibly. These forms include straight lines, curved lines, diagonal lines, and circles. Again, while the strokes can be taught in isolation from actual letters, the integration of instruction on strokes with instruction on specific letter forms will be more likely to reinforce writing progress. Cohen and Plaskon (1980) present several excellent examples of single story statements that correspond to the fundamental manuscript strokes (Figure 6.9).

As students are becoming ready for writing and are refining their fine motor skills, a progression can be followed to facilitate this process.

For example, students may first begin with writing exercises on the chalkboard with no lines to restrict letter and word formation. Subsequently, the use of newsprint may be appropriate for some children, with the student moving from writing in unlined fashion initially and later following the lines of the columns on the paper; crayons or markers would be most appropriate for this exercise. The next step in the sequence would logically be wide-lined paper and standard utensils. It is the decision of the teacher as to whether this sequence needs to be followed with individual students or whether they can forgo these procedures and begin writing on regular paper. The above sequence, however, does provide options if needed for specific students who experience difficulty in adjusting to the restrictions of standard utensils and standard lined paper.

Manuscript Instruction

For the majority of students in school, initial instruction focuses on manuscript writing. Although some controversy exists about the benefits of manuscript versus cursive as an initial strategy and although some programs that combine these two styles have gained popularity, most teachers will be following a curriculum that has an initial emphasis on manuscript writing. A subsequent section in this chapter discusses the relative merits of beginning instruction in manuscript or cursive form.

The most effective approach to teaching specific strokes, letters, and words is one in which teachers follow a consistent sequence of presentation. Most programs are based on the acknowledgment that these forms are probably best taught in isolation but that opportunities must be provided and reinforced for their use in the context of actual writing exercises. Varied, yet sequential, activities are more appropriate for the acquisition of letter forms (Cohen & Plaskon, 1980; Fauke, Burnett, Powers, & Sulzer-Azaroff, 1973; Graham & Miller, 1980).

Graham and Miller (1980) provide an excellent review of effective instructional techniques that facilitate letter formation in beginning writers. The following discussion represents an adaptation of the specific steps these writers presented for handwriting instruction. As in virtually all specialized instruction in most curricular areas, the first step is based on teacher *demonstration* of the formation of specific letters. During this phase, the student should be observing the specific strokes involved in the formation of the letter. Students' attention should be directed to the *distinctive features* of specific letters and to how they compare and/or contrast with letters previously learned. As the student begins to actually transcribe the letters, the teacher should use the strategies of *prompting* and *tracing* to facilitate the student's task. These strategies can include manual guidance of the student's hand during writing, directionality arrows included within the word to be written, and other forms of cues such as color or grids. By using tracing, the tactile sense is introduced and may yield increased effectiveness with individual students; letters made of felt and letters written in sand or clay can also serve as helpful tactile adjuncts.

Once the student no longer has need for intrusive prompting by teacher and tracing exercises, letter and word formation instruction becomes a function of *copying*. For many students this includes copying from *near-point* (i.e., from a paper on the student's desk) followed by *far-point* (i.e., from the blackboard). Throughout the copying stage, and as a transition into writing from memory, students should be encouraged to engage in *self-instruction* by describing the letter and verbalizing to themselves what writing procedures they are following.

Once a letter can be written from memory, there is a need for *continued repetition* of the form to ensure acquisition and enhance maintenance. Finally, *corrective feedback* from the teacher, *extrinsic reinforcement*, and/or *self-correction* strategies can be used to ensure that the letter is retained and that increased legibility is effected.

Manuscript instruction requires the selection of a logical sequence of letters to be presented. These can be grouped in a variety of ways. An example of a possible grouping of lower case and upper case manuscript letters is presented in Figure 6.10.

Cursive Writing

Once the student has made appropriate progress in acquiring competence in the formation of manuscript letters, transition to cursive is begun, usually in the third grade in most school divisions. When individual decisions to transfer are made, indicators of readiness include manuscript proficiency, ability to write all letters from memory, and self-initiated imitation of cursive forms linked to an apparent desire to learn that style (Mandell & Gold, 1984).

The switch in focus to cursive instruction should stress the key aspects of the style that will afford smooth transition for the learner. Among the characteristics of cursive that should be discussed and illustrated for the student are positioning of the paper, writing utensil staying on the paper throughout the writing of individual words, all letters starting at the baseline, establishment of a basic left to right rhythm, appropriate slant to the right, connection of most letters, and spaces allowed only between words. The student should be encouraged to begin with basic manuscript strokes and letters which can evolve respectively into cursive forms and letters. For example, the word *cat* in

FIGURE 6.10. Manuscript Letters Instructional Sequence

A. Lower case

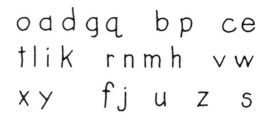

B. Upper case

From Polloway, E. A., Payne, J. S., Patton, J. R., & Payne, R. S. (1985). *Strategies for teaching retarded and special needs learners.* Columbus, OH: Charles E. Merrill, pp. 269–270. Reprinted with permission.

manuscript form is very similar to its cursive counterpart and thus presents a good beginning point for cursive instruction. By stressing similarities in strokes, the visual memory demands of learning a new style will be somewhat lessened. Figure 6.11 provides an illustration of a transitional alphabet that can assist in the introduction of cursive letters.

FIGURE 6.11. Manuscript to Cursive: Transitional Letters

From Anderson, P. S. (1972). *Language skills in elementary education,* New York: Macmillan, p. 189. Reprinted with permission.

The instructional procedures discussed in the previous section on manuscript writing are equally valid for cursive instruction. In particular, given the loops and flourishes of many letters and the unique forms of specific letters, attention to distinctive graphic features will become even more critical. Obviously, the major difference is in the instructional

FIGURE 6.12. Cursive Letters Instructional Sequence

A. Lower case

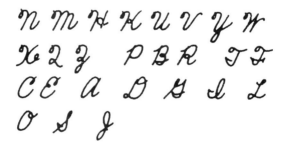

B. Upper case

From Polloway, E. A., Payne, J. S., Patton, J. R., & Payne, R. S. (1985). *Strategies for teaching retarded and special needs learners.* Columbus, OH: Charles E. Merrill, pp. 269–270. Reprinted with permission.

sequence followed for the introduction of letters. Again, there is no proven system that needs to be followed in cursive instruction. The sequence presented in Figure 6.12 presents one alternative to sequencing both lower and upper case letters.

Maintenance, Proficiency, and Generalization

Regardless of whether instruction has focused on manuscript or cursive writing, there will be a need for instructional procedures beyond the acquisition stage of learning. Several approaches have been developed that can increase the likelihood of maintenance of skills learned, increase proficiency in terms of legibility, and promote generalization from the handwriting program to appropriate penmanship within written compositions and other language products.

One technique, originally reported by Lovitt (1975), is called *selective checking*. This approach is most appropriate for refinement in formation of individual letters and/or words that have previously been taught to students in either manuscript or cursive form. The approach is tied to regular, preferably daily, writing assignments such as in-class themes or dictations. Using selective checking, the teacher selects a specific letter to be evaluated at the end of a given daily assignment; students typically would not be informed as to the selection prior to task completion. A model is provided to the student with an inherent established criterion as to what constitutes acceptable legibility. At the end of the assignment, a quick review is made of each of the specific examples of the letter-of-day with ongoing written work. Illegibility then is used as a basis for assigning additional practice exercises, while correct formation of the letter can become the basis for reinforcement.

The selective checking approach could be used across various ability levels in handwriting. Initially the teacher can select which lower case or upper case letters might be indicated. Later, short words of a specified length (i.e., three letters), longer words (e.g., six letters), and perhaps specific, common words might provide focus (e.g., *the*, *was*, *to*).

Contingency management programs can also be useful for the development of handwriting proficiency. Reinforcement schedules based on tangible rewards or on free time and activities can be helpful in encouraging students to improve their legibility (Hopkins, Schutte, & Garton, 1971; Salzburg, Wheeler, Devar, & Hopkins, 1971).

Success of any maintenance, proficiency, or generalization program will ultimately be based on the active involvement of the students themselves. Therefore, teachers should move in the direction of self-regulation as the most effective long-term procedure to follow. In the case of writing, appropriate procedures would include self-monitoring of letter or word formation, self-evaluation of how the individual letter word compares to the established criterion, and ultimately self-reinforcement for successful performance. Several procedures have been reported in the literature.

Kosiewicz, Hallahan, Lloyd, and Graves (1982) reported on the efficacy of self-instructional and self-correction procedures with a 10-year-old learning disabled boy. Their procedures were subsequently presented as a teaching tactic by Lovitt (1984). The program is based on two copying tasks: one from words in isolation and the other from a paragraph for self-instruction. The student was encouraged to use the following procedures (these would incorporate assistance for spelling as well):

> (a) Say aloud the word to be written. (b) Say the first syllable. (c) Name the letters in the first syllable three times. (d) Write the first syllable and say each letter as it is written. (e) Repeat steps b through d for each succeeding syllable. (These instructions may be written on a flash card and kept on the student's desk.) (Lovitt, 1984, p. 217)

For self-correction, the student in Kosiewicz et al.'s (1982) research was trained to correct his own errors from a previous day's writing before beginning a new assignment. This was accomplished first with teacher monitoring, eventually shifting to less frequent evaluation accompanied by periodic praise for good writing and accurate self-management.

Graham (1983) also reported on a self-instructional procedure. The student was trained, following the teacher's lead, to verbally describe letters as the student made them, thus attending to each step in letter formation. Graham (1983) reported moderate success but indicated a need for further study of the amount of training needed by individual students and for an analysis of the interaction between self-verbalization and specific motor movements.

One major problem with maintenance and proficiency is the degree of motivation that students, especially adolescents, may have for producing legible writing. To increase motivation, Davis and Miller (1983) stress that students need to have reasons to learn to write and that this can be best accomplished through connections with daily living skills and pursuits. Some examples offered by Davis and Miller (1983) include writing job applications, developing an address book, keeping schedules of upcoming times and places for social events, and writing recipes for cooking. They also encourage teachers to consider *calligraphy*. Calligraphy can be defined as "the act of creating print that possesses specific style and beauty. The word comes from 'Kallos' meaning beautiful, and 'graphein' meaning to write" (D'Angelo, 1982, p. 23). As D'Angelo notes, calligraphy can have a positive effect on the quality of writing by improving legibility and assisting students in developing a personally unique handwriting style. The artistic qualities of calligraphy encourage neatness as students develop a skill that can be both practical and pleasurable.

Finally, a decision should be made as to whether direct instruction of handwriting skills should be continued or whether students are ready for maintenance and proficiency programs. Towle (1978) has designed a useful set of assessment tools that provide objective measures of legibility and speed as a basis for such decisions. For example, she identifies the following criterion for far-point copying: 40 legibly formed letters in correct sequence per minute with two or fewer illegibilities. Performance above criterion would indicate need for maintenance, with below-criterion performance indicative of the need for further instruction and/or directed practice.

Cursive versus Manuscript

In education, and specifically in the field of learning disabilities, there has been a continuing debate over the relative merits of manuscript versus cursive writing as an initial handwriting style. Of course, the usual procedure in schools, as discussed earlier, has been for instruction to begin in manuscript writing, with a transition to cursive made at approximately the second or third grade level. However, although this is traditional practice, it is not a process that is based on empirical evidence. Very limited data are available on handicapped students, and thus judgments are likely to be based on custom or on professional perspective or bias.

Individuals who argue that cursive alone should be taught to handicapped students (again, primarily learning disabled students) base their arguments on the following:

❑ Cursive writing encourages rhythm in writing.

❑ Cursive encourages a view of words as wholes and coincidentally eliminates many of the problems that may be created in spacing within words.

❑ Cursive eliminates problems with reversals.

❑ Cursive emphasizes left to right directionality.

❑ If cursive is taught initially, there is no need for transfer and for learning divergent letter forms.

❑ Cursive is required or at least encouraged for personal signatures.

❑ There are social reasons to encourage cursive writing, and many students will consider it to be "grown-up" writing.

❑ Cursive is consistent with integration goals in that it will probably be the preferred writing form in the regular classroom beyond the third grade.

❏ Cursive is a more automatic form of writing and hence may provide fewer distractions from the actual communicative, conceptual act of writing.

On the other hand, equally committed manuscript proponents argue that problems in transition to cursive writing could best be handled by teaching manuscript alone. Such proponents present the following arguments:

❏ Manuscript writing tends to be easier to learn due to the simpler strokes that are necessary.

❏ Manuscript is closer to the printed word and provides reciprocal reinforcement for reading and writing skills.

❏ Teaching manuscript alone eliminates the necessity for transfer.

❏ Manuscript tends to be more legible for many individuals. At least in some cases, manuscript can be equally as fast as cursive, although the issue of speed has not been resolved in the literature (Early et al., 1976).

❏ Cursive can result in different forms for the same letter, while manuscript is consistent across letters.

❏ Manuscript writing is likely to be developmentally easier for children to acquire (Barbe, Milone, & Wasylyk, 1983).

Certainly, discussion regarding cursive versus manuscript writing is most critical for children at the elementary level, since older students will probably decide on their own which style to use. For special educators, the issue is often moot, since most students will already have been taught cursive writing prior to the referral for special services. Therefore, as Otto et al. (1973) note, the question is not whether manuscript should be taught—it already has been in most cases—but when and if transition to cursive should be made. It is logical to conclude that students who have had a great deal of difficulty learning the manuscript alphabet will have an equal amount of difficulty learning cursive; this would seem to argue for the acquisition of one style that is functional for the student rather than placing on the student the additional burden of learning a second style. On the other hand, if an individual has had serious problems with the reversal of letters and words, the shift in instruction to the cursive style may indeed be warranted.

In recent years, the cursive versus manuscript argument has been diverted due to the development of other options that acknowledge the relative merits of both forms. Several of these alternative approaches are discussed in the following paragraphs.

Mixed Scripts. Consistent with common practice in writing, Mullins, Joseph, Turner, Zawadski, and Saltzman (1972) suggest that instruction for disabled learners should focus on a combination form. Such an approach could be successful, since it would take advantage of the primary benefits of both manuscript and cursive writing. Essentially, their mixed script is a manuscript form with lines drawn to simulate cursive, thus enhancing rhythm while avoiding spacing problems. All capital letters are in print form, and the flourishes, loops, and other unnecessary strokes of cursive writing have been eliminated. Readers interested in reviewing the actual model script should consult the journal article or Polloway and Smith (1982).

Several other programs based on mixed manuscript and cursive forms have also been developed. Hagin's (1983) *Write—Right or Left* program uses manuscript letters as a lead-in to a simplified cursive style. Connections between letters are taught as natural movements to the next vertical downstroke. Hagin (1983) claims that the program combines the legibility benefits of manuscript with the speed of cursive. Finally, Connell (1983) recommends a return to Chancery Cursive, the traditional writing style of western civilization, again simplified to be more similar to manuscript.

D'Nealian Program. Another program that acknowledges the value of blending cursive and manuscript forms is the D'Nealian approach. Developed by Thurber and Jordan (1978), the D'Nealian approach attempts to make handwriting a more pleasant experience for students while providing classroom teachers a more logical teaching program.

The premise of the program is that handwriting should be taught as a continuous skill progression (Thurber, 1983). Thurber believes the circle-and-stick method of teaching handwriting is improper, since beginners do not have the hand-eye coordination required to put circles and sticks together into letters. Traditional handwriting methods also overlook development of a flowing stroke, rhythm, and slant; these are stressed in the D'Nealian Program. Letters are taught in sequences of groups of letters with similarity of stroke (e.g., *a, o, c, e*). Beyond minimum standards of form size and slant, the student is allowed a great deal of flexibility in writing style.

The D'Nealian program is suitable for learners at the point of readiness through eighth grade, and the authors believe the program is also well suited for learning disabled students. The greatest disadvantage of this method is that a child must be taught entirely with the program; the child who does not have prerequisite or final training will be at a disadvantage. The benefits of the program are the logical progression of skills which make the transfer to cursive writing easily and the great degree of flexibility for the individual learner.

Left-Handedness

The special demands that writing makes upon left-handed children and adolescents warrant the attention of teachers. Anyone who has ever gone through a simulation of writing with the left hand has learned to appreciate the special problems that confront the left-handed writer—having to cover their writing as they write, risking the smudging of the ink, and having to push rather than pull the utensil. Because approximately 10% of the general population is left-handed—and this number may be higher in special education programs—teachers should be prepared to make modifications in instruction for individual students. As Rubin (1975) notes, teachers must realize that "writing with the left hand is strictly a teaching problem, not a pupil problem. Where teachers understand how to help these beginning writers, pupils write successfully, with great speed and ease" (p. 332).

Two excellent sources available to teachers who are working with left-handed students are Harrison (1981) and Graham and Miller (1980). Some of the modifications these authors suggest to facilitate instruction are included in the following list:

❏ Group left-handed students together to facilitate instruction appropriate to their needs.

❏ Provide a left-handed model (e.g., a teacher, aide, or peer) who writes legibly.

❏ Direct students to grasp the utensil approximately 1 to 1½ inches from the end and to point it toward their left shoulder.

❏ Select a proper position for the paper (see Graham and Miller, 1980, for a diagram of alternatives).

❏ Provide writing exercises that encourage the student to practice sliding the utensil toward the right.

❏ Provide a model cursive script illustrating the preferred vertical backward slant as an option to the forward slant advocated for right-handed writers (see Figure 6.13 for an example).

❏ Encourage students to eliminate any loops and flourishes that may impede the writing process.

FIGURE 6.13. Model Cursive Alphabet for Left Handers

From Harrison, S. (1981). Open letter from a left handed teacher: Some sinistral ideas on the teaching of handwriting. *Teaching Exceptional Children, 13,* 119. Copyright 1981 by Stephanie Harrison. Reprinted with permission.

❏ Consider the special needs of left-handed writers for equipment such as desks and scissors.

Technical Alternatives

In addition to the basic approaches to handwriting which have been previously discussed, increasing attention has been given to nonwriting alternatives. These options (e.g., typing) can provide alternatives to the complex motoric demands of writing for the student with severe writing problems. Such nonwriting alternatives can also motivate reluctant learners who may find the physical aspects of written communication difficult or intimidating. Bain (1982) notes that the possibilities for compensatory strategies in writing are limitless; she did, however, offer these two cautions:

❏ Compensatory approaches should not be seen as substitutes for carefully designed programs of remediation; and

❏ regardless of compensatory procedure, instructional time and supervision must be provided to ensure mastery.

The discussion that follows focuses on the use of typing as well as on possible computer applications. In addition, Chapter 11 provides some other technical alternatives for visually handicapped and hearing impaired students.

Typing. One popular alternative to writing is typing. It has been used as an alternative or adjunct to handwriting for learning disabled, sensory impaired, moderately handicapped, and slow learning students (Calhoun, 1985). A variety of advantages have been reported for typing, including legibility, promotion of a responsive and reinforcing work environment, provision of practice for letter recognition, transfer of benefits to reading, motoric ease of production, potential for speed, and appearance of the final product (Calhoun, 1985). Typing has clear benefits for instructional demands at the secondary and postsecondary levels as well as in job-related duties. In addition, it offers handicapped students the opportunity to develop a product that has essentially the same physical qualities as that of any other person; the benefits of this fact for job acquisition are apparent.

Computer Applications. Computer usage has applications for disabled students in providing alternative forms of expressive output and in word processing. With reference to the former, the opportunity for a complete bypass of writing can be of critical importance to individuals with very serious motor problems, especially those with physical handicaps. The uses of computers to provide a mode for communication for severely handicapped learners are further discussed in Chapters 9 and 10.

Word processing represents an advance over typing in terms of the capabilities it offers the user for constructing written expressive communication. In addition to the advantages previously noted for typing, word processing can also offer advanced potential for editing written products and for developing multiple copies of the same or slightly revised text. Hasselbring (1985) succinctly describes word processing and summarizes the benefits of its use for students:

> A word processing program is an electronic word handler: words are typed into the computer through the keyboard and displayed on the monitor as they are being typed. When the text is complete, the computer can save it permanently on a disk and/or type it on paper using a printer.

As Hagen (1983) noted, written language skills for the handicapped are among the most difficult to acquire. They include the tedious effort that goes into the organization of thoughts, the laborious task of writing them down, searching for the right words, revising and rewriting. Revision often means copying over and over again. Revising, reworking, and recopying, can inhibit anyone, but to handicapped learners they may present an almost insurmountable barrier that can crush the process of composition and expression.

With a word processing program many of these writing barriers can be eliminated. A word processor allows changes in the written text with simple editing commands. Words can be inserted and deleted, sentences and paragraphs rearranged, punctuation changed, and spelling checked. Rewriting an assignment means altering only affected words and sentences, not retyping the entire assignment. The completed text can then be permanently saved to disk and printed out in a clear, readable form (p. 166).

Programs such as the Bank Street Writer offer children a chance to utilize word processing with a minimum of the complexity often found in business-oriented word processors.

BEST PRACTICES

While some curricular domains such as reading can boast of empirically validated methodologies that can be matched to the needs of individuals or to groups of learners, this luxury is not available in the area of handwriting. Although the discussion of instruction in this chapter has drawn from the existing literature, there are clearly significant limitations that must be acknowledged. Of particular note is the fact that virtually all of the empirical research available in handwriting has included only students within regular programs. The literature on exceptional students essentially is restricted to anecdotal reports or general observations. In spite of these deficiencies, it is nevertheless possible to derive some central considerations that represent best practices for instruction for handicapped and remedial learners in handwriting.

Primary attention must be given to legibility rather than to other quality indicators that reflect greater concerns for the aesthetics of writing. Therefore, instruction should focus on those specific skills that foster effective communication. The classic study reported by Quant (1946) provides some direction for this instruction: Legibility is most dependent on good letter formation; thus, this aspect of writing warrants the greatest attention of teachers. Of secondary importance are compactness in style (referring to a reduction in spacing) and regularity of slant. On the other hand, the weight of the line and the evenness of the alignment are factors that are not critical to legibility and are thus of less instructional value.

Readiness presents a paradox to the teacher. While obviously not all children are developmentally ready to begin formal instruction in writing, most children will profit more from writing instruction than from nonvalidated training in prerequisite skills. The most defensible position to take is that once students have established a preferred hand (or at least have developed motoric competence in one hand), have acquired the necessary fine motor skills to grasp the utensil, and possess the necessary cognitive abilities to understand the communication act, then time spent on actual writing instruction will be far more productive than that spent on nonlinguistic fine motor

training exercises. The needs of students who have more serious difficulties with motor demands can be met better through adaptations in the utensil, the grip, the writing surface, or in the assignment rather than stressing prerequisites.

In the absence of empirical support of either cursive or manuscript as an initial approach to writing, the teacher is best advised to follow the traditional sequence practiced in most schools—beginning with manuscript and then shifting to cursive. However, to simplify the transition for handicapped learners, the adoption of a mixed script as an alternative to standard cursive should be seriously considered. Given the fact that most adolescents and adults will evolve their own style regardless of instruction, and given that this style in many cases will be likely to contain elements of cursive and manuscript, there can be tangible benefits to teaching the modified form and forgoing the emphasis on standard cursive style.

Finally, the importance of motivation should not be overlooked. Educators should select methodologies and modify curriculum in order to present programs that will increase the likelihood of positive responding by students. The use of free time or other contingencies for accurate writing, the availability of background music during writing period, the emphasis on writing for functional purposes, and the use of typewriters, word processors, and other supplementary compensatory tools and technologies can all contribute to an enhanced attitude toward written communication.

7

SPELLING

$\mathbf{S}$pelling is a valued skill within our society, and good spellers are accorded respect as intelligent persons. Although intellectual ability and spelling ability are not parallel, it is recognized that most problem learners have difficulty spelling. In fact, spelling has been cited as the most evident problem of learning disabled adults, presenting itself in 80% of the cases (Bookman, 1984; Fraueheim, 1978). Spelling deficiencies have recently been examined as evidence of problems in general cognitive development and of linguistic problem solving, emphasizing the link between observed spelling performance and underlying learning problems.

The demands of the spelling process, which require the speller to *discriminate, recall,* and *reproduce* an exact letter sequence, are among the learning traits often identified as areas of difficulty for learning disabled, mildly mentally retarded, and emotionally disturbed students. Mildly handicapped learners are frustrated in their attempts to spell not only by their own learning deficiencies but also by the numerous phoneme-grapheme inconsistencies in the English language. Since there usually is only one way to spell any particular word, all other attempts, even close approximations, must be considered incorrect.

The inconsistencies in the language reflect historical and geographical influences. Our Anglo-Saxon ancestors were not particularly concerned with regularity. In fact, before the advent of printing, spelling

---

Portions of this chapter have appeared previously in Cohen, S. B., & Plaskon, S. P. (1980). *Language arts for the mildly handicapped.* Columbus, OH: Charles E. Merrill, pp. 321–360.

the same word differently was an acceptable practice. Popular use of the printing process brought with it the need to standardize the language form for the common reader. The practical demands of printing a common language form created a need for a regularity in English spelling which persists today.

The student of English orthography must meet the requirements of acceptable spelling in order to communicate in written language. The question of whether English orthography follows a generally consistent pattern with predictable grapheme-phoneme associations is often debated. Hanna and colleagues examined the 3,000 most frequently used words in children's writings and found that the grapheme-phoneme associations were consistent almost 80% of the time (Moore, 1951). In a later study, Hanna expanded his research to include 17,000 words. Again, the results showed a high percentage of consistency when phonological factors such as position in syllables, internal constraints, and stress are considered (Hodges & Rudolf, 1966). Despite Hanna's work, many language experts question the spelling consistency of the language, and, therefore, the search for the appropriate instructional approach continues.

The consistency of grapheme-phoneme relationships provides stability in spelling of both familiar and unfamiliar words. Yet, due to the numerous phonetic possibilities for spelling most words, the correct spelling of a word can only be assured after examination of the word pattern. Revisualization, the ability to reproduce a spelling pattern after it has been seen, is a significant aspect of the spelling process. Yet educators and language experts have continually debated whether spelling competence can be achieved through persistent use of spelling generalizations (i.e., rules). More recently, attention has been given to the developmental aspects of learning to spell as learners increase their orthographic knowledge.

We believe that spelling is a developmental task and that instruction for remedial learners should be based on a combined approach offering the gradual introduction and accumulation of necessary vocabulary as well as the incorporation of the most useful generalizations. Regularities of sound-to-letter relationships that the mildly handicapped learner can efficiently learn should be taught to promote spelling independence. However, beyond formal spelling instruction, emphasis must be given to daily language participation, allowing each learner to observe, produce, and correct spelling words.

WHAT IS SPELLING?

Spelling a word is a complex act involving the interaction of several skills. The definition of spelling relates to the recognition, recall, and

FIGURE 7.1. The Spelling Process

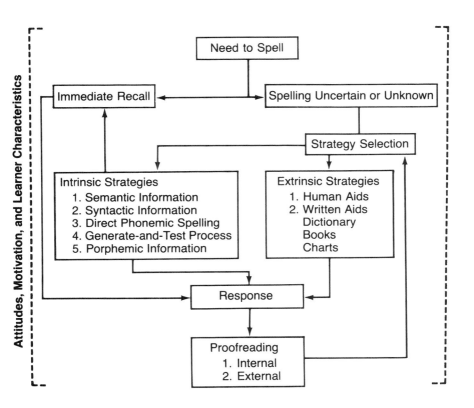

From Graham, S., & Miller, L. (1979). Spelling research and practices: A unified approach. *Focus on Exceptional Children.* *12*(2), Reprinted with permission of Love Publishing Company.

reproduction of correct letter sequences, while the process of spelling includes motivation to spell, intrinsic and extrinsic strategies to generate letter patterns, responding either orally or in writing, and proofreading techniques (Graham & Miller, 1979). The relationship among these components is illustrated in Figure 7.1. Spellers do not always use all the intrinsic and extrinsic strategies available to them when producing a spelling word. The task of spelling instruction for problem learners is to help the speller access the most effective strategy at any one time.

SPELLING GOALS

Mildly handicapped learners need to learn to spell the words they will use in practical everyday situations during their school years and as adults working in the mainstream of society. Spelling should not be considered an academic subject in its own right but rather an essential tool subject to the broader area of written expression. Although often relegated to a brief isolated period of study during the academic day, spelling is a skill that can and should be incorporated into the general writing program.

The major goal of a spelling program for exceptional students is to develop writers who will not make themselves conspicuous through spelling errors. Although a good number of spelling errors would be necessary before writing becomes unreadable, the frequency and type of spelling errors made by the writer influence the reader's acceptance of the message as well as his or her view of the writer.

Since spelling is a learned skill, it follows that it is one that is amendable by instruction. Those students whose written work is free of spelling errors can concentrate on sequencing, clarity, and expressiveness and as a result have a better chance for positive achievement. A writer who is able to spell without too much difficulty will be aided by a better self-concept, greater ease of communication, and more efficient acquisition of related language arts skills. Cohen and Plaskon (1980) list three basic objectives of the spelling program:

1. To accurately spell the most frequently used words that the child needs to write now and in the future.

2. To develop self-correction skills for adjusting spelling errors.

3. To develop the ability to locate the correct spelling of unfamiliar words. (p. 328)

THE PROBLEM SPELLER

Why are there good spellers and poor spellers? What are the differences in abilities between these two groups and, what difference has instruction made in the development of each? Research aimed at answering questions such as these has led to information that has helped to reshape our thinking about the spelling process and how best to teach spelling to handicapped learners.

The prevalence of spelling disabilities has not been reported in the literature, and other than a general recognition of their widespread existence, there have apparently been no attempts to quantify the presence of these disabilities. What is known is that there are two basic categories of spelling disabilities: (a) specific spelling skill deficits and (b) difficulties that are the result of a general pattern of language and learning problems (Polloway & Smith, 1982). Students in both categories are also often negatively influenced by poor instructional techniques. In the former category, the chance of correction is dependent upon appropriate diagnosis and remediation of the particular spelling problem, while the latter grouping represents a more serious educational concern. Spelling is so closely linked to other areas of language arts that its relevance can be appreciated only within the total communication framework. That is, spelling exists as a means for the child to translate spoken language or cognition into written language. A problem in any language-related area may be reflected in the student's spelling performance. There appears to be consensus among professionals working with children with reading and spelling problems that there is a strong relationship between spelling and reading difficulties and that spelling deficiencies are the most difficult to remediate.

The combination of the complexity of the spelling process and the language-related deficiencies experienced by many mildly handicapped learners results in a slower acquisition of spelling skills. Stephens (1977) makes several generalizations about the causes of spelling difficulties manifested by handicapped learners.

1. Poor spellers often have lower intellectual ability. Spelling is a cognitive function that depends on multisensory skills such as visual and auditory acuity, discrimination, imagery, and motor adequacy.

2. Poor spellers commonly have revisualization problems and are unable to reproduce word patterns. The ability to visualize a word in one's mind is an effective means of improving spelling through self-correction.

3. Poor spellers have difficulty using phonetic skills to learn sound-symbol associations.

4. Poor spellers may mispronounce words when speaking and then attempt to spell the words as they say them.

5. Poor spellers may rely so heavily on phonetic generalizations that they are unable to spell irregular words.

6. Poor spellers may be unfamiliar with word meanings and as a result may have difficulty spelling words that sound alike but have different meanings (e.g., knead/need).

In addition to the characteristics mentioned above that result in spelling inadequacies, Haring, Lovitt, Eaton, and Hansen (1978) detail three difficulties common to problem learners working in traditional spelling basal programs: (a) the difficulty of reading written directions related to spelling practice exercises; (b) the wide range of activities, which tend to confuse rather than focus; and (c) the lack of individualization within the content and approaches used. As a result these students tend to depend on teacher assistance to a greater extent and to become bored and frustrated with established programs.

DEVELOPMENT OF SPELLING SKILLS

When children learn to speak, a recognized developmental pattern is followed that allows them to respond in an organized manner to the world around them. As children grow and participate more and more in the environment, language advances qualitatively. Spelling research has provided evidence that, similar to language development, learning to spell is a developmental language process. Advances in the child's cognitive knowledge (i.e., orthographic understanding) are associated with an increased ability to spell. There appears to be a general sequence that is followed when one learns to spell (Beers & Henderson, 1977; Gentry, 1984; Reed & Hodges, 1982). Beginning with early invented spelling, the learner seeks to understand the relationship of sounds, letters, and written language. During the preschool and early primary years, children create their own spelling strategies to meet their early writing needs. A child's first spelling words may be at a prephonetic or beginning phonetic stage in which a personal theory of grapheme-phoneme association is tested. Such early spelling systems are based on a developing knowledge of phonology and are evidenced by consonant and vowel sounds represented by the letter the name of which comes closest to the sound (e.g., *tip* for *type*). Although incorrectly spelled, these written word attempts (known as invented spellings) are as relevant in the learning sequence as the child's early attempts at language.

Invented spellings are defined as word patterns conceived from a child's use of various cognitive strategies at different points in development. As the child's knowledge of orthography increases, changes in spelling patterns, known as error types, systematically and predictably occur. These qualitative changes are the direct result of the learner's experiences with written language.

The progression in invented spellings can be associated with five identified strategies corresponding to five developmental stages: precommunicative, semiphonetic, phonetic, transitional, and correct (Gentry, 1982). Although the labels given to these stages may vary according to author, the application of the cognitive strategies they represent is fairly consistent. In line with the developmental nature of the spelling process, children progress at varying rates of achievement and may fluctuate between an advanced strategy for high-frequency words and a less sophisticated strategy for low-frequency words. Phonetically spelled sentences of a young child and of a mildly handicapped child are illustrated in Figure 7.2.

A classification system for identifying developmental spelling errors is as follows:

1. Precommunicative spelling. Spellers randomly string together letters of the alphabet without regard to letter-sound correspondence. Example: OPSPO = eagle; RTAT = eighty.

2. Semiphonetic spelling. Letters represent sound but only some of the letters are represented. Example: E = eagle; A = eighty.

3. Phonetic spelling. Words are spelled like they sound. The speller represents all of the phonemes in a word, although the spelling may be unconventional. Example: EGL = eagle; ATE = eighty.

4. Transitional spelling. A visual memory of spelling patterns is apparent. Spellings exhibit conventions of English orthography: vowels in every syllable, e-marker and vowel digraph patterns, correctly spelled inflectional endings, and frequent English letter sequences. Example: EGUL = eagle; EIGHTEE = eighty.

5. Correct spelling. The word is spelled correctly. (Gentry, 1984, pp. 15–16)

The experiences young children have with exposure to printed words and their opportunities for spelling performance provide nurturance for correct spelling. As the child progresses from letter-sound mapping (phonetic spelling) to letter-sound matching (transitional spelling), more demands are made on the visual memory of sound and word patterns. Ultimately, visual memory becomes the most important ability in the spelling of unknown words (Frith & Frith, 1980). During transition from phonetic to correct spelling, children must be given the opportunity to compare their spellings with the standard word forms. A self-discovery method (self-checking) allows children to refine and generalize their spellings. As morphemic structure (e.g., prefixes, suffixes, and root words) is better understood, the awareness of word patterns significantly increases.

In normal learners the transition to standard spelling is generally completed by the third grade, when a higher level of English orthography is employed for correct spelling (Gentry, 1978). The application of findings related to developmental spelling is not limited to non-handicapped populations. Preliminary evidence suggests that learning

FIGURE 7.2. Children's Writing Samples Showing Invented Spellings*

i LØt tˍoReD qn D
Cqn tL the tIm.

(I learned to read and I can tell the time.)
Katie, age 5.11

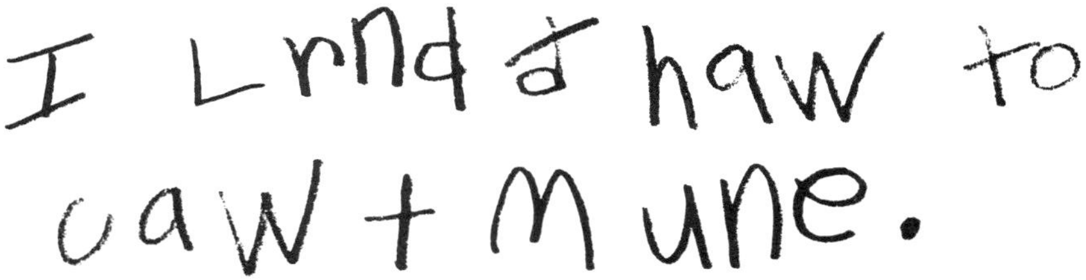

I Lrnd ə haw to
uaw t M une.

(I learned how to count money.)
Tim, age 5.10

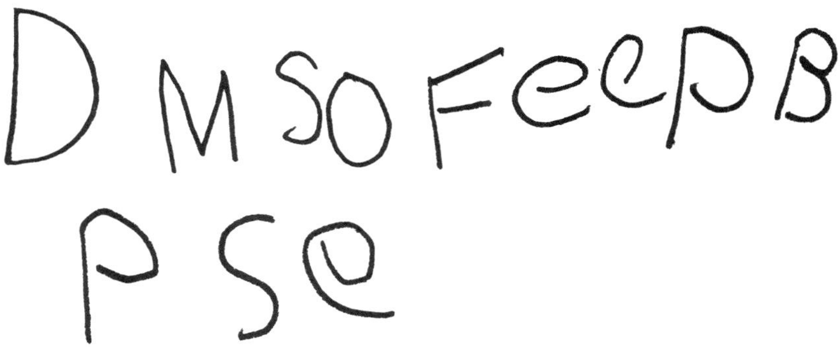

D M SO FeePB
P SØ

(I like to do puzzles and do housekeeping.)
Pat, age 6, mildly handicapped

*Each child was asked to write what he or she had learned in school this year and then to read the sentence to the teacher.

disabled children employ the same sequence of developmental strategies but at a delayed rate of progress (Carpenter & Miller, 1982; Gerber & Hall, 1985). These mildly handicapped learners are using error patterns similar to those of younger nonhandicapped learners.

Researchers who have examined the developmental aspects of spelling have generally concluded that spelling instruction should not be limited to the formal framework that is so often advocated in commercial and specified school district programs. To this effect, Hodges (1981) has made several recommendations, which are summarized below.

1. Spelling instruction should be incorporated within the foundation of general language study to provide students opportunities to examine the relationship between spoken and written language and to apply this understanding to spelling. Students should learn to perceive spelling as an integrated system by exploring word development and usage.

2. Differences in the styles and rates of learners should be accommodated through a variety of materials and approaches.

3. The natural curiosity of children should be highlighted in spelling instruction through regular writing activities, allowing them to apply a growing knowledge of orthography.

4. All spelling approaches must include multiple opportunities for students to assess their own spellings and to learn from their errors as they apply new orthographic knowledge.

The advances in understanding the process that the young speller goes through—that is, viewing spelling from the ways the learner learns—have resulted in the integration of spelling into the total language arts curriculum. The new emphasis upon writing as both a learning process and a product has focused attention on spelling within the writing situation. Current thinking recognizes the writer's use of spelling both during the initial stage of written thought generation and in the concluding stage of editing. As for all children, but especially for problem learners, the mere activity of checking one's spelling will not lead to spelling growth. Instead, a plan of error correction must be instituted in order to learn the proper spelling.

ASSESSMENT OF SPELLING SKILLS

A child who displays uncertainty as to the correct spelling of a word and is unable to make use of appropriate problem-solving strategies (i.e., strategies based on previously acquired information related to letter sequence and orthographic generalizations) is experiencing a spelling problem. Difficulties in spelling, as in any other language-related area, should be assessed to locate the source, or sources, of the problem and to outline a program of sequential remediation. Assessment should be aimed at determining whether the difficulty is related to an isolated word or set of words or is more seriously centered on the child's inability to solve spelling problems (Shores & Yee, 1973).

Formal Assessment of Spelling

To gain information about a child's spelling ability, the teacher may choose from a variety of test options, either formal or informal in nature. Many standardized achievement tests have spelling sections that provide an objective means of obtaining age and grade-level norms. Unfortunately, these norms are little more than gross estimates of the child's spelling ability. Specifically, such figures indicate whether students are spelling above or below their average peers. This information is of little use for the remediation of spelling difficulties and provides limited information for instructional decision making.

Standardized achievement tests that include spelling subsections are listed in Table 7.1. As the table indicates, there are essentially two techniques employed to measure spelling ability. The *dictated-word* format requires the child to write words orally presented. *Proofreading* presents the student with a series of words that may or may not be correctly spelled. After examining the words the speller must decide whether or not each word pattern is acceptable. A variation on this format (*multiple choice*) asks the student to select the correctly spelled stimulus word from several possible spellings of that word (e.g., *knee* or *nee*).

One notable exception among standardized tests is the *Test of Written Spelling* (Larsen & Hammill, 1986). Known as the TWS–2, this achievement test focuses upon spelling and provides accurate information regarding the student's spelling level and areas of manifest difficulty. The test words, selected because they appeared in 10 commonly used basal spelling programs, are presented with validity coefficients and difficulty levels. The TWS–2 was constructed to incorporate the two theories that (a) mastery of a certain number of spelling rules is necessary for spelling independence and (b) words that do not conform to standard generalizations must be learned through rote memorization. Reflecting these constructs, the test words are classified as either *predictable* or *unpredictable*. Scores on this dictated test are given for each subtest as well as for total achievement. Although the TWS–2 is recommended as an individually given test, it can easily be adapted for group administration and scoring.

A caution must be given on the administration of the TWS–2 with mildly handicapped learners. The standardized sample used to establish the TWS–2 test scores, as in most standardized tests, did not include handicapped students, and, therefore, its generalizability to this population is not certain. Also, it has been claimed that the use of the test with normal learners has resulted in a large percentage who exceed the scores of the standardization range (Gerber & Cohen, 1985), indicating that the norm may not represent typical achievement. Despite this concern, the TWS–2 is a progressive step in the assessment of spelling problems. When used in conjunction with other informal measures, the TWS–2 can provide a great deal of easily interpretable information.

Informal Assessment of Spelling Ability

Informal spelling procedures can represent assessment materials that are either commercially produced or teacher-made but which lack the standardization of more formal measures. The advantage of the informal tools is that they are designed to reveal specific spelling skill difficulties and are more adaptable to individual diagnostic needs. The major dimensions of informal spelling assessments, presented in Figure 7.3, are useful formats for understanding the diversity of assessment approaches.

The traditional weekly spelling test given on Friday morning to assess the students' familiarity with a prescribed list of words is an example of a dictated format. Words can be given either in isolation or within the context of a sentence. Either way, this procedure has been recognized by some as the most valid and effective type of spelling assessment (Cartwright, 1969; Cohen & Plaskon, 1980). In contrast to the dictated format in which the child must generate the word pattern, the recognition test structure, also referred to as proofreading, presents the learner with spelling options. Variations of the procedure include having the students correct spelling errors as they find them or indicating the correct spelling from a set of words. Both dictation and recognition tests may be timed or untimed, and both may use words in context or in isolation.

Although the use of spelling tests such as these has been widely accepted, these tests have not been without some criticism. Dictated tests, as they are given in the weekly exam, rely mainly on rote recall of selected words. As such, they do not demonstrate the student's ability in any true aspect of the spelling process. Recognition tests also present

TABLE 7.1. Selected Standardized Achievement Tests with Spelling Subsections

Test	Publisher	Appropriate Grade/Age	Administration	Relevant Format
California Achievement Test (CTB/McGraw-Hill, 1978)	CTB & McGraw-Hill	Grades 1–5 to 12	Group	Proofreading
Comprehensive Tests of Basic Skills (CTBS, 1977)	CTB & McGraw-Hill	Grades 2–5 to 12	Group	Proofreading
Iowa Tests of Basic Skills (ITBS) (Hieronymous, Lindquist, & Hoover, 1982)	Science Research Associates	Grades 1–8	Group or Individual	Proofreading
Metropolitan Achievement Tests: Survey Battery (Balow, Hogan, Farr, & Prescott, 1978)	Psychological Corporation	Grades 2–5 to 9–5	Group	Dictation
Peabody Individual Achievement Tests (PIAT) (Dunn & Markwardt, 1970)	American Guidance Services	Grades K–12	Individual	Multiple choice

TABLE 7.1. Continued

Test	Publisher	Appropriate Grade/Age	Administration	Relevant Format
SRA Achievement Series (Naslund, Thorpe, & Lefever, 1978)	Science Research Associates	Grades 1–5 to 10	Group	Proofreading
Stanford Achievement Tests (SAT) (Gardner, Rudman, Karlsen, & Merwin, 1982)	Psychological Corporation	Grades 1–5 to 9–5	Group	Proofreading
Test of Written Spelling–2 (TWS–2) (Larsen & Hammill, 1986)	PRO-ED	Grades 1–9	Group or Individual	Dictation
Wide Range Achievement Test (WRAT–R) (Jastak & Jastak, 1984)	Jastak	Ages 5–Adult	Individual	Dictation

FIGURE 7.3. Spelling Tests: Major Dimensions

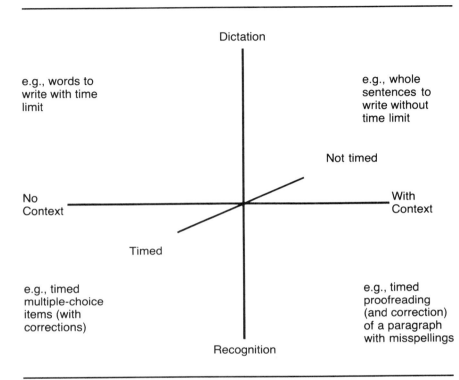

e.g., words to write with time limit

e.g., whole sentences to write without time limit

e.g., timed multiple-choice items (with corrections)

e.g., timed proofreading (and correction) of a paragraph with misspellings

From Gerber, M. M., & Cohen, S. B. (1985). Assessment of spelling skills. In A. F. Rotatori & R. Fox (Eds.), *Assessment for regular and special education teachers*, p. 261. Austin, TX: PRO-ED. Reprinted with permission.

concerns because of their disregard for the fact that spelling is a generating process that encompasses all spelling subskills, resulting in the speller independently producing a word. Proofreading, although an essential subskill, is only one component of the spelling process and in a natural context is used when the writer does not know in advance that there are incorrect spellings to be found. The contrived nature of the recognition tests allows for only a limited assessment of spelling ability.

The assessment information gathered from timed versus untimed tests is in a large part a matter of interpretation of performance. When a speller is forced to perform under a timed situation (referred to as a speed test), the information conveyed is the speller's performance relative to other students with the time variable held constant. Untimed tests, on the other hand, provide an assessment of the learner's power, or absolute ability. The decision to apply a time element to an assessment will relate to the questions the teacher wishes to answer concerning the student's spelling performance.

The truest test of spelling performance is the spontaneous production of a written product. As such, spelling assessment may be done as a routine part of almost any other written activity included in the academic program. Whether it is an assignment for written expression, social studies, or science is of consequence only in regard to the technical words that may be necessary. In cases where difficult technical words are pertinent to the writing, the teacher may choose to assist the writer by providing oral or visual prompts such as lists of key words. Gerber and Cohen (1985) specify five easily used measures of spelling ability that can be applied to any written passage.

1. Percentage of total number of words spelled correctly.

2. Percentage of total number of different words spelled correctly.

3. Percentage of errors that are spontaneously self-corrected (or improved).

4. Average number of sounds, letters or syllables per words attempted correctly.

5. Number of correct words per minute. (p. 263)

Observation. When informal spelling assessment strategies are to be used, it is important that the teacher decide whether the purpose of the assessment is to ascertain the presence or absence of a particular skill or to determine the spelling progress being made over time. In the first case the assessment involves *summary observations* in which the speller's strengths or weaknesses in any of the subskills are scrutinized. The use of checklists or scope and sequence charts in commercial spelling series is appropriate for this purpose. The teacher must have a clear understanding of what the spelling subskills are and how they relate to the overall spelling process. A child who is achieving 85% or higher on such observations is considered a capable speller, while a child who is performing below the 60% level is in need of a focused spelling program.

A second type of observation approach is *systematic observation*, in which the teacher follows the student's progress in a certain skill over a period of time. This is achieved through repeated observations, which are often designed by the teacher to evaluate the effectiveness of spelling instruction. The teacher may wish to monitor the student's mastery of a specific spelling skill, a designated series of word lists, or a particular instructional technique.

One approach to spelling assessment is to use a systematic spelling observation guide. Figure 7.4 illustrates one possible form, which is

FIGURE 7.4. Systematic Spelling Observation Guide

Name _____   Current spelling placement:

Date _____   Level _____
                                            Series _____
                                            Lesson # _____

I. General orientation toward spelling	Too seldom		Too often	
a. Attends to teacher appropriately	1	2	3	4
b. Follows directions	1	2	3	4
c. Asks appropriate questions when directions are not understood	1	2	3	4
d. Pronounces words accurately	1	2	3	4
e. Repeats seven word sentences	1	2	3	4
f. Average speaking vocabulary	1	2	3	4
g. Copies letters accurately	1	2	3	4
h. Copies words accurately	1	2	3	4
i. Knows alphabet	1	2	3	4
j. Spells name:				
—first	1	2	3	4
—last	1	2	3	4
k. Spells some words from memory	1	2	3	4
l. Asks how to spell new words	1	2	3	4
m. Handwriting is legible:				
—manuscript	1	2	3	4
—cursive	1	2	3	4

II. Behavior during dictation   Average % correct words _____

a. Pauses to think before spelling	1	2	3	4
b. Spells word completely without pause	1	2	3	4
c. Response to error-making				
—recognizes most errors immediately	1	2	3	4
—backtracks to check/correct	1	2	3	4
—changes letters in the course of spelling word	1	2	3	4
—erases errors	1	2	3	4
—crosses out errors	1	2	3	4
—writes over errors	1	2	3	4
—rewrites whole word	1	2	3	4
—frequent partial spellings before complete spelling	1	2	3	4

FIGURE 7.4. Continued

		Too seldom		Too often
d.	Repeats words/letters before writing	1	2	3 4
e.	"Sounds out" while spelling	1	2	3 4
f.	Asks for repetition frequently	1	2	3 4
g.	Cheats or continuously watches others	1	2	3 4
h.	Rubs/closes eyes, becomes restless, looks fatigued	1	2	3 4
i.	Negative emotional outbursts	1	2	3 4
j.	Writes whole sentences when asked	1	2	3 4
k.	Content with performance	1	2	3 4

III. Behavior during natural writing   Average % correct words _____

a.	Initiates stories, poems, picture captions, etc.	1	2	3 4
b.	Writes more than one sentence	1	2	3 4
c.	Response to error-making			
	—recognizes most errors immediately	1	2	3 4
	—backtracks to check/correct	1	2	3 4
	—changes letters in the course of spelling word	1	2	3 4
	—erases errors	1	2	3 4
	—crosses out errors	1	2	3 4
	—writes over errors	1	2	3 4
	—rewrites whole word	1	2	3 4
	—frequent partial spellings before complete spelling	1	2	3 4
d.	Uses words learned in other areas of curriculum (e.g., reading, math, social studies, etc.)	1	2	3 4
e.	Attempts to read finished written work to self, friends, teacher, parents	1	2	3 4
f.	Proud of work	1	2	3 4
g.	Finishes writing projects	1	2	3 4
h.	Sought by others for spelling help	1	2	3 4
i.	Asks teacher for help	1	2	3 4
j.	Rubs/closes eyes, becomes restless, looks fatigued	1	2	3 4
k.	Negative emotional outbursts	1	2	3 4

From Gerber, M. M., & Cohen, S. B. (1985). Assessment of spelling skills. In A. F. Rotatori & R. Fox (Eds.), *Assessment for regular and special education teachers,* pp. 269–270. Austin, TX: PRO-ED. Reprinted by permission.

appropriate either as an initial screening device or as a record of continuous progress.

Word Lists. One of the most direct forms of spelling assessment is the use of word lists in which the student is required to spell each word and a percentage of correct responses is noted. In general, word lists are developed from three categories of words: (a) survival or high-utility words for the individual student, (b) basic vocabulary words and, (c) rule exemplar words. Spelling programs that are commercially produced are generally based on the use of word lists. Some survival words may apply to all students (e.g., *danger*, *exit*, and *walk*), while others are unique to a single student (e.g., the child's name and address). The basic vocabulary words taught at each grade level are those thought to be most commonly used by students at the grade. Rule exemplar words are included to assess the speller's ability to generalize rules to produce previously unknown spellings.

Assessment of survival words and basic vocabulary word lists will determine if the child has learned a given set of words and is able to produce the words without assistance. Errors in either of these two types of word lists commonly indicate a need to reteach the words, making the necessary decision as to whether to change the instructional strategy. The rule exemplar list offers a different piece of assessment information. The teacher examines these words in an attempt to determine the student's ability to apply orthographic knowledge to solve spelling problems. When errors are made on these types of words, the teacher can apply an error analysis and determine which generalizations are in need of instruction.

Informal Spelling Inventories. Informal spelling inventories (ISIs) are another technique that can be easily developed and evaluated. Similar to their reading counterparts, ISIs are designed to establish the child's basic skill deficiencies and to assist in placing the learner with the correct spelling material. In essence, ISIs are a variation on spelling list assessments, which allow teachers to construct their own composite list aimed at answering a spelling assessment question. If a teacher chooses to use a basal spelling program as the basis of the ISI, Mann and Suiter (1974) have provided a procedure that can easily be followed:

1. From a basal spelling series select a random sample of 20 words from each grade level.

2. Randomization can be done in many ways. The simplest way is to divide the total number of words in the level by 20 (e.g., if there were 100 words in the set, you would select every 5th word for the ISI).

3. Begin testing at two grade levels below the child's actual grade placement. For first and second grade begin at level one.

4. Test each word by saying the word, using it in a sentence, and saying the word again.

5. Encourage students to attempt to spell each test word. This can be done by telling them to put down any sound they know in the word.

6. Testing ends at the level in which the student misses seven words in the list.

7. It is not necessary to complete the whole inventory in one sitting. Breaking up the assessment time may alleviate frustration and boredom for some children.

Correct Letter Sequence.   A more recent development in the assessment of spelling knowledge has been the focus on the number of correct letter sequences (CLS). Created by Deno, Mirkin, Lowry, and Kuehnle (1980) as a formative evaluation procedure, this technique has been shown to reliably predict standardized achievement test performance in both normal and learning disabled populations. The concreteness of the approach makes it extremely easy and accessible for teachers. CLS is a technique for scoring spelling production by counting correct letter pairs within word patterns. Credit is also given for correctly beginning and ending a word. An example of a CLS applied to three different spellings of the same word is:

Spelling 1	^p^n^e^u^m^o^n^i^a^	10 correct
Spelling 2	^n^u^m^o^n^i a	6 correct
Spelling 3	n^e w m^o^n y a^	4 correct

The carets signify a correct sequence within the word and are also used to represent the appropriate beginning and ending letters. The CLS measure can be applied to any word list and is a reliable tool for systematic observation of spelling progress. Use of a CLS system will reduce the problems associated with a "right or wrong" assessment, which can potentially mask improvements in spelling ability.

Error Analysis.   Regardless of the assessment strategy selected for use, the teacher may wish to employ error analysis as a means of categorizing any spelling problems. Error analysis provides more information than a mere percentage score and verifies if any consistent difficulty is evident. Its use as a procedure is based on the evidence that spelling errors tend to be consistent, demonstrating nonrandom attempts at sequencing word patterns. The effectiveness of an error analysis approach depends upon two factors: (a) the student's consistency in error production and (b) the teacher's consistency in its application to a remedial program. The consistency in types of spelling errors made by learning disabled students has been verified in a study by DeMaster, Crossland, and Hasselbring (1986). They conclude "that there is legitimate basis for using diagnostic error analysis in connection with individualized prescriptive teaching" (p. 95).

Error analysis will also help the teacher to determine the child's classification within a developmental spelling framework (i.e., prephonetic, phonetic, transitional, correct, or deviant). The application of this information to the instructional program will allow the teacher to appropriately match the selection of spelling material to the child's functional level.

Whatever assessment technique is used, it is important for teachers to understand that the goal is appropriate instructional decision making and not just scoring (i.e., classification) of student responses. Assessment in its formative stages is a means to further student achievement by clarifying the need for instructional changes. Assessment information that is gathered but not used in this manner is simply a waste of time.

TEACHING SPELLING SKILLS

During the school day most students engage in writing activities that require the production of spelling words. How these words are acquired depends on several interacting factors, including the student's learning capacity, the oral environment that surrounds the student, the focus on vocabulary development through reading and writing activities, and the instructional sequence for learning spelling words and generalizations. There is no one spelling approach suitable for all learners nor is any one approach rated significantly higher than any other. The teacher must, therefore, be familiar with a repertoire of approaches and capable of adapting the program to fit group and individual needs.

A survey conducted by the editors of *Academic Therapy* (1984) examined the materials and techniques most commonly used by readers to teach spelling to LD students. The results indicated that few state-approved spelling programs were being implemented for this student population. However, there were a number of commercial programs employed that used approaches based on a multisensory method. The techniques and ideas commonly shared were:

❑ Assign words from basal reader stories.

❑ Assign words that had been misspelled in the student's writing assignments.

❑ Use finger spelling (kinesthetic approach).

❑ Design weekly spelling lists which closely follow the reading program's introduction of vocabulary.

❑ A pre-test is given before the weekly spelling test.

❑ Words used in more than one class subject seem to be most often spelled correctly.

❑ Students make their own flashcards.

❑ Students trace the correct spelling of words they miss, saying each letter as they trace it and pronouncing the word each time it is completed. (p. 77)

These findings suggest that teachers are trying a variety of approaches to teach spelling to problem learners. However, the findings seem to indicate that while teachers are intent on increasing the ratio of correct spellings to incorrect spellings made by students, there appears to be little emphasis on the quality of spellings. It is the product rather than the process that is of concern. Taking this approach gains little insight into the student's orthographic problem-solving skills. Teachers need to use more diagnostic-prescriptive techniques in their instructional programs.

The variety of techniques used to teach spelling allows a teacher to select the most appropriate method for a particular student's needs. A study by Hammill, Larsen, and McNutt (1977) examined spelling instructional methodologies and found that basal programs based on linguistic theory were the most commonly used.

Linguistic Spelling Approach

The English language is based on a number of consistencies known as linguistic generalizations. These can be taught to mildly handicapped children as they learn grapheme-phoneme associations. Although the utility of teaching grapheme-phoneme generalizations is often debated, it is possible to achieve some success if the child is taught only one sound-symbol association for each written symbol. All other forms of the phoneme are taught as irregular words, which are learned through a visual process.

The linguistic approach generates spellings from a bottom-up orientation. That is, the speller concentrates on producing word spellings by attending to one phoneme at a time and applying knowledge of sound-symbol relationships. The difficulty for many mildly handicapped learners is in applying sound segmentation skills. In addition, the number of graphemes representing a single phoneme is also a stumbling block. However, the teacher needs to understand the importance of linguistic spelling for spelling generalization and to incorporate elements of the linguistic approach whenever possible.

Formalized spelling instruction in most commercial programs begins at the end of first or the beginning of second grade. When the reading and spelling programs do not conform to the same sequence of linguistic principles, it is advisable to modify the spelling program to match the linguistic reading sequence. This ensures consistency across subject areas and eliminates the confusion caused when a child is instructed in two conflicting programs. A suggested sequence for a linguistic spelling program is provided in Table 7.2. The following section on spelling rules also contains information relevant to a linguistic spelling approach.

Visual Spelling Approach

The difficulties experienced by the problem learner when learning to spell often result from the inconsistencies in the English orthography and the number of graphemes that can be associated with a phoneme. Therefore, whenever a letter pattern is produced, the final test of its correctness is whether it "looks right." Spelling can be viewed as a visual process in which the speller must continually validate letter sequences against a mental image of the previously seen word. This need for revisualization is why so many of us use the strategy of writing out an uncertain word in three or four possible configurations and selecting the one that appears to be correct. If the writer has never before encountered the word, it is virtually impossible for him or her to be certain of its correct spelling. At best in such cases, a good attempt can be made at phonetically deciphering the spelling. It is interesting to note that this comparison of a newly produced spelling and the visual image may be done either in written form or in the "mind's eye."

The visual approach concentrates on the development of a visual word image. It is significant that the whole word is the important unit rather than any one segment or sound-symbol association. The goal in teaching the visual approach is to create an impression of the word which the child can automatically reproduce in a writing task. Word study habits that result in strong visual word images will lead to improved spelling ability. The prescribed study method which follows is an adaptation of a method developed by Horn (1954) and is designed to stress the visual elements of a word and to prevent inappropriate spelling habits. This learning strategy can be applied to all new spelling words as a regular feature of a spelling program.

TABLE 7.2. Suggested Linguistic Spelling Program

General guidelines:
1. Teach 2–5 words per week.
2. Follow a weekly plan of instruction (such as the one suggested later in this chapter).
3. Integrate the week's spelling words in as many other classroom activities as possible (e.g., reading and writing).
4. Teach one related word group at a time. Not all words need to be taught in one lesson.
5. Review past words frequently.
6. Include one sight word in each lesson.

Lessons:
1. CVC (Consonant-vowel-consonant)
   a. Short *a* families (bat, hat, cat, sad, mad, had)
   b. Short *i* families (hit, bin, lid)
   c. Short *o* families (son, hot, mob)
   d. Short *u* families (but, pun, fun, sun)
   e. Short *e* families (bet, pen, fed, set)
2. CVCC (having short vowel sounds and ending in double letters)
   a. *ll* words (hell, sell, tell)
   b. *ss* words (kiss, moss, less)
3. CCVC (with short vowel sounds)
   a. Two-letter initial blends (*sh*-ship, *bl*-blend, *sw*-swim)
   b. Digraphs (*ch*-chat, *sh*-shot, *wh*-when)
4. CCCVC (three-letter blends with short vowel sounds) (*str*-string, *spr*-spring)
5. CVCV (long vowel sound, silent final *e*)
   a. Long *a* (make, cape, date)
   b. Long *i* (hike, bite, mile)
   c. Long *o* (joke, some, mode)
   d. Long *u* (cute, duke, tune)
   e. Long *e* (Pete)
6. CCVCV (with long vowel sounds)
   a. Two-letter initial blends (*sp*-spade, -stick)
   b. Digraphs (*sh*-shame, *wh*-while)
7. CCCVCV (three-letter blends with long vowel sounds) (*str*-stroke, spr-sprite)
8. Alternate (soft) sounds of *c* and *g* (city, gear)
9. R controlled vowels (*ar*-car, *er*-her, *ir*-sir, *ur*-fur)
10. Vowel digraphs (*ee*-teen, *ay*-say, *ai*-braid, *ea*-bead)
11. Silent letters (knee, knot, honor, listen)
12. Irregular words (the, said)
13. Root words
14. Prefixes and suffixes
15. Homonyms

Adapted with permission from Mann, P., and Suiter, P. (1974). *Handbook in diagnostic teaching: A learning disabilities approach.* Boston: Allyn & Bacon, pp. 130–131.

❑ Look at the whole word.

❑ Say the word.

❑ Close your eyes and say the word.

❑ Say the letters as you look at the word.

❑ Close your eyes and say the letters.

❑ Check your spelling.

❑ Write the word without the model.

❑ Check your spelling.

❑ Repeat steps if an error is made at any point.

Repetition is essential if a visual method is employed as the primary teaching approach. The teacher should be certain to frequently check the student's spelling to prevent incorrect patterns from forming a strong visual image that will be difficult to break.

Regardless of the primary approach used in the spelling program, all irregularly spelled words must be learned through visual memory. It is difficult to say what element of a word will be particularly troublesome for any one student. Therefore, it is important to focus the student's attention on the whole word. Unless a specific weakness is noticed or a certain element, such as a prefix, is being applied to previously learned words, it is not generally advantageous to highlight word parts. The separation of elements hinders the development of a complete word image and does not promote successful reproducton of the spelling pattern.

Cognitive Spelling Approach

The information that has been gathered about the developmental aspects of spelling ability has focused attention upon a new approach to spelling instruction—cognitive problem solving. Hall (1984) describes three categories of cognitive behavior related to spelling: (a) automatic spellings, which are written without conscious attention paid to the process, (b) consciously recognized words, which, however, take some effort to generate the correct response (this is usually achieved after the speller lists several alternative spellings), and (c) unknown spellings, which cannot be correctly written without resorting to an external source (e.g., dictionary or teacher). Correct spelling often results from the writer's ability to compare either a word or a word part to mental images of word patterns based on one's past experiences, knowledge of how words are formed (i.e., rules), and/or an understanding of word groups. The speller's task is to solve the spelling problem by

> purveying, allocating, evaluating and generally orchestrating resources from both the data-driven (decoding) and the hypothesis-driven (recognitive) components of information processing. This suggests a third major component of processing, often referred to as the "executive" whose function it is to mediate between data-driven and hypothesis-driven information processing. The executive component enables the problem-solver (a) to reduce the scope of a problem by appropriately allocating cognitive resources according to some strategic plan, and (b) to decide when a solution, defined ultimately in terms of reduction of uncertainty (not necessarily a correct response), has been achieved. (Hall, 1984, pp. 70–71)

The importance of the information processing perspective for the teacher who is establishing a spelling program is in knowing that most problem learners follow the same logical sequence of spelling development as do normal learners. The fact that these problem learners are not random in their misspellings means that they possess orthographic information which they try to use. The problem often results from poorly formed or inefficient strategies for applying orthographic knowledge. The teacher who understands the developmental sequence will be able to assess the student's current functioning level, including the application of information, and will be able to predict where the student should be heading.

An additional advantage of the cognitive problem-solving approach is that it allows learners to take responsibility for monitoring their own spelling behavior. It is desirable to train the learner to use cognitive resources such as sound-symbol association, phonetic features such as tense, structural analysis, and proofreading strategies (see section on error detection and correction later in this chapter). Students learn to depend on their own abilities to solve orthographic problems.

A FUNCTIONAL SPELLING PROGRAM

The more often a child encounters a word, the more apt he or she is to spell it correctly. This is because of the increased visual association with the word as well as the fact that familiarity with a word increases the student's motivation to use (i.e., spell) it correctly. The child realizes the importance of a word for communication purposes. Spelling becomes recognized as a tool for effective written expression.

Children's speech centers around a limited number of high frequency words which have relevance to the children and their environment. In addition to general conversational vocabulary, frequently used

TABLE 7.3. Most Frequently Used Words in Children's Written Work

1. the	26. school	51. would	76. now
2. I	27. me	52. our	77. has
3. and	28. with	53. were	78. down
4. to	29. am	54. little	79. if
5. a	30. all	55. how	80. write
6. you	31. one	56. he	81. after
7. we	32. so	57. do	82. play
8. in	33. your	58. about	83. came
9. it	34. got	59. from	84. put
10. of	35. there	60. her	85. two
11. is	36. went	61. them	86. house
12. was	37. not	62. as	87. us
13. have	38. at	63. his	88. because
14. my	39. like	64. mother	89. over
15. are	40. out	65. see	90. saw
16. he	41. go	66. friend	91. their
17. for	42. but	67. come	92. well
18. on	43. this	68. can	93. here
19. they	44. dear	69. day	94. by
20. that	45. some	70. good	95. just
21. had	46. then	71. what	96. make
22. she	47. going	72. said	97. back
23. very	48. up	73. him	98. an
24. will	49. time	74. home	99. could
25. when	50. get	75. did	100. or

From Folger, S. (1946). The case for a basic written vocabulary. *The Elementary School Journal, 47.* As found in DeHaven, E., *Teaching and learning in the language arts.* Boston: Little, Brown, 1979, p. 287. Reprinted with permission.

content-oriented words which are an important part of the academic environment are considered functional to the learner. The foundation of a functional program can be either an established list of high-frequency words, such as the one found in Table 7.3, or a word list constructed from the child's own language experience. The overlap between these two methods should be evident.

Using the language experience method, the teacher has a direct means of determining the student's language orientation for significant words. The student is asked to write a story, which may be only a phrase or short sentence for young children. When a student wants to use a word of unknown spelling, he or she is told to attempt a spelling or leave a space where appropriate. The teacher then supplies the unknown word, and it is added to the student's "Words to be Learned List."

A functional spelling approach establishes the content of the spelling program but does not specify the learning method. Words may be studied by a linguistic, visual, cognitive, or eclectic approach. The functionality of the program relates to the word frequency and the implicit meaningfulness of the spelling task. The positive aspect of the technique results from the child's own motivation to spell a word.

REMEDIAL SPELLING TECHNIQUES

Spelling programs for the majority of learners are based on traditional group-centered approaches such as those found in the basal spelling series. For many disabled spellers, these programs may not provide the necessary (a) individualization, (b) emphasis on word study, or (c) repetitive practice. The alternative is to use a remedial spelling technique.

Several remedial spelling techniques have been developed and researched. Each method focuses upon a plan for word study that systematically allows the child to learn the needed word. Graham and Miller (1979) suggest that an effective word study approach concentrates on the whole word and requires pronunciation, visual imagery, auditory feedback, and practice in recall. Table 7.4 details several appropriate techniques from which the teacher may choose.

TEACHING SPELLING RULES

Any teacher who has ever tried to teach spelling rules to problem learners has experienced the frustration associated with getting a learner to remember the rule and to appropriately apply it. The question of whether it is worth the effort has been asked repeatedly. Specifically, educators have been interested in knowing to what extent spelling rules should be taught. Although this has primarily been examined for normal learners, these are still pertinent questions regarding the problem learner. Some mildly handicapped students may be unable to learn rules at all and, as a result, may rely on visual and auditory recall in order to produce letter sequences. Others will learn the generalization but be unable to apply the rule at the appropriate time. Still others may be capable of learning and applying only a limited number of rules.

TABLE 7.4. Remedial Spelling Techniques

Visual Sensory Method
1. The Teacher selects words that highlight linguistic principles and color codes phonetic elements.
2. Child traces the word while saying it.
3. Child visualizes the word while saying it in a sentence.
4. Child writes the word.

Fernald Method (Fernald, 1943)
1. Teacher writes and says the word for the child (using a grease pencil or crayon is advocated)
2. Child traces the word repeatedly while saying it.
3. Child says the word while writing it from model.
4. Child writes the word without the model.
5. If correct, a new word is begun. If incorrect, steps 2 through 4 are repeated.

Cover and Write Method (Graham & Miller, 1979)
1. Look at word, say it.
2. Write word two times.
3. Cover and write one time.
4. Check work.
5. Write word two times.
6. Cover and write one time.
7. Check work.
8. Write word three times.
9. Cover and write one time.
10. Check work.

Horn Method (Horn, 1954)
1. Pronounce each word.
2. Look at each part of the word as you pronounce it again.
3. Spell the letter sequence.
4. Visualize the word, spell it.
5. Check your spelling recall.
6. Write the word.
7. Check your spelling.
8. If incorrect, repeat all steps.

Gillingham and Stillman Method (Gillingham & Stillman, 1970)
1. Child learns sound-symbol associations using a visual-auditory-kinesthetic-tactile (VAKT) approach.
2. Child learns visual letter patterns (VAKT).
3. Child learns word patterns (VAKT).

Phonovisual Method (Schoolfield & Timberlake, 1960)
1. Consonants are introduced by association with word pictures.
2. Vowels are introduced by association with word pictures.
3. Child says the word and keys the visual image of the letter sound.

TABLE 7.5. High-Utility Spelling Rules

Rule	Function
Final *e* rule	Drop the *e* at the end of a word if you are adding a suffix that begins with a vowel.
Plural rule	The majority of nouns form their plural by adding *s*.
Plural variation	Nouns ending in *s*, *x*, *sh*, and *ch* are pluralized by adding *es* to the end of the word.
Plural variation	If a word ends with a *consonant = y* combination you add *es*.
q-u rule	Always follow a *q* with a *u*.
i-e rule	The *i* goes before the *e*, except after *c*, or when you hear the sound *a* as in neighbor and sleigh.
Contractions	A contraction combines two words and always has a missing part. Show the missing part by using an apostrophe.
Possessive rule	Possessives of singular nouns and irregular plural nouns are formed by adding 's.
y-to-*i* rule	If a consonant precedes the final *y*, change *y* to *i* when adding a morphograph that does not begin with *i*.

A manageable way to approach this issue is to establish a limited number of the most frequently used rules as part of the spelling program. If rules are emphasized too heavily within the program, they are apt to lose their functionality and become a burden to the learner. However, the learning of a limited number of rules may be a component of any spelling approach. In any case, rules should be taught one at a time and only when there is a need for them. Periodic review of the previously learned rules and practice in rule application will increase retention and lead to generalization. As often as possible, the teacher should point out the rule or word pattern similarity to previously learned words (e.g., *ring*, *sing*, *fling*). The teacher needs to direct attention to words that exemplify the rule in order to achieve rule generalization.

Several of the rules deemed to have the highest utility are listed in Table 7.5. Although for nonhandicapped learners an inductive teaching approach is often advocated for establishing rules, this may not be the most desirable approach for problem learners. An inductive method encourages students to discover spelling generalizations by analyzing several words that share a common linguistic property. Following this analysis the students are asked to apply the generalization when spelling unfamiliar words. The cognitive abilities necessary for induction are of a higher order than those exhibited by some mildly handicapped learners. A more direct deductive method may be most effective. The rule, along with exemplars, is provided to the learner, who is then given numerous opportunities to (a) discriminate the use of the rule and (b) apply the rule in new situations. The choice of an instructional approach should be guided by the teacher's decision as to whether the student is capable of learning and applying rules and whether the student learns best from inductive or deductive experiences.

ERROR DETECTION AND CORRECTION

No matter how well conceived and developed the spelling program is, there will be a certain number of errors made by all students, with an increased number made by problem spellers. Teachers can reduce the rate of spelling errors by taking preventive measures and by employing monitoring and correction procedures.

Spelling Demons

Many words do not conform to linguistic patterns and as a result are troublesome to learn. Commonly referred to as "spelling demons," these words can present a particular problem to the handicapped learner. Figure 7.5 lists the most frequently misspelled words in the elementary grades. A practical use of a list such as this is as a preventive tool. The teacher should select those words that are appropriate to the child's speaking vocabulary level and begin an intensive program of word study.

Mnemonic Devices

Concentrated instruction and repetitive practice, such as advocated in a study method, will increase the visual image and help the student learn the "spelling demons." The use of mnemonic devices is another strategy that can assist some students in learning the spelling of difficult words. The demands of learning a whole list of mnemonics should not be

FIGURE 7.5. Spelling Instruction

about	come	has	Mar.	said	think
address	coming	have	maybe	Santa Claus	thought
afternoon	couldn't	haven't	me	Saturday	through
again	cousin	having	Miss	saw	time
all right	daddy	he	morning	school	to
along	day	hear	mother	schoolhouse	today
already	Dec.	hello	Mr.	send	together
always	didn't	her	Mrs.	sent	tomorrow
am	dog	here	much	sincerely	tonight
an	don't	him	my	snow	too
and	down	his	name	snowman	toys
answer	Easter	home	nice	some	train
anything	every	hope	Nov.	something	truly
anyway	everybody	hospital	now	sometime	two
April	father	house	nowadays	sometimes	until
are	Feb.	how	o'clock	soon	vacation
arithmetic	fine	how's	Oct.	stationery	very
aunt	first	I	off	store	want
awhile	football	I'll	on	studying	was
baby	for	I'm	once	summer	we
balloon	fourth	in	one	Sunday	weather
basketball	Friday	isn't	our	suppose	well
because	friend	it	out	sure	went
been	friends	it's	outside	surely	were
before	from	I've	party	swimming	we're
birthday	fun	Jan.	people	teacher	when
bought	getting	just	play	teacher's	white
boy	goes	know	played	Thanksgiving	will
boys	going	lessons	plays	that's	with
brother	good	letter	please	the	won't
brought	good-by	like	pretty	their	would
can	got	likes	quit	them	write
cannot	grade	little	quite	then	writing
can't	guess	lots	receive	there	you
children	had	loving	received	there's	your
Christmas	Halloween	made	remember	they	you're
close	handkerchiefs	make	right	they're	yours

From Fitzgerald, James A. (1951). *A basic life spelling vocabulary.* Milwaukee: Bruce, pp. 144–150. Reprinted by permission of the Glencoe Press.

placed on some students who find them difficult to remember. However, even for these students such lists can be used as a means of motivating interest in the study of words and their structure. Examples of a few mnemonic spelling devices are: (a) The princi*pal* is your *pal*, (b) a princip*le* is a ru*le*, (c) a secret*ary* is station*ary* at her desk, and (d) On Sat*ur*day we can have f*un*.

Imitation of Errors

Contingent imitation of a student's spelling errors has been shown to be an effective technique for reducing the inappropriate response pattern. For example, a study by Kauffman, Hallahan, Hass, Brame, and Boren (1978) compared the effectiveness of providing a child who has made a spelling error with a correct model of the word versus imitating the child's error ("This is how you spelled the word . . .") and then giving the model ("This is the right way to spell the word . . ."). In each case the child was expected to rewrite the word. The "Imitation Plus Model" technique was the most effective, especially when used with errors made on nonphonetic words. The researchers speculated that the results were due to the learning principle that examples of "not concepts" need to be provided when teaching a basic concept. The appropriate teaching sequence is to provide a negative concept example followed by a positive concept example and opportunity to practice the correct response. Imitation, modeling, and practice will reduce the chance of repeated errors occurring. This imitation plus modeling approach has since been used in a computer study (Hasselbring, 1984) in which LD students were reported to increase their ability to learn word lists.

Proofreading Skills

No speller needs to be able to recall the correct spelling of every word produced in a writing task. Instead, the writer must be able to recognize when a letter pattern may be incorrect and then apply corrective measures. This editing process, referred to as *proofreading*, allows the speller to scan the writing and to detect obvious inaccuracies. Once an error is located (even if the student simply suspects the error), intrinsic and extrinsic strategies may be applied.

Many problem spellers have difficulty proofreading their own writing to detect spelling errors. To the frustration of many teachers, some students will incorrectly spell words that they have spelled accurately on spelling tests or on other activities. Often the teachers attribute the errors to carelessness. For some students this may very well be the case, but carelessness will not account for all editing errors. Many writers who claim to have proofread their work will miss spelling errors due to the fact that they have no systematic approach to detecting and then correcting errors.

In order to perform complex integrated skills, all learners must be able to respond to feedback received from their own performance. However, the inability to monitor their own responses has been noted as a trait of many problem learners. Educators working with the learning disabled have reported that this group exhibits deficits in monitoring errors in spelling four times as often as normal students (Alley, Deshler, & Warner, 1979). Remediation of this problem, therefore, must depend on the development of a systematic strategy.

When asked to proofread a written product, the learner should be instructed on (a) what to do when a suspected error is located and (b) how to correct the misspelling. Known as a learning strategy, the procedure will allow the writer to independently monitor his or her own work. The following strategy should be taught using materials with controlled errors and then transferred to writing generated by the student. The writer is told to review his or her work, applying each step in the strategy until a correct spelling is found.

1. Read each sentence separately.

2. Circle any suspected spelling error.

3. Examine the word within the context to determine if the word should be capitalized.

4. Try to sound out the word applying sound-symbol associations and/ or morphemic elements.

5. Generate alternative spellings of the word, selecting the one that looks (and feels) the most accurate.

6. If the word still appears incorrect, seek external assistance such as from a word list, a dictionary, or the teacher.

In the case of the very young writer or the severely disabled speller, the teacher may wish to modify the strategy in order to maintain the monitoring function while simplifying the spelling task. To do this, instruct the student to circle all uncertain words prior to handing in the writing paper. The teacher then can provide a list of accurate spellings for all circled words, which the student uses to correct the paper. The important thing is that the child is still responsible for detecting spelling errors and is developing rudimentary proofreading skills.

Dictionary Skills

A major component of any spelling program should be the use of extrinsic references such as a dictionary, glossary, or graded word list. The dictionary is a basic spelling tool with which all learners working at or above the third grade level should be familiar. For the young or disabled learner, the use of alphabetized word lists should be encouraged over the more traditional dictionary. A variation on this is the individual spelling dictionary or word book which acts as a personal reference source.

The common lament of, "How can I look it up if I can't spell it?", is one all teachers are familiar with. Dictionary use is possible when several subskills come together and allow for independent problem solving. It is not enough to know the beginning sound of the word if the remaining unknown phonemic parts do not correspond to a single grapheme. For instance, knowing that *experience* begins with an *e* sound will not be enough if the child is unsure as to the next letter (is it *x*, *k*, or *c*?), what grapheme corresponds to the *i* sound (is it *i*, *ei*, or *ee*?), or what is the proper way of spelling the final morphemic element *ence* (*ence*, *ents*, or *ense*?). The speller must be able to meld a variety of intrinsic strategies in order to develop a close approximation of the word before using the dictionary as a spelling checker.

Skills necessary for dictionary use are: (a) alphabetizing, (b) using guide words, (c) locating words of uncertain spelling, (d) locating word meanings, and (e) interpreting diacritical markings. Within the spelling program the dictionary should be emphasized as a feedback source that is most helpful when used with words with few uncertain elements.

ESTABLISHING THE WEEKLY SPELLING PROGRAM

The creation of an effective spelling program will depend upon its integration with the general writing program. To compartmentalize these two aspects of the language arts is to reduce the impact of spelling as a functional skill. The motivation received from writing has a direct influence on growth in spelling.

The basic components of a sound spelling program include (a) a selected word list, (b) a pretest-posttest procedure, (c) a word study program (including instructional procedures), (d) review activities and tests, and (e) evaluation and feedback procedures.

Techniques often used in spelling programs that have not been substantiated as effective include presenting syllabicated word forms, repeatedly writing words without any other word study format, studying word "hard spots," individualizing time allocations for spelling

TABLE 7.6. Weekly Spelling Program

Day	Activity
Monday	Pretest Word analysis
Tuesday	Word study Vocabulary development
Wednesday	Spelling activities for word practice
Thursday	Practice test Word study of missed words
Friday	Evaluation and feedback

study, writing the words in the air, overemphasizing phonic rules, and giving initial word presentation in sentence or paragraph form (Allred, 1984). The teacher should note these unvalidated practices and seriously attempt to eliminate them from the spelling program.

The amount of time that should be given to the spelling program within the weekly routine of the regular classroom has been commonly cited as between 60 and 75 minutes per week (Allred, 1984). This is based on research conducted as early as 1897 (Rice, 1897) and verified by Jarvis in 1963. However, this time allotment is specified for the study of word lists and may need to be expanded when word study encompasses additional activities. Although the problem learner may actually need a longer period of study, this does not necessarily mean that any one session should extend over more than 15 minutes. In such cases, planning for fewer words or for word study more than once a day may be appropriate. The question of time allotment is closely tied to the meaningfulness of the activity students engage in. The most effective activities are ones that relate to learning about words and the direct application of words in written experiences.

The organization of the spelling program around a weekly routine should contain the essential elements listed above. A suggested spelling program is provided in Table 7.6.

SPELLING ACTIVITIES

It is an unfortunate fact of many programs that spelling is a deadly subject for most mildly handicapped learners. This need not be the case given a carefully planned instructional program, an appropriate selection of games and spelling activities, and a careful integration of spelling into other areas of study. Feedback and conference sessions concerning the student's performance on specific spelling activities will help to promote spelling independence.

When selecting spelling activities and games, it is important to choose ones that focus attention on the spelling process rather than on significant features of the activity or game. The more involved the learners are in the activity, the more benefit they will receive from the spelling task. When students are minimally involved and acting as passive observers, their learning is reduced. Therefore, such games as spelling contests that have one student responding at a time should be avoided.

The following activities are suggestions that can be adapted to fit the class or an individual student's spelling program needs.

Editing

Editing activities can be varied to include self-correction, peer correction, and team approaches. The goal, however, remains the same: to develop independent and self-correcting spellers. To achieve this, it is important to establish the guidelines for editing procedures that the group will follow. These should include (a) what is to be edited and (b) what feedback is to be given (e.g., incorrect words are to be circled).

Visual Imagery

Visual imagery can be trained by assigning reading material to students that includes specified words that the student needs to learn. Early readings may even highlight these words by underlining or color coding them in order to draw the learner's attention.

A slightly different visual image approach is to present the learner with controlled reading material and ask the student to find words that contain certain letter patterns or orthographic generalizations. These words may then be used for further study.

Personal Dictionaries

Personal dictionaries may be used to focus students' attention on words that are important for their writing needs. Students may add to the dictionary based upon words that need to be learned, demon words, high-frequency words, or content-related words.

Spelling Cards

Spelling Cards is a game that can be played by pairs of learners having about the same spelling ability. Spelling words are written on individual cards, and there are approximately 20 cards to a deck. Each player receives six cards to begin with. A player reads a word and then says it in a sentence. The next player must spell the word. If the word is spelled correctly, the player is given the word card as a token. If the word is spelled incorrectly, the card remains with the original player. When one player is left without any cards, the other player wins.

Spelling Bingo

Spelling Bingo is played in a manner similar to the original Bingo game. Player cards are headed with columns that are numbered one to five (any square combination may be used such as 3 × 3 or 4 × 4). The squares below each column number are filled with phonemes (e.g., *e, ight, ay, bl, f*), and students are given a chance to cover a square when a word is called that contains a certain phoneme. A variation on this is to provide a word list and have students mark off the squares on their cards that contain phonemes which are in the words on the list.

Kinesthetic Spelling

Kinesthetic spelling allows the learner to develop the "feel" of the word pattern. This is done to help the student establish the movement (visualization is also important) of the letter forms during the writing process. Writing the word in a box of shallow sand or salt is one method. Another is to write or trace the word over a sheet of sandpaper. Painting over the letters as a tracing task will also increase the kinesthetic awareness. Kinesthetic techniques should be recognized as fun and used for the novelty effect they can have when incorporated into a well-developed program of study.

COMPUTER APPLICATIONS IN SPELLING

The advantages of microcomputers for disabled learners, including unlimited practice, immediate feedback, motivation, performance charting, record keeping, and active participation, are all relevant to the use of computers in spelling instruction. More and more studies using microcomputers are examining instructional practices in spelling. Early research in the late 1960s used computers to study the effect of repetitions and the distribution of practice on spelling performance. Knutson (1967) found that immediate and spaced repetitions on the microcomputer resulted in substantial word learning and that spaced repetition was consistently better than either no repetition or word practice. Findings by Fishman (1968) extended this research by demonstrating that computerized spelling drills using masss practice resulted in greater short-term performance, while distributed trials resulted in increased learning over a longer period of time.

How words are presented to the learner to study is another instructional variable that has been studied using computerized programs. Focusing upon the presentation methods of whole word versus word parts, Block, Tucker, and Butler (1974) examined the effects upon learning rates and retention levels. Their findings indicate that words displayed by letters were learned most rapidly, followed by words displayed by chunks and whole words, respectively. Interestingly, retention level was not affected by the presentation method.

The use of microcomputers with problem spellers has more recently become a research focus. Spelling, which has for a long time been recognized as a difficult subject to teach to mildly handicapped learners, has recently been provided with the technology to reverse this negative situation. The microcomputer allows the teacher to appropriately individualize spelling instruction to accommodate a range of individual differences. Studies that have focused upon problem learners have shown the computer's usefulness for remediating spelling difficulties. Learning small groups of spelling words rather than a single large list was shown to be an effective approach for low-ability students working on computerized lists (Hansen, 1966). These students did significantly better on short lists of 6 words each than on a unit list of 18 difficult words.

The development of microcomputer programs for effective instruction of spelling has been verified by Hasselbring (1982), Fisher (1984), and Rieth, Polsgrove, and Eckert (1984). Hasselbring designed the Computerized Spelling Remediation Program using an interactive format to teach via modeling, imitation, and feedback. The program functions without teacher monitoring of student responses and offers the student the opportunity to practice spelling skills independently.

Fisher (1984) also advocates the use of interactive programs that use speech synthesizers to present spelling words. This form of computer-assisted instruction eliminates the problem of continuously presenting a written model of the spelling word on the computer screen. In such programs the computer controls the audio component so that the rate of presentation, the instructions, and the feedback are appropriate.

Fisher specifies the advantages of speech synthesis interfaced with the computer for spelling instruction:

1. There is easy production of words or sentences that have been typed by the teacher or student or entered from files of previously learned words. Lists can be reconstituted to match individual needs.

2. Reinforcement and corrective feedback can be presented to the learner orally. A problem reader is more apt to respond when praised or corrected verbally than when forced to read comments.

3. Words can be repeated as many times as the speller needs to hear them in order to analyze the auditory components.

4. The student is given the chance to explore phonetic spellings when the computer repeats the word, phrase, or sentence the student has typed. This allows the student to experiment with spellings and to analyze the written word according to both auditory and visual feedback.

At Indiana University's Center for Innovation in Teaching the Handicapped (CITH), the focus in microcomputer spelling instruction has been to develop a program that is based directly on learning principles (Rieth, Polsgrove, & Eckert, 1984). The program incorporates automatic and continuous assessment in order to identify students' functioning levels and to track their spelling progress. The result is the *SPELLMASTER* system, which provides students with either a timed visually displayed spelling list or a Voltrax Type 'N Talk speech synthesized list. The *SPELLMASTER* consists of two components: the presentation of teacher-specified spelling lists (Spell) and a managing program which specifies participating students and individual criteria, creates and edits spelling lists, and reports student scores (Report).

Using the Report software component, teachers are able to mold individual programs by appropriately placing the students and establishing unique spelling lists and acceptance criteria for each learner. The adaptability of the system even allows the teacher to select the output mode (aural or visual), specify the number of learning trials, and direct the format of the correction procedure. Finally, the teacher is able to obtain daily progress reports.

The *SPELLMASTER* system is a good example of the use of current technology in spelling instruction. As the technology advances and the availability of microcomputers increases in the classroom, the likelihood of more and easier programs multiplies. Although the advantages of microcomputer instruction in spelling are considerable, two significant problems can occur. First, slow learners may, if left unmonitored, key in a letter string, letter by letter, decreasing the visual representation of the word pattern. Therefore, rehearsal of the letter sequence must be encouraged. Second, some children will not automatically make the transfer of the typed word pattern learned on the microcomputer to handwritten material. In such cases, an additional programming step is necessary to ensure the transfer (Peters, 1985).

The microcomputer has also been used for assessment of spelling ability. A computerized version of the *Test of Written Spelling* (TWS) resulted in shorter administration time due to the computer's ability to pace for individual rates and to automatically compute and record scores (Hasselbring & Crossland, 1982). However, in a second study designed to verify these results and examine the effects of the microcomputer on student performance and attitude, Varnhagen and Gerber (1984) found that students took less time and spelled more words correctly in the traditional written form of the TWS. The increased time needed for students to locate letters on the keyboard appeared to interfere with the cognitive processes being assessed by the test. The authors caution the use of the microcomputer for spelling assessment.

How future spelling software is programmed to meet individual students' needs will still largely be the responsibility of the classroom teacher and will to some extent depend upon that teacher's knowledge of spelling and spelling instruction.

BEST PRACTICES

There is little conclusive evidence to suggest the best method for teaching spelling. When research in spelling and spelling practices for nonhandicapped learners is combined with a basic understanding of the learning traits of problem learners, there emerge several factors that should result in higher spelling achievement.

1. The presentation of new spelling words is most efficiently and effectively done through the use of a word list. This method most directly introduces the novel words, shortening the instruction time, while increasing the retention and transfer of the words.

2. Word lists should be kept short when introducing new

words (5 to 8 words). The addition of review words should not significantly increase the weekly list.

3. The use of a pretest to determine the words the student needs to focus upon eliminates repetitive instruction and helps the student to recognize specific areas of difficulty that require attention. Pretests should be corrected immediately by the students themselves, allowing the students to discriminate correct from incorrect responses. This element of immediate self-correction and feedback has been found to be the single most important variable in teaching spelling relative to the allotted time given for instruction.

4. Systematic instruction of spelling which provides poor spellers with procedures for word study is preferable. Teachers are cautioned not to simply point out spelling errors but also to provide a corrective program.

5. Spelling performance and recall have been shown to improve by simple, contingent imitation of a spelling error followed by the correct word pattern.

6. The incorporation of verified principles of learning within the spelling program will result in better spelling ability. Such principles as reduced unit size, distributed and sufficient practice, and generalization training need to be more consistently applied to the spelling curriculum for problem learners.

7. Phonics instruction is supplemental to, not a substitute for, spelling. Teaching those generalizations that apply to a large number of words can be beneficial; however, too many generalizations may be detrimental to the learning process.

8. Teaching the words most frequently used by children will result in the greatest generalization. Since fewer than 300 words account for more than 50% of the words used in children's writings (Fitzgerald, 1951), this is not too enormous a task. Individual experiences (e.g., subject content, personal information, and current events) will dictate the selection of additional words.

9. Functional spelling skills increase as a result of involvement with words. The child who has numerous opportunities to read and write will be able to relate to the letter patterns and will increasingly be able to reproduce the spellings.

10. Improvements in spelling ability may be small, such as

increases in the number of correct letter pairs within words. Therefore, it is important to continually assess and record student performance.

There are many reasons why students misspell words. Diagnosis and classification of a learner's spelling ability are necessary before remediation can begin. Understanding a child's developmental spelling level will allow a teacher to plan an appropriate program. The differences in spelling ability and spelling dysfunctions mandate that no one method be used to teach spelling. Instead, a teacher must be able to adapt elements of various approaches to meet individual needs.

WRITTEN EXPRESSION

Written expression is the final language skill to be acquired. As the culmination of language learning, the acquisition of written language abilities must draw upon previous experiences within the areas of speaking, listening, and reading. Unfortunately, writing has often been allowed to take a back seat to these other language areas in education.

As recently as the spring of 1986, wire services reported that "American students' writing skills remained in dismal shape," with 62 to 80% of all 17-year-olds demonstrating poor writing across three areas of assessment. Although these data are based on studies in regular education, the relative neglect of writing has occurred to an even greater extent in special education, where emphasis has so clearly been placed on reading and mathematics. The purpose of this chapter is to provide an appropriate perspective on the importance of written expression and then to provide discussion of useful approaches to assessment and effective avenues for instruction.

It is helpful to begin with a set of initial considerations regarding writing. First, written language must be viewed by the writer as a process as well as a product. It is important for all students, including handicapped learners, to realize that the task of writing includes a series of steps and cannot be viewed as the simple, straightforward production of a polished form.

Second, writing must always be considered for its communicative properties. Therefore, it demands attention to the needs and characteristics of the audience. To achieve this the writer must develop a clear sense of purpose as he or she begins the task. While oral communication, in contrast, can support unclear ideas which can be clarified in the communication exchange between speakers, written expression dictates that the writer be able to clearly express ideas for an unseen and perhaps unknown audience (Hansen, 1978).

Third, writing must be tied to an emphasis on cognition. Obviously, clear writing demands clear thinking; otherwise, the central objective of communication cannot possibly be achieved. The implications for organization of thought and thus of writing are apparent.

Additionally, writing must be seen as a primary variable that will serve as a predictor for either success or failure in school, particularly for students in secondary and postsecondary settings. The demands of taking notes in class, responding to short answer and essay test items, and developing papers and projects all require the ability to write logically and coherently.

Finally, for many students there is more to the act of writing than just the concern for achievement. Rather, the expressive side of writing should also be considered for its possible contribution to the enhancement of personal attitudes and perhaps concept of self, especially in older students. Thus, writing can serve as an end as well as a means; while students are achieving specific skill goals in writing, it is likely that they can simultaneously achieve by-product objectives in the areas of personal and social adjustment.

DEVELOPMENT OF WRITTEN EXPRESSION

Written expression is best conceptualized as consisting of three stages: prewriting, writing, and postwriting. Although these stages should not be considered totally discrete, they nevertheless provide an accurate outline of the necessary steps that go into the successful act of writing.

Table 8.1 provides a sequence of specific tasks associated with written language. It is an expansion of the sequence for handwriting presented in Chapter 6, with specific focus on written expression. Although the list does not represent a precise schedule for the developmental acquisition of skills, it does illustrate the major elements necessary for successful writing. The table has been divided into the three stages as delineated above. As can be seen, the primary challenges

TABLE 8.1. Written Language Sequence

Prewriting

- possesses the requisite experiential background
- possesses the requisite oral receptive and expressive abilities
- possesses the necessary rudimentary reading skills
- writes (handwriting) legibly (or has developed requisite skill in alternative means)
- has the desire to communicate in written form

Writing

- writes simple phrases
- writes simple sentences
- writes compound and complex sentences
- begins sentences with a capital letter
- uses capital letters appropriately according to other rules
- ends sentences with appropriate punctuation
- uses punctuation marks appropriately according to other rules
- demonstrates simple rules for sentences
- demonstrates complex rules for sentences
- identifies parts of speech
- uses descriptive and varied vocabulary
- writes complete paragraphs
- writes notes and letters
- expresses creative ideas in writing
- takes effective lecture notes
- responds accurately to essay exam questions

Postwriting

- edits and revises for capitalization
- edits and revises for punctuation
- edits and revises for sentence structure
- edits and revises for word usage
- edits and revises for content and ideation
- edits and revises for overall organization

for the would-be writer during the prewriting stage concern motivational factors and the setting of purpose. Next, the writing stage subsumes the majority of the technical skills associated with the writing act itself. Finally, the postwriting stage includes the efforts made during revision or editing of the written work. The reader is referred to Hall (1981) for further information on the relationship of these three stages and to Polloway, Patton, and Cohen (1981, 1983) for a model of the writing process.

WRITING CHARACTERISTICS OF HANDICAPPED LEARNERS

A limited data base exists on the written language abilities of handicapped students. However, it is apparent that exceptional learners are likely to experience problems running the full gamut of skills within the written language domain. Certainly, many of the difficulties that disabled persons experience in writing may be residuals from the linguistic areas of speaking, reading, handwriting, and spelling discussed previously. Other problems, such as thought development and editing, may represent difficulties unique to the act of written expression.

A general initial concern regarding the characteristics and needs of exceptional learners in writing has to do with the nature of the writing act and the nature of the difficulties commonly experienced by mildly handicapped students. Included in this area for consideration are general abilities that underlie successful writing. First, the successful writer must be *actively involved* in the task and thus must demonstrate a cognitive awareness of the writing process. This ability is particularly important in writing, since it is clearly not something that can be done *to* students—it must be done *by* them. Second, the student must pay careful *attention* to task demands and details such as focusing on the various grammatical conventions of standard English. Third, the writer must be *reflective* and thus able to generate creative ideas or to consider the correct match between the mode of communication and the background or needs of the audience. These three abilities are significant because they are common problems experienced by handicapped learners. For example, the professional literature is replete with references to mildly handicapped students as inactive learners (e.g., Torgeson, 1977), as experiencing attentional deficits (e.g., Ross, 1976), and as displaying a learning style characterized more by impulsivity than reflectivity (e.g., Epstein, Hallahan, & Kauffman, 1975).

Although the above discussion presents some discouraging initial considerations relative to special written language instruction, it should coincidentally be encouraging to the teacher. While writing can frequently represent a deficit area for exceptional learners, at the same time it can be viewed as a potential vehicle for providing assistance that may activate the disabled learner, reinforce attention and focus, and develop a reflective learning style.

Specific Areas of Difficulty

Given that written language is the last verbal system that the child is asked to master, difficulties in writing may not be evident until the middle elementary years or even until high school. While structural skill deficits may be noted relatively early, late recognition might be especially common for those students whose difficulties lie in the formulation of ideas to be conveyed in written form.

Students may present a variety of achievement profiles in writing. Johnson and Myklebust (1967) cautioned that learning disabled children may, for example, function at age level in ideation but substantially below that in related writing skills. Disorders in formulation and syntax may exist separately, although more often disabled writers will present difficulties with both (Johnson & Myklebust, 1967).

No long-term inquiries into the specific written language skills of handicapped students have been reported in the literature that is comparable, for example, to the work of Loban (1963) with nonhandicapped children. Therefore, empirical data on the nature of specific problems found in mildly handicapped and remedial learners are somewhat limited. The relatively few studies that have been reported confirm what might be deemed typical expectations.

Myklebust (1973), investigating the writing skills of students identified as reading disabled, reports that deficiencies were commonly found in linguistic output (determined by the total number of words used and the overall number of sentences written), competence in syntax, and the ability to use abstractions in expressing thoughts. Poplin and her colleagues (Poplin, Gray, Larsen, Banikowski, & Mehring, 1980), using test data from the *Test of Written Language*, reported greater deficits in those areas that reflect the conventional aspects of grammar and spelling than in those areas more indicative of ideation.

A study reported by Hermreck (1979) compared the written essays of learning disabled and nonhandicapped students across several grades and reported differentiated totals of words used. Hermreck found that nondisabled students wrote on an average of 42% more words per essay than did their disabled peers.

Deshler (1978) identified another problem. He reported that learning disabled students detected only one-third of the errors they made in writing, which he compared to nonhandicapped students who identified twice as many of their own errors. Deshler classified this deficiency as a monitoring deficit which could result in the student failing to correct both externally-produced and self-generated errors. Academic and post-school implications are apparent with this problem.

Related clinical and anecdotal data verify these trends in writing difficulties in handicapped students. Wiig and Semel (1980), for example, reported that middle and secondary school disabled students often had a series of difficulties that could interfere with performance and encoding language. Common problems they identified that might be present included difficulties in semantics (e.g., minimal elaboration, restricted writing and word use, and limited word meanings), syntax (e.g., limited use of tense variants and complex sentences), and memory (e.g., inefficiency in retaining and retrieving words). The problems that Wiig and Semel (1980) identified clearly would become more significant as students are faced with demands of secondary and postsecondary education. Several studies (e.g., Davis, 1975; Wells, 1974) provide good illustrations of the difficulties that may confront disabled students after high school. This body of research is discussed in detail in Chapter 14, which focuses specifically on language problems in disabled adults.

ASSESSMENT OF WRITING SKILLS

It should be clear from the brief review above that handicapped learners can experience a myriad of problems in writing. Therefore, assessment activities must focus on the specific deficits as well as talents that individual students have within this domain. In a review of key approaches to assessment, the following sections discuss both formal and informal methods for collecting data on students' writing performance. Since the emphasis is on assessment information that can provide a sound basis for subsequent instructional programming, particular attention is given to the use of informal assessment tools.

Formal Assessment

A limited number of comprehensive tools are available for the formal evaluation of writing skills. Nevertheless, a number of formal tests are general in scope and include subtests focusing on the evaluation of written expression. Table 8.2 lists the commercial tests and relevant subtests that provide possible sources of assessment data.

A variety of formats have been used to assess writing skills. *Contrived* test items present the student with a series of choices and instructions to select the correct response (e.g., the item that is grammatically accurate). This type of item is the most commonly used format for group standardized writing tests as well as some subtests of individual evaluative instruments.

Writing samples provide a preferable alternative to contrived formats for analyzing writing ability, since data can be obtained directly from the student's own work. Samples may be taken from a variety of written

TABLE 8.2. Formal Tests of Written Language

Test	Publisher	Appropriate Ages/Grades	Administration	Relevant Subtests or Focus of Assessment
SRA Achievement Series (Thorpe, Lefever, & Hasland, 1974)	Science Research Associates	Grades 2 to 9	Group	Usage including capitalization
Stanford Achievement Test (SAT) (Madden, Gardner, Rudman, Karlsen, & Merwin, 1973)	Psychological Corporation	Grades 1-5 to 9-5 Language subtests, 3-0 to 9-5	Group	Capitalization Punctuation Usage
Metropolitan Achievement Tests (Durost, Bixler, Wrightstone, Prescott, & Balow, 1971)	Harcourt Brace Jovanovich	Grades K to 9-5 Language Components, 3-5 to 9-5		Punctuation Capitalization Usage
Test of Adolescent Language–2 (TOAL–2) (Hammill, Brown, Larsen, Wiederholt, 1987)	PRO-ED	Ages 11-0 to 18-5	Individual	Writing/Vocabulary Writing/Grammar
Picture Story Language Test (Myklebust, 1965)	Western Psychological Services	Ages 7-0 to 17-0	Individual and/or Group	Scoring areas include the following scales: Productivity, Syntax, Abstract-Concrete
Test of Written Language (TOWL) (Hammill & Larsen, 1983)	PRO-ED	Ages 8-6 to 14-5	Individual	Vocabulary Thematic Maturity Word Usage Style Spelling Handwriting

FIGURE 8.1. Written Language Sample

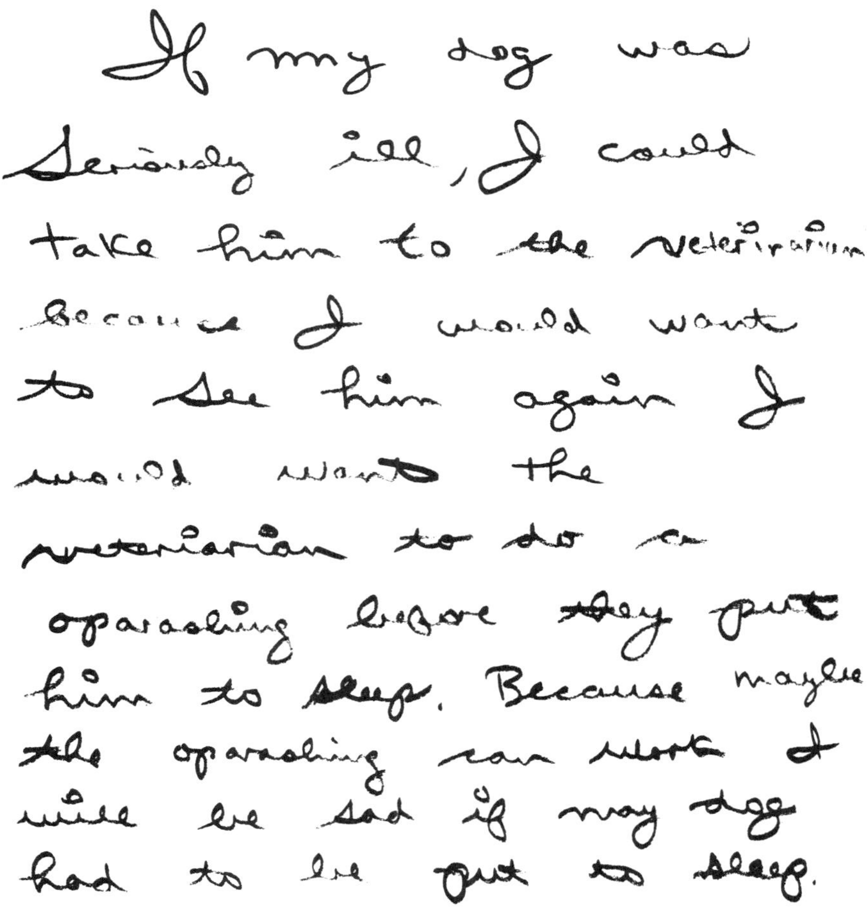

If my dog was Seriously ill, I could take him to the veterinarian Because I would want to See him again I would want the veterarian to do a oparashing before they put him to sleep. Because maybe the oparashing can work I will be sad if may dogg had to be put to sleep.

The authors acknowledge the assistance of the children in Ms. Debra Zimmerman and Ms. Judi Sherry's class for providing samples of written work.

assignments such as compositions, letters, reports written for specific content areas, and daily journals (see Figure 8.1). Typically, the assessment information generated from writing samples is evaluated either in terms of the analysis of *specific skills and attributes* (e.g., sentence length, grammatical structure) or viewed *holistically*, wherein samples are appraised in a general sense and given an overall ranking. These aspects of assessment of writing samples are further elaborated on in the following section on informal assessment.

Informal Assessment

A variety of approaches are available for informal assessment of the multifaceted skills associated with writing. This discussion of assessment includes the three general areas of content (with a focus on ideation and conceptualization), vocabulary, and form (including mechanical skills). In addition, discussion in this section also includes the holistic scoring of writing.

Content. The area of content as used here is defined as the ideas, concepts, and overall integrity of the written product. Cartwright (1969) divided this area for assessment purposes into the three concerns of accuracy, ideas, and organization. His scale for evaluation is presented in Table 8.3. Dependent on the specific writing sample to be evaluated, these three areas may warrant attention. Although this approach is not completely objective, it does provide foundational guidelines for the evaluation of content in writing; the more precisely these guidelines are designated, the more reliable will be the appraisal. Although the three areas are somewhat arbitrarily selected, they nevertheless illustrate major content concerns. Cartwright (1969) suggests several patterns that might emerge that have instructional implications.

> A number of different patterns of strengths and weaknesses may emerge when using the rating scheme. For example, a particular student might be rated fairly high in accuracy and ideas, and low in organization. This pattern might indicate that the student should practice outlining and writing from an outline. A pattern of low accuracy and moderate to high ideas and organization could indicate good organization of some original ideas but a minimal command of relevant factual information. (Evidence for the validity of this particular pattern can be obtained from anyone who has read essay examinations of students who have not committed themselves to much study prior to the examination.) (pp. 105–107)

Vocabulary. The purpose of assessment in vocabulary is to evaluate the strength and variety of a child's lexicon. There are several procedures available that can provide useful information of instructional relevance.

One technique that has often been used to measure the overall variety of words is the *type-token ratio*. This procedure takes its name from the fact that it provides a comparison of the different words used

TABLE 8.3. Content Evaluation Scale

Area of Assessment	Score
Accuracy (appropriate for all forms of discourse)	
The composition completely satisfies all the objectives of the assignment. All the necessary facts and concepts included and correctly interpreted.	10
	9
	8
Most of the relevant concepts are included. The composition satisfies most of the objectives of the assignment.	7
	6
Several relevant facts or concepts omitted. Some assignment objectives not satisfied.	5
	4
Superficial coverage of topic; factual content very limited.	3
	2
Exhibits little or no understanding of the topic. Composition does not meet any of the objectives of the assignment.	1
	0
Ideas (increases in importance as form of discourse proceeds from narration to exposition or argumentation)	
Ideas suggested are pertinent to the topic, and/or represent a high degree of originality. No clichés or hackneyed phrases are present.	10
	9
	8
	7
Presents a variety of good but standard ideas.	6
	5
Ideas not clear or are inadequate. Often resorts to clichés.	4
	3

TABLE 8.3. Continued

Area of Assessment	Score
	2
Exhibits neither originality nor understanding of the task. Does not meet any objectives of the written assignment. Presents only clichés or restatement of the ideas of others.	1
	0

Organization (necessary for all types of discourse)

Ideas developed in logical sequence. Appropriate emphasis given to different ideas when necessary. Paragraphing is appropriate to content. Successful use of topic sentences, suspense, and climax if relevant to type of discourse.	10
	9
	8
	7
Some improvement could be shown in sequence of idea development. Paragraphing not always consistent with content.	6
	5
Does not carry out a logical progression of ideas. Paragraphing and overall organization indicates haziness in thinking, although parts of the composition show some internal relationship.	4
	3
	2
	1
Very poor arrangement of ideas; no logical relationship between sections or ideas. Paragraphing nonexistent or inappropriate to content. Sentences bear little relationship with each other or with paragraphs. Unimportant or irrelevant ideas emphasized.	0

From Cartwright, G. P. (1969). Written expression and spelling. In R. M. Smith (Ed.), *Teacher diagnosis of educational difficulties.* Columbus, OH: Charles E. Merrill, pp. 106–107.

(types) to the overall number of words in a passage (tokens). The computation is straightforward: type/token = ratio. In the writing sample shown in Figure 8.1, the total number of words (tokens) is 55, while the number of different words (types) is 35; hence, the ratio would be .63.

The type-token ratio provides a measure of maturity of writing style. Increased diversity of usage as indicated by an increase in the ratio illustrates improvement in the student's varied word choices. When used as a pre/post measure, teachers can simply select a 50- or 100-word sample at the beginning of the intervention program and a like-sized sample subsequently for comparative purposes.

An alternative procedure for assessing vocabulary is the *index of diversification*. This measure compares the total number of words used to the number of occurrences of the most frequently used word. Referring again to the sample in Figure 8.1 with a total of 55, the number of occurrences of "to" is 6, so the index would be 55/6 = 9.2. As Polloway and Patton (1982) noted, increases in the index indicate a broader vocabulary base.

A third approach for assessing word usage is an informal one that focuses on the use of *unusual or atypical words*. In this case, the measure is simply a frequency count of words used that have not commonly been a part of a student's writing vocabulary. Again referring to Figure 8.1, the words "veterinarian," "oparashing" (operation), and "seriously" might be designated as unusual or atypical words. By keeping a running list of new words, this procedure could be used to systematically identify new words being used and thus serve as an indicator of vocabulary gains.

Form. Two approaches are helpful relative to the evaluation of written language form or structure. *Average sentence length* (ASL) provides a measure of maturity of writing by focusing on the increasing complexity of sentences generated by students. The ASL is essentially an arithmetical average of the number of words per sentence. In the sample in Figure 8.1, there are four sentences; therefore, the ASL would be 55/4 = 13.8.

Error analysis is the most commonly used assessment procedure in written language. As noted previously, it involves a comparison of errors found with a list of basic grammatical skills (see Table 8.1 for a brief list). In the sample in Figure 8.1, specific errors that can be identified include the presence of a sentence fragment and the absence of a comma after the initial subordinate clause. All efforts related to error analysis should be tied to educational programming. There is little to be gained, and perhaps a risk of attitudinal damage, from giving feedback to students about errors made for which instruction has not previously been provided. This concern is further discussed in the section later in this chapter dealing with the remediation of structural difficulties.

Holistic Scoring. According to Mishler and Hogan (1982), holistic scoring is the oldest method of evaluating written essays. With this approach, raters are asked to compare a student's writing sample to samples that represent various levels of writing. A single overall judgment of quality is given which may be based on a variety of grammatical areas (e.g., word choice, spelling, organization, sentence structure, and imagination). Multiple raters, typically a group of teachers who are trained on a set of *anchor points*, are most commonly used to evaluate a set of papers, that is, papers preselected to illustrate various points along the scoring scale. Mishler and Hogan (1982) report from their review of studies using holistic scoring that reliability for ratings has been well within the acceptable range. They note that the use of this approach with handicapped students could provide a means of evaluating overall progress in learning to write while also providing data useful for comparison to other handicapped and/or nonhandicapped students. Because the procedure is extremely efficient (trained raters can evaluate approximately one paper per minute), holistic scoring is particularly attractive for use with large groups of students.

TEACHING WRITTEN EXPRESSION

The following discussion focuses on specific strategies that are appropriate for the three stages of prewriting, writing, and postwriting. Instructional methods as well as curricular programs are included in the discussion.

Prewriting Stage

Three interrelated concerns have been associated with prewriting: stimulation, motivation, and purpose (Polloway et al., 1981). Although these concerns represent somewhat arbitrary distinctions, there are several essential points concerning the teacher's role across these three aspects of the prewriting stage.

Stimulation.   Stimulation is concerned with the input that provides the necessary basis for student output. As Johnson and Myklebust (1967) noted, "All children, with the exception of the most creative, benefit from stimulation and encouragement before they write. Creativity does not emerge in a vacuum" (p. 232).

Key considerations related to stimulation include (a) the need for input from the two receptive domains of reading and listening; (b) the need for the opportunity to discuss and clarify ideas and concepts; and (c) the need for the development of thought patterns on a specific topic.

A basic assumption is that stimulation develops only within a supportive, conducive atmosphere.

During the prewriting stage, students can also be stimulated to draw on a variety of experiences. Tompkins and Friend (1986) list the following five strategies that may be helpful: *observing* objects and events and jotting down descriptive words that apply; *sensory exploration* of possible topics leading to the generation of words that draw from the unique contribution of each of the senses; *mapping* or diagramming a topic in order to organize key words and thoughts before writing by using the visual dimension; using *markings* or strategies that encourage students to draw on past experiences in order to collect and organize their own ideas for writing on a topic (e.g., "things to keep secret"); and *interviewing* (e.g., by developing a set of questions for peers, adults, or family).

Finally, it is useful to consider that, as Phelps-Gunn and Phelps-Terasaki (1982) note in their review of research, the stress on oral language, as one way to stimulate writing, does by itself not ensure improvement in specific task skills. However, stimulation does provide the prerequisite orientation and conceptualization regarding the general task ahead for the writer.

Motivation. The key element of motivation is instilling the desire to communicate. It naturally corresponds to the oral language equivalent of intention previously discussed in the chapter on speaking. A transactional view of language (e.g., McLean & Snyder-McLean, 1978) dictates that the social base for language is critical to development—it is of similar importance in the area of written language.

Motivation can be considered from two perspectives. In one perspective, motivation is seen as flowing from within the writer. In this case, the task of the teacher is to create the desire to write by providing the student with relevant, interesting, and exciting tasks to write about. To accomplish this, topics and themes of particular interest to the individual or the group of students should be provided. Table 8.4 is a list of possible topics; the reader is referred to Carlson (1970), Petty and Bowen (1967), Polloway and Smith (1982), and Polloway et al. (1985) for additional ideas. In a related vein, motivation can also be enhanced by helping the student initiate the writing task. Specific ways that this can be achieved include providing a sentence to begin a story; providing a lengthy introduction to a story to which the student must write the conclusion; setting up a hypothetical situation and having the writer respond to it; and inventing a series of circumstances that require the student to consider alternatives in order to complete the plot of the story.

While considering the various ways that teachers can develop motivation by providing interesting topics, it is important to consider the cautionary note about instructional programming provided by Graves (1985):

> The most pernicious aspect of teacher interventions is that children begin to learn early on that others need to supply topics because they come to the page with nothing in their heads. A focus on skills and form to the exclusion of child-initiated meaning further confirms their lack of fit with the writing process. (p. 38)

The discussion to this point has been based on the assumption that motivation flows from within the writer, since students' desire to write can be cultivated from their basic intention, which is already well developed. However, when this scenario cannot validly be assumed, as is often true with handicapped learners and in particular adolescents, then straightforward motivational strategies may simply be insufficient. Rather, there may be a need for what Phelps-Gunn and Phelps-Terasaki (1982) term *motivational remediation*.

If writing does not flow from within, the necessity of providing reinforcement programs provides a second perspective on the enhancement of motivation. Specific techniques are discussed later in this chapter as they relate to the effects of reinforcement programs on specific writing skill areas. It is sufficient to note here that the teacher will want to consider utilizing a reinforcement strategy that sets up contingencies tied to the achievement of particular written language goals.

Alley and Deshler (1979) provide several good points which serve as a summary to the concerns for motivation. They identify attitude as a key concern for teachers working on writing with adolescent disabled learners, and they suggest that the following might prove helpful: Encourage students to focus initially on ideas rather than mechanics so that they first feel comfortable with writing before trying to achieve perfection (thus sensing failure) with mechanical skills; expose students to a variety of experiences to build their knowledge base for writing; use tape recorders as an initial way to record thoughts with later efforts to transcribe and revise these thoughts; and have students write daily or weekly journals with no corrective feedback provided.

Although motivation is clearly a critical concern in writing, it is important to add that, as with stimulation, developing the desire to write does not automatically translate into having the ability to write (Phelps-Gunn & Phelps-Terasaki, 1982). Therefore, motivational techniques must be paired with systematic instructional procedures in order to accomplish meaningful improvement in writing ability. Neither the provision of relevant and exciting topics nor the establishment of powerful reinforcement contingencies alone can result in mature writing.

TABLE 8.4. Topics for Writing Assignments

1. Loneliness.
2. What will you be doing in 1991?
3. Pollution: What is it? Why? What can we do about it?
4. What would you do if you were invisible for 48 hours?
5. Love.
6. Happiness.
7. Fight.
8. War.
9. Peace.
10. I am a raindrop.
11. I am a snowflake.
12. Death.
13. What is your favorite sport and why?
14. Describe what it is like to be fog. How does it change things?
15. What bugs you?
16. Describe someone you like. Why?
17. Write a spooky Halloween story.
18. Describe television commercials—one you like and one you don't.
19. Excitement is . . .
20. Be an animal.
21. What is your favorite television show? Why?
22. 'Twas the night before Christmas and you were in a haunted house.
23. You are a checker at a supermarket.
24. You are a shoe. Where have you been and what have you seen?
25. What scares you?
26. Pretend you are a yo-yo.
27. Pretend you are a flower.
28. Pretend you are the wind.
29. A day in the life of an ice cream cone.
30. A day in the life of a lollipop.
31. A day in the life of a pencil.
32. A day in the life of a balloon.
33. Pretend you are a magician.
34. You wake up and you are the only one left on earth.
35. A day in the life of a cup of coffee.
36. Pretend you are 20 years old.
37. Pretend you are a book.
38. Pretend you are a bank.
39. Pretend you are a teacher.
40. Pretend you are a leaf.
41. Pretend you are a television.
42. Pretend you are a pumpkin.
43. Pretend you are a skeleton.
44. How could you make someone happy?
45. How can you make the world a better place to be?
46. I am a tough kid.
47. I am a smart kid.
48. Sometimes I have trouble remembering things.
49. A day in the life of a hot dog.
50. I am a toad.
51. I am a scarecrow.
52. I am invisible.
53. If I were president.
54. If I were a python.
55. If I were a dolphin.
56. How a snowman feels when he melts.
57. If I were a star.
58. If I were being attacked by an octopus.
59. If I were a frogman.
60. If I were a caveman.
61. If I were a hunter.
62. What I see when I look out the window.
63. Tell about a fight.
64. If I were weightless.
65. Describe a classmate and have the class guess who it is.
66. Describe a funny made up animal and draw it.
67. Invent a new invention.
68. You are an inventor. What did you invent? What does it do? How does it work?

TABLE 8.4. Continued

69. A new labor-saving device – what it does, how it works.
70. An advertisement.
71. A treasure chest.
72. Ouch!
73. I can fly.
74. I am an old man.
75. Wow!
76. I am a doctor.
77. Look out!
78. Don't.
79. It was midnight.
80. The mysterious stranger.
81. An old wooden bucket.
82. It was as big as a . . .
83. My greatest wish is to . . .
84. I am the proud owner of . . .
85. You have just become champion of . . . How did it happen? How do you feel?
86. A great day for a turtle.
87. It was an autumn day. I was burning leaves when . . .
88. The time you thought something terrible might happen to you.
89. That special day.
90. The day I climbed the mountain to see the volcano.
91. A shipwreck.
92. An African safari.
93. A strange night.

94. Fire!
95. It was a dark, foggy night.
96. Have you ever spent a night on the desert?
97. A tall tale.
98. Lost!
99. When dinosaurs lived.
100. A caterpillar won't hurt you, or will it?
101. A camping trip.
102. The train wreck.
103. You spent the night in a cave. How did you get there? How did you feel? How did you get home – or did you?
104. To soar like an eagle.
105. Life in a shell.
106. Hey! Wait a minute.
107. Why! I think I'm great.
108. What I want to be.
109. The exciting night when the grizzly bear came.
110. I am a quarter.
111. An adventure story.
112. A day in the life of a Big Mac.
113. From the tallest tree I can see . . .
114. Inside a bottle.
115. Pretend you are a gum ball.
116. A day in the life of a hand.
117. A tack.
118. Sweetie, the all day sucker.
119. A drop of glue.

120. A hot rod racer.
121. A message in a bottle.
122. Cartoons.
123. A mystery.
124. A funny thing that happened.
125. A wug is
126. The Loch Ness Monster.
127. A doorknob.
128. Motorcyclist.
129. Motorbike.
130. Pilot.
131. The wild, wild west.
132. A candy bar.
133. A made up word.
134. Darkness.
135. Robin Hood.
136. I am a zipper.
137. Where teachers go after school and what they do.
138. How do you get up on a Saturday morning?
139. A bucket of chicken.
140. A fly is in my soup.
141. A soft drink.
142. A hammer.
143. Hey look! I'm a drum.
144. Ugh!
145. Watch out for that bucket of paint!

From Cady, J. L. (1975). Pretend you are . . . an author. *Teaching Exceptional Children, 8,* 30–31. Reprinted with permission.

Purpose. The third aspect of the prewriting stage concerns the setting of purpose. It is critical that all writers, and this certainly would include handicapped students, have a clear understanding of their reason for writing. Generally, specific tasks are tied to the achievement of objectives classified as either creative or functional writing. Building from this general foundation for purpose, students should then be shown that the specific task in which they are engaged may equate to a relatively flexible assignment with primary emphasis on personal expression or, on the other hand, may require a highly structured format tied to a specific utilitarian rationale.

After determination of the general purpose in writing, students subsequently need to consider specific goals for individual writing assignments. For functional writing, which is clearly transactional in nature, such objectives might include careful consideration of the background and interests of the audience, close attention to correct format to communicate the intended message, and an appropriate arrangement of the output to achieve this basic goal. For creative writing, the student can more often be encouraged to pursue a greater degree of flexibility in arrangement with increased emphasis on personal interests and with individual preference for organization and perhaps format.

Writing Stage

The writing stage is obviously the core of the process that faces the would-be writer. Included herein are the traditional skills associated with the written language domain such as vocabulary development, sentence structure, and word usage.

The primary issue to be addressed by the instructor at the writing stage concerns the overall teaching approach that will be used. The key question essentially is whether to teach writing skills apart from, or tied to, the individual student's own writing. The succeeding discussion on grammar instruction illustrates the implications of this decision.

Traditional grammar instruction has often focused on the structural features of language and thus has included attention to the parts of speech, diagramming of sentences, and various exercises and worksheets related to specific aspects of grammar. In spite of the tendency of many teachers to stress this approach, little evidence exists in support of the efficacy of such procedures (Sherwin, 1969).

As an alternative to the traditional skills training focus, Graves (1985) argues for a writing process approach that places primary emphasis on the expression of meaning by the child.

> Most teaching of writing is pointed toward the eradication of error, the mastery of minute, meaningless components that make little sense to the

child. Small wonder. Most language arts texts, workbooks, computer software, and reams of behavioral objectives are directed toward the "easy" control of components that will show more specific growth. Although some growth may be evident on components, rarely does it result in the child's use of writing as a tool for learning and enjoyment. Make no mistake, component skills are important; if children do not learn to spell or use a pencil to get words on paper, they won't use writing for learning any more than the other children drilled on component skills. The writing-processing approach simply stresses meaning first, and then skills in the context of meaning. Learning how to respond to meaning and to understand what teachers need to see in texts takes much preparation. (p. 43)

Reflecting a similar perspective, Barenbaum (1983) indicates that grammar instruction for disabled learners is most effective when it is ultimately tied to the student's own writing samples rather than being taught apart from it. In the absence of proven effectiveness with both nonhandicapped and handicapped learners, it is of questionable merit to proceed with an emphasis on instruction in specific writing skills isolated from the writing act itself.

Given the possible problems with separate grammar instruction, skills instruction is more likely to be effective if provided in a way integrated with the students' own writing. To accomplish this, initially students must be provided with an opportunity to write. Second, they need to be sequentially taught appropriate skills while being shown how and when to apply them to specific writing tasks. Third, teachers should provide selective feedback on a limited number of skills that have been previously taught; it is reasonable to conclude that the heavy marking of all errors on papers should be avoided and replaced with a focus on feedback on those skills currently being taught. An overemphasis on correction may lead to writing styles characterized by safe, repetitive, and frequently unimaginative sentences (e.g., I like to play baseball. I like to go fishing. I like to go to school!) while coincidentally having a negative effect on student attitudes toward writing in general and toward creative production in particular.

The discussion below highlights particular areas of written language instruction for handicapped learners. Since the subjects of spelling and handwriting were discussed in previous chapters, they are not addressed here. However, it is important to remember that these basic skills are tools that cannot be divorced from the written expression process.

Vocabulary Development. The primary objective of instruction in vocabulary building is to expand the lexical options available to students in their composing efforts. Such expansion should include efforts to increase the variety of words used while enhancing the complexity and descriptiveness of the written language efforts of students. Several approaches that can prove helpful in vocabulary development are discussed below.

A good basis for the development of vocabulary is to relate it to the student's oral language. The language experience approach (LEA), discussed in Chapter 5 in the section on developmental reading approaches, offers a natural lead-in by combining lessons that include attention to listening, speaking, reading, and writing. With this approach students dictate stories which teachers transcribe for subsequent reading. By then having students rewrite and revise the stories, the transition from oral to written expression can be achieved. LEA can assist by shaping the strength of students' writing vocabulary in the direction of the size of their speaking vocabulary.

Within the context of specific writing tasks, several strategies may prove helpful. Students can generate specific words that might be needed in a writing assignment, and the teacher might write them on the blackboard for illustration and later reference. A list of words can be kept on the bulletin board or on a piece of chart paper from which students can copy and compile the words in a notebook for later use; this can be especially helpful with high-frequency words that are troublesome to spell. Ultimately, the goal is to play down the importance of accurate spelling during the actual writing task. Since the demands of spelling can produce a conceptual break in the writing task for poor spellers, it is more significant initially to reinforce word use rather than correct spelling. By providing the accurate spelling of words that are likely to be used before the task begins or by encouraging students to correct their spelling during the postwriting stage, further interruptions in the conceptualization process necessary for coherent composing can be avoided.

Instructional activities should also focus on enhancing the development of descriptive language. For example, students can brainstorm alternative words for usage in a specific instance and then systematically replace the words in their own written compositions. This exercise can be done with synonyms as well as with a variety of adjectives and adverbs in order to increase descriptiveness of an individual composition or essay.

The use of reinforcement contingencies as mentioned earlier in this chapter can also prove helpful in developing a broader lexicon. The variety of vocabulary words used by the student can be analyzed in a variety of ways such as via a type-token ratio or through the tallying of the number of unusual words used by the student. Reinforcement contingencies can then be set up based on the strength of the ratio or on the frequency of words counted that are not a part of the student's typical compositions.

Several research studies have focused on the use of contingency management to improve writing. An approach that proved successful in enhancing vocabulary development was reported by Ballard and Glynn (1975). Primary-aged students were taught the nature of descriptive and action words and then encouraged to use them during story time. Each day a 20-minute period was scheduled for writing. After completion of the assignment, the students were then asked to list the descriptive and action words that were used and to compare that list to previous compilations to ascertain which ones were new. Using this self-monitoring system, students could then award themselves points contingent on the number of new words written. The points were exchangeable for various free time activities. Ballard and Glynn's (1975) program also resulted in an increase in the number of sentences in compositions and improvement in the overall quality of the stories written. It is interesting to note that the quality of the stories was highest when the rewards were contingent on the number of different action words produced.

Other applied behavior analysis reports have also illustrated the value of contingencies on writing skills. Van Houten, Morrison, Jarvis, and MacDonald (1974) provided elementary school students feedback and social recognition through public data display based on the number of words in their compositions. They report that this strategy resulted in a doubling of the rate of words written. Similar benefits were also reported for programs focused on the total number of words and the number of new or different words (Brigham, Graubard, & Stans, 1972), unusual uses for words (Glover & Gary, 1976), and different adjectives and action words used (Maloney & Hopkins, 1973).

Finally, it is helpful to consider a cautionary note relative to vocabulary development. Cohen and Plaskon (1980) indicate that it is preferable to develop a smaller, accurately used vocabulary in lieu of a larger, perhaps apparently impressive one. In this way, fluency would not be sacrificed for improvements in overall lexicon. For some students, and especially for those who are functioning at lower levels and/or have limited writing ability, the most appropriate goal would be to assist them in acquiring and correctly using a limited number of words. This consideration is particularly apt when the curricular focus is on functional writing.

Sentence Structure. Sentence formation is frequently a major problem area facing handicapped learners and thus should be considered as the critical element in the teaching of grammar. The typical difficulties experienced by disabled learners can be illustrated by the prevalence of rambling prose relatively free of formal sentence structure or by the use of short, highly repetitive sentences that may be geared primarily to the prevention of errors.

To develop good sentence sense, students first need to be made aware of the components of sentences and then must learn how to extend and expand simple sentences to more complex ones. This has traditionally been done through provision of skill instruction on the parts of speech. However, for many students good sentence structure can better be accomplished by focusing on the functional nature rather than the descriptive terminology of the respective parts of speech. Building from work done with the Fitzgerald Key with deaf students, Phelps-Terasaki and Phelps (1980) developed a sentence guide to assist teachers in providing instruction in this area. Its focus includes sentence generation, elaboration, and ordering.

Regardless of whether or not a formal sentence production program is used, it is beneficial for instruction to emphasize the development of grammatically accurate and increasingly complex sentences. Figure 8.2 provides an example of how a sentence extension guide can be presented for student use. The questions in the table present an alternative to the direct teaching of terms for the specific parts of speech, as noted in the preceding paragraph.

Essentially, sentence extension can be accomplished by breaking sentences down into the specific components as a basis for expanding them from simple phrases to more complex constructions. This can be done in two ways: analytically or synthetically. The former approach would proceed by taking an individual sentence, analyzing it across the chart as illustrated by Figure 8.2, then demonstrating for students how to break it down according to specific questions. The synthetic approach proceeds in the opposite manner by providing words in each of the columns and then having students put the words together to form meaningful sentences. In addition to teaching sentence structure, this approach also provides an excellent way of further developing vocabulary by focusing attention on alternative word choices. Basically, this organizational framework provides a system for having students move from individual lexical items to enhanced sentence usage, sentence sense, and subsequently sentence generation.

Another approach to developing writing skills that has implications for sentence structure as well as motivation is the CATS method suggested by Giordano (1982). As noted in Figure 8.3, the acronym CATS stands for copy, alter, transform, and supply a response. The copy stage is self-evident. *Alter* refers to the substitution of one word in a sentence previously copied; *transform* refers to grammatical modification in tense, number, or gender or into negative or interrogative forms; and *supply* a response is based on a teacher-generated question that is copied and answered.

Sentence combining strategies represent a logical progression from the approaches discussed above. Sentence combining allows the writer to embed one statement or a series of statements within another one. Such efforts may yield benefits in terms of syntactic maturity, memory, and organization.

FIGURE 8.2. Sample Phelps Sentence Guide

THE PHELPS SENTENCE GUIDE:					SAMPLE STAGE 1 SENTENCES				
First? Second? Then? Next? Finally? Last? At Last? Later?	Which? How many? What kind of?	Who? What?	How much? Which? How many? What kind of?	Doing? (is, are, was, were, am, have, had, do, did, does)	What?	For what? To what? To whom? For whom?	When?	Where?	How? Why? If? So? Because? So that? Since?
	The fat	boy		is eating	cake				because I'm the teacher
		The man in the long scarf		is driving	a sports car				
		The rocket		is flying				to the moon	
	The funny	clown		is juggling	bottles				
		The boy on the raincoat		is riding	his bike		at night		
		The man in the boots		is riding	the horse			in the street	
	The two	girls		are giving	the dog	a bath			
		The ghost		is scaring	the boy				
	The pretty	lady		is wearing	a long dress				
		The pitcher		is throwing	the ball	to the catcher			
		The bird		is building	a nest			in the tree	

From Phelps-Terasaki, D., & Phelps, T. (1980). *Teaching written expression: The Phelps sentence guide program.* Novato: CA: Academic Therapy, pp. 16–17. Reprinted with permission.

FIGURE 8.3. Sample CATS Exercise

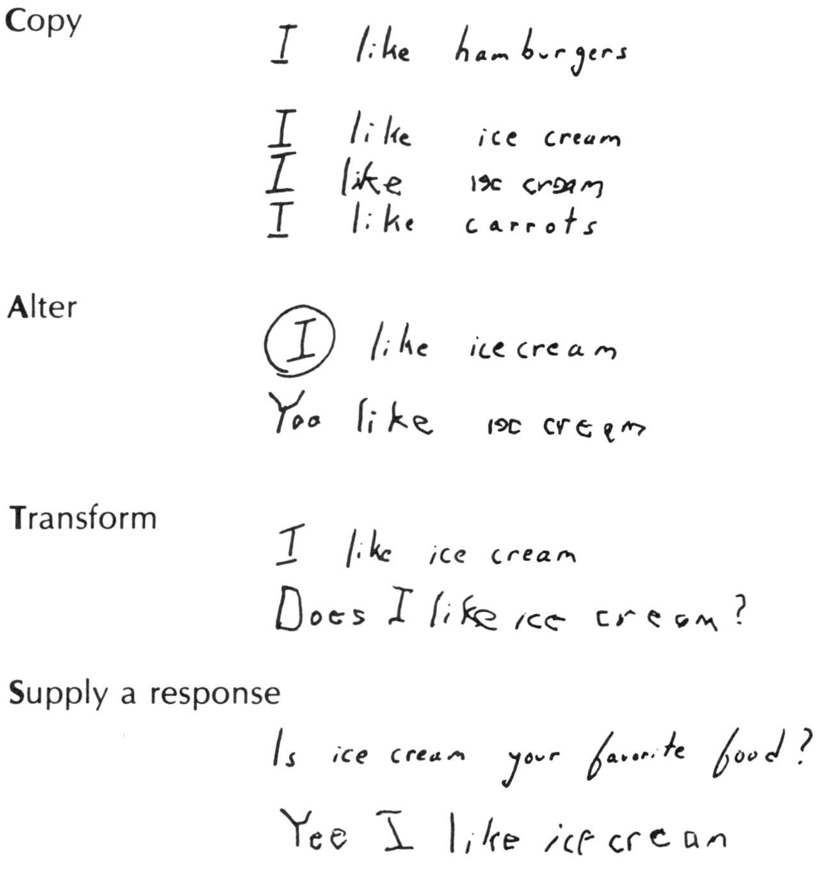

Copy

I $like$ $hamburgers$

I $like$ ice $cream$
I $like$ ice $cream$
I $like$ $carrots$

Alter

(I) $like$ $ice cream$
You $like$ $ice cream$

Transform

I $like$ ice $cream$
$Does$ I $like$ ice $cream$?

Supply a response

Is ice $cream$ $your$ $favorite$ $food$?
Yee I $like$ $ice cream$

From Giordano, G. (1982). CATS exercises: Teaching disabled writers to communicate. *Academic Therapy, 18,* 236. Reprinted with permission.

A simple way to facilitate the process of sentence combining is to teach students key connecting words such as *and, but, when, after,* and *because* and then show the students when and how to apply them. However, a full program such as the one developed by Strong (1983) should be considered as an alternative.

Strong's (1983) program is based on a self-teaching method in which small kernel sentences are combined to make longer sentences and subsequently paragraphs. His book provides ten phases, and within each phase are topic suggestions for the specific paragraph(s). The phases are as follows:

❑ Phases 1 through 4 provide kernel sentences for the student to combine to make a paragraph. The kernel sentences are numbered to help the student combine those with the same number into an individual sentence.

❑ Phases 5 and 6 provide kernels, but the student now must arrange them into an order that makes a coherent sentence and then a paragraph.

❑ Phases 7 and 8 provide kernels to be arranged in more than one paragraph with each paragraph showing a unit of meaning.

❑ Phases 9 through 20 offer kernels taken from the works of contemporary authors with the student encouraged to write his or her own paragraph and then compare it to the original work.

Figure 8.4 provides a sample exercise from Strong's (1983) *Sentence Combining* program. In addition to Strong's (1983) formal program for teaching sentence combining, the skill can also be developed through informal means. For example, Reutzel (1986) has presented an excellent discussion of how basal readers can be used as sentence combining composing books.

While developing grammatical skills through the writing of sentences, several other concerns need to be addressed. Students should be taught error awareness so that they can begin to make correct choices on individual word usage. Awareness can be encouraged by sample exercises that include choosing the correct sentence from a group of sentences, correcting a previously prepared sentence or paragraph, or listening to a teacher's dictation with mistakes to be corrected. However, to be successful such exercises must always be closely applied to the student's own writing. Students should be encouraged to engage in self-correction where they can write and then read aloud to themselves in order to listen for possible errors.

A related concern is skill maintenance. Once a particular skill has been acquired, it is important that it be continually reinforced by the teacher so that it will remain within the student's writing repertoire. An effective way to accomplish this is to use *selective checking*, a procedure discussed earlier in the chapter on handwriting. With selective checking, an individual skill is randomly chosen on a given day, and reinforcement is made contingent on the fact that it was done correctly. For example, capitalization of the first word in a sentence or correct usage of a particular punctuation mark could be selected for a given day.

FIGURE 8.4. Sentence Combining: Sample Exercise Number 1

VALUE JUdGMENT

1.1. Carol was working hard on her test.
1.2. Sue slipped her a note.

2.1. She unfolded the paper carefully.
2.2. She didn't want her teacher to see.

3.1. The note asked for help on a question.
3.2. The question was important.

4.1. Carol looked down at her paper.
4.2. She thought about the class's honor system.

5.1. Everyone had made a pledge.
5.2. The pledge was not to cheat.

6.1. Carol didn't want to go back on her word.
6.2. Sue was her best friend.

7.1. Time was running out.
7.2. She had to make up her mind.

8.1. Her mouth felt dry.
8.2. Her mouth felt tight.

INVITATION: Finish the story. Explain the reasons behind Carol's value judgment.

From Strong, W. R. (1983). *Sentence combining: A composing book* (2nd ed.). New York: Random House, p. 4. Reprinted with permission.

Another important consideration worth reiterating is the fact that excessive correction can have a negative effect on the development of writing ability and motivation. The teacher should be particularly aware of written errors that reflect primarily dialectical differences, of correcting unreasonable standards or debatable grammatical rules, or of correcting errors related to skills not previously taught to the student.

Finally, it is necessary to consider the element of time commitment. Graves (1985) indicates that disabled students need to write at least four days per week in order to see appreciable change in their writing. He suggests that infrequent writing "merely reminds them that they can't write" (p. 39). While Graves' comments refer to the development of writing ability in general, certainly they are applicable also to improvement in structural skills.

Paragraph Development. The development of cohesive paragraphs represents a transition from the individual sentence to the full composition, essay, or other written product. Paragraph instruction provides training in organizational skills and thus can provide the basis for developing the student's ability to improve the overall integrity of the manuscript to be produced.

As Otto and colleagues (Otto, McMenemy, & Smith, 1973; Otto & Smith, 1980) note, the key to successful paragraph writing is to make specific assertions and then to elaborate on them. In order to learn paragraphing skills, students can be shown how to form a prototypical paragraph. At first, the teacher can provide a topical sentence that introduces the core thought for the paragraph. Then the student's task is defined as adding two or three sentences that describe this topical sentence and provide further elaboration on it. A summary or "clincher" sentence can be used when appropriate or when deemed necessary. While clearly not all paragraphs do or should follow this format, this approach to instruction nevertheless can provide a good illustration of what paragraphs should accomplish. While it would be inaccurate to teach students that all paragraphs have, or even need, formal topical sentences, such paragraphs nevertheless are worth teaching, because they can assist the student in organizing the writing product. This structure reinforces the fact that every paragraph makes a statement and/or contains a series of sentences dealing with a unified set of ideas. Thus, paragraphs become units of thought regarding certain statements (Otto & Smith, 1980).

A helpful way to begin instruction in paragraphing is to assign students short, functional writing tasks. For example, students can be asked to write a simple letter to a mail order company in order to purchase a particular item. In this case the initial sentence, or the topical sentence, would state what the individual wants to buy. The subsequent three or four sentences would then describe the item, discuss the form of payment, provide the address to send the item to, and end with a simple closing.

Paragraphs can eventually provide a basis for expansion to composition construction. When tied to outlines, attention to the information to be covered in individual paragraphs can assist in this transition by providing a means of laying out the entire product. Such an approach also assists in the development of transition between paragraphs and between major sections of a composition. Ultimately, it can guide students in the enhancement of logical thinking, the organization of details and main ideas, and the study of new material. A structured presentation of the usage of outlining can be taught as a basis for subsequent student writing activities (Mandell & Gold, 1984). A summary of outlining techniques is presented in Figure 8.5.

Postwriting Stage

The goal of the postwriting stage is to teach students that the revision of writing can lead to greater personal satisfaction with the final product. In order to be successful, instruction at the postwriting stage requires a nonthreatening environment so that students can develop a positive association with the process of proofreading, thus disassociating it from its frequent use as a punitive measure. Proofreading necessitates the active involvement of students. Therefore, for handicapped students, simply telling them to proofread their material will rarely be sufficient. Rather, students must learn the concept of the working draft, realize that all writers work through a series of efforts before arriving at their completed product, and then learn the specific ways that this revision process can be accomplished.

Since proofreading requires specific skills and active involvement, it is an ability that must be taught and then subsequently applied to written tasks. To establish a basic understanding of the concept, several approaches can be used. For example, students can be provided with anonymous commercially produced papers written by other students and instructed to identify correct or incorrect sentences, find individual spelling errors, and/or find all capitalization errors. After this initial objective of awareness is achieved, then students should be shifted to the editing of their own work. This shift to application is a frequently overlooked part of many commercial curriculums. Initially, students should be focusing on only one or two skills at a time. Thus, for example, proofreading may begin as simply an effort to peruse one's own manuscript and identify and correct specific punctuation errors such as the addition of periods at the ends of declarative sentences.

FIGURE 8.5. Summary of Outlining Techniques

Type	Description	Example
Pictorial outlining	Writers make spontaneous sketches to recall and organize details.	Child draws 3–5 illustrations (spontaneous and a minimum number of strokes) and then arranges them in sequence.
Topical outlining	Writers record only those details of an incident that can be related to a specified topic.	Topic is identified before the experience and items randomly recorded (e.g., a reporter's notebook or notebook on sports).
Charting	Writers arrange details so as to reflect an incident's temporal or spatial structure.	Time lines teach temporal relations; spatial relations are taught by quadrants or by left-right, bottom-top.

Type	Description	Example
Question sets	Writers respond to narrative or taxonomical sets of questions.	Teacher asks: Who? When? Where? What happened? Why you feel the way you do?
Question generation	Writers devise a list of questions: arrange them from general to specific.	Student asks: Why did Jim get hurt? Who started the fight? How could it have been prevented?
Predication outlining	Writers identify an incident's central character and indicate whether that person was the initiator or recipient of actions.	

Type	Description	Example
Hierarchical outlining	Writers designate progressively superordinate categories under which to group details of an incident.	Traditional outline: I. A. 1. a.

Adapted with permission from Giordano, G. (1984). *Teaching writing to learning disabled students*. Rockville, MD: Aspen Publications, pp. 59–63.

When a series of skills have been learned, all the skills can be employed simultaneously. A helpful procedure for assisting students in proofreading is to use the acronym COPS, developed by the Learning Disabilities Institute of the University of Kansas (Schumaker et al., 1981) for teaching adolescent disabled learners. The letters refer to the following: C for capitalization (especially names, I, and the first letter of a sentence), O for overall appearance of the paper (for example, spacing, legibility, general neatness, complete sentences, paragraph indentation, and clarity of writing), P for punctuation (with attention primarily to periods, question marks, and commas in a series), and S for spelling.

Beyond the initial utilization of proofreading skills, the process can be expanded when students develop the ability to apply more advanced skills. Krause (1983) suggests the following questions for students to focus their attention on the comprehensive revision of sentences and paragraphs:

Sentence Revision Checklist
1. Is my subject specific enough?
2. Do I need adjectives or other modifiers to create a better image?
3. Do I need words (adverbs or phrases) to tell how, when or where?
4. Have I used capital letters and punctuation marks correctly?
5. Do my subjects and verbs agree?

Paragraph Revision Checklist
1. Where is my most important sentence? Does it stand out?
2. Do all of my other sentences tell about the important sentence?
3. Can I combine some short sentences to make them sound better?
4. Are all of my pronouns clear?
5. Do all of the verbs refer to the same time?
6. Is the first line indented? Is every sentence using proper capitalization and punctuation? (p. 30)

If successful, postwriting strategies not only represent a way to achieve better writing but also provide a vehicle for encouraging independence and active involvement and a shift toward an internal locus of control in academic tasks. Again, the key element is that students realize that all writing products require their attention beyond the initial draft stage and that further improvements can result in greater satisfaction with their writing efforts.

WRITING APPLICATIONS

The possible activities and products that should be considered for inclusion in the written language curriculum are quite extensive. To illustrate this, consider as a brief sample the list that Hansen (1978) presents based on a report of the National Council of Teachers of English which identified the forms of writing that may occur in a school evaluation or in adulthood.

1. Writing directions, announcements, and minutes of a meeting.
2. Writing reports about articles or stories.
3. Summarizing data from reading, oral, and written reports as well as class discussions.
4. Communicating personal experiences.
5. Writing imaginative compositions.
6. Writing letters for social and business purposes.
7. Writing for the school magazine or newspaper.
8. Writing which requires special competencies in the organization and development of ideas. (p. 115)

In this section, several of these forms of possible written products are discussed. They represent topics of particular significance or interest for instruction in special programs.

Composition Writing

Previous discussion has highlighted the varied skills necessary for successful composition writing. The model that is implicit in this chapter has focused on the specific areas that students must attend to throughout the three stages of writing. However, without attention to the formulation of ideas, little of consequence is likely to be accomplished by would-be writers.

A key element that must therefore be focused on is the development of ideation. A useful model developed by Johnson and Myklebust (1964) suggests a developmental progression from concrete to abstract thought. The model's four stages are summarized in Table 8.5. Embedded within the structure of this model are clear implications for instructional programming.

An alternative to composition writing as a means of developing expressive or creative skills is poetry. A variety of approaches to poetry writing are available and have been reported in the literature. One technique that can be particularly effective with disabled students is that of developing unrhymed poems. Figure 8.6 includes some samples of student efforts of this type.

TABLE 8.5. A Sequential Progression for Building Ideation

1. *Concrete/Descriptive*
   Labeling
   Simple sentences

2. *Concrete/Imaginative*
   Inferences
   Based on relatively simple events and simple sentences

3. *Abstract/Descriptive*
   Move from the concrete
   Write stories

4. *Abstract/Imaginative*
   Open-ended plots
   Speculative, hypothetical
   More involved exercises

Adapted from Johnson, D. J., & Myklebust, H. R. (1967). *Learning disabilities: Educational principles and practices.* New York: Grune & Stratton.

Notetaking

Taking appropriate notes is an increasingly important skill for students in secondary and postsecondary settings. Although research on the process has not demonstrated a specific strategy to be more effective than another, Saski, Swicegood, and Carter (1983) report that most researchers and educators have concluded that any strategy for taking notes is better than none at all. Although no substantial data base has developed relative to teaching this skill to disabled learners, educational practice has identified some useful approaches to developing notetaking skills. Some suggestions include:

1. Teacher supplies completed notes; students copy into format.

2. Teacher directs specific notetaking exercise and pauses during lectures/text activities to tell students what information to write.

3. Students practice identifying relevant/irrelevant ideas through paraphrasing and summarizing.

4. Teacher supplies students with topic sentences and has them complete the rest of notes on their own.

5. Teacher supplies study guide or an advance organizer before a lecture so students know what to attend to in lecture.

FIGURE 8.6. Unrhymed Poetry Samples

Two-Word Poems

Two-word poems are intended to be just two words to a line. They can have as many lines as you want them to but there can be only two words on a line. The poems can be about anything including weather, love, friends or food. Some samples:

My bike,	My car,	My boyfriend,
Goes fast,	Goes fast,	Is older,
Painted orange,	Painted pink,	Much taller,
White pads,	Big wheels,	Very nice,
White seat,	Ford Mustang.	Loves cars.
White grips,		
Big wheels,		
Schwinn Motorcross		

Color Poems

When you think about *colors,* which one comes into your mind first? Now from where you are sitting look around the room and find your color in as many places as you can. Once you listed them, your color poem will begin to write itself.

Blue	Blue
Blue is on the bulletin board.	Blue is on a book I see.
Blue is on Kevin's shirt.	Blue is in a picture I see.
Blue is the color of my jeans.	Blue is the color of my shoes.
Blue is the color I like and why	Blue is the color of the ocean.
don't you write about the color	
you like?	

Noun and Verb Poems

Noun and verb poems can be arranged in a way that provides a picture of their meanings. To write one of these poems, just arrange the letters of a word or words in the form of its meaning. Since verbs often show action, your poem can do the same.

Name Poems

You can describe yourself, make up a funny poem about yourself, or tell a story using name poems. Write your name in a column and follow the letters with words that tell something about you. For example:

C Creative	J Jealous	R Righteous
O One-and-only	E Evil	O Organized
R Rebellious	N Numerous	B Big
N Nice	N Noble	E Excellent
E Exciting	I Intelligent	R Real
L Loyal	E Excellent	T Tall
I Intelligent		
U Unique		
S Smooth		

The authors appreciate the assistance given by Michael Boryan in sharing these samples of student-written poetry from his middle school learning disabilities class.

FIGURE 8.7. Notetaking Formats

Format Number 1

OLD INFORMATION	NEW INFORMATION	QUESTIONS
2″	5″	1″
(Previously studied information; connections between old and new information)	(Basic notetaking column)	(Comments about notes that need to be elaborated on or which are important for future assignments)

Format Number 2

TOPIC SENTENCE _____

BASIC IDEAS	BACKGROUND INFORMATION	QUESTIONS
5″	2″	1″
(Basic notetaking column; stress on information for tests, reports, etc.)	(Related or interesting information)	(Comments about notes that need to be elaborated on or which are important for future assignments)

From Saski, J., Swicegood, P., & Carter, J. (1983). Notetaking formats for learning disabled adolescents. *Learning Disability Quarterly, 6,* 269. Reprinted with permission.

6. Student notes are monitored periodically to check for accuracy and completeness.

To assist with the notetaking process, Saski et al. (1983) report on two formats that have proved useful in classroom settings with handicapped learners. These two formats are shown in Figure 8.7.

As can be noted in Figure 8.7, both formats are columnar. Three columns are provided to students as a basis for taking notes, particularly for use in lecture-oriented secondary school classes and for notetaking from textbooks. In the first format, columns include *new information,* wherein the majority of data are noted (e.g., facts, figures, and dates); *old information* for notes from previously learned material to serve as a connection to the new information; and *questions,* where students can work in information that needs clarification or indicate information likely to be on a test. The second format includes room for a *topic sentence* related to the material to be covered; *basic ideas* (the core of the material being presented); *background* to focus on topics of particular interest to the students; and *questions* (again, for unclear information).

To use either of these strategies, Saski et al. (1983) also provide a list of guidelines for teachers and students. These suggestions are a good illustration of how to operationalize notetaking procedures.

1. Teachers supply students with completed notetaking formats, students copy the notes onto blank formats, and follow their copied notes in a lecture or textbook activity.

2. Teachers direct specific notetaking, pausing during lecture or textbook activities to tell students what to write down in their notes.

3. Students identify relevant and irrelevant information from lecture or textbook activities, either during lectures or from completed notes supplied by the teacher.

4. Students use Format 2, with topic sentences supplied by the teacher, to complete their own notes from lecture or textbook activities. Teacher cues students on relevant and important information to be included in their notes.

5. Students use Format 2, with topic sentence supplied by the teacher, to complete their own notes from lecture or textbook activities without cues from the teacher.

6. Students use Format 2 to select two to four topics during a lecture or textbook activity but do not fill in notes.

7. Students use Format 2 to select topics and complete their own notes from lecture or textbook activities.

8. Students use Format 1 or 2 to complete the basic notetaking column, then rewrite notes according to specific topics, and complete the remaining columns with teacher assistance.

9. Students use Format 1 or 2 to complete all three columns. Afterwards the teacher checks their notes.

10. Students use Format 1 or 2 to engage in independent notetaking. (p. 270)

Essay Exams

Increasing attention to the quandaries faced by disabled adolescents in academic programs has resulted in a greater emphasis on the specific elements of the regular classroom that will be problematic for the student with written language deficits. Certainly, one of these areas involves successful responding to classroom tests. While several techniques have been developed to assist in the maximizing of students' performance on various forms of tests (e.g., the SCORER system for objective tests; see Alley & Deshler, 1979), our concern is for essay exams that require more advanced levels of responses. As Polloway et al. (1981, 1983) note, the effects of the essay test can be "devastating" on the student with written language problems. They offer the following suggestions to mitigate this problem:

1. Nurture a positive, success-oriented attitude toward the impending test situation.

2. Encourage students to use their time effectively, both prior to the test when preparing and during the test itself.

3. Have students perform triage on the essay questions—responding first to the questions to which they know the answers, and postponing the more difficult ones.

4. Instruct students on recognizing and understanding certain "task-demand" clue words such as *compare*, *elaborate*, and *list*.

5. Encourage students to outline the answer to each essay question before giving any written response. This helps not only the testee but the examiner as well.

6. Incorporate the use of mnemonic aids in test preparation and test taking (for example, the taxonomic breakdown of Kingdom, Phylum, Class, Order, Genus, Species may be remembered more readily through the mnemonic phrase, "King Peter Comes of Good Stock").

7. Use alternative means of evaluation with students who encounter greater difficulty with written form, as their performance on essay-type tests may not accurately reflect their competence or knowledge. (Polloway et al., 1981, pp. 13–14)

COMPUTER APPLICATIONS IN WRITTEN EXPRESSION

The possible use of computer technology in the written language domain has been referred to in the two previous chapters. The most prominent applications for written expression instruction are in the areas of computer-assisted instruction (CAI) programs to enhance specific skills and word processing to support the development of composition writing.

CAI programs have been developing at a rapid pace in all areas of curriculum, and written language is no exception. The most recent edition of the Specialware Directory (LINC Associates, 1986) of software designed for exceptional children lists in excess of 60 programs that relate to various aspects of the written language domain. Although many of these programs doubtlessly serve as simply an electronic alternative to traditional ditto exercises for grammar and vocabulary, there are numerous programs currently available and in development that present effective and interesting tutorial, drill and practice, gaming, and simulation activities to the disabled learner. Since software is an ever-changing commercial market, the reader is referred to the Specialware Directory—which is regularly revised—for specific information and brief reviews on available programs.

CAI programs, at their best, represent opportunities to improve writing in a somewhat contrived situation. A more promising avenue for computer usage is through word processing. Morocco and Neuman (1986) clearly state the advantages of word processing for enhancing writing. They reviewed the literature in this area and report that microcomputers through word processing programs have been successful in helping disabled students in the three key areas of planning, composing, and editing. Specifically, such programs can be of benefit in the daily management of mechanics through the facility in erasing and replacing words, promoting collaboration with peers, and providing a channel for personal expression for students with social deficits. Morocco and Neuman (1986) provide a summary of the potential contribution of word processing:

> A pencil is a private writing tool which the individual child uses to translate thoughts onto paper. Although a word processor also functions as an individual's writing tool, it creates a special kind of writing environment. It makes the individual's writing process more "permeable"—teachers can more easily see what strategy a child is using at any particular moment, and when the strategy has broken down. Other people can read the child's writing at the same time that the child is reading or writing it, and can make suggestions, or react with their own related ideas and experiences. It also makes the writing process more visible because it brings into sharp relief processes that are less apparent with paper and pencil.
>
> As a "permeable" writing environment, word processors create possibilities for teacher-child interactions which would be intrusive if the child were writing with pencil. Prompting; reinforcing the child's ideas; observing revision processes; offering strategies for generating ideas, managing spelling, organizing ideas and revising; stimulating re-reading; mirroring an

audience's viewpoint; and taking dictation from the child—these teacher intervention techniques are more possible and less obtrusive when the writing is on a word processor. This kind of writing environment can transform the writing experience of the learning disabled child providing it is used to reinforce the child's self-image as author and to help the child acquire writing strategies that will help him be productive in the mainstream classroom. (pp. 246–247)

Several word processing programs are available that were written specifically for handicapped students. One of the most widely used in both regular and special education is the Bank Street Writer program, published by Scholastic. As reviewed by LINC (1986), the program is an easy-to-use system with jargon-free directions for students. Through the use of simple commands, students can edit their own work and add and delete words, phrases, sentences, and paragraphs. Teachers interested in this or any word processing program are advised to evaluate its applicability for students before considering a purchase.

BEST PRACTICES

Written expression deficits in handicapped children and adolescents have recently begun to receive the degree of attention in the professional literature that they deserve. It has been the primary purpose of this chapter to identify models and practices that represent the most promising approaches to conceptualizing, assessing, and teaching students who are experiencing problems in this domain.

A separate and distinct written language curriculum does not exist for handicapped learners; therefore, it has been a common observation that no other curricular area evidences the same degree of congruence between general and special education with regard to teaching strategies (e.g., Haring & Bateman, 1977; Kirk & Johnson, 1951; Polloway & Smith, 1982; Wallace & McLoughlin, 1976). Nevertheless, exceptional students do bring special needs to the task of learning to write, thus modifications in instructional programming will certainly be necessary. Given this fact, the following discussion briefly highlights the major implications for teaching that stem from the previous discussion on the stages of writing.

The teaching activities that take place during the *prewriting stage* must acknowledge the reality of the way that handicapped students present themselves for instruction. In particular, no assumptions can be made that these individuals will have had the necessary experiential prerequisites to develop ideation, have a desire to communicate via written means, and have an understanding of their purpose in writing and the nature of their intended audiences. Each of these factors should be addressed in the planning and implementation of instruction.

The actual teaching of writing reflects a long history of variant focuses. Throughout, there has consistently been an emphasis placed by many educators on instruction in the structural features of language—at times to the exclusion of having children actually write. We have found no data base to support such a position with nonhandicapped students, let alone with those who have been identified as having learning deficits. Instruction during the *writing stage*, therefore, should tie together the regular opportunity to write with the periodic teaching of specific skills that can be directly applied to students' own work.

The third stage, *postwriting*, has traditionally been the least emphasized of the components of written expression. However, proofreading can provide not only an opportunity to learn valuable skills with immediate applicability but also some benefits regarding attitude change. If taught correctly, the supervised process of editing and revising can promote in disabled students the willingness to receive constructive feedback and the ability to sense how to achieve improvement in their own work. For those disabled students whose regular school programs have been replete with failure, such an emphasis has the potential of providing direction toward the development of strategies for overcoming specific difficulties while learning how to compensate for others.

Part Three

ADAPTATIONS FOR EXCEPTIONAL POPULATIONS

PRESCHOOL HANDICAPPED CHILDREN

by Sherryl Edwards

Prior to the early 1970s, young children who had serious developmental disabilities were frequently institutionalized. Those children who were not placed in institutions were typically kept at home and cared for, but rarely were structured educational measures attempted or, in many cases, even available. With the passage of Public Law 94–142, all handicapped children, including those who had been considered untrainable by many educational professionals, were to be accorded all of the educational perquisites given to nonhandicapped children. This major legislative initiative had significant implications for special education programs, and, although it did not provide for federal support to all states for preschool children, it nevertheless reinforced state efforts to serve all children.

For speech/language development specialists and teachers of handicapped children, the introduction of this population into school programs presented a dilemma. The language model with which they had previously worked primarily consisted of grammatic structure, syntax, and articulation. Clearly, such an approach to language development was not going to be appropriate for younger and more severely involved children. Additionally, the oral system had been the basis upon which all communication was developed. It became apparent that some of these children would not be verbal, at least not an initial basis. To underscore this point, it is instructive to consider that it has been estimated that more than 5% of mentally retarded children and 50% of autistic children will fail to acquire speech (Shane, 1985).

The purpose of this chapter is to discuss language programming for preschool handicapped children. A particular concern will be with those youngsters who experience severe developmental disabilities manifested in serious difficulties in the acquisition of oral language. In the succeeding chapter, further discussion of the language needs of older severely handicapped students will be provided.

CONSIDERATIONS IN EARLY LANGUAGE TRAINING

There are several predictors that have been used in determining the population of young children at risk for severe language disabilities. Shane (1985) postulated that if a child has not developed spontaneous speech by 4 years of age, it is highly unlikely that oral speech will be a primary mode of communication for that child. In addition, since there is a close relationship between the severity of mental retardation and the ability to develop speech, cognitive deficits are always quite apparently predictive of problems. Neuromuscular competency, vocal repertoire, and eating skills also are of help in identifying children who are at risk for the development of speech. As stated by Shane and Bashir (1980), "persistent oral reflexes suggest an extremely poor prognosis for speech development. We view these factors as an early predictor of failure to develop speech and one which leads to election of an augmentative communication system" (p. 409). The vowels, and a few of the consonant sounds, require only gross movements of the oral structures. Production of other sounds requires precise articulatory movement (McDonald, 1980). These precise movements are beyond the capacity of some severely mentally and/or physically handicapped children.

The question, then, becomes how to change the language development intervention model to meet the needs of these special children. In recent years, theories of language development and training have undergone major revisions. Methods of training have taken two major directions: operant conditioning and naturalistic or environmental training. In addition, other questions have involved the oral/nonoral approach and aided/nonaided gestural communication. It is these programming questions that are addressed in this chapter.

For those children who have severe handicaps, communication involves interaction with a narrow circle of people. Those with whom the young child has the opportunity to interact generally include immediate family members, most often the mother. Within the classroom, the teacher and aide are the primary caregivers, and there will also be some communication among members of the child's class. Assuming the child lives at home, these persons then frame the parameters of his or her communicative environment. Beginning communication is most often between the child and the primary caregiver who knows him best and will see communicative cues that others might miss. Therefore, the focus of communication training must be closely related to the interactions between the child and primary caregiver.

Verbal language is one aspect of communication, simply a single behavior along a continuum (Rogers-Warren & Warren, 1984). Other forms of communication introduced in recent years include far more primitive means, including eye blinks, eye gazes, other gestures, communication boards, computers, and signs (Shane, 1985). As noted in Chapter 10, language is now considered in its functional form, as pragmatics, rather than solely as a formal structure to be learned and used.

Language usage depends upon cognitive ability, social skills, and some degree of physical mobility. Cognitive and social skills are to some extent directly related. For example, children who are severely involved often will also be severely physically impaired. This compounds the difficulties presented in the development of language skills, because the severe impairment of gross and fine motor development impedes motoric exploration and manipulation. Assuming visual function is intact, visual attending is critical in the development of prelinguistic skills. In order to communicate, children must be able to attend and to indicate that they are attending (Rogers-Warren & Warren, 1984). This ability to indicate engagement provides the cue which the caregiver must see to interact. It provides the context for the natural development of communication by allowing for topics of discussion. It provides for the caregiver an indication of those objects or activities that the child finds reinforcing. When some idea is given of what the child finds pleasurable, the caregiver can more easily create the environment for learning. Interaction is the primary and most essential element in the development of communication (Rogers-Warren & Warren, 1984).

Practice indicates that by beginning with prelinguistic skills at the young child's developmental level, communication training is viable. The question posed concerns which methods and which tools will most successfully meet the child's needs in developing these skills.

An apt summary to this discussion of considerations for early language training can be drawn from Bryen and Joyce's (1985) review of 43 studies of language development in severely handicapped children. They concluded that in any such program, the handicapped individual must first have the desire to interact. The purpose of communication must be understood, involving turn taking and communicative intent. Motor requirements must be addressed for a successful program to be developed. The goals that are established must be attainable for that particular child. An obvious first concern in designing appropriate programs is the collection of assessment data.

ASSESSMENT

The assessment of language in preschool handicapped children must be a multifaceted process. The discussion below highlights some basic considerations that should be part of evaluative efforts and reviews some available instruments.

Basic Considerations

Assessment for children with a very limited repertoire of skills must begin with some basic areas of concern. For example, children who have not mastered chewing, sucking, and swallowing will not have the necessary muscular control to develop oral communication skills. It then becomes necessary to assess for the most appropriate alternative means of communication. As McDonald (1980) notes, several areas should be considered in determining whether a child is to be considered a candidate for an alternative communication system:

❑ The history of the pregnancy, birth, and neonatal period in order to secure any indications of brain damage, for example, anoxia, low Apgar, seizures, or early feeding difficulties.

❑ Developmental delays, particularly in the area of speech development.

❑ Findings from examination, including abnormal reflexes, or muscle tone, inappropriate suck or swallow, or inadequate efforts at chewing.

There are certain prerequisites for the development of any systematic communication system. It must first be determined that the child has developed *object permanence*, that is, ability to remember an object if it is removed from sight. If this has not developed, each time the object is seen, the child would view it as if it were new and would have to relearn it, along with the symbol. The ability to seek and maintain eye contact is also a prerequisite, as is attending to task. The child must also have a desire to communicate. If assessment determines that these skills are lacking or incompletely acquired, they must first be developed before a more advanced communicative system can be attempted (Harris-Vanderheiden, 1975).

In the assessment of young children, it is important to determine, if possible, the preferred sensory modality for attending (Moores, 1980). While some children are auditory attenders, others may be primarily visual attenders. This is often seen with autistic children. It is apparent that teaching a child only through the auditory mode will serve little purpose if that child primarily responds to visual stimuli, attending little or not at all to auditory cues.

It is also important to observe the child's communicative attempts, both vocal and nonvocal. Many behaviors that are not vocal can nevertheless be considered to be communicative. For example, does the child look at his or her parent or teacher, and then toward a particular object? Does he or she become more active or suddenly still when near an object of interest? If the child is physically handicapped, is there any part of his or her body, including eyebrows and toes, that can be used communicatively?

Observing children in their natural environments on several occasions is necessary and will provide invaluable information in assessing communicative skills. Parent interviews are also of critical importance in assessment, especially when assessing a child with whom the tester is not familiar. For example, many young and severely involved children often respond well only to others who are significant to them.

Formal Instruments

It is difficult to find tests that provide an unbiased assessment of communication skills in preschool handicapped children. A few warrant special mention, however. Table 9.1 provides an overview of a number of available assessment instruments. Several of these are further discussed below.

The *Developmental Communication Curriculum Inventory* (Hanna, Lippert, & Harris, 1982) was created to assess the communicative skills of very low functioning individuals. It involves direct interaction with the child in assessing general demeanor, behavioral style, spontaneous language, and personality. This observation should yield information concerning the behaviors that precede symbolic development of language; the amount and form of communicative interactions the child

TABLE 9.1. Assessments of Communication Skills for Preschool Handicapped Children

Test	Publisher	Area Assessed/Mental Age
Carolina Picture Vocabulary Test (Layton & Holmes, 1978)	Modern Education	Receptive test specifically designed for children who use American Sign Language as their primary mode of communication.
Developmental Communication Curriculum Inventory (Hanna, Lippert, & Harris, 1982)	Charles E. Merrill	General demeanor, behavioral style, spontaneous language, and personality are assessed. Includes nonvocal communicative interactions.
Cognitive, Linguistic, and Social Communicative Scales (Tanner & Lamb, 1983)	Modern Education	Uses parent interview to assess preschool age children.
Early Language Milestone Scale (ELM) (Coplan, 1983)	Modern Education	Language screener for MA 0–36 months. Assesses auditory expressive, auditory receptive, and visual.
Environmental Language Inventory and Environmental Prelanguage Battery (Horstmeier & McDonald, 1978)	Charles E. Merrill	Intended for prelanguage training of children of any age who are severely language delayed.

TABLE 9.1. Continued

Test	Publisher	Area Assessed/Mental Age
Initial Communication Process (Schery & Wilcoxen, 1982)	Publishers Test Service	Used in assessing communication levels of severely handicapped children whose language levels are between 0 and 36 months. Administered by observation over at least two weeks.
Preverbal Assessment-Intervention Profile (Connard, 1984)	ASIEP	Assesses preintentional verbal skills of SPH/MH children. Based on Piagetian theory.
Program for the Acquisition of Language with the Severely Impaired (PALS) (Owens, Jr., 1982)	Charles E. Merrill	Uses informal observation and caregiver interview in assessing presymbolic and symbolic language skills of severely handicapped individuals, preschool through adult age.
Receptive-Expressive Emergent Language Scale (REELS) (Bzoch & League, 1970)	Assorted Publications	Tests developing receptive and expressive language of children who are developmentally between ages 0 and 36 months.
Verbal Language Development Scale (Mecham, 1971)	American Guidance Service	Assesses a child's communicative activities within the normal environmental setting, ages 1 month to 6 years.

performs, such as vocalizations, eye movements, and signs; and stimulability, such as the acquisition of gestures, understanding of physical prompts, and generalization. A parent interview is an integral part of this test, allowing for parent or significant caregiver to assist in the determination of the presence or emergence of various skills as an equal partner with the examiner. A well-developed curriculum guide is provided for the development of intervention programs.

Initial Communication Process (Schery & Wilcoxen, 1982) is an instrument created for use in assessing the communication levels of severely handicapped children whose language levels are considered to be between birth and 30 months. It is intended to be used in the creation of appropriate instructional objectives. It is to be administered primarily through observational techniques over a period of at least 2 weeks and in several environmental contexts. No special training or materials are required for administration.

The *Preverbal Assessment-Intervention Profile* (PAIP) (Connard, 1984) is intended to provide an adequate means of assessing the preintentional verbal skills of severely/profoundly/multiply handicapped children. It is based on Piagetian theory and utilizes his sensorimotor stages 1 through 4. Results of the evaluation provide preliminary placement and an indication of need for further diagnostics, functioning levels across several developmental areas of language, a descriptive section to provide a narrative of current level of function, and a list of goals to be implemented.

The *Pre-Speech Assessment Scale* (PSAS) (Evans-Morris, 1984) is a comprehensive scale intended to provide the examiner with a view of the prespeech behavior of the neurologically impaired child who is cognitively between the ages of 0 and 24 months. There are 27 areas evaluated, which are included in six categories: feeding behavior, sucking, swallowing, biting and chewing, respiration-phonation, and sound play.

This scale provides an in-depth account of the child's abilities in the prespeech area. Originally, the assessment was created for the use of therapists who had been trained in its use. Recently, however, it has become available to other educators without the prerequisite training session. The assessment is quite involved, however, and much practice is necessary before the examiner will feel competent in its use.

The *Program for the Acquisition of Language with the Severely Impaired* (PALS) (Owens, 1982) was developed to assess and provide an intervention model for use with individuals who have severe language delays. It is divided into presymbolic and symbolic skills. PALS is a two-step evaluation consisting of an informal observation and caregiver interview. This is followed by a more in-depth Developmental Assessment Tool. These are administered over several sessions.

The *Receptive-Expressive Emergent Language Scale* (REEL) (Bzoch & League, 1970) is intended to test the developing receptive and expressive language of children who are developmentally between the ages of 0 and 36 months. It can be administered by caretaker interview and/or observation.

It is hoped that as understanding of the skills and needs of young and severely handicapped children continues, more assessments that test the full range of communication and communicative intent will be developed. The need is felt especially keenly in testing children who cognitively function in the profound range of mental retardation. In-depth assessment is the key to developing the most suitable communication system for each handicapped child.

INSTRUCTIONAL APPROACHES

With many children, communication training truly "begins at the beginning." Thus, for many severely or profoundly motorically and/or cognitively handicapped children, positioning is a fundamental concern in programming (Musselwhite & Saint Louis, 1982). Positioning provides for more adequate breath control for eating, swallowing, and vocalization. An increase in vocalizations is often seen in children during eating (Evans-Morris, 1981). In most situations, positioning the child in a sitting position, feet supported, shoulders protracted, and head in midline, will increase the possibilities for vocalization. It is important to provide all necessary support. If a child is fighting to maintain postural placement, he or she will be less able to attend or to respond. Adequate equipment for positioning is essential and should be available. In working with the child's physical therapist, appropriate placement and positioning can be determined. Depending upon the child's individual needs, many adaptive chairs and supports are available to aid in providing adequate positioning.

Head control, visual tracking, and scanning are prerequisites to more involved levels of communication. According to Musselwhite and St. Louis (1982), these are areas with future possibilities of expressive communication, especially important because they lead to communication skills other than speech if speech is not a viable alternative. Care should also be taken to define and work toward eliminating interfering behaviors such as self-stimulatory and self-injurious behaviors.

Evans-Morris (1981) stresses the importance of incorporating communication training into the feeding schedule with severely handicapped children. In studying normal communication between nonhandicapped infants and caregivers, many communicative signals are noted.

Among them are crying or agitated movement indicating hunger, eye gaze and movements directed toward the caregiver while eating, and facial grimace or refusal of foods if, for example, they are disliked or if the infant is full. These behaviors are communicative and developmental. Some specific behaviors developed through feeding interaction as described by Evans-Morris (1981) are: turn taking, or reciprocal communication, during which the child indicates a need to which the caregiver responds; causality, in which the child learns that specific behaviors on his or her part elicit specific responses on the part of the caregiver, as in receiving the next bite of food when the child vocalizes; object permanence, seen when the child searches for food that has fallen, or makes sucking movements when he or she sees an empty bottle; and gaze behaviors, which indicate interest, the desire to communicate, and waiting for a response. The gaze often indicates that about which the child wishes to communicate, such as which food he or she wants to have in the next spoonful, or the aversion of gaze may indicate that the child is full or that the caregiver needs to pause before continuing feeding. Thus, caregivers and trainers should not miss the opportunity to develop eye gaze, turn taking, yes/no decisions, choice making, and vocalizations throughout this highly motivating time for the child. Eventually, pictorial representations for the foods can be introduced at feeding and then play time.

Because the severely handicapped child's signals may be unclear, they are often misread or overlooked, which can result in lack of reinforcement (Evans-Morris, 1981). For example, the child with cerebral palsy—often thrust into extension by the cuddling efforts of the parent or in positions resulting from reflexive head and arm movements—may signal rejection to the parent or caregiver. It also often becomes difficult for the caregiver to differentiate unregulated movements from intended signals due to the child's lack of control over the degree of movement. It is of utmost importance, therefore, that the caregiver learn to read the child's communicative signals. This comes through careful observation over a period of time.

In working with young children with severe developmental disabilities, no matter what mode of communication training is being undertaken, a carefully selected core lexicon must be the objective. Words chosen for communication training must reflect the individual child's needs based upon an intensive evaluation of environment and daily living, including basic needs and interests. Words that allow children to make choices will be highly motivational and will enrich their ability to control their environment. Frequent choices for initial training are yes/no, words connected with eating and drinking, favorite toys, dressing, and toileting. These should be presented gradually rather than as a blitz of words to learn. Words with concrete referents are easier to understand and learn. For example, *drink* or *cup* are easier to learn, since they each have a visual referent, than would be *here*, which has none.

Nonvocal Approaches

Nonvocal communication systems are introduced when it is felt that because of gross abnormality of the oral structures, inadequate breathing mechanism, and/or severe cognitive limitations, oral communication will not be probable. A good example of such an approach is the communication board. Communication boards can vary in complexity and can be based on very limited communicative concepts. The cognitive and physical limitations of the child and the limitations of space on the board are factors that must be considered in its development. In developing such a system, care must be taken to provide for the child's cognitive and motoric level of development. While some children will be able to point to or move a hand toward the picture desired, others may be able only to operate a headstick or a light pointer which is attached to the head (St. Louis, 1985).

Harris and Vanderheiden (1980) set forth two techniques of language board communication that are appropriate to young severely handicapped children. One technique is direct selection, and the other is scanning. Direct selection involves pointing in some way directly to the representation on the board. This requires that the child have good range of motion in order to be able to accurately indicate the picture or object desired. Scanning requires less ability. The individual observes a scanner which moves from one representation on the board to another. The child gestures in some way when the scanner is on the representation desired. Other forms such as encoding and point/scan require more cognitive ability and the ability to understand alphabet and numbers; the reader is encouraged to consult Harris and Vanderheiden (1980) for further information.

Communication boards can range from clock-face dials, which the child uses to make choices, to intricately gridded boards that contain a picture or symbol in each square. As the child progresses communicatively, the board can be sectioned to provide more choices. Originally, the board could be designed for as few as two choices, such as yes/no or eat/drink (Flanagan, 1982).

In order to effectively use a communication board, the child must first understand that the pictures represent objects or actions. There are many symbol systems available. However, in selecting a system, the teacher must consider whether the symbols are within the child's ability to understand or are too abstract for him or her to use effectively

(Flanagan, 1982). Initially, actual objects or photographs may be affixed to the board.

In assessing nonvocal communication systems, several general factors must be taken into account. The questions below are ones that should be considered:

1. Can the child use the board or system quickly enough to maintain the receiver's interest while completing his or her thought?

2. Does the system provide a way for the child to initiate a conversation?

3. Is the device accepted by the child and his or her family as an appropriate and effective communication aid?

4. Can the system be expanded to allow for additional content to be developed and displayed?

St. Louis (1985) has established some more specific questions to be asked by the teacher before actually designing the communication board.

1. What are the goals for the use of the language board?

2. Where are the child's communication environments?

3. What does the child need to communicate (customized vocabulary, headstick, etc.)?

4. What are the child's motor skills?

5. Which symbol systems are the most appropriate for the child?

6. Which style of board fits the child's goals?

7. How will the child learn to communicate with the board?

8. How can the board's effectiveness be measured?

It is important to assess the effectiveness of various communication techniques early in order to effectively build upon the mode that is judged to be most promising. These would include communication boards for which can be chosen a variety of representations, including small objects, photographs, or symbols such as Blissymbols or Rebus symbols. Also taken into consideration should be the use of signed speech or total communication, which is the combination of sign and oral speech (also see Chapter 11). In addition, other aided devices, including computer-assisted communication, have recently begun to have a major impact on the field. These are discussed below.

Aided Communication Devices.   In increasingly frequent use with severely involved children are aided or electromechanical devices for communication. While the more sophisticated computer language systems have proven to be of invaluable assistance to those children who are severely physically impaired but intellectually of normal ability, they are far too involved for the child who is extremely cognitively limited. As one option, there are toys which are available or which can be constructed for these children that are both motivating and reinforcing. Children who may be otherwise unresponsive can learn that they can to some extent control their environment (Flanagan, 1982). Another option is switches which can teach concepts of cause and effect, yes/no responses, and choice making. These can range from the simple pressure switch, which results in the playing of a musical toy or tape, to computer software, which can be designed to teach these skills (Hanline, Hanson, Veltman, & Spaeth, 1985).

The use of computers has gained impetus in recent years in communication training with handicapped children. Their use with mildly handicapped children in teaching many skills has frequently been observed (Bowe, 1984) and has been discussed in previous chapters. However, since computers provide interaction naturally as a consequence of the child's actions, and provide both visual and auditory stimulation, clearly more severely impaired children can also benefit from computers and electromechanical toys. For example, this writer had a program designed that first taught a child to press and release the pressure plate by rewarding him or her with large colorful pictures and music for a correct response or a specified amount of blank screen and silence for noncompliance. Once this was taught, the program used a cursor of variable size which moved at variable speed over from two to eight screens to teach identification and choice making.

There are several companies that provide software for severely handicapped children and that also offer various devices that enable the child with limited range of motion to activate computers (see Table 9.2 for a list). For example, the Koala Pad by Koala Technologies Corporation is a device that allows individuals to draw using varied strokes and colors. This is excellent for the child with good range of motion but poor fine motor control. The design of the pad allows for placement of the hand for stability while using the finger to control what appears on the screen. *Logo* is a computer language that uses a graphic called a "turtle." The child becomes in control by directing the turtle. Use of this program has been effective in teaching attending skills with autistic and severely mentally retarded children (Gray, 1984).

Battery-operated toys can also be used interactively between children or between child and teacher. Children who are too motorically involved to manipulate the toys by hand can still benefit from them by

TABLE 9.2. Sources of Computer Software and Equipment

Aspen Systems Corporation
P.O. Box 6018
Gaithersburg, MD 20877

Crestwood Company
P.O. Box 0406
Milwaukee, WI 53204

Don Johnston
Developmental Equipment
981 Winnetka Terrace
Lake Zurich, IL 60047

EKEG Electronics Co., Ltd.
P.O. Box 46199
Station G
Vancouver, BC V6R 4G5

Graphic Learning Corporation
P.O. Box 4649
Richmond, VA 23229

Institute on Technology
P.O. Box 1155
Brookline, MA 02146

Intellectual Software
798 North Avenue
Bridgeport, CT 06606

Koala Technologies Corp.
3100 Patrick Henry Drive
Santa Clara, CA 95950

Laureate Learning Systems, Inc.
One Mill Street
Burlington, VT 05401

Parrot Software
190 Sandy Ridge Road
State College, PA 16803

Prentke Romich Company
8769 Township Road 513
Shreve, OH 44676-9421

Quest Publishers and Distrib-
  utors, Inc.
P.O. Box 7952
Richmond, VA 23221

Softkey Systems, Inc.
4737 Hibiscus Avenue
Edina, MN 55435

Street Electronics Corp.
1140 Mark Avenue
Carpinteria, CA 93013

Unicorn Engineering Co.
6201 Harwood Avenue
Oakland, CA 94618

using any of a number of adapted switches which can be activated by as simple a movement as an eye blink or slight head movement. For example, a switch can be adapted to activate a battery-powered toy animal, which the child can engage as the teacher verbalizes creatively about the toy, directing the child to move the toy from place to place during the play activity (Musselwhite, 1985).

Electromechanical toys can easily be constructed using battery-operated toys and such easily procured items as electrical tape, solder, subminiature phone jacks, and needle-nose pliers. *More Homemade Battery Devices for Severely Handicapped Children with Suggested Activities* (Burkhart, 1982) is an excellent source for such devices. By constructing toys that can be operated by switches, the child can interact with toys through the use of whatever motion is available. Switches can be adapted that activate the toys through, for example, the lifting of the head, turning of the head, movement of the arm toward or away from the child, and the foot.

Such interaction can create within the child the motivation to continue to interact, because the toy provides feedback through movement. It gives children the feeling of control over their environment. Their movements cause the toy to go or stop. It provides a powerful reinforcer for children through visual and/or auditory stimulation. It teaches cause and effect through the provision of consequences for the child's efforts at movement. The feedback provided is natural and directly related to the child's action, rather than contrived by others (Hanline et al., 1985). This is also an excellent yet natural means for providing interactive communicative play between two children in a natural environment.

Hanline et al. (1985) describe several electromechanical toys which can be constructed easily. They include a weight-bearing board that teaches the child to bear weight on extended arms while in the prone position, providing lights as a reinforcer; a Reach-and-Grasp Wheel, which provides visual reinforcement for bimanual reach/grasp; and a "kickpanel," which can be attached to any of several reinforcers, such as radio or tape recorder, and activated when the child, lying supine, extends his or her foot.

These are a few of many toys that can be adapted or designed for specific needs. Imagination and simple tools can result in activities intended to develop a specific skill for a specific child. Many of these switches and toys can also be ordered through adaptive equipment catalogs. Table 9.3 provides a list of information sources that can assist in these efforts.

In considering questions regarding the evaluation of assisted communication programs, it is instructive to consider the findings reported by Bryen and Joyce (1985). They indicate in their review of research that, while most of the 43 programs they investigated that used unaided

TABLE 9.3. Sources of Computer-Assisted Programming

Bulletin on Science and Technology for the Handicapped
AAAS
1515 Massachusetts Avenue, NW
Washington, DC 20005

Closing the Gap
P.O. Box 68
Henderson, MN 56044

Communication Enhancement Clinic
The Childrens Hospital
300 Longwood Avenue
Boston, MA 02115

Communication Outlook
Artificial Language Laboratory
Computer Science Department
Michigan State University
East Lansing, MI 48824

Department of Speech Pathology and Audiology
University of South Alabama
Mobile, AL 36688

Journal of Special Education Technology
Exceptional Child Center
Utah State University
Logan, UT 84322

LINC Resources, Inc.
1875 Morse Road, Suite 225
Columbus, OH 43299

Software Registry
CUSH
James Fitch, Editor
Department of Speech Pathology and Audiology
University of South Alabama
Mobile, AL 36688

The Handicapped Source
101 Route 46 East
Pine Brook, NJ 07058

Trace Center International Software/Hardware Registry
University of Wisconsin–Madison
314 Waisman Center
1500 Highland Avenue
Madison, WI 53706

communication systems with severely/profoundly impaired children were considered moderately successful, the majority of the communication programs that did involve devices to aid in communication were not successful in developing self-initiated language. Some possible explanations for this finding could be that the symbols involved in the aided systems were too abstract to be understood and used. The artificiality of pictures or symbols in relation to actual objects could also be a factor. These systems were also less portable and therefore more restrictive. Also to be considered is the increased amount of involvement and understanding required on the part of the listener (Bryen & Joyce, 1985). Each of these factors should be considered in program design and/or implementation.

Gestural Facilitation in Language Intervention. Many educational centers that were once adamantly oral in their approach to language training are now incorporating Total Communication into their programs. This change appears to be due primarily to the failure of oral programs to effectively develop speech in many severely handicapped children. Possibly the traditional obvious reluctance to use signed speech results from a belief that this emphasis may impede the development of oral communication.

Interest in the total communication approach was aroused when studies with deaf children born to hearing parents and deaf children born to deaf parents were compared for language use and structure. The children whose deaf parents incorporated both oral and gestural language training were found to have more intricately developed language patterns (Moores, 1980).

Several studies have been conducted to research the use of verbal cues as opposed to verbal cues with gestures. A study conducted by Romski and Ruder (1984) followed a group of Down Syndrome children reared at home who were offered speech only and speech plus gestures in language training. The amount of generalization provided following the training was used as the determinant. While overall the two systems did not differ significantly in either learning or generalization, it was noted that one child learned only when speech was accompanied by gestures and that four other children learned more effectively during speech/sign instruction. One child's learning was not observed to be facilitated by the combination of speech and sign. Also, it was seen that the combination form seemed to assist in training prepositions. Apparently, a visual cue for *in* or *on* resulted in a more concrete concept for these children.

Another study reported by Sisson and Barrett (1984) revealed very dramatic differences in results between total communication and oral presentations. While those presented with a total communication program mastered 100% of forms, the children presented oral stimuli alone mastered none. These results indicate that total communication can facilitate the development of communication in severely handicapped children.

An attempt was made by Abrahamson, Cavallo, and McCluer (1985) to determine whether signing maintains an advantage over oral speech in language development. Preverbal children were presented sign-accompanied speech. Both speech and sign were offered for acquisition. The children showed a definite preference for the initial use of sign. Results of this study indicate that vocabulary and two-morpheme combinations developed earlier in sign than in oral speech. Larger vocabularies developed in children to whom language was presented bimodally. Children with Down Syndrome were overall much more able to acquire signs than words. Signs were most often developed first, but in children who developed language, the advantage of sign over speech disappeared as speech increased. These findings strongly support the fact that sign has much more significance during the prelinguistic period of development. Since many individuals with severe developmental disabilities remain at this level, sign must be strongly considered as an alternative. Many children who have failed to acquire speech can nevertheless master some vocabulary through signs.

Variables that seem to have a bearing on the learnability of signs include the number of hands used, the symmetry of hand motion in these signs, the amount of body contact made by the hands, and the repetitiveness and visibility of the signs. Two-handed signs were easier for children to master (Luftig, 1984), as were symmetrical signs and those produced with body contact. More repetitive signs were easier to master also. Luftig also determined that more concrete referents were more easily mastered, and the frequency with which the referent occurred in the child's environment affected its acquisition. It is important also that if sign is to be the mode of choice, the adults who are significant to the child's environment must incorporate sign into their everyday life.

While it appears that there are children for whom gestural facilitation will not be an effective technique, most severely handicapped children appear to benefit significantly by its inclusion in a language intervention program. Furthermore, some signs are more easily learned than others by such children.

Discussion. It is important to remember that before communication skills are developed, through whatever method is judged most appropriate for the child, there are prerequisite skills that must be present. For example, Shane (1985) indicates that specific hand movements are necessary for the formation of signs. Dexterity can be enhanced through the use of manipulatives such as Play-Doh and tiny objects which require the development and use of the pincer grasp. Attending skills must be developed before interaction can take place. Overall, in deciding what communication system is most appropriate to the child, it is imperative that the child's communicative prerequisites, such as range of motion, fine motor skills, and attending, be assessed and whatever gaps that exist be systematically addressed.

It must also be remembered that alternative communication systems do not of themselves preclude the future development of speech; if it is within the child's cognitive and physical capacity to develop oral communication, he or she will probably do so. Rather, these systems enhance the development of communication. They provide a bridge over the communication barrier and at times aid in the development of oral speech.

Why are these methods of communication training successful? Fristoe and Lloyd (1977) provide some possible answers:

1. The use of a nonspeech communication system removes the pressure for speech as the only means of communication.

2. The visual component of alternative communication circumvents the short-term auditory deficit that is related to speech.

3. When necessary, shaping of specific responses is possible with alternative systems.

4. Observation of the message is possible, whether signed or displayed on a screen or board.

5. Visual attention is included rather than auditory only.

6. Alternative communication provides a multimodal approach — tactile and visual as well as auditory.

Operant Conditioning Techniques

Programs that have been developed according to operant conditioning techniques are teacher-directed. They involve training a specific response and providing rewards for that response. Rewards are typically edibles such as candy, fruit, or juice, flashing lights, or the use of an object that the child likes. Many training programs involve having the child choose his or her reward from a selection or "menu." Such programs have been used in the development of gross motor imitation, increased vocalization, development of gestural communication, and increased use of words and phrases. A host of studies have been conducted concerning the effectiveness of the operant conditioning technique; several representative examples are discussed below. Although these studies are not all concerned with preschool handicapped children, they nevertheless provide the flavor of the types of intervention efforts associated with operant learning and are thus relevant to our discussion.

Duker and van Grinsven (1983) used operant conditioning in comparing the development of verbalizations using verbal cues alone and verbal cues paired with gestures. The results indicate 48% success with verbal cues and 49% success with verbal and gestural cues. Sisson and Barrett (1984) conducted a similar study pairing oral methods against oral and gestural attempts at training language using operant techniques. Children were drilled in a "therapy room," which was free of distractions, and candy and praise were used for reinforcers when one of a set of six picture cards was correctly named. The results of this study indicate 100% mastery of the words using total communication and 0% mastery using words alone. Of interest, however, is the finding that no generalization of these concepts was observed other than being able to name the pictures themselves within the therapy room setting.

Operant conditioning has been used in the development of gross motor imitation. Guess, Sailor, and Baer (1976), however, discovered that the use of motor imitation as an antecedent to communication development might not be beneficial. Forty percent of the children with whom this system was used never developed the ability to imitate sounds.

Snyder, Lovitt, and Smith (1975) compiled 23 studies which had been conducted using operant techniques since 1968. The studies involved severely retarded subjects, most of whom were institutionalized. The results of the studies are mixed in the area of generalizability. While some indicate moderate success with generalizability of concepts, others indicate that no generalization had occurred. There is some indication of generalization across stimuli, although not across settings.

Neef, Walters, and Egel (1984) conducted a comparison study of operant and environmental procedures in the training of yes/no responses in severely retarded children. Use of intensive drill in a contrived environment yielded no generalization of yes/no responses. The Mand-Model technique developed by Rogers-Warren and Warren (1980), resulted in all of the children involved generalizing yes/no to other areas of their environment. This technique is addressed later in this chapter.

Bricker and Dennison (1978) proposed using operant techniques incorporated into the daily routine of the child. This requires teaching imitation of sounds during play, eating, diapering, and bathing. This system involves first imitating the child and then requiring the child to imitate the caregiver through providing edible or physical rewards. This and other programs that integrate the two approaches serve to teach the child the function of language. These approaches are closer to a pragmatic approach, although they are still caregiver directed.

Overall, while operant conditioning techniques have proven effective in some specific situations, research has indicated that they may have limitations in language development intervention programs, especially in the area of generalization. Nevertheless, operant efforts clearly must be considered, especially with severely cognitively delayed children. Continuing efforts toward the achievement of generalization characterize more recent research efforts, and this issue will deserve more attention in the future. We now move to consideration of the environmental model that addresses the issue of training and generalization from a different focus.

Environmental Language Intervention Techniques

Another basic method of language intervention, that of environmental or naturalistic training, takes a very different approach. Where operant training requires a basically empty room with no distractions, the environmental model utilizes the home or classroom and the objects and people within it that are interesting to the child. Rather than selecting from a menu of reinforcers, the object requested or the fact of having gotten the caregiver's attention serve as the reinforcers. The environment is often contrived to increase the opportunities for communication (Halle, Alpert, & Anderson, 1984).

In this system, the child is considered to be the initiator. Often, this is difficult to achieve, especially with a child whose previous attempts at attention-getting have been unnoticed. The environment is arranged in such a way as to increase the opportunities for the child to be successful in these attempts at getting attention. By doing this, there is no need for transference of any learned concepts from the training setting to the normal environment. The significant others in the child's life are exposed to, and therefore involved in, the training of the child's language skills. This involvement assists in increasing the actual number of interactions for the child. The communication that is developed is functional, because it is created out of the needs the child perceives within the natural setting. Functional consequences of interaction are also of primary importance to this program (Halle et al., 1984).

Some prerequisites that must be considered for language training within this model include content, the social and physical environment, and the communicative repertoire necessary for the child (Halle et al., 1984). In considering content, it must be remembered that the child must have something of interest to him or her about which to communicate. Socially, the caregiver must interact with the child in ways that will encourage the child to respond. The physical arrangement of the area must necessitate requesting on some level. The child's repertoire could include ways to signal pleasure and pain, wetness or hunger, or, on a more advanced level, greetings and requests. This can take many forms, including quieting activity, purposeful movement such as eye blinks or arm movements, smiles, vocalizations, gestures, or signs.

The context in which the interaction occurs enables the child to attach meaning to what is being taught. By providing this social basis for interaction rather than a clinical background, motivation is introduced. Communication is then an ongoing interaction with others who are significant to the child (Bryen & Joyce, 1985). Certain considerations that should be taken into account initially include how easily the system implemented for the child will be understood by significant others, how easily the system can be produced by the child, and how easily the system can later be converted to a more developed system of communication (Halle et al., 1984).

Because previous attempts at communication by the child may have been ignored, focusing attention is often the first consideration. In order to achieve this, the teacher attends to the child. If the caregiver interprets any activity or gaze as communicatively intended, the child is rewarded with the caregiver's attention. Initially, these may often be unintentional signals, but by rewarding them it is hoped that they will become communicative. Reacting to nonintentional interaction leads to the child's understanding and intent in subsequent actions. Gradually, the program works toward more sophisticated interaction. The caregiver gradually changes his or her responses and expectations, which places on the child the demand for improvement of skills (Rogers-Warren & Warren, 1984). To develop more expanded language, the caregiver can prompt the child with questioning or modeling. This modeling or prompting should be concise and simple, with reinforcers being the object requested and/or verbal reinforcement (Cavallaro, 1983).

The relationship between the child and the caregiver is of the utmost importance in the environmental model. The child must see a social reason for communicating, which is developed through reactions received from the caregiver. It is critical for the caregiver to interpret the child's behaviors as communicative. As in the nonhandicapped child's acquisition of language, unintentional behaviors are originally rewarded. Initially, the caregiver interprets actions and vocalizations. Later, utterances or actions are paralleled by the caregiver, who is expanding the child's behavior. Eventually, the caregiver models and prompts. The model provided is one of "progressive interchanges" (Rogers-Warren & Warren, 1984). It requires that the caregiver not match the child's signals, as would be expected in normal language development, but that the caregiver provide signals that are slightly in advance of the developmental level of the child.

Mand-Model Procedures. Within the environmental intervention model are three basic systems of development. The first to be developed is the Mand-Model Procedure (Rogers-Warren & Warren, 1980). In this model, the caregiver interprets the object or action that the child desires. The caregiver then makes a request, such as, "Tell me what this is." If the child responds with the desired response, based upon his or her developmental level and goals, the teacher rewards verbally and provides the object or action. If the response is not forthcoming, the caregiver models, "You want the _____." Gradually, more complex response structures are required of the child. Use of this model has resulted in increased verbalizations and complexity of generalization across activities. Also, increased maintenance has been observed following the fading of the model (Halle et al., 1984). This model has been utilized primarily in the development of speech, but shows indications of adaptability to other methods of interaction. A weakness that appears to be inherent in this model is that it fails to teach the child to initiate.

Time-Delay Procedure. A second approach to the environmental intervention model is the Time-Delay Procedure. It has been found to be instrumental in teaching the child to initiate interactions (Halle et al., 1984). In implementing this program, the caregiver watches the child closely, noting the child's attention to a specific item. The adult then delays in providing the item in order to assist the child in cuing. Any cue that is given is then praised, and the object of interest is provided. If no cue is given, a verbal prompt is given. This activity is used throughout the day, in delaying providing food, activities, or materials, in order to elicit a cue. Gradually, the cuing system is faded as the child increases requests. This can be used in combination with the Mand-Model after the original request is taught (Halle et al., 1984).

Incidental Teaching Procedure. A third model is the Incidental Teaching Procedure. While the Mand-Model and the Time-Delay procedures teach the child to respond and to initiate, this model teaches the child to expand on communication skills. The environment is arranged to encourage requests. Once an appropriate response or request is firmly established, the caregiver begins to require a slightly more complex form. Halle et al. (1984) report significant increases in generalizations to other situations using this model.

Inherent in this basic model is the necessity for the caregiver to be aware of those things and activities that are of special interest to the child. It is also important to gradually increase the expectations for interaction. This model is based on the child's signals and requires attending skills on the part of the child in order to be instituted. It requires that stimuli provided be slightly beyond the child's level. Interactions must also be with individuals who are significant to the child. It involves initially responding to unintentional communication, then to intentional interaction. Prompts are utilized, then gradually faded. Modeling is provided, as is imitation. The focus is on interaction with the child's natural environment, with emphasis on the arrangement of that environment to facilitate interaction.

No program can be considered effective if generalization to other activities cannot be provided. Cavallaro (1983) reports that the use of incidental teaching has been shown to be effective in convincing the child that he or she has some degree of control over the environment and in reinforcing and thereby creating continually more appropriate forms of communication. Generalization must take into account the child's developmental skills and the context in which these skills will be used. Horner and Budd (1985) found that training language in the setting in which it was expected to occur resulted in generalization across time, setting, and individuals. A further finding was that with the acquisition of signed communication, a significant reduction of self-stimulatory behavior was observed.

PARENTAL INVOLVEMENT

Parental involvement is critical for carry-over of any learning in young and severely handicapped children and thus is especially important in the area of language. Therefore, a close working relationship must be maintained between the teacher and parents. Any skills being taught in the classroom must also be taught in the home in order for generalization to occur. The only way this can be accomplished is through constant communication between the parents and the teacher. Frequent classroom visits by the parents should be encouraged. The teacher must be available to provide the parents with any training necessary to meet the child's needs. Parents will not automatically feel comfortable with signing or with communication boards. This will become easier for them if they are shown the ways in which the alternative communication system or language training method has proven helpful to their child. The teacher can also provide the parents with activities they can do at home with the child in order to enhance generalization.

BEST PRACTICES

Language clearly relates to all aspects of daily living. It is imperative, therefore, that every child be provided a system for communicating to the extent of his or her cognitive and motoric ability. While early systems of language development required the individual to be oral, it has now been established that other options are available. Studies recently have been investigating the method of language intervention and the form of communication that will best meet the needs of each individual child. The operant technique has traditionally been most frequently used among severely handicapped children. The results are seen to be more mechanical and less generalizable to other situations than language skills developed through the environmental intervention approach. A system that more closely resembles the daily life of the individual can be viewed as having some key positive points, including the familiarity of the environment and objects around which the model builds, the inclusion of those individuals who are significant to the child, and the ease with which the model can cross activities and situations. Results indicate greater generalization through the use of this model. It appears that the setting of functional goals in language development results in functional development.

The use of signing in addition to verbal prompts has been shown to be significant in the development of communication in some children and certainly must be considered in the assessment of each child. This system is shown to be especially important in the development of more abstract concepts such as prepositions.

Finally, care should be taken in the development of aided systems. It must be determined that this will be a viable solution to the difficulty the child has with language. Adaptive equipment such as switches, toys, and software, however, have been shown to be important in the development of early prelinguistic forms of development such as cause/effect and yes/no, by teaching children that they can have control over their environment.

Through thorough understanding of the models and communications systems available, and thorough assessment of each child's cognitive, social, and motoric skills, the caregiver will be better able to provide the most viable system of communication for the child. Further research will continue to develop and refine systems that will improve communicative skills for young handicapped children who experience significant delays in language acquisition and development.

SEVERELY
HANDICAPPED
LEARNERS

by Jo Webber

Understanding the causes and characteristics of severe communication disorders is the first step toward effective instruction. Autistic, deaf-blind, and severely retarded students often exhibit similar language characteristics and problems with somewhat similar manifestations. Most of these students have multiple language deficits requiring intensive educational intervention. Their language disorders vary in magnitude and multiplicity, so each assessment and each educational plan must reflect an individualized approach.

Students who are severely handicapped may show deficits in both receptive (understanding) language and expressive (communicative) language. These deficits may range from a total absence of language understanding and production to speech and grammar problems. A broad range of language difficulties is possible and may include mutism, echolalia, perseveration, inappropriate and useless remarks, idiosyncratic use of words and phrases (Wing, 1969), noncommunicative language, omission or incorrect use of function words (Ricks & Wing,

1975), deviant pronunciation or articulation of speech sounds (Cunningham, 1968), and distortion in pitch, rhythms, intonation, and stress patterns (Wing, 1969).

These language problems usually fall into two areas: language content and language use (Bloom & Lahey, 1978). Language *content* refers to *what* we talk about, or the meaning of our language (James, 1982), while language *use* refers to how we use our language to communicate. Deficits in language *form* (the connection of sound and meaning) have usually been considered a secondary problem for severely handicapped students (James, 1982).

PREVERBAL/LOW VERBAL LANGUAGE DISORDERS

Some students have little or no speech and may show limited desire to communicate. These students may be labeled as *mute*. Any sounds such students make are seemingly not meaningful and are often unintelligible. No effort is made to refer to an object, place, or event. These students may use vocalizations in a nonfunctional manner, preferring to "play" with the sounds rather than to communicate (Donnellan-Walsh, Gossage, LaVigna, Schuler, & Traphagen, 1976). Most of these students have poor receptive language, although absence of speech does not preclude receptive understanding—particularly if the mutism is the result of physical disabilities.

Low Cognition

One aspect that seems to characterize preverbal individuals is their apparent lack of knowledge about their immediate environment. They do not attend to individuals around them, they make little eye contact, they do not play with toys, and they appear to be in their "own little world" (Wing, 1969). One explanation for this may be found in the cognitive development literature. It is believed that cognitive functioning serves as a readiness for language development (Flavell, 1977). Kahn (1976) suggests that individuals who had reached Stage 6 (Sensorimotor) of the Piagetian developmental levels measured by the Uzgiris and Hunt (1975) scales exhibited meaningful expressive language, while the pre-Stage 6 group did not.

The literature supports the premise that the *sensorimotor period* (Piaget, 1954; Piaget & Weil, 1951) seems to be closely linked to early language development (Corrigan, 1978; Ingram, 1978). During this period (0–2 years), a normal child will actively explore and learn about his or her environment. Children use their senses to experience the world around them. It is understandable that a child who has sensory or motor impairment will not proceed through this period without some assistance. Cognitive delay for mentally retarded children also prevents normal progress through this stage. It is puzzling, however, that autistic children who seemingly have no sensory, motor, or cognitive deficits also fail to proceed through the sensorimotor period and develop language. Nevertheless, cognitive intervention strategies will often need to accompany or, in some cases, precede language training for preverbal or low verbal students.

Competing Behaviors

Another major characteristic of preverbal, low verbal, and verbal students with severe language problems is the presence of a variety of bizarre and inappropriate behaviors. These behaviors often interfere with language acquisition. Inappropriate behavior clusters often develop in the absence of socially acceptable forms of communication (Polloway & Smith, 1982). Tantrums, opposition, screaming, biting, hitting, hair pulling, vomiting, twirling, hand flapping, and self-abuse may all be presenting behaviors of the severely handicapped student. Some of these behaviors may be self-stimulatory in nature, while some may be inappropriate attempts at communication (Talkington, Hall, & Altman, 1971). A student who has been told to sit down may hit someone. This often means, "No, I don't want to sit down." The challenge is "to expand these primitive efforts at communication into preferred language forms" (Polloway & Smith, 1982, p. 41).

Oppositional students (those students refusing to comply with requests or commands) present a particularly complex set of problems. It is very difficult to assess cognitive development and language acquisition (receptive or expressive) when each teacher command is met with either a refusal to comply, avoidance, or some other inappropriate response. For instance, a student may be told, "Give me the red card." The student may then pick up the green card and crush it. What exactly does this behavior mean in terms of intelligence and receptive language? Or a student may be instructed, "Look at me," a simple attention task and a prerequisite for language training. The student may continue to engage in self-stimulatory behavior and act as though he or she did not hear. This same student will often attend beautifully if the teacher is holding a piece of candy.

Competing behavior and cognitive deficits impair learning. In preverbal and low verbal students, all three characteristics (language deficits, cognitive deficits, and competing behaviors) may be present, implying that all three areas must be addressed in the classroom. Behavior that appears to result from cognitive delay may in fact be due to opposition or withdrawal. Precious time may be wasted with an intervention program aimed only at environmental exploration when a good contingency management or compliance training program could suffice.

Physical Disorders

Many severely handicapped students are interactive, nonoppositional, and have the intellectual capacity for simple language but cannot communicate due to physical impairments. Cerebral palsy may cause articulation to be a virtually impossible endeavor. Pointing or meaningful gestures may also be difficult to a student with spasticity, rigidity, or atrophied muscles. Historically, students who were physically prevented from communicating in traditional ways were invariably and most often inaccurately considered profoundly retarded. Today, sign language (Moores, 1980), communication boards, and electrical/electronic equipment (Carlson, 1981; Vanderheiden & Harris-Vanderheiden, 1976) allow individuals with cerebral palsy to communicate effectively with others.

VERBAL LANGUAGE DISORDERS

Some severely handicapped students have speech or manual signs (form) and have something to say (content), but they do not realize that language can be used to serve a variety of functions (use) (James, 1982). These students may be able to name objects and people but fail to use language to get what they need or want. Additionally, they do not initiate conversations, preferring instead to answer only when prompted.

Often severely handicapped children use their language inappropriately. Their content does not match the content of the preceding statement or the context in which it is delivered. Upon arriving at school, a student's first verbalization of the day may be, "Is that a red shirt?", when requested to take his or her seat. A child may talk about the washing machine when trying to communicate that he or she wants to go home. Since communication involves both a sender and a receiver, communication has not occurred if the receiver is confused. Nonfunctional language patterns are found in many severely handicapped students. When other people do not understand what the student intends to communicate, it can impair the student's social and intellectual development.

Echolalia

One language pattern often found in severely handicapped verbal students is *echolalia*. Echolalia is the parroting of words, phrases, or sentences in a nonmeaningful format (Donnellan-Walsh et al., 1976). For example, a teacher may ask a student, "What's your name?" The student responds, "Your name." This type of echolalia—words repeated immediately after the prompt—is known as *immediate echolalia* (Risley & Wolf, 1967). Lovaas (1977) suggests that immediate echolalia may be a form of self-stimulation. Students who exhibit immediate echolalia may also have trouble with reversals of pronouns. They may repeat personal pronouns exactly as they hear them, referring to another person as *I* and themselves as *you*. This is a particularly difficult problem to correct and is often a challenge for the teacher (Ross, 1974).

A student who will repeat previously heard television commercials, nursery rhymes, poems, songs, or sentences with no apparent communicative intent is exhibiting *delayed echolalia*. Delayed echolalia may also be a form of self-stimulation, oppositional behavior (Donnellan-Walsh, Gossage, LaVigna, Schuler, & Traphagen, 1976), or metaphorical communication (language with private meanings) (Kanner, 1973.) The important point is that even though this type of repetition may be entertaining, it is often nonfunctional language and has limited usefulness as a communication tool.

Perseveration

Some students will choose a word, phrase, or sentence and repeat it over and over, often at a high rate of speed. This phenomenon is called *perseveration*. In normal language development, a child who learns a new word may want to play with the word by repeating it several times. Severely handicapped individuals may continue to exhibit perseverative language and behavior patterns as they mature. If perseveration becomes a task-avoidance or self-stimulatory behavior and prevents functional communication, then it may need to be eliminated while functional language training is initiated.

Echolalia and perseveration seem to increase in frequency as a student's anxiety increases (Donnellan-Walsh et al., 1976). Often, providing a student with words to communicate frustration ("Please stop") or confusion ("I don't know") will decrease the incidence of echolalia and perseveration. In sum, students identified as severely handicapped will exhibit more than one of the characteristics that have been described. Obviously, individualized programming for severely handicapped students is a necessity. The first step in this programming is the process of comprehensive individualized assessment.

ASSESSMENT

The purpose of a comprehensive communication assessment is to gather information that can lead to effective communication intervention. Assessment is a process of designating the level of a student's ability as compared to a predetermined sequence of behaviors in several developmental areas. The accuracy with which a teacher is able to pinpoint a student's ability level and diagnose deficit areas is directly related to the success of the subsequent instruction. Assessment (both initial and ongoing) is an integral part of the teaching process.

Severely handicapped students exhibit delays and deficits in several areas that relate to communication. These areas include cognition, socialization, sensorimotor skills, and receptive and expressive language. Since this population tends to show limited abilities in each of these areas, accurate assessment depends on astute observation and interview skills. This type of assessment "requires input from a number of persons, each viewing the problem from an individual sphere of expertise" (Fairweather, Haun, & Finkle, 1983, p. 6). Thus, the special educator, speech pathologist, psychologist, physical therapist, parent, medical expert, and the individual student may all be important sources of assessment information. This *multidisciplinary* team approach requires each team member to determine abilities and deficits in his or her particular area of expertise (Table 10.1). The data provided by each team member provide the basis for instructional decision making.

This section discusses various informal and formal techniques for evaluating the performance of severely handicapped students with regard to communication functions. Brown (1986) suggests that the environment determines which skills should be assessed and which skills are ultimately achieved, because language skills that are taught should be functional, span several domains, and be those that the student requires most often to achieve the highest level of independence. A comprehensive assessment should reflect the student's present ability in relation to the communication demands of his or her environment. Both the student and the environment need to be scrutinized.

Cognitive Variables

Cognitive variables that tend to correlate with language acquisition include imitation, means-end relationships, object permanence, and symbolic functioning (Bates, Bengni, Bretherton, & Volterra, 1979; Chappell & Johnson, 1976; Curcio, 1978; Kahn, 1976). Unfortunately, cognitive prerequisites are not always assessed for language intervention planning. Bryen and Joyce (1985) found that 48.9% of the language

TABLE 10.1. Multidisciplinary Team Member Functions

Team Member	Responsibilities
Child	To become actively involved in decision making when possible; to indicate preferences and needs; to implement suggestions; to recommend changes
Parent Caregiver	To give input on child's communication needs in the home and community; to instruct others about the aid; to indicate the practical applications of proposed systems
Occupational/Physical Therapist	To evaluate the child's physical condition and developmental functioning level including perceptual and motor abilities, ambulation, range of motion, abnormal physical reflexes, fatigue, endurance, and strength
Speech/Language Pathologist	To evaluate communication skills including prognosis for the development of speech, receptive and expressive language, present means of communication, and future communication needs
Teacher	To provide input on educational/scholastic skills, communication needs in classroom, social adjustment, and learning styles
Psychologist	To provide information about intelligence; to rate and style of learning and general observational data
Others as needed	Medicine, engineering, audiology, social work, physical education, teacher aid, consulting

Adapted with permission from M. Russell (1984). Assessment and intervention issues with the nonspeaking child. *Exceptional Children, 51,* 67. Copyright 1984 by The Council for Exceptional Children.

studies of severely handicapped that they reviewed indicated no evidence of cognitive assessment. As they concluded, "This neglect may have seriously reduced the effects of intervention efforts reported in these studies" (p. 12).

Assessing cognitive functioning in nonverbal students is difficult, because language and cognition are so intricately interrelated and because most standardized cognitive assessment instruments were developed for verbal children. However, the instruments developed for normal infants and young children may be adapted and used with severely handicapped students in order to obtain some information on cognitive functioning. Some instruments that might be useful include the *Ordinal Scales of Psychological Development* (Uzgiris & Hunt, 1975), based on Piaget's theory of intellectual development; *Bayley Scales of Infant Development* (Bayley, 1969); *Preschool Language Scale* (Zimmerman, Steiner, & Evatt, 1969); and the *McCarthy Scale of Children's Ability* (McCarthy, 1972). Information obtained from these scales might be examined closely. It is important to keep in mind that there is still much controversy concerning whether cognitive competence must precede language acquisition (Reichle & Keogh, 1986).

Observation of *imitative* behavior and actual training of various motor and verbal imitations (e.g., tongue thrusts, arm movements, babbling) may additionally be used to assess cognitive functioning. Sherman (1971) suggests that a child's ability to imitate is a primary factor in the acquisition of new vocal responses. However, it is evident that communicative behavior can be established in the absence of generalized imitative behavior (Reichle, Rogers, & Barrett, 1984).

Means-end relationships refer to the methods by which a child obtains desired objects or attention. Shane (1980) suggests that a means-end sensorimotor Stage 5 as assessed on the Uzgiris-Hunt Scales is a precondition for use of an augmentative communication system. Stage 5 represents the methods that a normal child, 12 to 18 months old, would use to obtain objects and attention. However, crying in earlier infancy appears to be an adequate method of obtaining attention (Reichle & Keogh, 1986), so this cognitive prerequisite may not be absolutely necessary for further language development.

Two ways of assessing an individual's acquisition method (means-end relations) are interviews and observational techniques. Figure 10.1 illustrates a checklist that can be used to pinpoint current communicative strategies and provide some information regarding cognitive functioning.

Object permanency refers to the ability of a person to retain the concept of an object even though the object is out of sight. "At present, the relationship between object permanency and language acquisition has not been satisfactorily resolved," (Reichle & Keogh, 1986, p. 202) but assessment in this area could produce useful information. Different assessment tasks, such as hiding objects under a cloth to observe whether the student will uncover it, can be used to indicate whether the student has obtained this cognitive construct. Consideration might be given, however, to the reinforcing value of the object. If the student does not care to have the object, he or she may not uncover it. This would not necessarily indicate a lack of the achievement of object permanence, but rather the student's feelings about that particular object.

It is important to realize the controversy concerning the relationship of cognition and language. Although it is recommended that cognitive variables be assessed, it is not evident that certain cognitive levels must be obtained before communication training can begin. Certainly, students who have imitative behavior, who can acquire desired objects through pointing or gesturing, who have obtained an understanding of object permanency, and who can match symbols to objects will probably acquire knowledge with more ease. However, there is no reason to exclude learners from language training until those cognitive variables are taught. Training both language and cognitive skills simultaneously can be of maximum benefit to the student.

Social Variables

The desire to interact is very important to the acquisition of language. Many severely handicapped students appear to exhibit no interactive or communicative behaviors. Autistic children, particularly, do not appear to use learned language to interact but produce speech responses only when cued and reinforced. Assessing social variables is most often accomplished through interviewing others who know the child and through observations of the child in several situations. The *Autism Screening Instrument for Educational Planning* (ASIEP) (Krug, Arick, & Almond, 1980) has a subtest specifically designed to assess a student's social interaction.

For the purpose of this particular assessment using ASIEP, an adult and the student are observed. The observer uses a time sampling procedure. Behaviors such as self-stimulation, crying, laughing, gestures, play, conversations, and tantrums are coded as to their interactive quality. The adult alternately cues and prompts the student, interacts with no cues or prompts, and totally refrains from initiating interaction in order to observe the student's desire to interact and methods of doing so. Preferably, these observations take place across settings and across caregivers in order to comprehensively assess all student-environment interactions.

Further informal observations may give the following information regarding social variables.

FIGURE 10.1. Communication Interview Form

Student: _____ School: _____

Examiner: _____ Date: _____

Functions

COMMENTS

1. Requests for affection/interaction

2. Requests for adult action

Cue Questions:

1. Requests for affection/interaction
   What if S wants:
   - adult to sit near?
   - peer to sit near?
   - nonhandicapped peer to sit near?
   - adult to look at him
   - adult to tickle him?
   - to cuddle/embrace?
   - to sit on adult's lap?
   - Other:

2. Requests for adult action
   What if S wants:
   - help with dressing?

	Crying	Aggression	Tantrums/Self Injury	Shakes "no"/Nods "yes"	Facial Expression	Passive Gaze	Gaze Shift	Proximity	Gestures/Pointing	Gives Object	Pulling Other's Hands	Touching/Moving Other's Face/Body	Grabs/Reaches	Enactment	Removes Self/Walks Away	Vocalization/Noise	Intonation	Inappropriate Echolalia	Appropriate Echolalia	One-Word Speech	One-Word Signs	Complex Speech	Combined Signs

to be read a book?																									
to play ball/a game?																									
to go outside/to store?																									
Other:																									
3. Requests for object, food, or things **What if S wants:**																									
an object out of reach?																									
a door/container opened?																									
a favorite food?																									
music/radio/tv?																									
keys/toy/book?																									
Other:																									
4. Protest **What if:**																									
common routine is dropped?																									
favorite toy/food taken away?																									
taken for ride without desire?																									
adult terminates interaction?																									
required to do something doesn't want to do?																									
Other:																									
5. Declaration/comment **What if S wants:**																									
to show you something?																									
you to look at something?																									
Other:																									

Column group headers:

3. Requests for object, food, or things

5. Protest

5. Declaration/comment

From Hedrick, D. L., Prathey, E. M., & Toben, A. R. (1975). *Sequenced Inventory of Communication Development.* Seattle: University of Washington Press, p. 51. Reprinted with permission.

1. Does the student initiate interaction? This initiation may be in the form of approaching, touching, offering objects, gesturing, vocalizing, signing, speech, or facial expressions.

2. Does the student respond to another's initiated interaction? This may be in the form of imitation, following directions, gesturing, speaking, vocalizing, or facial expressions.

3. Does the student maintain interaction (e.g., following, imitating, taking turns, offering objects, vocalizing, signing, speaking)?

4. Does the student terminate interaction by moving away, pushing, gesturing, speaking?

5. Does the student play? Is the play cooperative, parallel, or in isolation?

Through an analysis of these questions, the teacher may discover that the student is communicating in several ways, though it may not be readily apparent to people who do not know the student.

Further useful assessment information can be obtained during various interviews with significant adults (e.g., parents, siblings, psychologists). Interview information might include some of the following components.

1. A description of a situation in which the individual will be most socially interactive. How do they interact?

2. A list of situations in which the individual is most socially interactive with peers.

3. A list of situations in which the individual is most socially interactive with adults.

4. A list of activities that the individual most likes to do with other people.

Motor Variables

Information regarding prerequisite motor variables is necessary before deciding the type of communication instruction to employ. Bryen and Joyce (1985) suggest assessing (a) motor requirements for a vocal system, (b) fine motor coordination required for manual gestures, and (c) precise and sustained hand control essential for pointing or switch manipulation if using a communication board.

Physiological disorders may be a primary cause of a student's language difficulty. The diagnosis of *apraxia* (the inability to produce voluntary speech motions, even though the motor mechanisms are apparently functional) might dictate a nonoral intervention. Speech may also be impeded by *dysarthria*, a dysfunction of the central nervous system that immobilizes the tongue or the jaw. For a discussion of differential diagnosis of these motor impairments, refer to Shane (1980), who presents a review of current studies and provides recommendations for the observational diagnosis of nonoral individuals.

An individual's voluntary control over hand, arm, and finger movement can affect the future success of a manual communication system. The individual will need to be able to formulate single signs and signed sequences. Current motor functions and possible future functioning ability following physical therapy and maturation might also be considered. If an individual does not possess the manual dexterity required for manual communication, an alternative language system needs to be introduced.

Pointing, scanning, and encoding process (see the Language Intervention section later in this chapter for definitions) depend on varying levels of motor control; thus, "the type of communication board used and the method of designating information will be predicated on the available physical structures under voluntary control" (Shane, 1980, p. 220). Physical assessment might include observing the use of upper body control (including head, mouth, eyes, arms, fingers, and shoulders). Proper seating and positioning are dependent on lower body extremities. Additionally, assessment might include information on abnormal reflex patterns, range of motion, visual acuity, and auditory discrimination (Russell, 1984). It is the instructor's responsibility to provide an accessible communication system for each student. Current technology and ingenuity have the potential to overcome even the most severe physical impairments.

Nonverbal Communicative Strategies

Systematic observation and analysis of prelinguistic communicative strategies such as pointing, crying, nodding, and eye contact provide information concerning an individual's readiness for a formal language system (Bates et al., 1979; McLean & Snyder-McLean, 1978). Wilcox and Campil (1985) delineated several nonverbal behaviors that were perceived as being communicative. In their study, a student was videotaped in a school setting. Several primary caregivers (including the parents) were asked to observe the videotape and indicate the behaviors they saw as some form of communication. The following behaviors were listed: (a) head and neck movements (turns, shaking, nods); (b) mouth movements (tongue in and out, mouth open and shut); (c) facial expressions (smiles, frowns); (d) intentional vocalizations (sounds, crying, laughing); (e) upper extremity movements (arms, hands, fingers), and (f) total body movements (postural shifts).

A target for initial language intervention might be the behaviors that occur most frequently and are perceived as communicative by the most adults. Communication in the broadest sense includes primitive and sometimes inappropriate behavior. Assessing these behaviors provides insight as to communicative intent and current communicative ability. For many students, this is their only means of interaction with the environment.

Receptive and Expressive Language

Formal and informal assessment techniques can be used to determine an individual's receptive and expressive language skills. Observations, interviews, and direct training tasks are informal methods often employed with severely handicapped individuals. Donnellan-Walsh et al. (1976) suggest several questions to be answered during an observation that will assist in analyzing receptive language.

1. Does the student respond differently to various environmental sounds (e.g., sirens, refrigerator door opening, mother's voice, television, vacuum cleaner)?

2. Does the student respond to people who speak to him?

3. Does the student attend to conversation, music, television programs?

4. Does the student show any understanding of time, space, size, or quantity? (p. 585)

Directing a student through different tasks can also provide an assessment of the level of their receptive language. One-stage commands such as "Sit down," "Get your coat," "Go to the bathroom," or "Open the door" may be met with compliance or lack of understanding. If the student is physically impaired, the commands might be "Point to the ball," "Show me your nose," "Touch chair," "Give me the plate," and so forth. In this manner, the teacher can determine a student's understanding of an oral vocabulary. A string of commands might be given in order to assess memory skills. Again, cognition and language are interrelated and can be assessed simultaneously.

It is necessary during this informal assessment to distinguish between receptive language skills and oppositional behavior. Some students simply will not follow commands even though they understand what was said. In this case, a reinforcer may be given to the student for compliance with a few commands, and then the reinforcer may be faded for the more difficult receptive assessment tasks. It is important not to punish a student when he or she cannot perform a task, but it is also important not to misdiagnose cognitive deficits when in fact the student is merely willful and stubborn.

Expressive language is usually assessed through formal as well as informal measures (Table 10.2). For instance, the Sample of Vocal Behavior subtest of the ASIEP (Krug et al., 1980) establishes a process for analyzing spontaneous utterances in terms of variety, function, articulation, and length. Communicative gestures can also be evaluated. Most formal assessment instruments rely on someone's observation of the student's expressive and receptive language functions (both spontaneous and elicited). In this way, the student's knowledge of language meaning, usage, form, and some cognitive skills are assessed and documented. Comprehensive assessment information provides the initial step for language intervention and the data necessary for choosing an effective language system.

Because the environment is an integral part of the student's daily communication, environmental factors also need to be analyzed. Brown (1986) recommended several environmental questions for teachers to consider during the assessment process.

1. Are you assessing the skill in the appropriate places?

2. Are you assessing the skill at the appropriate times of the day?

3. Are you using materials that reflect those needed in the natural environment?

4. Are you assessing the student under natural conditions?

5. Are you assessing a sufficient range of skills that will be required in the natural environment?

6. Are you relying on artificial cues and consequences to elicit student behavior?

The implication is that any communicative behavior can only be understood in its context (Mishler, 1979). To observe a student's behavior in terms of communicative intent and function out of context might lead to invalid assumptions resulting in inappropriate language programming.

In terms of echolalia, current research is suggesting several communicative functions utilized in immediate and delayed echolalia (Dore, 1975; Halliday, 1975; Prizant, 1978; Prizant & Duchan, 1981; Prizant & Rydell, 1984). Receptive understanding, social variables, and language form can be observed in echolalic utterances.

TABLE 10.2. Assessment Instruments of Language Development for Use with Severely Handicapped Individuals

Instrument	Publisher
Autism Screening Instrument for Educational Planning (ASIEP) (Krug, Arick, & Almond, 1980)	ASIEP
Preverbal Assessment Intervention Profile (Connard, 1984)	ASIEP
Psychoeducational Profile (Schopler & Reichler, 1976)	Child Development Products
Sequenced Inventory of Communication Development (Hedrick, Prathey, & Toben, 1975)	University of Washington Press
Developmental Sentence Analysis (Lee, 1974)	Northwestern University Press
Environmental Language Inventory (MacDonald & Horstmeier, 1978)	Charles E. Merrill
Bzoch-League Receptive-Expressive Emergent Language Scale (REEL) and *Assessing Language Scales in Infancy* (manual) (Bzoch & League, 1971)	Tree of Life Press
Preschool Attainment Record (Doll, 1966)	American Guidance Service
Learning Accomplishment Profile (Giffen Sanford, 1985)	Chapel-Hill Outreach Program Kaplan Press
Peabody Picture Vocabulary Test–Revised (Dunn, 1981)	American Guidance Service
The Denver Developmental Screening Test (Frankenburg, 1970)	University of Colorado Medical Center
Goldman-Fristoe Test of Articulation (Goldman & Fristoe, 1969)	American Guidance Service
McCarthy Scale of Children's Abilities (McCarthy, 1972)	Psychological Corporation
TARC Assessment System (Sailor & Mix, 1975)	PRO-ED
Preschool Language Scale (Zimmerman, Steiner, & Evatt, 1969)	Charles E. Merrill

TABLE 10.2. Continued

Instrument	Publisher
Bayley Scales of Infant Development (Bayley, 1969)	Psychological Corporation
AAMD Adaptive Behavior Scale–Public School Version (Lambert, Windmiller, Cole, & Figueroa, 1975)	American Association on Mental Deficiency
Birth to Three Scales of Development (Bangs & Dodson, 1974)	DLM

> For both immediate and delayed echolalia, the salient dimensions include degree of comprehension of the repeated utterance, whether an utterance is produced interactively or noninteractively, and whether any structural changes are imposed in repetition. For delayed echolalia, an additional factor is the relevance of the utterance to the situational or conversational context. (Schuler & Prizant, 1985, p. 168)

Many behaviors, verbal and nonverbal, can be functional communication. Given a very broad definition of language, a comprehensive language assessment for severely handicapped students requires astute observation and interview skills and careful analytical skills.

In order for a skill to become functional as a communication tool, the student needs to demonstrate language competence spontaneously, across settings and people. If this is not the case, the skill must be taught during the intervention phase. Language intervention should consist of long-term goals (determined by the natural communication demands of the student's environment); short-term objectives (determined by a developmental sequence beginning at the student's present level of functioning); and a designated communication system (determined by the student's prerequisite skills, the availability of adaptive equipment, and the environment's tolerance of the communication system). Planning intervention and choosing a language system are difficult. However, this is a very important process. The next section will provide information on intervention to assist with that process.

LANGUAGE INTERVENTION

Communication is basic to almost every human endeavor. The challenge for teachers of severely handicapped students is to establish an effective mechanism through which the student can interact with others. Given comprehensive assessment information, the teacher must make several decisions about intervention. Furthermore, these decisions need to be well founded in current theory and research.

Historically, language intervention focused exclusively on the aural/oral modalities. This means that speech was equated with language, and almost all intervention focused on speech training. During the late 1970s the view of language shifted (Bryen & Joyce, 1985). Now language is also taught through the visual/motor modalities using sign language and other symbol systems (Romski, Sevcik, & Joyner, 1984). This broader view of language also considered the important interrelationship of social, cognitive, and linguistic abilities (Bates et al., 1979; Bruner, 1977; Sugarman-Bell, 1978). Assessment and intervention of only one or two of these variables produce, at best, only a partial language training program.

Finally, since the educational goal for all students is to foster independence and competence in our society, current literature suggests that language intervention should include functional and structural goals. Although syntax, grammar, and intelligibility are important, "language does not exist as an end in itself, but as a means to the achievement of some specific social/communicative function" (McLean & Snyder-McLean, 1978, p. 49).

This section focuses on the teacher decisions necessary for the development of an effective language intervention program for severely handicapped students. By delineating intervention goals, deciding on an intervention model, choosing a language system matching the child's abilities and needs, and determining subsequent language competence, the teacher can proceed systematically in this very important task. Failure to provide appropriate language intervention can undermine the student's motivation, promote feelings of failure, increase anxiety and tension, and retard social and intellectual development.

Intervention Goals

Setting individualized goals for severely handicapped students is prerequisite to any intervention program. Assessment information provides a picture of each student's abilities and deficit areas in relationship to environmental needs. Given this information, decisions concerning specific language goals can be formulated. These goals fall into two major categories: structural goals and functional goals.

Structural Goals. The structure or form of a language system is basic to effective communication. Structural components of language include a varied vocabulary, correct grammar, appropriate execution, and intelligible speech. Providing a severely handicapped individual with even minimal structural communication skills can make an enormous difference in the course of his or her life. The following paragraphs provide a number of suggestions in this regard.

First, the student needs to learn that words, signs, pictures, and symbols represent something else. This is called *referentiality* (Donnellan-Walsh et al., 1976). As the student performs various behaviors (e.g., eating, drinking, toileting), the teacher can present him or her with the correct words, signs, or corresponding pictures. In this way, the student can begin to make an association between the symbol and the actual event.

Second, vocabulary must be built that the student can master. An individual with a limited vocabulary needs words that are functional and that communicate what the individual does or wants to do most often. For a student who likes food, *eat* may be a good first vocabulary word. For a student who likes to play with a ball, *ball* may be a good first word. In order to help decide which vocabulary words to begin teaching, Donnellan-Walsh et al. (1976) list some sample words that are easily used vocally or nonvocally in a functional manner (Figure 10.2).

It is important to choose vocabulary words that will have meaning to the student. The student's vocabulary should be appropriate to his or her personality, situation, and developmental stages (Carlson, 1981). Having completed a thorough assessment, the teacher has a good idea of the individual's needs and the characteristics of his or her environment. A more comprehensive vocabulary list is delineated by Rittenhouse and Myers (1982) under the categories of:

action	activities
animals	body parts
clothing	colors
conditions	food
identities	linguistic
location	number and amount
self-care	school
time	

Carlson (1981) suggests a process for choosing vocabulary that is child-centered and situationally appropriate. First, the child's parents, teachers, and other significant adults are asked to specify in which settings the child spends time and how much time is spent in each setting. Second, the adults are asked to indicate observational and participatory activities that the child may experience in these settings. The objective is to find those words that the child may want to use in

FIGURE 10.2. Examples of Single-Word Utterances that May Be Useful as First Teaching Objectives

Food		Clothing		Playtime	
Lunch	Eat	Pants	Put on	Ball	Ride
Cookie	Drink	Shirt	Take off	Truck	Jump
Juice		Sweater		Car	
Ice Cream		Coat		Doll	
Candy		Shoes		Bike	
Milk		Pajamas		Blocks	
etc.		etc.		Book	
				etc.	

People/Socialization			Things Around Home			Body Parts
Own Name	Hug	Hi	TV	Sit	In	Nose
Mommy	Sit	Thanks	Bed	Look	Out	Face
Daddy		Help	Table	Sleep	Up	Eye
Jimmy			Chair			Ear
Debby			Toilet (potty)			Tummy
etc.			Cup			Arms
			Door			etc.
			Home			

Movement	Requesting	
Walk	Give me	more
Go	Want	
Come		
etc.		

From A. Donnellan-Walsh et al. (1976). *Teaching makes a difference.* Santa Barbara: Santa Barbara County Public Schools, p. 151. Copyright 1976 by Santa Barbara County Public Schools. Reprinted with permission.

a particular milieu in addition to those that the adults may want the child to use.

Third, the adults are asked to list words from selected settings by category (e.g., people, actions, places, feelings, etc.). Fourth, those words that are within the child's developmental experience (words regarding participatory rather than observational activities) and interest level (words eliciting the child's attention and pleasurable reactions) are the first words selected for expression. Receptive vocabulary can be developed from an interview with adults in the child's environment listing words used most often with the child.

Last, the evolution and expansion of the child's vocabulary is dependent on the variety of experiences offered the child (Carlson, 1981). The chosen vocabulary should be "open-ended and sensitive to developmental, environmental, and cultural changes" (Carlson, 1981, p. 244).

After one-word responses are regularly produced, the student may be ready to learn word combinations. Nouns are usually taught first, since abstract symbols are more easily understood when paired with a concrete object. Next, a few verbs such as want, give, go, and eat may be added so that the student can produce two-word combinations. Pronouns, particularly *I*, added to these two-word combinations form complete sentences (e.g., "I want juice"). Adjectives can be added as they are necessary. The rate and extent to which the teacher works on language structure will be dictated by the cognitive and functional level of the student. Some students may learn only one or two vocabulary words, while others may learn several hundred and be able to use correct grammar. The most important issue is that the child demonstrate both the desire and the functional ability to communicate in some fashion.

In a review of language training studies conducted with severely handicapped individuals, Bryen and Joyce (1985) found that 40% of those studies focusing only on establishing initial vocabulary were successful; 42.8% of those studies focusing only on expansion into combinational phrases and sentences were successful; but only 22% of the studies addressing both initial vocabulary and expansion into combinational phrases were successful. Thus, the scope of established structural goals may determine the success of the language program.

Intelligible language (speech or sign) is often a problem for students who also have physical handicaps. Certainly, having more people who can understand what the student is trying to communicate is desirable. However, spending an inordinate amount of time on articulation or mastering the exact hand movement may inhibit the desire to communicate. The teacher can continue to pronounce or sign correctly and prompt the correct word usage, but the primary structural goal should not overshadow the student's communicative intent.

Structural goals for language training for severely handicapped persons may include:

1. Creating an association between objects/activities and symbols for those objects and activities.

2. Choosing relevant and simple vocabulary. Begin usually with nouns having concrete and meaningful examples.

3. Pairing nouns and verbs or nouns and adjectives as nouns are mastered.

4. Making simple sentences of phrases as pronouns and proper nouns are added.

5. Working on intelligibility but not to the exclusion of the student's desire to communicate.

Research has shown that structural language behaviors "can be taught to severely handicapped persons" (Bryen & Joyce, 1985, p. 20). However, these learned structural behaviors need to lead to communicative functions that are useful to the entire development of the individual.

Functional Goals. The pragmatic functions of language for severely handicapped persons are often more important than the particular structure of language. Bruner (1974–75) defined pragmatic as the "directive function of speech (or other communicative signals) through which speakers affect the behavior of others in trying to carry out their intention" (p. 283). Communicative competence expands the uses of language so that linguistic structure assists an individual in obtaining functional goals derived from his or her own needs, desires, or intentions. "Functional goals refer to the many purposes for which the particular structures can be used" (Bryen & Joyce, 1985, p. 18).

Bates and colleagues (Bates et al., 1979) discuss communicative intent during the prelinguistic period, demonstrating that intentional and functional communication occurs before the emergence of language. Indeed, communicative competence may be a prerequisite for language development. For severely handicapped individuals, many of whom are prelinguistic, pointing, gestures, vocalizations, and eye contact may be their only form of communication.

Functional goals address the expansion of the uses of language so that the learner is better served. When determining individualized functional goals for students, the teacher needs to consider *spontaneous* and *self-initiated* language use, *elicited* language use, and *communicative intent*.

Most recent studies addressing language training for severely handicapped individuals report on the *elicited* functions being taught (Bryen & Joyce, 1985). For example, teachers present specific pictures or questions, and the student provides the correct label or response. This training, although effective in eliciting language production, is usually conducted in a clinical-type setting and often has little resemblance to the conversational functions found in more normal environments. In conversation, the communicative functions are initiated by the learners' own desires, needs, and intentions rather than having the communicative function predetermined by specific materials or trainers.

Spontaneous and *self-initiated* language use is a very important consideration for severely handicapped students. Sometimes the only spontaneous communication present is crying or screaming. Since this communication is spontaneous, it might be considered as a starting point for subsequent instruction. Harris and Vaderheiden (1980) suggest that a spontaneous language training program

> should be a gradual, evolutionary one that introduces advanced communicative and interactive skills as natural extensions of existing skills and activities; where new communicative forms or techniques are introduced to help the child better express already mastered or learned functions; and where new functions would initially be introduced within the content of already mastered physical and cognitive skills. (p. 240)

When both elicited and spontaneous communication skills are present, the primary functional goal for severely handicapped students becomes that of increasing *communicative intent*. The learner must be provided with the motivation to communicate. This is best done during interactions with significant others in natural contexts where together they encounter objects and people. During these natural, relevant interactions, requests are made, objects are recognized, and undesirable events are rejected. Communication occurs in a natural environment, and the student is provided a means for letting someone else know his or her intentions.

Too often, spontaneous self-initiated language with communicative intent is not systematically taught in lieu of contrived, elicited language programs. Research findings support "the primacy of developing communicative competence rather than learning isolated language behaviors that fail to serve the various intents, desires, and needs of the learner" (Bryen & Joyce, 1985, p. 26). Bryen and Joyce (1985) further determined from their review that in 4.3% of the studies addressing only elicited functional goals were there successful outcomes, whereas 87.5% of the studies addressing the goal of spontaneous usage of learned structures showed successful outcomes.

Some examples of functional language goals might include:

. Increasing the frequency and variety of interactive experiences for each student.

. Encouraging spontaneous and self-initiated communication.

. Expanding communicative intent by facilitating requests, rejection, and descriptions of objects and/or people.

. Increasing natural conversational interaction by teaching social conventions (e.g., "thank you" or "you're welcome") or nonverbal communicative symbols (e.g., smiles, eye contact, etc.) (Higginbotham & Yoder, 1982).

In summary, goal determination seems to be a primary discriminating factor in establishing successful language training.

> If the goals that are selected for severely handicapped students are restricted, poorly formulated, or not reflective of the complexity of the behaviors to be learned by the student, then assessment, intervention methods and measures of student success are also likely to be restricted or distorted. (Bryen & Joyce, 1985, p. 25)

Having formulated both structural and functional language goals based on a comprehensive assessment of the student's current functional level, the teacher is ready to choose an intervention model.

Intervention Models

Two primary intervention models have been found effective in teaching communication to severely handicapped students. These models are the *interactive model*, based on the view that language is learned through social interactions, and the *operant model*, based primarily on the work of Skinner. The intervention model chosen, or the subsequent combination of models, depends on the structural and functional goals formulated for each child. The models can be used in combination provided the teacher has a clear understanding of the underlying theories and their prescribed components.

Interactive Model. The interactive model is based on the theory that language develops through social interactions that begin at birth. Freedle and Lewis (1977) state that "to understand the growth of language one must look at language as it is used in naturalistic, interactive sequences of peer with peer or Mother with child" (p. 157). Normal language does not develop in isolation or in contrived situations. In normal development during feeding, bathing, or diaper changes, the mother interacts with the infant using facial expressions, speech, physical contact, humming, and so forth. In turn, the child begins to make facial expressions and verbal noises. Crying communicates distress, and smiles begin to communicate contentment.

In the same way, severely handicapped individuals can develop language. However, these particular students show "reduced or inconsistent ability to interact with their environment; reduced or inconsistent ability to engage in vocal or motor play with others; the inability to express emotions, needs and thoughts; and the inability to develop control of normal communication mechanisms" (Harris & Vanderheiden, 1980, p. 234). Thus, teachers need to provide more deliberate interaction opportunities and more systematic language training than found in normal infant stimulation.

Applying the interactive model in a classroom dictates that the student be provided various opportunities to interact with different people and objects. Individualized functional goals should reflect these activities. During these interactions, prelanguage and language goals are addressed. Specific linguistic skills are introduced and developed through nonlinguistic activities like play. For example, pointing to a communication board may be developed as an extension of a play activity, and only later is the pointing skill applied to a board for communication purposes (Harris & Vanderheiden, 1980).

Teachers are cautioned against introducing higher level tasks to the student too soon. It might be inappropriate to expect a student who is functioning at a low cognitive level to learn a new visual graphic system or vocal system simultaneously with symbolic communication. Interactive activities are planned with regard to the student's physical and cognitive abilities and to the student's interests. Communication skills are added as an extension of existing skills and activities. "It is critically important to keep interaction in mind and focus upon providing the (student) with efficient ways to interact using current skills (or with slight modifications to them) and to resist trying to jump ahead to the introduction of more advanced techniques or skills (e.g., symbolic communication via augmentative physical modes)" (Harris & Vanderheiden, 1980, p. 241).

The environmental context in which language is taught has been recognized as a very important factor for successful language development (Sailor & Guess, 1983). Language training might take place on the playground, in the bedroom, during meals, and in the community as well as in the classroom. Additionally, the inclusion of various people significant to the student (e.g., parents, siblings) in the language training program seems to increase the functionality and durability of learned language. As the opportunity for interaction increases, the possibilities for effective language training also increase. Thus, the teacher of severely handicapped students might work communication skills into every activity, provide for a wide variety of interaction activities throughout the day, and encourage all significant people in the student's life to do the same.

Harris and Vanderheiden (1980) suggest three areas to be addressed consistent with the interactive model of language development with severely handicapped individuals.

1. *The development of physical mechanisms for the expression of communication and interaction with others.* These might include eye gazes, pointing, head shaking, and verbal noises. Remember that these mechanisms need to be developed as an extension of already existing skills demonstrated in play or high-interest activities. They can be connected to a

direct symbolic communication system once interaction ability is dem
onstrated.

2. *The development of general interaction ability and of motivation and
intent to communicate.* Attention should be given to already existing
interactive skills, even though they may be primitive. Adaptive play
techniques matching the student's motoric abilities and special position
ing techniques may be necessary to maximize interactive opportunities
Additionally, allowing the student some environmental control (e.g.
choosing or rejecting food and toys, activating bells and lights by head
movements, or other gross motor movements) can be beneficial. In thi
way prelinguistic cognitive skills are developed that later can be used
to master a symbolic communication system.

3. *The development of cognitive skills required for symbolic communica
tion.* More opportunities provided for the student to explore and contro
the environment allow for further prelinguistic cognitive development
For students who are limited motorically and perceptually, this mean
that creative experiences developed by the teacher are very important
Particularly important are imitative skills that are forerunners of sym
bolic functioning (Bates et al., 1979; Hurd, 1972; Piaget, 1954). Any
attempts by the student to interact with people or objects or to imitate
others' behavior should be encouraged and facilitated by parents, care
givers, siblings, and teachers. In this way, the student can develop the
cognitive skill necessary to accommodate a symbolic language system.

As the student interacts, symbolic language (words, pictures, signs
symbols) may be paired with the particular objects or activities engag
ing the student. Any reaction by the student to these various languag
systems may be an indicator of which system or combination of system
to teach. The notion that normal language development is an evolution
ary process involving many nonlinguistic behaviors before speech
mastery seems to also hold true for severely handicapped students
regardless of the specific language system finally employed (Harris &
Vanderheiden, 1980). These nonlinguistic skills can be developed throug
social interaction. This model does not, however, preclude use of th
operant model that is discussed in the next section.

Operant Model. The operant or behavioral model is based on th
assumption that human behavior (including language) is learned throug
environmental conditioning. In other words, the environment elicit
behavioral responses through some form of stimulus and strengthen
that response through reinforcement (Skinner, 1957). A *stimulus* is th
antecedent or cue that elicits a certain behavioral response from a
individual. A *response* is any observable or measurable act of an indivi
ual. *Reinforcement* is any consequence occurring after a behavior tha
increases or maintains the probability of that behavior recurring.

A teacher, by controlling the stimulus and reinforcement, can teach language responses even to animals. The student's role in this model is somewhat passive. Since the teacher controls the stimuli, language responses are elicited rather than self-initiated. The responses are discrete and observable, and each elicited response is counted to illustrate the acquisition of correct language usage given certain environmental conditions. After correct responses, the student is reinforced with social praise, food, a favorite toy, smiles, hugs, and so forth.

The operant model dictates a step-by-step teaching sequence, usually in short training settings using one-to-one instruction in a quiet, segregated setting. The student is taught a behavior or class of behaviors. Mass trials and data collection are an integral part of the operant model. According to Reichle and Keogh (1986), a typical training sequence might include the following things.

1. Establishing attending skills.
2. Achieving generalized motor imitation.
3. Shaping generalized vocal/verbal/manual imitation.
4. Receptive labeling, or comprehension of object names.
5. Expressive labeling or producing object names. (p. 204)

Rather than a student communicating because of a need or desire, the student responds to the teacher's model, cue, or prompt in order to receive the reinforcer. The operant model produces little spontaneous language, and the learned language has frequently been found not to generalize well (Reichle & Keogh, 1986). *Generalization* refers to the expansion of language skills to different settings, with different people, under different circumstances or stimuli.

A typical teaching session using the operant model might be described as follows:

Teacher: "O.K. it's time for our lesson. (Holds up shoe) What's this?"

Child: (No response)

Teacher: "Say shoe."

Child: "Shoe."

Teacher: "Good talking. (Puts away shoe. Gives child candy. Pauses. Then holds up sock.) What's this?"

Child: "Shoe."

Teacher: "No! (Puts away sock. Pauses. Holds up sock again.) What's this? Say sock."

> **Child:** "Sock."
>
> **Teacher:** "Good talking." (Puts away sock. Gives child candy.) (Carr, 1985, p. 46)

The sequence might be repeated 50 times while prompts and cues are faded out.

Note that in this sequence, the *stimuli* are the teacher commands, instructions, and the objects (e.g., shoe and sock). The *response* was the verbal label by the child. The *consequences* were the statements "Good talking," "No!", and candy.

Although criticism of the use of an operant model alone has increased in the field, behavioral methods have been empirically validated in the teaching of productive and receptive labels, grammatical morphemes, and sentence structures (Carr, 1985). Operant procedures have also resulted in decreased inappropriate language (e.g., some forms of echolalia and idiosyncratic use of words) (Lovaas et al., 1966).

The question seems to center around whether the operant model alone has increased functional communication in daily living (Lord, 1985). Currently, it is recommended that the interactive model or pragmatic approach be combined with behavioral theory to offer more generalizable and functional language training.

Components of an Interactive/Operant Approach. The best of both the interactive and the operant models seems to provide for the most effective language training of severely handicapped individuals. Reichle and Keogh (1986) state that, "speech, signing, and graphics, or any communication of language skills needs to be taught within the framework of functional communication exchanges" (p. 206). However, they further suggest that this framework "should not be interpreted to mean that one-to-one instruction is artificial, outdated, or ineffective" (p. 206). Hart and Rogers-Warren (1978) advocate that any language use, regardless of form, be reinforced so that the child will learn the communication function. Mulligan, Guess, Holvoet, and Brown (1980) have developed the Individualized Curriculum Sequencing Mode to assure that functional learning generalizes across settings and people.

The interactive model dictates a shift away from massed-trial, out-of-context instruction to instruction that incorporates naturally occurring events and interactions. The emphasis is on the functionality of language and communicative intent. Spontaneous language and the generalization of communication across settings, people, and materials are of primary importance.

The operant model offers evidence that direct instruction can "offer the teacher a better opportunity to focus the learner's attention on criterion-related cues" (Reichle & Keogh, 1986, p. 207). The teacher might also utilize reinforcement (social and tangible) for any communication attempts by the student to help shape correct language structure and language use as the student progresses. Student responses can still be recorded by the teacher for evaluative purposes. The stimuli in this combination model are the naturally occurring activities that have meaning to the student in addition to the teacher-induced stimuli.

The teacher, by arranging for natural events and interactions, can stimulate functional language in severely handicapped students. These language responses, socially reinforced and shaped into structurally correct forms, provide the student with a communication tool that can be used in various situations. By using child-centered stimuli with teacher/environmentally controlled consequences and deliberate attention to generalization, the teacher can achieve both structural and functional goals for each student.

LANGUAGE SYSTEMS

The process of deciding which language system to present to a severely handicapped child is a difficult one. Controversy is widespread regarding which system is the most effective and which decision method teachers should incorporate (Reichle & Keogh, 1986). Once a language system or combination is selected, the student usually receives only that designated training. If the system is determined to be inappropriate, precious training time has been wasted in addition to the time lost in active communication and the development of social and cognitive skills. Also, given no language system, the child may regress, showing more maladaptive behavior and fewer cognitive milestones. For these reasons, the teacher assumes a great deal of responsibility in this decision process.

Hedrick and Kemp (1984) observe that the responsibility for language training of severely handicapped individuals falls with the public schools. This is especially problematic considering the dearth of pre-service training curricula that address "procedures for developing strategies to be used when planning language programs" (Hedrick & Kemp, 1984, p. 58).

The currently available language programs from which to choose "represent various theoretical approaches and incorporate a range of training strategies intended for a variety of populations" (Warren & Rogers-Warren, 1980, p. 134). Teachers, with little training, are asked to make crucial decisions about a child's language acquisition with few clear guidelines and apparently many possible choices. There are no easy answers. Reichle and Keogh (1986) recommend that teachers keep sight of one important guideline. The entire planning/teaching process revolves around the assumption that speech or any language system would be "immediately functional to the learner" (Reichle & Keogh, 1986, p. 207). The teacher is encouraged to use several criteria in the planning process: (a) comprehensive assessment data including both the student and his or her environment, (b) the subsequent structural and functional goals, and (c) the response of the student once the system is introduced.

This section discusses several language systems used with severely handicapped students. The selection of the best system for an individual student might be facilitated by knowledge of the strengths and weaknesses of several systems. Ultimately, the teacher must strive for an individual match between the student and a particular language mode. The consequences of this decision can affect the student's entire life.

Unaided Language Systems

A language system that the student can utilize without relying on physical aid is called an *unaided system*. The two unaided language systems used with severely handicapped students are speech training and manual communication (sign language).

Speech Training. "Speech is the combination of particular sounds to create socially agreed upon symbols as part of a spoken linguistic code" (Bryen & Joyce, 1985, p. 9). In speech training, the goal is to teach the student to initiate understandable vocal symbols, respond to vocal messages, and to use vocal symbols in order to request, describe, and/or reject or protest. Since spoken language requires some knowledge of language rules, cognitive development is often intertwined in the teaching process.

Most often, speech training for severely handicapped students is conducted in a clinic or laboratory setting where a therapist, utilizing the operant sequencing model, provides a sequence of activities designed to facilitate the learner reaching a specific goal (e.g., labeling objects and pictures). Reinforcement is provided for correct vocal responses (or approximations). One-word labels are expanded to two- and three-word phrases as descriptions, requests, or rejections. The speech therapist or teacher provides the cue, and the training consists of several trials with the same cue and response until the student provides correct vocal symbols at a predetermined rate. The vocabulary and language functions are chosen based on the relevancy to the particular student. Once the teacher or therapist knows which activities the student is likely to engage in, the activity can be made contingent upon a verbal request. For example, a student who likes to play with a ball needs to say "Ball" or "Want ball" before being allowed to have the ball. This method incorporates both structural and functional language goals.

Currently, it is recommended that language be taught in natural contexts "spread across a wider time span, with use of multiple trainers, and provision of natural cues and consequences" (Sailor & Guess, 1983, p. 268). Guess and Mulligan (1982) have formulated a language training program that is combined with instruction in other skill areas. Suggested sequences for speech training can be found in several sources (Gray & Ryan, 1973; MacDonald & Horstmeir, 1978; Sailor & Guess, 1983; Sailor, Guess, & Baer, 1973). The beginning teacher may refer to simple sequences for general guidelines, but the students' individual differences will dictate deviations.

Teaching the first spoken words. If the student does not imitate verbal sounds, then instruction in verbal imitation is recommended as the first step. The model in Figure 10.3 is based on an operant approach (Donnellan-Walsh et al., 1976). Sounds that the student already utters should be chosen. These sounds are subsequently shaped into words. It is very difficult for the teacher to successfully prompt vocal responses.

Attaching meaning to words. Next, meaning must be attached to words by following these steps.

1. Teach requesting behaviors.
   a. Connect natural consequences to speaking (e.g., say "Milk" and then let the student receive milk upon the correct response).
   b. Teach a second request word (e.g., say "Sandwich," followed by natural consequences).
   c. Teach differentiation between first and second words (e.g., "What do you want?" Hold up the milk and sandwich. Give the natural consequences for responses).
   d. Teach additional words.

2. Teach protesting behaviors.
   a. Establish "No" or head shake.
   b. Present student with something he or she doesn't want (e.g., lemon slice).
   c. Ask "Do you want this lemon?" Prompt to say "No."
   d. Take the lemon away contingent on student's "No."
   e. Create situations throughout the day that require the student to protest.

3. Teach labeling.
   a. Ask "What is this?" and point to an object or a picture.
   b. Prompt correct response.

FIGURE 10.3.   An Operant Model for Early Language Learning

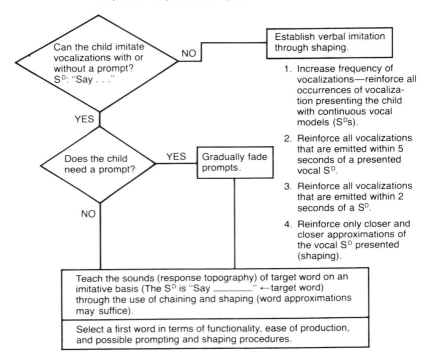

HOW TO ESTABLISH THE FIRST SPOKEN WORDS

Prerequisites: Attending
A repertoire of spontaneous speech-like vocalizations

Can the child imitate vocalizations with or without a prompt? S^D: "Say . . ."

NO → Establish verbal imitation through shaping.

1. Increase frequency of vocalizations—reinforce all occurrences of vocalization presenting the child with continuous vocal models (S^Ds).

2. Reinforce all vocalizations that are emitted within 5 seconds of a presented vocal S^D.

3. Reinforce all vocalizations that are emitted within 2 seconds of a S^D.

4. Reinforce only closer and closer approximations of the vocal S^D presented (shaping).

YES

Does the child need a prompt?

YES → Gradually fade prompts.

NO

Teach the sounds (response topography) of target word on an imitative basis (The S^D is "Say _____" ←target word) through the use of chaining and shaping (word approximations may suffice).

Select a first word in terms of functionality, ease of production, and possible prompting and shaping procedures.

S^D: Discriminative Stimulus

From A. Donnellen-Walsh et al. (1976). *Teaching makes a difference.* Santa Barbara: Santa Barbara County Public Schools, p. 161. Copyright 1976, Santa Barbara County Public Schools. Reprinted with permission.

   c. Reinforce correct response and fade prompt.
   d. Teach second labeling response.
   e. Establish discrimination by alternating the two objects or pictures.
   f. Teach additional words.
   g. Ask, "What am I doing?" and repeat steps *b* and *c*.
   h. Ask, "What are you doing?"

i. Ask, "What is (another student) doing?" At this point, the teacher may introduce pictures as the stimuli rather than using people if the student is ready for symbolic representation.

Teaching word combinations. Once the student has acquired 10 to 20 words, word combinations can be introduced. Determine whether the combination will further communicate intent and functionality.

1. Teach imitation of "want."

2. Require "want" plus noun and verb.

3. Require "I want" plus noun and verb.

4. Require "I want _____" in response to the question, "What do you want?"

Teaching receptive skills. It is helpful to issue specific instructions that the student must follow.

1. Give commands such as "Sit down," "Come here," "Get your lunch," "Go to the bathroom," prompt correct behavior, reinforce and fade prompt.

2. Add commands such as "Give me," "Show me," "Point to," "Touch," followed by objects and people in the child's environment (include the names of the child's body parts).

3. Give more complicated commands requiring discrimination skills (e.g., "Give me the spoon and knife," "Show me the little blue ball").

Possible word combinations are offered in Figure 10.4.

Prompting nonecholalic responses. Students who exhibit echolalia may require additional consideration in order for the student to learn to use language for communicative purposes. Although Prizant (1978) delineated several functional categories of communication in echolalic responses, nonecholalic responses are the most desirable goal for students. If asked a question requiring a one-word response, the echolalic student may repeat the entire question. This response may actually mean *yes*, but few people would understand the true meaning. Donnellen-Walsh et al. (1976) recommend the following prompts to attempt to eliminate echolalic responses.

1. Ask the question in a low voice, but prompt (verbally) the correct response in a loud voice (e.g., What is this? CANDY). Gradually decrease the volume of the prompt and use a normal voice for the question.

FIGURE 10.4. Word Combinations

ATTRIBUTE + NOUN

	Variable	Fixed	Examples
Carrier phrase:	Color	Noun	Green/blue cup
"Give me . . ."	Size	Noun	Big/little cup
	Noun	Color	Green cup/bowl
	Noun	Size	Big cup/bowl
or	(Color + size + noun)		Big yellow block
	(Size + color + noun)		Little red cup

POSSESSIVE + NOUN

	Variable	Fixed	Fixed	Variable
"Point to . . ."	Jimmy's	Nose	Jimmy's	Nose
	Mary's	Nose	Jimmy's	Toes
			Jimmy's	Teeth

AGENT + ACT

	Variable	Fixed	Fixed	Variable
"Point to . . ."	Girl	is sitting	Mary	is sitting
	Boy	is sitting	Mary	is walking
	Mary	is sitting	Mary	is jumping

PREPOSITION + NOUN

	Fixed	Variable	Fixed	Variable
"Put"	Under	Block	In	Box
	Under	Chair	Under	Box
	Under	Table	On top of	Box
			Next to	Box

The crucial thing is to stress that one word can be substituted by another. For example, one noun (cup) can be combined with a number of attributes and one attribute (big) with a number of nouns, or schematically:

$$\text{(Attribute)} \times \begin{matrix} 1 \\ 2 \\ 3 \\ N \end{matrix} + \text{Noun; Attribute} + \times \begin{matrix} 1 \\ 2 \\ 3 \\ N \end{matrix}$$

After two-word combinations are mastered, three-word combinations can be presented such as "big yellow block."

---

2. Only whisper the prompt.

3. Only ask the question without a verbal prompt.

4. If necessary, place fingers on the student's mouth to prevent echoing until the prompt has been presented.

5. Fade all prompts (physical and verbal).

Carr, Schreibman, and Lovaas (1975) suggest that teaching students appropriate responses to confusing situations (e.g., "I don't know" or "I don't want to") will decrease echolalic behavior. Garber and David (1975) state that echolalic children demonstrate more appropriate responses when they understand the question or command and can offer an appropriate verbal response. Schuler and Prizant (1985) suggest that mitigated echolalia (e.g., echolalia with a structural change) may span the gap between noncommunicative echolalia and functional language. For instance, a student who uses the phrase, "Do you want a sandwich?" to request everything he or she wants may be taught to substitute different direct objects (e.g., "Do you want a *walk*?") while retaining the majority of the echoing behavior. In this way the student is given a functional method of communicating without having to totally eliminate the echolalic behavior. Currently, new theories are emerging concerning the cause and treatment of echolalia (Schuler & Prizant, 1985). Even though the echoing behavior may never be totally eradicated, primitive echoing responses may be altered to provide more productive and flexible language forms.

It is important to conduct speech training in the natural environment (i.e., school, home, bus, etc.). Severely handicapped students do not generalize well with any skill. Thus, language training conducted in clinical settings does not tend to carry over to the places in which the child needs or wants most to communicate (Bryen & Joyce, 1985). This does not preclude any clinical training. Some skills are best taught one-to-one in an isolated format, but "language develops out of the continuous, ongoing process of an individual's daily interactions with others in the environment, not through occasional or infrequent efforts" (Bryen & Joyce, 1985, p. 17).

In sum, many severely handicapped students fail to learn to communicate from a "speech only" program, because they cannot imitate vocally or because they lack the necessary prerequisite physiological and cognitive skills (Reichle & Keogh, 1986). In the mid-1970s there was a shift away from speech only training to alternative language modes. Unfortunately, there is a paucity of research on the effectiveness of these alternative systems. This lack of research may be due to the fact that the alternative language systems were teacher-initiated because of frustration with speech only training programs (Reichle & Keogh, 1986).

Manual Communication. If a student has severe auditory impairment or neuromuscular disorders which prevent the development of a vocal language system, a nonvocal system may be employed to substitute for the vocal system (Chapman & Miller, 1980). This may also be true for students who have unintelligible speech or who have failed repeatedly in speech and language therapy with few functional verbalizations (Carrier, 1973; Carrier & Peak, 1976). Nonvocal systems have been employed to *augment* vocal production and sometimes are faded to leave only a functional vocal system (Chapman & Miller, 1980). Harris-Vanderheiden, Brown, MacKenzie, Reinen, and Scheibel (1975) and others (Creedon, 1976; Schaeffer, 1980) have postulated that nonvocal systems have actually facilitated speech. Apparently, manual communication fosters spontaneity which transfers to speech (Schaeffer, 1980).

The literature, however, reflects some reservations about advocating manual communication. Sailor and Guess (1983) pointed out that sign language tends to prohibit integrated placements for severely handicapped individuals, because interpreters are needed in the community at large. They recommend sign language only for severely handicapped, hearing-impaired students who will likely be placed with other individuals who comprehend sign language. On the other hand, others (e.g., Harris, Lippert, Yoder, & Vanderheiden, 1977; McDonald & Schultz, 1973; McNaughton, Kates, & Silverman, 1978) have found that an augmentation language mode does not impede the development of vocal language systems and may provide a communication tool while an individual learns the more complex vocal mode.

Bryen and Joyce (1985), in their language intervention review, reported that 34.9 percent of the programs used sign language with severely handicapped individuals. Another 16.2 percent used sign and spoken language combined. They cited two concerns regarding sign language. First, sign language and speech rely on linguistic rules thus requiring the learner to attain certain complex cognitive strategies. Second, sign language relies on sufficient motor skills for an individual to be able to execute the system. Often, severely handicapped students have neither of these prerequisites.

Despite the reservations, several manual language systems have been tried with severely handicapped students. These include the American Manual Alphabet, American Sign Language, Amer-Ind, Seeing Essential English, Signed English, Signing Exact English, mime, nonsense signs, and Ontario Sign Language. Generally, it has been found that the "less sophisticated level of representation may facilitate the acquisition of a communicative system and form the developmental basis for the use of arbitrary symbols" (Romski et al., 1984, p. 69).

Utilizing a similar sequence as discussed in the speech training section, mentally retarded individuals have been successful in producing a sign vocabulary of one to 400 words, two-word sign combinations, or linking signed symbols with vocal utterances (Creedon, 1973; Kopchick, Rombach, & Karlan, 1975; Miller & Miller, 1973; Richardson, 1975). Physical prompting is easier with manual presentations than with the vocal mode. Additionally, the student is required to rely on visual access and visual discrimination skills.

The important goal, again, is to provide the individual with a functional communication system. A manual language system may provide that opportunity. However, given the lack of universal understanding of signs and the cognitive and physiological prerequisites, the trend in language training has been toward aided symbol systems made accessible through sophisticated and creative technology.

Aided Language Systems

Aided language systems require the individual to rely on some equipment in addition to the body in order to communicate. Symbols such as the written word, pictures, or established symbol sets are introduced in some format that the student can physically manipulate. The student can point to, or indicate in some other fashion, a symbol combination that, in turn, communicates intent, desire, recognition, or some other function. A discussion of the symbol sets and delivery formats follows.

Symbol Sets. Several symbol sets have been used to provide a language system for severely handicapped students. These include Blissymbols (Archer, 1977); Lexigrams (Rumbaugh, 1977); Rebus System (Clark & Woodcock, 1976); *Non-Speech Language Initiation Program* (Non-SLIP) (Carrier & Peak, 1975); pictures; and the written word. These sets are visually based and require the learner to select a symbol from a display using recognition memory. Selection strategies vary depending on individual abilities. Direct selection, scanning, or encoding can be used to access symbols. Direct selection requires the individual to point to the elements of the message. *Scanning* is a process of presenting symbols to the learner sequentially until the student indicates by using yes/no responses which symbols have been chosen. *Encoding* is a learner-controlled process whereby the user indicates a message through patterning multiple symbols which are memorized or looked up on a chart (Romski et al., 1984). The various symbol sets demand varying cognitive prerequisites. It is important to remember that they are to be used to enhance communication and not as an end in themselves.

Blissymbols is a graphic communication system that potentially can be arranged to provide many communicative functions. Historically, Blissymbols have been used with children who, because of cerebral palsy, required an alternative expressive language system, even though their receptive language was developed at the appropriate level (Kates & McNaughton, 1975). Charles K. Bliss, the originator of this system, intended to construct "a simple system of 100 logical pictorial symbols which can be operated and read like 1 + 2 = 3 in all languages" (Bliss, 1965, p. 3).

Blissymbols are derived from basic geometric shapes (Figure 10.5). These shapes are combined to form line drawings resembling actual objects or depicting ideas. The symbols are always presented with written captions so that the user can communicate with people lacking knowledge of the system.

The beginning learner is presented symbols on 3″ × 3″ cards. Gradually the symbols are reduced in size until they can be arranged on a grid in 1″ × 1″ squares. The grid must be adapted so that the student can have access to it at all times. For those students in wheelchairs, a communication board can be developed and attached to the chair. For ambulatory students, a portable display is necessary.

A student must be able to comprehend that "a visual symbolic representation can serve as a communication signal" (McNaughton & Kates, 1980, p. 318) and must have the physical skills to select a symbol before being introduced to Blissymbols. Silverman, McNaughton, and Kates (1978) report that Blissymbolics users demonstrated improved communication abilities, hand control, head control, level of motivation, attentiveness, and showed less hyperactivity and aggression than nonusers. However, Blissymbols are often perceived as complicated and difficult, and the vocabulary tends to be more applicable to adults (McNaughton & Kates, 1980). Fristoe and Lloyd (1979) conclude that despite the constraints, Blissymbols can serve a wide range of individual ability levels, because they do not require syntactical rules.

Lexigrams (Rumbaugh, 1977), based on the same theory as Blissymbolics, are composed of nine geometric elements that can be used singly or in combination to communicate. "Meanings are randomly assigned to the configurations from an available symbol pool" (Romski et al., 1984, p. 69).

The *rebus system* uses 818 pictographic symbols found in the *Standard Rebus Glossary* (Clark, Davies, & Woodcock, 1974). Sailor and Guess (1983) consider this "communication board/booklet expressive system to be a major innovative development in severely handicapped students to amass increasingly complex and useful linguistic skills" (p. 271). The rebus symbols seem to be easier to learn than Blissymbols because of their simplicity and phonetic base (Clark & Woodcock, 1976). They have been used to initiate reading skills with students exhibiting communication disorders (Moores, 1980).

FIGURE 10.5. Sample Blissymbols

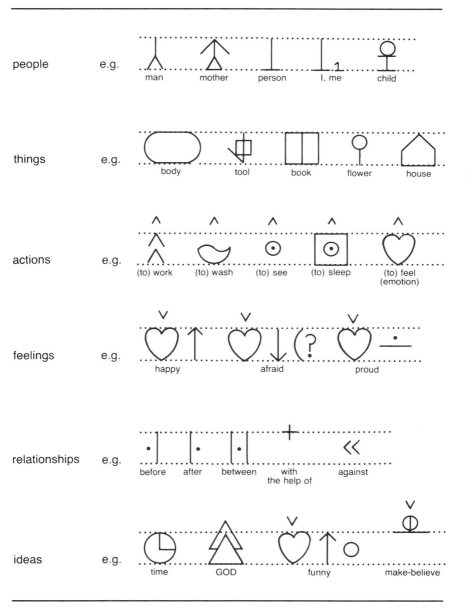

From H. Silverman, S. McNaughton, & B. Kates. (1978). *Handbook of Blissymbolics.* Copyright 1978 by Blissymbolics Communication Institute, p. 10. Blissymbolics used herein derived from the symbols described in the work, *Semantography,* original copyright © C. K. Bliss, 1949.

The *Non-Speech Language Initiation Program* (Non-SLIP), developed by Carrier and Peak (1975), uses symbols that vary across many attributes. Sixty different colored plastic forms are used to symbolize language functions. The students arrange the chips in a sentence frame to convey specific meaning. The colors represent the syntactic class (i.e., nouns are one color, verbs another, etc.). The authors intended this program to allow students to circumvent speech while learning semantic and syntactic language properties (Woolman, 1980). The trainer presents a picture card, and the student identifies the picture by placing the correct chip or chip combinations on the picture.

McLean and McLean (1974) concluded that for autistic students with no speech, the use of an abstract symbol system like Non-SLIP may be the only means of developing expressive language. Clark (1981) used Blissymbols, Rebus, and Non-SLIP with 36 normal preschool children to compare learning rates. She discovered that the children found Rebus the easiest to learn, followed by Blissymbols and Non-SLIP. Kuntz (1974) found, however, that severely retarded persons showed no difference in learning rates between Rebus and Non-SLIP. Porter and Schroeder (1980) found that 11 students who had been taught Non-SLIP showed gains in speech performance. These same students maintained skills in Non-SLIP symbol usage three years after the program was initiated. Determining which mode may work best for an individual student may entail some trial and error. All of these systems offer communicative potential, but some require higher level prerequisites than do others.

One drawback to any abstract symbol system is its limited usefulness. The symbols are difficult to keep at the students' disposal, and the general population does not understand the system. For that reason, printed words should accompany the symbols whenever possible. Great potential lies in these systems if they facilitate manual sign or speech acquisition. One advantage of the symbol sets is that the student does not have to rely on recall in order to communicate, since the symbols are visually displayed. The sequence remains visually displayed, which assists the student in finding the next element of the sequence, and the student can refer to the sequence many times in the course of a conversation.

Simple *pictures* representing various people, places, things, and actions may also be used for students who cannot effectively utilize abstract symbols. The complexity of the picture, the size, and the number of pictures presented will depend on an individual student's cognitive and physical functioning levels. It has been suggested that the sensorimotor stage 5 means-end performance should be considered a prerequisite for the implementation of a picture communication system (Chapman & Miller, 1980). Communication pictures may be teacher-made artwork or photographs or may be commercially developed (e.g.,

Picture Communication Symbols, Mayer-Johnson Co., Box 86, Stillwater, MN 55082).

Once it is determined that the student can relate to pictures, the teacher should pick pictures that are as representational of actual objects and people as possible. Included should be people of personal significance to the student, favorite objects and places, functional objects and places (e.g., body parts, clothes, classroom, etc.), numbers and colors, and common verbs and adjectives if cognitively appropriate.

The required picture size should be determined by beginning with large pictures (5–6″) and gradually decreasing the size until a 1″ × 1″ minimum is reached. Smaller pictures can fit easily on communication boards and are easier to transport in larger quantities. For students with visual impairment, small pictures or glossy prints may not be appropriate. Pictures usually need to be protected from possible damage during everyday activities.

Pictures might be presented only in pairs until it is evident that the student can choose pictures from a larger field. Pictures may be arranged on a communication board, in book format, on a fold-over grid, or on a key ring—whichever allows the student the greatest access. The important variable is to promote spontaneous and generalized use of the language system.

Written words, phrases, and sentences are sometimes used as a communication system for severely handicapped students. Naturally, the comprehension of written words requires a higher level of cognition than some of the other symbol systems. For students with cerebral palsy or autism who cannot acquire speech but who possess a relatively high level of receptive language, the written mode may be appropriate.

Printed messages may be shared with a majority of the population, but unless the student can write, there is a problem of accessibility. Since most severely handicapped students cannot write, the written "system is not generalizable" (Moores, 1980, p. 35). However, the written mode has a one-to-one relationship to English and circumvents the difficulty of learning phonetic rules.

Words, phrases, and sentences should be chosen carefully to maximize functional communication for the student. Since the teacher often constructs the word cards, communication boards, booklets, and so forth, the student's communicative potential is dependent on teacher-initiated vocabulary. Access should be provided to vocabulary that expresses the individual's interests, needs, and desires. Pictures and written words are often arranged in a noun-verb-object order to facilitate the scanning and encoding procedures.

All symbol sets have the potential of either supplementing or augmenting verbal communication. The effectiveness of symbol systems depends on the individual's motoric, cognitive, and sociocommunicative abilities and on the teacher's skill. Functional goals must be stressed. The purpose is not just to train a language system but to provide the student a vehicle for communication.

Delivery Formats. Having determined an effective symbol set, the teacher must decide on an effective delivery format. Some aided symbol sets are available in computer software packages. All of the symbol sets can be arranged on various types of communication boards, and most of the sets can be adapted in a format conducive to students who are ambulatory and who need to communicate in several settings.

Communication boards. Communication boards can be developed for any symbol set and will allow the student to use direct selection, scanning, and/or encoding during communication. Communication boards range from a simple three-picture set to complex electronic devices. They can be affixed to wheelchairs or beds, lie horizontally or stand vertically, be rigid or flexible, and be transparent or opaque. Since the communication board often offers students their only means of communication, it is imperative that the board be functional and accessible even to those with varying degrees and types of disabilities. "The child's communication board must be viewed as a dynamic medium that can be changed and enlarged rapidly as the child advances in learning and socialization" (McDonald, 1980, p. 66).

Numerous sources provide information pertaining to the development of communication boards (Davies, 1973; Dixon & Curry, 1973; Goldberg & Fenton, 1960; McDonald & Schultz, 1973; Vanderheiden & Grilley, 1976). Commercially developed communication boards might generally be avoided, because a child's language grows daily from interaction with the environment. Initially, the board may contain only a few symbols (e.g., a cup, a TV, a toilet) but will expand as the student acquires new vocabulary. Print or symbol sets may be combined with pictures at first to instruct the student and help him or her learn the symbol system. The pictures are then faded out, for symbols usually allow more comprehensive communication and incorporate concepts and affective variables. Some communication boards contain the alphabet and "most used" words so that the student who can learn to spell and read will be provided a mechanism with which to communicate.

For students whose manual control and dexterity permits pointing, a direct selection process might be incorporated. For instance, the student can point using his or her extremities, a head pointer, or triggering an electronic device to indicate the picture, symbol, letter, or word of choice.

If the student has little or no mobility, a *scanning* procedure is recommended. The teacher presents pictures or words one at a time, until the student signals and the desired element is selected. The student may signal by moving his or her eyes, head, or an arm or leg. This procedure is slower than direct selection but can be used for students with multiple and/or severe disabilities.

A third procedure that might be used for signaling with students who have limited ability to control body parts is *encoding*. This procedure requires the student to point only to combinations of numbers, which in turn indicate specific messages. For instance, pointing to numbers 1 and 3 indicates the item next to 13, or *Dad*. This procedure requires less range of motion to access messages. Combinations of these three procedures (i.e., direct selection, scanning, and encoding) can be developed to accommodate various physical constraints while allowing for maximum communicative potential.

Communication boards have made it possible for severely handicapped individuals to interact with their environments in new ways. But "even with a communication board, a handicapped person cannot share ideas and feelings with himself" (McDonald, 1980, p. 76). That is, an individual cannot communicate in isolation; he or she needs to be exposed to real-life situations in the company of various people. In this way, the boards become functional, and the student can advance socially, emotionally, and cognitively.

Computers. Recently, computer assisted formats have been developed for use with severely handicapped individuals. Speech synthesizers provide vocal output when prompted by a direct selection procedure and a keyboard. Expanded keyboards allow physically handicapped individuals access and can be outfitted with pictures or words. Romski et al. (1984) and Romski, Sevcik, White, and Rumbaugh (1983) used a computer-based system to instruct severely mentally retarded students to highlight chosen symbols on a display panel, relocate symbols with little effort, and project symbols on the monitor for recall and reference. Some computers have printed output, allowing the student to directly select or encode on the keyboard and produce a tape with a printed message (one such system is SPEECHPAC/SCANPAC, John Long Associates, P.O. Box 29465, San Antonio, TX 78229).

Present computer technology seems to limit adequate generalization of language skills. Monitors and keyboards do not travel easily from place to place. However, engineers and technicians have joined educators in the search for effective augmentation devices to facilitate communication through creative use of computer technology.

Assistive devices. In order for severely handicapped students to be able to utilize communication boards and computers, they may need physical assistance. Assistive devices allow automatic or muscular control of the direct selection, scanning, or encoding procedures. Pointers and switches of various construction can fit on different parts of the body to make it possible to activate automatic selectors and scanners or to specifically indicate messages on communication boards and keyboards. Vanderheiden (1978) has compiled the *Non-Vocal Communication*

Resource Book with illustrations, descriptions, and ordering information related to various communication aids and assistive devices. It is the professional's responsibility to adequately assess what type of device might be required to help the student become an effective, independent communicator.

The development and selection of mechanisms through which students can interact, respond, and express themselves is the primary goal of language intervention. Assistive devices and communication aids may provide a new learning potential for the student who has previously been physically incapable of producing language. Harris and Vanderheiden (1980) describe communication aids ranging from "communication boards to portable independent aids with calculator-type displays, built in strip printers, television displays and typewriter controllers" (p. 275). The technology for overcoming physical limitations and hearing/vision impairments is impressive. However, more work seems necessary in the development of simpler formats and aids for children who are very young, extremely active, or who have severe cognitive impairments (Harris & Vanderheiden, 1980).

BEST PRACTICES

Unaided and aided language systems vary in the level of physical, cognitive, and sociocommunicative prerequisites that are required. Unaided systems can be utilized with no additional physical assistance. Unaided systems include speech training and manual communication. These systems can be taught individually or in combination. The literature reflects the current controversy over which system may be the best one for severely handicapped individuals. Perhaps the key word is *individual*. Successful language training seems to be tied to the match among the system chosen, the student's various abilities, and the instructional skill of the teacher.

Aided systems are those that assist the student who cannot otherwise communicate. Different symbol sets replace verbal and manual communication, and various aids and devices allow physically handicapped students to access the symbol sets and make them understandable to others. Engineering and computer technology have increased the communicative potential of many more severely handicapped students.

The process of choosing which system to teach a student and/or which aids to utilize is a difficult one. The danger lies in choosing one particular language mode and leaving the student with no communication system during the instruction period. An additional consideration is that the system chosen may not ultimately be the most functional one, and precious training time may be lost. Finally, unless the chosen symbol is a verbal one, it may not generalize well across settings. This is a particular problem for manual signs and symbol sets.

Reichle and Keogh (1986) have suggested that an alternative to the process of choosing the "best" communication system might be to train language skills in all systems. This would allow for situation specificity when one language mode would be better suited to different learning needs or conditions and would also help relieve the pressure on the teacher to select the *one* system that can meet all of the individual's communicative needs. This mixed mode strategy advocates the instruction of different systems in different learning contexts.

In a mixed mode system, assessment information would consist of identifying comprehension requirements in the learner's environment. Thus,

if no one in the home understands sign language, graphic communication may be a better option in that setting. If specific signs are not understood easily, then graphic representations might be used. Incorporating "universal" signs (e.g., *yes*, *no*, *stop*, etc.) into the instruction of verbal students may assist them while they struggle to master speech. The benefits of a mixed mode system are "increasing potential listener participation, and improving message understandability" (Reichle & Keogh, 1986, p. 197). Simultaneous instruction in several language systems may offer the learner many of the advantages of each system while alleviating many of the respective disadvantages.

Reichle and Keogh (1986) delineated three issues from the 1970s and '80s that are still unresolved. The first is that decision rules for the selection of communication systems for severely handicapped individuals are discrepant and controversial. Second, the integration of "cognitive prerequisites" and "functional prerequisites" for language acquisition is still debatable. A third consideration is that intervention technology needs to amalgamate factors pertaining to communication environments, how the communication is delivered, and what exactly is being communicated. Reichle and Keogh's (1986) recommendations for the future center on the instruction of a mixed mode of expression that will make selection of one language mode over another a false issue. They emphasize function over form by advocating that new learners be taught to *describe* and *request*. These functions are not dependent on the comprehension of complex graphic, signing, or speech systems. Finally, they advise against teaching cognitive prerequisites as separate units from functional communication.

Bryen and Joyce (1985) cited trends that characterized successful interventions. Subject characteristics prior to intervention did not differentiate between successful and unsuccessful programs. By assessing cognitive, social, and motor prerequisites, and using the information in instructional planning, the probability of success was increased. These researchers found that studies using speech training or manual communication were moderately successful and that sign language training was no more successful than speech training. Aided systems (e.g., Blissymbols, premade symbols, etc.) were found generally to be unsuccessful.

Studies that incorporated ongoing environmental intervention were much more successful than those employing isolated training sessions. Studies that had the functional goal of spontaneous communication were

much more successful than those specifying only structural goals or elicited language goals. In regard to teaching methods, those studies using an interactional process alone or in conjunction with operant methods were generally more successful than were studies using only operant methods. Finally, the successful studies showed positive effects in addition to the specified language goals. These effects included (a) the acquisition of speech even when nonvocal systems were taught, (b) gains on test scores, (c) more instances of adaptive behavior, (d) more desire by the handicapped student to interact, and (e) positive effects on the instructors. In conclusion, Bryen and Joyce (1985) reiterated their most important finding as a future recommendation.

> Teaching isolated skills that have little or no functional utility to severely handicapped people should be seriously questioned. This is especially critical when it comes to language and communication. For if we, even inadvertently, reduce or distort these students' ability to communicate, in doing so we have deprived them of one of their most fundamental and powerful possessions. (p. 35)

The new generation of language programs for the severely handicapped will probably contain parts of traditional programs while adding new content, generalization techniques, and environmental analysis (Warren & Rogers-Warren, 1980). Educators and clinicians are urged to incorporate programs that enhance the generalization of language skills and to utilize generalization assessments to ensure that it occurs.

Russell (1984) advocates the assessment of an individual's cognitive, physical, linguistic, and environmental factors emphasizing interactional needs. Semantics, syntax, and form must be combined with the teaching of functional communication. Sailor and Guess (1983) recommend a continuing education model for the severely handicapped "until such time that the student has attained competitive employment and independent living status" (p. 339). An effective language intervention program is the basis for this endeavor.

For severely handicapped individuals, any services or training should provide for optimal assistance in helping them achieve the fundamental right of successful integration into their community. Jean Itard (1972), writing in 1806 to France's Minister of the Interior, makes an articulate case for the education and care of severely handicapped individuals.

> Finally, my lord, from whatever point of view one looks at this long experiment, whether one sees it as the methodical education of a wild man, or whether one restricts oneself to considering it as the physical and moral treatment of one of those creatures born ill-favored, rejected by society and abandoned by medicine, the care that has been lavished on him, the care that is still his due, the changes that have taken place, those one hopes are still to come, the voice of humanity, the interest aroused by so cruel a desertion and so strange a fate, all these things combine to commend this extraordinary young man to the attention of scholars, the solicitude of our administrators and the protection of the government. (p. 179)

SENSORY HANDICAPPED STUDENTS

Hearing and seeing are usually considered vital in almost every aspect of an individual's educational, vocational, and social development. The ability to hear and see is certainly basic to growth in any of the language arts skills. Consequently, children with sensory handicaps, those with hearing or visual impairments, are often at a distinct disadvantage in school unless special adaptations are made.

The specialized techniques that have been developed for teaching either hearing impaired or visually impaired students are many and crucial. Some of the methods and materials are so unique that teaching these groups of handicapped students is often considered the most special of all areas of special education. Nonetheless, the majority of both groups are educated in public schools and are often found in regular classrooms.

This chapter provides an overview of definitions for both hearing impaired and visually impaired. The language arts characteristics of these populations are discussed, and the various instructional adaptations used to educate both groups of handicapped children are described. Instructional techniques for developing all of the language arts skills of hearing impaired and visually impaired students serve as a focus of this chapter.

DEFINITIONS

The following paragraphs offer various definitions of visual and hearing impairment and related handicaps.

Hearing Impaired

The term *hearing impaired* is used to describe individuals who need special education services because of a hearing loss. Individuals with hearing impairments are generally classified as *deaf* or *hard of hearing*. However, various professionals tend to define these groups quite differently. Those with a physiological orientation base their definitions on the measurable degree of hearing loss. The intensity or loudness of sound is measured in *decibels* (dB), with 0 dB representing the faintest sound an individual with normal hearing can detect. Any hearing loss above 27 dB to approximately 90 dB is usually considered hard of hearing, while any loss beyond 90 dB is usually categorized as deaf.

On the other hand, professionals with an educational orientation base their definitions on the student's ability to speak and develop language. The definition of the Conference of Executives of American Schools for the Deaf, for example, follows:

> A *deaf* person is one whose hearing disability precludes successful processing of linguistic information through audition, with or without a hearing aid.

> A *hard-of-hearing* person is one who, generally with the use of a hearing aid, has residual hearing sufficient to enable successful processing of linguistic information through audition. (Report of the Ad Hoc Committee to Define Deaf and Hard of Hearing, 1975, p. 509)

In addition, a hearing impairment can be described in terms of the time at which a hearing loss occurs. *Prelingual hearing impairment* refers to loss of hearing that occurs before the development of speech and language, while *postlingual hearing impairment* describes a loss that occurs after speech and language skills have been acquired. Heward and Orlansky (1984) point out that the educational program for a prelingually hearing impaired child usually focuses upon the acquisition of language and communication. The maintenance of intelligible speech and appropriate language patterns is usually the educational focus for the postlingually hearing impaired student.

Visually Impaired

Although there is no universally accepted definition of blindness, the term *visually impaired* is used to describe all degrees of visual handicaps within this highly heterogeneous group (Jan, Freeman, & Scott, 1977). The two most common ways of describing visual impairment are the legal and educational definitions.

The legal definition involves measurements of visual acuity and field of vision. With normal visual acuity being 20/20, an individual is classified as legally blind with visual acuity of 20/200 or less in the better eye after the best possible correction or field of vision no greater than 20 degrees. The partially sighted are legally defined as those with visual acuity between 20/70 and 20/200 in the better eye after correction.

The educational definition of visual impairment, on the other hand, considers the extent to which a child's vision affects learning and makes special methods or materials necessary. Educators differentiate between blind and low-vision students. *Blind* usually refers to those who do not have sufficient vision to learn to read print and must use braille as the reading medium. Low-vision students, on the other hand, can learn through the visual channel by using optical aids or large-print books. According to Bryan and Jeffrey (1982), 75 to 80% of the school-age visually impaired population are classified as low-vision students.

LANGUAGE ARTS CHARACTERISTICS

It is important for all educators to recognize that the sensory impaired student has abilities, interests, and needs that are for the most part quite similar to those of all students (Hanninen, 1975). However, a number of instructional needs are unique to those students who are either hearing impaired or visually handicapped. As we will note, a hearing loss or a visual impairment can severely affect some areas of language arts development and essentially have no effect on other language arts skills.

Characteristics of Hearing Impaired Individuals

The most seriously affected area of development in hearing impaired individuals is their difficulty in understanding and using spoken language. The problems that the hearing impaired have with spoken language also severely impede the adequate development of reading skills.

In terms of both listening and speaking, young hearing impaired children are at an obvious disadvantage in receiving auditory feedback when they make sounds, in receiving verbal reinforcement from adults, and in adequately hearing an adult language model (Hallahan & Kauffman, 1986). Consequently, with few exceptions, the hearing impaired child is quite handicapped in his or her ability both to listen and to use spoken language as a means of communication. In response to these problems, there has recently been a tremendous increase in the number of early intervention programs for the young hearing impaired child. Moores (1982) points out that these programs involve a much wider range of services than traditionally is associated with educators. In addition to language, speech, and pre-academic training, most programs include parent and family counseling and training in communication techniques.

According to King and Quigley (1985), the hearing impaired child is likely to arrive at beginning reading with a very limited knowledge base, inadequately developed cognitive and linguistic skills, and little or no comprehension of English figurative language. More specifically, Hart (1978) notes that, in reading, hearing impaired individuals are characterized by a limited sight vocabulary, difficulty in learning abstract words, wild guessing at unknown words, difficulty in understanding complex language forms, and constantly requiring help and guidance. In addition, most hearing impaired children do not enjoy reading and seldom choose to read on their own.

Characteristics of Visually Impaired Individuals

It is a generally accepted conclusion that the academic achievement of visually impaired students is not affected as greatly as that of hearing impaired students (Hallahan & Kauffman, 1986). Since hearing seems to be more important for school learning than seeing, visually handicapped students do not usually experience the depth of language arts difficulties evidenced by those with hearing impairments. Nevertheless, blind or low-vision pupils will usually require special instruction in some areas of the language arts.

It is usually essential that visually impaired students increase the efficiency of their other senses to compensate for their lack of sight (Holland, 1973). The development of listening skills, in particular, is an important instructional consideration, because listening is often used as a means for learning various academic material. Bischoff (1967), for example, found that visually handicapped students can be taught to increase their listening skills through a sequence of listening lessons.

Visual impairments will also contribute to slower language development in many children. Consequently, Hanninen (1975) notes that it is vital for the development of language in visually handicapped children that they be afforded verbal contact while still infants. As children grow older and can understand what others are saying, Hanninen recommends deliberately explaining and demonstrating many tasks and experiences that are often taken for granted in sighted children.

Although more visually impaired children read print than read braille, reading and writing are still skills that often require special instructional adaptations for the blind or low-vision student. The use of various optical aids, large print materials, the Perkins Brailler, or typing, which are subsequently discussed in this chapter, are all important considerations in helping the visually impaired become proficient in both reading and writing.

While these adaptations play a prominent role in the education for some visually impaired students, it is more important to keep in mind that there are virtually no limits on the extent to which a visually handicapped child may participate in a complete, well-rounded language arts program.

INSTRUCTIONAL ADAPTATIONS

Some of the unique methods and materials used in the education of both hearing impaired and visually impaired students are described in this section.

Adaptations for Hearing Impaired Students

Educational opportunities for hearing impaired students in regular public schools have become widespread only in recent years. At the present time, approximately 92% of hearing impaired students are receiving special services (Trybus, 1985). Nonetheless, communication problems among these children continue to be the major instructional consideration for educators. In addition, the challenge of selecting the most appropriate communication system continues to be a major controversy in this field. The chief communication methods for hearing impaired students, along with a number of recent technological advances, are discussed in the following paragraphs.

Sign Language. Signing is a communication method that uses manual gestures, known as signs, to represent words, ideas, and concepts.

Instead of speech sounds being used as a conventional set of signals, signs are used for the same purpose (Quigley & Paul, 1984). There are actually many different sign languages, used by deaf people in various countries throughout the world. In the United States and Canada, most individuals use American Sign Language (usually referred to as ASL and Ameslan). Heward and Orlansky (1984) note that ASL has its own syntax, vocabulary, and grammatical rules which do not correspond exactly to spoken or written English. They point out that in ASL the hands' shape, location, and movement, the intensity with which motions are made, and the signer's facial expression all communicate meaning and content.

Fingerspelling. Fingerspelling is a means for representing the 26 letters of the English alphabet by various finger positions on one hand (see Figure 11.1). Fingerspelling and sign language have traditionally been called the manual approach to teaching communication skills to the hearing impaired. In communicating manually, most deaf individuals generally use both methods together. Fingerspelling, for example, is used for spelling out proper names for which no signs exist, and often for clarification.

Auditory Training. Auditory training is the process that teaches hearing impaired individuals to make use of their residual hearing. As noted by Ross (1981), almost all hearing impaired individuals have much more "hearing potential" than they actually use. Consequently, participation in auditory training programs often can effectively develop whatever residual hearing the individual may have.

Generally, auditory training programs include at least four categories of tasks: (a) *awareness*, in which children must respond to the presence or absence of sound; (b) *sound discrimination*, in which children must learn a specific response, depending on the particular auditory training unit, and accomplish this response with a variety of sounds; (c) *speech discrimination*, in which children must learn a specific response, again depending on the auditory training unit, and generalize the response to a variety of vocalizations, including pitch sounds, directions, inflectional patterns, and words that are sung; and (d) *fine speech discrimination*, in which tasks are similar to speech discrimination tasks, except that more subtle discriminations are required (Lowenbraun, Appleman, & Callahan, 1980). Some examples of more specific auditory training units are listed in Table 11.1.

Speechreading. Speechreading (sometimes called lipreading) is the process of teaching hearing impaired individuals to use all available visual cues for undertaking spoken language. Speechreading and auditory

FIGURE 11.1. Fingerspelling Alphabet

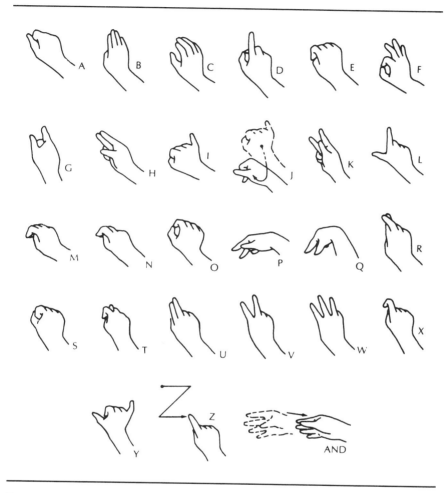

From Fant, L. J. (1971). *Say it with hands.* Silver Springs, MD: National Association for the Deaf, pp. 1–2. Reprinted with permission.

training have traditionally been called the oral approach to teaching communication skills to the hearing impaired.

Although speechreading can be a valuable additional skill for the hearing impaired, it is difficult to learn and has many limitations. Some speech sounds, called *homophenes*, have lip movements that are indistinguishable from other lip movements (e.g., *p*at, *m*at, *b*at). In addition, speechreading is made difficult by the rapidity of some speakers' speech

TABLE 11.1. Examples of Auditory Training Units

Sound Discrimination Tasks	Speech Discrimination Tasks	Fine Speech Discrimination Tasks
I. Gross sound discrimination using common noisemakers	I. Discrimination of simple one-part directions	I. Discrimination of mastered vocabulary words in carrier sentences
II. Discrimination of fast versus slow rhythms	II. Discrimination of two-part directions	II. Discrimination of mastered vocabulary words in isolation
III. Discrimination of loud versus quiet sounds	III. Discrimination of high versus low, voiced pitch sounds	III. Discrimination of individual phonetic elements
IV. Discrimination and counting of beats	IV. Discrimination of spoken versus sung speech	IV. Discrimination of individual phonetic sounds and matching them to alphabet letters
V. Auditory-Sequential memory	V. Discrimination of people's voices	V. Discrimination of phonetic elements within words
VI. Discrimination of long versus short sounds	VI. Discrimination of inflectional patterns for statements, questions and exclamations	VI. Discrimination of words differing by one phonetic element, including rhyming words
VII. Discrimination of high versus low pitch sounds	VII. Discrimination of rhythmic phrasing within speech patterns	
VIII. Auditory-sequential memory for high versus low pitch sounds		
IX. Discrimination of common safety sounds		
X. Discrimination of common household sounds		
XI. Discrimination of common human sounds		

TABLE 11.1. Continued

Sound Discrimination Tasks	Speech Discrimination Tasks	Fine Speech Discrimination Tasks
XII. Discrimination of common animal sounds		
XIII. Discrimination of common transportation sounds		
XIV. Localization of sounds		

From Lowenbraun, S., Appleman, K. I., & Callahan, J. L. (1980). *Teaching the hearing impaired: Through total communication.* Columbus, OH: Merrill, p. 108. Reproduced with permission.

movements, regional differences in speech, and minimal mouth movements of some speakers.

Cued Speech.   Cued speech is a method of supplementing speechreading. It involves manual representation of the phonetic elements of speech that are not readily visible for speechreading. The system makes use of eight different hand shapes used in four different positions near the mouth and larynx. The method cannot function alone as a manual system of communication, since it carries no meaning without an accompanying speech signal (Cornett, 1967). Although cued speech is a relatively new approach, some evidence indicates that it is a successful means for improving the communication skills of hearing impaired individuals (Nicholls & Ling, 1982).

Total Communication.   The total communication approach actually serves as a philosophy that advocates the use of both oral and manual methods of communication. When total communication is used as a teaching method, students are usually taught to use residual hearing along with instruction in signing, fingerspelling, auditory training, and speechreading. The total communication approach was the most common method of communication in the Jordan, Gustason, and Rosen (1979) study of hearing impaired classes.

Hearing Aids. Hearing aids are an important part of the educational program for many hearing impaired students. Although there are many different types of hearing aids, the basic function of any hearing aid is to amplify sound.

The various kinds of hearing aids, according to Hallahan and Kauffman (1986), range from wearable hearing aids to group training units used by a number of pupils at the same time. The efficiency of the wearable hearing aids has been tremendously improved since the development of miniature transistors. They are now available in models that can be worn behind the ear, within the ear, or built into eyeglasses.

Group auditory trainers are often used in the classroom to provide amplification for students. Most systems available today use a wireless FM frequency which permits greater mobility for both the teacher and students.

Although hearing aids are widely recommended for the hearing impaired and are used by approximately 79% of hearing impaired students at least some time in the classroom (Karchmer & Kirwin, 1977), it is important to note certain limitations of these devices. Heward and Orlansky (1984) note that hearing aids do not necessarily make sounds clearer. Some hearing impaired students will continue to hear sounds with distortions with or without a hearing aid because of the type of hearing loss they have. In addition, Kirk and Gallagher (1986) observe that hearing aids can be tiring to use and sometimes break down or malfunction. Most important, however, hearing aids will not "cure" a hearing loss and must be used in conjunction with planned programs for developing various communication skills.

Technological Advances. Recent technological advances in both electronics and computers have provided hearing impaired individuals with increased communication opportunities. The teletypewriter (TTY), for example, enables individuals to send and receive immediate written messages over telephone lines. However, Hallahan and Kauffman (1986) point out that very few people other than the deaf have reason to own a TTY. Nonetheless, the TTY has helped to make the telephone more accessible to some hearing impaired individuals.

In addition to the TTY, television captioning is another technological advancement of recent years. With closed captions, hearing impaired individuals are able to read captions on the television screen through special decoding device. This allows the deaf to watch current entertainment and news programs on television which use closed captioning.

Adaptations for Visually Impaired Students

A wide variety of specialized materials and devices have been developed and modified for the instruction of visually impaired students. Nonetheless, most educators agree that visually impaired students should b educated in the same general way as sighted students. The major difference is that visually impaired students will rely on sensory modalities other than vision to acquire information. Many of the specialized materials discussed in the following paragraphs were developed with this consideration in mind.

Braille. Braille, a system of reading and writing, is probably the best known of all the specialized materials used with the blind. Braille consists of tactually distinguishable, raised-dot patterns which represent the graphic symbols of our language, including the alphabet, numbers, and scientific, mathematical, and musical notations. As noted in Figure 11.2, braille involves different combinations of the basic unit of the six-dot cell. In the United States, two grades of braille are commonly used. Braille grade 1 uses full spelling and consists of the letters of the alphabet, numbers, punctuation, and composition signs. Braille grade 2 is a contracted system which consists of grade 1 plus 189 contractions and abbreviated words. Braille grade 2 is used for all of a student's printed materials and is the official system for English-speaking countries.

Learning to read braille is recognized as a much more difficult task than learning to read print. Braille reading is also complicated by a number of factors, including the multiple use of signs where one-dot configurations in braille may represent a letter, word, or punctuation mark. In addition, some braille symbols are easily reversed, since they are mirror images of each other, and, while most basal readers rely heavily on illustrations, braille books of course do not contain pictures. Braille materials can also be in short supply in many locations.

A recent technological advancement has been the development of *VersaBraille*, a system that records braille on cassette tape. Information sent from the tape through a microcomputer is displayed to the student either in print or in braille.

Braille writing instruction is usually initiated in first grade at the same time that braille reading is introduced (Hanninen, 1975). Among the available devices for braille writing, the *Perkins Brailler* and the *slate and stylus* are probably the most widely used. The Perkins Brailler, which resembles a typewriter, consists of only six keys corresponding to the six dots of the braille cell. Depressing the appropriate key embosses the desired combination of six dots on paper. The slate and stylus, which is smaller and quieter than the brailler, is used to punch out the braille dots by hand. The slate and stylus is slower to use, because the braille dots are written one at a time and from right to left.

Optacon. The *Optacon* is an electronic device that converts print into a form that can be felt with the fingers. A small camera is moved along

FIGURE 11.2. Braille Alphabet and Numerals

The six dots of the braille cell are arranged
and numbered thus: 1 ● ● 4
                       2 ● ● 5
                       3 ● ● 6
The capital sign, dot 6, placed before a letter
makes it a capital. The number sign, dots 3,
4, 5, 6, placed before a character, makes it a
figure and not a letter.

1	2	3	4	5	6	7	8	9	0
a	b	c	d	e	f	g	h	i	j

k	l	m	n	o	p	q	r	s	t

u	v	w	x	y	z	Capital sign	Number sign	Period	Comma

From The Division for the Blind and Physically Handicapped, Library of Congress
Washington, DC 20542.

the print line, and letters are reproduced on a tiny screen of vibrating
pins over which the reader places his or her finger. Reading speed with
the Optacon is quite slow, because the machine displays only one letter
of a word at a time. Nevertheless, Rhyne (1981) points out that the
Optacon allows accessibility to the printed word and immediacy to
printed information which would not otherwise be available to the
student.

Kurzweil Reading Machine. The *Kurzweil* is actually a small computer that
converts printed material into spoken English. Reading material is placed
face down on a scanner, and a synthetic voice is subsequently heard
reading the material. The student can regulate the speed and tone of

the voice or have the machine spell out words letter by letter. Although the Kurzweil is expensive for individual purchase, the machine is being widely used in various libraries, universities, and other agencies.

Large-Print Books. Enlarged print is sometimes recommended as an effective instructional adaptation for the low-vision student (Hanninen, 1975). Type size for large-print books ranges up to 30-point, whereas material for sighted individuals is usually printed in 10-point type. However, Heward and Orlansky (1984) recommend that visually impaired students use the smallest print size that they can comfortably read. These researchers point out that equally important factors to consider, beside the size of print, are the quality of the printed material, the contrast between print and page, the spacing between lines, and the illumination of the setting in which the student reads.

In terms of large-print computers, software programs are available that allow production of large print on conventional microcomputers and specially designed hardware configurations. According to Goodrich (1984), the advantage of large-print computers is that they provide sufficient magnification to be used by many partially sighted individuals at one time on the same monitor.

Optical Aids. There are a variety of optical aids available to assist the visually impaired. The use of optical aids helps low-vision students to perform better at certain tasks and to use their vision to the greatest possible degree. According to Hanninen (1975), the following are useful optical aids: (a) *High plus lenses* can help with great magnification; (b) the *loupe* is an ordinary convex lens used as a hand reading glass; (c) *spectacle magnifiers* are ordinary glasses fitted to give one or both eyes a closer focus; (d) *telescopic aids* are appliances that can clip over the lens of an ordinary eyeglass; and (e) *projection enlargers* are used in the classroom in the magnification of opaque material by projectors.

Optical aids are also an effective means of gaining access to computers, because they do not require changes in the computer itself (Goodrich, 1984). In addition, these aids usually cost less than specially designed software or hardware.

TEACHING LANGUAGE ARTS

Achieving academic success is closely dependent upon the adequate development of spoken and written language skills. Proficiency in listening, speaking, reading, and written expression provide all individuals with many diverse avenues for learning essential academic skills.

It is no wonder, then, that the language arts are a necessary focus in teaching both hearing impaired and visually handicapped students. Some of the unique instructional considerations in teaching each of the language arts skills to these special populations are described in the following sections.

Listening

Developing the skill of listening is one of the most essential areas of instruction for both the hearing impaired and the visually impaired. In addition to serving as a foundational skill for all the language arts, the ability to listen adequately enters into life's activities for almost all adults (Bischoff, 1979). Some of the more important considerations in developing listening skills among the sensory handicapped are discussed in the following sections.

Teaching Listening Skills to Hearing Impaired Students. As previously noted, auditory training is the process of teaching hearing impaired students to make better use of their residual hearing regardless of the extent of hearing loss. Through amplification and the use of various educational procedures, students can improve their listening ability and especially to discriminate among speech sounds.

The first step in an auditory training program is developing an *awareness* of sound, a prerequisite skill for the more complex discrimination tasks. Lowenbraun, Appleman, and Callahan (1980) mention that thorough work in awareness tasks is appropriate for preschoolers or children not experienced in auditory training. The two basic components of the training program for the development of awareness of sound proposed by these writers are (a) a sound the teacher makes and (b) a response to that sound by the child. Different sound sources might include a piano, bell, horn, clap, or voice, while responses might include putting a peg in a pegboard, a block in a box, or raising a hand.

The next level of experience once the child is aware of sound is that of *discrimination* of sounds. This is a more complicated skill than awareness and involves noting the differences in two or more sounds. Some examples of sound discrimination tasks involve discriminating gross noisemaker sounds, fast-slow rhythms, loud-soft sounds, high-low pitches, and common environmental sounds (Lowenbraun, Appleman, & Callahan, 1980).

The *recognition* of sound follows sound discrimination. At this level, students must not only differentiate among sounds, but they must be able to identify, label, or reproduce the sound through listening. This level requires some prior listening experiences.

Some of the following instructional activities can also be included in various auditory training sessions:

☐ Have children discriminate among prerecorded common household sounds (e.g., telephones, toilet flushing, doorbell, alarm clock, etc.).

☐ The piano is an excellent tool for teaching rhythm, pitch, and inflection. Also, the imitation of piano tones is helpful for the child whose voice is too high or too low (Cassie, 1976).

☐ Have children indicate specific locations of sounds (e.g., right, left, under, in the back, in the front, etc.).

☐ Combine auditory training with vision and/or touch whenever possible.

☐ Have children match various sounds (animals, transportation, etc.) to specific pictures representing these sounds.

☐ Performing short plays before the class is an excellent opportunity for children to listen carefully to each other and to improve inflection and natural rhythm in speech (Cassie, 1976).

Teaching Listening Skills to Visually Impaired Students. The development of listening skills for the visually impaired is considered a very important part of the educational program for these students. Listening is a crucial skill for the visually impaired, because much of the information processed in and out of school is received through listening. Despite the emphasis on the development of listening skills, Hatlen (1976) points out that teachers of visually impaired students are still depending too much on the automatic development of listening skills while students are mainstreamed in regular classrooms.

A structured program for developing listening skills should be initiated early in the school career of visually impaired children. The program outlined by Bishop (1971), for example, suggests beginning with simple sound identification such as the sound of a spoon in a cup, or of a book being closed. Further listening discrimination is developed with taped recordings of a telephone ringing or a clock ticking, followed by identification of the voices of different speakers; exercises in tone and volume discrimination include recognition of the differences between near and far, high and low, and loud and soft sounds. The discrimination of words that sound similar but are not identical can be a means for leading into a phonics program.

A number of other listening tips have been offered by Johnson (1959).

1. Tie in listening improvements with everyday listening.

2. Make pupils "sound conscious."

3. Give listening tests.

4. Analyze pupil listening habits.

5. Give listening exercises on a graduated scale.

6. Make certain that pupils know why they are to listen, what they are to listen for, and how they are to listen.

7. Teach listening directly and indirectly.

8. Do not expect complete learning in one presentation.

9. Remove potential distractions to good listening and help pupils adjust to those that cannot be avoided.

10. Develop criteria for good listening habits (e.g., attention, quiet, courtesy, etc.).

The use of devices that allow language to be either compressed or accelerated is another important consideration for enhancing the listening skills of visually impaired individuals. Compressed speech is a technique that speeds speech electronically by deleting nonessential sounds without losing clarity (Kirk & Gallagher, 1986). Accelerated speech, on the other hand, increases the word rate by running a tape at a higher than normal speed. However, this technique results in the unpleasant "Donald Duck effect." Nevertheless, many visually impaired individuals depend on these aids for acquiring information through talking books or tapes.

Many of the following activities can also be used for developing the listening skills of the visually impaired student.

❑ Have children identify recordings of various animal sounds, household appliances, vehicles, and so forth.

❑ Have students select the one word that does not belong in a group of words read to them (e.g., woman, girl, flower, lady).

❑ "Simon Says" games are excellent for listening and following specific directions.

❑ Read a short story to a child and have him or her retell it in sequential order.

❑ Have children verbally repeat the sound or rhythm from drum beats, clapping, or rhythm-band instruments (Bishop, 1971).

❑ Read various riddles to a group and have children guess answers.

❑ Use commercial programs (e.g., *Listen and Think, Durrell Listening-Reading Series*, etc.) which have been adapted for use with the visually handicapped by the American Printing House for the Blind.

Speaking

Spoken language skills serve as an essential prerequisite to all phases of academic achievement. Children with difficulties in this area are consequently hampered in learning most school subjects. For visually impaired students, the lack of vision fortunately does not alter the ability to understand and use language. However, as noted in this section, the comprehension and production of spoken language is, by far, the most severely affected area for development in hearing impaired individuals (Hallahan & Kauffman, 1986).

Teaching Speaking Skills to Hearing Impaired Students. An individual's hearing impairment, as previously noted, is usually described as *mild, moderate, severe,* or *profound.* The specific degrees of hearing loss will usually have differing effects upon a student's speech and language development and considerations for educational programs. Table 11.2 lists some examples of the effects of various degrees of hearing impairment on speech and language skills.

Among the variety of methods and materials used to teach speech and language skills to the hearing impaired, the principles of *Visible Speech* have had a tremendous influence on speech and language methods used with this population. Visible Speech, a system designed to represent any sound the human mouth can utter, has been used as the basis for a number of different methods. The *Northhampton Charts* (Yale, 1939), also called the *Yale Charts,* are commonly used in hearing impaired classrooms to teach vowel and consonant sounds (Moores & Maestas y Moores, 1981).

A so-called "natural" approach to the development of speech among the hearing impaired is the TVA (tactile, visual, auditory) method. According to Moores (1982), the emphasis in this informal approach is on encouraging spontaneous communication and utilizing a whole-word technique as opposed to drills in elements and syllables. Rhythm and voice qualities also receive attention with this approach.

Auditory training procedures are used to help children make better uses of their residual hearing. The various technological advances in hearing aids are also important factors in the development of spoken language skills of the hearing impaired. Auditory training and hearing aids have even been of benefit for children with severe and profound hearing impairments.

TABLE 11.2. Effect of Hearing Loss on Various Language Arts Skills

Faintest Sound Heard	Effect on the Understanding of Language and Speech	Probable Educational Needs and Programs
Slight 27 to 40 dB	• May have difficulty hearing faint or distant speech. • Will not usually have difficulty in school situations.	• May benefit from a hearing aid as loss approaches 40 dB. • Attention to vocabulary development. • Needs favorable seating and lighting. • May need speechreading instruction. • May need speech correction.
Mild 41 to 55 dB	• Understands conversational speech at a distance of 3 to 5 feet (face to face). • May miss as much as 50% of class discussions if voices are faint or not in line of vision. • May have limited vocabulary and speech anomalies.	• Should be referred to special education for educational follow-up. • May benefit from individual hearing aid by evaluation and training in its use. • Favorable seating and possible special class placement, especially for primary age children. • Attention to vocabulary and reading. • May need speechreading instruction. • Speech conservation and correction, if indicated.
Moderate 56 to 70 dB	• Conversation must be loud to be understood. • Will have increasing difficulty with school group discussions. • Is likely to have defective speech. • Is likely to be deficient in language use and comprehension. • Will have limited vocabulary.	• Will need resource teacher or special class. • Should have special help in language skills, vocabulary development, usage, reading, writing, grammar, etc. • Can benefit from individual hearing aid by evaluation and auditory training. • Speechreading instruction. • Speech conservation and speech correction.

TABLE 11.2. Continued

Faintest Sound Heard	Effect on the Understanding of Language and Speech	Probable Educational Needs and Programs
Severe 71 to 90 dB	• May hear loud voices about 1 foot from the ear. • May be able to identify environmental sounds. • May be able to discriminate vowels but not all consonants. • Speech and language defective and likely to deteriorate. • Speech and language will not develop spontaneously if loss is present before 1 year of age.	• Will need full-time special program for deaf children, with emphasis on all language skills, concept development, speechreading, and speech. • Program needs specialized supervision and comprehensive supporting services. • Can benefit from individual hearing aid by evaluation. • Auditory training on individual and group aids. • Part-time in regular classes as profitable.
Profound 91 dB or more	• May hear some loud sounds but is aware of vibrations more than tonal pattern. • Relies on vision rather than hearing as primary avenue for communication. • Speech and language defective and likely to deteriorate. • Speech and language will not develop spontaneously if loss is prelingual.	• Will need full-time special program for deaf children, with emphasis on all language skills, concept development, speechreading, and speech. • Program needs specialized supervision and comprehensive supporting services. • Continuous appraisal of needs in regard to oral or manual communication. • Auditory training on individual and group aids. • Part-time in regular classes only for carefully selected children.

From Heward, W. L., & Orlansky, M. D. (1984). *Exceptional children* (2nd ed.). Columbus, OH: Charles E. Merrill, pp. 234–235. Reprinted with permission of Merrill Publishing Co.

Teaching Speaking Skills to Visually Impaired Students. Although the spoken language development of visually impaired children has not been studied extensively, most experts in this area believe that the intellectually normal visually impaired do not differ from sighted individuals in spoken language skills (Civelli, 1983; McGinnis, 1981). This is not surprising, since the visually impaired child is still able to hear language and, as noted by Hallahan and Kauffman (1986), may be even more motivated than the sighted student to use language, because it is the main channel through which he or she communicates with others.

One feature of visually impaired students' language that has engendered considerable debate is their use of *verbalisms*. The work of Cutsforth (1951) suggests that the vocabulary of blind individuals often includes words for which they have not had adequate concrete experiences. This phenomenon is called verbalism, and it occurs because visually impaired individuals must often rely on visually oriented verbal descriptions from sighted individuals. In Harley's (1963) study of verbalisms, he found that the older, the more experienced, and the more intelligent a visually impaired individual is, the less he or she uses poorly conceptualized verbal expressions. Nonetheless, it is usually recommended that instruction for visually impaired students include as much concreteness as possible to avoid falling into a pattern of unreality and verbalisms (Lowenfield, 1952).

Reading

Reading is frequently the most difficult academic subject for hearing impaired and visually impaired students. The difficulties in reading encountered by these groups usually affect other academic areas, since reading is considered the common denominator for success in most school subjects. A number of reading techniques used with sensory impaired students are described in this section.

Teaching Reading Skills to Hearing Impaired Students. All national surveys, individual studies of reading achievement, and studies of specific aspects of the reading process indicate that most hearing impaired children have difficulty with reading (Quigley & Paul, 1984). These authors point out that hearing impaired students lack the experiential, cognitive, and linguistic base needed to learn to read fluently. As previously noted, hearing impaired readers are often characterized by poor word attack skills and by difficulties in comprehending complex language and abstractions.

Generally, the reading methods and materials used with hearing impaired students are similar to those used with hearing children. No single material or technique is considered best for the hearing impaired. Adapting specific materials and approaches to meet individual needs, interests, and abilities of each hearing impaired student is usually recommended (Hart, 1978).

A basal-type reading series that has been developed for the hearing impaired is *Reading Milestones* (Quigley & King, 1981). The eight levels of this series include 10 reading books, 10 workbooks, and a teacher's guide at each level. The language of the reader is controlled based upon research results with deaf students. In addition, longer sentences in each of the first three levels use a "chunking" or phrase format (e.g., The house of sticks / falls / down). Nonetheless, the material is used similarly to most traditional basal reading approaches.

In terms of word attack skills, it is usually recommended that all of the various techniques (e.g., context, structure, etc.) be introduced to hearing impaired students. However, Hart (1978) indicates that phonics is probably best used with those hearing impaired students with usable residual hearing and with children beyond the primary level. Ultimately, Hart believes that children should develop enough versatility and flexibility to know which particular approaches are most appropriate for a given word in a particular context.

Developing the comprehension skills of hearing impaired students will usually require a great deal of careful teacher guidance and help. Oral questions are usually easier for hearing impaired students to handle than written comprehension questions. Hart (1978), for example, recommends allowing the hearing impaired child to respond through words, gestures, actions, or pictures, since these responses will more accurately reveal the quality of a child's reading experience. Hart believes that one of the best techniques for checking comprehension is to engage in dramatic play with the child, acting out selected portions of the story.

Some additional instructional suggestions in teaching reading to the hearing impaired follow.

❏ Present new vocabulary in writing, pronouncing the words and using them in several sentences. New words should be written on a list for the child to take home for study with parents or tutors (Lapp & Flood, 1983).

❏ Experiences in and outside school may be recorded simply on charts illustrated with pictures, drawings, or photographs. Figure 11.3 is an example of this activity (Hart, 1978).

❏ Play charades by using sentences that can be acted out by the child (e.g., The boy got very tired while mowing the grass).

❏ Match sentences to pictures taken from workbooks, magazines, and so forth.

❏ Provide students with a word that has multiple meanings, such as *run*. Have the students use the word in a sentence, employing as many different meanings as possible (Wallace & Kauffman, 1986).

FIGURE 11.3. An Experience Story with Photographs for Hearing Impaired Students

| Making Jello | *Photograph*

Mary got a bowl. | *Photograph*

Henry got a cup. |

| *Photograph*

Ruth put the Jello in the bowl. | *Photograph*

Michael put a cup of water in the bowl. | *Photograph*

Andrea put a cup of water in the bowl, too. |

| *Photograph*

Sarah mixed. | *Photograph*

Howie mixed, too. | *Photograph*

Mrs. B. put the bowl in the refrigerator. |

| *Photograph*

We all ate the Jello. Mmmm! It was good. |

From Hart, B. O. (1978). *Teaching reading to deaf children.* Washington, DC: The Alexander Graham Bell Association for the Deaf, p. 44. Reprinted with permission.

❑ Provide practice in differing question forms, one at a time and in sequence (e.g., who, what, when, where, what color, how many, how often, how long) (Hart, 1978).

Teaching Reading Skills to Visually Impaired Students. Most experts recommend that visually impaired children read print rather than braille, since only a minority of those who are legally blind would have no usable residual vision (Hanninen, 1975). The use of print actually provides the student with a great advantage over braille in speed of reading, use of pictures and diagrams, and accessibility to reading material.

Basically, the low-vision student will follow the same progression of steps in learning to read as does the sighted student (Rhyne, 1981). The only differences in instructing the low-vision student are those material and optical aid modifications that are included to make print easier to see. In addition, reading readiness activities for visually impaired students are usually more varied and intensive due to often limited experiences and reduced interactions of these students with the environment (Lowenfield, 1973). According to Rhyne (1981), field trips, hands-on experiences, and a constant barrage of verbal translation of visual events contribute to the acquisition of concepts that would normally be acquired by sighted children in an incidental fashion.

Young visually impaired children should also be presented with many concrete objects to touch and manipulate. In addition, Burns and Broman (1983) suggest that verbal explanations should accompany tactile experiences, describing shape, size, weight, hardness, texture, pliability, and temperature. Tape recorders can also be used for presenting information.

As noted previously in this chapter, various optical aids that make the task of reading printed material more pleasant and more efficient are often used with visually impaired students. In fact, Hanninen (1975) emphasizes that the use of appropriate magnifiers to aid low vision can improve dramatically the ability of some visually impaired pupils to see print and can replace the use of large print for some students.

On the other hand, students who learn braille usually require practice in the mechanical components related to braille reading. The development of tactual discrimination, finger dexterity, hand and finger movements, light finger touch, the concept of book and page positions, and page turning skills are considered prerequisites for later braille reading (Rhyne, 1981).

Some additional instructional activities for teaching reading to visually impaired students are described in the following list.

❑ A nature walk with emphasis on smells, shapes, and textures wherein children are asked to verbalize how things smell and feel helps to build oral language fluency and create an appreciation for the fact that there is more to objects than what they look like (Lapp & Flood, 1983).

❑ Use an integrated language arts approach with emphasis on the relationship of listening, speaking, and writing to various reading skills.

❑ For developing auditory skills, have students identify sounds on a tape, listen and respond to stories or poems read to them, and/or keep a diary classifying various sounds heard at different times, in different places, and so forth.

❑ Have students note likeness and difference in forms, objects, and symbols, along with discriminating various sizes, shapes, and spatial positions.

❑ For developing a sight vocabulary, label familiar objects in the classroom with large, dark, and clear letters (or with braille, if appropriate).

❑ Line markers or "peep cards" (cards with rectangular holes cut out and large enough to view an entire line at one time) can assist low-vision students in keeping their places (Bishop, 1971).

Handwriting

Handwriting instruction for hearing impaired students is similar to that used for all students, since hearing impaired pupils usually encounter minimal difficulties in this area. For visually impaired students, however, the development of handwriting skills becomes progressively more important as visual acuity increases (Hanninen, 1975).

Handwriting instruction for blind students, for example, usually consists of learning to write their own signatures so that they can assume responsibilities such as maintaining a bank account, registering to vote, and applying for a job (Heward & Orlansky, 1984). On the other hand, students with low vision are often taught handwriting skills using the same procedures as those with normal vision, except the size of the lettering used may be modified, and writing utensils that produce a broader line are sometimes used. The resulting combination of large symbols and dark bold lines provides maximum visibility and readability.

As noted previously in this chapter, the Perkins Brailler and the slate and stylus are important communication tools for the blind student. Typing instruction, too, is a prominent part of the curriculum for visually impaired students. Typing is usually taught to visually impaired pupils quite early in the school program, since it often provides a means for communicating with sighted individuals. In addition, typing is usually faster and more legible than a visually impaired student's handwriting.

Typing instruction for blind and low-vision students is not very different from instruction used with sighted individuals. Specific adaptations for developing typing proficiency may include typing from large print or braille texts, or using a tape version of the text and a foot pedal. In addition, Rhyne (1981) mentions that, for blind students, side margins can be indicated on the page with paper clips, and bottom margins can be noted by placing a second sheet of paper with a line of braille dots under the typing paper. Finally, Hanninen (1975) notes that visually impaired students are usually responsive to learning to use a typewriter, and most find it an interesting and useful skill.

Spelling

Spelling is the one area of the language arts in which neither hearing impaired nor visually impaired students encounter unusual difficulties.

In fact, there is no conclusive evidence of a greater incidence of spelling difficulties among either group when compared to the general population.

The field of vision of some low-vision students may prohibit them from seeing a full word at one glance. In these cases, Bishop (1971) recommends specifically teaching the pupil to write out a word in order to mentally visualize the entire word.

The blind student who uses braille for spelling should be made aware of the correct letter spelling for various words in addition to the braille contractions used in Grade 2 braille. Hanninen (1975) mentions that some teachers have students write words in Grade 1 braille followed by the contrasted form for each word, while others routinely ask the pupil to spell out each word orally.

Written Expression

Instructional programs for developing written communication skills have historically been an important curriculum component for sensory impaired students. For visually impaired students, emphasis is usually placed on the mechanical aspects of written expression, including the learning of braille writing and typing. Unfortunately, the quality of ideas expressed and the manner in which these ideas are expressed have been only minimally discussed in the literature on visual impairment. Notwithstanding the importance of braille writing and typing for visually impaired students, we feel that productivity, syntax, content, and organization of thoughts should also be integral parts of the written communication program for this population.

In contrast, Moores and Maestas y Moores (1981) point out that intensive efforts have been devoted to the development of written language skills of the hearing impaired. Consequently, many different techniques and materials have been developed for the purpose of helping hearing impaired children acquire and use written language (Heward & Orlansky, 1984).

Language instruction programs for the hearing impaired are generally labeled *analytical* or *natural*. According to Moores and Maestas y Moores (1981), analytical approaches are designed to provide a student with correct speech and language structures by the building up of elements on a systematic basis. The most commonly used analytical system for teaching language to the hearing impaired is the Fitzgerald Key (Fitzgerald, 1929), usually referred to as the Key.

The Key was developed to provide children with rules by which they could generate correct English sentences as well as find and correct their own errors in composition. Instruction in the Key involves placing individual words under appropriate headings, such as *who, what, where, with*, *when*, and so forth. Children are initially provided practice in correct word order. Sentence complexity is gradually increased to include more detailed structure, such as possession, transitive verbs and objects, and so forth. The Key often can be found along a wall in classrooms for hearing impaired students. Children also work exercises at their seats with Key paper containing the various elements of the Key.

Another analytical program that is widely used is a generative-transformational grammar program developed at the Rhode Island School for the Deaf by Blackwell, Eugen, Fischgrund, and Zarcadoolas (1978). This program consists of an entire curriculum from preschool through secondary school. It was designed to integrate principles of language development with Piagetian developmental psychology. Lessons are based on five basic sentence patterns: (a) noun phrase + verb (The baby cries); (b) noun phrase + verb + noun phrase (The baby drinks the milk); (c) noun phrase + linking verb + adjective (The baby is cute); (d) noun phrase + linking verb + noun phrase (The baby is a boy); and (e) noun phrase + linking verb + adverbial (The baby is in the crib). More complex patterns are systematically introduced as the program progresses (Moores, 1982).

Natural language approaches, on the other hand, emphasize language development in the context of everyday "natural" communication. Instead of using formal drills and exercises, the proponents of natural methods feel that language principles are best presented to children in natural situations which provide spontaneous learning for the child (Moores & Maestas y Moores, 1981). Games and stories provide subsequent practice in the language principles learned.

Today, most language programs for the hearing impaired use a combination of analytical and natural methods. Generally, Moores and Maestas y Moores (1981) believe the tendency is to employ natural methods with young hearing impaired children and replace this method with more structured lessons as the children become older and difficulties in English become more apparent and more specific.

BEST PRACTICES

Due to the fact that we live in a literate society, hearing impairments and visual handicaps can have a profound impact on a student. Surveys of the hearing impaired, for example, show that only about one-half of this handicapped group are able to read at the mid-fourth-grade level (Hallahan & Kauffman, 1986). Similar studies with the visually impaired suggest that both low-vision and blind children are behind sighted peers in mental age (Suppes, 1974). Consequently, a well-planned instructional program in all areas of the language arts is an absolute necessity for sensory handicapped pupils.

The specific language arts skills taught to hearing impaired and visually handicapped students will be the same as those taught to all children, but teaching materials and instructional techniques will usually have to be adapted to the special needs and problems of both populations.

Language arts materials that include natural language familiar to the child are usually recommended for the sensory impaired. In addition, Burns, Roe, and Ross (1984) suggest listening to stories, composing and reading language experience stories, playing language games, and oral discussion as activities that help sensory impaired children develop receptive and expressive language skills.

A coordinated approach to language arts instruction will provide a broader range of academic experiences and skill development for both hearing impaired and visually impaired students. An integrated program of study that makes maximal use of recent technological advances in these fields actually capitalizes on each student's language arts strengths while developing specific areas of need. In addition, an integrated program probably provides the best learning opportunity for sensory impaired children to reach their maximum potential in each of the language arts.

VARIANT LANGUAGE SPEAKERS

Language arts instruction for children whose language does not conform to the standard English used within the mainstream of American society has been the subject of a great many papers, books, debates and, more recently, research studies in education. The language these children display differs in some way from the language of the common educational system. Consequently, there is an occasional need for alteration of instruction in order to achieve the goal of education, which is to create productive, self-sufficient citizens who can contribute to the society at large.

The linguistic forms that make up current American English usage are numerous and varied. Although English is the accepted language, there is no single standard English dialect. A wide range of language behavior is acceptable within what is commonly regarded as standard English. English language patterns vary on a continuum across regions, ethnic backgrounds, and socioeconomic levels. These differences, along

An earlier version of this chapter first appeared in Cohen, S. B., & Plaskon, S. P. (1980). *Language arts for the mildly handicapped*. Columbus, OH: Charles E. Merrill.

with the natural versatility of language, provide a great deal of variation and reflect the pluralism of the general society.

Persons using nonstandard speech patterns in 20 to 30% of their conversations are generally considered variant speakers (Labov, 1967) and often are stereotyped by the language they use. This occurs even within the existing wide range of acceptable speech patterns. A person's language plays an important role in interactions with other members of the immediate environment and in ultimate acceptance by society.

Language usage is a key factor in establishing identification with one's own community. Later, as the individual seeks social mobility and acceptance by a new segment of the society, language continues to play a vital role. The interrelatedness of language and society has been incorporated into the growing field of sociolinguistics.

Teachers of variant English speaking children should be aware of how environment and culture influence children's language patterns and their performance on language-related academic tasks. Two distinct groups of learners whose language separates them from their mainstreamed peers as well as from each other are native English speakers, whose cultural differences are reflected in their use of a variation of the standard language form, and children of immigrant backgrounds, whose primary language is not English and who are recognized as being "limited in English proficiency" (O'Malley, 1982).

Throughout this chapter the terms *variant English*, *nonstandard English*, and *dialect* are used to denote persons using a different English language form. There is no intent to imply a substandardization of any English language form used by a specific segment of society or to segregate a group on the basis of dialectical differences. The intent is only to emphasize the reality of language variation. The following statement prepared by the National Council of Teachers of English emphasizes the philosophical base of this chapter by underscoring the rights of children whose language presents a different pattern from the majority.

> We affirm the students' right to their own patterns of and varieties of language—the dialects of their nurture or whatever dialects in which they find their own identity and style. Language scholars long ago denied that the myth of a standard American dialect has any validity. The claim that any one dialect is unacceptable amounts to an attempt of one social group to exert its dominance over another. Such a claim leads to false advice for speakers and writers, and immoral advice for humans. A nation proud of its diverse heritage and its cultural and racial variety will preserve its heritage of dialects. We affirm strongly that teachers must have the experiences and training that will enable them to respect diversity and uphold the rights of students to their own language.

IDENTIFICATION OF VARIANT ENGLISH SPEAKERS

Differences in children's English speech patterns result from geographic location, social class, age, race, and national origin. Each variable may influence the person's pronunciation, word selection, and sentence construction. The following statements illustrate differences in each of these essential language components:

Pronunciation: De boy rode on de train.
(The boy rode on the train.)
Expression: Mash the button.
(Press the button down.)
Structure: She be happy.
(She is always happy.)

Differences in pronunciation and expression which are commonly associated with regional parts of the country are easily recognized by everyone, and although listeners may have certain biases either in favor or against certain dialects, there is not necessarily a preconception of the speaker as having lower ability or specific class identification. However, differences in structural components will trigger such assumptions as evidenced in a statement by Petty and Jensen (1980): "In contrast to differences in pronunciation and vocabulary, differences in grammar are generally indices of dialects spoken by the socially and educationally disadvantaged" (p. 34).

Language Disorder Versus Language Difference

The language exhibited by the mildly handicapped child is of great interest to the classroom teacher and should be considered during instructional planning. Language plays an essential role in the learning process, and a breakdown or variation in language production may impede the child's acquisition of new skills. However, the extent of the interference and the means of instruction vary according to whether the child demonstrates a language *disorder* or a language *difference*.

The term *language disorder* refers to a broad classification of communication difficulties, including delayed speech, vocabulary disorders, syntactical abnormalities, and poor comprehension. The child who has a language disorder may not be able to remember words (dysnomia) and may substitute "whatchamecallit" for unknown names and objects. Another child may have the appropriate vocabulary but may not be able to organize words into a comprehensible sequence. As a result the simple sentence, "This is my book," may be spoken as, "My this book is." Disorders such as these, reflected in the process of producing language, are known as expressive disorders or expressive aphasia.

Receptive language disorders (receptive aphasia) are manifested as poor comprehension. Some children may have difficulty understanding small units of a word (*ed* as in *walked*), while others will be unable to comprehend whole word meanings or more complex units such as sentences. For instance, in "The boy ran after the girl," it may be difficult for certain children to comprehend who was doing the chasing.

Speech disorders are also of concern to the classroom teacher in that they can interfere with the flow of communication and make learning more difficult. A speech disorder refers to problems of voice, articulation, and fluency and can be differentiated from the larger category of language disorders. A child who stutters, consistently mispronounces the initial *r* sound, or speaks in an extremely high-pitched voice has a speech disorder.

Language differences may also affect the child's learning ability. However, the "problem" in this case is based upon sociolinguistic variation rather than clinical pathology. Children who come from homes and communities where the primary language is other than English or a variant form of English are considered language different. In most cases, language-different children are not language deficient. Their language development and language usage are appropriate for their environment, and there is no implication of existing language deficits or inferior language abilities.

The differential between the child's language system and standard English may result in learning problems. Language-different children have been shown to experience difficulty in learning language-related skills, especially in reading skill development (Shuy, 1972). Teachers working with variant English speaking children on language arts skills need to display a positive and accepting attitude toward the children and their culture and to understand the effect the children's language difference has on the learning process.

Although language differences and language disorders are not necessarily associated, a child may be both language different and language disordered. Such a child is a variant English speaker who demonstrates a particular language problem. Among the mildly handicapped student population, many children may actually be representative of these two language classifications.

Identification of Handicapped Variant Speakers

To begin to understand the instructional needs of the handicapped, variant English speaker, it is necessary to establish guidelines for identifying such children. Identification starts with the determination of a handicapping condition and then is extended to include any child whose language is recognizably different from the standard English speaker in pronunciation, vocabulary, or grammar. A variant-English speaker is one whose language differences are not solely the result of pathological difficulties.

Handicapped children from several major ethnic and socioeconomic groups may be expected to use a variation of English in their communication processes. Special classes and services are often used as placement for mildly handicapped children whose primary language is considered nonstandard. Among others, these populations include

1. Black children in both northern urban centers and rural southern regions

2. Chicano Americans (of Mexican, Puerto Rican, and Spanish descent)

3. Children of Chinese background

4. Poor, rural white children (e.g., many Appalachian children)

5. Children of Asian background

Although there are common features in the English language variations within each of these groups, not all children will use all of the features. The frequency of any feature is unique to the individual child and his or her personal environment. The importance of becoming linguistically familiar with the language differences of the children you are teaching cannot be underestimated. A teacher who is linguistically naive may be unable to differentiate among a student's learning problems, true language problems, and variant speech usage.

The problems presented by the handicapped, nonstandard English speaking child are unique, therefore, the instructional program must be adjusted to best serve the child. It is not sufficient to attend to the child's learning problem regardless of variant language framework, nor is it appropriate to assume that language orientation is solely responsible for the child's learning failures. The teacher must develop instructional plans for the learning deficits with consideration and attention given to the language variation. Unfortunately, debate concerning the best course of action still rages, and many of the pedagogic problems remain unsolved.

Variant Language Development

The development of communication skills is the primary concern of the language arts classroom. The variant English speaker is a child who possesses an intact language system. Such speakers should not be classified as intellectually inferior, immature in language acquisition, genetically deviant, or naturally representative of lower-class homes. Persons subscribing to any of these myths commonly assigned to nonstandard English speakers succumb to a *deficit* model of language development.

Deficit Model of Language Development. The deficit model of language development holds that nonstandard English speakers lack facility with the standard language form due to a cognitive limitation which makes them unable to reason and to make use of abstract thinking. The deficit model was illustrated by Bereiter and Engelmann's (1966) conclusions that variant speakers are unable to use causal logic because of the lack of an if-then structure and the use of double negation and unspecified plural forms. The misconception is not in the language usage of the variant speaker, but in the assumption that such usage implies a cognitive limitation.

An example of an erroneous assumption would be:

Child: I didn't do nothing.
Interpretation: I did do something.

Those believing in the cognitive deficit theory would not recognize the negative element of the statement but would postulate that the double negatives cancel each other out resulting in a positive statement (i.e., *I did something*). However, familiarity with the rules of variant English would disprove this assumption and verify the child's use of the negative form.

Difference Model of Language Development. The difference model of variant language development is a second and more acceptable theory (Baratz & Shuy, 1969; Cohen & Cooper, 1972). According to this model, English language variations are considered as systematic and structured as standard dialect, and persons using variant English are recognized as able to communicate and to think successfully. The stigma of cognitive dysfunction or inferiority is not present. With both standard and nonstandard English the deep structures of sentences and the rules that operate on them are the same (Dale, 1976). Neither language form can be considered more effective than the other. The child's language context within the difference model is recognized as a rich instructional resource, because the child already understands and speaks an acceptable English form.

SHIFTING LANGUAGE STYLES

Throughout their daily routines all speakers tend to shift back and forth from informal to more formalized speech. The language form that is

FIGURE 12.1. Selection of the appropriate style

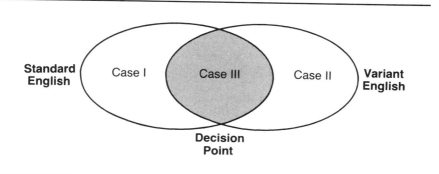

From Cohen, S. B., & Plaskon, S. P. (1980). *Language arts for the mildly handicapped.* Columbus, OH: Charles E. Merrill.

used is based on the speaker's perception of the audience and the purpose for the communication. When speaking to a group of college students in a lecture hall, the professor is likely to present a formal, highly structured language pattern. The same instructor coincidentally meeting a student on the street would be less apt to speak as formally and would be even more informal during a casual conversation in the home of a friend who happens also to be a student in the lecture class.

Style shifting is a natural aspect of language competence and should be expected and encouraged in the variant speaker who is learning to adjust to appropriate uses of standard English. The child must learn to differentiate situations that require a more formalized oral or written communication from those that allow an informal approach.

The important element of style shifting, the discrimination among situations requiring a decisive selection of speech form, is illustrated in Figure 12.1. Case I represents situations in which only standard English is appropriate and any other language form would be counterproductive, for instance, a job interview or a business letter. Case II, however, signifies the opposite end of the continuum where the variant language is the practical and acceptable form. Speaking to a close friend or writing an informal note to a parent would exemplify Case II situations. In both Cases I and II, language structure should be automatic. Finally, the importance of the child's ability to move along the language continuum and determine the appropriateness of either standard or nonstandard language for a given situation is illustrated in Case III. Examples of Case III would be meeting new people or a social engagement with a business associate.

TABLE 12.1. Comprehension Errors

Sentence	Error Form	Comprehension Problems
When I passed by, I read the posters. (Labov, 1967)	Without the past-tense marker *ed*, it becomes: *When I pass by, I read the posters.*	Use of the past-tense marker in the word *passed* influences the pronunciation of the word *read*.
This is John's street.	Without the possessive form of the proper noun, the sentence changes to: *This is John Street.*	Absence of the possessive marker in *John's* could change the sentence meaning to imply that the name of the street is *John*.
You'll like this movie.	The removal of the future-tense marker *you'll* leaves the sentence as: *You like this movie.*	Without the future-tense marker, the sentence can be interpreted as either an interrogative sentence or a declarative present-tense sentence, depending on inflection.

From Cohen, S. B., & Plaskon, S. P. (1980). *Language arts for the mildly handicapped.* Columbus, OH: Charles E. Merrill.

INSTRUCTIONAL OBJECTIVES AND PROGRAMMING

The instructional focus of a language arts program for any child whose language differs from the norm is to develop appropriate communication skills to the extent that the individual may ultimately be mainstreamed into the larger society. The difficulty in achieving this goal is compounded when the child possesses both a handicapping condition and a language background that differs from standard English.

The majority of nonstandard speech forms present little or no problem to the listener or reader. In addition, most differences will not deter the child's own comprehension. However, in some cases the child's variant language ultimately affects comprehension, as, for example in the absence of past-tense markers, possessives, and future-tense markers. Table 12.1 contains examples of nonstandard English sentence forms and explanations of the possible comprehension errors that may result.

The examples in Table 12.1 clearly show that the teacher must pay close attention to the child's semantic intentions. Another area of miscommunication may result from phonological differences, such as *toe* for *toll*; *pin* for *pen*; and pronouncing *marry, merry,* and *Mary* similarly. It may be necessary either to have children expand upon their statements in order to clarify their intention for the listener (teacher) or to restate what they "heard" the teacher say. In this way, comprehension can be checked and misunderstanding can be avoided.

In addition to the instructional objectives developed for all language arts learners, variant English speaking students require a special focus on skills ranging from the development of general communication to communication in standard English forms. Therefore, sociolinguists such as Labov (1967) have developed a series of objectives for these students which include the ability to (1) understand spoken English in order to learn from the teacher; (b) read and comprehend printed material; (c) communicate to others in spoken English; (d) express themselves in writing; (e) spell correctly; (f) use standard English in oral communication; and (g) use appropriate pronunciation in order to avoid stigmatization.

Several important principles for language development and language arts curricula are suitable for instruction of the mildly handicapped child who speaks variant English. Although listed as separate points, these principles should be considered with the understanding that language is an integrated function.

❑ There is no "perfect" or standard English speech form. English is flexible and has a range of acceptable speech patterns.

❑ English instruction must be based on description and use of English as it exists today and not upon strict rules of the past. The language of the child's environment and the acceptance of bidialectalism should be established at an early age and should be part of the instructional plan throughout the school years.

The child's cultural identity, attitudes, and feelings of self-worth are of primary consideration in the development of an instructional program. It is unfortunate that teachers and others within society often discriminate on the basis of language variation. Many negative connotations, such as *poor, wrong,* and *bad,* are applied to variant English forms. The effect of such bias on the teaching process for the mildly handicapped nonstandard speaker can be very detrimental. The problem learner's feelings of insecurity in the learning situation are serious enough to warrant attention without the additional problems of prejudice. A teacher with a negative attitude will be unsuccessful in motivating and instructing these children.

Instructional Alternatives

The question of which instructional approach is appropriate for teaching the mildly handicapped minority speaker is very difficult. Although often debated, there are at present four possible approaches for teaching nonstandard speakers:

1. Eradication of the nonstandard language form

2. Complete acceptance of the variant language form

3. Bidialectalism

4. Bilingualism

A closer examination of each of these choices for the mildly handicapped child may prove helpful.

Eradication. The child comes to school speaking and comprehending the language of the family environment. This language is purposeful and well established. Beyond the early school years, the peer group continues to exert the most substantial influence on the child's language, and in the majority of cases the peer group represents the variant language. At the end of each school day, the child returns to this same environment where use of the variant language form is functional for all members of the community. Therefore, there will always be situations in which the variant language form is appropriate, and its eradication would be a disservice.

The mildly handicapped child may be even more likely to need the social acceptance of peers who use the same variant language. Thus, a firm commitment to maintaining the nonstandard language form may need to be made. It would be unwise to underestimate the child's need for social acceptance and to try to remove this tangible bond. In fact, it may even be considered impossible to eradicate evidence of the variant language.

Acceptance of the Variant Language. The ultimate goal of the educational process is for the mildly handicapped child to assimilate as much as possible into the general society. Complete maintenance of the variant language limits the child's eventual social and economic rewards. The child's language system should be accepted along with the child; however, stylistic variations must be introduced and the child made aware of social needs and alternative speech patterns.

Bidialectalism. This third alternative is most commonly preferred, because it allows the child to adapt effectively to meet the language demands of specific occasions. Bidialectalism is not easily established and may be an added frustration to the mildly handicapped child who is already experiencing language problems. The effective teacher will help the child to learn the major elements of standard English and to gradually shift the language pattern.

Not everyone agrees with the approach of bidialectalism. Some parents and professionals feel that it is an unnecessary language requirement that places too many needless demands on the child. They believe that the teaching of bidialectalism suggests that the language and culture of the variant speaking child are wrong and that the child must learn the right way to communicate. This bias can be avoided by teaching bidialectalism in a manner that suggests that both standard and variant English are useful and correct given the appropriate situation.

Bilingualism. Bilingualism is the ability to speak two languages. Although the level of fluency does not need to be equal, there is an assumption of language proficiency in both languages. The child who speaks a language other than standard English at home may not be bilingual upon school entrance. Some children may have no English at all (known as non-English speaking (NES)), while others may be considered limited English speaking (LES). This second group is the one most commonly found in the schools, as most children have acquired some English background through such experiences as television, movies, music, and peer interactions.

The problems within the school program that these children experience are many. In particular they do not have the advantage of learning language arts from an English speaking background. The failure they experience may result from many different factors, among which Thonis (1976) delineates the following:

1. Lack of experiences in the dominant culture from which concepts specific to the English speaking community may be acquired.

2. Inadequate oral command of the English language which is the language of the instructional program.

3. Lowered sense of self-esteem resulting from repeated feelings of inadequacy.

4. Unrealistic curriculum which imposes reading and writing English before listening comprehension and speaking fluency have been established. (p. 1)

The intent of education for the child who is first developing English proficiency is two-fold: (a) to gain mastery of standard English and (b) to learn the content of the standard school curriculum at an appropriate rate. Baca and Cervantes (1984) interpret this dual focus to mean that English, or any second language, is not the primary goal of bilingual education; rather, it is to teach concepts, information, and skills through the language that the child is most comfortable with. These skills are then reinforced through the second language. The debate that has embroiled educators for decades is how to best achieve this objective. Should instruction be presented in English in the hope that the child will quickly learn enough language to advance in intellectual and academic functioning, or is it preferable to teach the basic curriculum in the child's native language while also providing structured English language instruction?

A 1974 landmark decision of the United States Supreme Court (*Lau v. Nichols*) ruled that primary instruction in English to children who could not understand English was discriminatory. The decision was the result of a class action suit brought on behalf of 1,800 children of Chinese descent who were non-English speaking. The plaintiffs claimed that the San Francisco schools provided programs that were insufficient to meet the linguistic needs of these children. As English is the language of instruction, the court asserted that the children were not being given the chance for full participation in the school program. The former Department of Health, Education and Welfare (HEW) was charged with the task of developing guidelines for instructional programs. These guidelines, now known as Lau guidelines, developed more extensive programs for NES and LES students by stipulating that language programs were necessary if schools were to meet the educational needs of language minority children. The Education for All Handicapped Children Act enacted by Congress in 1975 followed the spirit of the Lau decision by requiring nondiscriminatory testing and evaluation procedures for the placement of handicapped minority children.

Bilingual education is defined by LaBouve (1977) as an educational program in which two languages are used for instruction. The major thrust has been on transitional programs in which instruction in the child's first language is used to bridge the learning process until the child's English proficiency has reached an acceptable level. The three most common elements in transitional programs are: (a) instruction is provided in both English and the first language; (b) the cultural heritage associated with the first language is included in the curriculum; and (c) there is an emphasis on developing the child's self-esteem and self-concept (DiStefano, Dole, & Marzano, 1984).

A second type of approach, and the one most favored by bilingual educators (Gollnick & Chinn, 1986), is what is termed a *maintenance program*. Maintenance programs are based on a pluralistic approach aimed at helping the child achieve comfort in both bilingual and bicultural environments. While both English and the child's native language are taught, there is also an attempt to teach English culture along with the native culture. At the present time few exemplary programs are of this type.

Although bilingual education is under federal court mandate, it is still a controversial topic. It is important to remember that: (a) the bilingual population of this country is not heterogeneous; (b) cutbacks in educational spending are jeopardizing many worthy educational programs; and (c) many citizens believe that being an American means immediate and total immersion in the language and the culture of the society. At the present time, the predominant point of view is that total immersion is not the answer. The track record of such programs is poor. Children who have been placed in these programs often experience confusion, alienation, and failure. It may take as many as five to seven years for bilingual children to develop the necessary language for the academic and cognitive tasks required in a school placement (Cummins, 1980). As a result, these children may demonstrate lower initial achievement than their English-speaking classmates (Esquivel & Yoshida, 1985). The advantages of promoting the child's self-esteem and maintaining an appropriate intellectual curve override the problems associated with bilingual education.

The question of which language is appropriate for the child who has been diagnosed as having a language disorder is more clear-cut. Ortiz (1984) found that such children benefited from instruction given in the language of the predominant community. Langdon (1983) found supporting results emphasizing the importance of instruction in only the child's native language rather than a bilingual orientation.

Oral Language Instruction

At the early stages of oral language instruction it is important for children to first feel comfortable as speakers. They must be able to stand in front of a group to present information or exchange intimacies in a conversation without feeling overly anxious, stammering, or becoming confused. *The child's natural language in its variant form should be the springboard for oral expression.* Lessons for developing more acceptable language patterns should be structured around practical and meaningful situations.

Variant English seldom causes oral communication problems in the classroom. Bryen, Hartman, and Tait (1978) stress that the majority of classroom oral communication problems are attitudinal.

> Many teachers constantly correct the language and speech of their youngsters until these youngsters view communication as yielding, at best corrective measures and, at worst, punitive ones. As a result, these youngsters may feel that the safest course is to use minimal language in the classroom. (pp. 231–232)

Oral language transition occurs with appreciation of language variation, and that language may acceptably shift depending on the specific social situation. Therefore, it is important that the child be given both structured and spontaneous speech situations in order to learn how and when to transfer from informal variant speech to formal standard speech. Correcting random errors in oral language is an unsystematic and almost useless task. On the other hand, starting at the very beginning of language development and building a new language system fails to make use of the child's enormous amount of language achievement (Burling, 1973). The dilemma can be resolved by systematic instruction of the oral language using:

❑ Appropriate modeling

❑ A comparative program of parallel language sequencing

❑ Activities for planned practice of standard speech forms

Mildly handicapped children need a great deal more practice to reorient their speech patterns. Emphasis should be placed on grammatical structuring rather than pronunciation differences. People in general will tolerate mispronunciation to a greater extent than other language variations. Oral language should be carefully modeled for the child, but there should be no attempt to correct the child's speech by having him or her repeat the proper form. For instance:

Teacher: Alice likes you. She is willing to share her ball with you.

Child: She a friend.

Teacher: Yes, she is a good friend.

In this case the teacher presented the correct model and expanded the child's speech pattern without penalizing the student in any way.

When language is the primary objective of the activity, corrective feedback and immediate reinforcement are essential.

Teacher: Look at this picture of the boy. What is the boy doing?
Child: He jumpin'.

Teacher: Yes, he is jumping. Can you say that the way I did?

Child: He is jumping.

Teacher: Very good.

It is important and probably more effective to call as little attention as possible to standard speech when language is spontaneous. Children are more likely to imitate teachers, peers, and others that they admire and whose respect they seek. The content of the message should receive the most attention with less emphasis given to standard usage. In this way, emotional stress is avoided, communication is developed, and self-confidence can be established. Each of these three elements is particularly sensitive to the needs of the problem learner.

Oral language skills can be developed using a variety of activities such as the following:

1. *Name the action.* A child selects a picture card that represents an activity or movement. The child must describe the action using standard English. The student who successfully states the activity selects the next card, also using standard English.

2. *Sell it.* The teacher selects two children to role-play a salesperson and a customer. The teacher tells the salesperson what to sell or gives the salesperson something to sell. The task is to convince the customer that he or she really needs and wants the selected object.

3. *Sentence completion.* Each student in the room begins a sentence, stopping in the middle for the next person to pick up and complete. Sample sentences might be:

   > Yesterday I . . .
   > He was a very . . .
   > I went to the store and . . .

4. *Motivation.* Brainstorm all the situations that require the speaker to use standard English. Keep a class list and review it often. Use the situations on the list to motivate the child to want to learn standard speech.

5. *Role play.* Develop a series of situations that require either standard (formal) speech or nonstandard (informal) speech. The child must decide which is the appropriate speech form and act out the situation using that form. Sample situations are:

   ❑ Trying to convince the baseball team coach to let you pitch the big game

   ❑ Telling a friend about a movie you watched on TV last night

   ❑ Explaining your art project to a panel of judges

6. *Say it another way.* The teacher or an appointed child begins by saying a sentence in either standard or nonstandard speech form. The next child must repeat the sentence, translating it into the other speech form. For example:

Standard: People are not ready for winter yet.
(Peop'es ain't ready fouh winner, ya know.)

Standard: I have lived here.
(I have live here.)

Nonstandard: He be workin'.
(He is always working.)

The purpose of activities such as these is to provide the variant speaking child with practice in using standard English, making decisions about using an appropriate speech form, and paralleling and accepting standard and variant language patterns. The complexity of the task will need to be adjusted to match the skills of the mildly handicapped learner.

Written Language Instruction

There has been very little research or literature related to the process of teaching writing skills to the variant speaker. What there is closely ties writing to speaking and reading skill development. Burling (1973) presents an explicit comparison of the writing styles and corresponding instructional techniques of standard speakers (Style I) and nonstandard speakers (Style II). Table 12.2 illustrates five techniques presently used to reach what Burling refers to as the acceptable, "literary," style (Style III). The chart commentaries are based on Burling's explanations of each technique as it applies to the nonstandard speaker.

A major conclusion of Burling's (1973) discussion is that Style I and Style II speakers are often differentially treated for instructional purposes. Style II speakers commonly exhibit difficulties which are increased by the negative attitudes of teachers. An implication for the mildly handicapped, variant speaker is that instructional methods may be similar to those used with other mildly handicapped children with two exceptions. First, the teacher's expectations and attitude must convey a positive approach to children concerning their colloquial expressions and culture. Second, the necessary time frame for writing achievement must be extended to allow for the gradual acquisition of the new language form.

The techniques described by Burling (1973) refer to the written language style. The underlying conflict is between determining "good" writing from mechanically "correct" writing. Bryen et al. (1978) discuss this point with direct implication for the variant speaker.

The assumption can be made that the speakers of variant dialects are faced with no greater handicaps in learning to write a "good" composition than are speakers of standard dialects. What might be expected, however, is a greater incidence of a mechanically "incorrect" composition because of the divergence between syntactical and phonological structures of variant dialects and those structures which have come to be accepted as "correct." (p. 214)

Following Burling's (1973) analysis, the reader should be aware of differences in approaching the teaching of writing to variant and to standard speakers. It becomes necessary to systematically examine the effects of variant language on specific mechanical writing practices, such as spelling and word usage. Other writing conventions remain relatively unaffected by the language difference and therefore will not be covered in this section. Refer to Chapter 8 (Written Expression) for a review of instruction in writing conventions. The information provided here expands on the methods already discussed.

Spelling. The presentation on spelling instruction in Chapter 7 established the lack of a perfect phoneme-grapheme correspondence of the English spelling system. Yet there is enough consistency that the child who can use a sound-symbol relationship will have an advantage in learning to spell. For the nonstandard speaking child, many phonological features will not be accurately represented in standard written form. Table 12.3 examines several phonological elements that may cause difficulty for black variant speakers in learning how to spell.

The teacher must be alert to the variability of the children in the class in order to differentiate between a child whose spelling difficulties are the direct result of nonstandard speech and a child whose problems are of a more serious nature. For some mildly handicapped children, this may be a very difficult task indeed.

The child who spells *sing* as *sin* has probably not pronounced the final phoneme *g* and therefore has left it off the written word. Each phoneme that was pronounced was spelled. In this case, it would be appropriate to say that the child has a pronunciation problem and not a spelling problem. However, the child who spells *house* as *dleus* has a spelling difficulty—the inability to associate appropriate graphic symbols with letter sounds.

A major difficulty arises when the teacher uses a different pronunciation than the student. The teacher needs to be sensitive to the student's own pronunciation. This involves careful listening, fine tuning to variations among children, and conscious probing. A series of questions and pointers for identification of different pronunciations are listed in Table 12.4. As shown, three techniques can be used to have a child identify speech sounds: picture stimulus, questioning, or repetition.

Spelling for a variant speaking child whose pronunciation does not correspond with the grapheme-phoneme regularities of standard English

TABLE 12.2. Techniques for Teaching Written Expression

Technique	To Style I (Standard) Speakers	To Style II (Nonstandard) Speakers	Commentary
Teach new spoken forms to young children, believing that these are prerequisites to learning to read.	Never	Sometimes	An attempt is made to switch Style II speakers to a more standard oral form before writing is begun. It is a false assumption in such cases to believe that the standard spoken and written forms are the same.
Correct the written work of small children vigorously when it reflects their colloquial style.	Rarely	Often	Style II writers are more often criticized for mechanical and colloquial expressions than are Style I speakers. The reality is that the expressive power of the written content is often secondary to the standardization of writing conventions and expressions.
Expect literary style to be unconsciously absorbed from reading.	Yes	Yes	Teacher can do little to directly assist a child in absorbing a language form through the reading process. However, we do know that Style II speakers tend to read more poorly and therefore read less often. The result is a slower absorption process.
Rephrase difficult passages into "different words" (into a colloquial style) when that helps a child to understand.	Yes	No	When a Style II speaker has difficulty comprehending, teachers seldom will rephrase the expression into variant English form. The teacher's attitude against the variant form along with a lack of

TABLE 12.2. Continued

Technique	To Style I (Standard) Speakers	To Style II (Nonstandard) Speakers	Commentary
			understanding of the linguistic nature prevent rephrasing into the Style II colloquial expression. Although teachers may restate the phrase in a second standard form, it is not always helpful to the Style II speaker.
Leave until high school, or even college, deliberate instruction in overcoming colloquialisms in written style.	Usually	No	Written compositions of most Style I speakers are not evaluated for expression other than to assist the child in clarity and writing mechanics. Style II speakers are often edited for colloquialisms at a much earlier age and with a much more concerted effort.

Adapted with permission from Burling, R. (1973). *English in black and white.* New York: Holt, Rinehart and Winston, pp. 151–155.

is a much more difficult task. This is mainly due to the large number of speech sounds which do not exist within the variant language form and the increased number of homophones generally found in such speech. These techniques will help the teacher establish what words the child says as homophones as well as what sounds (and in what position) the child leaves out of his or her speech. In many cases, the child will not even be able to differentiate the phoneme differences when heard. For instance, a child who says *walk* instead of *walked* may not be able to recognize, let alone repeat, the final sound.

Spelling instruction becomes largely a visual memory task. The child must learn to portray the graphic symbols of sounds which are not said (*dumb* for *dum*) or which are said alike but spelled differently

TABLE 12.3. Black Dialect Influences on Spelling

Phonological Feature	Standard English	Variant English
r-lessness	skirts teenagers sore	skits teenages saw
l-lessness	always help school	aways hep schoo
a/an article	an apple	a apple
n/ing	everything going	everythin goin
consonant cluster simplification	understand test closest	understan tes closes
e-i merger	pen	pin

From Bryen, D. N., Hartman, C., Tait, P. E. (1978). *Variant English*. Columbus, OH: Merrill, p. 216. Reprinted with permission.

(*peel* and *pail*). In many cases the child will need to be given additional instruction in learning to differentiate words based on meaning. *Words that are being taught visually must be taught in context.* Only in this way will the child learn to associate the visual representation with the appropriate word meaning.

Usage. Other major writing problems of the variant language speaker are the selection of words and the construction of expressions. Although many of the variant language forms found in spoken language are not found in written compositions (e.g., *ain't*, often said, is seldom written), many other variant phrases are present in writing. Ross (1976) believes that certain expressions do not appear because they are so deeply opposed in the school environment. Children may recognize the relative formality of writing as opposed to the informality of speaking.

Many of the differences of variant speakers are consistent grammatical changes. Instruction for such errors can be centered upon teaching bidialectalism—that is, parallel forms of standard and nonstandard English. The teacher should present the child with the alternative way of saying (writing) a phrase or sentence. Gladney (1972) presented the

TABLE 12.4. Procedures for Identification of Different Pronunciations

Technique	Procedure
Picture stimulus	Show the child a set of pictures or words and ask him or her to identify them. For example, numeral three and a tree or single picture such as a *school* (does the child leave off the final *l*?).
Questioning	Ask the child to answer specific questions to establish variability.
	• What number comes after three? (*four* or *foe*)
	• People who have no money are _____? (*poor* or *pour*)
	• When you have a cut is it called a _____? (*sore* or *saw*)
	• The person at the back of the line is _____? (*las* or *last*)
Repetition	Have the child repeat a series of sentences after you or tell you a story using certain key words. (Attend to the possible spelling, not the grammatical errors.)
	Teacher: I had a cold last week.
	Child: (I have a *coal las* week.)
	Teacher: The answers on the test were all right.
	Child: (The answers on the *tes* was *arat*.)

two forms as *school talk* and *everyday talk*. The bidialectical language program devised for the Chicago schools incorporated spoken and written language as well as reading. The children were introduced to school talk (standard language) as an alternative way of getting their message across. Children were taught to translate (again both in speaking and writing) from one form to the other.

For the variant English speaker, writing can be a very frustrating activity if it is consistently "red penciled" and considered wrong. The teacher should establish the purpose of the writing exercise and make corrections accordingly. The mildly handicapped variant speaker may be even more reluctant to produce a written product because of past failures. Encouragement and motivation are essential. Allow the child to write freely, reinforcing the meaning of the expression while teaching appropriate usage separately. At a later time, "good" writing and "correct" writing can be merged.

Problems in Reading Achievement

Causes of reading failure among variant English speakers have drawn a great deal of attention among professional educators, linguists, and sociologists. The controversy that centers on the influence of language variance on reading achievement has not been fully resolved, and the research thus far has resulted in conflicting points of view.

Discussion of language interference in reading ability has centered on several significant factors. Some writers contend that the frequent mismatch between the teacher's dialect and the child's dialect causes conflict when the teacher tries to get the child to pronounce each word as the teacher would say it. The teacher's reaction to variant language translations as reading errors handicaps the child in learning to read (Cunningham, 1976–77; Rigg, 1978). Whether or not the child differentiates the pronunciation between *oil* and *all* or *since* and *cents* in the same manner as the teacher is of little importance. The child who reads, "I had eight since in my pocket," understands that the reference is to money and not time. The child does not need to be corrected because of phonological differences. The child whose language varies from the teacher's is as accurate in pronunciation as the teacher may be. The purpose of reading is meaning, not simply the sounding of letters and words. Grapheme-phoneme associations are simply a means to comprehending the printed word.

Miscues.   Dialect differences often result in miscues—differences between the printed words and the reader's oral presentation. Goodman (1965) first presented the idea that the difference between the reader's dialect and the language of the printed material can cause miscues and that this conflict may affect reading success. Miscues, which occur because authors and readers have dialect differences, can appear in pronunciation, syntax, and semantics. The important element to look for when a miscue is noted is that comprehension remains intact regardless of the variation between the reader's language and the author's writing. Phonological mismatches between the child's language and the standard printed form are not to be considered reading errors any more than are teacher-student dialect mismatches. In most cases teachers can, and do, ignore mispronunciations if they are consistent with the student's reading level and nonstigmatizing common speech. For instance, "I had ice cream an cake las night," will generally be acceptable. However, "Dat boy et my food" will present a more noticeable stigma and will be corrected by most teachers as a reading error. In both instances the reader understood the author's intent and derived accurate meaning from the reading, yet one example is considered more of a variation than the other.

Syntactic and semantic miscues are more often attended to by teachers who are naive in linguistic training and reading instruction. The child may read, "He jump up high" for "He jumped up high," or "Dana mother cook a good dinner" for "Dana's mother cooked a good dinner." These changes do not influence the deep structural meaning of the sentences. The teacher needs to be aware that the child who is translating from the author's dialect into variant English is going through a complex process of recognizing the graphic symbol and then rearranging verbal output to fit natural expression. The child has presented the writing in a manner that is simply more comfortable.

Miscues occurring in oral reading do not affect comprehension. The question of comprehension during silent reading has also been researched, unfortunately with inconclusive results. Comparisons of children's reading comprehension on material printed in standard English and nonstandard English were reported to show no significance by Simons and Johnson (1974) and Liu (1974–76). Both of these studies, however, had methodological problems which must be considered when interpreting the results. Harber (1977), on the other hand, found a significantly higher achievement in standard orthography when children were reading standard English material than when they were reading nonstandard English.

It is interesting to compare these reading comprehension findings with those of listening comprehension tasks, which show no significant differences according to standard or variant language form (Harber, 1977; Levy & Cook, 1973). The implications are that variant language speakers may be receptively bidialectical at a fairly early age due to mass media, school instruction, and community interaction. Listening comprehension skills for standard English, contrary to reading comprehension skills, may be spontaneously acquired for the variant language speaker.

Methods for Reducing Reading Problems. Several alternatives have been suggested for ameliorating the reading problems that often result from the inconsistencies between spoken and written language. The most commonly referred to alternatives are:

1. Teaching standard English prior to beginning reading instruction

2. Developing and using materials printed in nonstandard language forms

3. Teaching children to read materials with certain neutralized features

4. Using standard materials but allowing children to read a nonstandard form

The discussion that follows is limited to direct implications of each alternative for teaching reading to nonstandard English speakers.

Teaching standard English prior to beginning reading instruction. The development of standard language must begin at a very early age to avoid the delay of reading instruction. Many prescribed studies, such as those conducted by Bereiter and Engelmann (1966), although highly structured and somewhat successful, failed to carry over into the primary school years. In addition, this alternative is associated with a cognitive deficit approach and provides little benefit.

Developing and using materials printed in variant English. It has been suggested that dialect-based reading materials be used for initial reading instruction. Gradually, a transition to standard materials would be programmed. "The rationale behind this approach is that the task of beginning reading involves decoding the written word as being representative of already meaningful spoken language" (Bryen et al., 1978, p. 197).

Somervill (1975), among others, has suggested that there is no need to use anything other than traditional orthography (standard spelling), since all children learn to read words that are phonetically inconsistent. At present there is no evidence to either support or dispute this contention, and the disagreement has resulted in a weakening of advocacy for the approach.

Some success has been achieved with the method of developing and using materials printed in nonstandard English, primarily because of the confidence it provides the early reader by eliminating a mismatch between the reader and the printed material. However, disadvantages do exist. Teachers must be very well versed in linguistic variance, since not all children in a class may have the same dialect. Also, the teacher will need to be able to create additional reading materials when necessary.

Teaching children to read using materials with neutralized features. This is a less extreme approach than developing and using materials printed in nonstandard English. It is also primarily an initial teaching approach which emphasizes the similarities between the standard and nonstandard language forms. The major disadvantage is that the many differences among dialects render it almost impossible to decide which features should or should not be neutralized.

Use standard materials but allow children to read in a variant English form. Dialect reading of existing materials is the most practical solution, because it requires no additional or alternative materials. The early discussion of miscues is applicable to this alternative. The teacher instructs the child in grapheme-phoneme correspondence and allows the child to transpose the instruction into dialect. The child is able to make use of natural language while learning to gain meaning from the printed page.

Somervill (1975) cautions, however, that certain children who may have no trouble in pronunciation differences may be confused by having to make "a mental translation of grammatical features while attempting to read" (p. 254). In fact, it may be that only fluent readers can make dialect translations during oral readings. A teacher, therefore, should not be too concerned about a child who is able to make dialect switches— this may be an encouraging feature.

Other Considerations. A great deal more research needs to be done before any one approach can be endorsed. The relationship between reading ability and language variation is still uncertain. The major point for instructional emphasis, however, should be to achieve comprehension in both oral and silent reading. The approaches discussed relate directly to oral reading only. The specific purpose of oral reading is diagnosis. Before diagnosing a true reading problem of a variant English speaker, the teacher must understand the language variation used by the child and be able to differentiate between actual reading problems and language miscues.

Other than adaptations to the basic reading material, a variety of methodological approaches have and can be successfully used to teach reading to language variant children. The two most common instructional options are the *language experience approach* (LEA) and the *direct instruction model* (e.g., Distar Reading Program by SRA). Both of these approaches are discussed in detail in other parts of this text, and the reader is advised to review this information. Although there may be little choice in selecting reading materials for the classroom, the teacher can make a real difference in the nature of reading instruction. A positive attitude toward working with children whose language is linguistically different is the key factor. The teacher must understand and accept both the child's culture and language and must be able and willing to incorporate basic linguistic principles into sound instructional practices.

Another significant area of concern in the selection of reading material is the existence of racial or cultural stereotyping or bias. Since the content of the books children read do influence attitudes, it is necessary for the teacher to be aware of any bias presented by the author as well as to understand the effect on the developing child's self-concept. An early but important study into the development of children's ideas about foreigners was done by Piaget and Weil (1951), who concluded that children formed stereotypes at a relatively young age. These researchers identified three stages of developing attitudes:

1. Stage 1, *Egocentric stage*: The child sees the world as revolving around himself.

2. Stage 2, *Sociocentric stage*: The group the child belongs to is the focus around which everything revolves.

3. Stage 3, *Stage of reciprocity*: The child realizes that certain people are foreigners within a country or larger population and foreigners have feelings about belonging to their own homeland.

To combat the problems of bias in texts, Saunders (1982) recommends teaching children to use *critical reading* techniques which will help the reader learn to ask appropriate questions and to fairly judge the materials. Robinson (1964) details 12 critical reading components. As explained by Saunders (1982), these are:

1. Recognizing and discriminating between judgments, facts, opinions, and inferences.

2. Comprehension of implied ideas.

3. Interpretation of figurative and other non-literal language.

4. Detection of propaganda.

5. Formation of and reaction to sensory images.

6. Anticipation of outcomes.

7. Generalization within the limits of acceptable evidence.

8. Making logical judgments and drawing conclusions.

9. Comparison and contrast of ideas.

10. Perception of relationships of time, space, sequence, and cause and effect.

11. Identification of the author's point of view or bias.

12. Reaction to such literary forms as satire, irony and cynicism. (p. 115)

BEST PRACTICES

Mildly handicapped, variant English language speakers are found in almost every special education classroom or placement. Although the educational goals for these learners vary little from the general special education population, the instructional techniques and the philosophical bases behind them are somewhat different. The alternatives available to the teacher will depend on the type of language variation the child displays and the language arts subject area in which instruction is being offered.

Standard English is seen as a continuum of language forms with a range of acceptability. Variant English speakers may range from children who demonstrate dialectical differences to limited English speakers (LES) or even non-English speaking (NES) individuals. The intent of instruction is to allow the child greater access to the general language community of this country. To do this it is necessary to (a) instruct the child in language arts skills that will lead to greater academic achievement and (b) motivate the child toward learning and using standard speech when the situation calls for it.

Theoretical models behind instruction for nonstandard speakers include the deficit model and the difference model. The support for the difference model has grown enormously. The debate emphasized today in educational circles is not related as much to dialectical differences and their cognitive base as it is to the appropriate bilingual approach for LES and NES learners. The influx of foreign-language speakers in the classroom has influenced the teaching of the language arts as well as other areas of the curriculum.

The influence of language differences on the teaching of the three major language arts areas of speaking, writing, and reading must be recognized by the teacher. A teacher who is linguistically naive may be unable to detect the influence of the variant language pattern on the child's learning and performance. As a result, inappropriate decisions may be made concerning instructional objectives and techniques. In addition, it is important for the teacher to accept the child's language and culture in order to promote the child's healthy self-concept.

GIFTED AND TALENTED STUDENTS

The emphasis throughout this book has been on providing an appropriate instructional program for students who are handicapped in learning any of the language arts. Due to the inappropriate nature of the traditional language arts curriculum for these handicapped learners, we have often recommended special educational materials and methods.

Pupils at the other extreme of the continuum, those who are gifted and talented, also present perplexing instructional problems for the teacher of language arts. Many of these students will require special educational challenges and opportunities if they are to learn most effectively and reach their individual potential.

This chapter provides an overview of definitions of the gifted, along with the language arts characteristics of this population, identification and assessment procedures, and various approaches to educating the gifted. Our emphasis, however, will be on instructional techniques for best meeting the language arts needs of gifted and talented students in our schools.

DEFINITIONS

Through the years, a number of very different definitions of the term gifted have been suggested. One of the earliest definitions was proposed by Terman (1925), who defined gifted students as those who score in the top 2% on standardized tests of intelligence. Since that time, however, a number of other proposals have been made which attempt to broaden the concept of giftedness by including other dimensions of ability besides intelligence.

One widely accepted definition of the gifted which has been used in federal legislation was proposed by Marland (1972). This definition follows.

> Gifted and talented children are those identified by professionally qualified persons who, by virtue of outstanding abilities, are capable of high performance. These are children who require differential educational programs and services beyond those normally provided by the regular classroom in order to realize their contributions to self and society. Children capable of high performance include those with demonstrated achievement and/or potential ability in any of the following areas:
> 1. General intellectual ability
> 2. Specific academic aptitude
> 3. Creative or productive thinking
> 4. Leadership ability
> 5. Visual and performing arts (p. 10)

Although this definition has been useful in demonstrating that a wide variety of abilities should be incorporated into any definition of giftedness, it has a number of limitations. Renzulli (1978), for example, points out that the definition fails to account for motivational factors, and the lack of specificity in terminology may result in misinterpretation. The alternative definition offered by Renzulli (1978) has consequently gained considerable attention. We feel that his "three-ring" definition, which includes above-average ability, task commitment, and creative expression, is necessary for identifying gifted students. The Renzulli definition states that

> giftedness consists of an interaction among three basic clusters of human traits—these clusters being above average general abilities, high levels of task commitment, and high levels of creativity. Gifted and talented children are those possessing or capable of developing this composite set of traits and applying them to any potentially valuable area of human performance. Children who manifest or are capable of developing an interaction among the three clusters require a wide variety of educational opportunities and services that are not ordinarily provided through regular instructional programs. (p. 184)

Fortunately, both of these widely-accepted definitions move away from the narrow concept of giftedness as an IQ score. As noted by Swassing (1985), the first definition stresses areas of giftedness, while the Renzulli definition emphasizes three important clusters of traits. In addition, both definitions emphasize that achievement, either realized or potential, requires educational opportunities beyond the curriculum and instructional practices of regular education.

LANGUAGE ARTS CHARACTERISTICS OF GIFTED STUDENTS

As noted in the preceding section, giftedness is a complex concept covering a wide range of abilities and traits (Swassing, 1984). Because few students are gifted in exactly the same ways and because their divergent gifts permit them to grow rapidly in different ways, it is often difficult to characterize the gifted child in relation to the language arts (West, 1980). It is possible, nonetheless, to list a number of general distinguishing features of gifted students. However, as noted by Swassing (1984), the list reflects characteristics of the group and not any single individual. Their giftedness makes these students unique, and this uniqueness sometimes defies attempts to categorize them into well-ordered compartments.

In terms of the language arts, an early signal that a child is gifted may be early reading. Burns, Roe, and Ross (1984) point out that extremely bright children frequently teach themselves to read without any formal instruction and often are able to read materials designed for beginning reading before they enter school. These authors note that approximately half of the children classified as gifted by intelligence tests could read at the kindergarten level, and nearly all of them could read at the beginning of first grade.

Gifted children will also very often begin to use language at an earlier age than most children, since intelligence affects both the ability to mimic verbal symbols and to understand the meanings of them (Ausubel & Sullivan, 1970). In fact, McCarthy (1960) found that accelerated language development is one of the most striking characteristics of intellectually gifted children. Most will be accelerated in vocabulary usage and understanding, in choice of words, and in use of longer and more complex sentences (Knight, 1974). Such children also tend to express ideas originally and effectively.

As in oral expression, gifted students will often demonstrate some early and unique talents in creative writing. Many will begin to write independently without formal instruction by keeping diaries, journals, or by writing creative stories. It is important to note, however, that the mechanical aspects of writing (i.e., punctuation, handwriting, etc.) will not always be at the advanced level of thought evidenced in the content of stories. Gifted children will often require specific instruction in various mechanical aspects of writing.

Some additional language arts characteristics that have been noted (Burns & Broman, 1983; Rupley & Blair, 1983; Sisk, 1977) include:

1. A rich and well-developed vocabulary and interest in words

2. High level of abstract thinking

3. Frequent use of information sources (e.g., dictionary, encyclopedia, etc.) to explore areas of interest

4. Comprehension abilities at early grade levels that go beyond the literal level and are evidenced by understanding of the relationship of story ideas

5. Ability to understand complex concepts, perceive relationships, and think critically

6. Long attention span combined with initiative and the abilities to plan and set goals

It is important to reiterate that the preceding listing and discussion of language arts skills is not characteristic of all gifted students. Hallahan and Kauffman (1986) point out that it is not unusual for gifted children to go unrecognized by school personnel or to become unpopular with teachers and fellow students because of their inquisitiveness, unusual knowledge or wit, or boredom with unchallenging school work. Perhaps the one safe generalization regarding this population is that the gifted student is likely to adapt most rapidly and most successfully to the total environment, and, by adapting quickly to responsive and receptive environments, such students often became popular and accepted leaders (West, 1980).

IDENTIFICATION AND ASSESSMENT

Most educators agree that no single indicator is sufficient to identify gifted children. According to Swassing (1984), identification usually involves a combination of procedures, including (a) intelligence tests, (b) creativity measures, (c) achievement measures, (d) teacher nomination, (e) parent nomination, (f) self-nomination, and (g) peer nomination. Kirk and Gallagher (1986) believe that any program for identifying gifted students should include both subjective and objective methods of evaluation and that subjective measures should be checked by standardized tests and other objective measures of ability.

Although it is not the purpose of this chapter to examine in depth the techniques for the identification and assessment of gifted children, it should be noted that teacher rating scales and observations are currently being advocated as convenient and useful methods for identifying gifted students in the language arts. The *Scales for Rating Behavioral Characteristics of Superior Students* (Renzulli, Smith, White, Callahan, & Hartman, 1976), for example, has the teacher rate each student on a series of four-point scales related to various classes of characteristics, including learning, motivation, creativity, leadership, artistic abilities, dramatic skills, communication, and planning. The items on which the teacher rates students were derived from research studies of the characteristics of the gifted. Kirk and Gallagher (1986) mention that later testing of intelligence shows that most students who have achieved high ratings on this type of scale are shown to be gifted. Table 13.1 lists several sample items from a teacher rating scale of superior students.

Teacher observation of students is another important assessment technique that has been recently included as part of the total appraisal process of gifted individuals. We feel that systematic observation provides much valuable data concerning the learning and development of specific students. A large part of this information can be used in planning instructional programs for gifted students.

In guiding observations of language arts behavior of the gifted, West (1980) suggests that the following kinds of questions are valuable:

Language

1. Is the student acquainted with and responsive to fluent, imaginative, creative, and colorful language?

2. Does the student's language conform to the model respected in the subculture (which may be different from standard classroom models)?

3. Is the student confident in expressing ideas in the familiar subcultural environment?

Composition

1. Has the student developed the basic mechanical skills which provide freedom and confidence for additional growth?

2. Does the student make and support observations and opinions beyond the capacity of peers?

3. Does the student write independently (diaries, journals, imaginative writing, etc.)?

TABLE 13.1. Sample Items from *Scales for Rating Behavioral Characteristics of Superior Students*

Learning Characteristics	1. Has quick mastery and recall of factual information. 2. Reads a great deal on his own; usually prefers adult level books; does not avoid difficult material; may show a preference for biography, autobiography, encyclopedias and atlases.
Motivational Characteristics	1. Prefers to work independently; requires little direction from teachers. 2. Likes to organize and bring structure to things, people, and situations.
Creativity Characteristics	1. Is a high risk taker; is adventurous and speculative. 2. Nonconfusing; accepts disorder; is not interested in details; is individualistic; does not fear being different.
Leadership Characteristics	1. Is self-confident with children his own age as well as adults; seems comfortable when asked to show his work to the class. 2. Seems to enjoy being around other people; is sociable and prefers not to be alone.
Artistic Characteristics	1. Incorporates a large number of elements into art work; varies the subject and content of art work. 2. Is particularly sensitive to the environment; is a keen observer — sees the unusual, what may be overlooked by others.
Dramatics Characteristics	1. Effectively uses gestures and facial expressions to communicate feelings. 2. Can readily identify himself with the moods and motivations of characters.
Communication Characteristics — Precision	1. Speaks and writes directly and to the point. 2. Is able to express ideas in a variety of alternate ways.
Communication Characteristics — Expressiveness	1. Uses voice expressively to convey or enhance meaning. 2. Uses colorful and imaginative figures of speech such as puns and analogies
Planning Characteristics	1. Grasps the relationships of individual steps to the whole process. 2. Establishes priorities when organizing activities.

From Renzulli, J., Smith, L., White, A., Callahan, C., & Hartman, R. (1976). *Scales for Rating Behavioral Characteristics of Superior Students.* Mansfield Center, CT: Creative Learning Products. Reprinted with permission.

4. Does the student respect writing and choose to engage in it for various purposes?

Reading

1. Is the student confident of word analysis, phonics, vocabulary from context, and other reading skills?

2. Does the student have listening, reading, writing, and speaking vocabularies beyond those of peers?

3. Does the student possess abilities in comprehension, interpretation, evaluation, and rate beyond those of peers?

4. Does the student have independent study, library, dictionary, and research skills?

Speaking

1. Is the student confident in initiating purposeful conversations with peers, adults, and strangers?

2. Does the student enjoy participating in discussions and conversations and in delivering brief announcements and literary selections?

3. Is the student comfortable with the courtesies and conventions of social intercourse?

4. Does the student use and appreciate humor in speech?

Special Interests

1. Does the student work independently and persistently over a period of time on individually chosen personal projects?

2. Does the student seek details of and application for self-chosen areas of interest?

The identification and assessment of the gifted is a complicated matter. All gifted students will not be superior in the language arts, and exceptional ability in one aspect of the language arts does not necessarily mean that an individual is gifted (Barbe & Milone, 1985). Consequently, it is recommended that a cautious yet flexible appraisal of gifted students be made using a combination of both objective and subjective measures of performance.

INSTRUCTIONAL APPROACHES

The varied characteristics found among gifted students are also reflected in the many different types of curriculums and instructional adaptations

TABLE 13.2. Educational Approaches for the Gifted

Enrichment	Ability Grouping	Acceleration
Field trips	Seminars	Early school admission
Book and/or hobby clubs	Minicourses	Grade skipping
Tutors or mentors	Cluster grouping	Advanced placement classes
Summer programs	Resource rooms	
Guest lectures	Team teaching	Early admission to college
New curriculum	Special Saturday classes	Independent study
Community programs		Additional courses
Student exchanges	Honors programs	Nongraded classes

presently being utilized with gifted students in our schools. Most of the adaptations are designed to bring gifted students together for some period of time. According to Kirk and Gallagher (1986), adaptations are included in the education of the gifted for the following reasons:

❑ to provide gifted students with an opportunity to interact with one another, to learn and be stimulated by their intellectual peers;

❑ to reduce variance with the group on instructionally relevant dimensions (e.g., past achievement) in order to make it easier for the teacher to provide instructionally relevant materials; and

❑ to place gifted students with an instructor who has special expertise in working with gifted students or in a relevant content area.

The three most common types of educational adaptations for the gifted are enrichment, ability grouping, and acceleration. A number of approaches for implementing these adaptations are listed in Table 13.2.

Enrichment usually allows a student to study an area of interest in much more depth than is usually possible in the regular classroom. After students have mastered basic skills, Swassing (1985) points out that enrichment activities may include field trips, library work, science experiments, creative writing, or various art projects. Although enrichment has been a widely used method, it has also been criticized as random, haphazard, and lacking an adequate research base (Swassing, 1985).

A model of enrichment that was developed to guide the planning of enrichment activities for the gifted is called the Enrichment Triad Model (ETM) (Renzulli, 1977, 1982). It is based on three levels, or types, of enrichment. Type I activities are designed to interest students in topics that are not a part of the regular curriculum and encourage exploration of these topics. In Type II activities students are involved in exercises designed to provide the skills, knowledge, and attitudes necessary for future in-depth study, to learn how to learn within a subject or content area. Type III activities of the ETM emphasize the investigation of real problems. Real problems have meaning in light of the subject matter and circumstances in which the problems have been defined.

Ability grouping is another type of educational provision for the gifted in which the students are homogeneously grouped according to their abilities. Students may spend all (e.g., special classes) or part (e.g., resource rooms, seminars, etc.) of their time in the special groups. Hallahan and Kauffman (1986) point out that proponents of ability grouping argue that only when gifted students are grouped together can they be provided truly effective instruction, while opponents argue that ability grouping is an undemocratic process which fosters an intellectual elite.

Acceleration is an educational approach for the gifted designed to move the student through school more rapidly than usual. Included among the adaptations of this approach are early admission to school, grade skipping, credit by examination, and advanced placement. A number of experts (Pressey, 1962) believe that acceleration is an excellent educational approach for reducing the time spent in training and providing additional years of productivity. Nonetheless, acceleration has had limited implementation because of the fear of social and emotional adjustment problems often incorrectly attributed to it.

The social and emotional skills of each student, together with his or her intellectual abilities, will help to determine the most appropriate approach for educating each gifted pupil. Regardless of whether enrichment, ability grouping, or acceleration is emphasized, the most important consideration in teaching language arts skills to the gifted is the particular instructional experience offered each pupil. Consequently, the following sections of this chapter focus on specific methods, materials, and approaches for teaching each of the language arts skills to this population.

TEACHING LANGUAGE ARTS TO GIFTED STUDENTS

The emphasis that schools give to the language arts underscores their importance within our society (Barbe & Milone, 1985). There are, of course, important academic advantages of the various language arts skills; however, proficiency within each area also provides enjoyable recreational experiences (e.g., reading), along with a means for self-expression (e.g., speaking and writing). It should not be surprising then that the language arts have been recognized as favorite subjects of gifted students (Gallagher, 1975).

Generally, a language arts instructional program for the gifted should provide considerable opportunity for these students to put their advanced thinking to work in the free-flowing give-and-take of ideas through speaking, reading, and writing activities (Knight, 1974). In addition, Gallagher (1975) believes that gifted students should be encouraged to express themselves with imagination, to develop original and unusual ideas, and to learn the skills that will provide them with the mechanisms for more effective expression.

In designing a language arts program for gifted students, strong consideration should be given to integrating as many of these skills as possible into a coordinated unit of study. One approach, as described by Burns and Broman (1983), would be to supply the classroom with a variety of books and allow the pupils to read widely. Four follow-up techniques which might arise from this type of setting would be (a) storytelling to classmates and other classes; (b) dramatization of stories read; (c) illustrating favorite books or making murals, posters, and dioramas about books; and (d) establishing a literature club in which pupils set their own goals and rules.

Language arts experiences for gifted students should be an integral part of all subject areas. Kaplan (1979), for example, recommends that the content and skills of the language arts should be introduced and practiced as they relate to other subject areas for different purposes and varied times. The examples in Table 13.3 illustrate how various types of writing can be easily integrated into mathematics, social studies, science, and art.

Listening

As the most used language arts skill, listening is considered basic to the development of proficiency in speaking, reading, and writing. However, as noted in Chapter 3, listening is also the least taught language arts skill, and its development is often left to chance.

Gifted children usually possess considerable skill in listening, and a child's abilities in this area are often an early characteristic of superior intellect and language skills. In fact, listening involves a good deal of high-level mental activity. Devine (1981) points out, for example, that listening to a speaker's main idea, listening for a speaker's inferences,

TABLE 13.3. Examples of Integrating Writing with Various Content Areas

Types of Writing	Mathematics	Social Studies	Science	Art
Responsive writing	Speech about a class-determined mathematical problem	Letters requesting information	Editorial about a specific need or problem	Poetry evoked from something observed
Descriptive writing	Dictionary of terms	Lyrics for song about a historic event	News article about a discovery	Advertisement for an "opening"
Technical writing	Directions to perform an operation	Interview with an individual	Labels for a display	Recipe for a process
Reflective writing	Diary of a number: "The Life of a Million."	Memoirs of a famous individual	Journal article about a scientific discovery	Monologue of an artist about his or her works

From Kaplan, S. N. (1979). Language arts and social studies curriculum in the elementary school. In A. H. Passow (Ed.), *The gifted and talented: Their education and development* (p. 159). Chicago: National Society for the Study of Education. Reprinted with permission of the Society.

or listening to predict outcomes may simply be thinking processes used in an oral-aural context. He believes that, at its higher levels, listening seems to involve much critical thinking and is actually much like thinking.

Although surveys of actual classroom practices indicate that little time is devoted to listening instruction, teachers must teach students to listen. This means, for example, that teachers must prepare pupils for classroom talk by presenting an overview and explaining difficult concepts and vocabulary in advance, by giving student listeners something to anticipate, by personalizing presentations, by teaching note-taking and outlining skills to more advanced groups, by using visual aids, by encouraging responses during and after the talks, and by teaching specific listening skills (Devine, 1981).

In teaching listening skills to gifted students, an excellent technique for individualization is the learning center approach. Burns and Broman (1983) point out that learning centers allow for differences in ability, learning rate, mode of learning, and interest. They outline the following steps in planning a listening learning center:

1. Identifying the content area
2. Pretesting to diagnose strengths and weaknesses of pupils in the area
3. Determining the skills to be learned at the center
4. Establishing the sequence of tasks from easiest to most difficult
5. Identifying different kinds of instructional materials to use and devising different ways to present these in tasks of graduated difficulty
6. Posttesting to evaluate each major segment of the center

Table 13.4 lists some examples of tasks and materials to be used in a listening center focusing on literal, interpretive, and critical listening skills for intermediate grade level pupils.

Some additional instructional activities for enhancing the listening skills of the gifted are provided in the following paragraphs.

❑ Provide opportunities for children to hear, use, and discuss various idiomatic expressions of the English language (e.g., "a wolf in sheep's clothing") (Knight, 1974).

❑ Tell students in advance that there will be at least five factual errors in a talk and have them listen for the specific errors.

❑ Have students prepare in advance detailed directions for completing an activity in class (e.g., drawing a simple map representing a familiar area). Give the class time to follow the directions and to then talk about their success or failure (Devine, 1981).

❑ Read a short story and stop periodically, asking the student to predict what will happen next.

❑ Use simple riddles to describe familiar people, places, and animals. Ask students to use the description to guess the identity. Have them think of riddles to ask other students (Wallace & Kauffman, 1986).

❑ Have students make predictions on what is yet to be said, based on what has already been said. Progress from omitting a conclusion to omitting more and more of the speech (Knight, 1974).

❑ To develop the skill of following spoken directions, have each student plan a two-minute talk on "How to Put on an Overcoat." As the directions are spoken, have volunteers do *exactly* what the speaker says (Devine, 1981).

TABLE 13.4. Listening Skills and Materials for the Intermediate Grades

Skills	Tasks	Materials Needed
Detail	Find answers to specific questions	Tapes of graded difficulty, questions to answer
Sequence	Establish sequence	Set of sequential pictures to arrange according to a taped story
Directions	Construct according to directions	Arts and crafts materials, set of directions to be read aloud by a student
Rhyme and rhythm	Mark stress in a sonnet	Poetry record, copy of poem to mark stressed and unstressed syllables
Images	Illustrate or describe the "picture" communicated	Lyric poem read aloud by a student
Moods	Contrast poems written in differing moods	Poetry tape, crayons, finger paint, paper
Bias or prejudice	Compare reports of the same incident	Teacher-made tape from two newspaper accounts
Validity of information	Analyze commercials on television	Television, list of "bandwagon" techniques
Fact or opinion	Detect clues for opinion	Television documentary, clues to "opinions"

From Burns, P. C., & Broman, B. L. (1983). *The Language arts in childhood education* (5th ed.). Boston: Houghton Mifflin, p. 125. Reprinted with permission.

❏ Have students listen to the reading of a poem and then retell it in prose form.

❏ Make constructive criticisms of oral presentations of student peers in such areas as:
   a. choice of words and clarity
   b. ease of identification of main point or purpose
   c. development and substantiation of ideas
   d. general appeal to an audience. (Knight, 1974)

Speaking

The acquisition of language, especially spoken language, is probably the most remarkable intellectual accomplishment of a human being. In order for children to develop a linguistic system that is adequately functioning, as noted in Chapter 4, they must master the rules of phonology, morphology, syntax, and semantics, all of which are components of spoken language. And all of which are developed quite early in the gifted.

Most gifted children are quite advanced in the area of spoken language. As early as in the first two years, a small but positive relationship seems to exist between the observed level of infant language and later measures of intelligence (Winitz, 1964). Moreover, in an analysis of all forms of language used by a wide cross-section of elementary-age students, Loban (1963) found the highest correlation to be between the results of an intelligence test and an oral vocabulary test.

Gifted children tend to express themselves quite well, and, as noted by Knight (1974), gifted children usually have an advanced vocabulary and fluency of speech that is beyond their peers. In addition, Burns and Broman (1983) mention that gifted children are often accelerated in understanding of vocabulary, in maturity of sentence structure, and in originality of expression.

Gifted students will nonetheless require a variety of instructional approaches to maximize their spoken language skills. According to Polloway and Smith (1982), instructional programs can be based on commercial materials, an individually designed program, or, most often, a combination of both. Regardless of which approach is selected, the following teaching guidelines will be effective in planning instructional programs.

1. Work with students at their own level of language rather than using words suggested by methods and word lists (Wood, 1969).

2. Teach language in various natural settings (e.g., classroom, playground, etc.) and not only in isolated groups.

3. Always give students the feeling that you are interested in what they are saying.

4. Attempt to teach spoken language skills in connection with other curriculum content (Wiig & Semel, 1984).

5. Spoken language skills are generally enhanced by a fluency of ideas and a propensity for problem solving (Knight, 1974).

A number of teaching activities, games, or materials designed to meet specific objectives are usually included in any instructional program for increasing the spoken language skills of gifted students. A number of these activities are described in the following paragraphs.

❑ Provide students opportunities to practice impersonations. Encourage them to imitate each other's voice qualities and word patterns (Polloway et al., 1985).

❑ After reading a story, have a student retell it to another pupil using his or her own words.

❑ Emphasize cognitive strategies by teaching students to use self-monitoring, verbal rehearsal, and error analysis. Lerner (1985) recommends that students be involved in setting goals and in developing learning strategies to reach these goals.

❑ Encourage various kinds of dramatizations by utilizing pantomime to act out stories and poems, making use of puppets to dramatize the events of a story, or following up a story with an impromptu production employing dialogue (Knight, 1974).

❑ Set aside time for role-playing activities, including such topics as asking for a favor, procedures to follow during an emergency, handling an embarrassing moment, dealing with an angry person, and extending an invitation (Cohen & Plaskon, 1980).

❑ Develop skills related to the analysis and judgment of propaganda by having students listen to political speeches and television commercials for such things as name calling, generalities, bandwagoning, and sidetracking (Lamb, 1967).

❑ Begin to develop the skills of parliamentary procedure by having students learn the precise steps to conducting an orderly meeting. Extend the idea to other related activities such as a mock political convention (Knight, 1974).

❑ Give students the opportunity to conduct interviews. Have them practice interviewing and evaluating the information gained and the kinds of questions that produced the greatest amount of information. Schedule interviews with individuals from the school and community (Haley-James & Hobson, 1980).

❑ Create a mock radio station by using the public address system available on some tape recorders and stereos. Let students choose jobs on a rotating basis as a class or school radio station is put into operation (Polloway et al., 1985).

Reading

Through the years, there has been a continuing interest in teaching reading to the gifted. Terman's early work studied the reading ability and interests of the gifted, while Strang (1955, 1961) and Witty (1955) provided insights into specific instructional procedures for teaching reading to the gifted. Of course, this interest is not unexpected, since gifted students almost by definition are very good readers, and, as previously noted, many enter school already reading. In addition, gifted readers usually possess large vocabularies, can reason and think on an abstract level beyond the level of their peers and, most important, tend also to be highly motivated to read.

Nonetheless, gifted students do need reading instruction. As noted by Trezise (1977), this instruction usually should not be the kind that focuses on basic decoding skills but should include objectives appropriate to the needs and learning styles of this particular group of pupils. Carr (1984) believes that the reading program should be differentiated in terms of content covered, methods taught, and pacing of instruction for gifted readers. Some of the general features of an instructional program for gifted readers have been described by Barbe, Renzulli, Labuda, and Callahan (1971) and Cassidy (1981). They include the following:

1. Differentiation of instruction is imperative.

2. There should be many opportunities to relate and apply concepts acquired through reading to other subject areas.

3. An ever-increasing range of reading material should be made available in the classroom to the gifted student.

4. Opportunities should be made available to develop long-range interests in given topics through various resource materials.

5. Gifted students need continuity in reading instruction throughout their school careers.

6. Instruction and experience is needed to develop research skills with an emphasis on reading (e.g., library skills, dictionary skills, etc.).

Many instructional programs for gifted readers include a wide variety of literature which taps the differing interests of this population. Trezise (1977) observes that good readers are always author-conscious, and a reading program for the gifted should increase the student's awareness of who is writing, what is being written, what the themes are, and what the author's style is.

Nonetheless, it is not always a simple task to provide a balanced literature program for gifted readers. It is important that teachers be familiar with the best of children's literature themselves so that they may provide appropriate guidance. In this regard, Mangieri and Issacs (1983) have compiled a summary of interesting children's books for the gifted reader which should be beneficial to a teacher in this regard.

The Junior Great Books Reading and Discussion Program is another plan to bring classic literature to gifted readers. The program was developed by the Great Books Foundation and is described by Winkley and Rhoads (1968) as an approach that uses discussion to increase the group's knowledge of a book and to guide the group in thinking reflectively. Discussion focuses on the universal themes in the books as well as on the author, particular content, and style of writing. The teacher is expected to guide students through questioning rather than simply imparting information. On the other hand, students are responsible for carefully reading the selection before the discussion, hearing others' opinions, giving reasons for their own opinions and conclusions, and asking questions of other members of the group (Norton, 1985).

Another instructional strategy used with gifted readers in the third through sixth grades is inquiry reading (Cassidy, 1981). In this approach, the student conducts independent research on topics of special interest to them. The approach usually takes about four weeks. During the first week, the students learn the procedure, identify appropriate resources for their topic, and develop contracts with deadlines for completing the task. The second and third weeks are spent working independently. For example, students can interview resource people or read reference works in the library during this time. The fourth week is used to complete the project, prepare and give presentations, and evaluate the inquiry.

Many of the following activities can also be used in attempting to develop the reading skills of gifted pupils.

❑ Select a current news topic and compare coverage on it from at least three different printed news sources. Comparison may be suggested in terms of:
   a. Objectivity—facts or opinions;
   b. Words used—neutral or emotion-laden;
   c. Slant—direction if one exists;
   d. Feelings after reading each source (Cushenbury & Howell, 1974).

❑ Have students compare two or more books by the same author and discuss writing style, characters, and general themes.

❑ Encourage a group of gifted readers to rewrite a classic children's story using current expressions and settings.

❑ Publish books by student authors. Set up a review board, negotiate contracts, select illustrators, and arrange for publicity. The books can be placed in the school library (Wright, 1983).

❑ Use *Non-Stop Stories* (Hollands, 1985), which are stories that do not stop where the stories end. Each selection is a unique problem-solving activity. Participants receive some, but not all of, the information needed to describe a crime, catastrophe, or unusual event. By generating possible solutions, the students uncover missing elements and "solve" the story by making it complete.

❑ Instead of writing a standard book report, Wright (1983) recommends these alternatives: (a) write a letter recommending the book to a friend, (b) for a historical book, make a time line that illustrates the events in sequence, (c) compose a telegram giving the essence of the book in a certain number of words, or (d) prepare a radio announcement or TV commercial to advertise the book.

❑ Form small groups of gifted students to discuss material read or for teaching higher-level comprehension skills.

❑ Use the Directed Reading-Thinking Activity (DRTA) described in Chapter 5 to increase the gifted reader's use of critical thinking skills through prediction and problem solving.

❑ Encourage students to read contemporary poetry, black literature, modern rhetoric, folklore, myths, fables, plays, and other nonstandard writings.

Handwriting

Handwriting is indispensable for most written expression. Wallace and Larsen (1978) note that regardless of how well organized the written passage may be, it will not convey a thought adequately unless it is presented in a legible fashion. Nonetheless, it is important to keep in mind that good handwriting is only a tool for achieving effective communication, and that the ideas expressed are the primary consideration.

Although some gifted children will enter school already proficient in handwriting, Knight (1974) points out that many gifted students are not particularly good at handwriting. He, too, feels that these pupils should be expected to learn at least the minimum of handwriting mechanics—not at the expense of fluency or imagination, but as an important tool relevant to the communication of their ideas through writing.

In teaching handwriting to gifted students, we suggest that teachers follow the general instructional procedures recommended for effective programming for all students as outlined in Chapter 6.

The sequence for teaching manuscript and cursive writing as presented to all students in school should be followed with the gifted. However, for some gifted children, providing early instruction in cursive writing may serve as a motivating factor for the child. Similarly, teaching the student to use calligraphy can have a positive effect on the quality of writing by improving legibility and assisting pupils in developing a personally unique handwriting style (D'Angelo, 1982). Teaching gifted students to use some of the mixed scripts discussed in Chapter 6 can also be an alternative to using either manuscript or cursive writing.

Microcomputers are another effective alternative for helping gifted students. Young pupils can learn to use the microcomputer keyboard with the aid of software called typing tutors. Some of the typing tutors are designed as games for use with younger children, while others are designed for drill and practice in teaching typing skills to older students.

In addition to the teaching suggestions listed in Chapter 6, many of the following handwriting activities can be used in instructing the gifted student.

❑ Provide pupils with the opportunity to practice handwriting skills in personal notes and letters, in formal letters, and on job applications.

❑ Have a graphologist speak to the class about various handwriting styles.

❑ Study the history of handwriting by finding early examples in books (e.g., Egyptian hieroglyphics).

❑ Collect and study the handwriting styles of famous individuals.

❑ Promote self-evaluation of handwriting by using an opaque or overhead projector (Knight, 1974).

❑ Have students keep minutes of class meetings, seminars, and guest speakers.

❑ Record an orally read paragraph on a unique topic and have students copy it in legible handwriting (Greene & Petty, 1975).

❑ Have students research the history of various handwriting instruments that have been used through the years.

❑ Have students write a word as many times as they can using a different writing form each time (upper case, cursive, lower case, etc.) (Wulpe, 1968).

Spelling

Although spelling is considerd one of the most basic and essential skills within the language arts curriculum, the ability to spell is nevertheless recognized as a complex and multifaceted process. Spelling is believed to be a more difficult task than reading for all students, since the opportunity to draw on peripheral clues is greatly reduced (Wallace & Kauffman, 1986).

Generally, gifted spellers will have developed a "spelling consciousness." They tend to note the way others spell words, to double-check their own spelling, to look up words in the dictionary, to keep personal spelling lists, and to carefully proofread papers they produce in and out of class (Devine, 1981).

As noted in Chapter 7, there is no single spelling method that is suitable for all learners nor is any single approach rated significantly higher than any other. However, spelling instruction for gifted students should be closely associated with other facets of the language arts, especially reading and written expression. An integrative approach to spelling instruction places the emphasis on both functional and individual words, which has a greater sense of meaning for the gifted pupil. In addition, spelling instruction for gifted students is usually initiated earlier in their school careers because of correspondingly advanced reading and written expression skills.

It is usually recommended that teachers use a pretest approach with gifted students so that pupils do not have to waste class periods on words they can already spell. Thus, Norton (1985) believes that the gifted speller can take part in a spelling period without excessive boredom.

Some authors have suggested that teachers of the gifted move beyond the word lists found in basic graded spellers. Knight (1974), for example, recommends the use of advanced spelling basals with those students whose spelling skills merit such an approach or the use of a thesaurus for learning synonyms and antonyms for words in the basic list.

On the other hand, Devine (1981) indicates that spelling lists, whether organized by frequency, difficulty, or common patterns, are artificial and irrelevant to the interests and practices of students. He recommends personal lists of spelling words for each pupil. Words on the list can be those that have been misspelled in the past or those used in creative writing or in various subject areas. Figure 13.1 lists another alternative for those students who need a special spelling challenge.

Spelling instruction for gifted students is often linked with vocabulary study and vocabulary-building activities. Norton (1985), for example, suggests that students can find synonyms for overworked words and discover when a sentence's meaning would improve with the use of a more exacting synonym. Interesting lessons and strategies may also be developed for using roots and affixes through word-building contests, homonym games, making word families, scrambling and unscrambling

FIGURE 13.1. An Alternative Approach to Spelling for Gifted Students

---

CHALLENGE SPELLING

MONDAY: Give the pretest to whole class. Those who make *no* errors are eligible to try to become "Challenge Spellers" for the week.

TUESDAY: 1. Give phrase test using several list words from the lesson in each phrase to the persons who made no errors on the pretest. Those making no errors on this phrase test become "Challenge Spellers." *All* words in the phrases must be correct.
2. Those who made errors on the pretest do exercises from speller to learn the word list.

WEDNESDAY: 1. The "Challenge Spellers" find ten words they need to learn to spell and work on them.
2. All others take phrase test described above.

THURSDAY: 1. The "Challenge Spellers" take an individual test from the ten-word lists.
2. All others take sentence dictation test.

NOTE: A bulletin board graph can be kept to show the number of "Challenge Spellers" from the class each week to help increase incentive to become a "Challenge Speller."

From Knight, L. N. (1974). *Language arts for the exceptional: The gifted and the linguistically different.* Itasca, IL: F. E. Peacock, p. 88. Reprinted with permission.

---

polysyllabic words, making and solving crossword puzzles, and creating new words from old roots and affixes (Devine, 1981).

The following instructional activities are also recommended for helping to make spelling a meaningful tool for the gifted.

❑ Proofreading activities are often useful in enhancing spelling skills. Graham and Miller (1980) suggest the following: providing a short list of words that includes misspelled words to be located, providing a passage with spelling errors ranging from those that are obvious to various spelling demons, having students find the total number of words purposely misspelled in a written composition, and identifying the correctly spelled word from a series of alternatives.

❑ Have students build a Spelling Box. Each time a student misspells a word, he or she writes it on a card and deposits it in the box. The contents of the box subsequently become the source for weekly reviews, drills, and tests (Devine, 1981).

❏ Make a list of words that can be spelled more than one way (e.g., theatre/theater, dialog/dialogue, program/programme) (Knight, 1974).

❏ Have students invent new words by blending two familiar words and providing definitions for the new words. For example, *squirabbit* might be a cross between a squirrel and a rabbit, and *glup* might be a glass and cup combination (Wallace & Kauffman, 1986).

❏ Have students research the history of certain words.

❏ Provide pupils with bonus words to spell from various subject areas.

❏ Have students find words with different pronunciations of the same spelling pattern (e.g., *ough* in *tough, bough, cough, hiccough,* etc.) (Knight, 1974).

❏ Have students keep unusual or colorful words in a special notebook. Encourage students to use those words in their written assignments (Wallace & Kauffman, 1986).

❏ Introduce students to anagrams by having them spell as many words as possible from the scrambled letters of one word.

Written Expression

Written expression is a highly complex and multidimensional skill. The ability to convey thoughts in writing adequately depends upon the successful acquisition of all previous stages of language development and the development of skills in speaking, reading, spelling, handwriting, capitalization, punctuation, word usage, and grammar.

While reading and writing are related processes, Mason and Au (1986) point out that studies indicate that individual children are not necessarily at the same overall level of development in both reading and writing. Teachers often report, for example, that the students who are the best readers in the class are not necessarily the best writers. These authors also state that children who are already reading in kindergarten will vary in their writing development. Consequently, gifted students will often require instruction in the mechanics of writing along with help in communicating their ideas in their writing.

As noted previously in this chapter, by the time gifted children enter school they will have an advanced vocabulary, will probably know the relationship between oral and written language, and will know the rudiments of handwriting. Given this stage of development, Barbe and

Milone (1985) recommend that writing instruction begin at the same time that reading instruction is initiated in school and that writing and reading be equally emphasized in the curriculum. These authors outline an instructional process whereby gifted students dictate stories as a first step for teaching the composing process. Dictation is followed by more structured written expression where the pupil is provided many types of reinforcement for writing. Barbe and Milone (1985) recommend establishing a writing center where activities are based on students' interests, skills that need reinforcement, different learning styles, and ease of implementation.

Teaching editing skills is another important consideration in working with gifted students (Polette, 1982). In teaching children to edit, the emphasis is on making the work better by providing corrective examples rather than just proofreading the work. Polette points out that the best editors of gifted children's work are other gifted children. Editing each other's work provides young writers with readers, which, of course, is a primary objective for any written product.

Any approach for teaching writing to the gifted should include the following guidelines (Devine, 1981).

1. Prepare students for writing by defining the specific writing job to be done, helping students specify their possible readers, pointing out sources of information about the topic, teaching or reteaching useful patterns of organization, helping individuals to select the pattern most appropriate for their purpose, listing transitional words and phrases in advance, and providing plans or formats to guide writers as they develop their first drafts.

2. Provide time in class for writing so that students receive guidance while they are writing rather than later.

3. Emphasize rewriting and the fact that the first draft is a tentative attempt to organize ideas for specific readers.

4. Be sure that a student's writing is read.

Some additional instructional activities for promoting writing among the gifted are listed in the following paragraphs.

❑ Use story boxes for creative writing by putting different slips of paper in three boxes. Box 1 contains seasons of the year; Box 2, places; and Box 3, actions. The student selects one slip from each box and writes a story (Knight, 1974).

❑ Provide many opportunities for writing, including keeping a journal, writing letters, preparing a class newspaper, or writing poetry and plays.

❑ Encourage students to write a letter to the editor of a newspaper expressing their opinion on a local, state, or national issue (Wiener, 1981).

❑ Introduce students to various poetry forms (free verse, haiku, etc.) and have them experiment with writing poems.

❑ Have students write plays to illustrate some real or imagined event or problem, or base the play on a literary selection (Knight, 1974).

❑ Use progressive writing exercises in which the objective is to pick up where a classmate has left off and write for two or three minutes. Improvements and corrections can be made at the conclusion of the exercise (Polloway et al., 1985).

❑ Introduce students to cliches, metaphors, parodies, puns, similes, and figurative language and have them practice writing examples of each (Polette, 1982).

❑ Have students practice writing limericks and riddles and share them with the rest of the class.

❑ Invite local authors to speak to students and have them guide pupils through a writing exercise.

BEST PRACTICES

Gifted students are similar to all exceptional pupils in that they will require special educational provisions to reach their full potential. More specifically, a language arts program for gifted students should be characterized by a differentiated curriculum that denotes higher cognitive concepts and processes, instructional strategies that accommodate the learning styles of the gifted, and special grouping arrangements appropriate to the needs of the gifted (e.g., enrichment, acceleration, etc.).

Identifying the gifted and designing an instructional program to meet the learning needs of this population are usually accomplished through the use of a variety of formal and informal assessment procedures. Intelligence tests, achievement tests, creativity measures, the students' actual performance in the language arts program, peer nomination procedures, and teacher observations are usually used for this purpose.

It is usually recommended that a wide variety of literature be used in programs for the gifted in order to tap the varying interests and abilities of these students. Heilman, Blair, and Rupley (1986) point out that the use of literature can be integrated with all the language arts. Literature serves as an excellent foundation for the development of skills in listening, speaking, reading, and written expression.

The development of critical thinking skills is another frequently used strategy in developing the language arts of the gifted (Polette, 1982). Writing, for example, is frequently taught as a thinking process whereby skills are developed in planning, forecasting, problem solving, decision making, and evaluation.

Although many gifted students will have acquired a number of language arts skills before they have entered school, we strongly believe that the gifted nonetheless require direct instruction. In order for these pupils to reach their potential, we recommend a well-planned instructional program that challenges and maximizes the language capabilities of gifted and talented students.

DISABLED ADULTS

by James R. Patton

Concerted efforts to address the needs of adults with various learning problems are a recent reality. Certainly, there have been dedicated individuals who have worked with this population over the years. Yet it is only recently that major professional attention has been directed this way. Much has happened for children with special needs over the course of the last 20 years, as evidenced by the proliferation of services for children identified as handicapped. Most of the handicapped students who receive special education in the public schools are considered mildly or moderately disabled; categorically, we refer to them as learning disabled, retarded, and behaviorally disordered.

Until recently very little attention has been given to what happened to these identified students once they left lower education. Moreover, little concern has been focused on students who had learning-related problems but did not qualify for special services while they were in school. However, it has become increasingly clear that the problems that many of these students displayed while in school did not go away when they left high school. Various professionals in postsecondary settings noticed that these students were matriculating at their institutions along with a large number of other nontraditional students. Others realized that many of these young adults had problems adjusting to community living, often due to their vocational and academic limitations. Unfortunately, there was very little research or literature about this group to which professionals could turn. Within the last few years, the situation has changed dramatically. Programs for adults with learning problems now exist, and more are being established. Nevertheless, there is a great deal that remains to be done.

This chapter is about disabled adults and many of the language-related problems which they have. Much of what is presented will focus on the problems that are evident in postsecondary educational settings (i.e., institutions of higher education), although many of the procedures can affect performance in employment settings as well. This chapter does not address the more specific clinical forms of language disorders such as aphasia or the language problems associated with dementia and head injury. The focus is on more academically-related aspects of language such as reading, writing, listening, and oral expression.

BASIC CONSIDERATIONS

Adults with learning problems represent a heterogeneous group of individuals whose needs run the gamut from mild to severe. Some have difficulties that are obvious, while others fall through the cracks (Smith, 1985). Swanson and Yeannakis (1982) reflect the sentiments of other professionals by indicating that this group is often difficult to reach and consequently difficult to teach. It is also important to point out that adults with learning problems are not "grown up children with learning problems" (Polloway, Smith, & Patton, 1984); rather, they are adults with adult needs and must be addressed as such. This means that we must follow these guidelines:

❑ be sensitive to the fact that they are adults and many of the techniques appropriate for use with children will not be appropriate for this group;

❑ be cognizant of the principles of adult learning;

❑ be ready to capitalize on two powerful aids to learning for adults: adult insight and economic motivation (Nelson, 1978);

❑ be aware that the primary needs of some adults are not academic— they very well may be personal or social.

It is difficult to say for sure how many adults have learning problems that cause some degree of discomfort in their lives. This is not to say that estimates do not exist. For the sake of helping to understand the extent of the problem as seen from various vantage points, selected

TABLE 14.1. Estimates of Learning Problems in Adults

Groups	Concern	Number	Source
Adults (general)	Illiteracy	27 million	—
	Learning problems	13–16 million	Moss (1980)
Adult Education	Percentage of students who function at eighth grade level or below and who have learning problems	50%	Weisel (1980)
College Students	Community college students with learning disabilities	2–3%	Cooper (1980)
	1985 entering freshman class—students with learning disabilities	1.1%	Higher Education Research Institute (1985)
	Entering freshmen who have difficulty reading textbooks	50%	Lieberman & Cohen (1982)

figures are presented in Table 14.1. As can be seen, there is considerable variation in the type of information cited due in great part to whether we are talking about illiteracy, identifiable learning disabilities, or learning problems in general. Furthermore, the extent of the problem varies greatly as well. Yet the message is clear: A significant number of adults are experiencing learning problems.

Definitions

To date there is no definition of adults with learning problems that enjoys general professional acceptance. The term *learning disability* (LD) is often used to describe this populaton and may be an acceptable concept to use with adults. However, the child-based definition of LD as is typically used in public schools is plagued with ambiguity and can lead to confusion. As a result, various attempts to define LD and learning problems in adults have been made; a sampling of these is presented below.

Adults with exceptional learning problems have a disorder, or disorders, in one or more of the basic processes involved in learning. These include difficulties in selective attention, information processing, memory retention and retrieval, utilization of feedback and carrying out intentions. Learning problems may be manifested in difficulties with listening, talking, reading, writing, arithmetic and interpersonal communication. They may include such conditions referred to as learning disabilities, perceptual or neurological handicaps, minimal brain dysfunction, dyslexia, organizational problems and developmental delay. Included also are the minimal visual and auditory dysfunctions that occur due to aging, unusual occupational conditions or physiological problems. (National Association for Public Continuing and Adult Education, 1980)

A specific learning disability refers to disorders in which an individual exhibits a significant/severe discrepancy between the current level of developed intellectual abilities and academc performances despite regular instruction and educational opportunity, as currently measured by professionally recognized diagnostic procedures. Academic performance refers to achievement in the following areas: listening comprehension, oral expression, written expression, basic reading skills, reading comprehension, mathematical calculation and reasoning. Specific Learning Disabilities are often due to constitutional, genetic and/or neurological factors and are not primarily due to: visual or auditory sensory deficits, motor handicaps, severe emotional disturbance, environmental or economic disadvantage, cultural/language difference, or mental retardation. (California Association of Postsecondary Educators of the Disabled, 1982)

Both of these definitions suggest that adults with learning problems may encounter difficulties in a number of academic areas. For purposes of this chapter, the focus will be on individuals who display problems in the various language-related areas. Whether they meet the exact criteria of "learning disabled" will not be a major concern.

Adulthood Needs

As inferred early in this chapter, the unique concern of learning disabled adults is that their needs are acknowledged. Polloway and colleagues (Polloway et al., 1984) have argued that the needs of adults with learning disabilities should be examined throughout their life span, paying close attention to significant life events. Sedita (1980) has suggested that there are two major categories into which the learning-related needs of most adults can be grouped:

❏ *basic literacy skills* necessary for successful community living (e.g., functional reading and math, job applications, money management);

❑ *higher level skills* essential for successful performance in postsecondary education and certain types of employment (e.g., well-developed ability to listen, express oneself orally, read critically, and write effectively).

These latter skills as well as other study skills will be covered in subsequent sections of this chapter.

CHARACTERISTICS OF DISABLED ADULTS

A large body of research and knowledge about adults with learning problems does not currently exist. Much of what we do know about this population has come from two major sources: anecdotal reports about the lives of certain individuals and follow-up data which have been collected after a given period of time on groups of individuals (Patton & Polloway, 1982). There are inherent problems in both types of information. The anecdotal reports, while useful in giving us insight into the specific types of problems these adults have faced and continue to encounter, do not allow us to draw conclusions that can be generalized with certainty to the larger group. The follow-up studies that actually looked at adult outcomes are limited in the following ways. First, there have been few of these studies (for a review of those that have been conducted, see Horn, O'Donnell, & Vitulano, 1984); and in those studies that have been conducted, few have included control groups of adults without major learning-related disabilities to gauge the learning status of adults in general. Second, there has been some inconsistency in the selection of dependent variables (e.g., what data should be examined). What is clear is that few data have been collected on the learning-related characteristics of this group; most of what has been obtained relates to demographics and occupational status.

Another source of information with more relevance to the learning needs of adults is beginning to emerge. With the influx of these individuals into postsecondary educational settings has come a number of research efforts that have looked at students' skills across academic areas. Most notable has been the attention given to written language, which will be highlighted later in this chapter.

One note of caution is warranted. It should be stressed that it is unlikely that any one individual will display all of the characteristics presented in the following paragraphs. The objective of this section is to give the reader an overall picture of what this population looks like. As Gray (1981) notes, it is important to consider the needs of each person on an individual basis.

General Characteristics

Many of the characteristics described in this section are problematic for certain adults, because such deficits can significantly interfere with everyday life. Blalock (1981) observes that many of these characteristics which may have been problems during school years remain so in adulthood.

> It seems that the type of learning may change with different demands, but the inability to profit from experience remains a problem even when a "curriculum" is no longer an obstacle. Many of these people might be viewed as special education "successes" because of their skill levels, but they continue to experience difficulty learning and fulfilling their potentials and goals. (p. 45)

The general characteristics of this population are presented in Table 14.2, which is an adaptation of a similar table originally developed by Patton and Polloway (1982). Principal changes involve additional information which was obtained from other sources (Mangrum & Strichart, 1983a, 1984; Vaillancourt, 1979).

Language Characteristics

For adults who are continuing to pursue educational goals, the most critical deficits are in the area of language. It has been estimated that over 80% of those adults who experience learning difficulties have written language problems (Blalock, 1981; Cordoni, 1979; Gregg, 1983). Washington (1981) provides an interesting example of one community college student's written responses (presented below) to a history assignment. The student was asked to describe the Incas, Sir Francis Drake, and John Cabot.

> INCAS—was a Sounh anaina tlid of rausad the 1500 who was caner by sheips arnada dancing the aztecs.
> SIR FRANCIS DRAKE—was a spiese a potie in the late 1500's.
> JOHN CABT—he was a Englis nan of Round the late 1400's and a Expoler who wooder have descver Anein. (p. 1)

It is quite clear that writing problems as evidenced above are likely to cause much agony for this student and for his instructors over the course of his college career.

For other adults with language problems, employment and even everyday living can be seriously affected (see Clarke, 1973; Cox, 1977;

TABLE 14.2. Characteristics of Learning Disabled Adults

Type of Characteristic	Associated Behavior
Personal	disorganization, sloppiness, carelessness, difficulty in following directions, poor decision-making skills, inadequate independent functioning skills, few hobbies and interests
Emotional	frustration, anxiety, fear, anger, short temper, sense of helplessness, insecurity, guilt, poor self-concept, embarrassment, lack of self-confidence, neurotic and borderline psychotic symptoms
Social	social imperception (difficulty relating to people and situations appropriately), poor peer relationships (meeting people, making friends, keeping friends), poor family relationships, inappropriate social behaviors
Behavioral	impulsivity/disinhibition, restlessness, hyperactivity
Cognitive	problems with the following tasks—attention (selecting important features of task and sustaining attention thereafter), use of cognitive strategies, sequencing, memory, reasoning, organization of ideas, generalization
Academic	underachievement, difficulties in language (written and spoken), reading, math, spelling
Study Skills	poor work habits, disorganized, inefficient management of time, poor note-taking and outlining skills, problems in goal setting, difficulty in using various resources (e.g., library) and reference materials (e.g., dictionary), inefficient test-taking skills, test anxiety
Vocational	below average career success, problems finding and keeping jobs, poor work habits (following directions, attitude), poor work skills (inefficiency, errors), problems with specific work skills (e.g., taking phone messages), numerous job changes

Lenkowsky & Saposnek, 1978; Miller, 1973; Schwartz, Gilroy, & Lynn, 1976; Simpson, 1979). For example, the range of job possibilities can be very restricted if one is not able to read. Moreover, consider how frustrating it must be to be unable to read to your children or when they, at a very young age, are able to read better than you.

Some of the language characteristics often displayed by adults with learning problems are presented in Table 14.3. If more detailed information related to any of the language areas is desired, the reader is encouraged to consult the references listed in column three of the table.

It should also be noted that language problems can influence performance in other areas as well. Blalock (1981) found that poor reading ability and memory difficulties of some college students probably affected their scores on certain arithmetic measures. Some individuals have learned to compensate for their weaknesses; many others have not.

Characteristics of Adult Learners

There is no "typical" adult with learning problems; similarly, there is no "typical" adult learner. However, as Best (1977) indicates, there are certain general characteristics that many adult learners demonstrate. These characteristics are noteworthy, because they differ from those of children and adolescents. Unfortunately, many instructional efforts with adults are based on child models. More important, if we are concerned about adults who have had a history of frustration with learning-related tasks, we should be sensitive to the following characteristics.

Adult learners:

❑ need to maintain dignity;

❑ are often doubtful of their ability to learn;

❑ are strongly goal-oriented;

❑ have many experiences upon which to draw;

❑ usually have outside work and family responsibilities;

❑ may require more time for learning tasks—learning rate and reaction time decline with increasing age although learning ability may not;

❑ find that their adult learning experience is more heterogeneous in terms of age, interests, and experiences of classmates than the learning environment to which they were exposed as children;

❑ may become more sensitive to their physical environment as they age. (Best, 1977, pp. 2–6)

Knowledge of these features of adult learners and how they relate to people with special needs is essential to the development of appropriate services.

ASSESSMENT

Although more attention is being given to the needs of adults with learning disabilities, there have been few developments in the area of assessment. A number of years ago, Marsh and colleagues (Marsh, Gearhart, & Gearhart, 1978) remarked that assessment measures specifically designed for adults were scarce. Even though today there are instruments that have an adult focus, most of them generate derived scores (e.g., grade or age equivalents) and little else. Diagnostic measures which are generally much more instructionally valuable are virtually nonexistent. It has become apparent to those professionals who work with adults that more than just achievement scores is needed prior to the initiation of intervention. That is, we need to develop new diagnostic measures or enhance the skills of those who must do diagnostic work. Vogel (1982) comments that "the scarcity of standardized, reliable, and valid diagnostic instruments for the assessment of LD adults requires the diagnostician to be very skillful in eliciting important qualitative information during the testing" (p. 522).

Examination of programs that serve adults with learning problems reveals that batteries of tests are typically used. The exact composition of these batteries varies across settings, but certain areas of functioning are regularly investigated (Mangrum & Strichart, 1983b; Poell, 1982). These areas include:

❑ Cognitive abilities

❑ General achievement (i.e., academic skills)

❑ Reading

❑ Mathematics

❑ Oral and written language

❑ Affective/social/emotional levels

❑ Specific abilities (e.g., auditory or visual perception)

❑ Study skills and habits

❑ Career awareness and aptitude

❑ Learning style

In her study of postsecondary level institutions that serve adults with learning disabilities, Poell (1982) found that a number of formal as well as informal measures were used. Ostertag and associates (Ostertag, Baker, Howard, & Best, 1982), in their study of California community

TABLE 14.3. Language-Related Characteristics

Language Arts Area	Areas of Difficulty	References
Listening	• understanding what is said orally • attentional skills • memory • auditory discrimination • auditory comprehension • notetaking	Blalock (1981) Johnson (1980) Mangrum & Strichart (1984)
Speaking	• pronunciation of multisyllabic words • clarity of verbalizations • application of rules for using language • word retrieval and usage • formulation of ideas	Blalock (1981) Johnson (1980) Mangrum & Strichart (1984)
Reading	• application of phonetic rules • automaticity in decoding • reading rate • comprehension skills (literal and critical) • techniques for enhancing comprehension	Blalock (1981) Mangrum & Strichart (1984) Vogel (1985a)
Handwriting	• establishing a personal style • legibility • rate • proper grip	
Spelling	• [one of the most noticeable problems] • regular and irregular words • perception of letter-sound relationship	Blalock (1981) Cohen (1984) Mangrum & Strichart (1984) Vogel (1985a) Vogel & Moran (1982)

TABLE 14.3. Continued

Language Arts Area	Areas of Difficulty	References
Spelling	• memory (rules and specific words) • self-checking techniques	
Writing (Expressive)	• [80–90% of learning disabled college students have problems] • word usage • quality of essays • syntactic complexity (certain aspects) • mechanics (capitalization and punctuation) • overall sense of structure within and between sentences • organization and sequencing of ideas • proofing skills	Blalock Gregg (1982, 1985) Vogel (1985b) Vogel & Moran (1982) Wiig & Fleischmann (1980)

colleges that operated formal programs for learning disabled students, noted a consistency across programs in the procedures that were used to identify and diagnose students who might qualify for such services. The most frequently used formal tests as found in this study included *Wide Range Achievement Test* (WRAT), *Peabody Individual Achievement Test* (PIAT), *Peabody Picture Vocabulary Test–Revised* (PPVT–R), *Detroit Tests of Learning Aptitude* (DTLA), *Woodcock-Johnson Psychoeducational Test Battery*, *Wepman Auditory Discrimination Test*, *Weschler Adult Intelligence Scale–Revised* (WAIS–R), *KeyMath Diagnostic Mathematics Test*, *Woodcock Reading Mastery Test* (WRMT), and *Bender Visual-Motor Gestalt Test*. The frequency of use of these measures is corroborated by others as well (Mangrum & Strichart, 1983b; Poell, 1982).

Because there are so few instruments available to postsecondary personnel to help them diagnostically, it has been a common practice to use tests designed for use with younger students with this older group. Tests like the PIAT and WRMT were developed for students in kindergarten through grade 12; the KeyMath is designed for preschool through grade 6. Using tests like these with adults may be justified on the basis of the information obtained when the tests are conducted by a skilled diagnostician; however, caution is advised in using any derived scores from such measures with individuals for whom the tests are not designed. It is also suggested that the technical features (reliability, validity, and standardization) of formal tests be considered before utilization.

The next two sections examine various methods that have been developed to measure the language characteristics of adults. One major distinction has been made; the instruments that are described have been classified as either formal or informal. For the purposes of this chapter, *formal* refers to tests that have been standardized. That is, they provide set procedures for administration and scoring, have been normed on a selected population, and furnish the diagnostician with a variety of derived scores (e.g., age/grade levels, percentiles, standard scores). *Informal* refers to measures that can be conceptualized as "structured observations that appraise the student's performance without reference to other students" (Compton, 1984, p. 3).

Formal Measures

The fact that a common core of tests is typically given to adults has already been discussed. Unfortunately, many of these tests of high-frequency use are not diagnostically useful, and some are not age-appropriate for adults. In this section, an attempt is made to focus on those formal instruments that contain language dimensions. The various measures presented have been further categorized according to whether they have been developed (a) with adult populations in mind or (b) for younger students but with diagnostic utility for older individuals.

Several formal measures are available that either have been developed specifically for adults or include norms with upper ranges that include adults. A list of the more commonly used measures is presented in Table 14.4. There are no evaluative statements about these tests; therefore, it is up to the reader to explore each of these and make an independent determination of appropriateness and usefulness.

As mentioned above, inclusion in Table 14.4 does not imply endorsement. The purpose is to present those instruments that are currently available and in use in selected educational settings. It is strongly suggested that certain features of these tests such as technical adequacy and their appropriateness with adults with learning problems be considered. For example, some of the technical features of the *Tests of Adult Basic Education* have been called into question (Donlon, 1978). Similarly, Raynor (1978) has challenged the appropriateness of using the *Nelson Denny Reading Test* with students who are not highly skilled readers.

These two examples reflect only two of the concerns of which postsecondary personnel need to be aware.

It is also common practice to use tests that were not designed for adult populations to gain diagnostic information. This is acceptable as long as it is done on an "informal" basis. In other words, the administration of age-inappropriate tests is valid only when the information obtained is used to better understand an individual's strengths and weaknesses and not to determine program eligibility. Some potentially useful tests that fall into this category are suggested in Table 14.5.

Informal Measures

Due to the paucity of formal instruments that have a direct diagnostic utility with adults, informal techniques are often used by themselves or as supplements to formal procedures to screen, identify, and diagnose learning problems. The attractiveness of informal measures can be attributed to their flexibility. They can be used in a variety of ways and can be tied closely to curriculum. Barsch (1980) notes that such measures can be used to assess students on a continuous basis—a concept that currently is receiving much popularity in the literature related to special learners.

Informal techniques can take many forms, three of which are discussed in this section. First, there are commercially available tests, selected examples of which are presented in Table 14.6. The second type of informal measure includes techniques that have been used in various research projects and that show promise in clinical/educational settings as well. Examples include the T-unit analysis, which is a part of *The Diagnostic Evaluation of Expository Paragraphs* (DEEP) developed by Moran (1981); the *Syntactic Density Scoring Index* (SDS) (Golub & Kidder, 1974), a computerized procedure for examining oral and written language samples; and the analysis of specific types of textual cohesion (i.e., grammatical ties, transitional ties, and lexical ties) in students' writing samples (Gregg, 1985).

The third type of informal procedure is the use of checklists. Although less exact and not as qualitatively valuable as either of the preceding two choices, checklists can serve one valuable purpose—that of initial screening or identification. Checklists have been used with faculty members from various disciplines to help locate students who might have significant learning problems. This is particularly noteworthy, because, if done early enough, some problems can be avoided and needed services can be delivered. Usually checklists request information on many different domains, of which language is only one. Examples of comprehensive checklists have been published elsewhere (Bingham, 1978; Mangrum & Strichart, 1984; Vaillancourt, 1979).

TABLE 14.4. Formal Instruments Appropriate for Adults

Test	Publisher	Target Group	Administration	Language-Related Subtests
Adult Basic Learning Examination (ABLE) (1967)	Harcourt Brace Jovanovich	adults[a]	Group	Vocabulary Reading Spelling
Bender Visual Motor Gestalt Test (Bender, 1946)	American Orthopsychiatric Association	15–50 yrs[b]	Individual or Group	
Diagnostic Analysis of Reading Errors (DARE)[c] (1979)	Jastak Associates	gr 6–jr college	Individual or Group	
Diagnostic Spelling Potential Test (DSPT) (1982)	Academic Therapy Publications	7 yrs–adult	Individual or Group	Spelling Word Recognition Visual Recognition Auditory-Visual Recognition
Environmental Language Inventory (ELI)[d] (MacDonald, 1978)	Psychological Corporation	2 yrs–adult	Individual	
Goldman-Fristoe-Woodcock Test of Auditory Discrimination (GFW) (Goldman, Fristoe, & Woodcock, 1970)	American Guidance Service (1970)	4–70 yrs	Individual	

TABLE 14.4. Continued

Test	Publisher	Target Group	Administration	Language-Related Subtests
Lindamood Auditory Conceptualization Test (LAC)[e] (1971)	Teaching Resources Corporation	preschool–adult	Individual	
Nelson Denny Reading Test (1981)	Riverside	gr 9–adult	Group	Vocabulary Comprehension/Rate
Peabody Picture Vocabulary Test–Revised (PPVT–R) (Dunn & Dunn, 1981)	American Guidance Service	2½–40 yrs	Individual	
Stanford Diagnostic Reading Test (SDRT) (Beatty, Madden, Gardner, & Karlsch, 1977)	Harcourt Brace Jovanovich	gr 1–jr college	Group	Reading Comprehension Word Meaning Word Parts Phonetic Analysis Structural Analysis Scanning and Skimming Fast Reading
Tests of Adult Basic Education (TABE)[f] (1976)	CTB/McGraw-Hill	adult	Group	Reading (vocabulary and comprehension)

TABLE 14.4. Continued

Test	Publisher	Target Group	Administration	Language-Related Subtests
Woodcock-Johnson Psychoeducational Battery (WJPEB)[h] (Woodcock & Johnson, 1977)	DLM	3 yrs–adult	Individual	[Reading Cluster] Letter-Word Identification Word Attack Passage Comprehension [Written Language Cluster] Dictation Proofing
Wide Range Achievement Test (WRAT) (Jastak & Wilkinson, 1984)	Jastak		Individual or Group[i]	Reading Spelling

[a]3 levels
[b]Pascal & Suttell Scoring System
[c]DARE is a spelling test
[d]measures expressive language
[e]measures auditory discrimination and sounds in sequence
[f]three levels (F, M, D)
[h]Part Two: Tests of Achievement
[i]Spelling and Arithmetic subtests can be given in a group format

The Diagnostic Procedure

A sequence of activities that constitutes the diagnostic process for adult populations has been discussed by Weisel (1980). Her model is illustrated in Figure 14.1. The major steps identified in Figure 14.1 do not require elaborate explanation. However, additional comments related to each step are offered below.

❏ *Step 1:* Note that direct observation of a student may not always be possible; nevertheless, the development of hypotheses should still be accomplished.

❏ *Step 2:* The value of interviewing the students early in this sequence results from (a) getting them actively involved in the diagnostic process and (b) giving the diagnostician an opportunity to begin collecting information (e.g., oral language sample). This would be an excellent time to request a writing sample as well.

❏ *Step 3:* The selection, administration, and interpretation of appropriate diagnostic measures as well as a sensitivity to adult needs require a sophisticated level of competence on the part of diagnosticians, without which their effectiveness will be severely limited.

❏ *Step 4:* Weisel's (1980) comments regarding the assessment process should serve as a general guideline for working with adults: "Diagnosis is something we do *with* students, not something we do *to* them" (p. 33).

❏ *Step 5:* It is extremely important for the diagnostician to be able to interpret the assessment information correctly and to make the transition "from testing to teaching."

❏ *Step 6:* It is critical to continue to involve students in this process so that their educational plans reflect their personal goals, individual situations, and adulthood needs.

❏ *Step 7:* All educational plans should be considered tentative, as ongoing evaluation may indicate that revisions are in order.

With an introduction to various formal and informal techniques for assessing adult learners and with a framework for visualizing this assessment process (Figure 14.1), it seems only natural to now examine instructional techniques for addressing the various language areas which are characteristically problematic for learning disabled adults. Before embarking on such a task, it is useful to remember that assessment and instruction are not two distinctly separate endeavors. It is highly desirable to have assessment practices intertwined with instruction (i.e.,

TABLE 14.5. Formal Instruments Not Designed for Adults that Can Be Used Diagnostically

Test	Publisher	Target Group	Administration	Language-Related Subtests
Clinical Evaluation of Language Functions (CELF) (Semel & Wiig, 1980)	Psychological Corporation	gr K–12	Individual	[Language-Processing] Word and Sentence Structure Word Classes Linguistic Concepts Relationships and Ambiguities Oral Directions Spoken Paragraphs [Language-Production] Word Series Confrontation Naming Word Associations Model Sentences Formulated Sentences
Detroit Tests of Learning Aptitude–Revised (DTLA–2) (Hammill, 1985)	PRO-ED	6–17 yrs	Individual	Word Opposites Sentence Imitation Oral Directions Word Sequences Story Construction Symbolic Relations Conceptual Matching Word Fragments Letter Sequences

TABLE 14.5. Continued

Test	Publisher	Target Group	Administration	Language-Related Subtests
Expressive One-Word Picture Vocabulary Test (EOWPVT) (1979)	Academic Therapy Publications	2–12 yrs	Individual	
Myklebust Picture Story Language Test (Myklebust, 1965)	Grune & Stratton	7–17 yrs	Individual or Group	
Peabody Individual Achievement Test (PIAT) (Dunn & Markwardt, 1970)	American Guidance Service	gr K–12	Individual	Reading Recognition Reading Comprehension Spelling
Test of Adolescent Language–2 (TOAL–2) (Hammill, Brown, Larsen, & Wiederholt, 1987)	PRO-ED	11–18½ yrs	Individual or Group	Listening/Vocabulary Listening/Grammar Speaking/Vocabulary Speaking/Grammar Reading/Vocabulary Reading/Grammar Writing/Vocabulary Writing/Grammar

TABLE 14.5. Continued

Test	Publisher	Target Group	Administration	Language-Related Subtests
Test of Reading Comprehension (TORC) (Brown, Hammill, & Wiederholt, 1986)	PRO-ED	6½–14½ yrs	Individual or Group	[3 core subtests] General Vocabulary Syntactic Similarities Paragraph Reading [5 supplemental subtests]
Test of Written Language (TOWL) (Hammill & Larsen, 1983)	PRO-ED	gr 2–12	Individual or Group	Vocabulary Thematic Maturity Handwriting Spelling Word Usage Style
Test of Written Spelling (TWS–2) (Larsen & Hammill, 1986)	PRO-ED	5–15 yrs	Individual or Group	Predictable Words Unpredictable Words
Woodcock Reading Mastery Tests (WRMT) (Woodcock, 1973)	American Guidance Service	gr K–12	Individual	Letter Identification Word Identification Word Attack Word Comprehension Passage Comprehension

FIGURE 14.1. Steps in the Diagnostic Process

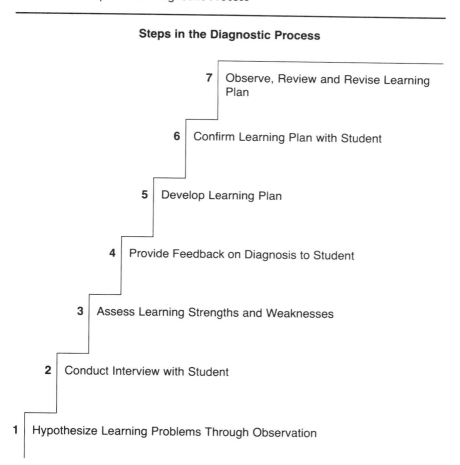

Steps in the Diagnostic Process

7 | Observe, Review and Revise Learning Plan

6 | Confirm Learning Plan with Student

5 | Develop Learning Plan

4 | Provide Feedback on Diagnosis to Student

3 | Assess Learning Strengths and Weaknesses

2 | Conduct Interview with Student

1 | Hypothesize Learning Problems Through Observation

curricularly based) in order to regularly monitor the performance of students and to make instructional decisions based on this information.

INSTRUCTIONAL APPROACHES

Overall philosophy concerning how to deal with adults with learning problems dictates the types of services they receive. Blalock and Dixon (1982) have identified two major orientations that are operative in most

TABLE 14.6. Informal Measures Appropriate For Adults

Test	Publisher	Target Group	Administration	Language-Related Subtests
Adult Basic Education/ Learning Disabilities Screening Test (Vaillancourt, 1979)		adults	Individual or Group	Word Recognition Spelling Writing Sample Reading Comprehension
Brigance Diagnostic Inventory of Essential Skills (Brigance, 1981)	Curriculum Associates	gr 4–12	Individual or Group[a]	Reading • Word Recognition • Oral Reading • Comprehension • Analysis • Reference Writing Spelling
Diagnostic Evaluation of Expository Paragraphs (DEEP) (Moran, 1981)	University of Kansas	—	Group	[Scoring procedure assesses:] Mechanics Spelling Conventions Complexity & Variety of Sentence Structure Word Selection

TABLE 14.6. Continued

Test	Publisher	Target Group	Administration	Language-Related Subtests
London Procedure (Weisel, 1977)	—	ABE student	Individual	Comprehension (listening) Sequential Memory of Random Numbers & Words in Context Alphabet Days of the Week Months of the Year Auditory to Motor Reading of Single Words
Malcomesius Specific Language Disability[b] (1967)	Educators Publishing Service	gr 6–8	Group	[10 subtests]
Reading Evaluation–Adult Diagnosis (READ) (1972)	Literacy Volunteers of America	—	Individual	[3 parts:] Sight Words Word Analysis Skills Reading/Listening Inventory

[a]Some subtests can be given in a group format
[b]This is an extension of the Slingerland Screening Tests for Identifying Children with Specific Language Disability

postsecondary educational settings: (a) change the student to match the demands of the institution or (b) change the institution to match individual student needs. More frequently, it is the former orientation that predominates. As Patton and Polloway (in press) stress, "prudence suggests that LD students are well-advised to do whatever they can to succeed in *existing* environments" (p. 3).

Two major instructional approaches exist for preparing adults with various problems to deal successfully with the demands of their everyday environments. The first orientation is the *remedial* approach. Some professionals (Lieberman & Cohen, 1982; Roueche, Baker, & Roueche, 1984) have criticized the use of this approach in adult reading programs because of the lack of documented evidence indicating that students prosper from such efforts. Others (Polloway et al., 1986) offer a more optimistic perspective on the effectiveness of remedial programming with older students, suggesting that remedial efforts should not be forsaken in all cases. It is important to recognize that the effectiveness of a given remedial program will depend on the organizational structure of the program, the methodology used, and the competence of the key personnel.

The second instructional orientation is the *compensatory* approach. This approach involves the utilization of nontraditional methods for dealing with areas that are problematic for adults with learning problems. It can be useful in educational settings (e.g., changes in the way instruction is presented) and in community living (e.g., alternative ways for filling in a job application). Recent technological advances allow many individuals to cope relatively easily with some of their learning-related problems. For example, the availability and increasing use of microcomputers for word processing offer persons with spelling problems an attractive way to check their written efforts through the use of spelling programs. In this section of the chapter, both of the instructional orientations introduced above are considered.

The remaining portion of this section presents selected teaching techniques, compensatory strategies, and, when applicable, programs for the following language-related skill areas: listening, speaking, reading, writing, and study skills. (For a detailed listing of specific instructional materials in these areas, see Vaillancourt, 1979.) Some of the suggestions presented in earlier chapters may be relevant for adult populations as well. However, suggestions offered in this chapter are specifically appropriate for adults. The suggestions under each skill area represent only selected examples and should not be considered an exhaustive list.

Teaching Listening Skills to Adults

Perhaps more than any other of the language arts areas discussed in this chapter, listening is the most neglected from an instructional point of view. This is unfortunate if, as some have suggested (Schnell, 1977), listening is the most used of the language arts skills; certainly, the importance of this skill in most college-level courses is apparent.

Alley and Deshler (1979) organized listening skill instruction according to the sequential stages of prelistening, listening, and postlistening strategies. This model as well as many of their suggestions are used below.

Prelistening strategies

❑ Encourage review of previous notes or readings.

❑ Show how to be prepared for effective listening by selecting a proper seating arrangement and having appropriate materials.

❑ Students should acquire advanced organizers (e.g., outlines of lectures) and become familiar with new vocabulary.

❑ Consider the characteristics of the speaker to whom one has to listen.

Listening strategies

❑ Have students use visual aids as much as possible. Some instructors may have developed graphic models of the key concepts. See Reinhardtsen (1982) for some interesting ideas for putting graphic models on slides so that students can use them in conjunction with tape recordings at later dates.

❑ Students need to be shown how to use organizational, verbal, and nonverbal cues employed by the speaker.

❑ Instruction on summarizing the main points of a speech may be needed.

❑ Skills in question asking must be taught.

❑ More efficient methods for remembering information are usually worth presenting. Alley and Deshler (1979) suggest teaching rehearsal, visual imagery, and coding/clustering techniques.

❑ Various methods of note-taking (e.g., mind-mapping) may have to be presented. (More on this topic is presented in the section on study skills later in this chapter.)

❑ Have students use the margin of their notes to record notes to themselves that emerge from the listening activity (e.g., things they need to do).

❑ Some students should be instructed to concentrate totally on what is being presented and not to take notes. They are better off getting a copy of someone else's notes—someone who takes good notes—or using a tape recorder.

❑ To actively engage students in the listening process, it is often useful to give them much experience in directed listening/thinking activities.

Postlistening strategies

❑ Instill the need to review as soon as possible what was just listened to. This might mean jotting down the main points, reviewing one's notes, or acting on the margin messages as suggested above.

❑ A useful activity is to summarize the information that was acquired.

Teaching Speaking Skills to Adults

Being able to orally express oneself is most valued within a social context. However, this aspect of communication is needed in other facets of everyday life, too. It seems that an assumption that adults have adequate speaking skills has been made, as there are few commercially available programs that address this area. A listing of suggestions for developing more facility in this area is presented below.

❑ Focus instruction on real applications, particularly social settings (pragmatic language).

❑ Not much can be done to compensate for the need to communicate orally. However, one can avoid situations where speaking skills are necessary for success (e.g., seminar classes, jobs such as receptionist, salesperson, or teacher).

❑ Teach adults to think before they talk. Alley and Deshler (1979) encourage teaching students to develop the use of "wait time" (see Chapter 4).

❑ Provide instructional activities that require students to generate words that describe various items, situations, or pictures.

❑ Show students how to combine simple sentences into more complex ones. Then give them much practice doing so.

❑ Create many opportunities for students to orally express themselves: sharing activities, interviews, descriptions of movies they saw.

❑ Use brainstorming sessions as a way for students to contribute to a discussion without feeling uncomfortable. It is crucial that the instructor know how to conduct such an activity.

Teaching Reading Skills to Adults

Most of the attention given to the high rates of illiteracy has centered on reading. The statistics presented in Table 14.1 support the concern that currently exists about the large number of people who either cannot read or who read so poorly that their lives are affected. For those who are in postsecondary educational settings, adequate reading skills become the essential factor for academic success. Unfortunately, for those who do not read well, the textual material they will encounter may prove to be their downfall. The suggestions found below reflect the two approaches discussed earlier: remediation and compensation.

This section is broken down into three parts: basic skills, comprehension skills, and miscellaneous suggestions.

Basic reading skills

❑ Attention may need to be given to phonetic and structural analysis. Students may have a very difficult time with multisyllabic words. Many educators of adults have difficulty teaching in this area, as they have little background in the teaching of reading. The use of systematic reading/language programs which teach these skills may be indicated (see Table 14.7).

❑ Language experience approaches can be very useful for working on basic skills, because they capitalize on the older student's interests, experiences, and oral language abilities.

❑ Provide many opportunities for detecting the meaning of words. Alley and Deshler (1979) suggest that instruction include words with straightforward meanings, words with multiple meanings, technical words, and infrequently used words. Skills related to using the dictionary and to using contextual cues are important as well.

Comprehension skills

❑ Show students how to use a variety of techniques that have been found to increase comprehension: prediction strategies, graphic-aid strategies, and questioning strategies (see Polloway et al., 1985 for examples of these strategies).

❑ Help students to develop ways of using visual imagery for remembering the content of what they read.

❑ Provide students with a checklist for monitoring their reading (Clary, 1984).

❑ Spend some time clarifying the confusion associated with qualifying words such as *only, always, never, except,* especially as they appear in questions.

TABLE 14.7. Selected Reading Programs Appropriate for Adults

Program	Publisher/Reference	Components	Features
Adult Basic Reading Program	Vaillancourt (1979)		• structured, sequential program in basic vowel patterns • multisensory
Bourn Sound Method	Kenneth Bourn (820 Bradley Rd., Joppa, MD 21085)		• coded sound-symbol approach • reading taught through spelling and writing • 9 "attack steps" used with every word that is a problem
Corrective Reading Program	SRA	• Teacher's book–Guide and Presentation sections • student's book • placement test	• 2 strands: decoding and comprehension • 3 levels (A, B, C) • very structured & sequential program • teacher-directed and independent activities • record-keeping system • reinforcement system

TABLE 14.7. Continued

Program	Publisher/Reference	Components	Features
Individually Prescribed Instructional System	PACE Learning Systems	• instructional modules	• programmed materials • individualized • coordinated by "learning managers" • self-paced • performance contracting
Monterey Reading Program	Monterey Learning Systems	• Teacher's manual • Program books (2 binders) • Student response booklets	• highly structured • development of decoding skills • much oral responding
Multi-Sensory Approach to Language Arts	Slingerland (1971)	• Teacher's manuals—three levels • supplementary classroom materials (e.g., pocket wall chart)	• multisensory • small group format • highly structured • phonetic, alphabetic program for teaching, reading, writing, and spelling • daily format of lessons includes auditory and visual approaches

TABLE 14.7. Continued

Program	Publisher/Reference	Components	Features
New Streamlined English Series	Laubach, Kirk, & Laubach (1973)	• 5 skillbooks • 5 correlated readers • Teacher's manuals	• basic reading and writing course • memory techniques (pictures and superimposed letters) • includes dictation, writing practice, and homework
Steck-Vaughn Adult Reading	Steck-Vaughn	• Teacher's guide • Student books level 1: 7 books level 2: 8 books • audio cassette component (optional)	• self-correcting format • individualized • Level 1: prereading, word recognition, word attack • Level 2: comprehension • criterion–referenced testing throughout
The Writing Road to Reading	Spalding & Spalding (1969)	• Teacher's book • phonogram cards	• structured • total language arts system ("unified phonics") • teaches 70 phonograms and 45 basic sounds • prescribed instruction • multisensory

❑ Show students how to use study guides and how to highlight reading material effectively.

❑ Teach the skills of skimming (i.e., getting an idea or overview of the material) and scanning (i.e., searching for specific information).

Miscellaneous suggestions

❑ Locate reading material that appeals to adults but is written at lower levels.

❑ Help students to buy used textbooks that have been highlighted well by their previous users.

❑ Have students use taped materials. Schumaker, Deshler, and Denton (1984) have developed a strategy called SOS (Survey, Obtain, and Self-test) in which each of these substrategies has students engage textual/tape materials in a certain way.

❑ Make students aware that many of them may qualify for the services of Recordings for the Blind.

Some of the commercially available programs for teaching reading to adult populations are presented in Table 14.7. Remember that inclusion in this table does not imply endorsement nor is there any attempt to evaluate the quality of any of these programs.

Teaching Writing Skills to Adults

To a great many adults, writing poses their greatest challenge. For some, writing can be avoided to a certain extent, although not totally. However, for others, particularly those adults who are in educational settings, it is a major hindrance. Myklebust (1965) and others have postulated that writing is the highest level of language skill development. The following suggestions are selected examples of ways for helping adults improve or cope with their written language problems.

Handwriting

❑ The ultimate criterion for acceptable handwriting of adults is legibility. Determine whether manuscript or cursive is more useful.

❑ Advise persons with poor handwriting to use a word processor or typewriter.

❑ To systematically teach handwriting skills to adults, one might want to consult a program like *The Writing Road to Reading* (described in Table 14.7).

Spelling

❑ Instruct students in ways to spell both regularly and irregularly spelled words. Deductive approaches are advised over inductive ones.

❑ Multisensory programs that have been suggested as appropriate for use with adults include *A Multi-Sensory Approach to Language Arts for Specific Language Disability Children* (Slingerland, 1971); *Remedial Techniques in Basic School Subjects* (Fernald, 1943); and *The Writing Road to Reading* (Spalding & Spalding, 1969).

❑ It may also be advisable to teach mnemonic strategies for recall of irregularly spelled words.

❑ Show students how to use compensatory aids such as *The Bad Speller's Dictionary* (Krevisky & Linfield, 1967). This resource first provides a phonetic spelling of the word and then presents the correct spelling.

Written expression

❑ As Alley and Deshler (1979) stress, it is important to improve the adolescent's attitude toward the writing process. This is true for adults as well.

❑ Clarify the different purposes for expressive writing and various target audiences (see Polloway et al., 1981).

❑ Give students practice with various functional writing tasks such as copying from other sources and dictation/note-taking.

❑ Capitalize on the adult student's interests, experiences, and curiosity when approaching expressive writing tasks.

❑ Teach students these prewriting skills: identifying topics to write about, researching a topic, organization, and outlining.

❑ Teach students these writing skills: choosing appropriate vocabulary and using words appropriately; analyzing sentences using graphic techniques (i.e., diagramming) (Zink, 1982); sentence combining (i.e., making complex sentences from simple sentences); selecting topic and supporting sentences; awareness of transition words and phrases (this can be done through lists and associated instructional activities); sequencing paragraphs; and facility with capitalization and punctuation.

❑ Teach students these postwriting skills: proofreading for structural changes (techniques of error monitoring like COPS—C = capitalization; O = overall appearance; P = punctuation; S = spelling—are promising) (see Schumaker, Deshler, Alley, Warner, Clark, & Nolan, 1982); and proofreading for ideation changes.

❑ Utilize the services of writing labs and/or writing centers. According to Harris (1981), the focus of labs is on the product, while centers focus more on students' skills and the process of writing.

Teaching Study Skills to Adults

It is extremely important for any number of reasons that adults possess efficient study skills. The general impression is that these skills are relevant only to educational situations. This is hardly the case, as many of these skills are used regularly in our everyday lives. Yet, as Towle (1982) indicates, these skills "belong to an invisible curriculum" (p. 90). Educators infrequently teach study skills to students in any systematic manner, assuming that the skills will be picked up incidently. A listing of which study skills need to be addressed and some specific suggestions and techniques for teaching them are presented below.

Organizational skills

❑ Show students how to manage their time. Provide time sheets if necessary.

❑ Review the way students organize their daily lives. Based on this analysis, suggest ways to improve their systems (e.g., carry small notebook for writing down important information or use stick-on notes to remind them to do something).

❑ Examine students' study habits and make necessary suggestions.

Locational skills

❑ Teach students how to use dictionaries and other reference materials.

❑ Go to the library and show students how to use it.

❑ Provide instruction on the use of graphs, charts, diagrams, tables, figures, and pictures.

Textual material skills

❑ Demonstrate how to use the typical components of textbooks (table of contents, glossary, index).

❏ Present systematic techniques for surveying textual material. Systems like SQ3R (survey, question, read, recite, review) (Robinson, 1946) may be effective. See Clary (1984) for an overview of various survey techniques.

Note-taking skills

❏ Provide examples of effective ways of taking notes. Distribute prepared sheets designed for this task.

❏ Practice having students take notes in a controlled situation, eventually approximating the conditions of the regular classroom.

❏ Consider presenting alternative techniques for taking notes (e.g., mind-mapping).

Memory skills

❏ Match various techniques (e.g., clustering, association, mnemonics, imagery) with the strengths of the student.

❏ Encourage the use of various visual imagery strategies for enhancing memory ability.

❏ Practice the strategies under controlled conditions.

Test-taking skills

❏ In preparing for tests, Alley and Deshler (1979) suggest having students do the following: determine precisely what will be covered on the test; obtain copies of previous tests (if possible); develop a study schedule; become knowledgeable of different testing terms (e.g., *compare, contrast,* etc.); and create in oneself a positive mental attitude.

❏ Teach students to be efficient test takers. The use of a strategy like SCORER (S = schedule time, C = clue words, O = omit difficult questions, R = read carefully, E = estimate answers, R = review answers) can be of great help (Carman & Adams, 1972).

❏ For some students, test anxiety can inhibit their ability to do the best that they are capable of doing. Decker, Polloway, and Decker (1985) summarize three approaches for dealing with this problem: (a) teach appropriate study and test-taking skills; (b) teach relaxation techniques to the student; and (c) change the student's inappropriate expectations.

❏ Cronin and Currie (1984) have put together an excellent guide to materials for the instruction of study skills.

BEST PRACTICES

When working with adults who display a range of learning-related problems, it is essential to keep certain points in mind. First, professionals must be cognizant of the needs of adults. The characteristics of adult learners (Best, 1977) discussed earlier in this chapter highlight the fact that teaching adults is different from teaching children or adolescents. Adults with learning problems raise some additional concerns, because they have most likely experienced years of frustration which may complicate some of the characteristics cited by Best (1977). It is essential that professionals be sensitive to the unique needs of adults, treat them as adults at all times, and use age-appropriate material with them.

Instructionally, there are some encouraging findings resulting from research with learning disabled adolescents and young adults. Deshler, Schumaker, and Lenz (1984) have summarized what seem to be the major components of an effective skills acquisition program. Although much of the research on this system has been conducted with adolescents, the findings appear to have relevance for adults as well. The eight-step procedure is as follows:

❏ task-related pretest

❏ teacher provided rationales for using a skill and description of the skill

❏ teacher modeling of the skill

❏ student verbal rehearsal of the steps involved in the skill to a mastery recall level

❏ controlled practice (or ability-level practice)

❏ advanced practice (or grade-appropriate practice)

❏ positive and corrective feedback throughout practice

❏ task-related post-test (p. 112)

It will also be necessary to use existing services with adult populations as much as possible. Within postsecondary educational settings, these resources might include counseling services, writing labs/centers, various diagnostic clinics, and consultation with specific faculty and staff. In community settings, these services would involve adult basic education classes, mental health centers, private tutoring/educational agencies, and other training facilities. There are two realities associated with these suggestions: (a) In many areas of the country, these options do not exist or are not appropriate; and (b) there are very few professionals trained to work with adults with learning-related problems.

The overriding goal is to provide adults with the skills and knowledge that they desire and that they might need to deal successfully with the demands of everyday living. It has become obvious that "consideration of learning problems can no longer be restricted to the school-age individual" (Patton & Polloway, 1982, p. 86). Ultimately, we want adults to be as independent as possible, as Bacigalupo (1981) has suggested. However, they may need some assistance along the way.

REFERENCES

Abrahamsen, A., Cavallo, M., & McCluer, J. (1985). Is the sign advantage a robust phenomenon? From gesture to language in two modalities. *Merrill-Palmer Quarterly, 31*, 177–209.

Academic Therapy (1984). *20*(1), 77–81.

Alberto, P., Jobes, N., Sizemore, A., & Doran, D. (1980). A comparison of individual and group instruction across response tasks. *Journal of the Association for the Severely Handicapped, 5*, 285–293.

Alberto, P. A., & Troutman, A. C. (1986) *Applied behavior analysis for teachers* (2nd ed.). Columbus, OH: Charles E. Merrill.

Algozzine, B., & Korinek, L. (1985). Where is special education for students with high prevalence handicaps going? *Exceptional Children, 51*, 388–394.

Algozzine, B., Mirkin, P., Thurlow, M., & Graden, J. (1981, October). *Opportunity to learn as a function of what your teacher thinks of you—practice, practice, practice: An update on the work of the Minnesota Research Institute.* Paper presented at the Third Annual Conference of the Council for Learning Disabilities, Houston, TX.

Allen, R. V., & Allen, C. (1982). *Language experience activities* (2nd ed.). Boston: Houghton Mifflin.

Alley, G. R., & Deshler, D. D. (1979). *Teaching the learning disabled adolescent: Strategies and methods.* Denver, CO: Love Publishing.

Alley, G., Deshler, D., & Warner, M. (1979). Identification of learning disabled adolescents: A Bayesian approach. *Learning Disability Quarterly, 2* (2), 76–83.

Allred, R. A. (1984). *Spelling trends, content, and methods.* Washington, DC: National Education Association.

Anastasi, A. (1982). *Psychological testing* (5th ed.). New York: Macmillan.

Anderson, P. L. (1983). *Denver handwriting analysis.* Novato, CA: Academic Therapy Press.

Anderson, P. S. (1972). *Language skills in elementary education.* New York: Macmillan.

Apple, N. C. (1979). *A study of the literature objectives of the Pittsburgh Scholars Program in English, Grades 10 and 11.* Unpublished doctoral dissertation, University of Pittsburgh.

Archer, L. (1977). Blissymbols—A nonverbal communication system. *Journal of Speech and Hearing Disorders, 42*, 568–579.

Aukerman, R. C. (1981). *The basal reader approach to reading.* New York: John Wiley.

Aukerman, R. C., & Aukerman, L. R. (1981). *How do I teach reading?* New York: John Wiley.

Aulls, M. W. (1982). *Developing readers in today's elementary school.* Boston: Allyn & Bacon.

Ausubel, D. P., & Sullivan, E. V. (1970). *Theory and problems of child development.* New York: Grune & Stratton.

Baca, L. M., & Cervantes. H. T. (1984). *The bilingual special education interface.* St. Louis: C. V. Mosby.

Bachara, G. (1976). Empathy in learning disabled children. *Perceptual and Motor Skills, 43,* 541–542.

Bacigalupo, M. (1981). Identification and accommodation of the college qualified learning disabled student. In S. H. Simon (Ed.), *The accessible institution of higher education: Opportunity, challenge, and response.* Ames, IA: Association on Handicapped Student Service Programs in Postsecondary Education. (ERIC Document Reproduction Service No. ED 216 486)

Bain, A. M. (1982). Written expression: Assessment and remediation for learning disabled students. *Learning Disabilities, 1*(5), 49–61.

Ballard, K. D., & Glynn, T. (1975). Behavioral self-management in story writing with elementary school children. *Journal of Applied Behavior Analysis, 8,* 387–398.

Bandura, A. (1977). *Social learning theory.* Englewood Cliffs, NJ: Prentice-Hall.

Baratz, J. C., & Shuy, R. W. (Eds.). (1969). *Teaching black children to read.* Washington Center for Applied Linguistics.

Barbe, W. B. (1975). *Barbe Reading Skills Check Lists.* Honesdale, PA.

Barbe, W. B., & Milone, M. N. (1985). Reading and writing. In R. H. Swassing, *Teaching gifted children and adolescents* (pp. 276–313). Columbus, OH: Charles E. Merrill.

Barbe, W. B., Milone, M. N., & Wasylyk, T. M. (1983). Manuscript is the "write" start. *Academic Therapy, 18,* 397–405.

Barbe, W. B., Renzulli, J. M., Labuda, M., & Callahan, C. (1971). Innovative reading programs for the gifted and creative. In P. A. Witz (Ed.), *Reading for the gifted and creative student.* Newark, DE: International Reading Association.

Barenbaum, E. M. (1983). Writing in the special class. *Topics in Learning and Learning Disabilities, 3*(3), 12–20.

Barsch, J. (1980). Community college: New opportunities for the LD child. *Academic Therapy, 15,* 467–470.

Bartel, N. R., & Bryen, D. N. (1982). Problems in language development. In D. D. Hammill, & N. R. Bartel (Eds.), *Teaching students with learning and behavior problems* (pp. 283–376). Boston: Allyn & Bacon.

Bates, E. (1976). *Language and context: The acquisition of pragmatics.* New York: Academic Press.

Bates, E., Bengni, L., Bretherton, I., & Volterra, V. (1979). *The emergence of symbols: Cognition and communication in infancy.* New York: Academic Press.

Bauer, R. H. (1977). Memory processes in children with learning disabilities: Evidence for deficient rehearsal. *Journal of Experimental Child Psychology, 24,* 415–430.

Bayley, N. (1969). *Bayley Scales of Infant Development.* New York: The Psychological Corp.

Beck, I. L. (1977). Comprehension during the acquisition of decoding skills. In J. T. Guthrie, (Ed.), *Cognition, curriculum, and comprehension* (pp. 113–156). Newark, DE: International Reading Association.

Becker, H. J. (1983). How schools use microcomputers. *Classroom Computer Learning, 4*(2), 41–44.

Becker, W. C. (1977). Teaching reading and language to the disadvantaged: What have we learned from field research. *Harvard Educational Review, 47,* 518–543.

Becker, W. C., & Carnine, D. W. (1980). Direct instruction. In B. B. Lahey & A. E. Kazden (Eds.), *Advances in clinical child psychology* (Vol. 3, pp. 429–473). New York: Plenum Press.

Becker, W. C., Engelmann, S., & Thomas, D. R. (1975). *Teaching 2: Cognitive learning and instruction.* Chicago: Science Research Associates.

Beers, J. W., & Henderson, E. (1977). A study of developing orthographic concepts among first graders. *Research in the Teaching of English, 11,* 133–148.

Behrmann, M. (1984). *Handbook of microcomputers in special education.* San Diego: College Hill Press.

Bereiter, C., & Engelmann, S. (1966). *Teaching disadvantaged children in the preschool.* Englewood Cliffs, NJ: Prentice-Hall.

Berger, N. S. (1978). Why can't Johnny read? Perhaps he's not a good listener. *Journal of Learning Disabilities, 11,* 633–638.

Berko, J. (1958). The child's learning of English morphology. *Word, 14,* 150–177.

Bernstein, B. (1961). Social class and linguistic development: A theory of social learning. In H. A. Halsey, J. Floud, & C. A. Anderson (Eds.), *Education, economy, and society* (pp. 288–314). New York: Free Press.

Best, G. C. (1977). *The problems of the adult learner: A handbook for teachers.* Palatine, IL: William Raney Harper College. (ERIC Document Reproduction Service No. ED 194 705)

Betts, E. A. (1956). *Foundations of reading instruction.* New York: American Book Co.

Biberdorf, J. R., & Pear, J. J. (1977). Two-to-one versus one-to-one student-teacher ratios in the operant verbal training of retarded children. *Journal of Applied Behavior Analysis, 10,* 506.

Bingham, G. (1978). *Working with adult exceptional learners: A handbook of suggestions for assessment, educational planning and instructional strategies.* New Brunswick, NJ: Center for Adult Development, Rutgers University. (ERIC Document Reproduction Service No. ED 167 725)

Bischoff, R. W. (1967). Improvement of listening comprehension in partially sighted students. *Sight Saving Review, 37,* 3.

Bischoff, R. W. (1979). Listening: A teachable skill for visually impaired persons. *Journal of Visual Impairment and Blindness, 73,* 59–67.

Bishop, P., & French, R. (1982). Effects of reinforcers on attending behavior of severely handicapped boys in physical education. *Journal for Special Educators, 18,* 48–57.

Bishop, V. E. (1971). *Teaching the visually limited child.* Springfield, IL: Charles C. Thomas.

Blackwell, P., Eugene, E., Fischgrund, J., & Zarcadoolas, C. (1978). *Sentences and other systems.* Washington, DC: Alexander Graham Bell Association.

Blalock, G., & Dixon, N. (1982). Improving prospects for the college-bound learning disabled. *Topics in Learning & Learning Disabilities, 2*(3), 69–78.

Blalock, J. W. (1981). Persistent problems and concerns of young adults with learning disabilities. In W. Cruickshank & A. Silvers (Eds.), *Bridges for tomorrow: The Best of ACLD* (Vol. 2, pp. 137–157). Syracuse, NY: Syracuse University Press.

Blalock, J. W. (1982). Persistent auditory language disorders in adults with learning disabilities. *Journal of Learning Disabilities, 15,* 604–609.

Bliss, C. K. (1965). *Semantography—Blissymbolics.* Sydney, Australia: Semantography Publications.

Block, K. K., Tucker, S. A., & Butler, P. A. (1974). *Spelling, learning and retention under variations in focal unit of word presentation in a computer assisted spelling drill.* Pittsburgh: Learning Research and Development Center, University of Pittsburgh.

Block, K., Tucker, S., & Peskowitz, N. (1972). *Drill-and-practice in CAI spelling: Word ratings and instructional treatment.* Project Interim Report No. 1. Pittsburgh: Learning Research and Development Center, University of Pittsburgh.

Bloom, L., & Lahey, M. (1978). *Language development and language disorders.* New York: John Wiley.

Bloomfield, L. (1933). *Language.* New York: Holt, Rinehart and Winston.

Bond, G. L., Tinker, M. A., & Wasson, B. B. (1979). *Reading difficulties: Their diagnosis and correction* (4th ed.). Englewood Cliffs, NJ: Prentice-Hall.

Bookman, M. (1984). Spelling as a cognitive-developmental linguistic process. *Academic Therapy, 20*(1), 21–31.

Bootzin, R. R., Bower, G. H., Zajonc, R. B., & Hall, E. (1986). *Psychology today: An introduction* (6th ed.). New York: Random House.

Borus, J. F., Greenfield, S., Spiegel, B., & Daniels, G. (1973). Establishing imitative speech employing operant techniques in a group setting. *Journal of Speech and Hearing Disorders, 38,* 533–541.

Bos, C. S. (1982). Getting past decoding: Assisted and repeated readings as remedial methods for learning disabled students. *Topics in Learning and Learning Disabilities, 1,* 51–57.

Boucher, C. R. (1984). Pragmatics: The verbal language of learning disabled and non-disabled boys. *Learning Disability Quarterly, 7,* 266–270.

Bourque, M. L. (1980). Specifications and validation of reading skill hierarchies. *Reading Research Quarterly, 15,* 237–267.

Bowe, F. (1984). Micros and special education. *Popular Computing, 3*(13),121–128.

Bower, E. M. (1981). *Early identification of emotionally handicapped children in school* (3rd ed.). Springfield, IL: Charles C. Thomas.

Bricker, D., & Dennison, L. (1978). Training prerequisites to verbal behavior. In M. Snell (Ed.), *Systematic instruction of the moderately and severely handicapped* (pp. 157–178). Columbus, OH: Charles E. Merrill.

Brigham, T., Graubard, P., & Stans, D. (1972). Analysis of the effects of sequential reinforcement contingencies on aspects of composition. *Journal of Applied Behavior Analysis, 5,* 421–429.

Brophy, J., & Good, T. (1986). Teacher behavior and student achievement. In (Eds.), *Handbook of research on teaching* (3rd ed., pp. 328–375).

Brown, F. (1986, January). Functional assessment tool subcommittee report. *TASH Newsletter,* 2–3.

Brown, L., Hermanson, J., Klemme, H., Hanbrich, P., & Ora, J. P. (1986). Using behavior modification principles to teach sight vocabulary. *Teaching Exceptional Children, 2,* 120–128.

Brown, R. (1973). *A first language: The early stages.* Cambridge, MA: Harvard University Press.

Brown, V. L., Hammill, D. D., & Wiederholt, J. L. (1986). Test of Reading Comprehension. Austin, TX: PRO-ED.

Bruner, J. (1972). The course of cognitive growth. In A. Cashden & E. Grugion (Eds.), *Language in education: A source book* (p. 165). London: Routledge & Kegan Paul.

Bruner, J. S. (1974–75). From communication to language—A psychosocial perspective. *Cognition, 3,* 255–287.

Bruner, J. S. (1977). Early social interaction and language acquisition. In H. R. Schaffer (Ed.) *Studies in mother-infant interaction.* New York: Academic Press.

Bruner, J. S. (1978). Learning the mother tongue. *Human Nature, 1*(9), 42–49.

Bryan, T. (1974). An observational analysis of classroom behaviors of children with learning disabilities. *Journal of Learning Disabilities, 7,* 26–34.

Bryan, T. (1979). *Let's go, cabbagehead: Syntactics and pragmatics of learning disabled children's communication.* Paper presented to the American Psychological Association, New York.

Bryan, T. (1983, October). *The hidden curriculum: Social and communication skills.* Paper presented at Lynchburg College, Lynchburg, VA.

Bryan, T. L., Donahue, M., & Pearl, R. (1981). Studies in learning disabled children's pragmatic competence. *Topics in Learning and Learning Disabilities, 1*(2), 29–39.

Bryan, W. H., & Jeffrey, D. L. (1982). Education of visually handicapped students in the regular classroom. *Texas Tech Journal of Education, 9,* 125–131.

Bryen, D. N., Hartman, C., & Tait, P. E. (1978). *Variant English.* Columbus, OH: Charles E. Merrill.

Bryen, D., & Joyce, D. (1985). Language intervention with the severely handicapped: A decade of research. *Journal of Special Education, 19,* 7–36.

Buchanan, C. (1966). *Programmed reading.* New York: McGraw-Hill.

Burkhardt, L. (1982). *More homemade battery devices for severely handicapped children with suggested activities.* Millville, PA: Author.

Burling, R. (1973). *English in black and white.* New York: Holt, Rinehart and Winston.

Burns, P. C. (1974). *Diagnostic teaching of the language arts.* Itasca, IL: F. E. Peacock.

Burns, P. C. (1980). *Assessment and correction of language arts difficulties.* Columbus, OH: Charles E. Merrill.

Burns, P. C., & Broman, B. L. (1983). *The language arts in childhood education* (5th ed.). Boston: Houghton Mifflin.

Burns, P. C., & Roe, B. D. (1985). *Informal Reading Inventory.* Boston: Houghton Mifflin.

Burns, P. C., Roe, B. D., & Ross, E. P. (1984). *Teaching reading in today's elementary schools.* Boston: Houghton Mifflin.

Bush, C. L., & Huebner, M. H. (1979). *Strategies for reading in the elementary school* (2nd ed.). New York: Macmillan.

Bzoch, K., & League, R. (1970). *Receptive-Expressive Emergent Language Scale.* Bainesville, FL: Assorted Publications.

Calhoun, M. L. (1985). Typing contrasted with handwriting in language arts instruction for moderately retarded students. *Education and Training of the Mentally Retarded, 20,* 48–52.

Carlson, F. (1981). A format for selecting vocabulary for the nonspeaking child. *Language, Speech, and Hearing Services in the Schools,* XII, 240–245.

Carlson, R. K. (1970). *Writing aids through the grades.* New York: Teacher's College Press.

Carman, R. A., & Adams, W. R. (1972). *Study skills: A student's guide for survival.* New York: John Wiley.

Carpenter, D., & Miller, L. J. (1982). The spelling of reading disabled students and able readers. *Learning Disability Quarterly, 5,* 65–70.

Carr, E. G. (1985). Behavioral approaches to language and communication. In E. Schopler (Ed.), *Communication problems in autism* (pp. 37–58). New York: Plenum Press.

Carr, E., Schreibman, L., & Lovaas, O. I. (1975). Control of echolalic speech in psychotic children. *Journal of Abnormal Child Psychology, 3,* 331–351.

Carr, K. S. (1984). What gifted readers need from reading instruction. *The Reading Teacher, 38,* 144–146.

Carrier, J. K., Jr. (1973). *Application of functional analysis and nonspeech response mode to teaching language* (Report No. 7). Parsons, KS: Kansas Center for Research in Mental Retardation and Human Development.

Carrier, J. K., Jr., & Peak, T. (1975). *Nonspeech language initiation program.* Lawrence, KS: H & H.

Carrow, E. (1974). *Carrow elicited language inventory.* Austin, TX: Learning Concepts.

Cartwright, G. P. (1969). Written expression and spelling. In R. M. Smith (Ed.), *Teacher diagnosis of education difficulties* (pp. 95–117). Columbus, OH: Charles E. Merrill.

Cassidy, J. (1981). Inquiry reading for the gifted. *Reading Teacher, 35,* 17–21.

Cassie, D. (1976). *The auditory training handbook for good listeners.* Danville, IL: Interstate.

Cavallaro, C. (1983). Language interventions in natural settings. *Teaching Exceptional Children, 16,* 65–71.

Chall, J. S. (1983). *Stages of reading development.* New York: McGraw-Hill.

Chapman, R. S., & Miller, J. F. (1980). Analyzing language and communication in the child. In R. Schiefelbusch (Ed.), *Nonspeech language and communication: Analysis and intervention* (pp. 159–190). Austin, TX: PRO-ED.

Chappell, G. E., & Johnson, G. A. (1976). Evaluation of cognitive behavior in the young nonverbal child. *Language, Speech and Hearing Services in the Schools, 7,* 17–27.

Charles, C. M. (1974). *Teacher's petit Piaget.* Belmont, CA: Fearon.

Charlop, L., & Thibodeau, M. (1985). Increasing spontaneous verbal responding in autistic children using a time delay procedure. *Journal of Applied Behavior Analysis, 18,* 155–166.

Childs, S. B., & Childs, R. (1971). *Sound spelling.* Cambridge, MA: Educators Publishing Service.

Chomsky, N. (1967). The formal nature of language. In E. Lenneberg (Ed.), *Biological foundations of language* (pp. 397–442). New York: John Wiley.

Civelli, E. (1983). Verbalism in young children. *Journal of Visual Impairment and Blindness, 77,* 61–63.

Clark, C. (1981). Learning words using traditional orthography and the symbols of Rebus, Bliss, and Carrier. *Journal of Speech and Hearing Disorders, 46,* 191–196.

Clark, C., Davies, M., & Woodcock, R. (1974). *Standard rebus glossary.* Circle Pines, MN: American Guidance Service.

Clark, C., & Woodcock, R. (1976). Graphic systems of communication. In L. L. Lloyd (Ed.), *Communication assessment and intervention strategies* (pp. 549–605). Baltimore: University Park Press.

Clarke, L. (1973). *Can't read, can't write, can't talk too good either.* New York: Penguin.

Clary, L. M. (1984). The application of study techniques with learning disabled adolescents. In W. M. Cruickshank & J. M. Kliebhan (Eds.), *Early adolescence to early adulthood* (pp. 49–60). Syracuse: Syracuse University Press.

Cohen, J. (1984). The learning disabled university student: Signs and initial screening. *NSAPA Journal, 21*(3), 22–31.

Cohen, S. A., & Cooper, T. (1972). Seven fallacies: Reading, retardation, and the urban disadvantaged reader. *Reading Teachers, 26,* 38–45.

Cohen, S. B., & Plaskon, S. P. (1980). *Language arts for the mildly handicapped.* Columbus, OH: Charles E. Merrill.

Compton, C. (1984). *A guide to 75 tests for special education.* Belmont, CA: Fearon.

Connard, P. (1984). *Preverbal Assessment Intervention Profile.* Portland, OR: ASIEP.

Connell, D. (1983). Handwriting: Taking a look at the alternatives. *Academic Therapy, 18,* 413–420.

Cooper, L. R. (1980). The preparation of teachers for developmental studies programs. *Community College Review, 7,* 36–40.

Coplan, J. (1983). *Early Language Milestone Scale.* Tulsa, OK: Modern Education Corp.

Corbin, R. (1966). *The teaching of writing in our schools.* New York: Macmillan.

Cordoni, B. (1979). Assisting dyslexic college students: An experimental program design at a university. *Bulletin of the Orton Society, 29,* 263–268.

Cornett, O. (1967). Cued speech. *American Annals of the Deaf, 112,* 3–13.

Corrigan, R. (1978). Language development as related to Stage 6 object permanence development. *Journal of Child Language, 5,* 173–189.

Cox, S. (1977). The learning disabled adult. *Academic Therapy, 13,* 79–86.

Crabtree, M. (1963). *Houston test of language development.* Chicago: Stoelting.

Creative growth through handwriting (2nd ed.). (1978). Columbus, OH: Zaner-Bloser.

Creedon, M. P. (1973). Language development in nonverbal autistic children using a simultaneous communication system. Paper presented at Society for Research in Child Development Meeting, Philadelphia. In R. Schiefelbusch (Ed.) *Nonspeech language and communication: Analysis and intervention* (p. 43). Austin, TX: PRO-ED.

Creedon, M. P. (1976, July). *The David School: A simultaneous communication model.* Paper presented to the National Society for Autistic Children meeting, Oak Brook, IL.

Cronin, M. E., & Currie, P. S. (1984). Study skills: A resource guide for practitioners. *Remedial and Special Education, 5*(2), 61–69.

Cummins, J. (1980). Psychological assessment of emigrant children: Logic or intuition? *Journal of Multilingual and Multicultural Development, 1,* 97–111.

Cunningham, M. A. (1968). A comparison of the language of psychotic and non-psychotic children who are mentally retarded. *Journal of Child Psychology and Psychiatry, 9,* 229–244.

Cunningham, P. M. (1976–1977). Teacher's correction responses to black-dialect miscues which are non-meaning-changing. *Reading Research Quarterly, 4,* 637–653.

Cunningham, P. M., & Cunningham, J. W. (1976). Improving listening in content area subjects. *NASSP Bulletin, 60*(404), 26–31.

Curcio, F. (1978). Sensorimotor functioning and communication in mute autistic children. *Journal of Autism and Childhood Schizophrenia, 3,* 281–292.

Cureton, L. R., Dunn, M. M., Grossman, D. L., Johnston, C. A., Lunsford, D. B., Mejia-Gjiurdici, C., & Swanson, P. S. (1983). *Developmental language curriculum.* Fairfax, VA: Fairfax County Public Schools.

Cushenberry, D. C., & Howell, H. (1974). *Reading and the gifted child: A guide for teachers.* Springfield, IL: Charles C. Thomas.

Cutsforth, T. D. (1951). *The blind in school and society.* New York: American Foundation for the Blind.

Dahl, P., & Samuels, S. J. (1977). Teaching children to read using hypothesis test strategies. *The Reading Teacher, 30,* 603–606.

Dale, P. S. (1976). *Language development: Structure and function* (2nd ed.). New York: Holt, Rinehart and Winston.

D'Alonzo, B. J. (1981). Time compressed speech and the listening comprehension of educable mentally retarded students. *Mental Retardation, 19*(4), 177–179.

D'Angelo, K. (1982). Developing legibility and uniqueness in handwriting. *Language Arts, 59,* 23–27.

Davies, G. H., (1973). Linguistics and language therapy: The sentence construction board. *Journal of Speech and Hearing Disorders, 38,* 205–214.

Davis, D., & Miller, B. (1983). Why should I learn to write? *Academic Therapy, 18,* 431–435.

Davis, V. I. (1975). *Including the language learning disabled student in the college English class.* Paper presented at 26th annual meeting of the Conference on College Composition, St. Louis. (ERIC Document Reproduction Service No. ED 114 823)

Decker, T. W., Polloway, E. A., & Decker, B. B. (1985). Help for the LD college student. *Academic Therapy, 20,* 339–345.

DeHaven, E. P. (1983). *Teaching and learning the language arts* (2nd ed.). Boston: Little, Brown.

DeMaster, V., Crossland, C., & Hasselbring, T. (1986). Consistency of learning disabled students' spelling performance. *Learning Disability Quarterly, 9*(1), 84–88.

Denham, C., & Lieberman, A. (1980). *Time to learn.* Washington, DC: National Institute of Education.

Dennis, W. (1960). Causes of retardation among institutional children: Iran. *Journal of Genetic Psychology, 96,* 47–59.

Deno, S. L., Mirkin, P. K., Lowry, L., & Kuehnle, K. (1980). *Relationships among simple measures of spelling and performance on standardized achievement tests* (Research Report No. 21). Minneapolis: University of Minnesota, Institute for Research on Learning Disabilities.

Deshler, D. D. (1978). Psychoeducational aspects of learning disabled adolescents. In L. Mann, L. Goodman & J. L. Wiederholt (Eds.), *Teaching the learning disabled adolescent* (pp. 48–74). Boston: Houghton Mifflin.

Deshler, D. D., Schumaker, J. B., & Lenz, B. K. (1984). Academic and cognitive interventions for LD adolescents: Part I. *Journal of Learning Disabilities, 17,* 108–117.

DeStefano, J. S. (1978). *Language, the learner, and the school.* New York: John Wiley.

Devine, T. G. (1981). *Teaching study skills: A guide for teachers.* Boston: Allyn & Bacon.

Dexter, B. L. (1977). *Special education and the classroom teacher: Current perspectives and strategies.* Springfield, IL: Charles C. Thomas.

Dieterich, T., Freeman, C., & Griffin, P. (1978). *Assessing comprehension in a school setting.* Arlington, VA: Center for Applied Linguistics.

DiStefano, P., Dole, J. A., & Marzano, R. J. (1984). *Elementary language arts.* New York: John Wiley.

Dixon, C. C., & Curry, B. (1973). Some thoughts on the communication board. *Journal of Speech and Hearing Disorders, 38,* 73–88.

Dolch, E. W. (1953). *The Dolch basic sight word list.* Champaign, IL: Gerrard.

Donahue, M., & Bryan, T. (1984). Communicative skills and peer relations of LD adolescents. *Topics in Language Disorders, 4*(2), 10–21.

Donlon, T. F. (1978). Review of Test of Adult Basic Education. In O. K. Buros (Ed.), *The eighth mental measurements yearbook.* Highland Park, NJ: Gryphon Press.

Donnellan-Walsh, A., Gossage, L. D., LaVigna, G. W., Schuler, A., & Traphagen, J. D. (1976). *Teaching makes a difference: A guide for developing successful classes for autistic and other severely handicapped children.* Santa Barbara, CA: Santa Barbara Public Schools.

Dore, G. (1975). Holophrases, speech acts, and language universals. *Journal of Child Language, 2,* 21–40.

Downing, J. (1965). *The initial teaching alphabet experiment.* Chicago: Scott Foresman.

Dudley-Marling, C. (1985). The pragmatic skills of learning disabled children: A review. *Journal of Learning Disabilities, 18,* 193–199.

Duker, P., & van Grinsven, D. (1983). The effect of gestural facilitation on the acquisition of noun-verb labeling responses with severely retarded individuals. *Journal of Special Education Technology, 6,* 20–27.

Dunn, L. (1968). Special education for the mildly retarded: Is much of it justifiable? *Exceptional Children, 35,* 5–22.

Durrell, D. D., & Catterson, J. H. (1980). *Durrell Analysis of Reading Difficulty* (3rd ed.). Cleveland, OH: Psychological Corp.

Durost, W. N., Bixler, H. H., Wrightstone, J. W., Prescott, G. A., & Balow, I. H. (1971). *Metropolitan achievement test.* New York: Harcourt, Brace, Jovanovich.

Dwyer, C. A. (1978). Woodcock Reading Mastery Test. In O. K. Buros (Ed.), *The eighth mental measurements yearbook*, (Vol. II, pp. 1303–1305). Highland Park, NJ: Gryphon Press.

Early, G. H., Nelson, D. A., Kleber, D. J., Treegoob, M., Huffman, E., & Cass, C. (1976). Cursive handwriting, reading, and spelling achievement. *Academic Therapy, 12*(1), 67–84.

Edmark Associates (1972). *Edmark reading program*. Bellevue, WA: Authors.

Ekwall, E. E. (1985). *Locating and correcting reading difficulties* (4th ed.). Columbus, OH: Charles E. Merrill.

Ekwall, E. E., & Shanker, J. L. (1983). *Diagnosis and remediation of the disabled reader* (2nd ed.). Boston: Allyn & Bacon.

Elium, M. D., & McCarver, R. B. (1980). *Group vs. individual training on a self-help skill with the profoundly retarded*. (ERIC Document Reproduction Service No. ED 223 060)

Engelmann, S., Becker, W. C., Hanner, S., & Johnson, G. (1980). *Corrective reading program*. Chicago: Science Research Associates.

Engelmann, S., & Bruner, E. (1969). *Distar: An instructional system*. Chicago: Science Research Associates.

Engelmann, S., & Bruner, E. (1984). *Reading mastery: Distar*. Chicago: Science Research Associates.

Engelmann, S., & Osborn, J. (1971, 1972, 1976). *Distar: An instructional system* (for language). Chicago: Science Research Associates.

Epstein, M. H., Hallahan, D. P., & Kauffman, J. M. (1975). Implications of the reflectivity-impulsivity dimension for special education. *Journal of Special Education, 9*, 11–25.

Esquivel, G. B., & Yoshida, R. K. (1985). Special education for language minority students. *Focus on Exceptional Children, 18*(3) 1–8.

Evans-Morris, S. (1981). Communication/interaction development at mealtimes for the multiply handicapped child? Implications for the use of augmentative communication systems. *Language, Speech and Hearing Services in the Schools, 12*, 216–233.

Evans-Morris, S. (1984). *Pre-Speech Assessment Scale: A rating scale for the measurement of pre-speech behaviors from birth through two years*. Clifton, NJ: J. A. Preston.

Fairweather, B. C., Haun, D. H., & Finkle, L. J. (1983). *Communication systems for severely handicapped persons*. Springfield, IL: Charles C. Thomas.

Farr, R. (1969). *Reading: What can be measured?* Newark DE: International Reading Association.

Fauke, J., Burnett, J., Powers, M. A., & Suzer-Azaroff, B. (1973). Improvement of handwriting and letter recognition skills: A behavior modification procedure. *Journal of Learning Disabilities, 6*, 296–300.

Favell, J. E., Favell, J. E., & McGimsey, J. F. (1978). Relative effectiveness and efficiency of group vs. individual training of severely retarded persons. *American Journal of Mental Deficiency, 83*, 104–109.

Fernald, G. M. (1943). *Remedial techniques in basic school subjects*. New York: McGraw-Hill.

Filer, P. S. (1981). Conversations with language delayed children: How to get them talking. *Academic Therapy, 17*, 57–62.

Fink, W. T., & Sandall, S. R. (1978). One-to-one vs. group academic instruction with handicapped and nonhandicapped preschool children. *Mental Retardation, 16,* 236–240.

Fink, W. T., & Sandall, S. R. (1980). A comparison of one-to-one and small group instruction strategies with developmentally disabled preschoolers. *Mental Retardation, 18,* 34–35.

Fisher, F. (1984). Spelling by speech synthesis: A new technology for an old problem. *Annual Review of Learning Disabilities, 2,* 150–151.

Fishman, E. (1968). Massed versus distributed practice in computerized spelling drills. *Journal of Educational Psychology, 59,* 290–296.

Fitzgerald, E. (1929). *Straight language for the deaf.* Staunton, VA: McClure.

Fitzgerald, J. (1951). *A basic life spelling vocabulary.* Milwaukee, WI: Bruce.

Flanagan, K. (1982). Computer needs of severely mentally retarded persons. *Journal of Special Education Technology, 5,* 47–50.

Flavell, J. H. (1977). *Cognitive development.* Englewood Cliffs, NJ: Prentice-Hall.

Fokes, J. (1976). *Fokes sentence builder.* New York: Teaching Resources.

Forness, S. R., & Kavale, K. A. (1984). Education of the mentally retarded: A note on policy. *Education and Training of the Mentally Retarded, 19,* 239–245.

Frankel, F., & Graham, V. (1976). Systematic observation of classroom behavior of retarded and autistic preschool children. *American Journal of Mental Deficiency, 81,* 73–84.

Fraueheim, J. (1978). Academic achievement characteristics of adult males who were diagnosed as dyslexic in childhood. *Journal of Learning Disabilities, 11*(8) 476–483.

Freedle, R., & Lewis, M. (1977). Prelinguistic conversations. In M. Lewis & L. A. Rosenblum (Eds.), *Interaction, conversation, and the development of language* (pp. 157–186). New York: John Wiley.

Fristoe, M., & Lloyd, L. (1977). Manual communication for the retarded and others with severe communication impairment: A resource list. *Mental Retardation, 15*(5), 18–21.

Fristoe, M., & Lloyd, L. (1979). Nonspeech communication. In N. R. Ellis (Ed.), *Handbook of mental deficiency: Psychological theory and research* (pp. 401–430). Hillsdale, NJ: Erlbaum.

Frith, V., & Frith, C. (1980). Relationships between reading and spelling. In J. F. Kavanagh & R. L. Venezky (Eds.), *Orthography, Reading, and Dyslexia* (pp. 287–296). Austin, TX: PRO-ED.

Gallagher, J. J. (1975). *Teaching the gifted child* (2nd ed.). Boston: Allyn & Bacon.

Garber, N. B., & David, L. C. (1975). Semantic considerations in the treatment of echolalia. *Mental Retardation, 13,* 8–11.

Gates, A. I., & McKillop, A. S. (1962). *Gates-McKillop Reading Diagnostic Tests.* New York: Bureau of Publications, Teachers College Press, Columbia University.

Gates, A. I., McKillop, A. S., & Horowitz, E. C. (1981). *Gates-McKillop-Horowitz Reading Diagnostic Test.* Scranton, PA: Harper & Row.

Genishi, C. (1981). Language across the contexts of early childhood. *Theory into Practice, 20*(2), 109–115.

Gentry, J. R. (1978). Early spelling strategies. *Elementary School Journal, 79,* 88–92.

Gentry, J. R. (1982). An analysis of developmental spelling in GNYS AT WRK. *The Reading Teacher, 36*, 192–200.

Gentry, J. R. (1984). Developmental aspects of learning to spell. *Academic Therapy, 20*(1), 11–19.

Gerber, A., & Bryen, D. (1984). *Language and learning disabilities.* Austin, TX: PRO-ED.

Gerber, M. M. (1984). The Department of Education's sixth annual report to Congress on PL 94-142: Is Congress getting the full story? *Exceptional Children, 51*, 209–224.

Gerber, M. M., & Cohen, S. B. (1985). Assessment of spelling skills. In A. F. Rotatori & R. Fox (Eds.), *Assessment for regular and special education teachers* (pp. 249–278). Austin, TX: PRO-ED.

Gerber, M. & Hall, R. (1985). *The development of spelling in learning disabled and normal students* (Monograph No. 1). Austin, TX: Society for Learning Disabilities and Remedial Education.

Gerston, R., Brockway, M. A., & Henares, N. (1983). The Monterey DI Program for students with limited English (ESL). *Association for Direct Instruction News, 2*(4), 8–9.

Gettinger, M. (1984). Applying learning principles to remedial spelling instruction. *Academic Therapy, 20*(1), 41–47.

Gillespie-Silver, P. (1979). *Teaching reading to children with special needs.* Columbus, OH: Charles E. Merrill.

Gillingham, A., & Stillman, B. (1970). *Remedial training for children with specific difficulty in reading, spelling, and penmanship* (7th ed.). Cambridge, MA: Educators Publishing Service.

Gilmore, J. V., & Gilmore, E. C. (1968). *Gilmore Oral Reading Test.* New York: Harcourt Brace Jovanovich.

Giordano, G. (1982). CATS exercises: Teaching disabled writers to communicate. *Academic Therapy, 18*, 233–237.

Gladney, M. R. (1972). A teaching strategy. In R. E. Hodges & E. H. Rudorf (Eds.), *Language and learning to read* (pp. 73–83). Boston: Houghton Mifflin.

Glover, J., & Gary, A. L. (1976). Procedures to increase some aspects of creativity. *Journal of Applied Behavior Analysis, 9*, 79–84.

Goldberg, H. R., & Fenton, G. (1960). *Aphonic communication for those with cerebral palsy: Guide for the development and use of a communication board.* New York: United Cerebral Palsy of New York State.

Gollnick, D. M., & Chinn, P. C. (1986). *Multicultural education in a pluralistic society* (2nd ed.). Columbus, OH: Charles E. Merrill.

Golub, L. S., & Kidder, C. (1974). Syntactic density and the computer. *Elementary English, 51*, 1128–1131.

Goodman, K. (1965). Dialect barriers to reading comprehension. *Elementary English, 41*, 853–860.

Goodman, K. S. (1972). Reading: The key is in children's language. *The Reading Teacher, 25*, 505–508.

Goodman, K. S. (1973). Miscues: windows on reading. In K. S. Goodman (Ed.), *Miscue analysis.* Urbana, IL: ERIC Clearinghouse.

Goodman, Y. M., & Burke, C. I. (1972). *Reading Miscue Inventory: Manual procedure for diagnosis and remediation.* New York: Macmillan.

Goodrich, G. L. (1984). Applications of microcomputers by visually impaired persons. *Journal of Visual Impairment and Blindness, 78,* 408–414.

Graham, S. (1982). Measurement of handwriting skills: A critical review. *Diagnostique, 8,* 32–42.

Graham, S. (1983). The effect of self-instructional procedures on LD students' handwriting performance. *Learning Disability Quarterly, 6,* 231–234.

Graham, S. & Miller, L. (1979). Spelling research and practice: A unified approach. *Focus on Exceptional Children, 12*(2), 1–16.

Graham, S. & Miller, L. (1980). Handwriting research and practice: A unified approach. *Focus on Exceptional Children, 13*(2), 1–16.

Graves, D. H. (1985). All children can write. *Learning Disabilities Focus, 1*(1), 36–43.

Gray, B., & Ryan, B. P. (1973). *A language program for the nonlanguage child.* Champaign, IL: Research Press.

Gray, G. (1975). Education service delivery. In W. V. Cegelka (Ed.), *Educating the 24-hour retarded child.* National Training Meeting on Education of the Severely and Profoundly Mentally Retarded. Arlington, TX: National Association of Retarded Citizens.

Gray, L. (1984). Logo helps remove children's handicaps. *Educational Computer, 4,* 33–37.

Gray, R. A. (1981). Service for the LD adult: A working paper. *Learning Disability Quarterly, 4,* 426–434.

Gray, W. S., & Robinson, H. M. (Eds.). (1967). *Gray Oral Reading Test.* Indianapolis: Bobbs-Merrill.

Greene, H. A., & Petty, W. T. (1975). *Developing language skills in the elementary schools* (5th ed.). Boston: Allyn & Bacon.

Gregg, K. N. (1983). College learning disabled writers: Error patterns and instructional alternatives. *Journal of Learning Disabilities, 16,* 334–338.

Gregg, K. N. (1985). College learning-disabled, normal, and basic writers: A comparison of frequency and accuracy of cohesive ties. *Journal of Psychoeducational Assessment, 3,* 223–231.

Gregory, R. P., Hackney, C., & Gregory, N. M. (1982). Corrective reading programme: An evaluation. *British Journal of Educational Psychology, 52,* 33–50.

Gresham, F. M. (1982). Misguided mainstreaming: The case for social skills training with handicapped children. *Exceptional Children, 48,* 422–433.

Groff, P. J. (1961). New speeds of handwriting. *Elementary English, 38,* 564–656.

Grossman, H. J. (1973, 1977). *Manual on terminology and classification in mental retardation.* Washington, DC: American Association on Mental Deficiency, Special Publication No. 2.

Grossman, H. J. (1983). *Classification in mental retardation.* Washington, DC: American Association on Mental Deficiency.

Guerin, G. R., & Maier, A. S. (1983). *Informal assessment in education.* Palo Alto, CA: Mayfield.

Guess, D., & Mulligan, M. (1982). The severely and profoundly handicapped. In E. L. Meyen (Ed.), *Exceptional children and youth* (pp. 262–303). Denver: Love Publishing.

Guess, D., Sailor, W., & Baer, D. (1976). Children with limited language. In R. L. Schiefelbusch (Ed.), *Language intervention strategies* (pp. 101–143). Baltimore: University Park Press.

Hagin, R. A. (1983). Write right or left: A practical approach to handwriting. *Journal of Learning Disabilities, 16,* 266–271.

Haig, J. H., & Patterson, B. H. (1980, March). *An overview of adult learning disabilities.* Paper presented at the 13th annual meeting of the Wester College Reading Association, San Francisco. (ERIC Document Reproduction Service No. ED 197 563)

Haley-James, S., & Hobson, C. (1980). Interviewing: A means of encouraging the drive to communicate. *Language Arts, 57,* 497–502.

Hall, B. O. (1978). *Teaching reading to deaf children.* Washington, DC: The Alexander Graham Bell Association for the Deaf, Inc.

Hall, J. K. (1981). *Evaluating and improving written expression: A practical guide for teachers.* Boston: Allyn & Bacon.

Hall, R. J. (1984). Orthographic problem-solving. *Academic Therapy, 20*(1), 67–75.

Hallahan, D. P., & Kauffman, J. M. (1976). *Introduction to learning disabilities: A psycho-behavioral approach.* Englewood Cliffs, NJ: Prentice-Hall.

Hallahan, D. P., & Kauffman, J. M. (1977). Labels, categories, behaviors: ED, LD, and EMR reconsidered. *Journal of Special Education, 11,* 129–149.

Hallahan, D. P., & Kauffman, J. M. (1986). *Exceptional Children: Introduction to special education* (3rd ed.). Englewood Cliffs, NJ: Prentice-Hall.

Halle, J., Alpert, C., & Anderson, S. (1984). Natural environment language assessment and intervention with severely impaired preschoolers. *Topics in Early Childhood Special Education, 4,* 36–55.

Halliday, M. A. K. (1975). *Learning how to mean.* New York: Elsevier/North Holland.

Hammill, D. D. (1986). Correcting handwriting deficiencies. In D. D. Hammill & N. R. Bartel (Eds.), *Teaching students with learning and behavior problems* (4th ed., pp. 155–177). Boston: Allyn & Bacon.

Hammill, D. D., & Bartel, N. R. (1986). *Teaching students with learning and behavior problems* (4th ed.). Boston: Allyn & Bacon.

Hammill, D. D., Brown, V. L., Larsen, S. C., & Wiederholt, J. L. (1980). *Test of adolescent language.* Austin, TX: PRO-ED.

Hammill, D. D., & Larsen, S. C. (1974). The effectiveness of psycholinguistic training. *Exceptional Children, 41,* 5–14.

Hammill, D. D., & Larsen, S. C. (1974). The relationship of selected auditory perceptual skills and reading ability. *Journal of Learning Disabilities, 7,* 429–435.

Hammill, D. D., & Larsen, S. C. (1983). *Test of Written Language.* Austin, TX: PRO-ED.

Hammill, D. D., Larsen, S. C., & McNutt, G. (1977). The effects of spelling instruction: A preliminary study. *The Elementary School Journal, 78,* 67–72.

Hammill, D. D., & Newcomer, P. L. (1982). *Test of Language Development– Intermediate.* Austin, TX: PRO-ED.

Hamre-Nietupski, S., Nietupski, J., & Rathe, T. (1986). Letting the data do the talking: Selecting the appropriate nonverbal communication system for severely handicapped students. *Teaching Exceptional Children, 18,* 130–134.

Handleman, J. S., & Harris, S. L. (1983). A comparison of one-to-one versus couplet instruction with autistic children. *Behavioral Disorders, 9,* 22–26.

Hanline, M., Hanson, M., Veltman, M., & Spaeth, D. (1985). Electromechanical teaching toys for infants and toddlers with disabilities. *Teaching Exceptional Children, 18,* 20–29.

Hanna, R., Lippert, E., & Harris, A. (1982). *Developmental communication curriculum inventory.* Columbus, OH: Charles E. Merrill.

Hanninen, K. A. (1975). *Teaching the visually handicapped.* Columbus, OH: Charles E. Merrill.

Hansen, C. L. (1978). Writing skills. In N. G. Haring, T. C. Lovitt, M. D. Eaton, & C. L. Hansen (Eds.), *The fourth R: Research in the classroom* (pp. 93–126). Columbus, OH: Charles E. Merrill.

Hansen, D. N. (1966). *Applications of computers to research on instruction.* Paper read at National Society of College Teachers of Education meeting, Feb. 17, 1966.

Harber, J. (1977). Influences of presentation dialect and orthography form on reading performance of black inner-city children. *Educational Research Quarterly, 2*(2), 9–16.

Haring, N. G., & Bateman, B. (1977). *Teaching the learning disabled child.* Englewood Cliffs, NJ: Prentice-Hall.

Haring, N. G., Lovitt, T. C., Eaton, M. D., & Hansen, C. L. (1978) *The fourth R: Research in the classroom.* Columbus, OH: Charles E. Merrill.

Harley, R. K. (1963). *Verbalism among blind children.* New York: American Foundation for the Blind.

Harper, J. R. (1977). Influence of presentation dialect and orthography form on reading performance of black inner-city children. *Educational Research Quarterly, 2*(2) 9–16.

Harris, A., & Sipay, E. R. (1980). *How to increase your reading ability* (7th ed.). New York: Longman.

Harris, A., & Sipay, E. R. (1985). *How to increase your reading ability* (8th ed.). New York: Longman.

Harris, D., Lippert, J., Yoder, D., & Vanderheiden, G. (1977). Blissymbols: An augmentative symbol communication system for nonvocal severely handicapped children. In R. York and E. Edgar (Eds.), *Teaching the severely handicapped* (Vol. IV, pp. 238–262). Seattle, WA: Special Press.

Harris, D., & Vanderheiden, G. (1980). Augmentative communication techniques. In R. Schiefelbusch (Ed.), *Nonspeech language and communication: Analysis and intervention* (pp. 259–302). Austin, TX: PRO-ED.

Harris, M. (1981). Process and product: Dominant models for writing centers. In T. Hawkins & P. Brooks (Eds.), *Improving writing skills.* San Francisco: Jossey-Bass.

Harris-Vanderheiden, D. (1975). Blissymbols and the mentally retarded. In G. Vanderheiden & K. Grilley (Eds.), *Nonvocal communication techniques and aids for the severely handicapped* (pp. 120–131). Austin, TX: PRO-ED.

Harris-Vanderheiden, D., Brown, W. P., MacKenzie, P., Reinen, S., & Scheibel, C. (1975). Symbol communication for the mentally handicapped. *Mental Retardation, 13,* 34–37.

Harrison, S. (1981). Open letter from a left handed teacher: Some sinistral ideas on the teaching of handwriting. *Teaching Exceptional Children, 13,* 116–120.

Hart, B. O. (1978). *Teaching reading to deaf children.* Washington, DC: The Alexander Graham Bell Association for the Deaf.

Hart, B., & Rogers-Warren, A. (1978). Milieu teaching approaches. In R. Schiefelbusch (Ed.), *Language intervention strategies* (pp. 193–236). Austin, TX: PRO-ED.

Hasselbring, T. (1982). Remediation of spelling problems in learning handicapped students through the use of microcomputers. *Educational Technology, 22,* 15–16.

Hasselbring, T. S. (1984). Using a microcomputer for imitating student errors to improve spelling performance. *Computers, Reading, and Language Arts, 1*(4), 12–14.

Hasselbring, T. S. (1985). Microcomputer applications to instruction. In E. A. Polloway, J. S. Payne, J. R. Patton, & R. A. Payne (Eds.), *Strategies for teaching retarded and special needs learners* (3rd ed., pp. 154–175). Columbus, OH: Charles E. Merrill.

Hasselbring, T. S., & Crossland, C. L. (1982). Application of microcomputer technology to spelling assessment of learning disabled students. *Learning Disability Quarterly, 5,* 80–82.

Hatlen, P. (1976). Priorities in educational programs for visually handicapped children and youth. *DVH Newsletter, 20,* 1.

Heber, R. F., & Garber, H. (1971). An experiment in prevention of cultural-familial mental retardation. In D. A. Primrose (Ed.), *Proceedings of the Second Congress of the International Association for the Scientific Study of Mental Deficiency.* Warsaw: Polish Medical Publishers.

Heckleman, R. G. (1969). The neurological impress method of remedial reading instruction. *Academic Therapy, 4,* 277–282.

Hedrick, D. L., & Kemp, J. C. (1984). Guidelines for communication intervention with younger retarded children. *Topics in Language Disorders, 4*(1), 58–65.

Hedrick, D. L., Prathey, E. M., & Toben, A. R. (1975). *Sequenced Inventory of Communication Development.* Seattle: University of Washington Press.

Hegge, T. G., Kirk, S. A., & Kirk, W. D. (1955). *Remedial reading drills.* Ann Arbor, MI: George Wahr.

Heilman, A. W., Blair, T. R., & Rupley, W. H. (1986). *Principles and practices of teaching reading* (6th ed.). Columbus, OH: Charles E. Merrill.

Hennings, D. G. (1979). Revised edition of Russell, D., Russell, E., & Hennings, D. G. (1959) *Listening aids: Throughout the grades.* New York: Teachers College Press, Columbia University.

Hermreck, L. A. (1979). *A comparison of the written language of LD and non-LD elementary children using the inventory of written expression and spelling.* Unpublished master's thesis, University of Kansas.

Heward, W. L., & Orlansky, M. D. (1984). *Exceptional children* (2nd ed.). Columbus, OH: Charles E. Merrill.

Higginbotham, D. G., & Yoder, D. E. (1982). Communication within natural conversational interaction: Implications for severe communicatively impaired persons. *Topics in Language Disorders, 2*(2), 1–19.

Higher Education Research Institute. (1985). *American freshman: National norms for Fall 1985*. Los Angeles: Graduate School of Education, University of California.

Hill, J. W. (1984, March). *Unrecognized learning disabilities in adulthood: Implications for adult education*. Paper presented at the 108th Annual Meeting of the American Association of Mental Deficiency, Minneapolis. (ERIC Document Reproduction Service No. ED 253 983)

Hixon, T. J., Shriberg, J. D., & Saxman, J. H. (1980). *Introduction to communication disorders*. Englewood Cliffs, NJ: Prentice-Hall.

Hodges, R. (1981). *Learning to spell: Theory and research into practice*. Urbana, IL: National Council of Teachers of English.

Hodges, R. E., & Rudolf, H. E. (1966). Searching linguistics for cues for the teaching of spelling. *Research on handwriting and spelling*. Champaign IL: National Council of Teachers of English.

Holland, L. E. (1973). Foreword. In C. S. Stocker, *Listening for the visually impaired: A teaching manual*. Springfield, IL: Charles C. Thomas.

Hollands, J. W. (1985). *Non-stop stories*. New York: Irvington.

Hopkins, B. L., Schutte, R. C., & Garton, K. L. (1971). The effects of access to a playroom on the rate and quality of printing and writing of first and second-grade students. *Journal of Applied Behavior Analysis, 4*, 77–87.

Horn, E. (1954). *Teaching spelling*. Washington, DC: American Research Association.

Horn, W. F., O'Donnell, J. P., & Vitulano, L. A. (1984). Long-term follow-up studies of learning disabled persons. In J. K. Torgesen & G. M. Senf (Eds.), *Annual review of learning disabilities* (Vol. 2, pp. 77–90). New York: Professional Press.

Horner, R., & Budd, C. (1985). Acquisition of manual sign use: Collateral reduction of maladaptive behavior, and factors limiting generalization. *Education and Training of the Mentally Retarded, 20*, 39–47.

Horstmeier, D., & McDonald, J. (1978). *Environmental Language Inventory and Environmental Prelanguage Battery*. Columbus, OH: Charles E. Merrill.

Hoskins, B. (1983). Semantics. In C. T. Wren (Ed.), *Language learning disabilities: Diagnosis and remediation* (pp. 85–112). Rockville, MD: Aspen Systems.

Idol, L. (Ed.). (1988). Grace Fernald's *Remedial techniques in basic school subjects*. Austin, TX: PRO-ED.

Ingram, D. (1978). Sensorimotor intelligence and language development. In A. Lock (Ed.), *Action, gesture, and symbol: The emergence of language*. New York: Academic Press.

Itard, J. (1972). *The wild boy of Aveyron*. (E. Fawcett, P. Ayrton, & J. White, Trans.). London: NLB, 7 Carlisle St. (Original work published 1801).

James, S. L. (1982). Language disorders in autistic children. In P. Knoblock (Ed.), *Teaching and mainstreaming autistic children* (pp. 155–175). Denver, CO: Love.

Jan, J. E., Freeman, R. D., & Scott, E. P. (1977). *Visual impairment in children and adolescents*. New York: Grune & Stratton.

Jarvis, O. T. (1963). How much time for spelling? *Instructor, 73*, 59.

Jenkins, J. R., Mayhall, W. F., Peschka, C. M., & Jenkins, J. M. (1974). Comparing small group and tutorial instruction in resource rooms. *Exceptional Children, 40*, 245–251.

Johnson, D. (1986). Persistent auditory disorders in young dyslexic adults. *Bulletin of the Orton Society, 30,* 268–276.

Johnson, D. D. (1971). The Dolch list reexamined. *The Reading Teacher, 24,* 455–456.

Johnson, D. J. (1980). Persistent auditory disorders in young dyslexic adults. *Bulletin of the Orten Society, 30,* 268–276.

Johnson, D. J., & Myklebust, H. R. (1967). *Learning disabilities: Educational principles and practices.* New York: Grune & Stratton.

Johnson, E. W. (1959). *The improvement of listening skills.* Columbus, OH: Department of School Services and Publications, American Educational Publications.

Johnson, J. L., Flanagan, K., Burge, M. E., Kaufman-Debriere, S., & Spellman, C. R. (1980). Interactive individualized instruction with small groups of severely handicapped students. *Education and Training of the Mentally Retarded, 15,* 230–237.

Johnson, K. R. (1969). When should standard English be taught to speakers of non-standard Negro dialect? *Language Learning, 20,* 19–30.

Jordan, I., Gustason, G., & Rosen, R. (1979). An update on communication trends in programs for the deaf. *American Annals of the Deaf, 124,* 350–357.

Kahn, J. (1976). Relationship of Piaget's sensorimotor period to language acquisition of profoundly retarded children. *American Journal of Mental Deficiency, 79,* 640–643.

Kaluger, G., & Kolson, C. J. (1978). *Reading and learning disabilities* (2nd ed.) Columbus, OH: Charles E. Merrill.

Kaminsky, S., & Powers, R. (1981). Remediation of handwriting difficulties: A practical approach. *Academic Therapy, 17,* 19–25.

Kamm, K., Miles, P. J., Van Blaricom, V. L., Harris, M. L., & Stewart, D. M. (1972). *Wisconsin Tests of Reading Skill Development.* Minneapolis: National Computer Systems.

Kanner, L. (1973). *Childhood psychosis: Initial studies and new insights.* Washington, DC: V. H. Winston.

Kaplan, S. N. (1979). Language arts and social studies curriculum in the elementary school. In A. H. Passow (Ed.), *The gifted and talented: Their education and development* (pp. 155–168). Chicago: The National Society for the Study of Education.

Karchmer, M. A., & Kirwin, L. A. (1977). *The use of hearing aids by hearing impaired students in the United States.* Washington, DC: Office of Demographic Studies, Gallaudet College.

Karlin, R. (1980). *Teaching elementary reading: Principles and practices* (3rd ed.). New York: Harcourt Brace Jovanovich.

Karlsen, B., Madden, R., & Gardner, E. F. (1974, 1977). *Stanford Diagnostic Reading Tests.* New York: Harcourt Brace Jovanovich.

Kates, B., & McNaughton, S. (1975). *The first application of Blissymbolics as a communication medium for non-speaking children (1971–1974).* Toronto, Ontario, Canada: Blissymbolics Communication Institute.

Kaufman, A. S., Zalma, R., & Kaufman, N. L. (1978). The relationship of hand dominance to the motor coordination, mental ability, and right-left awareness of young normal children. *Child Development, 49,* 885–888.

Kauffman, J. M. (1985). *Characteristics of children's behavior disorders* (3rd ed.). Columbus, OH: Charles E. Merrill.

Kauffman, J. M., Hallahan, D. P., Hass, K., Brame, T., & Boren, R. (1978). Imitating children's errors to improve their spelling performance. *Journal of Learning Disabilities, 11,* 33–38.

Kavale, K., & Forness, S. (1985). *The science of learning disabilities.* San Diego, CA: College-Hill Press.

Kazdin, A. E., & Erickson, L. M. (1975). Developing responsiveness to instructions in severely and profoundly retarded residents. *Journal of Behavior Therapy and Experimental Psychiatry, 6,* 17–21.

Kean, J. M., & Personke, C. (1976). *The language arts: Teaching and learning in the elementary school.* New York: St. Martin's Press.

Kerr, M. M., & Nelson, C. M. (1983). *Strategies for managing behavior problems in the classroom.* Columbus, OH: Charles E. Merrill.

King, C. M., & Quigley, S. P. (1985). *Reading and deafness.* San Diego, CA: College-Hill.

Kirk, S. A., & Gallagher, J. J. (1986). *Educating exceptional children* (5th ed.). Boston: Houghton Mifflin.

Kirk, S. A., & Johnson, G. O. (1951). *Educating the retarded child.* Cambridge, MA: Houghton Mifflin.

Kirk, S. A., Kirk, W. D., & Minskoff, E. H. (1985). *Phonic remedial reading lessons.* Novato, CA: Academic Therapy Publications.

Kirk, S. A., Kliebhan, S. J. M., & Lerner, J. W. (1978) *Teaching reading to slow and disabled learners.* Boston: Houghton Mifflin.

Kirk, S. A., McCarthy, J. J., & Kirk, W. (1968). *Illinois Test of Psycholinguistic Abilities.* Urbana, IL: University of Illinois Press.

Knight, L. N. (1974). *Language arts for the exceptional: The gifted and the linguistically different.* Itasca, IL: F. E. Peacock.

Knight-Arest, I. (1984). Communicative effectiveness of learning disabled and normally achieving 10- to 13-year-old boys. *Learning Disability Quarterly, 7,* 237–245.

Knutson, J. (1967). *Spelling drills using a computer-assisted instructional system.* Technical Report No. 112. Stanford, CA: Institute for Mathematical Studies in the Social Sciences, Stanford University.

Kohl, F. L., Wilcox, B. L., & Karlan, G. R. (1978). Effects of training conditions on the generalization of manual signs with moderately handicapped students. *Education and Training of the Mentally Retarded, 13,* 327–335.

Kopchick, G. Rombach, D., & Karlan, G. (1975). A total communication environment in an institution. *Mental Retardation, 13,* 22–23.

Kosiewicz, M. M., Hallahan, D. P., Lloyd, J., Graves, A. W. (1982). Effects of self-instruction and self-correction procedures on handwriting performance. *Learning Disability Quarterly, 5,* 71–78.

Kotsonis, M., & Patterson, C. (1980). *Comprehension monitoring in learning disabled youngsters* (Technical Report No. 19). Charlottesville, VA: University of Virginia Learning Disabilities Research Institute.

Krause, L. A. (1983). Teaching the second "r". *The Directive Teacher, 5*(1),30.

Krevisky, J., & Linfield, J. L. (1967). *The bad speller's dictionary.* New York: Random House.

Krug, D. A., Arick, J. R., & Almond, P. J. (1980). *Autism Screening Instrument for Educational Planning (ASIEP)*. Portland, OR: ASIEP.

Kuntz, J. B. (1974). *A nonvocal communication program for severely retarded children*. Unpublished doctoral dissertation, Kansas State University, Manhatten.

LaBouve, B. W. (1977). *Bilingual education: A position paper*. National Council of State Supervisors of Foreign Languages.

Labov, W. (1966) *The social stratification of English in New York City*. Washington, DC: Center for Applied Linguistics.

Labov, W. (1967). Some sources of reading problems for Negro speakers of nonstandard English. In A. Frazier (Ed.), *New directions in elementary English*. Champaign, IL: National Council of Teachers of English.

Lamb, P. (1967). *Guiding children's language learning*. Dubuque, IA: William C. Brown.

Langdon, H. W. (1983). Assessment and intervention strategies for the bilingual language-disordered student. *Exceptional Children, 50*, 37–46.

Lapp, D., & Flood, J. (1983). *Teaching reading to every child* (2nd ed.). New York: Macmillan.

LaPray, M., & Ross, R. (1969). The graded word list: Quick gauge of reading ability. *Journal of Reading, 12*, 305–307.

Larsen, S., & Hammill, D. (1986). *Test of Written Spelling*. Austin, TX: PRO-ED.

Laughton, J., & Hasenstab, M. S. (1986). *The language learning process*. Rockville, MD: Aspen.

Layton, T., & Holmes, D. (1978). *Carolina Picture Vocabulary Test*. Tulsa, OK: Modern Education Corp.

Lee, L. L. (1974). *Developmental Sentence Analysis*. Evanston, IL: Northwestern University Press.

Lenkowsky, L. K., & Saposnek, D. T. (1978). Family consequences of parental dyslexia. *Journal of Learning Disabilities, 11*, 59–65.

Lenneberg, E. H. (1966). The natural history of language. In F. Smith & G. Miller (Eds.), *The genesis of language* (pp. 219–252). Cambridge, MA: MIT Press.

Lent, J. R. (1968). Mimosa Cottage experiment in hope. *Psychology Today, 2*, 51–58.

Lerner, J. W. (1985). *Learning disabilities: Theories, diagnosis, and teaching strategies* (4th ed.). Boston: Houghton Mifflin.

Levy, B. B., & Cook, H. (1973). Dialect proficiency and auditory comprehension in standard and black nonstandard English. *Journal of Speech and Hearing Research, 16*, 642–649.

Liebermann, J. E., & Cohen, B. (1982). Five contemporary fallacies: Remedial reading at the community college level. *Adult Literacy and Basic Education*, 91–99.

LINC Associates. (1986). *Specialware directory: A guide to software for special education* (2nd ed.). Columbus, OH: Author.

Lindsley, O. R. (1964). Direct measurement and prosthesis of retarded behavior. *Journal of Education, 147*, 62–81.

Liu, S. S. F. (1975–76). An investigation of oral reading miscues made by nonstandard dialect speaking black children. *Reading Research Quarterly, 11*, 193–197.

Lloyd, J. W., Epstein, M. H., & Cullinan, D. (1981). Direct teaching for learning disabilities. In J. Gottlieb, & S. S. Strichart (Eds.), *Developmental theory and research in learning disabilities* (pp. 278–309). Baltimore: University Park Press.

Loban, W. D. (1963). *The language of elementary school children.* NCTE Research Report No. 1. Champaign, IL: National Council of Teachers of English.

Lord, C. (1985). Contribution of behavioral approaches. In E. Schopler (Ed.), *Communication problems in autism* (pp. 257–282). New York: Plenum Press.

Lovaas, O. I. (1977). *The autistic child: Language development through behavior modification.* New York: Irving.

Lovaas, O. I., Berrberich, J., Perloff, B., & Schaeffer, B. (1966). Acquisition of imitative·speech by schizophrenic children. *Science, 151,* 705–707.

Lovitt, T. C. (1975). Applied behavior analysis and learning disabilities: Part I. *Journal of Learning Disabilities, 8,* 432–443.

Lovitt, T. C. (1975). Applied behavior analysis and learning disabilities: Part II. *Journal of Learning Disabilities, 8,* 504–518.

Lovitt, T. C. (1977). *In spite of my resistance—I've learned from children.* Columbus, OH: Charles E. Merrill.

Lovitt, T. C. (1984). *Tactics for teaching.* Columbus, OH: Charles E. Merrill.

Lowenbraun, S., Appleman, K. I., & Callahan, J. L. (1980). *Teaching the hearing impaired through total communication.* Columbus, OH: Charles E. Merrill.

Lowenfeld, B. (1952). The child who is blind. *Exceptional Children, 19,* 96–102.

Lowenfeld, B. (1973). *The visually handicapped child in school.* New York: John Day.

Lucas, E. V. (1980). *Semantic and pragmatic language disorders: Assessment and remediation.* Rockville, MD: Aspen.

Luftig, L. (1984). An analysis of initial sign lexicons as a function of eight learnability variables. *Journal of the Association for Persons with Severe Handicaps, 9,* 193, 200.

Lundsteen, S. (1979). *Listening: Its impact on reading and the other language arts* (rev. ed.). Urbana, IL: National Council of Teachers of English.

MacDonald, J., & Horstmeier, D. (1978). *Environmental language intervention program.* Columbus, OH: Charles E. Merrill.

Madden, R., Gardner, E. F., Rudman, H. C., Karlsen, B., & Merwin, J. C. (1973). *Stanford Achievement Test.* New York: Psychological Corporation.

Maddux, C. D. (1984). Using microcomputers with the learning disabled: Will the potential be realized? *Educational Computer, 4*(1), 31–32.

Maloney, J. B., & Hopkins, B. L. (1973). The modification of structure and its relationship to subjective judgments of creative writing. *Journal of Applied Behavior Analysis, 6,* 425–433.

Malson, L. (1972). *Wolf children* (E. Fawcett, P. Ayrten, & J. White, Trans.). London: NLBB, 7 Carlisle St. (Original work published 1964)

Mandell, C. J., & Gold, V. (1984). *Teaching handicapped students.* St. Paul, MN: West.

Mann, P. H., & Suiter, P. (1974). *Handbook in diagnostic teaching: A learning disabilities approach.* Boston: Allyn & Bacon.

Mangieri, J. N., & Issacs, C. W. (1983). Recreational reading for gifted children. *Roeper Review, 5,* 11–14.

Mangieri, J. N., & Readence, J. E. (1977). Mainstreaming implications for the teaching of reading. *Reading Improvement, 14,* 165–167.

Mangrum, C. T., & Strichart, S. S. (1983a). College possibilities for the learning disabled: Part one. *Learning Disabilities, 2*(5), 57–68.

Mangrum, C. T., & Strichart, S. S. (1983b). College possibilities for the learning disabled: Part two. *Learning Disabilities, 2*(6), 69–81.

Mangrum, C. T., & Strichart, S. S. (1984). *College and the learning disabled student: A guide to program selection, development, and implementation.* Orlando, FL: Grune & Stratton.

Manzo, A. J. (1975). Guided reading procedure. *Journal of Reading, 7,* 287–291.

Marge, M. (1972). The general problem of language disabilities. In J. V. Irwin & M. Marge (Eds.), *Principles of childhood language disabilities* (pp. 75–98). Englewood Cliffs, NJ: Prentice-Hall.

Markgraf, B. (1957). *An observational study determining the amount of time that students in the tenth and twelfth grades are expected to listen in the classroom.* Unpublished master's thesis, University of Wisconsin, Madison, WI.

Marland, S. P. (1972). *Education of the gifted and talented.* Washington, DC: U.S. Office of Education.

Marlowe, W., Egner, K., & Foreman, D. (1979). Story comprehension as a function of modality and reading ability. *Journal of Learning Disabilities, 12,* 194–197.

Marsh, G. E., II, Gearheart, C. K., & Gearheart, B. R. (1978). *The learning disabled adolescent.* St. Louis: C. V. Mosby.

Martorella, P. A. (1986). Teaching concepts. In J. Cooper (Ed.), *Classroom teaching skills* (pp. 181–223). Lexington, MA: D. C. Heath.

Mason, J. N., & Au, K. H. (1986). *Reading instruction for today.* Glenview, IL: Scott, Foresman.

Matson, J. L., DiLorenzo, T. M., & Esveldt-Dawson, K. (1981). Independence training as a method of enhancing self-help skills acquisition of the mentally retarded. *Behavior Research and Therapy, 19,* 399–405.

Matthes, C. (1972). *How children are taught to read.* Lincoln, NE: Professional Educator.

McCarthy, D. (1960). Language development. *Monographs of Social Research and Child Development, 25,* 5–14.

McCarthy, N. (1972). *McCarthy Scale of Children's Abilities.* New York: Psychological Corp.

McCullough, C. M. (1963). *McCullough Word Analysis Tests.* Boston: Ginn.

McDonald, E. T. (1980). Early identification and treatment of children at risk for speech development. In R. Schiefelbusch (Ed.), *Nonspeech language and communication: Analysis and intervention* (pp. 49–80). Austin, TX: PRO-ED.

McDonald, E. T., & Schultz, A. R. (1973). Communication boards for cerebral palsied children. *Journal of Speech and Hearing Disorders, 39,* 71–85.

McGinnis, A. R. (1981). Functional linguistic strategies of blind children. *Journal of Visual Impairment and Blindness, 75,* 210–214.

McLean, J. E., & Snyder-McLean, L. K. (1978). *A transactional approach to early language training.* Columbus, OH: Charles E. Merrill.

McLean, L., & McLean, J. (1974). A language training program for nonverbal autistic children. *Journal of Speech and Hearing Disorders, 39,* 186–193.

McNaughton, S., & Kates, B. (1980). The application of Blissymbolics. In R. L. Schiefelbusch (Ed.), *Nonspeech language and communication: Analysis and intervention* (pp. 305–321). Austin, TX: PRO-ED.

McNaughton, S., Kates, B., & Silverman, H. (1978). *Handbook of Blissymbolics.* Toronto, Ontario, Canada: Blissymbolics Communication Institute.

Mecham, M. (1971). *Verbal Language Development Scale.* Circle Pines, MN: American Guidance Service.

Medley, D. M. (1977). *Teacher competence and teacher effectiveness: A review of process-product research.* Washington, DC: American Association of Colleges for Teacher Education.

Mercer, C. D. , & Mercer, A. R. (1985). *Teaching students with learning problems* (2nd ed.). Columbus, OH: Charles E. Merrill.

Mercer, J. R. (1973). *Labeling the mentally retarded.* Berkeley: University of California Press.

Miller, A., & Miller, E. (1973). Cognitive-developmental training with elevated boards and sign language. *Journal of Autism and Childhood Schizophrenia, 3,* 65–86.

Miller, J. (1973). What happened to those who got away? *Academic Therapy, 9,* 47–55.

Miller, J. F. (1981). *Assessing language production: Experimental procedures.* Austin, TX: PRO-ED.

Mishler, C., & Hogan, T. P. (1982). Holistic scoring of essays: Remedy for evaluating the third R. *Diagnostique, 8*(1), 4–16.

Mishler, E. (1979). Meaning in context: Is there any other kind? *Harvard Educational Review, 49,* 1–21.

Monroe, M. (1951). *Growing into reading.* New York: Scott, Foresman.

Moore, J. T. (1951). *Phonetic elements appearing in a three thousand word spelling vocabulary.* Unpublished doctoral dissertation, Stanford University, Stanford, CA.

Moores, D. F. (1980). Alternative communication modes: Visual-motor systems. In R. Schiefelbusch (Ed.), *Nonspeech language and communication: Analysis and intervention* (pp. 27–48). Austin, TX: PRO-ED.

Moores, D. F. (1982). *Educating the deaf: Psychology, principles and practices* (2nd ed.). Boston: Houghton Mifflin.

Moores, D. F., & Maestas y Moores, J. (1981). Special adaptations necessitated by learning impairments. In J. M. Kauffman & D. P. Hallahan (Eds.), *Handbook of special education* (pp. 576–592). Englewood Cliffs, NJ: Prentice-Hall.

Moos, R. (1976). *The human context: Environmental determinants of behavior.* New York: John Wiley.

Moran, M. R. (1981). *The diagnostic evaluation of expository paragraphs* (Research Report No. 34). Lawrence, KS: University of Kansas, Institute for Research in Learning Disabilities.

Moray, N. (1969). *Listening and attention.* Baltimore, MD: Penguin.

Morocco, C. C., & Neuman, S. B. (1986). Word processors and the acquisition of writing strategies. *Journal of Learning Disabilities, 19,* 243–247.

Morsink, C. V. (1984). *Teaching special needs students in regular classrooms.* Boston: Little, Brown.

Moss, J. R. (1980). Guest editorial. *Adult Learning Problem Notes.*

Mulligan, M., Guess, D., Holvoet, J., & Brown, F. (1980). The individualized sequencing model (I): Implications from research on massed distributed and spaced trial learning. *Journal of the Association for the Severely Handicapped, 5,* 325–336.

Mullins, J., Joseph, F., Turner, C., Zawadzski, R., & Saltzman, L. (1972). A handwriting model for children with learning disabilities. *Journal of Learning Disabilities, 5,* 306–311.

Muma, J. R. (1971). Language intervention: Ten techniques. *Language, Speech, and Hearing Services in Schools, 2*(5), 7–17.

Muma, J. (1978). *Language handbook: Concepts, assessment, intervention.* Englewood Cliffs, NJ: Prentice-Hall.

Muma, J. R., & Pierce, D. E. (1981). Language intervention: Data or evidence. *Topics in Learning and Learning Disabilities, 1*(2), 1–11.

Musselwhite, C. R., & St. Louis, K. (1982). *Communication programming for the severely handicapped: Vocal and non-vocal strategies.* San Diego, CA: College Hill Press.

Musselwhite, C. (1985, November). *Enhancing communication skills with the young severely handicapped.* Paper presented at Lynchburg College, Lynchburg, VA.

Myklebust, H. R. (1965). *Development and disorders of written language: Picture Story Language Test* (Vol. 1). New York: Grune & Stratton.

Myklebust, H. R. (1973). *Development and disorders of written language: Studies of normal and exceptional children.* New York: Grune & Stratton.

Neef, N., Walters, J., & Egel, A. (1984). Establishing generative yes/no responses in developmentally disabled children. *Journal of Applied Behavior Analysis, 17,* 453, 460.

Neff, H., & Pilch, J. (1976). *Teaching handicapped children easily.* Springfield, IL: Charles C. Thomas.

Nelson, G. (1978, July). *A proposed system for developing individualized education programs for learning disabled adults at Vancouver Community College, King Edward Campus.* Paper presented at the First World Congress on Future of Special Education, Stirling, Scotland (ERIC Document Reproduction Service No. ED 158 521)

Nelson, K. E. (1977). Facilitating children's syntax acquisition. *Developmental Psychology, 13,* 101–107.

Nelson, N. W. (1981). An eclectic model of language intervention for disorders of listening, speaking, reading, and writing. *Topics in Language Disorders, 1*(2), 1–24.

Nevin, A., & Thousand, J. (in press). Avoiding/limiting special education referrals: Changes and challenges. In M. C. Wang, M. C. Reynolds, & H. C. Walberg (Eds.), *The handbook of special education: Research and practice.* Oxford, England: Pergamon Press.

Newcomer, P. L., & Hammill, D. D. (1976). *Psycholinguistics in the schools.* Columbus, OH: Charles E. Merrill.

Newcomer, P. L., & Hammill, D. D. (1982). Test of Language Development– Primary. Austin, TX: PRO-ED.

Newland, T. E. (1932). An analytical study of the development of illegibilities in handwriting from the lower grades to adulthood. *Journal of Educational Research, 26,* 249–258.

Nicholls, G. H., & Ling, D. (1982). Cued speech and the reception of spoken language. *Journal of Speech and Hearing Research, 25,* 262–269.

Norton, D. E. (1980). *The effective teaching of language arts.* Columbus, OH: Charles E. Merrill.

Norton, D. E. (1985). *The effective teaching of language arts* (2nd ed.). Columbus, OH: Charles E. Merrill.

Oliver, P. R. (1983). Effects of teaching different tasks in group versus individual training formats with severely handicapped individuals. *Journal of the Association for the Severely Handicapped, 8,* 79–91.

Oliver, P. R., & Scott, T. L. (1981). Group versus individual training in establishing generalization of language skills with severely handicapped individuals. *Mental Retardation, 19,* 285–289.

O'Malley, J. M. (1982). *Children's English and services study: Educational needs assessment for language minority children with limited English proficiency.* Rosslyn, VA: National Clearinghouse for Bilingual Education.

Orelove, F. P. (1982). Acquisition of incidental learning in moderately and severely handicapped adults. *Education and Training of the Mentally Retarded, 17,* 131–136.

Ortiz, A. (1984). Language and curriculum development for exceptional bilingual children. In P. C. Chinn (Ed.), *Education of culturally and linguistically different exceptional children* (pp. 77–100). Reston, VA: Council for Exceptional Children.

Orton, S. (1937). *Reading, writing, and speech problems in children.* New York: Norton.

Osborn, J., & Becker, W. (1980). Direct instruction language. In D. Bricker (Ed.), *Language intervention with children* (pp. 79–95). San Francisco: Jossey-Bass.

Ostertag, B. S., Baker, R. E., Howard, R. F., & Best, L. (1982). Learning disabled programs in California community colleges. *Journal of Learning Disabilities, 15,* 535–538.

Otto, W. (1973). Evaluating instruments for assessing needs and growth in reading. In W. H. MacGinitie (Ed.), *Assessment problems in reading* (pp. 14–20). Newark DE: International Reading Association.

Otto, W., McMenemy, R. A., & Smith, R. J. (1973). *Corrective and remedial teaching* (2nd ed.). Boston: Houghton Mifflin.

Otto, W., & Smith, R. J. (1980). *Corrective and remedial teaching* (3rd ed.). Boston: Houghton Mifflin.

Owens, R., Jr. (1982). *Program for the acquisition of language with the severely impaired.* Columbus, OH: Charles E. Merrill.

Pasanella, A. L. & Volkmor, C. B. (1977). *Teaching handicapped students in the mainstream: Coming back or never leaving* (2nd ed.). Columbus, OH: Charles E. Merrill.

Patton, J. R., & Polloway, E. A. (1982). The learning disabled: The adult years. *Topics in Learning and Learning Disabilities, 2*(3), 79–88.

Patton, J. R. & Polloway, E. A. (in press). Academic planning for the LD college student: Course analysis and selection. *Academic Therapy*.

Payne, J. S., Polloway, E. A., Smith, J. E., & Payne, R. A. (1981). *Strategies for teaching the mentally retarded* (2nd ed.). Columbus, OH: Charles E. Merrill.

Peters, M. L. (1985). *Spelling: Caught or taught?* Boston: Routledge & Kegan Paul.

Petty, W. T., & Bowen, M. E. (1967). *Slithery snakes and other aids to children's writing*. New York: Appleton-Century-Crofts.

Petty, W. T., & Jensen, J. M. (1980). *Developing children's language*. Boston: Allyn & Bacon.

Phelps-Gunn, T., & Phelps-Terasaki, D. (1982). *Written language instruction: Theory and remediation*. Rockville, MD: Aspen.

Phelps-Terasaki, D., & Phelps, T. (1980). *Teaching written expression: The Phelps sentence guide program*. Novato, CA: Academic Therapy.

Piaget, J. (1954). *The construction of reality in the child*. New York: Basic Books.

Piaget, J., & Weil, A. M. (1951). The development in children of the idea of homeland and relations with other countries. *International Social Science Bulletin*, III, 561, 578.

Poell, L. W. (1982). *The assessment of learning disabled students at the postsecondary level*. Unpublished master's paper. University of Hawaii, Honolulu.

Polette, N. (1982). *3Rs for the gifted*. Little, CO: Libraries Unlimited.

Polloway, E. A. (1985). Review of *Test of Written Language*. In J. V. Mitchell (Ed.), *Ninth Mental Measurements Yearbook* (pp. 1600–1602). Lincoln, NE: Buros Institute of Mental Measurements.

Polloway, E. A. (in press-a). Review of *Denver Handwriting Analysis* by P. L. Anderson (1982). In J. V. Mitchell (Ed.), *Tenth Mental Measurements Yearbook*. Lincoln, NE: Buros Institute of Mental Measurements.

Polloway, E. A. (in press-b). Review of *Diagnosis and remediation of handwriting problems* by D. H. Stott, F. A. Moyes, & S. E. Henderson (1985). In J. V. Mitchell (Ed.), *Tenth Mental Measurements Yearbook*. Lincoln, NE: Buros Institute of Mental Measurements.

Polloway, E. A., Cronin, M. E., & Patton, J. R. (1986). The efficacy of group versus one-to-one instruction: A review. *Remedial and Special Education, 1*, 22–30.

Polloway, E. A., Epstein, M. H., Polloway, C. H., Patton, J. R., & Ball, D. W. (1986). Corrective reading program: An analysis of effectiveness with learning disabled and mildly retarded students. *Remedial and Special Education, 7*(4), 41–47.

Polloway, E. A., & Patton, J. R. (April 16, 1982). *Written language and the mildly handicapped: Problems and instructional strategies*. Paper presented at the 60th annual international conference of the Council for Exceptional Children, Houston, TX.

Polloway, E. A., Patton, J. R., & Cohen, S. B. (1981). Written language for mildly handicapped students. *Focus on Exceptional Children, 14*(3), 1–16.

Polloway, E. A., Patton, J. R., & Cohen, S. B. (1983). Written language. In E. L. Meyen, C. A. Vergason, R. J. Whelan (Eds.), *Promising practices for exceptional children: Curriculum Implications* (pp. 285–320). Denver, CO: Love Publishing.

Polloway, E. A., Payne, J. S., Patton, J. R., & Payne, R. A. (1985). *Strategies for teaching retarded and special needs learners* (3rd ed.). Columbus, OH: Charles E. Merrill.

Polloway, E. A., & Smith, J. D. (1983). Changes in mild mental retardation: Population, programs, and perspectives. *Exceptional Children, 50,* 149–159.

Polloway, E. A., & Smith, J. D. (in press). Current status of the mild mental retardation construct: Identification, placement, and programs. In M. C. Wang, M. C. Reynolds, & H. C. Wahlberg (Eds.), *The Handbook of Special Education: Research and Practice.* Oxford, England: Pergamon Press.

Polloway, E. A., Smith, J. D., & Patton, J. R. (1984). Learning disabilities: An adult development perspective. *Learning Disability Quarterly, 7,* 179–186.

Polloway, E. A., & Smith, J. E. (1982). *Teaching language skills to exceptional learners.* Denver, CO: Love Publishing.

Poplin, M., Gray, R., Larsen, S., Banikowski, A., & Mehring, T. (1980). A comparison of components of written expression abilities in learning disabled and non-learning disabled children at 3 grade levels. *Learning Disability Quarterly, 3,* 46–53.

Porter, P. B., & Schroeder, S. R. (1980). Generalizations and maintenance of skills acquired in nonspeech language initiation program training. *Applied Research in Mental Retardation, 1,* 71–84.

Pressey, S. L. (1962). Educational acceleration: Occasional procedure or major issue? *Personnel and Guidance Journal, 41,* 12–17.

Prizant, B. . (1978). *An analysis of the functions of immediate echolalia in autistic children.* Unpublished doctoral dissertation, State University of New York, Buffalo.

Prizant, B., & Duchan, J. F. (1981). The functions of immediate echolalia in autistic children. *Journal of Speech and Hearing Disorders, 46,* 241–249.

Prizant, B. M., & Rydell, P. (1984). An analysis of the functions of delayed echolalia in autistic children. *Journal of Speech and Hearing Research, 27,* 183–192.

Quant, L. (1946). Factors affecting the legibility of handwriting. *Journal of Experimental Education, 14,* 297–316.

Quay, H. C. (1966). *Empirical-experimental approach to the nature and remediation of conduct disorders of children.* (ERIC Document Reproduction Service No. ED 021 896)

Quigley, S., & King, C. (1981). *Reading milestones.* Beaverton, OR: DorMac.

Quigley, S. P., & Paul, P. V. (1984). *Language and deafness.* San Diego, CA: College-Hill.

Radabaugh, M. T., & Yukish, J. F. (1982). *Curriculum for the mildly handicapped.* Boston: Allyn & Bacon.

Ramsey, W. (1967). The value and limitations of diagnostic reading tests for evaluation in the classroom. In T. C. Barrett (Ed.), *The evaluation of children's reading achievement* (pp. 65–77). Newark, DE: International Reading Association.

Ranieri, L., Ford, A., Vincent, L., & Brown, L. (1984). 1:1 versus 1:3 instruction of severely multihandicapped students. *Remedial and Special Education, 5*(5), 23–28.

Rankin, P. (1930). Listening ability: Its importance, measurement and development. *Chicago Schools Journal, 12,* 177–179.

Rashotte, C. A., & Torgesen, J. K. (1985). Repeated reading and fluency in learning disabled children. *Reading Research Quarterly, 20,* 180–188.

Raynor, A. L. (1978). Review of Nelson Denny Reading Test. In O. K. Buros (Ed.), *The eighth mental measurement yearbook.* Highland Park, NJ: Gryphon Press.

Reed, C., & Hodges, R. E. (1982). Spelling. *Encyclopedia of educational research.* New York: Macmillan.

Reichle, J., & Keogh, W. J. (1986). Communication instruction for learners with severe handicaps: Some unresolved issues. In R. H. Horner, L. H. Meyer, & H. D. B. Fredreick (Eds.), *Education of learners with severe handicaps: Exemplary service strategies* (pp. 189–218).

Reichle, J., Rogers, H., & Barrett, C. (1984). Communication of non-oral persons. In R. Schiefelbusch (Ed.), *Nonspeech language and communication: Analysis and intervention* (pp. 197–224). Austin, TX: PRO-ED.

Reid, D. H., & Favell, J. E. (1984). Group instruction with persons who have severe disabilities: A critical review. *Journal of the Association for Persons with Severe Handicaps, 9,* 167–177.

Reinhardtsen, J. (1982). *Special education courses for the learning disabled.* Ellenburg, WA: Central Washington University.

Renzulli, J. S. (1977, 1982). *The enrichment triad model: A guide for developing defensible programs for the gifted and talented.* Mansfield Center, CT: Creative Learning Press.

Renzulli, J. S. (1978). What makes giftedness? Reexamining a definition. *Phi Delta Kappan, 261,* 180–184.

Renzulli, J. S., Smith, L., White, A., Callahan, C., & Hartman, R. (1976). *Scales for rating the behavioral characteristics of superior students.* Mansfield Center, CT: Creative Learning Press.

Report of the Ad Hoc Committee to Define Deaf and Hard of Hearing. (1975). *American Annals of the Deaf, 120,* 509–512.

Reschly, D. J. (in press). Minority MR overrepresentation: Legal issues, research findings, and reform trends. In M. C. Wang, M. C. Reynolds, & H. C. Wahlberg (Eds.), *The handbook of special education: Research and practice.* Oxford, England: Pergamon Press.

Reutzel, D. R. (1986). The reading basal: A sentence combining composing book. *The Reading Teacher, 39,* 194–199.

Rhyne, J. M. (1981). *Curriculum for teaching the visually impaired.* Springfield IL: Charles C. Thomas.

Rice, J. M. (1897). The futility of the spelling grind–II. *Forum, 23,* 409–419.

Richards, J. (1978). *Classroom language: What sorts?* London: George Allen and Unwin.

Richardson, T. (1975). Sign language for the SMR and PMR. *Mental Retardation, 13,* 17.

Richek, M. A., List, L. K., & Lerner, J. W. (1983). *Reading problems: Diagnosis and remediation.* Englewood Cliffs, NJ: Prentice-Hall.

Ricks, D., & Wing, L. (1975). Language, communication, and the use of symbols in normal and autistic children. *Journal of Autism and Childhood Schizophrenia, 5,* 191–221.

Rieth, H., Polsgrove, L., & Eckert, R. (1984). A computer-based spelling program. *Academic Therapy, 20*(1), 59–65.

Rigg, P. (1978). Dialect and/in/for reading. *Language Arts, 55,* 285–290.

Rincover, A., & Koegel, R. L. (1977). Classroom treatment of autistic children: II. Individualized instruction in a group. *Journal of Abnormal Child Psychology, 5,* 113–126.

Risley, T. R., & Wolf, M. (1967). Establishing functional speech in echolalic children. *Behavior Research and Therapy, 5,* 73–88.

Rittenhouse, R. K., & Myers, J. J. (1982). *Teaching sign language: The first vocabulary.* Normal, IL: Illinois Associates.

Robinson, F. P. (1946). *Effective study.* New York: Harper.

Robinson, F. P. (1961). *Effective study.* New York: Harper & Row.

Robinson, H. M. (1964). Developing critical readers. In R. G. Stauffer (Ed.), *Dimensions of critical reading.* Newark, DE: International Reading Association.

Rogers-Warren, A., & Warren, S. (1980). Hands for verbalization: Facilitating the display of newly taught language. *Behavior Modification, 4,* 361–382.

Rogers-Warren, A., & Warren, S. (1984). The social basis of language and communication in severely handicapped preschoolers. *Topics in Early Childhood Special Education, 4,* 57–72.

Romski, M., & Ruder, K. (1984). Effects of speech and sign instruction on oral language learning and generalization of action + object combinations by Down's Syndrome children. *Journal of Speech and Hearing Disorders, 49,* 293–302.

Romski, M. A., Sevcik, R. A., & Joyner, S. E. (1984). Nonspeech communication systems: Implications for language intervention with mentally retarded children. *Topics in Language Disorders, 5*(1), 66–81.

Romski, M. A., Sevcik, R. A., White, R. A., & Rumbaugh, D. M. (1983, May). *Acquisition of symbolic communication in four severely retarded individuals: A preliminary report.* Paper presented at the meeting of the American Association on Mental Deficiency, Dallas, TX.

Rosenshine, B. V. (1977). *Academic engaged time, content covered, and direct instruction.* Paper presented at the American Education Research Association Annual Meeting, New York.

Ross, A. D. (1974). *Psychological disorders of children: A behavioral approach to theory, research, and therapy.* New York: McGraw-Hill.

Ross, A. O. (1976). *Psychological aspects of learning disabilities and reading disorders.* New York: McGraw-Hill.

Ross, M. (1981). Review, overview, and other educational considerations. In M. Ross & L. W. Nober (Eds.), *Educating hard of hearing children.* Reston, VA: Council for Exceptional Children.

Ross, S. B. (1976). On syntax of written black English. *TESOL Quarterly, 10,* 115–122.

Roueche, J. E., Baker, G. A., & Roueche, S. D. (1984). College responses to low-achieving students: A national study. *American Education, 20*(5), 31–34.

Rubin, D. (1975). *Teaching elementary language arts.* New York: Holt, Rinehart and Winston.

Ruddell, R. B. (1974). *Reading-language instruction: Innovative practices.* Englewood Cliffs, NJ: Prentice-Hall.

Rumbaugh, D. M. (Ed.). (1977). *Language learning by a chimpanzee: The LANA project.* New York: Academic Press.

Rupley, W. H., & Blair, T. R. (1983). *Reading diagnosis and remediation: Classroom and clinic* (2nd ed.). Boston: Houghton Mifflin.

Russell, M. (1984). Assessment and intervention issues with the nonspeaking child. *Exceptional Children, 51,* 64–71.

Sailor, W., & Guess, D. (1983). *Severely handicapped students: An instructional design.* Boston: Houghton Mifflin.

Sailor, W., Guess, D., & Baer, D. M. (1973). An experimental program for teaching functional language to verbally deficient children. *Mental Retardation, 11,* 27–35.

Salzberg, B. H., Wheeler, A. J., Devar, L. T., & Hopkins, B. I. (1971). The effects of intermittent feedback and intermittent contingent access to play on printing of kindergarten children. *Journal of Applied Behavior Analysis, 4,* 163–171.

Samuels, S. J. (1979). The method of repeated readings. *The Reading Teacher, 32,* 403–408.

Sapona, R. H. (1985). *Writing productivity of learning disabled students: The effects of using a word processing program.* Unpublished doctoral dissertation, University of Virginia, Charlottesville, VA.

Saski, J., Swicegood, P., & Carter, J. (1983). Notetaking formats for learning disabled adolescents. *Learning Disability Quarterly, 6,* 265–272.

Saunders, M. (1982). *Multicultural teaching: A guide for the classroom.* New York: McGraw-Hill.

Savage, J. F., & Mooney, J. F. (1979). *Teaching reading to children with special needs.* Boston: Allyn & Bacon.

Schaeffer, B. (1980). Spontaneous language through signed speech. In R. L. Schiefelbusch (Ed.), *Nonspeech language and communication: Analysis and intervention* (pp. 422–446). Austin, TX: PRO-ED.

Schery, T., & Wilcoxen, A. (1982). *Initial communication process.* Monterey, CA: Publishers Test Service.

Schiffman, G., Tobin, D., & Buchanan, B. (1982). Microcomputer instruction for the learning disabled. *Journal of Learning Disabilities, 15,* 557–559.

Schnell, T. R. (1977). Listening instruction in college reading programs. *Reading Horizons, 17,* 260–263.

Schoolfield, L. D., & Timberlake, J. B. (1960). *The phonovisual method.* Washington, DC: Phonovisual Products.

Schreiber, P. A. (1980). On the acquisition of fluency. *Journal of Reading Behavior, 12,* 177–186.

Schuler, A. L., & Prizant, B. M. (1985). Echolalia. In E. Schopler & G. B. Mesibo (Eds.), *Communication Problems in Autism* (pp. 163–186). New York: Plenum Press.

Schumaker, J. B., Deshler, D. D., Alley, G. R., Warner, M. M., Clark, F. L., & Nolan, S. (1982). Error monitoring: A learning strategy for improving adolescent academic performance. In W. M. Cruickshank & J. W. Lerner (Eds.), *Coming of age: The best of ACLD* (Vol. 3, pp. 170–183). Syracuse, NY: Syracuse University Press.

Schumaker, J. B., Deshler, D. D., & Denton, P. H. (1984). An integrated system for providing content to learning disabled adolescents using an audio-taped format. In W. M. Cruikshank & J. M. Kliebhan (Eds.), *Early adolescence to early adulthood* (pp. 79–107). Syracuse: Syracuse University Press.

Schumaker, J. B., Deshler, D. D., Denton, P. H., Alley, G. R., Clark, F. L., & Warner, M. M. (1981). *Multipass: A learning strategy for improving reading comprehension* (Research Report No. 33). Lawrence, KS: University of Kansas, Institute for Research in Learning Disabilities.

Schwartz, M. L., Gilroy, J., & Lynn, G. (1976). Neuropsychological and psychosocial implications of spelling deficit in adulthood: A case report. *Journal of Learning Disabilities, 9,* 144–148.

Sedita, J. (1980). *Help for the learning disabled college student.* Prides Crossing, MA: Landmark School.

Semel, E., & Wiig, E. (1980). *Clinical evaluation of language functions.* Columbus, OH: Charles E. Merrill.

Shane, H. (1980). Approaches to assessing the communication of non-oral persons. In R. L. Schiefelbusch (Ed.), *Nonspeech language and communication: Analysis and intervention* (pp. 197–224). Austin, TX: PRO-ED.

Shane, H. (1985, May). *Alternative communications: A means to an end.* Paper presented at conference for teachers of the severely and profoundly handicapped, Charlottesville, VA.

Shane, H. C., & Bashir, A. F. (1980). Election criteria for the adaptation of an augmentative communication system: Preliminary considerations. *Journal of Speech and Hearing Disorders, 48,* 408–414.

Sherman, J. (1971). Imitation and language development. In H. W. Reese (Ed.), *Advances in child development and behavior* (Vol. 6, pp. 239–272). New York: Academic Press.

Sherwin, J. S. (1969). *Four problems in teaching English: A critique of research.* Scranton, PA: International Textbook for National Council of Teachers of English.

Shores, J., & Yee, A. (1973). Spelling achievement tests: What is available and needed? *Journal of Special Education, 7,* 301–309.

Shuy, R. W. (1972). Speech differences and teaching strategies: How different is enough? In R. E. Hodges & E. H. Rudorf (Eds.), *Language and learning to read* (pp. 55–72). Boston: Houghton Mifflin.

Siegel, E., & Gold, R. (1982). *Educating the learning disabled.* New York: Macmillan.

Silverman, H., McNaughton, S., & Kates, B. (1978). *Handbook of Blissymbolics.* Toronto: Blissymbolics Communication Institute.

Simons, H. D., & Johnson, K. R. (1974). Black English syntax and reading interference. *Research in the Teaching of English, 8,* 339–358.

Simpson, E. (1979). *Reversal: A personal account of victory over dyslexia.* Boston: Houghton Mifflin.

Sisk, D. A. (1977). What if your child is gifted? *American Education, 13,* 23–26.

Sisson, L., & Barrett, R. (1984). An alternating treatments comparison of oral and total communication training with minimally verbal retarded children. *Journal of Applied Behavior Analysis, 17,* 559–566.

Skeels, H. M. (1966). Adult status of children with contrasting early life experiences. *Monograph of the Society for Research in Child Development, 31*(3), 1–65.

Skeels, H. M., & Dye, H. B. (1939). A study of the effects of differential stimulation on mentally retarded children. *Convention Proceedings American Association on Mental Deficiency, 44,* 114–136.

Skinner, B. F. (1957). *Verbal behavior.* New York: Appleton-Century-Crofts.

Slavin, R. E., Madden, N. A., & Leavey, M. (1984). Effects of cooperative learning and individualized instruction on mainstreamed students. *Exceptional Children, 50,* 434–443.

Slingerland, B. H. (1971). *A multi-sensory approach to language arts for specific language disability children.* Cambridge, MA: Educators Publishing Service.

Slingerland, B. H. (1974). *A multi-sensory approach to language arts for specific language disability children: A guide for primary teachers.* Cambridge, MA: Educators Publishing Service.

Slosson, R. L. (1963). *Slosson Oral Reading Test.* East Aurora, NY: Slosson Educational Publications.

Smith, E. B., Goodman, K. S., & Meredith, R. (1976). *Language and thinking in school.* New York: Holt, Rinehart and Winston.

Smith, J. E., & Payne, J. S. (1980). *Teaching exceptional adolescents.* Columbus, OH: Charles E. Merrill.

Smith, J. E., Polloway, E. A., & Smith, J. D. (1978). The continuing dilemma of the mildly handicapped. *Special Children, 4*(2), 52–63.

Smith, M. E. (1926). An investigation of the development of the sentence and the extent of vocabulary in young children. *University of Iowa Studies in Child Welfare, 3*(5).

Smith, M., & Meyers, A. (1979). Telephone-skills training for retarded adults: Group and individual demonstrations with and without verbal instruction. *American Journal of Mental Deficiency, 83,* 581–587.

Smith, S. L. (1985). Falling through the cracks: Learning disabled adults at night school. *The Pointer, 30*(1), 25–27.

Snyder, L., Lovitt, T., Smith, J. (1975). Language training for the severely retarded: Five years of behavior analysis research. *Exceptional Children, 42,* 7–15.

Somervill, M. A. (1975). Dialect and reading: A review of alternative solutions. *Review of Educational Research, 45,* 247–262.

Spache, G. D. (1981). *Diagnostic Reading Scales.* Monterey, CA: CTB/McGraw-Hill.

Spache, G. D., & Spache, E. B. (1986). *Reading in the elementary school* (5th ed.). Boston: Allyn & Bacon.

Spalding, R. B., & Spalding, W. T. (1969). *The writing road to reading* (2nd ed.). New York: Morrow Quill Paperbacks.

Spekman, N. J., & Roth, F. P. (1984). Intervention strategies for learning disabled children with oral communication disorders. *Learning Disability Quarterly, 7,* 7–18.

Spelling Survey. Ed. Staff. (1984). *Academic Therapy, 20,* 77.

St. Louis, K. (1985, May). *Communications systems: Language boards.* Paper presented at conference for teachers of the severely and profoundly handicapped, Charlottesville, VA.

Stauffer, R. (1975). *Directing the reading-thinking process.* New York: Harper & Row.

Stebbins, L. B., St. Pierre, R. G., Proper, E. C., Anderson, R. B., & Cerva, T. R. (1977). *Education as an experimentation: A planned variation model* (Vol. IV-A). Cambridge, MA: Abt Associates.

Stephens, T. M. (1977). *Teaching skills to children with learning and behavior disorders.* Columbus, OH: Charles E. Merrill.

Stevens, R., & Rosenshine, B. (1981). Advances in research on teaching. *Exceptional Education Quarterly, 2*(1), 1–9.

Stokes, F., & Baer, D. M. (1977). An implicit technology of generalization. *Journal of Applied Behavior Analysis, 10,* 349–367.

Storm, R. H., & Willis, J. H. (1978). Small group training as an alternative to individual programs for profoundly retarded persons. *American Journal of Mental Deficiency, 83,* 282–288.

Stott, D. H., Moyes, F. A., & Henderson, S. E. (1985). *Diagnosis and remediation of handwriting problems.* Guelph, ONT: Brook Educational Publishing.

Strang, R. (1955). Psychology of gifted children and youths. In W. Cruickshank, *Psychology of exceptional children and youth* (pp. 64–86). Englewood Cliffs, NJ: Prentice Hall.

Strang, R. (1961). Creative writing. In L. Fliegler, *Curriculum planning for the gifted* (pp. 184–212). Englewood Cliffs, NJ: Prentice-Hall.

Strong, W. (1983). *Sentence combining: A composing book* (2nd ed.). New York: Random House.

Sugarman-Bell, S. (1978). Some organizational aspects of preverbal communication. In I. Markova (Ed.), *The social context of language.* New York: John Wiley.

Suppes, P. (1974). A survey of cognition in handicapped children. *Review of Educational Research, 44,* 145–175.

Swanson, R. B., & Yeannakis, C. (1982). The use of a resource program model in work with adult problem learners. *Education and Training of the Mentally Retarded, 17,* 156–159.

Swassing, R. H. (1984). Gifted and talented children. In W. L. Heward & M. D. Orlansky, *Exceptional children.* Columbus, OH: Charles E. Merrill.

Swassing, R. H. (1985). *Teaching gifted children and adolescents* (pp. 365–395). Columbus, OH: Charles E. Merrill.

Taber, F. M. (1983). *Microcomputers in special education.* Reston, VA: Council for Exceptional Children.

Tadlock, D. F. (1978). SQ3R—Why it works, based on an information processing theory of learning. *The Journal of Reading, 22,* 110–116.

Tagartz, G. E., Otto, W., Klausmeier, H. J., Goodwin, W. L., & Cook, D. M. (1968). Effect of three methods of instruction upon the handwriting performance of third- and fourth-graders. *American Educational Research Journal, 5,* 81–90.

Talkington, I. W., Hall, S., & Altman, R. (1971). Communication deficits and aggression in the mentally retarded. *American Journal of Mental Deficiency, 76,* 235–237.

Talmy, S. (1984). Computing for the handicapped. *Creative Computing, 10,* 180–181.

Tanner, D., & Lamb. W. (1983). *Cognitive, Linguistic, and Social Communicative Scales.* Tulsa, OK: Modern Education.

Taylor, S. (1973). *Listening: What research says to the teacher.* Washington, DC: National Education Association.

Temple, C., & Gillet, J. (1984). *Language arts: learning processes and teaching practices.* Boston: Little, Brown.

Terman, L. (1925). *Genetic studies of genius* (Vol. 1). Stanford, CA: Stanford University Press.

Thonis, E. (1976). *Literacy for America's Spanish speaking children.* Newark, DE: International Reading Association.

Thorpe, L. P., Lefever, D. E., & Haslond, R. A. (1974). *SRA achievement series.* Chicago: Science Research Associates.

Thurber, D. N. (1983). Write on! With continuous stroke point. *Academic Therapy, 18,* 389–395.

Thurber, D. N., & Jordan, D. R. (1978). *D'Nealian handwriting.* Glenview, IL: Scott, Foresman.

Thurlow, M. L., Ysseldyke, J. E., Graden, J. L., & Algozzine, B. (1983). What's "special" about special education resource rooms for learning disabled students? *Learning Disability Quarterly, 6,* 283–288.

Thypin, M. (1979). Books for low reading level. *Journal of Learning Disabilities, 12,* 428–430.

Tompkins, G. E., & Friend, M. (1986). On your mark, get set, write! *Teaching Exceptional Children, 18,* 82–89.

Torgeson, J. K. (1977). The role of nonspecific factors in the task performance of learning disabled children: A theoretical assessment. *Journal of Learning Disabilities, 10,* 27–34.

Towle, M. (1978). Assessment and remediating of handwriting deficits. *Journal of Learning Disabilities, 11,* 370–377.

Towle, M. (1982). Learning how to be a student when you have a learning disability. *Journal of Learning Disabilities, 15,* 90–93.

Traub, N., & Bloom, F. (1970). *Recipe for reading.* Cambridge, MA: Educators Publishing Service.

Trezise, R. L. (1977). Teaching reading to the gifted. *Language Arts, 54,* 920–924.

Trybus, R. (1985). *Today's hearing impaired children and youth: A demographic and academic profile.* Washington, DC: Gallaudet Research Institute.

Ur, P. (1984). *Teaching listening comprehension.* New York: Cambridge University Press.

Uzgiris, I. C., & Hunt, J. M. (1975). *Assessment in infancy: Ordinal scales of psychological development.* Urbana, IL: University of Illinois Press.

Vaillancourt, B. (1979). *A special project for the development of assessment and educational programming techniques serving the adult basic education student with learning disabilities: Final report.* Palantine, IL: William Rainey Harper College. (ERIC Document Reproduction Service No. ED 193 433)

Vanderheiden, G. C. (Ed.). (1978). *Nonvocal communication resource book.* Baltimore: University Park Press.

Vanderheiden, G. C., & Grilley, K. (Eds.). (1976). *Non-vocal communication techniques and aids for the severely physically handicapped.* Austin, TX: PRO-ED.

Vanderheiden, G. C., & Harris-Vanderheiden, D. (1976). Communication techniques and aides for the nonvocal severely handicapped. In L. L. Lloyd (Ed.), *Communication assessment and intervention strategies* (pp. 423–500). Austin, TX: PRO-ED.

Vandever, T. R. , & Stubbs, J. C. (1977). Reading retention and transfer in TMR students. *American Journal of Mental Deficiency, 11,* 30–39.

Van Houten, R., Morrison, E., Jarvis, R., & MacDonald, M. (1974). The effects of explicit timing and feedback on compositional response rate in elementary school children. *Journal of Applied Behavior Analysis, 7,* 547–555.

Varnhagen, S., & Gerber, M. (1984). Use of microcomputers for spelling assessment: Reasons to be cautious. *Learning Disability Quarterly, 7,* 266–270.

Vogel, S. A. (1982). On developing LD college programs. *Journal of Learning Disabilities, 15,* 518–528.

Vogel, S. A. (1985a). Learning disabled college students: Identification, assessment, and outcomes. In D. D. Duane & C. K. Leong (Eds.), *Understanding learning disabilities: International and multidisciplinary views* (pp. 179–203). New York: Plenum Press.

Vogel, S. A. (1985b). Syntactic complexity in written expression of LD college writers. *Annals of Dyslexia, 35,* 137–157.

Vogel, S. A., & Moran, M. R. (1982). Written language disorders in learning disabled college students. In W. M. Cruickshank & J. W. Lerner (Eds.), *Coming of age: The best of ACLD* (Vol. 3, pp. 211–225). Syracuse: Syracuse University Press.

Vygotsky, L. S. (1962). *Thought and language* (ed. and trans. by E. Hanfman & G. Vakar). Cambridge, MA: MIT Press.

Walker, J. E., & Shea, T. M. (1984). *Behavior management: A practical approach for educators* (3rd ed.). St. Louis: Times Mirror/Mosby.

Wallace, G. (1981). Teaching reading. In J. M. Kauffman & D. P. Hallahan (Eds.), *Handbook of special education* (pp. 459–474). Englewood Cliffs, NJ: Prentice Hall.

Wallace, G., & Kauffman, J. M. (1986). *Teaching students with learning and behavior problems* (3rd ed.). Columbus, OH: Charles E. Merrill.

Wallace, G., & Larsen, S. C. (1978). *Educational assessment of learning problems: Testing for teaching.* Boston: Allyn & Bacon.

Wallace, G., & McLoughlin, J. A. (1979). *Learning disabilities: Concepts and characteristics.* Columbus, OH: Charles E. Merrill.

Walsh, B. J., & Lamberts, J. (1979). Errorless discrimination and picture fading as techniques for teaching sight words to TMR students. *American Journal of Mental Deficiency, 83,* 473–479.

Warren, S., & Rogers-Warren, A. (1980). Current perspectives in language remediation. *Education and Treatment of Children, 3,* 133–152.

Warren, S., & Rogers-Warren, A. (1983). A longitudinal analysis of language generalization among adolescents with severe handicapping conditions. *Journal of the Association for Persons with Severe Handicaps, 8,* 18–31.

Washington, M. H. (1981). *A comprehensive approach to assessing and remediating learning disabilities in learning disabled college students.* Northern Kentucky University. (ERIC Document Reproduction Service No. ED 218 839)

Webber, M. (1981). *Communication skills for exceptional learners.* Rockville, MD: Aspen.

Weisel, L. P. (1979). *The London Procedure: A screening, diagnosis and teaching guide for adult learning problems.* Columbus, OH: Instructional Materials Laboratory, The Ohio State University.

Weisel, L. P. (1980). *Adult learning problems: Insights, instruction, and implications.* Columbus, OH: ERIC Clearinghouse on Adult, Career, and Vocational Education. (ERIC Document Reproduction Service No. ED 193 534)

Wells, L. R. (1974). *Writing disorders and the learning disability student in the college English classroom.* (Doctoral dissertation, Northwestern University, 1973). *Dissertation Abstract International, 34,* 5764A-5765A. (University Microfilms No. 74-7846, 230)

West, W. W. (1980). *Teaching the gifted and talented in the English classroom.* Washington, DC: National Education Association.

Westling, D. L., Ferrell, K., & Swenson, K. (1982). Intraclassroom comparison of two arrangements for teaching profoundly mentally retarded children. *American Journal of Mental Deficiency, 86,* 601-608.

Wiederholt, J. L., & Bryant, B. R. (1986). *Gray Oral Reading Tests–Revised.* Austin, TX: PRO-ED.

Wiederholt, J. L., Hammill, D. D., & Brown, V. (1978). *The resource teacher: A guide to effective practices.* Austin, TX: PRO-ED.

Wiener, H. (1981). *The writing room.* New York: Oxford University Press.

Wiig, E. H., & Fleischmann, N. (1980). Prepositional phrases, pronominalization, reflexivization, and relativization in the language of learning disabled college students. *Journal of Learning Disabilities, 13,* 571-576.

Wiig, E. H., & Harris, S. (1974). Perception and interpretation of nonverbally expressed emotions by adolescents with learning disabilities. *Perceptual and Motor Skills, 38,* 239-245.

Wiig, E. H., & Semel, E. M. (1976). *Language disabilities in children and adolescents.* Columbus, OH: Charles E. Merrill.

Wiig, E. H., & Semel, E. M. (1980). *Language assessment and intervention for learning disabled.* Columbus, OH: Charles E. Merrill.

Wiig, E. H., & Semel, E. M. (1984). *Language assessment and intervention for learning disabled* (2nd ed.). Columbus, OH: Charles E. Merrill.

Wilcox, M. G., & Campil, P. (1985, November). *Developing communication skills in young children with severe handicaps.* Paper presented at the meeting of the American Speech and Hearing Association.

Wilson, C. R. (1983). Teaching reading comprehension by connecting the known to the new. *The Reading Teacher, 36,* 382-390.

Wilson, J. (1982). Selecting educational materials and resources. In D. D. Hammill & N. R. Bartel (Eds.), *Teaching children with learning and behavior problems* (3rd ed., pp. 409-419). Boston: Allyn & Bacon.

Wilt, M. (1950). Study of teacher awareness of listening as a factor in elementary education. *Journal of Educational Research, 43,* 626-636.

Wing, L. (1969). The handicaps of autistic children: A comparative study. *Journal of Child Psychology and Psychiatry, 10,* 1-40.

Winitz, H. (1964). Research in articulation and intelligence. *Child Development, 35,* 287-297.

Winkley, C. K., & Rhoads, D. (1968). Junior great books discussion programs. In *Ivory, apes, and peacocks: The literature point of view.* Newark, DE: International Reading Association.

Wiseman, D. E., Hartwell, L. K., & Hannafin, M. J. (1980). Exploring the reading and listening skills of secondary mildly handicapped students. *Learning Disability Quarterly, 3,* 56-61.

Witty, P. A. (1955). Enriching the reading of the gifted child. *Library Journal, 20,* 2622.

Wolff, P. H. (1969). The natural history of crying and other vocalizations in early infancy. In B. M. Foss (Ed.), *Determinants of infant behavior* (Vol. 4). London: Methuen.

Wood, B. J. (1976). *Children and communication.* Englewood Cliffs, NJ: Prentice Hall.

Wood, N. (1969). *Verbal learning.* Belmont, CA: Fearon.

Woodcock, R. W. (1973). *Woodcock Reading Mastery Tests.* Circle Pines, MN: American Guidance Service.

Woolman, D. H. (1980). A presymbolic training program. In R. L. Schiefelbusch (Ed.), *Nonspeech language and communication: Analysis and intervention* (pp. 327–356). Austin, TX: PRO-ED.

Wren, C. (1983). *Language learning disabilities.* Rockville, MD: Aspen.

Wright, J. D. (1983). *Teaching the gifted and talented in the middle school.* Washington, DC: National Education Association.

Wulpe, W. W. (1968). A form constancy technique for spelling proficiency. In J. I. Arena (Ed.), *Building spelling skills in dyslexic children* (pp. 13–14). San Rafael, CA: Academic Therapy Publications.

Yale, C. (1939). *Formation and development of elementary English sounds.* Northampton, MA: Clarke School for the Deaf.

Yawkey, T., Askov, E., Cartwright, C., Dupuis, M., Fairchild, S., & Yawkey, M. (1981). *Language arts and the young child.* Itasca IL: F. E. Peacock.

Zaner-Bloser (1979). *Creative growth with handwriting.* Columbus, OH: Author.

Zentall, S. (1983). Learning environments: A review of physical and temporal factors. *Exceptional Education Quarterly, 4*(2), 90–109.

Zimmerman, I. L., Steiner, V. G., & Evatt, R. L. (1969). *Preschool Language Scale.* Columbus, OH: Charles E. Merrill.

Zink, K. E. (1982). *Let me try to make it clearer.* Ellenburg, WA: Instructional Media Center, Central Washington University.

Zweig, R. L., & Associates. (1971). *Fountain Valley Teacher Support System in Reading.* Huntington Beach, CA: Richard L. Zweig.

AUTHOR INDEX

SUBJECT INDEX